Seat Ibiza
Owners Workshop Manual

Martynn Randall

Models covered

(4889 - 320)

Ibiza Hatchback
Petrol: 1.2 litre (1198cc) & 1.4 litre (1390cc)
Turbo-Diesel: 1.4 litre (1422cc) & 1.9 litre (1896cc)

Does NOT cover models with 1.6, 1.8 or 2.0 litre petrol engines or 1.9 litre non-turbo diesel engine
Does NOT cover Cupra models, or new model range introduced May 2008

© Haynes Publishing 2010

ABCDE
FGHIJ
KLMNO
PQRST

A book in the **Haynes Owners Workshop Manual Series**

ISBN **978 1 84425 889 5**

British Library Cataloguing in Publication Data
A catalogue record for this book is available from the British Library.

Printed in the USA

Haynes Publishing
Sparkford, Yeovil, Somerset BA22 7JJ, England

Haynes North America, Inc
861 Lawrence Drive, Newbury Park, California 91320, USA

Haynes Publishing Nordiska AB
Box 1504, 751 45 UPPSALA, Sverige

Contents

Contents

The Seat Ibiza range covered by this manual was introduced to the UK market in April 2002. Using the same new A04 platform as its Seat Group sister cars, the Skoda Fabia and VW Polo, the car represents a substantial update on the preceding Ibiza range. At its launch, the car drew praise for its build quality and 'big-car feel' – not surprising, since it is nearly as big as a Mk 3 VW Golf.

The 1.4 litre petrol engines are derived from well-proven units which have appeared in many VW vehicles, but there's a new 1.2 litre 3-cylinder unit appearing for the first time in the Ibiza.

The diesel engines are all familiar units from the VW range: the 1.9 litre PD (Pumpe Duse)

TDI unit and the 1.4 litre PD (Pumpe Duse) unit. Both engines are turbocharged and have an intercooler.

All the engines are of overhead camshaft design, mounted transversely, with the transmission mounted on the left-hand side. All models have a five- or six-speed manual transmission, or four-speed automatic transmission.

All models have fully-independent front suspension, mounted on a subframe. The rear suspension is semi-independent, with suspension struts, trailing arms and a 'self-steering' torsion beam axle. The compact rear springs are mounted separately from the shock absorbers, to minimise intrusion into

the rear loadspace. The new speed-sensitive power steering system fitted to all models has an electric hydraulic pump, rather than an engine-driven one.

A wide range of standard and optional equipment is available within the Ibiza range to suit most tastes. All models have electric mirrors, tinted glass, four airbags, power steering and ABS as standard, with central locking, electric windows and air conditioning available further up the range.

Provided that regular servicing is carried out in accordance with the manufacturer's recommendations, the Seat Ibiza should prove a reliable and economical small car. The engine compartment is well-designed, and most of the items needing frequent attention are easily accessible.

Your Seat Ibiza manual

The aim of this manual is to help you get the best value from your car. It can do so in several ways. It can help you decide what work must be done (even should you choose to get it done by a garage). It will also provide information on routine maintenance and servicing, and give a logical course of action and diagnosis when random faults occur. However, it is hoped that you will use the manual by tackling the work yourself. On simpler jobs it may even be quicker than booking the car into a garage and going there twice, to leave and collect it. Perhaps most important, a lot of money can be saved by avoiding the costs a garage must charge to cover its labour and overheads.

The manual has drawings and descriptions to show the function of the various components so that their layout can be understood. Tasks are described and photographed in a clear step by step sequence. The illustrations are numbered by the Section number and paragraph number to which they relate – if there is more than one illustration per paragraph, the sequence is denoted alphabetically.

References to the 'left' or 'right' of the car are in the sense of a person in the driver's seat, facing forwards.

Acknowledgements

Thanks are due to Draper tools Limited, who provided some of the workshop tools, and to all those people at Sparkford who helped in the production of this manual.

This manual is not a direct reproduction of the vehicle manufacturer's data, and its publication should not be taken as implying any technical approval by the vehicle manufacturers or importers.

We take great pride in the accuracy of information given in this manual, but car manufacturers make alterations and design changes during the production run of a particular car of which they do not inform us. No liability can be accepted by the authors or publishers for loss, damage or injury caused by any errors in, or omissions from, the information given.

Working on your car can be dangerous. This page shows just some of the potential risks and hazards, with the aim of creating a safety-conscious attitude.

General hazards

Scalding

• Don't remove the radiator or expansion tank cap while the engine is hot.
• Engine oil, automatic transmission fluid or power steering fluid may also be dangerously hot if the engine has recently been running.

Burning

• Beware of burns from the exhaust system and from any part of the engine. Brake discs and drums can also be extremely hot immediately after use.

Crushing

• When working under or near a raised vehicle, always supplement the jack with axle stands, or use drive-on ramps.
Never venture under a car which is only supported by a jack.
• Take care if loosening or tightening high-torque nuts when the vehicle is on stands. Initial loosening and final tightening should be done with the wheels on the ground.

Fire

• Fuel is highly flammable; fuel vapour is explosive.
• Don't let fuel spill onto a hot engine.
• Do not smoke or allow naked lights (including pilot lights) anywhere near a vehicle being worked on. Also beware of creating sparks (electrically or by use of tools).
• Fuel vapour is heavier than air, so don't work on the fuel system with the vehicle over an inspection pit.
• Another cause of fire is an electrical overload or short-circuit. Take care when repairing or modifying the vehicle wiring.
• Keep a fire extinguisher handy, of a type suitable for use on fuel and electrical fires.

Electric shock

• Ignition HT voltage can be dangerous, especially to people with heart problems or a pacemaker. Don't work on or near the ignition system with the engine running or the ignition switched on.

• Mains voltage is also dangerous. Make sure that any mains-operated equipment is correctly earthed. Mains power points should be protected by a residual current device (RCD) circuit breaker.

Fume or gas intoxication

• Exhaust fumes are poisonous; they often contain carbon monoxide, which is rapidly fatal if inhaled. Never run the engine in a confined space such as a garage with the doors shut.
• Fuel vapour is also poisonous, as are the vapours from some cleaning solvents and paint thinners.

Poisonous or irritant substances

• Avoid skin contact with battery acid and with any fuel, fluid or lubricant, especially antifreeze, brake hydraulic fluid and Diesel fuel. Don't syphon them by mouth. If such a substance is swallowed or gets into the eyes, seek medical advice.
• Prolonged contact with used engine oil can cause skin cancer. Wear gloves or use a barrier cream if necessary. Change out of oil-soaked clothes and do not keep oily rags in your pocket.
• Air conditioning refrigerant forms a poisonous gas if exposed to a naked flame (including a cigarette). It can also cause skin burns on contact.

Asbestos

• Asbestos dust can cause cancer if inhaled or swallowed. Asbestos may be found in gaskets and in brake and clutch linings. When dealing with such components it is safest to assume that they contain asbestos.

Special hazards

Hydrofluoric acid

• This extremely corrosive acid is formed when certain types of synthetic rubber, found in some O-rings, oil seals, fuel hoses etc, are exposed to temperatures above 400ºC. The rubber changes into a charred or sticky substance containing the acid. *Once formed, the acid remains dangerous for years. If it gets onto the skin, it may be necessary to amputate the limb concerned.*
• When dealing with a vehicle which has suffered a fire, or with components salvaged from such a vehicle, wear protective gloves and discard them after use.

The battery

• Batteries contain sulphuric acid, which attacks clothing, eyes and skin. Take care when topping-up or carrying the battery.
• The hydrogen gas given off by the battery is highly explosive. Never cause a spark or allow a naked light nearby. Be careful when connecting and disconnecting battery chargers or jump leads.

Air bags

• Air bags can cause injury if they go off accidentally. Take care when removing the steering wheel and/or facia. Special storage instructions may apply.

Diesel injection equipment

• Diesel injection pumps supply fuel at very high pressure. Take care when working on the fuel injectors and fuel pipes.

⚠️ *Warning: Never expose the hands, face or any other part of the body to injector spray; the fuel can penetrate the skin with potentially fatal results.*

Remember...

DO

• Do use eye protection when using power tools, and when working under the vehicle.

• Do wear gloves or use barrier cream to protect your hands when necessary.

• Do get someone to check periodically that all is well when working alone on the vehicle.

• Do keep loose clothing and long hair well out of the way of moving mechanical parts.

• Do remove rings, wristwatch etc, before working on the vehicle – especially the electrical system.

• Do ensure that any lifting or jacking equipment has a safe working load rating adequate for the job.

DON'T

• Don't attempt to lift a heavy component which may be beyond your capability – get assistance.

• Don't rush to finish a job, or take unverified short cuts.

• Don't use ill-fitting tools which may slip and cause injury.

• Don't leave tools or parts lying around where someone can trip over them. Mop up oil and fuel spills at once.

• Don't allow children or pets to play in or near a vehicle being worked on.

The following pages are intended to help in dealing with common roadside emergencies and breakdowns. You will find more detailed fault finding information at the back of the manual, and repair information in the main chapters.

If your car won't start and the starter motor doesn't turn

- ☐ If it's a model with automatic transmission, make sure the selector is in P or N.
- ☐ Open the bonnet and make sure that the battery terminals are clean and tight.
- ☐ Switch on the headlights and try to start the engine. If the headlights go very dim when you're trying to start, the battery is probably flat. Get out of trouble by jump starting (see next page) using a friend's car.

If your car won't start even though the starter motor turns as normal

- ☐ Is there fuel in the tank?
- ☐ Has the engine immobiliser been deactivated? This should happen automatically on inserting the ignition key. However, if a replacement key has been obtained, other than from a Seat dealer, it may not contain the transponder chip necessary to deactivate the system.
- ☐ Is there moisture on electrical components under the bonnet? Switch off the ignition, then wipe off any obvious dampness with a dry cloth. Spray a water-repellent aerosol product (WD-40 or equivalent) on electrical connectors like those shown in the photos. Pay special attention to the DIS ignition module's wiring connector. (Note that diesel engines don't usually suffer from damp.)

A Check the condition and security of the battery connections.

B Check the fuses and fusible links in the fusebox located on top of the battery.

Check that electrical connections are secure (with the ignition switched off) and spray them with a water-dispersant spray like WD-40 if you suspect a problem due to damp.

C Check the wiring to the ignition coils beneath the engine top cover (petrol models only).

D Check that all engine wiring is secure and undamaged.

Jump starting

When jump-starting a car using a booster battery, observe the following precautions:

✔ Before connecting the booster battery, make sure that the ignition is switched off.

✔ Ensure that all electrical equipment (lights, heater, wipers, etc) is switched off.

✔ Take note of any special precautions printed on the battery case.

✔ Make sure that the booster battery is the same voltage as the discharged one in the vehicle.

✔ If the battery is being jump-started from the battery in another vehicle, the two vehicles MUST NOT TOUCH each other.

✔ Make sure that the transmission is in neutral (or PARK, in the case of automatic transmission).

 Jump starting will get you out of trouble, but you must correct whatever made the battery go flat in the first place. There are three possibilities:

1 *The battery has been drained by repeated attempts to start, or by leaving the lights on.*

2 *The charging system is not working properly (alternator drivebelt slack or broken, alternator wiring fault or alternator itself faulty).*

3 *The battery itself is at fault (electrolyte low, or battery worn out).*

1 Connect one end of the red jump lead to the positive (+) terminal of the flat battery

2 Connect the other end of the red lead to the positive (+) terminal of the booster battery.

3 Connect one end of the black jump lead to the negative (-) terminal of the booster battery

4 Connect the other end of the black jump lead to a bolt or bracket on the engine block, well away from the battery, on the vehicle to be started.

5 Make sure that the jump leads will not come into contact with the fan, drive-belts or other moving parts of the engine.

6 Start the engine using the booster battery and run it at idle speed. Switch on the lights, rear window demister and heater blower motor, then disconnect the jump leads in the reverse order of connection. Turn off the lights etc.

Wheel changing

⚠️ **Warning:** *Do not change a wheel in a situation where you risk being hit by other traffic. On busy roads, try to stop in a lay-by or a gateway. Be wary of passing traffic while changing the wheel – it is easy to become distracted by the job in hand.*

Preparation

☐ When a puncture occurs, stop as soon as it is safe to do so.
☐ Park on firm level ground, if possible, and well out of the way of other traffic.
☐ Use hazard warning lights if necessary.

☐ If you have one, use a warning triangle to alert other drivers of your presence.
☐ Apply the handbrake and engage first or reverse gear (or Park on models with automatic transmission).

☐ Chock the wheel diagonally opposite the one being removed – a couple of large stones will do for this.
☐ If the ground is soft, use a flat piece of wood to spread the load under the jack.

Changing the wheel

1 The spare wheel and tools are stored in the luggage compartment. Lift out the jack and wheel changing tools from the centre of the spare wheel.

2 Unscrew the retainer and lift out the wheel.

3 Use the wire hook and wheel brace to remove the wheel trim, or the centre cap on some alloy wheels. Where applicable, use the plastic puller from the tool kit to remove the cover from each wheel bolt, including the anti-theft bolt.

4 Slacken each wheel bolt by half a turn (using the special splined adapter for the anti-theft bolt).

5 Locate the jack below the reinforced point on the sill (don't jack the vehicle at any other point of the sill) and on firm ground, then turn the jack handle clockwise until the wheel is raised clear of the ground.

6 Unscrew the wheel bolts and remove the wheel. Fit the spare wheel, and screw in the bolts. Lightly tighten the bolts with the wheelbrace then lower the vehicle to the ground.

7 Securely tighten the wheel bolts in the sequence shown then refit the wheel trim/ hub cap. Stow the punctured wheel back in the spare wheel well. Note that the wheel bolts should be tightened to the specified torque at the earliest possible opportunity.

8 When refitting the centre cap, ensure the tab engages correctly with the cut-out in the wheel centre.

Finally . . .

☐ Stow the jack and tools in the spare wheel.
☐ Check the tyre pressure on the wheel just fitted. If it is low, or if you don't have a pressure gauge with you, drive slowly to the nearest garage and inflate the tyre to the correct pressure.

Note: *If a temporary 'space-saver' spare wheel has been fitted, special conditions apply to its use. This type of spare wheel is only intended for use in an emergency, and should not remain fitted any longer than it takes to get the punctured wheel repaired. While the temporary wheel is in use, ensure it is inflated to the correct pressure, do not exceed 50 mph, and avoid harsh acceleration, braking or cornering.*

Identifying leaks

Puddles on the garage floor or drive, or obvious wetness under the bonnet or underneath the car, suggest a leak that needs investigating. It can sometimes be difficult to decide where the leak is coming from, especially if the engine bay is very dirty already. Leaking oil or fluid can also be blown rearwards by the passage of air under the car, giving a false impression of where the problem lies.

 Warning: Most automotive oils and fluids are poisonous. Wash them off skin, and change out of contaminated clothing, without delay.

 The smell of a fluid leaking from the car may provide a clue to what's leaking. Some fluids are distinctively coloured. It may help to clean the car carefully and to park it over some clean paper overnight as an aid to locating the source of the leak.
Remember that some leaks may only occur while the engine is running.

Sump oil

Engine oil may leak from the drain plug...

Oil from filter

...or from the base of the oil filter.

Gearbox oil

Gearbox oil can leak from the seals at the inboard ends of the driveshafts.

Antifreeze

Leaking antifreeze often leaves a crystalline deposit like this.

Brake fluid

A leak occurring at a wheel is almost certainly brake fluid.

Power steering fluid

Power steering fluid may leak from the pipe connectors on the steering rack.

Towing

When all else fails, you may find yourself having to get a tow home – or of course you may be helping somebody else. Long-distance recovery should only be done by a garage or breakdown service. For shorter distances, DIY towing using another car is easy enough, but observe the following points:

☐ Use a proper tow-rope – they are not expensive. The vehicle being towed must display an ON TOW sign in its rear window.

☐ Always turn the ignition key to the 'On' position when the vehicle is being towed, so that the steering lock is released, and the direction indicator and brake lights work.

☐ A rear towing eye is provided below the right-hand side of the rear bumper. The front towing eye is located in the tool kit, and is screwed into position behind the vent/cover on the right-hand side of the front bumper. Undo the bolt and remove the cover. The eye has a **left-hand thread**, which means it screws in **anti-clockwise**.

☐ Before being towed, release the handbrake and select neutral on the transmission. On models with automatic transmission, special precautions apply. If in doubt, do not tow, or transmission damage may result.

☐ Note that greater-than-usual pedal pressure will be required to operate the brakes, since the vacuum servo unit is only operational with the engine running.

☐ Because the power steering will not be operational, greater-than-usual steering effort will also be required.

☐ The driver of the car being towed must keep the tow-rope taut at all times to avoid snatching.

☐ Make sure that both drivers know the route before setting off.

☐ Only drive at moderate speeds and keep the distance towed to a minimum. Drive smoothly and allow plenty of time for slowing down at junctions.

Introduction

There are some very simple checks which need only take a few minutes to carry out, but which could save you a lot of inconvenience and expense.

These *Weekly checks* require no great skill or special tools, and the small amount of time they take to perform could prove to be very well spent, for example:

☐ Keeping an eye on tyre condition and pressures, will not only help to stop them wearing out prematurely, but could also save your life.

☐ Many breakdowns are caused by electrical problems. Battery-related faults are particularly common, and a quick check on a regular basis will often prevent the majority of these.

☐ If your car develops a brake fluid leak, the first time you might know about it is when your brakes don't work properly. Checking the level regularly will give advance warning of this kind of problem.

☐ If the oil or coolant levels run low, the cost of repairing any engine damage will be far greater than fixing the leak, for example.

Underbonnet check points

◄ **1.2 litre petrol (1.4 litre similar)**

A *Engine oil level dipstick*

B *Engine oil filler cap*

C *Coolant expansion tank*

D *Brake (and clutch) fluid reservoir*

E *Screen washer fluid reservoir*

F *Battery*

◄ **1.4 litre diesel (1.9 litre similar)**

A *Engine oil level dipstick*

B *Engine oil filler cap*

C *Coolant expansion tank*

D *Brake (and clutch) fluid reservoir*

E *Screen washer fluid reservoir*

F *Battery*

Engine oil level

Before you start

✔ Make sure that the car is on level ground.
✔ Check the oil level before the car is driven, or at least 5 minutes after the engine has been switched off.

HAYNES HiNT *If the oil is checked immediately after driving the vehicle, some of the oil will remain in the upper engine components, resulting in an inaccurate reading on the dipstick.*

The correct oil

Modern engines place great demands on their oil. It is very important that the correct oil for your car is used (see *Lubricants and fluids*).

Car care

● If you have to add oil frequently, you should check whether you have any oil leaks. Place some clean paper under the car overnight, and check for stains in the morning. If there are no leaks, then the engine may be burning oil.
● Always maintain the level between the upper and lower dipstick marks. If the level is too low, severe engine damage may occur. Oil seal failure may result if the engine is overfilled by adding too much oil.

1 The dipstick is often brightly coloured for easy identification (see *Underbonnet check points* for exact location). Withdraw the dipstick and use a clean rag or paper towel to wipe the oil from it. Insert the dipstick into the tube as far as it will go, then withdraw it again.

3 Oil is added through the filler cap aperture. Unscrew the cap.

2 Note the level on the end of the dipstick. It is satisfactory for the level to be anywhere in the dotted area. The notches on the dipstick represent the absolute MAX and MIN marks.

4 Place some cloth rags around the filler cap aperture, then top-up the level. A funnel may help to reduce spillage. Add the oil slowly, checking the level on the dipstick frequently. Avoid overfilling (see *Car care*).

Coolant level

Warning: Do not attempt to remove the expansion tank pressure cap when the engine is hot, as there is a very great risk of scalding. Do not leave open containers of coolant about, as it is poisonous.

Car care

● With a sealed-type cooling system, adding coolant should not be necessary on a regular basis. If frequent topping-up is required, it is likely there is a leak. Check the radiator, all hoses and joint faces for signs of staining or wetness, and rectify as necessary.

● It is important that antifreeze is used in the cooling system all year round, not just during the winter months. Don't top up with water alone, as the antifreeze will become diluted.

1 The coolant level varies with the temperature of the engine. When the engine is cold, the coolant level should be between the MIN and MAX marks.

2 If topping-up is necessary, wait until the engine is cold. Slowly unscrew the cap to release any pressure present in the cooling system, and remove the cap.

3 Add a mixture of water and the specified antifreeze (see *Lubricants and fluids*) to the expansion tank until the coolant level is halfway between the level marks. Refit the cap and tighten it securely. Note that some antifreeze is supplied pre-mixed with water ('ready to use'), and that no more water should be added to it.

Brake (and clutch) fluid level

Note: *On manual transmission models, the fluid reservoir also supplies the clutch master cylinder with fluid.*

Before you start
✔ Make sure that the car is on level ground.
✔ Cleanliness is of great importance when dealing with the braking system, so take care to clean around the reservoir cap before topping-up. Use only clean brake fluid.

Safety first!
● If the reservoir requires repeated topping-up this is an indication of a fluid leak somewhere in the system, which should be investigated immediately.

● If a leak is suspected, the car should not be driven until the braking system has been checked. Never take any risks where brakes are concerned

⚠ **Warning: Brake fluid can harm your eyes and damage painted surfaces, so use extreme caution when handling and pouring it. Do not use fluid that has been standing open for some time, as it absorbs moisture from the air, which can cause a dangerous loss of braking effectiveness.**

1 The MIN and MAX marks are indicated on the reservoir. The fluid level must be kept between the marks at all times. Note that the level will drop naturally as the brake pad linings wear, but must never be allowed to fall below the MIN mark.

2 If topping-up is necessary, first wipe clean the area around the filler cap to prevent dirt entering the hydraulic system. Unscrew and remove the reservoir cap.

3 Carefully add fluid, taking care not to spill it onto the surrounding components. Use only the specified fluid (see *Lubricants and fluids*); mixing different types can cause damage to the system. On completion, securely refit the cap and wipe away any spilt fluid.

Screen washer fluid level

● Screenwash additives not only keep the windscreen clean during bad weather, they also prevent the washer system freezing in cold weather – which is when you are likely to need it most. Don't top-up using plain water, as the screenwash will become diluted, and will freeze in cold weather.

Caution: On no account use engine coolant antifreeze in the screen washer system – this may damage the paintwork.

1 The screenwash fluid reservoir is located on the left-hand side of the engine compartment, behind the headlight. Pull up the filler cap to release it from the reservoir.

2 When topping-up the reservoir, a screenwash additive should be added in the quantities recommended on the bottle.

Battery

Caution: Before carrying out any work on the vehicle battery, read the precautions given in 'Safety first!' at the start of this manual.

✔ Make sure that the battery tray is in good condition, and that the clamp is tight. Corrosion on the tray, retaining clamp and the battery itself can be removed with a solution of water and baking soda. Thoroughly rinse all cleaned areas with water. Any metal parts damaged by corrosion should be covered with a zinc-based primer, then painted.

✔ Periodically (approximately every three months), check the charge condition of the battery as described in Chapter 5A. A 'magic eye' charge indicator is fitted to the standard battery – if the indicator shows green, then the battery is in good condition and charged up. If the indicator turns darker, eventually to black, then the battery requires charging. If the indicator shows clear/yellow, then the electrolyte is low and in a critical condition, and should be topped-up with distilled water. If charging the battery does not return the eye to green, the battery should be scrapped

✔ If the battery is flat, and you need to jump start your vehicle, see *Roadside Repairs*.

1 The battery is located in the front left-hand corner of the engine compartment. Release the catch at the back and swing the battery cover (where fitted) upwards and forwards to gain access to the battery terminals.

2 Check the security and condition of all the battery and fuse connections. The exterior of the battery should be inspected periodically for damage such as a cracked case or cover.

3 If corrosion (white, fluffy deposits) is evident, remove the cables from the battery terminals (refer to Chapter 5A), clean them with a small wire brush, then refit them. Automotive stores sell a tool for cleaning the battery post . . .

4 . . . as well as the battery cable clamps. **Note:** *Seat specifically prohibit the use of grease on the battery terminals*.

Wiper blades

1 Check the condition of the wiper blades; if they are cracked or show any signs of deterioration, or if the glass swept area is smeared, renew them. For maximum clarity of vision, wiper blades should be renewed annually, as a matter of course.

2 To remove a windscreen wiper blade, pull the arm fully away from the screen until it locks. Swivel the blade through 90°, then slide the blade away from the windscreen and off the arm.

3 Where applicable, don't forget to check the tailgate wiper blade as well. To remove the blade, lift it off the glass and unclip it from the end of the arm.

Tyre condition and pressure

It is very important that tyres are in good condition, and at the correct pressure - having a tyre failure at any speed is highly dangerous. Tyre wear is influenced by driving style - harsh braking and acceleration, or fast cornering, will all produce more rapid tyre wear. As a general rule, the front tyres wear out faster than the rears. Interchanging the tyres from front to rear ("rotating" the tyres) may result in more even wear. However, if this is completely effective, you may have the expense of replacing all four tyres at once! Remove any nails or stones embedded in the tread before they penetrate the tyre to cause deflation. If removal of a nail does reveal that the tyre has been punctured, refit the nail so that its point of penetration is marked. Then immediately change the wheel, and have the tyre repaired by a tyre dealer.

Regularly check the tyres for damage in the form of cuts or bulges, especially in the sidewalls. Periodically remove the wheels, and clean any dirt or mud from the inside and outside surfaces. Examine the wheel rims for signs of rusting, corrosion or other damage. Light alloy wheels are easily damaged by "kerbing" whilst parking; steel wheels may also become dented or buckled. A new wheel is very often the only way to overcome severe damage.

New tyres should be balanced when they are fitted, but it may become necessary to re-balance them as they wear, or if the balance weights fitted to the wheel rim should fall off. Unbalanced tyres will wear more quickly, as will the steering and suspension components. Wheel imbalance is normally signified by vibration, particularly at a certain speed (typically around 50 mph). If this vibration is felt only through the steering, then it is likely that just the front wheels need balancing. If, however, the vibration is felt through the whole car, the rear wheels could be out of balance. Wheel balancing should be carried out by a tyre dealer or garage.

1 Tread Depth - visual check
The original tyres have tread wear safety bands (B), which will appear when the tread depth reaches approximately 1.6 mm. The band positions are indicated by a triangular mark on the tyre sidewall (A).

2 Tread Depth - manual check
Alternatively, tread wear can be monitored with a simple, inexpensive device known as a tread depth indicator gauge.

3 Tyre Pressure Check
Check the tyre pressures regularly with the tyres cold. Do not adjust the tyre pressures immediately after the vehicle has been used, or an inaccurate setting will result.

Tyre tread wear patterns

Shoulder Wear

Underinflation (wear on both sides)
Under-inflation will cause overheating of the tyre, because the tyre will flex too much, and the tread will not sit correctly on the road surface. This will cause a loss of grip and excessive wear, not to mention the danger of sudden tyre failure due to heat build-up.
Check and adjust pressures
Incorrect wheel camber (wear on one side)
Repair or renew suspension parts
Hard cornering
Reduce speed!

Centre Wear

Overinflation
Over-inflation will cause rapid wear of the centre part of the tyre tread, coupled with reduced grip, harsher ride, and the danger of shock damage occurring in the tyre casing.
Check and adjust pressures

If you sometimes have to inflate your car's tyres to the higher pressures specified for maximum load or sustained high speed, don't forget to reduce the pressures to normal afterwards.

Uneven Wear

Front tyres may wear unevenly as a result of wheel misalignment. Most tyre dealers and garages can check and adjust the wheel alignment (or "tracking") for a modest charge.
Incorrect camber or castor
Repair or renew suspension parts
Malfunctioning suspension
Repair or renew suspension parts
Unbalanced wheel
Balance tyres
Incorrect toe setting
Adjust front wheel alignment
Note: *The feathered edge of the tread which typifies toe wear is best checked by feel.*

Electrical systems

✔ Check all external lights and the horn. Refer to the appropriate Sections of Chapter 12 for details if any of the circuits are found to be inoperative.

✔ Visually check all accessible wiring connectors, harnesses and retaining clips for security, and for signs of chafing or damage.

If you need to check your brake lights and indicators unaided, back up to a wall or garage door and operate the lights. The reflected light should show if they are working properly.

1 If a single indicator light, brake light or headlight has failed, it is likely that a bulb has blown and will need to be renewed. Refer to Chapter 12 for details. If both brake lights have failed, it is possible that the brake light switch operated by the brake pedal has failed. Refer to Chapter 9 for details.

2 If more than one indicator light or headlight has failed, it is likely that either a fuse has blown or that there is a fault in the circuit (see *Electrical fault finding* in Chapter 12). The main fuses are in the fusebox beneath a cover on the right-hand end of the facia panel. Use a small screwdriver to prise off the cover. The circuits protected by the fuses are shown on the inside of the cover. Additional heavy duty fuses and fusible links are in the fusebox located on top of the battery.

3 To renew a blown fuse, pull it from its location in the fusebox, using the plastic pliers provided. Fit a new fuse of the same rating, available from car accessory shops. It is important that you find the reason that the fuse blew (see *Electrical fault finding* in Chapter 12).

Lubricants and fluids

Engine (petrol) . . . . Multigrade engine oil, viscosity SAE 5W/30 to 10W/40, meeting specification VW 501 01, 502 00, 504 00 or better

Engine (diesel)

Without particulate filter . . . . Multigrade engine oil, viscosity SAE 5W/30 to 10W/40, meeting specification VW 505 01, 506 01, 507 00 or better

With particulate filter (engine codes BMS and BMT) . . . . Multigrade engine oil, viscosity SAE 5W/30 to 10W/40, meeting specification VW 507 00 or better

Cooling system . . . . Seat G12 coolant (antifreeze and corrosion protection)

Manual transmission

5-speed transmission . . . . API GL4 gear oil, viscosity SAE 75W

6-speed transmission . . . . Seat synthetic gear oil, viscosity SAE 70W/75

Automatic transmission

Main transmission . . . . Seat ATF

Final drive . . . . Seat G50 synthetic gear oil, viscosity SAE 75W/90

Braking and clutch systems . . . . Hydraulic fluid to US FMVSS 116 or DOT 4

Power steering reservoir . . . . Seat hydraulic oil G 002 000

Tyre pressures

Note: *The recommended tyre pressures for each Ibiza are given on a sticker attached to the inside of the fuel filler flap. The pressures given are for the original-equipment tyres – the recommended pressures may vary if any other make or type of tyre is fitted; check with the tyre manufacturer or supplier for latest recommendations. The following pressures are typical.*

	Front	Rear
Normal load	2.0 bar (29 psi)	2.2 bar (32 psi)
Full load	2.2 bar (32 psi)	2.8 bar (41 psi)

Note: *Where a space-saver spare tyre is fitted, its pressure must be 4.2 bar (61 psi).*

Chapter 1 Part A:
Routine maintenance and servicing – petrol models

Contents

Degrees of difficulty

| Easy, suitable for novice with little experience | | Fairly easy, suitable for beginner with some experience | | Fairly difficult, suitable for competent DIY mechanic | | Difficult, suitable for experienced DIY mechanic | | Very difficult, suitable for expert DIY or professional | |

Lubricants and fluids . . . .   Refer to end of *Weekly checks* on page 0•16

Engine codes
1.2 litre . . . .   AZQ, BME, BXV
1.4 litre . . . .   AUB, BBY, BBZ, BKY and BXW

Capacities

Engine oil – including filter
1.2 litre . . . .   2.9 litres
1.4 litre . . . .   3.2 litres

Cooling system
1.2 litre . . . .   5.1 litres
1.4 litre . . . .   5.5 litres

Transmission
Manual transmission . . . .   1.9 litres
Automatic transmission . . . .   5.7 litres

Fuel tank (approximate) . . . .   45 litres

Cooling system
Antifreeze mixture:
  40% antifreeze . . . .   Protection down to -25°C
  50% antifreeze . . . .   Protection down to -35°C
Note: *Refer to antifreeze manufacturer for latest recommendations.*

Ignition system

Spark plugs:	Type	Electrode gap
1.2 litre	Bosch F7 HER2	0.9 mm
	NGK ZFR5P-G	0.8 mm
1.4 litre:		
Engine codes AUB, BBY, BBZ and BKY	NGK BKUR 6ET-10	1.0 mm
Engine code BXW	NGK ZFR6T-11G	N/A

Brakes
Brake pad minimum thickness:
  Including backing plate:
    Front . . . .   7.0 mm
    Rear . . . .   7.6 mm
  Friction lining only:
    Front and rear . . . .   2.0 mm
Rear brake shoe friction material minimum thickness . . . .   1.5 mm

Torque wrench settings

	Nm	lbf ft
Alternator mounting bolt	20	15
Automatic transmission level plug	15	11
Manual gearbox filler/level plug	25	18
Oil filter housing cap (1.2 litre engines)	25	18
Roadwheel bolts	120	89
Spark plugs	30	22
Sump drain plug	30	22

The maintenance intervals in this manual are provided with the assumption that you, not the dealer, will be carrying out the work. These are the minimum intervals recommended by us for cars driven daily. If you wish to keep your car in peak condition at all times, you may wish to perform some of these procedures more often. We encourage frequent maintenance, since it enhances the efficiency, performance and resale value of your car.

When the vehicle is new, it should be serviced by a dealer service department (or other workshop recognised by the vehicle manufacturer as providing the same standard of service) in order to preserve the warranty. The vehicle manufacturer may reject warranty claims if you are unable to prove that servicing has been carried out as and when specified, using only original equipment parts or parts certified to be of equivalent quality.

All Seat models are equipped with a service interval display indicator in the instrument panel. Every time the engine is started the panel will illuminate for approximately 20 seconds with service information. Once the service interval has been reached, the display will flash 'INSP' for a service.

Note that the following schedule is our recommendation for service intervals and service tasks.

Every 250 miles or weekly

☐ Refer to *Weekly checks*

Every 5000 miles or 6 months, whichever comes first

☐ Renew the engine oil and filter (Section 3)

Note: *Seat recommend that the engine oil and filter are changed every 10 000 miles or 12 months. However, oil and filter changes are good for the engine and we recommend that the oil and filter are renewed more frequently, especially if the vehicle is used on a lot of short journeys.*

Every 10 000 miles or 12 months, whichever comes first

Note: *In addition to the item given above.*

☐ Brake pad/lining check (Section 4)
☐ Check the condition of the exhaust system and its mountings (Section 5)
☐ Check all underbonnet components and hoses for fluid and oil leaks (Section 6)
☐ Check the condition of the auxiliary drivebelt (Section 7)
☐ Check the coolant antifreeze concentration (Section 8)
☐ Check the brake hydraulic circuit for leaks and damage (Section 9)
☐ Check the headlight beam adjustment (Section 10)
☐ Check the underbody protection for damage (Section 11)
☐ Check the condition of the driveshafts (Section 12)
☐ Check the steering and suspension components for condition and security (Section 13)
☐ Check the battery condition, security and electrolyte level (Section 14)
☐ Lubricate all hinges and locks (Section 15)
☐ Check the condition of the airbag unit(s) (Section 16)
☐ Check the operation of the windscreen/tailgate/ headlight washer system(s) (as applicable) (Section 17)
☐ Check the engine management self-diagnosis memory for faults (Section 18)
☐ Check the operation of the sunroof and lubricate the guide rails (Section 19)
☐ Carry out a road test and check exhaust emissions (Section 20)
☐ Reset the service indicator (Section 21)

Every 20 000 miles or 2 years, whichever comes first

☐ Renew the pollen filter element (Section 22)
☐ Check the manual transmission oil level (Section 23)

Every 40 000 miles or 4 years, whichever comes first

☐ Renew the air filter element (Section 24)
☐ Renew the spark plugs (Section 25)
☐ Check the power steering hydraulic fluid level (Section 26)
☐ Check the automatic transmission fluid level (Section 27)
☐ Renew the timing belt and tensioner roller – 1.4 litre engines only (Section 28)*

* *Seat specify timing belt inspection after the first 60 000 miles and then every 20 000 miles until the renewal interval of 120 000 miles. However, if the car is used mainly for short journeys, we recommend that this shorter renewal interval is adhered to. The belt renewal interval is very much up to the individual owner but, bearing in mind that severe engine damage will result if the belt breaks in use, we recommend the shorter interval.*

Every 2 years

☐ Renew the brake (and clutch) fluid (Section 29)
☐ Renew the coolant (Section 30)*

* *This work is not included in the Seat schedule, and should not be required if the recommended G12 coolant antifreeze/inhibitor is used.*

Underbonnet view of a 1.2 litre model (1.4 litre model similar)

1   Engine oil filler cap
2   Engine oil dipstick
3   Coolant expansion tank
4   Windscreen/headlight washer fluid reservoir
5   Power steering fluid reservoir
6   Ignition coils and spark plugs
7   Fuel injectors
8   Front suspension strut upper mountings
9   Brake/clutch master cylinder fluid reservoir
10 Brake ABS unit
11 Engine management ECM
12 Battery
13 Oxygen (lambda) sensor
14 Oil filter housing
15 Throttle body

Front underbody view of a 1.2 litre model (others similar)

1   Sump drain plug
2   Manual transmission oil filler/level plug
3   Rear engine mounting/link
4   Driveshaft
5   Anti-roll bar link
6   Front brake caliper
7   Steering track rod
8   Front suspension lower arm
9   Front suspension subframe
10 Auxiliary drivebelt
11 Air conditioning compressor
12 Cooling system drain plug
13 Oxygen sensor

Rear underbody view of a 1.2 litre model (others similar)

1 Rear axle assembly
2 Fuel tank
3 Rear brake hoses
4 Rear suspension coil springs
5 Handbrake cables
6 Rear suspension shock absorbers
7 Exhaust rear silencer and tailpipe
8 Fuel tank filler pipe
9 Fuel filter

Maintenance procedures

1 Introduction

This Chapter is designed to help the home mechanic maintain his/her car for safety, economy, long life and peak performance.

The Chapter contains a master maintenance schedule, followed by Sections dealing specifically with each task in the schedule. Visual checks, adjustments, component renewal and other helpful items are included. Refer to the accompanying illustrations of the engine compartment and the underside of the car for the locations of the various components.

Servicing your car will provide a planned maintenance programme, which should result in a long and reliable service life. This is a comprehensive plan, so maintaining some items but not others will not produce the same results.

As you service your car, you will discover that many of the procedures can – and should – be grouped together, because of the particular procedure being performed, or because of the proximity of two otherwise unrelated components to one another. For example, if the car is raised for any reason, the exhaust can be inspected at the same time as the suspension and steering components.

The first step in this maintenance programme is to prepare yourself before the actual work begins. Read through all the Sections relevant to the work to be carried out, then make a list and gather all the parts and tools required. If a problem is encountered, seek advice from a parts specialist, or a dealer service department.

2 Regular maintenance

1 If, from the time the car is new, the routine maintenance schedule is followed closely, and frequent checks are made of fluid levels and high-wear items, as suggested throughout this manual, the engine will be kept in relatively good running condition, and the need for additional work will be minimised.
2 It is possible that there will be times when the engine is running poorly due to the lack of regular maintenance. This is even more likely if a used car, which has not received regular and frequent maintenance checks, is purchased. In such cases, additional work may need to be carried out, outside of the regular maintenance intervals.
3 If engine wear is suspected, a compression test (refer to Chapter 2A or 2B) will provide valuable information regarding the overall performance of the main internal components. Such a test can be used as a basis to decide on the extent of the work to be carried out. If, for example, a compression test indicates serious internal engine wear, conventional maintenance as described in this Chapter will not greatly improve the performance of the engine, and may prove a waste of time and money, unless extensive overhaul work is carried out first.
4 The following series of operations are those most often required to improve the performance of a generally poor-running engine:

Primary operations

a) Clean, inspect and test the battery (See 'Weekly checks').
b) Check all the engine-related fluids (See 'Weekly checks').
c) Check the condition and tension of the auxiliary drivebelt (Section 7).
d) Renew the spark plugs (Section 25).
e) Check the condition of the air filter, and renew if necessary (Section 24).
f) Check the condition of all hoses, and check for fluid leaks (Section 6).

5 If the above operations do not prove fully effective, carry out the following secondary operations:

Secondary operations

All items listed under Primary operations, plus the following:

a) Check the charging system (see Chapter 5A).
b) Check the ignition system (see Chapter 5B).
c) Check the fuel system (see Chapter 4A).
d) Renew the ignition HT leads (where applicable).

3.2a Undo the bolts (arrowed) and remove the engine undershield

3.2b Pull the engine cover/air filter housing upwards from the rubber mountings . . .

3.2c . . . and disconnect the breather hose

Every 5000 miles or 6 months

3 Engine oil and filter renewal

1 Frequent oil and filter changes are the most important maintenance procedures which can be undertaken by the DIY owner. As engine oil ages, it becomes diluted and contaminated, which leads to premature engine wear.
2 Before starting this procedure, gather all the necessary tools and materials. Also make sure that you have plenty of clean rags and

3.3 Undo the engine oil drain plug (arrowed) with an Allen key or bit

HAYNES HiNT

Keep the drain plug pressed into the sump while unscrewing it by hand the last couple of turns. As the plug releases, move it away sharply so the stream of oil issuing from the sump runs into the container, not up your sleeve.

newspapers handy, to mop-up any spills. Ideally, the engine oil should be warm, as it will drain better, and more built-up sludge will be removed with it. Take care, however, not to touch the exhaust or any other hot parts of the engine when working under the car. To avoid any possibility of scalding, and to protect yourself from possible skin irritants and other harmful contaminants in used engine oils, it is advisable to wear gloves when carrying out this work. Access to the underside of the car will be greatly improved if it can be raised on a lift, driven onto ramps, or jacked up and supported on axle stands (see *Jacking and vehicle support*). Whichever method is chosen, make sure that the car remains level, or if it is at an angle, that the drain plug is at the lowest point. Where necessary, undo the retaining bolts and remove the engine undershield(s), then also remove the engine top cover **(see illustrations)**. Disconnect the breather hose from the cylinder head cover as the top cover is removed.
3 Using an Allen key or bit, slacken the drain plug about half a turn **(see illustration)**. Position the draining container under the drain plug, then remove the plug completely **(see Haynes Hint)**. Recover the sealing ring from the drain plug.
4 Allow some time for the old oil to drain, noting that it may be necessary to reposition the container as the oil flow slows to a trickle.
5 After all the oil has drained, wipe off the drain plug with a clean rag, and fit a new

sealing washer. Clean the area around the drain plug opening, and refit the plug. Tighten the plug to the specified torque.
6 If the filter is also to be renewed, move the container into position under the oil filter. On 1.2 litre engines, the filter is located beneath a cap on the front right-hand end of the engine. On 1.4 litre engines, the canister-type filter is located on the front of the engine.
7 On 1.2 litre engines, unscrew the cap several turns from the oil filter housing until its sealing face is level with the side peg. Leave the cap in this position for at least one minute, to allow the oil to drain from the filter and housing. Cover the alternator with cloth rags, to prevent entry of oil. Completely unscrew the cap and withdraw it together with the filter. If the filter is stuck to the cap, tap the cap bottom extension lightly on a wooden base to release the filter. Using a screwdriver, remove the O-ring seal from the cap and discard it – a new one must be used when refitting **(see illustrations)**.
8 On 1.4 litre engines, using an oil filter removal tool if necessary, slacken the filter initially, then unscrew it by hand the rest of the way. Empty the oil in the filter into the container. Check the old filter to make sure that the rubber sealing ring has not stuck to the engine. If it has, carefully remove it.
9 Use a clean rag to remove all oil, dirt and sludge from the filter housing and cap, or filter sealing area (as applicable).
10 On 1.2 litre engines, fit a new O-ring seal

3.7a Unscrew the cap and remove the oil filter

3.7b Tap the bottom extension of the cap to release the filter to the cap, then insert the new filter in the housing and screw on the cap. Tighten the cap to the specified torque. Wipe away any excess oil.

11 On 1.4 litre engines, apply a light coating of clean engine oil to the sealing ring on the new filter, then screw it into position on the engine. Tighten the filter firmly by hand only – do not use any tools. Wipe away any excess oil.

12 Remove the old oil and all tools from under the car. Refit the engine undershield(s), tighten the retaining bolts securely, then lower the car to the ground. Also refit the engine top cover where applicable.

13 Remove the dipstick, then unscrew the oil filler cap from the cylinder head cover. Fill the engine, using the correct grade and type of oil (see *Lubricants and fluids*). An oil can spout or funnel may help to reduce spillage. Pour in half the specified quantity of oil first, then wait a few minutes for the oil to run to the sump. Continue adding oil a small quantity at a time until the level is up to the maximum mark on the dipstick. Refit the filler cap.

14 Start the engine and run it for a few minutes; check for leaks around the oil filter seal and the sump drain plug. Note that

there may be a few seconds delay before the oil pressure warning light goes out when the engine is started, as the oil circulates through the engine oil galleries and the new oil filter (where fitted) before the pressure builds-up.

15 Switch off the engine, and wait a few minutes for the oil to settle in the sump once more. With the new oil circulated and the filter completely full, recheck the level on the dipstick, and add more oil as necessary.

16 Dispose of the used engine oil safely, with reference to *General repair procedures* in the Reference section of this manual.

Every 10 000 miles or 12 months

4 Brake pad/lining check

Front and rear disc brakes

1 The outer brake pads can be checked without removing the wheels, by observing the brake pads through the holes in the wheels **(see illustration)**. If necessary, remove the wheel trim. The thickness of the pad lining must not be less than the dimension given in the Specifications.

2 If the outer pads are worn near their limits, it is worthwhile checking the inner pads as well. Jack up car and support it on axle stands (see *Jacking and vehicle support*). Remove the roadwheels.

3 Use a steel rule to check the thickness of the brake pads, and compare with the minimum thickness given in the Specifications **(see illustration)**.

4 For a comprehensive check, the brake pads should be removed and cleaned. The operation of the caliper can then also be checked, and the condition of the brake disc itself can be fully examined on both sides. Refer to Chapter 9.

5 If any pad's friction material is worn to the specified minimum thickness or less, all four pads at the front or rear, as applicable, must be renewed as a set. Never renew the pads on just one wheel, as uneven braking will result.

6 On completion of the check, refit the roadwheels and lower the car to the ground.

Rear drum brakes

7 Chock the front wheels, then jack up the rear of the car and support it on axle stands (see *Jacking and vehicle support*).

8 For a quick check, the thickness of friction material remaining on one of the brake shoes can be observed through the hole in the brake backplate which is exposed by prising out the rubber sealing grommet. If a rod of the same diameter as the specified minimum friction material thickness is placed against the shoe friction material, the amount of wear can be assessed. An electric torch or inspection

light will probably be required. If the friction material on any shoe is worn down to the specified minimum thickness or less, all four shoes must be renewed as a set.

9 For a comprehensive check, the brake drum should be removed and cleaned. This will allow the wheel cylinders to be checked, and the condition of the brake drum itself to be fully examined (see Chapter 9).

10 On completion of the check, refit the roadwheels where removed, and lower the car to the ground.

5 Exhaust system check

1 With the engine cold (at least an hour after the car has been driven), check the complete exhaust system from the engine to the end of the tailpipe. The exhaust system is most easily checked with the car raised on a hoist, or supported on axle stands, so that the exhaust components are readily visible and accessible (see *Jacking and vehicle support*).

2 Check the exhaust pipes and connections for evidence of leaks, severe corrosion and damage. Make sure that all brackets and mountings are in good condition, and that all relevant nuts and bolts are tight. Leakage at any of the joints or in other parts of the system will usually show up as a black sooty stain in the vicinity of the leak.

4.1 The outer brake pads can be observed through the holes in the wheels

3 Rattles and other noises can often be traced to the exhaust system, especially the brackets and mountings. Try to move the pipes and silencers. If the components are able to come into contact with the body or suspension parts, secure the system with new mountings. Otherwise separate the joints (if possible) and twist the pipes as necessary to provide additional clearance.

6 Hose and fluid leak check

1 Visually inspect the engine joint faces, gaskets and seals for any signs of water or oil leaks. Pay particular attention to the areas around the camshaft cover, cylinder head, oil filter and sump joint faces. Bear in mind that, over a period of time, some very slight seepage from these areas is to be expected – what you are really looking for is any indication of a serious leak. Should a leak be found, renew the offending gasket or oil seal by referring to the appropriate Chapters in this manual.

H31925

4.3 The thickness (a) of the brake pads must not be less than the specified amount

HAYNES HiNT

A leak in the cooling system will usually show up as white- or antifreeze-coloured deposits on the area adjoining the leak.

2 Also check the security and condition of all the engine-related pipes and hoses. Ensure that all cable-ties or securing clips are in place and in good condition. Clips which are broken or missing can lead to chafing of the hoses, pipes or wiring, which could cause more serious problems in the future.

3 Carefully check the radiator hoses and heater hoses along their entire length. Renew any hose which is cracked, swollen or deteriorated. Cracks will show up better if the hose is squeezed. Pay close attention to the hose clips that secure the hoses to the cooling system components. Hose clips can pinch and puncture hoses, resulting in cooling system leaks.

4 Inspect all the cooling system components (hoses, joint faces, etc) for leaks **(see Haynes Hint)**. Where any problems of this nature are found on system components, renew the component or gasket with reference to Chapter 3.

5 Where applicable, inspect the automatic transmission fluid cooler hoses for leaks or deterioration.

6 With the car raised, inspect the petrol tank and filler neck for punctures, cracks and other damage. The connection between the filler neck and tank is especially critical. Sometimes a rubber filler neck or connecting hose will leak due to loose retaining clamps or deteriorated rubber.

7 Carefully check all rubber hoses and metal fuel lines leading away from the petrol tank. Check for loose connections, deteriorated hoses, crimped lines, and other damage. Pay particular attention to the vent pipes and hoses, which often loop up around the filler neck and can become blocked or crimped. Follow the lines to the front of the car, carefully inspecting them all the way. Renew damaged sections as necessary.

8 From within the engine compartment, check the security of all fuel hose attachments and pipe unions, and inspect the fuel hoses and vacuum hoses for kinks, chafing and deterioration.

9 Where applicable, check the condition of the power steering fluid hoses and pipes.

7 Auxiliary drivebelt check and renewal

Check

1 Apply the handbrake, then jack up the front of the car and support it on axle stands (see *Jacking and vehicle support*).

2 Using a socket on the crankshaft pulley bolt, turn the engine slowly clockwise so that the full length of the auxiliary drivebelt can be examined. Look for cracks, splitting and fraying on the surface of the belt; check also for signs of glazing (shiny patches) and separation of the belt plies. Use a mirror to check the underside of the drivebelt **(see illustration)**. If damage or wear is visible, or if there are traces of oil or grease on it, the belt should be renewed as follows:

Renewal

3 For improved access, apply the handbrake, then jack up the front of the car and support it on axle stands (see *Jacking and vehicle support*). Remove the right-hand front roadwheel and wheel arch liner.

4 On 1.2 litre engines, lever off the cover (where fitted) from the tensioner pulley, then use a Torx key or spanner (as applicable) to turn the pulley anti-clockwise against the tension spring **(see illustration)**. If necessary, the tensioner may be retained with a drill bit inserted through the hole in the pulley arm and body.

5 On 1.4 litre engines with air conditioning, use a spanner to turn the tensioner central bolt clockwise to release the tension on the drivebelt **(see illustration)**.

6 On 1.4 litre engines without air conditioning, a tensioner spring is fitted between the alternator and bracket to tension the drivebelt. Loosen the upper pivot bolt and lower tension bolt, then swivel the alternator towards the engine to release the tension on the drivebelt.

7 Note how the drivebelt is routed, then remove it from the crankshaft pulley, alternator pulley and air conditioning compressor pulley (where applicable).

8 On all except 1.4 litre engines without air conditioning, locate the new drivebelt on the pulleys, and release the tensioner. Check that the belt is located correctly in the multi-grooves in the pulleys.

9 On 1.4 litre engines without air conditioning, push the alternator towards the engine to locate the drivebelt on the pulley, then release it so that the spring tensions the drivebelt. Before tightening the mounting bolts, Seat state that the engine must be cranked with the starter approximately 10 turns (only a second or two's cranking). To do this without starting the engine, disable the ignition system by disconnecting the wiring plug from the DIS ignition module (engine code AUB) or ignition coils (engine codes BBY, BKY, BBZ and BXW). The drivebelt is now correctly tensioned. Tighten the lower mounting bolt followed by the upper mounting bolt to the specified torque.

10 Refit the wheel arch liner and roadwheel, and lower the car to the ground.

8 Antifreeze check

1 The cooling system should be filled with the recommended G12 antifreeze and corrosion protection fluid – do not mix this antifreeze with any other type. Over a period of time, the concentration of fluid may be reduced due to topping-up with water (this can be avoided by topping-up with the correct antifreeze mixture – see Specifications) or fluid loss. If loss of coolant has been evident, it is important to

7.2 Check the underside of the auxiliary drivebelt with a mirror

7.4 Use a spanner to turn the tensioner and release the auxiliary drivebelt – 1.2 litre engines

7.5 Auxiliary drivebelt removal – 1.4 litre engine with air conditioning

make the necessary repair before adding fresh fluid.

2 With the engine cold, carefully remove the cap from the expansion tank. If the engine is not completely cold, place a cloth rag over the cap before removing it, and remove it slowly to allow any pressure to escape.

3 Antifreeze checkers (hydrometers) are available from car accessory shops. Draw some coolant from the expansion tank and observe how many plastic balls are floating in the checker. Usually, 2 or 3 balls must be floating for the correct concentration of antifreeze, but follow the tool manufacturer's instructions.

4 If the concentration is incorrect, it will be necessary to either withdraw some coolant and add antifreeze, or alternatively drain the old coolant and add fresh coolant of the correct concentration (see Section 30).

9 Brake hydraulic circuit check

1 Check the entire brake hydraulic circuit for leaks and damage. Start by checking the master cylinder in the engine compartment. At the same time, check the vacuum servo unit and ABS units for signs of fluid leakage.

2 Raise the front and rear of the car and support it on axle stands (see *Jacking and vehicle support*). Check the rigid hydraulic brake lines for corrosion and damage.

3 At the front of the car, check that the flexible hydraulic hoses to the calipers are not twisted or chafing on any of the surrounding suspension components. Turn the steering on full lock to make this check. Also check that the hoses are not brittle or cracked.

4 Lower the car to the ground after making the checks.

10 Headlight beam adjustment

1 Accurate adjustment of the headlight beam is only possible using optical beam-setting equipment, and this work should therefore be carried out by a Seat dealer or service station with the necessary facilities.

2 Basic adjustments can be carried out in an emergency, and further details are given in Chapter 12.

11 Underbody protection check

Raise and support the car on axle stands (see *Jacking and vehicle support*). Using an electric torch or lead light, inspect the entire underside of the car, paying particular attention to the wheel arches. Look for any damage to the flexible underbody coating,

which may crack or flake off with age, leading to corrosion (note, however, that the Ibiza does without such a coating for much of the underbody, and has instead a pair of plastic underbody panels at the front).

Also check that the wheel arch liners are securely attached with any clips provided – if they come loose, dirt may get in behind the liners and defeat their purpose. If there is any damage to the underseal, or any corrosion, it should be repaired before the damage gets too serious.

12 Driveshaft check

1 With the car raised and securely supported on stands, slowly rotate the roadwheel. Inspect the condition of the outer constant velocity (CV) joint rubber gaiters, squeezing the gaiters to open out the folds. Check for signs of cracking, splits or deterioration of the rubber, which may allow the grease to escape, and lead to water and grit entry into the joint. Also check the security and condition of the retaining clips. Repeat these checks on the inner joints **(see illustration)**. If any damage or deterioration is found, the gaiters should be renewed (see Chapter 8).

2 At the same time, check the general condition of the CV joints themselves by first holding the driveshaft and attempting to rotate the wheel. Repeat this check by holding the inner joint and attempting to rotate the driveshaft. Any appreciable movement indicates wear in the joints, wear in the driveshaft splines, or a loose driveshaft retaining nut.

13 Steering and suspension check

1 Raise the front and rear of the car, and securely support it on axle stands (see *Jacking and vehicle support*).

2 Visually inspect the track rod end balljoint dust cover, the lower front suspension balljoint dust cover, and the steering rack-and-pinion gaiters for splits, chafing or deterioration. Any wear of these components will cause loss of lubricant, together with dirt and water entry, resulting in rapid deterioration of the balljoints or steering gear.

3 Check the power steering fluid hoses for chafing or deterioration, and the pipe and hose unions for fluid leaks. Also check for signs of fluid leakage under pressure from the steering gear rubber gaiters, which would indicate failed fluid seals within the steering gear.

4 Grasp the roadwheel at the 12 o'clock and 6 o'clock positions, and try to rock it **(see illustration)**. Very slight free play may be felt, but if the movement is appreciable, further investigation is necessary to determine the source. Continue rocking the wheel while

12.1 Check the condition of the driveshaft gaiters (arrowed)

an assistant depresses the footbrake. If the movement is now eliminated or significantly reduced, it is likely that the hub bearings are at fault. If the free play is still evident with the footbrake depressed, then there is wear in the suspension joints or mountings.

5 Now grasp the wheel at the 9 o'clock and 3 o'clock positions, and try to rock it as before. Any movement felt now may again be caused by wear in the hub bearings or the steering track rod balljoints. If the inner or outer balljoint is worn, the visual movement will be obvious.

6 Using a large screwdriver or flat bar, check for wear in the suspension mounting bushes by levering between the relevant suspension component and its attachment point. Some movement is to be expected as the mountings are made of rubber, but excessive wear should be obvious. Also check the condition of any visible rubber bushes, looking for splits, cracks or contamination of the rubber.

7 With the car standing on its wheels, have an assistant turn the steering wheel back-and-forth about an eighth of a turn each way. There should be very little, if any, lost movement between the steering wheel and roadwheels. If this is not the case, closely observe the joints and mountings previously described, but in addition check the steering column universal joints for wear, and the rack-and-pinion steering gear itself.

8 Check for any signs of fluid leakage around the front suspension struts and rear shock absorber. Should any fluid be noticed, the suspension strut or shock absorber is defective internally, and should be renewed. **Note:** *Suspension struts/shock absorbers*

13.4 Check for wear in the hub bearings by grasping the wheel and trying to rock it

should always be renewed in pairs on the same axle to ensure correct handling.

9 The efficiency of the suspension strut/shock absorber may be checked by bouncing the car at each corner. Generally speaking, the body will return to its normal position and stop after being depressed. If it rises and returns on a rebound, the suspension strut/shock absorber is probably suspect. Examine also the suspension strut/shock absorber upper and lower mountings for any signs of wear.

14 Battery check

1 The battery is located in the front, left-hand corner of the engine compartment. Release the clip at the back, then swing the battery cover upwards and forwards to gain access to the battery terminals (see illustration).
2 Where necessary, open the fuse holder plastic cover (squeeze together the locking lugs to release the cover) to gain access to the battery positive (+) terminal and fuse holder connections.
3 Check that both battery terminals and all the fuse holder connections are securely attached and are free from corrosion. Note: Before disconnecting the terminals from the battery, refer to Chapter 5A.
4 Check the battery casing for signs of damage or cracking and check the battery retaining clamp bolt is securely tightened. If the battery casing is damaged in any way the battery must be renewed (see Chapter 5A).
5 If the car is not fitted with a sealed-for-life maintenance-free battery, check the electrolyte level is between the MAX and MIN level markings on the battery casing. If topping-up is necessary, remove the battery (see Chapter 5A) from the car then remove the cell caps/cover (as applicable). Using distilled water, top the electrolyte level of each cell up to the MAX level mark then securely refit the cell caps/cover. Ensure the battery has not been overfilled then refit the battery to the car (see Chapter 5A).
6 Some models are fitted with a battery with a 'magic eye' which shows the state of the battery and level of electrolyte. The 'magic

14.1 Remove the battery cover

eye' is located on the top of the battery, near the negative terminal. If the eye is green, the battery is in good condition and charged up. If the eye is black, the battery is flat and should be charged. If the eye is colourless or yellow, the electrolyte is low and in a critical condition, and should be topped-up with distilled water. If charging the battery does not return the eye to green, the battery should be scrapped.
7 On completion of the check, clip the cover securely back onto the fuse holder and close up the cover.

15 Hinge and lock lubrication

1 Lubricate the hinges of the bonnet, doors and tailgate with a light general-purpose oil. Similarly, lubricate all latches, locks and lock strikers. At the same time, check the security and operation of all the locks, adjusting them if necessary (see Chapter 11).
2 Lightly lubricate the bonnet release mechanism and cable with a suitable grease.

16 Airbag unit check

Inspect the exterior condition of the airbag(s) for signs of damage or deterioration. If an airbag shows signs of damage, it must be renewed (see Chapter 12). Note that it is not permissible to attach any stickers to the surface of the airbag, as this may affect the deployment of the unit.

17 Windscreen/tailgate/ headlight washer system check

1 Check that each of the washer jet nozzles are clear and that each nozzle provides a strong jet of washer fluid.
2 The tailgate jet should be aimed to spray at the centre of the screen, using a pin.
3 The windscreen washer nozzles are fixed, and cannot be adjusted.
4 Especially during the winter months, make sure that the washer fluid concentration is sufficient to avoid freezing.
Caution: On no account use engine coolant antifreeze in the screen washer system – this may damage the paintwork.

18 Engine management self-diagnosis memory fault check

This work should be carried out by a Seat dealer or diagnostic specialist using special equipment. The diagnostic socket is located behind a hinged cover beneath the driver's side of the facia.

19 Sunroof check and lubrication

1 Check the operation of the sunroof, and leave it in the fully-open position.
2 Wipe clean the guide rails on each side of the sunroof opening, then apply lubricant to them. Seat recommend lubricant spray G 052 778. Close the sunroof on completion.

20 Road test and exhaust emissions check

Instruments and electrical equipment

1 Check the operation of all instruments and electrical equipment, including the air conditioning system, where applicable.
2 Make sure that all instruments read correctly, and switch on all electrical equipment in turn, to check that it functions properly.

Steering and suspension

3 Check for any abnormalities in the steering, suspension, handling or road 'feel'.
4 Drive the car, and check that there are no unusual vibrations or noises which may indicate wear in the driveshafts, wheel bearings, etc.
5 Check that the steering feels positive, with no excessive 'sloppiness', or roughness, and check for any suspension noises when cornering and driving over bumps.

Drivetrain

6 Check the performance of the engine, clutch (where applicable), gearbox/transmission and driveshafts.
7 Listen for any unusual noises from the engine, clutch and gearbox/transmission.
8 Make sure the engine runs smoothly at idle, and there is no hesitation on accelerating.
9 Check that, where applicable, the clutch action is smooth and progressive, that the drive is taken up smoothly, and that the pedal travel is not excessive. Also listen for any noises when the clutch pedal is depressed.
10 On manual gearbox models, check that all gears can be engaged smoothly without noise, and that the gear lever action is smooth and not abnormally vague or 'notchy'.
11 On automatic transmission models, make sure that all gearchanges occur smoothly, without snatching, and without an increase in engine speed between changes. Check that all the gear positions can be selected with the car at rest. If any problems are found, they should be referred to a Seat dealer or specialist.
12 Listen for a metallic clicking sound from the front of the car, as the car is driven slowly in a circle with the steering on full-lock. Carry out this check in both directions. If a

clicking noise is heard, this indicates wear in a driveshaft joint, in which case renew the joint if necessary.

Braking system

13 Make sure that the car does not pull to one side when braking, and that the wheels do not lock when braking hard.

14 Check that there is no vibration through the steering when braking.

15 Check that the handbrake operates correctly without excessive movement of the lever, and that it holds the car stationary on a slope.

16 Test the operation of the brake servo unit as follows. With the engine off, depress the footbrake four or five times to exhaust the vacuum. Hold the brake pedal depressed, then start the engine. As the engine starts, there should be a noticeable 'give' in the brake

pedal as vacuum builds-up. Allow the engine to run for at least two minutes, and then switch it off. If the brake pedal is depressed now, it should be possible to detect a hiss from the servo as the pedal is depressed. After about four or five applications, no further hissing should be heard, and the pedal should feel considerably harder.

17 Under controlled emergency braking, the pulsing of the ABS unit must be felt at the footbrake pedal.

Exhaust emissions check

18 Although not part of the manufacturer's maintenance schedule, this check will normally be carried out on a regular basis according to the country the car is operated in. Currently in the UK, exhaust emissions testing is included as part of the annual MOT test after the car is 3 years old.

21 Resetting the service interval display

1 After all necessary maintenance work has been completed, the service interval display must be reset. Seat technicians use a special dedicated instrument to do this, and a print-out is then put in the vehicle service record. It is possible for the owner to reset the display as described in the following paragraph.

2 To reset the display manually, switch off the ignition, then press and hold down the trip reset button beneath the speedometer. Switch on the ignition and observe the service interval, then hold the button down for 10 seconds until '- - -' appears, followed by the trip readout.

Every 20 000 miles or 2 years

22 Pollen filter element renewal

1 The pollen filter is located on the heater assembly, and is removed into the passenger footwell.

2 Reach under the glovebox, and slide the two retaining catches on the pollen filter lower cover towards each other, to release and remove the cover **(see illustrations)**.

3 Withdraw the filter downwards from the heater assembly, and remove from inside the car **(see illustration)**.

4 Separate the filter from the frame, noting the fitted direction of the airflow arrows, which should be towards the driver's side **(see illustration)**.

5 Fit the new filter to the frame, with the airflow arrows pointing as noted before, then insert it into the heater assembly. Refit the lower cover, and slide the catches apart to secure it.

23 Manual transmission oil level check

1 Park the car on a level surface. For improved access to the filler/level plug, apply the handbrake, then jack up the front of the car and support it on axle stands (see *Jacking and vehicle support*), but note that the rear of the car should also be raised to ensure an accurate level check. The oil level must be checked before the car is driven, or at least 5 minutes after the engine has been switched off. If the oil is checked immediately after driving the car, some of the oil will remain distributed around the transmission components, resulting in an inaccurate level reading.

2 As applicable, undo the retaining bolts and remove the engine undershield(s). Wipe clean the area around the transmission filler/level plug which is situated on the rear, inner face of the transmission, above the engine rear mounting/torque link **(see illustration)**.

3 To unscrew the filler/level plug, a special

22.2a Slide the catches (arrowed) towards each other . . .

22.2b . . . and remove the pollen filter lower cover

23.2 Manual transmission oil filler/level plug location (arrowed)

22.3 Withdraw the pollen filter into the passenger footwell

22.4 Separate the filter from the frame, noting the airflow arrows

multi-splined key will be needed (Seat tool number T20118, though alternatives may be available). Since the plug will almost certainly be very tight, badly-fitting substitute tools are unlikely to work, and damage may be caused to the plug's splines.

4 The oil level should reach the lower edge of the filler/level hole. A certain amount of oil will have gathered behind the filler/level plug, and

will trickle out when it is removed; this does not necessarily indicate that the level is correct. To ensure that a true level is established, wait until the initial trickle has stopped, then add oil as necessary until a trickle of new oil can be seen emerging. The level will be correct when the flow ceases; use only good-quality oil of the specified type.

5 If the transmission has been overfilled so

that oil flows out when the filler/level plug is removed, check that the car is completely level (front-to-rear and side-to-side), and allow the surplus to drain off into a suitable container.

6 When the oil level is correct, refit the filler/level plug and tighten it to the specified torque. Wipe off any spilt oil then refit the engine undershield(s), tighten the retaining bolts securely, and lower the car to the ground.

Every 40 000 miles or 4 years

24 Air filter element renewal

1.2 litre engines

1 The air filter element is incorporated into the engine top cover.

2 Lift the engine top cover from the rubber grommets, disconnect the crankcase ventilation hose (see illustrations 3.2b and 3.2c).

3 With the top cover upside down on the bench, undo the bolts and remove the cover, then withdraw the air filter element (see illustrations).

4 Fit the new air filter element, ensuring that the edges are securely seated.

5 Refit the cover and tighten the bolts.

6 Before offering the cover back on, refit the rubber seal which fits over the throttle body (see illustration). Reconnect the hoses, then press the top cover into the rubber grommets.

1.4 litre engines

Engine codes AUB, BBY, BBZ and BKY

7 The air filter element is incorporated into the engine top cover.

8 Lift the engine top cover from the rubber grommets and disconnect the hoses as necessary.

9 With the top cover upside down on the bench, undo the four bolts and remove the cover, then withdraw the air filter element and gasket. Check the gasket for condition and renew if necessary.

10 Fit the gasket and the new air filter element, ensuring that the edges are securely seated.

11 Refit the cover and tighten the bolts.

12 Reconnect the hoses then press the top cover into the rubber grommets.

Engine code BXW

13 Undo the bolts and lift the upper part of the air cleaner housing. Disconnect breather the hose as the cover is removed.

14 Remove the air filter element.

15 Fit the new element, ensuring the edges are correctly seated.

16 Refit the cover and tighten the bolts.

17 Reconnect the breather hose.

25 Spark plug renewal

1 The correct functioning of the spark plugs is vital for the correct running and efficiency of the engine. It is essential that the plugs fitted are appropriate for the engine (a suitable type is specified at the beginning of this Chapter). If this type is used and the engine is in good condition, the spark plugs should not need attention between scheduled renewal intervals. Spark plug cleaning is rarely necessary, and should not be attempted unless specialised equipment is available, as damage can easily be caused to the firing ends.

1.2 litre engines

2 Remove the engine top cover.

3 The HT coils must now be pulled from the tops of the spark plugs. Seat technicians use a special tool to do this as the coils are very tight in their holders, however, a length of strong welding rod or similar, bent at right-angles at one end, will do the task. Hook the rod under

24.3a Undo the bolts (arrowed) securing the filter cover

24.3b Release the clips . . .

24.3c . . . and remove the filter element

24.6 Refit the rubber seal

25.3a Use a bent rod to release the HT coils . . .

25.3b . . . then remove them from the cylinder head

25.7 Remove the spark plugs – 1.2 litre engine

25.12a If single-electrode plugs are being fitted, check the electrode gap using a feeler gauge . . .

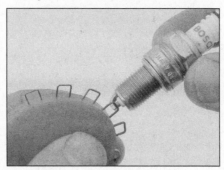

25.12b . . . or a wire gauge . . .

25.13 . . . and if necessary adjust the gap by bending the electrode

the wiring connector/HT coil then pull directly upwards **(see illustrations)**.

1.4 litre engines

Engine code AUB

4 Remove the engine top cover. Disconnect the HT leads from the spark plugs, taking care to pull on the connectors and not the leads.

Engine codes BBY, BKY, BBZ and BXW

5 Remove the engine top cover. The HT coils must now be pulled from the tops of the spark plugs. Seat technicians use a special tool to do this as the coils are very tight in their holders, however, a length of strong welding rod or similar, bent at right-angles at one end, will do the task. Hook the rod under the wiring connector/HT coil then pull directly upwards **(see illustrations 25.3a and 25.3b)**.

All engines

6 It is advisable to remove the dirt from the spark plug recesses using a clean brush, vacuum cleaner or compressed air before removing the plugs, to prevent dirt dropping into the cylinders.
7 Unscrew the plugs using a spark plug spanner, suitable box spanner or a deep socket and extension bar **(see illustration)**. Keep the socket aligned with the spark plug – if it is forcibly moved to one side, the ceramic insulator may be broken off. The use of a universal joint socket will be helpful. As each plug is removed, examine it as follows.
8 Examination of the spark plugs will give a good indication of the condition of the engine. If the insulator nose of the spark plug is clean

and white, with no deposits, this is indicative of a weak mixture or too hot a plug (a hot plug transfers heat away from the electrode slowly, a cold plug transfers heat away quickly).
9 If the tip and insulator nose are covered with hard black-looking deposits, then this is indicative that the mixture is too rich. Should the plug be black and oily, then it is likely that the engine is fairly worn, as well as the mixture being too rich.
10 If the insulator nose is covered with light tan to greyish-brown deposits, then the mixture is correct and it is likely that the engine is in good condition.
11 The spark plug electrode gap is of considerable importance as, if it is too large or too small, the size of the spark and its efficiency will be seriously impaired. On engines fitted with multi-electrode spark plugs, it is recommended that the plugs are renewed rather than attempting to adjust the gaps. On other spark plugs, the gap should be set to the value given by the manufacturer.
12 To set the gap on single electrode plugs, measure it with a feeler blade and then bend open, or closed, the outer plug electrode until the correct gap is achieved. The centre electrode should never be bent, as this may crack the insulator and cause plug failure, if nothing worse. If using feeler blades, the gap is correct when the appropriate-size blade is a firm sliding fit **(see illustrations)**. However, several models covered by this manual use spark plugs with multiple earth electrodes – *unless there is clear information to the contrary, no attempt should be made to adjust*

the plug gap on a spark plug with more than one earth electrode.
13 Special spark plug electrode gap adjusting tools are available from most motor accessory shops, or from some spark plug manufacturers **(see illustration)**.
14 Before fitting the spark plugs, check that the threaded connector sleeves are tight, and that the plug exterior surfaces and threads are clean. It's often difficult to screw in new spark plugs without cross-threading them – this can be avoided using a piece of rubber hose **(see Haynes Hint)**.

HAYNES HINT

It is very often difficult to insert spark plugs into their holes without cross-threading them. To avoid this possibility, fit a short length of rubber hose over the end of the spark plug. The flexible hose acts as a universal joint to help align the plug with the plug thread, the hose will slip on the spark plug, preventing thread damage to the aluminium cylinder head.

26.2 Unscrew the cap from the hydraulic fluid reservoir

26.3a The power steering fluid level must be between the upper and lower marks

26.3b Alternative power steering cap markings

15 Remove the rubber hose (if used), and tighten the plug to the specified torque using the spark plug socket and a torque wrench. Refit the remaining spark plugs in the same manner.

16 Reconnect the HT leads/ignition coils using a reversal of the removal procedure, then refit the engine top cover.

26 Power steering hydraulic fluid level check

1 Turn the front roadwheels to the straight-ahead position without starting the engine. If the car has been left standing for an hour or more, the power steering fluid will be cold (below 50°C), and the 'cold' level markings must be used. If, however, the engine is at normal temperature (above 50°C), the fluid will be hot, and the 'hot' level markings must be used.

2 The reservoir for the Electrically Powered Hydraulic Steering (EPHS) is located on the front left-hand corner of the engine compartment. **Note:** *On some models with a high-capacity battery, the battery and tray must be removed in order to access the reservoir filler cap.* The fluid level is checked

with the dipstick attached to the reservoir filler cap. Unscrew the cap from the hydraulic fluid reservoir, and wipe clean the integral dipstick with a clean cloth **(see illustration)**.

3 Screw on the cap hand-tight then unscrew it again and check the fluid level on the dipstick. The fluid level must be between the MIN (or lower) and MAX (or upper) marks **(see illustrations)**. If the fluid is cold (below 50°C), it must be at least above the lower level mark or MIN. If the fluid is hot (above 50°C), it must not be above the upper level mark or MAX.

4 If the level is above the maximum level mark, siphon off the excess amount. If it is below the minimum level mark, add the specified fluid as necessary (see *Lubricants and fluids*), but in this case also check the system for leaks. On completion, screw on the cap and tighten. Refit the battery and tray where removed.

27 Automatic transmission fluid level check

Note: *An accurate fluid level check can only be made with the transmission fluid at a temperature of between 35°C and 45°C, and if it is not possible to ascertain this temperature, it is strongly recommended that the check*

be made by a Seat dealer who will have the instrumentation to check the temperature and to check the transmission electronics for fault codes. Overfilling or underfilling adversely affects the function of the transmission.

1 Take the car on a short journey to warm the transmission slightly (see Note at the start of this Section), then park the car on level ground and engage P with the selector lever. Raise the front and rear of the car and support it on axle stands (see *Jacking and vehicle support*), ensuring the car is kept level. Undo the retaining bolts and remove the engine undershield(s) to gain access to the base of the transmission unit.

2 Start the engine and run it at idle speed until the transmission fluid temperature reaches 35°C.

3 Unscrew the fluid level plug from the bottom of the transmission sump **(see illustration)**.

4 If fluid continually drips from the level tube as the fluid temperature increases, the fluid level is correct and does not need to be topped-up. Note that there will be some fluid already present in the level tube, and it will be necessary to observe when this amount has drained before making the level check. Make sure that the check is made before the fluid temperature reaches 45°C. Check the condition of the seal on the level plug and renew it if necessary. Refit the plug and tighten to the specified torque.

5 If no fluid drips from the level tube, even when the fluid temperature has reached 45°C, it will be necessary to add fluid as follows while the engine is still running.

6 Using a screwdriver, lever off the cap from the filler tube on the front of the transmission. **Note:** *The locking device will be permanently damaged and a new cap must be obtained.*

7 With the cap removed, pull out the filler tube plug then add the specified fluid until it drips out of the level tube. Check the condition of the seal on the level plug and renew it if necessary. Refit the plug and tighten to the specified torque.

8 Refit the filler tube plug and the new cap.

9 Switch off the ignition then refit the engine undershield(s), tighten the retaining bolts securely, and lower the car to the ground.

10 Frequent need for topping-up indicates that there is a leak, which should be found and corrected before it becomes serious.

H31932

27.3 Automatic transmission fluid level check

1 Level plug
2 Level tube
3 Filler cap
4 Retaining clip

28 Timing belt and tensioner renewal (1.4 litre engines)

Refer to Chapter 2B.

Every 2 years

29 Brake (and clutch) fluid renewal

⚠️ *Warning: Brake hydraulic fluid can harm your eyes and damage painted surfaces, so use extreme caution when handling and pouring it. Do not use fluid that has been standing open for some time, as it absorbs moisture from the air. Excess moisture can cause a dangerous loss of braking effectiveness.*

1 The procedure is similar to that for the bleeding of the hydraulic system as described in Chapter 9, except that the brake fluid reservoir should be emptied by siphoning, using a clean poultry baster or similar before starting, and allowance should be made for the old fluid to be expelled when bleeding a section of the circuit. Since the clutch hydraulic system also uses fluid from the brake system reservoir, it should also be bled at the same time by referring to Chapter 6, Section 2.

2 Working as described in Chapter 9, open the first bleed screw in the sequence, and pump the brake pedal gently until nearly all the old fluid has been emptied from the master cylinder reservoir.

3 Top-up to the MAX level with new fluid, and continue pumping until only the new fluid remains in the reservoir, and new fluid can be seen emerging from the bleed screw. Tighten the screw, and top the reservoir level up to the MAX level line.

 HAYNES HINT *Old hydraulic fluid is often much darker in colour than the new, making it easy to distinguish the two.*

4 Work through all the remaining bleed screws in the sequence until new fluid can be seen at all of them. Be careful to keep the master cylinder reservoir topped-up to above the MIN level at all times, or air may enter the system and greatly increase the length of the task.

5 When the operation is complete, check that all bleed screws are securely tightened, and that their dust caps are refitted. Wash off all traces of spilt fluid, and recheck the master cylinder reservoir fluid level.

6 On models with a manual transmission unit, once the brake fluid has been changed the clutch fluid should also be renewed. Referring to Chapter 6, bleed the clutch until new fluid is seen to be emerging from the slave cylinder bleed screw, keeping the master cylinder fluid level above the MIN level line at all times to prevent air entering the system. Once the new fluid emerges, securely tighten the bleed screw then disconnect and remove the bleeding equipment. Securely refit the dust cap then wash off all traces of spilt fluid.

7 On all models, ensure the master cylinder fluid level is correct (see *Weekly checks*) and thoroughly check the operation of the brakes and (where necessary) clutch before taking the car on the road.

30 Coolant renewal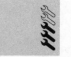

Note: *This work is not included in the Seat schedule, and should not be required if the recommended Seat G12 coolant antifreeze/inhibitor is used. However, if standard antifreeze/inhibitor is used, the work should be carried out at the recommended interval.*

⚠️ *Warning: Wait until the engine is cold before starting this procedure. Do not allow antifreeze to come in contact with your skin, or with the car's painted surfaces. Rinse off spills immediately with plenty of water. Never leave antifreeze lying around in an open container, or in a puddle in the driveway or on the garage floor. Children and pets are attracted by its sweet smell, but antifreeze can be fatal if ingested.*

Cooling system draining

1 With the engine completely cold, unscrew the expansion tank cap.

2 Firmly apply the handbrake then jack up the front of the car and support it on axle stands (see *Jacking and vehicle support*). Undo the retaining bolts and remove the engine undershield(s) to gain access to the base of the radiator.

3 Position a suitable container beneath the coolant drain plug which is located in the bottom hose fitting to the left-hand bottom end of the radiator. Unscrew the drain plug and pull it out slightly (there is no need to remove it completely) and allow the coolant to drain into the container **(see illustration)**. If desired, a length of tubing can be fitted to the drain outlet to direct the flow of coolant during draining. Where no drain outlet is fitted to the hose end fitting, remove the retaining clip and disconnect the bottom hose from the radiator to drain the coolant (see Chapter 3).

4 On engines with an oil cooler, to fully drain the system, also disconnect one of the coolant hoses from the oil cooler which is located at the front of the cylinder block.

5 If the coolant has been drained for a reason other than renewal then, provided it is clean, it can be re-used.

6 Once all the coolant has drained, securely tighten the radiator drain plug or reconnect the bottom hose to the radiator (as applicable). Where necessary, also reconnect the coolant hose to the oil cooler and secure it in position with the retaining clip. Refit the undershield(s), tighten the retaining bolts securely.

Cooling system flushing

7 If the recommended Seat coolant has not been used and coolant renewal has been neglected, or if the antifreeze mixture has become diluted, the cooling system may gradually lose efficiency, as the coolant passages become restricted due to rust, scale deposits, and other sediment. The cooling system efficiency can be restored by flushing the system clean.

8 The radiator should be flushed separately from the engine, to avoid excess contamination.

Radiator flushing

9 To flush the radiator, first tighten the radiator drain plug.

10 Disconnect the top and bottom hoses and any other relevant hoses from the radiator (see Chapter 3).

11 Insert a garden hose into the radiator top inlet. Direct a flow of clean water through the radiator, and continue flushing until clean water emerges from the radiator bottom outlet.

12 If after a reasonable period the water still does not run clear, the radiator can be flushed with a good proprietary cleaning agent. It is important that the manufacturer's instructions are followed carefully. If the contamination is particularly bad, insert the hose in the radiator bottom outlet, and reverse-flush the radiator.

30.3 Unscrew the drain plug and allow the coolant to drain into the container

30.18 Filling the cooling system

Engine flushing

13 To flush the engine, remove the thermostat (see Chapter 3).

14 With the bottom hose disconnected from the radiator, insert a garden hose into the thermostat housing. Direct a clean flow of water through the engine, and continue flushing until clean water emerges from the radiator bottom hose.

15 When flushing is complete, refit the thermostat and reconnect the hoses (see Chapter 3).

Cooling system filling

16 Before attempting to fill the cooling system, ensure the drain plug is securely closed and make sure that all hoses are securely connected and their retaining clips are in good condition. If the recommended Seat coolant is not being used, ensure that a suitable antifreeze mixture is used all year round, to prevent corrosion of the engine components (see following sub-Section).

17 Remove the coolant temperature sensor from the coolant distribution housing on the left-hand end of the cylinder head with reference to Chapter 3.

18 Remove the expansion tank filler cap and slowly fill the system with coolant **(see illustration)**, until bubble-free coolant runs from the temperature sensor hole, then refit the sensor immediately with reference to Chapter 3. Continue to fill the system until the level is up to the MAX level mark on the expansion tank. Help to bleed the air from the system by repeatedly squeezing the radiator bottom hose.

19 Refit the cap to the expansion tank, then run the engine at a fast idle speed until the cooling fan cuts in. Wait for the fan to stop then switch the engine off and allow the engine to cool.

20 When the engine has cooled, check the coolant level with reference to *Weekly checks*. Top-up the level if necessary, and refit the expansion tank cap.

Antifreeze mixture

21 If the recommended Seat coolant is not being used, the antifreeze should always be renewed at the specified intervals. This is necessary not only to maintain the antifreeze properties, but also to prevent corrosion which would otherwise occur as the corrosion inhibitors become progressively less effective.

22 Always use an ethylene-glycol based antifreeze which is suitable for use in mixed-metal cooling systems. The quantity of antifreeze and levels of protection are indicated in the Specifications.

23 Before adding antifreeze, the cooling system should be completely drained, preferably flushed, and all hoses checked for condition and security.

24 After filling with antifreeze, a label should be attached to the expansion tank, stating the type and concentration of antifreeze used, and the date installed. Any subsequent topping-up should be made with the same type and concentration of antifreeze.

25 Do not use engine antifreeze in the windscreen/tailgate washer system, as it will damage the paintwork. A screenwash additive should be added to the washer system in the quantities stated on the bottle.

Airlocks

26 If, after draining and refilling the system, symptoms of overheating are found which did not occur previously, then the fault is almost certainly due to trapped air at some point in the system, causing an airlock and restricting the flow of coolant; usually, the air is trapped because the system was refilled too quickly.

27 If an airlock is suspected, first try gently squeezing all visible coolant hoses. A coolant hose which is full of air feels quite different to one full of coolant, when squeezed. After refilling the system, most airlocks will clear once the system has cooled, and been topped-up.

28 While the engine is running at operating temperature, switch on the heater and heater fan, and check for heat output. Provided there is sufficient coolant in the system, any lack of heat output could be due to an airlock in the system.

29 Airlocks can have more serious effects than simply reducing heater output – a severe airlock could reduce coolant flow around the engine. Check that the radiator top hose is hot when the engine is at operating temperature – a top hose which stays cold could be the result of an airlock (or a non-opening thermostat).

30 If the problem persists, stop the engine and allow it to cool down completely before unscrewing the expansion tank filler cap or loosening the hose clips and squeezing the hoses to bleed out the trapped air. In the worst case, the system will have to be at least partially drained (this time, the coolant can be saved for re-use) and flushed to clear the problem.

Chapter 1 Part B:
Routine maintenance and servicing – diesel models

Contents

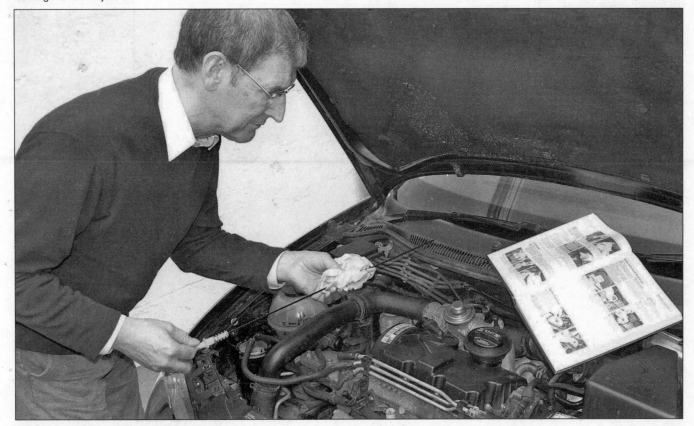

Degrees of difficulty

Easy, suitable for novice with little experience	**Fairly easy,** suitable for beginner with some experience	**Fairly difficult,** suitable for competent DIY mechanic	**Difficult,** suitable for experienced DIY mechanic	**Very difficult,** suitable for expert DIY or professional

Lubricants and fluids................................. Refer to end of *Weekly checks* on page 0•16

Engine codes
1.4 litre (3-cylinder)... AMF, BMS, BNM and BNV
1.9 litre (4-cylinder)... ATD, AXR, ASZ, BLT and BMT

Capacities

Engine oil (including filter)
1.4 litre engines .... 4.2 litres
1.9 litre engines .... 4.5 litres

Cooling system
1.4 litre engines .... 6.2 litres
1.9 litre engines .... 6.8 litres

Transmission
Manual transmission:
  1.4 litre engines .... 2.0 litres
  1.9 litre engines:
    Engine codes ATD, AXR and BMT .... 2.0 litres
    Engine codes ASZ and BLT .... 2.3 litres

Fuel tank (approximate)................................. 45 litres

Cooling system
Antifreeze mixture:
  40% antifreeze .... Protection down to -25°C
  50% antifreeze .... Protection down to -35°C
Note: *Refer to antifreeze manufacturer for latest recommendations.*

Brakes
Brake pad minimum thickness:
  Including backing plate:
    Front .... 7.0 mm
    Rear .... 7.6 mm
  Friction lining only:
    Front and rear................................... 2.0 mm
Rear brake shoe friction material minimum thickness .... 1.5 mm

Torque wrench settings

	Nm	lbf ft
Alternator mounting bolt.	20	15
Manual gearbox filler/level plug:		
5-speed transmission.	25	18
6-speed transmission:		
Hex-headed (Allen key) plug.	30	22
12-point splined plug.	45	33
Roadwheel bolts.	120	89
Sump drain plug.	30	22

The maintenance intervals in this manual are provided with the assumption that you, not the dealer, will be carrying out the work. These are the minimum intervals recommended by us for cars driven daily. If you wish to keep your car in peak condition at all times, you may wish to perform some of these procedures more often. We encourage frequent maintenance, since it enhances the efficiency, performance and resale value of your car.

When the vehicle is new, it should be serviced by a dealer service department (or other workshop recognised by the vehicle manufacturer as providing the same standard of service) in order to preserve the warranty. The vehicle manufacturer may reject warranty claims if you are unable to prove that servicing has been carried out as and when specified, using only original equipment parts or parts certified to be of equivalent quality.

All Seat models are equipped with a service interval display indicator in the instrument panel. Every time the engine is started the panel will illuminate for approximately 20 seconds with service information. Once the service interval has been reached, the display will flash 'INSP' for a service.

Note that the following schedule is our recommendation for service intervals and service tasks.

Every 250 miles or weekly
☐ Refer to *Weekly checks*

Every 6000 miles or 6 months, whichever comes first
☐ Renew the engine oil and filter (Section 3)
Note: *Seat recommend that the engine oil and filter are changed every 10 000 miles or 12 months. However, oil and filter changes are good for the engine and we recommend that the oil and filter are renewed more frequently, especially if the vehicle is used on a lot of short journeys.*

Every 10 000 miles or 12 months, whichever comes first
Note: *In addition to the item given above.*
☐ Fuel filter water draining (Section 4)
☐ Brake pad/lining check (Section 5)
☐ Check the condition of the exhaust system and its mountings (Section 6)
☐ Check all underbonnet components and hoses for fluid and oil leaks (Section 7)
☐ Check the condition of the auxiliary drivebelt (Section 8)
☐ Check the coolant antifreeze concentration (Section 9)
☐ Check the brake hydraulic circuit for leaks and damage (Section 10)
☐ Check the headlight beam adjustment (Section 11)
☐ Check the underbody protection for damage (Section 12)
☐ Check the condition of the driveshafts (Section 13)
☐ Check the steering and suspension components for condition and security (Section 14)
☐ Check the battery condition, security and electrolyte level (Section 15)
☐ Lubricate all hinges and locks (Section 16)
☐ Check the condition of the airbag unit(s) (Section 17)
☐ Check the operation of the windscreen/tailgate/ headlight washer system(s) (as applicable) (Section 18)
☐ Check the engine management self-diagnosis memory for faults (Section 19)
☐ Check the operation of the sunroof and lubricate the guide rails (Section 20)
☐ Carry out a road test and check exhaust emissions (Section 21)
☐ Reset the service indicator (Section 22)

Every 20 000 miles or 2 years, whichever comes first
☐ Renew the pollen filter element (Section 23)
☐ Renew the fuel filter (Section 24)
☐ Check the manual transmission oil level (Section 25)

Every 40 000 miles or 4 years, whichever comes first
☐ Renew the air filter element (Section 26)
☐ Check the power steering hydraulic fluid level (Section 27)
☐ Renew the timing belt and tensioner roller (Section 28)*
* *Seat specify timing belt inspection after the first 80 000 miles and then every 20 000 miles until the renewal interval of 100 000 miles. However, if the car is used mainly for short journeys, we recommend that this shorter renewal interval is adhered to. The belt renewal interval is very much up to the individual owner but, bearing in mind that severe engine damage will result if the belt breaks in use, we recommend the shorter interval.*

Every 80 000 miles
☐ Check the particulate filter – engine code BMT only (Section 29)

Every 100 000 miles
☐ Check the particulate filter – engine code BMS only (Section 29)

Every 2 years
☐ Renew the brake (and clutch) fluid (Section 30)
☐ Renew the coolant (Section 31)*
* *This work is not included in the Seat schedule, and should not be required if the recommended Seat G12 coolant antifreeze/inhibitor is used.*

Underbonnet view of a 1.4 litre model (1.9 litre model similar)

1　Engine oil filler cap
2　Engine oil dipstick
3　Oil filter
4　Coolant expansion tank
5　Fuel filter
6　Windscreen/headlight washer fluid reservoir
7　Master cylinder brake fluid reservoir
8　Valve block
9　Air cleaner housing
10　Engine management ECM
11　Battery
12　Alternator

Front underbody view of a 1.4 litre model (1.9 litre model similar)

1　Sump drain plug
2　Manual transmission drain plug
3　Engine rear mounting/link
4　Driveshaft
5　Front suspension subframe
6　Front suspension lower arm
7　Steering track rod
8　Front brake caliper
9　Front exhaust pipe
10　Intercooler hose to turbocharger
11　Air conditioning compressor
12　Radiator bottom hose

Rear underbody view

1 *Fuel tank*
2 *Rear axle assembly*
3 *Rear suspension coil spring*
4 *Rear shock absorber*
5 *Exhaust rear silencer*
6 *Handbrake cables*
7 *Hydraulic brake line*
8 *Fuel filler pipe*

Maintenance procedures

1 Introduction

This Chapter is designed to help the home mechanic maintain his/her car for safety, economy, long life and peak performance.

The Chapter contains a master maintenance schedule, followed by Sections dealing specifically with each task in the schedule. Visual checks, adjustments, component renewal and other helpful items are included. Refer to the accompanying illustrations of the engine compartment and the underside of the car for the locations of the various components.

Servicing your car will provide a planned maintenance programme, which should result in a long and reliable service life. This is a comprehensive plan, so maintaining some items but not others will not produce the same results.

As you service your car, you will discover that many of the procedures can – and should – be grouped together, because of the particular procedure being performed, or because of the proximity of two otherwise unrelated components to one another. For example, if the car is raised for any reason, the exhaust can be inspected at the same time as the suspension and steering components.

The first step in this maintenance programme is to prepare yourself before the actual work begins. Read through all the Sections relevant to the work to be carried out, then make a list and gather all the parts and tools required. If a problem is encountered, seek advice from a parts specialist, or a dealer service department.

2 Regular maintenance

1 If, from the time the car is new, the routine maintenance schedule is followed closely, and frequent checks are made of fluid levels and high-wear items, as suggested throughout this manual, the engine will be kept in relatively good running condition, and the need for additional work will be minimised.

2 It is possible that there will be times when the engine is running poorly due to the lack of regular maintenance. This is even more likely if a used car, which has not received regular and frequent maintenance checks, is purchased. In such cases, additional work may need to be carried out, outside of the regular maintenance intervals.

3 If engine wear is suspected, a compression test (refer to Chapter 2C) will provide valuable information regarding the overall performance of the main internal components. Such a test can be used as a basis to decide on the extent of the work to be carried out. If, for example, a compression test indicates serious internal engine wear, conventional maintenance as described in this Chapter will not greatly improve the performance of the engine, and may prove a waste of time and money, unless extensive overhaul work is carried out first.

4 The following series of operations are those most often required to improve the performance of a generally poor-running engine:

Primary operations

a) *Clean, inspect and test the battery (See 'Weekly checks').*
b) *Check all the engine-related fluids (See 'Weekly checks').*
c) *Drain the water from the fuel filter (Section 4).*
d) *Check the condition and tension of the auxiliary drivebelt (Section 8).*
e) *Check the condition of the air filter, and renew if necessary (Section 26).*
f) *Check the condition of all hoses, and check for fluid leaks (Section 7).*

5 If the above operations do not prove fully effective, carry out the following secondary operations:

Secondary operations

All items listed under *Primary operations*, plus the following:

a) *Check the charging system (see Chapter 5A).*
b) *Check the preheating system (see Chapter 5A).*
c) *Renew the fuel filter (Section 24) and check the fuel system (see Chapter 4B).*

3.2 Undo the bolts (arrowed) and remove the engine undershield

3.3 Sump drain plug (arrowed)

Every 6000 miles or 6 months

3 Engine oil and filter renewal

1 Frequent oil and filter changes are the most important preventative maintenance procedures which can be undertaken by the

HAYNES HINT

Keep the drain plug pressed into the sump while unscrewing it by hand the last couple of turns. As the plug releases, move it away sharply so the stream of oil issuing from the sump runs into the container, not up your sleeve.

DIY owner. As engine oil ages, it becomes diluted and contaminated, which leads to premature engine wear.

2 Before starting this procedure, gather all the necessary tools and materials. Also make sure that you have plenty of clean rags and newspapers handy, to mop-up any spills. Ideally, the engine oil should be warm, as it will drain better, and more built-up sludge will be removed with it. Take care, however, not to touch the exhaust or any other hot parts of the engine when working under the car. To avoid any possibility of scalding, and to protect yourself from possible skin irritants and other harmful contaminants in used engine oils, it is advisable to wear gloves when carrying out this work. Access to the underside of the car will be greatly improved if it can be raised on a lift, driven onto ramps, or jacked up and supported on axle stands (see *Jacking and vehicle support*). Whichever method is chosen, make sure that the car remains level, or if it is at an angle, that the drain plug is at the lowest point. Undo the retaining Torx bolts and remove the engine undershield(s), then also remove the engine top cover where applicable, by pulling it upwards at the front edge **(see illustration)**.

3 Slacken the sump drain plug about half a

turn. Position the draining container under the drain plug, then remove the plug completely **(see illustration and Haynes Hint)**. Recover the sealing ring from the drain plug.

4 Allow some time for the old oil to drain, noting that it may be necessary to reposition the container as the oil flow slows to a trickle.

5 After all the oil has drained, wipe off the drain plug with a clean rag, and fit a new sealing washer. Clean the area around the drain plug opening, and refit the plug. Tighten the plug securely.

6 Remove the engine top cover and packing (if not already done so) to gain access to the oil filter housing. Place absorbent cloths around the filter housing to catch any spilt oil.

7 Unscrew and remove the cap from the top of the oil filter housing using an oil filter strap or suitable spanner. Recover the large sealing ring from the cap, and the small sealing ring from the centre rod. Lift out the filter element **(see illustrations)**. Dispose of the element.

8 Using a clean rag, wipe all oil and sludge from the inside of the filter housing and cap(s).

9 Fit new sealing rings to the cap, then insert the new element and cap, and tighten securely **(see illustrations)**. Wipe up any spilt oil before refitting the engine top cover(s).

3.7a Unscrew the cap . . .

3.7b . . . and remove the filter element

3.7c Remove the sealing ring from the cap

10 Remove the old oil and all tools from under the car then refit the undershield(s) and lower the car to the ground. Also refit the engine top cover.

11 Remove the dipstick, then unscrew the oil filler cap from the cylinder head cover. Fill the engine, using the correct grade and type of oil (see *Lubricants and fluids*). An oil can spout or funnel may help to reduce spillage. Pour in half the specified quantity of oil first, then wait a few minutes for the oil to run to the sump (see *Weekly checks*). Continue adding oil a small quantity at a time until the level is up to the maximum mark on the dipstick. Refit the filler cap.

12 Start the engine and run it for a few minutes; check for leaks around the oil filter cap and the sump drain plug. Note that there may be a few seconds delay before the oil pressure warning light goes out when the engine is started, as the oil circulates through the engine oil galleries and the new oil filter before the pressure builds-up.

3.9a Lubricate the O-ring seal with engine oil

⚠️ **Warning: Do not increase the engine speed above idling while the oil pressure light is illuminated, as considerable damage can be caused to the turbocharger.**

13 Switch off the engine, and wait a few minutes for the oil to settle in the sump once

3.9b Insert the filter element together with the cap

more. With the new oil circulated and the filter completely full, recheck the level on the dipstick, and add more oil as necessary.

14 Dispose of the used engine oil safely, with reference to *General repair procedures* in the Reference section of this manual.

Every 10 000 miles or 12 months

4 Fuel filter water draining

Note: *This procedure is only applicable where a control valve is fitted to the top of the filter, fitted to 1.9 litre engines, and 1.4 litre engine code AMF.*

1 Periodically, the water collected from the fuel by the filter unit must be drained out.

2 The fuel filter is mounted on the right-hand inner wing (right as seen from the driver's seat) **(see illustration)**. At the top of the filter unit, release the clip and lift out the control valve, leaving the fuel hoses attached.

3 Slacken the bolt and raise the filter in its retaining bracket.

4 Position a container below the filter unit and pad the surrounding area with rags to absorb any fuel that may be spilt.

5 Unscrew the drain valve at the base of the filter unit, until fuel starts to run out into the container. Keep the valve open until about 100 cc of fuel has been collected.

6 Refit the control valve to the top of the filter and insert the retaining clip. Close the drain

valve and wipe off any surplus fuel from the nozzle.

7 Remove the collecting container and rags, then push the filter unit back into the retaining bracket and tighten the bracket securing bolt.

8 Run the engine at idle and check around the fuel filter for fuel leaks.

9 Raise the engine speed to about 2000 rpm several times, then allow the engine to idle again. Observe the fuel flow through the transparent hose leading to the fuel injection pump and check that it is free of air bubbles.

5 Brake pad/lining check

Front and rear disc brakes

1 The outer brake pads can be checked without removing the wheels, by observing the brake pads through the holes in the wheels **(see illustration)**. If necessary, remove the wheel trim. The thickness of the pad lining must not be less than the dimension given in the Specifications.

2 If the outer pads are worn near their limits, it is worthwhile checking the inner pads as well. Jack up car and support it on axle stands (see *Jacking and vehicle support*). Remove the roadwheels.

3 Use a steel rule to check the thickness of the brake pads, and compare with the minimum thickness given in the Specifications **(see illustration)**.

4 For a comprehensive check, the brake pads should be removed and cleaned. The operation of the caliper can then also be checked, and the condition of the brake disc itself can be fully examined on both sides. Refer to Chapter 9.

5 If any pad's friction material is worn to the specified minimum thickness or less, all four pads at the front or rear, as applicable, must be renewed as a set.

6 On completion of the check, refit the road-wheels and lower the car to the ground.

4.2 The fuel filter is mounted on the right-hand inner wing

5.1 The outer brake pads can be observed through the holes in the wheels

5.3 The thickness (a) of the brake pads must not be less than the specified amount

H31925

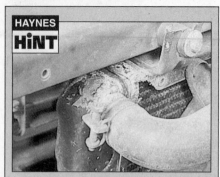

A leak in the cooling system will usually show up as white- or antifreeze-coloured deposits on the area adjoining the leak.

Rear drum brakes

7 Chock the front wheels, then jack up the rear of the car and support it on axle stands (see *Jacking and vehicle support*).

8 For a quick check, the thickness of friction material remaining on one of the brake shoes can be observed through the hole in the brake backplate which is exposed by prising out the rubber sealing grommet. If a rod of the same diameter as the specified minimum friction material thickness is placed against the shoe friction material, the amount of wear can be assessed. An electric torch or inspection light will probably be required. If the friction material on any shoe is worn down to the specified minimum thickness or less, all four shoes must be renewed as a set.

9 For a comprehensive check, the brake drum should be removed and cleaned. This will allow the wheel cylinders to be checked, and the condition of the brake drum itself to be fully examined (see Chapter 9).

10 On completion of the check, refit the road-wheels where removed, and lower the car to the ground.

6 Exhaust system check

1 With the engine cold (at least an hour after the car has been driven), check the complete exhaust system from the engine to the end of

8.2 Check the underside of the auxiliary drivebelt with a mirror

the tailpipe. The exhaust system is most easily checked with the car raised on a hoist, or supported on axle stands, so that the exhaust components are readily visible and accessible (see *Jacking and vehicle support*).

2 Check the exhaust pipes and connections for evidence of leaks, severe corrosion and damage. Make sure that all brackets and mountings are in good condition, and that all relevant nuts and bolts are tight. Leakage at any of the joints or in other parts of the system will usually show up as a black sooty stain in the vicinity of the leak.

3 Rattles and other noises can often be traced to the exhaust system, especially the brackets and mountings. Try to move the pipes and silencers. If the components are able to come into contact with the body or suspension parts, secure the system with new mountings. Otherwise separate the joints (if possible) and twist the pipes as necessary to provide additional clearance.

7 Hose and fluid leak check

1 Visually inspect the engine joint faces, gaskets and seals for any signs of water or oil leaks. Pay particular attention to the areas around the camshaft cover, cylinder head, oil filter and sump joint faces. Bear in mind that, over a period of time, some very slight seepage from these areas is to be expected – what you are really looking for is any indication of a serious leak. Should a leak be found, renew the offending gasket or oil seal by referring to the appropriate Chapters in this manual.

2 Also check the security and condition of all the engine-related pipes and hoses. Ensure that all cable-ties or securing clips are in place and in good condition. Clips which are broken or missing can lead to chafing of the hoses, pipes or wiring, which could cause more serious problems in the future.

3 Carefully check the radiator hoses and heater hoses along their entire length. Renew any hose which is cracked, swollen or deteriorated. Cracks will show up better if the hose is squeezed. Pay close attention to the hose clips that secure the hoses to the

8.5 On models with air conditioning, turn the tensioner (arrowed) clockwise . . .

cooling system components. Hose clips can pinch and puncture hoses, resulting in cooling system leaks.

4 Inspect all the cooling system components (hoses, joint faces, etc) for leaks **(see Haynes Hint)**. Where any problems of this nature are found on system components, renew the component or gasket with reference to Chapter 3.

5 With the car raised, inspect the fuel tank and filler neck for punctures, cracks and other damage. The connection between the filler neck and tank is especially critical. Sometimes a rubber filler neck or connecting hose will leak due to loose retaining clamps or deteriorated rubber.

6 Carefully check all rubber hoses and metal fuel lines leading away from the tank. Check for loose connections, deteriorated hoses, crimped lines, and other damage. Pay particular attention to the vent pipes and hoses, which often loop up around the filler neck and can become blocked or crimped. Follow the lines to the front of the car, carefully inspecting them all the way. Renew damaged sections as necessary.

7 From within the engine compartment, check the security of all fuel hose attachments and pipe unions, and inspect the fuel hoses and vacuum hoses for kinks, chafing and deterioration.

8 Check the condition of the power steering fluid hoses and pipes.

8 Auxiliary drivebelt check and renewal

Check

1 Apply the handbrake, then jack up the front of the car and support it on axle stands (see *Jacking and vehicle support*).

2 Using a socket on the crankshaft pulley bolt, turn the engine slowly clockwise so that the full length of the auxiliary drivebelt can be examined. Look for cracks, splitting and fraying on the surface of the belt; check also for signs of glazing (shiny patches) and separation of the belt plies. Use a mirror to check the underside of the drivebelt **(see illustration)**. If damage or wear is visible, or if there are traces of oil or grease on it, the belt should be renewed as follows:

Renewal

3 For improved access, apply the handbrake, then jack up the front of the car and support it on axle stands (see *Jacking and vehicle support*). Where applicable, remove the engine undershield.

4 Remove the right-hand front roadwheel, then remove the wheel arch liner.

5 The tensioner must now be turned clockwise to release the tension on the drivebelt. To do this, either use a spanner to turn the tensioner central bolt clockwise (models with air conditioning) **(see illustration)**, or

use a spanner on the square-shaped lug on the top of the tensioner (models without air conditioning). On the latter type, it is possible to retain the tensioner with a pin inserted through the holes provided.

6 Note how the drivebelt is routed, then remove it from the crankshaft pulley, alternator pulley, and air conditioning compressor pulley (where applicable) **(see illustration)**.

7 Locate the new drivebelt on the pulleys, then release the tensioner. Check that the belt is located correctly in the multi-grooves in the pulleys.

8 Refit the access panel and roadwheel, and lower the car to the ground.

9 Antifreeze check

1 The cooling system should be filled with the recommended G12 antifreeze and corrosion protection fluid – do not mix this antifreeze with any other type. Over a period of time, the concentration of fluid may be reduced due to topping-up with water (this can be avoided by topping-up with the correct antifreeze mixture – see Specifications) or fluid loss. If loss of coolant has been evident, it is important to make the necessary repair before adding fresh fluid.

2 With the engine cold, carefully remove the cap from the expansion tank. If the engine is not completely cold, place a cloth rag over the cap before removing it, and remove it slowly to allow any pressure to escape.

3 Antifreeze checkers are available from car accessory shops. Draw some coolant from the expansion tank and follow the checker manufacturer's instructions.

4 If the concentration is incorrect, it will be necessary to either withdraw some coolant and add antifreeze, or alternatively drain the old coolant and add fresh coolant of the correct concentration (see Section 31).

10 Brake hydraulic circuit check

1 Check the entire brake hydraulic circuit for leaks and damage. Start by checking the master cylinder in the engine compartment. At the same time, check the vacuum servo unit and ABS units for signs of fluid leakage.

2 Raise the front and rear of the car and support it on axle stands (see *Jacking and vehicle support*). Check the rigid hydraulic brake lines for corrosion and damage.

3 At the front of the car, check that the flexible hydraulic hoses to the calipers are not twisted or chafing on any of the surrounding suspension components. Turn the steering on full lock to make this check. Also check that the hoses are not brittle or cracked.

4 Lower the car to the ground after making the checks.

8.6 . . . and remove the auxiliary drivebelt

11 Headlight beam adjustment

1 Accurate adjustment of the headlight beam is only possible using optical beam-setting equipment, and this work should therefore be carried out by a Seat dealer or service station with the necessary facilities.

2 Basic adjustments can be carried out in an emergency, and further details are given in Chapter 12.

12 Underbody protection check

Raise and support the car on axle stands (see *Jacking and vehicle support*). Using an electric torch or lead light, inspect the entire underside of the car, paying particular attention to the wheel arches. Look for any damage to the flexible underbody coating, which may crack or flake off with age, leading to corrosion (note, however, that the Ibiza does without such a coating for much of the underbody, and has instead a pair of plastic underbody panels at the front).

Also check that the wheel arch liners are securely attached with any clips provided – if they come loose, dirt may get in behind the liners and defeat their purpose. If there is any damage to the underseal, or any corrosion, it should be repaired before the damage gets too serious.

13 Driveshaft check

1 With the car raised and securely supported on stands, slowly rotate the roadwheel. Inspect the condition of the outer constant velocity (CV) joint rubber gaiters, squeezing the gaiters to open out the folds. Check for signs of cracking, splits or deterioration of the rubber, which may allow the grease to escape, and lead to water and grit entry into the joint. Also check the security and condition of the retaining clips. Repeat these checks on the

13.1 Check the condition of the driveshaft gaiters (arrowed)

inner joints **(see illustration)**. If any damage or deterioration is found, the gaiters should be renewed (see Chapter 8).

2 At the same time, check the general condition of the CV joints themselves by first holding the driveshaft and attempting to rotate the wheel. Repeat this check by holding the inner joint and attempting to rotate the driveshaft. Any appreciable movement indicates wear in the joints, wear in the driveshaft splines, or a loose driveshaft retaining nut.

14 Steering and suspension check

1 Raise the front and rear of the car, and securely support it on axle stands (see *Jacking and vehicle support*).

2 Visually inspect the track rod end balljoint dust cover, the lower front suspension balljoint dust cover, and the steering rack-and-pinion gaiters for splits, chafing or deterioration. Any wear of these components will cause loss of lubricant, together with dirt and water entry, resulting in rapid deterioration of the balljoints or steering gear.

3 Check the power steering fluid hoses for chafing or deterioration, and the pipe and hose unions for fluid leaks. Also check for signs of fluid leakage under pressure from the steering gear rubber gaiters, which would indicate failed fluid seals within the steering gear.

4 Grasp the roadwheel at the 12 o'clock and

14.4 Check for wear in the hub bearings by grasping the wheel and trying to rock it

6 o'clock positions, and try to rock it (see illustration). Very slight free play may be felt, but if the movement is appreciable, further investigation is necessary to determine the source. Continue rocking the wheel while an assistant depresses the footbrake. If the movement is now eliminated or significantly reduced, it is likely that the hub bearings are at fault. If the free play is still evident with the footbrake depressed, then there is wear in the suspension joints or mountings.

5 Now grasp the wheel at the 9 o'clock and 3 o'clock positions, and try to rock it as before. Any movement felt now may again be caused by wear in the hub bearings or the steering track rod balljoints. If the inner or outer balljoint is worn, the visual movement will be obvious.

6 Using a large screwdriver or flat bar, check for wear in the suspension mounting bushes by levering between the relevant suspension component and its attachment point. Some movement is to be expected as the mountings are made of rubber, but excessive wear should be obvious. Also check the condition of any visible rubber bushes, looking for splits, cracks or contamination of the rubber.

7 With the car standing on its wheels, have an assistant turn the steering wheel back-and-forth about an eighth of a turn each way. There should be very little, if any, lost movement between the steering wheel and roadwheels. If this is not the case, closely observe the joints and mountings previously described, but in addition check the steering column universal joints for wear, and the rack-and-pinion steering gear itself.

8 Check for any signs of fluid leakage around the front suspension struts and rear shock absorber. Should any fluid be noticed, the suspension strut or shock absorber is defective internally, and should be renewed. **Note:** *Suspension struts/shock absorbers should always be renewed in pairs on the same axle to ensure correct handling.*

9 The efficiency of the suspension strut/shock absorber may be checked by bouncing the car at each corner. Generally speaking, the body will return to its normal position and stop after being depressed. If it rises and returns on a rebound, the suspension strut/shock absorber is probably suspect. Examine also the suspension strut/shock absorber upper and lower mountings for any signs of wear.

15 Battery check

1 The battery is located in the front, left-hand corner of the engine compartment. Release the clip at the back, then swing the battery cover upwards and forwards to gain access to the battery terminals (see illustration).

2 Where necessary, open the fuse holder plastic cover (squeeze together the locking lugs to release the cover) to gain access to the

15.1 Remove the battery cover

battery positive (+) terminal and fuse holder connections.

3 Check that both battery terminals and all the fuse holder connections are securely attached and are free from corrosion. **Note:** *Before disconnecting the terminals from the battery, refer to Chapter 5A.*

4 Check the battery casing for signs of damage or cracking and check the battery retaining clamp bolt is securely tightened. If the battery casing is damaged in any way the battery must be renewed (see Chapter 5A).

5 If the car is not fitted with a sealed-for-life maintenance-free battery, check the electrolyte level is between the MAX and MIN level markings on the battery casing. If topping-up is necessary, remove the battery (see Chapter 5A) from the car then remove the cell caps/cover (as applicable). Using distilled water, top the electrolyte level of each cell up to the MAX level mark then securely refit the cell caps/cover. Ensure the battery has not been overfilled then refit the battery to the car (see Chapter 5A).

6 Some models are fitted with a battery with a 'magic eye' which shows the state of the battery and level of electrolyte. The 'magic eye' is located on the top of the battery, near the negative terminal. If the eye is green, the battery is in good condition and charged up. If the eye is black, the battery is flat and should be charged. If the eye is colourless or yellow, the electrolyte is low and in a critical condition, and should be topped-up with distilled water. If charging the battery does not return the eye to green, the battery should be scrapped.

7 On completion of the check, clip the cover securely back onto the fuse holder and close up the cover.

16 Hinge and lock lubrication

1 Lubricate the hinges of the bonnet, doors and tailgate with a light general-purpose oil. Similarly, lubricate all latches, locks and lock strikers. At the same time, check the security and operation of all the locks, adjusting them if necessary (see Chapter 11).

2 Lightly lubricate the bonnet release mechanism and cable with a suitable grease.

17 Airbag unit check

Inspect the exterior condition of the airbag(s) for signs of damage or deterioration. If an airbag shows signs of damage, it must be renewed (see Chapter 12). Note that it is not permissible to attach any stickers to the surface of the airbag, as this may affect the deployment of the unit.

18 Windscreen/tailgate/ headlight washer system check

1 Check that each of the washer jet nozzles is clear and that each nozzle provides a strong jet of washer fluid.

2 The tailgate jet should be aimed to spray at the centre of the screen, using a pin.

3 The windscreen washer nozzles are fixed, and cannot be adjusted.

4 Especially during the winter months, make sure that the washer fluid concentration is sufficient to avoid freezing. *Caution: On no account use engine coolant antifreeze in the screen washer system – this may damage the paintwork.*

19 Engine management self-diagnosis memory fault check

This work should be carried out by a Seat dealer or diagnostic specialist using special equipment. The diagnostic socket is located behind a hinged cover beneath the driver's side of the facia.

20 Sunroof check and lubrication

1 Check the operation of the sunroof, and leave it in the fully open position.

2 Wipe clean the guide rails on each side of the sunroof opening, then apply lubricant to them. Seat recommend lubricant spray G 052 778.

21 Road test and exhaust emissions check

Instruments and electrical equipment

1 Check the operation of all instruments and electrical equipment including the air conditioning system.

2 Make sure that all instruments read correctly, and switch on all electrical equipment in turn, to check that it functions properly.

Steering and suspension

3 Check for any abnormalities in the steering, suspension, handling or road 'feel'.

4 Drive the car, and check that there are no unusual vibrations or noises which may indicate wear in the driveshafts, wheel bearings, etc.

5 Check that the steering feels positive, with no excessive 'sloppiness', or roughness, and check for any suspension noises when cornering and driving over bumps.

Drivetrain

6 Check the performance of the engine, clutch, gearbox and driveshafts.

7 Listen for any unusual noises from the engine, clutch and gearbox.

8 Make sure the engine runs smoothly at idle, and there is no hesitation on accelerating.

9 Check that the clutch action is smooth and progressive, that the drive is taken up smoothly, and that the pedal travel is not excessive. Also listen for any noises when the clutch pedal is depressed.

10 Check that all gears can be engaged smoothly without noise, and that the gear lever action is smooth and not abnormally vague or 'notchy'.

11 Listen for a metallic clicking sound from the front of the car, as the car is driven slowly in a circle with the steering on full-lock. Carry out this check in both directions. If a clicking noise is heard, this indicates wear in a driveshaft joint, in which case renew the joint if necessary.

Braking system

12 Make sure that the car does not pull to one side when braking, and that the wheels do not lock when braking hard.

13 Check that there is no vibration through the steering when braking.

14 Check that the handbrake operates correctly without excessive movement of the lever, and that it holds the car stationary on a slope.

15 Test the operation of the brake servo unit as follows. With the engine off, depress the footbrake four or five times to exhaust the vacuum. Hold the brake pedal depressed, then start the engine. As the engine starts, there should be a noticeable 'give' in the brake pedal as vacuum builds-up. Allow the engine to run for at least two minutes, and then switch it off. If the brake pedal is depressed now, it should be possible to detect a hiss from the servo as the pedal is depressed. After about four or five applications, no further hissing should be heard, and the pedal should feel considerably harder.

16 Under controlled emergency braking, the pulsing of the ABS unit must be felt at the footbrake pedal.

Exhaust emissions check

17 Although not part of the manufacturer's maintenance schedule, this check will normally be carried out on a regular basis according to the country the car is operated in. Currently in the UK, exhaust emissions testing is included as part of the annual MOT test after the car is 3 years old.

22 Resetting the service interval display

1 After all necessary maintenance work has been completed, the service interval display must be reset. Seat technicians use a special dedicated instrument to do this, and a print-out is then put in the car's service record. It is possible for the owner to reset the display as described in the following paragraph.

2 To reset the display manually, switch off the ignition, then press and hold down the trip reset button beneath the speedometer. Switch on the ignition and observe the service interval, then hold the button down for 10 seconds until '- - -' appears, followed by the trip readout.

Every 20 000 miles or 2 years

23 Pollen filter element renewal

1 The pollen filter is located on the heater assembly, and is removed into the passenger footwell. Undo the bolts and remove the panel above the footwell.

2 Reach under the glovebox, and slide the two retaining catches on the pollen filter lower cover towards each other, to release and remove the cover (see illustrations).

3 Withdraw the filter downwards from the heater assembly, and remove from inside the car (see illustration).

4 Separate the filter from the frame, noting the fitted direction of the airflow arrows, which should be towards the driver's side (see illustration).

5 Fit the new filter to the frame, with the airflow arrows pointing as noted before, then insert it into the heater assembly. Refit the lower cover, and slide the catches apart to secure it.

6 Refit the panel above the footwell.

24 Fuel filter renewal

1 The fuel filter is mounted on the right-hand inner wing (right as seen from the driver's seat). Position a container underneath the filter unit and pad the surrounding area with rags to absorb any fuel that may be spilt.

23.2a Slide the catches (arrowed) towards each other . . .

23.2b . . . and remove the pollen filter lower cover

23.3 Withdraw the pollen filter into the passenger footwell

23.4 Separate the filter from the frame, noting the airflow arrows

24.2 Release the clips and disconnect the hoses from the fuel filter. Note the arrows on the hoses indicating fuel flow

24.3a Spread the clips (arrowed) outwards . . .

24.3b . . . and lift the filter from the bracket

24.4 Push the clips (arrowed) apart slightly and lift the filter . . .

24.5 . . . slide out the retaining clip and lift out the control valve, leaving the fuel hoses attached

Note: *It may take a few seconds of cranking before the engine starts.*

11 Raise the engine speed to about 2000 rpm several times, then allow the engine to idle again. Observe the fuel flow through the transparent hose leading to the fuel injection pump and check that it is free of air bubbles.

Engine codes BNV, BNM and BMS

2 Note their fitted positions, then release the clips and disconnect the fuel hoses from the top of the filter **(see illustration)**.
3 Spread the 3 retaining clips and lift the filter from the bracket **(see illustrations)**.

All other engine codes

4 Push the 3 retaining clips apart slightly and lift the filter element a little from the bracket **(see illustration)**.
5 At the top of the filter unit, release the clip and lift out the control valve, leaving the fuel hoses attached to it **(see illustration)**.

6 Release the hose clips and pull the fuel supply and delivery hoses from the ports on the of the filter unit. Note the fitted position of each hose, to aid correct refitting later. Lift the filter from the bracket.
Caution: Be prepared for fuel spillage.
7 Fit a new fuel filter into the retaining bracket and tighten the securing bolts.
8 Refit the control valve to the top of the filter and insert the retaining clip.

All engine codes

9 Reconnect the fuel supply and delivery hoses, using the notes made during removal – note the fuel flow arrow markings next to each port. Where crimp-type hoses were originally fitted, use equivalent size worm-drive clips on refitting. Remove the collecting container and rags.
10 Start and run the engine at idle, then check around the fuel filter for fuel leaks.

25.4 On the 02R transmission, an Allen key or bit is needed on the filler/level plug

25 Manual transmission oil level check

1 Park the car on a level surface. For improved access to the filler/level plug, apply the handbrake, then jack up the front of the car and support it on axle stands (see *Jacking and vehicle support*), but note that the rear of the car should also be raised to ensure an accurate level check. The oil level must be checked before the car is driven, or at least 5 minutes after the engine has been switched off. If the oil is checked immediately after driving the car, some of the oil will remain distributed around the transmission components, resulting in an inaccurate level reading.
2 As applicable, undo the retaining bolts and remove the engine undershield(s). Wipe clean the area around the transmission filler/level plug which is situated on the front, left-hand end of the transmission **(see illustration)**.
Note: *On the 6-speed transmission, a new sealing washer will be needed for refitting.*
3 On the 6-speed transmissions, to unscrew the filler/level plug, a special multi-splined key will be needed (Seat tool number T20118, though alternatives may be available). Since the plug will almost certainly be very tight, badly-fitting substitute tools are unlikely to work, and damage may be caused to the plug's splines.
4 The 5-speed transmission has a hex fitting on its filler/level plug, which means it can be unscrewed with a large Allen key or bit **(see illustration)**. Ensure that the tool used is a good fit in the plug, and take care when loosening to avoid personal injury from surrounding components, as the plug will be tight.
5 The oil level should reach the lower edge of the filler/level hole. A certain amount of

25.2 Manual transmission oil filler/level plug location (arrowed)

H46068

oil will have gathered behind the filler/level plug, and will trickle out when it is removed; this does **not** necessarily indicate that the level is correct. To ensure that a true level is established, wait until the initial trickle has stopped, then add oil as necessary until a trickle of new oil can be seen emerging. The level will be correct when the flow ceases; use only good-quality oil of the specified type.

6 If the transmission has been overfilled so that oil flows out when the filler/level plug is removed, check that the car is completely level (front-to-rear and side-to-side), and allow the surplus to drain off into a suitable container.

7 When the oil level is correct, refit the filler/level plug and tighten it to the specified torque (on the 6-speed transmission, fit a new sealing washer). Wipe off any spilt oil then refit the engine undershield(s), tighten the retaining bolts securely, and lower the car to the ground.

Every 40 000 miles or 4 years

26 Air filter element renewal

1 The air filter is housed in the air cleaner, which is situated on the left-hand side of the inner wing, behind the battery.
2 Undo the four bolts and lift the cover from the top of the air cleaner body **(see illustration)**.
3 Lift out the air filter element **(see illustration)**.
4 Remove any debris that may have collected inside the air cleaner.
5 Fit a new air filter element in position, ensuring that the edges are securely seated.
6 Refit the air cleaner top cover and secure with the four bolts.

27 Power steering hydraulic fluid level check

1 Turn the front roadwheels to the straight-ahead position without starting the engine. If the car has been left standing for an hour or more, the power steering fluid will be cold (below 50ºC), and the 'cold' level markings must be used. If, however, the engine is at normal temperature (above 50ºC), the fluid will be hot, and the 'hot' level markings must be used.
2 The reservoir for the Electrically Powered Hydraulic Steering (EPHS) is located on the front left-hand corner of the engine compartment. **Note:** *On some models with a high capacity battery, the battery and tray must be removed in order to access the reservoir filler cap.* The fluid level is checked with the dipstick attached to the reservoir filler cap. Unscrew the cap from the hydraulic fluid reservoir, and wipe clean the integral dipstick with a clean cloth **(see illustration)**.
3 Screw on the cap hand-tight, then unscrew it again and check the fluid level on the dipstick. The fluid level must be between the MIN (or lower) and MAX (or upper) marks **(see illustrations)**. If the fluid is cold (below 50ºC), it must be at least above the lower level mark or MIN. If the fluid is hot (above 50ºC), it must not be above the upper level mark or MAX.
4 If the level is above the maximum level mark, siphon off the excess amount. If it is below the minimum level mark, add the specified fluid as necessary (see *Lubricants and fluids*), but in this case also check the system for leaks **(see illustration)**. On completion, screw on the cap and tighten. Refit the battery and tray where removed.

28 Timing belt and tensioning roller renewal

Refer to Chapter 2C.

26.2 Remove the cover . . .

26.3 . . . and lift out the air filter element

27.2 Unscrew the cap from the hydraulic fluid reservoir

27.3a The power steering fluid level must be between the upper and lower marks

27.3b Alternative power steering cap markings

27.4 Top-up the fluid level

Every 80 000 miles – engine code BMT

Every 100 000 miles – engine code BMS

29 Particulate filter check

Note: *Only 1.4 litre engine code BMS, and 1.9 litre engine code BMT are fitted with exhaust particulate filters.*

At approximately these mileages the remaining capacity of the particulate filter should be checked. Unfortunately, this can only be carried out using dedicated diagnostic equipment. Consequently, we recommend this task be entrusted to a Seat dealer or suitably-equipped specialist. If the capacity of the filter to absorb ash is exhausted, a new filter must be fitted as described in Chapter 4C.

Every 2 years

30 Brake (and clutch) fluid renewal

> ⚠ **Warning: Brake hydraulic fluid can harm your eyes and damage painted surfaces, so use extreme caution when handling and pouring it. Do not use fluid that has been standing open for some time, as it absorbs moisture from the air. Excess moisture can cause a dangerous loss of braking effectiveness.**

1 The procedure is similar to that for the bleeding of the hydraulic system as described in Chapter 9, except that the brake fluid reservoir should be emptied by siphoning, using a clean poultry baster or similar before starting, and allowance should be made for the old fluid to be expelled when bleeding a section of the circuit. Since the clutch hydraulic system also uses fluid from the brake system reservoir, it should also be bled at the same time by referring to Chapter 6, Section 2.

2 Working as described in Chapter 9, open the first bleed screw in the sequence, and pump the brake pedal gently until nearly all the old fluid has been emptied from the master cylinder reservoir.

3 Top-up to the MAX level with new fluid, and continue pumping until only the new fluid remains in the reservoir, and new fluid can be seen emerging from the bleed screw. Tighten the screw, and top the reservoir level up to the MAX level line.

HAYNES HINT *Old hydraulic fluid is often much darker in colour than the new, making it easy to distinguish the two.*

4 Work through all the remaining bleed screws in the sequence until new fluid can be seen at all of them. Be careful to keep the master cylinder reservoir topped-up to above the MIN level at all times, or air may enter the system and greatly increase the length of the task.

5 When the operation is complete, check that all bleed screws are securely tightened, and that their dust caps are refitted. Wash off all traces of spilt fluid, and recheck the master cylinder reservoir fluid level.

6 Once the brake fluid has been changed the clutch fluid should also be renewed. Referring to Chapter 6, bleed the clutch until new fluid is seen to be emerging from the slave cylinder bleed screw, keeping the master cylinder fluid level above the MIN level line at all times to prevent air entering the system. Once the new fluid emerges, securely tighten the bleed screw then disconnect and remove the bleeding equipment. Securely refit the dust cap then wash off all traces of spilt fluid.

7 Ensure the master cylinder fluid level is correct (see *Weekly checks*) and thoroughly check the operation of the brakes and clutch before taking the car on the road.

31 Coolant renewal

Note: *This work is not included in the Seat schedule, and should not be required if the recommended Seat G12 coolant antifreeze/ inhibitor is used. However, if standard antifreeze/inhibitor is used, the work should be carried out at the recommended interval.*

> ⚠ **Warning: Wait until the engine is cold before starting this procedure. Do not allow antifreeze to come in contact with your skin, or with the car's painted surfaces. Rinse off spills immediately with plenty of water. Never leave antifreeze lying around in an open container, or in a puddle in the driveway or on the garage floor. Children and pets are attracted by its sweet smell, but antifreeze can be fatal if ingested.**

Cooling system draining

1 With the engine completely cold, unscrew the expansion tank cap.

2 Firmly apply the handbrake then jack up the front of the car and support it on axle stands (see *Jacking and vehicle support*). Undo the retaining bolts and remove the engine undershield(s) to gain access to the base of the radiator.

3 Position a suitable container beneath the coolant drain plug which is located in the bottom hose fitting to the left-hand bottom end of the radiator. Unscrew the drain plug and pull it out slightly (there is no need to remove it completely) and allow the coolant to drain into the container **(see illustration)**. If desired, a length of tubing can be fitted to the drain outlet to direct the flow of coolant during draining. Where no drain outlet is fitted to the hose end fitting, remove the retaining clip and disconnect the bottom hose from the radiator to drain the coolant (see Chapter 3).

4 On engines with an oil cooler, to fully drain the system, also disconnect one of the coolant hoses from the oil cooler which is located at the front of the cylinder block.

5 If the coolant has been drained for a reason other than renewal, then provided it is clean, it can be re-used.

6 Once all the coolant has drained, securely tighten the drain plug or reconnect the bottom hose to the radiator (as applicable). Where necessary, also reconnect the coolant hose to the oil cooler and secure it in position with the retaining clip. Refit the undershield(s), tighten the retaining bolts securely.

Cooling system flushing

7 If the recommended Seat coolant has not been used and coolant renewal has been neglected, or if the antifreeze mixture has become diluted, the cooling system may gradually lose efficiency, as the coolant passages become restricted due to rust, scale deposits, and other sediment. The cooling system efficiency can be restored by flushing the system clean.

8 The radiator should be flushed separately from the engine, to avoid excess contamination.

31.3 Unscrew the radiator drain plug and allow the coolant to drain into the container

Radiator flushing

9 To flush the radiator, first tighten the radiator drain plug.

10 Disconnect the top and bottom hoses and any other relevant hoses from the radiator (see Chapter 3).

11 Insert a garden hose into the radiator top inlet. Direct a flow of clean water through the radiator, and continue flushing until clean water emerges from the radiator bottom outlet.

12 If after a reasonable period, the water still does not run clear, the radiator can be flushed with a good proprietary cleaning agent. It is important that the manufacturer's instructions are followed carefully. If the contamination is particularly bad, insert the hose in the radiator bottom outlet, and reverse-flush the radiator.

Engine flushing

13 To flush the engine, remove the thermostat (see Chapter 3).

14 With the bottom hose disconnected from the radiator, insert a garden hose into the thermostat housing. Direct a clean flow of water through the engine, and continue flushing until clean water emerges from the radiator bottom hose.

15 When flushing is complete, refit the thermostat and reconnect the hoses (see Chapter 3).

Cooling system filling

16 Before attempting to fill the cooling system, ensure the drain plug is securely closed and make sure that all hoses are securely connected and their retaining clips are in good condition. If the recommended Seat coolant is not being used, ensure that a suitable antifreeze mixture is used all year round, to prevent corrosion of the engine components (see following sub-Section).

17 Remove the coolant temperature sensor from the coolant distribution housing on the left-hand end of the cylinder head with reference to Chapter 3.

18 Remove the expansion tank filler cap and slowly fill the system with coolant **(see illustration)**, until bubble-free coolant runs

from the temperature sensor hole, then refit the sensor immediately with reference to Chapter 3. Continue to fill the system until the level is up to the MAX level mark on the expansion tank. Help to bleed the air from the system by repeatedly squeezing the radiator bottom hose.

19 Refit the cap to the expansion tank, then run the engine at a fast idle speed until the cooling fan cuts in. Wait for the fan to stop then switch the engine off and allow the engine to cool.

20 When the engine has cooled, check the coolant level with reference to *Weekly checks*. Top-up the level if necessary, and refit the expansion tank cap.

Antifreeze mixture

21 If the recommended Seat coolant is not being used, the antifreeze should always be renewed at the specified intervals. This is necessary not only to maintain the antifreeze properties, but also to prevent corrosion which would otherwise occur as the corrosion inhibitors become progressively less effective.

22 Always use an ethylene-glycol based antifreeze which is suitable for use in mixed-metal cooling systems. The quantity of antifreeze and levels of protection are indicated in the Specifications.

23 Before adding antifreeze, the cooling system should be completely drained, preferably flushed, and all hoses checked for condition and security.

24 After filling with antifreeze, a label should be attached to the expansion tank, stating the type and concentration of antifreeze used, and the date installed. Any subsequent topping-up should be made with the same type and concentration of antifreeze.

25 Do not use engine antifreeze in the windscreen/tailgate washer system, as it will damage the paintwork. A screenwash additive should be added to the washer system in the quantities stated on the bottle.

Airlocks

26 If, after draining and refilling the system, symptoms of overheating are found which did

31.18 Fill the cooling system

not occur previously, then the fault is almost certainly due to trapped air at some point in the system, causing an airlock and restricting the flow of coolant; usually, the air is trapped because the system was refilled too quickly.

27 If an airlock is suspected, first try gently squeezing all visible coolant hoses. A coolant hose which is full of air feels quite different to one full of coolant when squeezed. After refilling the system, most airlocks will clear once the system has cooled, and been topped-up.

28 While the engine is running at operating temperature, switch on the heater and heater fan, and check for heat output. Provided there is sufficient coolant in the system, any lack of heat output could be due to an airlock in the system.

29 Airlocks can have more serious effects than simply reducing heater output – a severe airlock could reduce coolant flow around the engine. Check that the radiator top hose is hot when the engine is at operating temperature – a top hose which stays cold could be the result of an airlock (or a non-opening thermostat).

30 If the problem persists, stop the engine and allow it to cool down **completely** before unscrewing the expansion tank filler cap or loosening the hose clips and squeezing the hoses to bleed out the trapped air. In the worst case, the system will have to be at least partially drained (this time, the coolant can be saved for re-use) and flushed to clear the problem.

Chapter 2 Part A:
1.2 litre petrol engine in-car repair procedures

Contents

Degrees of difficulty

Easy, suitable for novice with little experience	**Fairly easy,** suitable for beginner with some experience	**Fairly difficult,** suitable for competent DIY mechanic	**Difficult,** suitable for experienced DIY mechanic	**Very difficult,** suitable for expert DIY or professional

Specifications

General

Type	Three-cylinder in-line, chain-driven double overhead camshaft (DOHC), four-stroke, liquid-cooled
Cubic capacity	1198 cc
Manufacturer's engine codes*	AZQ, BME and BXV
Maximum power output:	
AZQ and BME	47 kW at 5400 rpm
BXV	51 kW at 5400 rpm
Maximum torque output	112 Nm at 3000 rpm
Bore	76.5 mm
Stroke	86.9 mm
Compression ratio	10.5 : 1
Compression pressures:	
New engine pressure	10 to 15 bar
Minimum compression pressure	7.0 bar
Maximum difference between cylinders	Approximately 3.0 bar
Firing order	1 – 2 – 3
No 1 cylinder location	Crankshaft pulley end
Direction of crankshaft rotation	Clockwise (when viewed from right-hand side of car)

* Note: See 'Vehicle identification' at the end of this manual for the location of engine code markings.

Lubrication system

Oil pump type	Chain-driven from crankshaft
Minimum oil pressure (oil temperature 80°C) at 2000 rpm	2.0 bar

Camshaft

Camshaft endfloat (maximum)	0.20 mm

Torque wrench settings

	Nm	lbf ft
Air conditioning compressor	23	17
Auxiliary drivebelt tensioner and guide pulley	40	30
Camshaft bearing caps:		
Stage 1	10	7
Stage 2	Angle-tighten a further 90°	
Camshaft position sensor	8	6
Camshaft sprocket:		
Stage 1	20	15
Stage 2	Angle-tighten by 90°	
Coolant pump pulley	22	16
Crankshaft pulley:*		
Stage 1	90	66
Stage 2	Angle-tighten a further 90°	
Cylinder head bolts:*		
Stage 1	30	22
Stage 2	Angle-tighten a further 90°	
Stage 3	Angle-tighten a further 90°	
Cylinder head cover/housing:		
Stage 1	10	7
Stage 2	Angle-tighten a further 90°	
Engine lifting eye	20	15
Flywheel bolts:*		
Stage 1	60	44
Stage 2	Angle-tighten a further 90°	
Left-hand engine mounting:*		
Mounting to body:		
Stage 1	50	37
Stage 2	Angle-tighten a further 90°	
Mounting to transmission:		
Stage 1	40	30
Stage 2	Angle-tighten a further 90°	
Oil filter cap	25	18
Oil filter housing	24	18
Oil level and temperature sender	8	6
Oil pressure switch	25	18
Oil pump	24	18
Oil pump chain tensioner	15	11
Oil pump sprocket:*		
Stage 1	20	15
Stage 2	Angle-tighten a further 90°	
Rear mounting link:*		
To transmission:		
Stage 1	30	22
Stage 2	Angle-tighten a further 90°	
To subframe:		
Stage 1	40	30
Stage 2	Angle-tighten a further 90°	
Right-hand engine mounting:*		
Pedestal to engine	45	33
Mounting to body:		
Stage 1	20	15
Stage 2	Angle-tighten a further 90°	
Intermediate bracket to pedestal:		
Stage 1	30	22
Stage 2	Angle-tighten a further 90°	
Sump bolts	9	7
Sump oil drain plug	30	22
Timing chain guide	15	11
Timing chain hydraulic tensioner	15	11
Timing cover (see illustration 5.19):		
Bolts 1, 2 and 3	50	37
Bolts 4 and 5	25	18
Bolts 6, 7, 8, 11 and 14, and all other bolts:		
Stage 1	8	6
Stage 2	Angle-tighten a further 90°	
Timing chain tensioner guide pivot	18	13

* Do not re-use

1 General information

How to use this Chapter

This Part of Chapter 2 describes those repair procedures that can reasonably be carried out on the engine while it remains in the car. If the engine has been removed from the car and is being dismantled, as described in Part D, any preliminary dismantling procedures can be ignored.

Note that while it may be possible physically to overhaul certain items while the engine is in the car, such tasks are not usually carried out as separate operations, and usually require the execution of several additional procedures (not to mention the cleaning of components and of oilways); for this reason, all such tasks are classed as major overhaul procedures, and are described in Part D of this Chapter.

Caution: The pistons, connecting rods and crankshaft must not be removed on these engines. If these components are excessively worn or damaged, the complete cylinder block and pistons must be renewed as an assembly.

Part D describes the removal of the engine/transmission from the car and the full overhaul procedures that can then be carried out.

Engine description

The engine is an in-line three-cylinder unit, which is mounted transversely at the front of the car, with the manual transmission bolted to the left-hand end of the engine. **Note:** *This engine is not available with automatic transmission.*

The engine is equipped with double overhead camshafts (DOHC, 12-valve), and incorporates a gear-driven balance shaft.

Caution: It is not permitted to dismantle the balance shaft and gears.

The cylinder block, cylinder head and valve cover are all cast in aluminium alloy. The cylinder bores are machined in the cylinder block. The crankshaft has four main bearings, and thrustwashers are fitted to number 3 main bearing to control crankshaft endfloat. A balance shaft is located in a housing beneath the cylinder block, and is driven by a gear located on the end of the crankshaft.

Camshaft drive is by chain from the crankshaft, and the chain is tensioned by a hydraulic tensioner. The valves are closed by coil springs and the camshafts actuate the valves by roller rockers and hydraulic tappets. The flywheel is located on a flange at the left-hand end of the crankshaft. The main bearings and the big-end bearings are of shell type, whilst the connecting rod small-end bearings are of the bronze bush type, being pressed into the connecting rod and reamed to suit.

The oil pump is chain-driven from the end of the crankshaft. Oil is drawn from the sump through a strainer and circulated through an externally-mounted filter to the various engine components.

Repairs with engine in car

The following work can be carried out with the engine in the car:
a) Compression pressure – testing.
b) Crankshaft pulley – removal and refitting.
c) Timing cover – removal and refitting.
d) Timing chain – renewal.
e) Timing chain tensioner and sprockets – removal and refitting.
f) Camshaft(s) and hydraulic tappets – removal and refitting.
g) Cylinder head – removal and refitting*.
h) Cylinder head – decarbonising.
i) Sump – removal and refitting.
j) Oil pump – removal, overhaul and refitting.
k) Crankshaft oil seals – renewal.
l) Engine/transmission mountings – inspection and renewal.
m) Flywheel – removal, inspection and refitting.

* Cylinder head dismantling procedures are detailed in Chapter 2D.

2 Compression test – description and interpretation

1 When engine performance is down, or if misfiring occurs which cannot be attributed to the ignition or fuel systems, a compression test can provide diagnostic clues as to the engine's condition. If the test is performed regularly, it can give warning of trouble before any other symptoms become apparent.
2 The engine must be fully warmed-up to normal operating temperature, the battery must be fully-charged, and the spark plugs must be removed (Chapter 1A). The aid of an assistant will also be required.
3 Remove fuse 25 from the fusebox. This is the fuse for the fuel injectors.
4 Fit a compression tester to the No 1 cylinder spark plug hole – the type of tester which screws into the plug thread is to be preferred.
5 Have the assistant hold the throttle wide open and crank the engine on the starter motor; after one or two revolutions, the compression pressure should build-up to a maximum figure and then stabilise. Record the highest reading obtained.
6 Repeat the test on the remaining cylinders, recording the pressure in each.
7 All cylinders should produce very similar pressures (see Specifications). Any one cylinder reading below 7.0 bar, or a difference of more than 3 bar between cylinders, suggests a fault.
8 Note that the compression should build-up quickly in a healthy engine; low compression on the first stroke, followed by gradually increasing pressure on successive strokes, indicates worn piston rings.
9 A low compression reading on the first stroke, which does not build-up during successive strokes, indicates leaking valves or a blown head gasket (a cracked head could also be the cause).
10 If the pressure in any cylinder is reduced to 7.0 bars or less, carry out the following test to isolate the cause. Introduce a teaspoonful of clean oil into that cylinder through its spark plug hole and repeat the test.
11 If the addition of oil temporarily improves the compression pressure, this indicates that bore or piston wear is responsible for the pressure loss. No improvement suggests that leaking or burnt valves, or a blown head gasket, may be to blame.
12 A low reading from two adjacent cylinders is almost certainly due to the head gasket having blown between them; the presence of coolant in the engine oil will confirm this.
13 If one cylinder is about 20 percent lower than the others and the engine has a slightly rough idle, a worn camshaft lobe could be the cause.
14 On completion of the test, refit the spark plugs, and refit the injectors fuse.

3 Engine assembly and valve timing marks – general information and usage

Note: *Seat TDC setting tools T10123 and T10121 will be required for this procedure. Alternatively, setting tools may be obtained from automotive tool manufacturers/suppliers.*
1 Top dead centre (TDC) is the highest point in its travel up-and-down its cylinder bore that each piston reaches as the crankshaft rotates. While each piston reaches TDC both at the top of the compression stroke and again at the top of the exhaust stroke, for the purpose of timing the engine, TDC refers to the No 1 piston position at the top of its compression stroke.
2 No 1 piston and cylinder are at the right-hand end of the engine. Note that the crankshaft rotates clockwise when viewed from the right-hand side of the car.
3 Disconnect the battery negative lead (see Chapter 5A). Remove all the spark plugs as described in Chapter 1A.
4 At the left-hand end of the cylinder head, unbolt the caps from the ends of the intake and exhaust camshafts. **Note:** *New O-rings must be fitted before refitting the caps (see illustration).*

3.4 Fit new O-rings before refitting the camshaft end caps

3.6a Fit the camshaft TDC tools . . .

3.6b . . . and tighten the bolts (arrowed)

3.6c Crankshaft TDC tool

3.6d Crankshaft TDC tool fitted through the cylinder block rear flange

5 Unbolt the crankshaft position/speed sender from the cylinder block rear flange.
6 Turn the engine with a socket on the crankshaft pulley bolt until the grooves at the left-hand ends of the camshafts are both horizontal. Now insert the tools T10123 into

the camshafts and secure with the bolts. The engine is now at TDC compression for No 1 cylinder and the remaining TDC tool can be inserted through the cylinder block rear flange into the hole in the flywheel (see illustrations).
7 If necessary, as a further check that No 1

cylinder is on its compression stroke, remove the TDC tools and turn the engine back a little from the position described in paragraph 6. Now turn the engine forwards again to TDC with a finger placed over No 1 spark plug hole. If No 1 piston is rising on a compression stroke, pressure will be felt building-up as the engine is turned forwards to TDC.
8 Once No 1 cylinder has been positioned at TDC on the compression stroke, TDC for any of the other cylinders can then be located by rotating the crankshaft clockwise 240° at a time and following the firing order (see Specifications).

4 Crankshaft pulley – removal and refitting

Removal

1 Pull up and remove the engine top cover and air filter (see illustration). Disconnect the vent hose as the cover is removed.
2 Raise the front of the vehicle and support it securely on axle stands (see *Jacking and vehicle support*). Undo the fasteners, remove the engine undershield and right-hand wheel arch liner (see illustration).
3 Mark the auxiliary drivebelt for normal rotation to ensure correct refitting. Note the routing of the drivebelt for ease of refitting.
4 Lever off the cover from the centre of the drivebelt tensioner roller, then use a Torx key to turn the tensioner anti-clockwise to the stop. Hold the tensioner in this position and remove the drivebelt from the pulleys. Release the tensioner or, if preferred, retain the tensioner in this position by inserting a suitable pin/drill bit through the hole provided.
5 Have an assistant engage 4th gear and apply firm pressure to the footbrake pedal, then loosen the crankshaft pulley bolt and remove it together with the pulley (see illustrations). Seat state that the bolt must be renewed whenever removed.

Refitting

6 Locate the pulley and new bolt on the end of the crankshaft, then tighten it to the specified torque and angle while holding it stationary using the method for removal (see illustration).
7 Locate the auxiliary drivebelt on the pulleys

4.1 Pull the engine top cover/air filter housing upwards from the rubber mountings

4.2 Undo the bolts (arrowed) and remove the engine undershield

4.5a Unscrew the crankshaft pulley bolt . . .

4.5b . . . and remove the crankshaft pulley

4.6 Angle-tightening the crankshaft pulley bolt

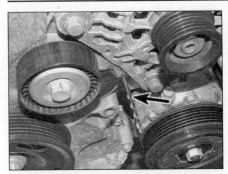

5.3 Insert a suitable pin/drill bit (arrowed) to retain the auxiliary drivebelt tensioner

5.9a Unscrew the crankshaft pulley bolt . . .

5.9b . . . and remove it together with the pulley

5.10a Undo the bolts . . .

5.10b . . . and remove the sump

5.11 Remove the oil level dipstick tube mounting bolt

while holding the tensioner against the spring pressure, then release the tensioner making sure that the ribs of the drivebelt locate correctly in the pulley grooves. Refit the cover to the centre of the tensioner roller.

8 Refit the engine undershield and lower the vehicle to the ground.

9 Refit the engine top cover and air filter as applicable.

5 Timing cover – removal and refitting

Removal

1 Pull up and remove the engine top cover and air filter **(see illustration 4.1)**. Disconnect the vent hose as the cover is removed.

2 Apply the handbrake, then jack up the front of the car and support it on axle stands (see *Jacking and vehicle support*). Remove the right-hand front roadwheel. Undo the fasteners, remove the engine undershield and the right-hand front wheel arch liner **(see illustrations 4.2)**.

3 Mark the auxiliary drivebelt for direction of rotation to ensure correct refitting. Lever off the cover from the centre of the drivebelt tensioner roller, then use a Torx key to turn the tensioner anti-clockwise to the stop. Hold the tensioner in this position and remove the drivebelt from the pulleys. Release the tensioner or, if preferred, retain the tensioner in this position by inserting a suitable pin/drill bit through the hole provided **(see illustration)**.

4 Hold the coolant pump pulley stationary

using an oil filter strap or similar tool, then unscrew the retaining bolts and remove the pulley from the drive flange.

5 On models with air conditioning, unbolt the auxiliary drivebelt guide pulley from the cylinder block, then unbolt the compressor and suspend it from the vehicle bodywork. There is no need to disconnect the refrigerant pipes.

6 Unbolt the auxiliary drivebelt tensioner and pulley from the cylinder block.

7 Remove the alternator as described in Chapter 5A.

8 Unclip the coolant expansion tank purge hose, and place it to one side.

9 Have an assistant engage 4th gear and apply firm pressure to the footbrake pedal, then use a multi-splined key to loosen the crankshaft pulley bolt and remove it together with the pulley. Alternatively, use a home-made tool to retain the pulley **(see illustrations)**. Seat state that the bolt must be renewed whenever removed.

5.12 Engine support bar attached to the right-hand end of the engine

10 Remove the sump as described in Section 9. If necessary, remove the exhaust front pipe as described in Chapter 4C to provide additional working space **(see illustrations)**.

11 Unbolt and remove the oil level dipstick tube **(see illustration)** and, where applicable, remove the oil level/temperature sender from the cylinder block.

12 The right-hand end of the engine must now be supported while the engine mounting is removed, and the engine then held in a safe position in order to carry out the remaining work. To do this, use a hoist or support bar attached to the engine lifting eyes – this is preferable to using a trolley jack beneath the engine **(see illustration)**. With the engine supported, remove the right-hand engine mounting with reference to Section 14.

13 Unbolt the PCV valve (crankcase ventilation) from the timing cover and recover the O-ring **(see illustration)**.

5.13 Remove the PCV valve (crankcase ventilation) from the timing cover

5.14a Remove the timing cover

5.14b If necessary, unscrew the bolts (arrowed) . . .

5.14c . . . and remove the oil separator from the timing cover

5.18a Apply the sealant to the timing cover

14 Progressively unscrew and remove all of the retaining bolts, then remove the timing cover from the engine. If necessary, tap the cover lightly to release the sealant, then withdraw the cover from the location dowels (see illustrations).

15 With the cover removed, slide the sleeve and O-ring from the end of the crankshaft. Note: *This is necessary as the sleeve must be assembled onto the crankshaft after refitting the timing cover.*

16 If the timing cover has been removed in order to carry out other work (ie, timing chain or cylinder head removal), the pistons must be positioned away from their TDC positions as a precaution against them touching the valves. To do this, temporarily refit the crankshaft pulley, then insert and tighten the crankshaft pulley bolt, using the TDC locking tool to hold the crankshaft stationary. Now, remove the locking tool and turn the crankshaft 45° anti-clockwise.

Refitting

17 Before refitting, carefully clean away all residues of sealant from the cover and engine. Also, check that the cover M6 retaining bolts still have thread sealant on their threads, and if not, renew them.

18 Apply a 3.0 mm diameter bead of sealant to the inside of the cover, making sure that the

5.18b Apply a bead of sealant as shown

A 3.0 mm bead
B Location dowels
C Joint between cylinder block and head

H45834

5.19 Timing chain cover bolt tightening sequence

H45836

6.3 Insert a 3.0 mm diameter drill bit (arrowed) in the hole to retain the timing chain tensioner piston

6.4a Hold the sprocket while loosening the bolt . . .

6.4b . . . then remove the bolt and sprocket

bead is on the inside of the bolt holes **(see illustrations)**. Do not forget the upper and lower centre holes. **Note:** *The timing cover must be refitted within 15 minutes of applying the sealant to the cylinder head.* Apply a little sealant to the joint between the cylinder head and block on the engine, at the front and rear points where the cover makes contact.

19 Carefully locate the timing cover on the engine, insert the bolts, and progressively tighten them to the specified torque in sequence **(see illustration)**.

20 Refit the sleeve to the end of the crankshaft together with a new O-ring. Seat state that the cover oil seal must not be lubricated with either oil or grease.

21 The remainder of refitting is a reversal of removal, remembering to tighten all fasteners to their specified torque, where given.

6 Timing chain, tensioner and sprockets – removal, inspection and refitting

Removal

1 Set the engine to TDC as described in Section 3 and insert the locking tools.

2 Remove the timing cover as described in Section 5 and position No 1 piston/crankshaft 45° anti-clockwise from its TDC position.

3 The timing chain tensioner rail must now be released from the chain, and the hydraulic tensioner locked. To do this, press the lower end of the rail rearwards so that it forces the piston into the hydraulic tensioner, then insert a suitable 3.0 mm diameter tool through the holes provided to retain the piston **(see illustration)**.

4 Identify the intake and exhaust camshaft sprockets for position, then unscrew and remove their retaining bolts and withdraw the sprockets, at the same time disengaging them from the timing chain. Seat state that it is in order to use their TDC tool to hold the camshafts stationary while loosening the sprocket retaining bolt, however, if pattern tools are used, we recommend that a sprocket retaining tool be made out of a length of metal bar, with two long bolts positioned to engage the holes in the sprocket **(see illustrations)**.

5 Unbolt the plastic cover from the oil pump, hold the sprocket stationary and unscrew the retaining bolt – discard the bolt as a new one must be used on refitting. Slide the small sprocket from the end of the crankshaft and place the chain and sprockets to one side. **Note:** *The sprocket is not keyed to the crankshaft.*

6 Slide the crankshaft sprocket together with the timing chain from the crankshaft **(see illustration)**. **Note:** *The sprocket is keyed to the crankshaft.*

7 Slide the tensioner rail from its upper pivot. If necessary, unbolt the remaining guide rail and hydraulic tensioner from the cylinder block **(see illustrations)**.

Inspection

8 Thoroughly clean all components, then examine the timing chain and oil pump drive chain for excessive wear. Also check

6.6 Remove the timing chain sprocket from the crankshaft

6.7b . . . then unbolt the remaining guide rail

the sprocket teeth for wear. If the engine has covered a high mileage, the chain and sprockets should be renewed as a matter of course.

9 The crankshaft pulley bolt must be renewed whenever removed.

Refitting

10 Check that the camshafts are still positioned at TDC with the locking tools fitted and the retaining bolts tightened. No 1 piston should still be positioned before TDC (see Section 5).

11 Slide the tensioner rail onto its upper pivot. Refit the guide rail and hydraulic tensioner, and tighten the mounting bolts to the specified torque.

12 Engage the crankshaft sprocket in the timing chain and locate the sprocket on the end of the crankshaft, making sure it is engaged with the groove.

6.7a Slide the tensioner rail from its upper pivot . . .

6.7c Remove the timing chain tensioner

6.18 Balance shaft gear alignment indents (arrowed)

13 Engage the oil pump drive sprocket (small) with the drive chain, then locate the sprocket on the end of the crankshaft. Engage the large sprocket in the chain, position the sprocket on the oil pump and screw on the new retaining bolt. Tighten the bolt to the specified torque while holding the sprocket stationary.

14 Refit the oil pump plastic cover and tighten the bolts.

15 Refit the sump with reference to Section 9.

16 Clean the contact surfaces of the camshafts and sprockets and engage the sprockets with the timing chain. Locate the sprockets on the end of the camshafts and insert the retaining bolts, loosely at this stage so that the sprockets can move freely on the locked camshafts.

17 Press the lower end of the timing chain tensioner rail rearwards, remove the locking tool, and release the rail to tension the timing chain.

18 Turn the crankshaft slowly clockwise 45° so that No 1 piston is at TDC, and insert

6.19 Mark the bolt and sprocket to apply the tightening angle

the locking tool through the cylinder block rear flange into the flywheel – note that the crankshaft should be turned slowly to the TDC position; if it is turned too far, turn it back and start again. The indents on the balance shaft gears must also be aligned with each other **(see illustration)**.

19 Apply slight anti-clockwise pressure to the camshaft sprocket with the holding tool (paragraph 4), then tighten the retaining bolt to the torque and angle given in the Specifications. The angle-tightening can be made by marking the bolt and sprocket with dabs of paint **(see illustration)**.

20 Turn the engine through two complete revolutions, then check that the TDC tools can be fitted to the camshaft and flywheel. Remove the tools.

21 Unbolt and remove the crankshaft pulley from the end of the crankshaft, then refit the timing cover with reference to Section 5.

7 Camshafts and hydraulic tappets – removal, inspection and refitting

Removal

1 Remove the timing cover as described in Section 5.

2 Remove the camshaft sprockets as described in Section 6.

3 Remove the ignition coils with the power output stage. Note that Seat technicians use a special tool (T10094) to remove the coils, however, a length of bent welding rod or similar hooked under the wiring plugs, may be used to extract the coils.

4 Unscrew the cylinder head cover bolts in the **reverse** order to that shown for tightening in paragraph 25, and remove them **(see illustration)**.

5 Remove the cylinder head cover complete with camshafts from the cylinder head **(see illustration)**. If it is tight, use a mallet or rubber hammer to tap the top of the cover in several places in order to release it from the locating dowels.

6 Clean away the sealant from the cylinder head and cover.

7 With the cylinder head cover on the bench, loosen the camshaft bearing cap/housing bolts in the **reverse** order to that shown for tightening in paragraph 20. Lift the caps/housings from the cover **(see illustration)**. Identify the caps/housings for location to ensure correct refitting.

8 Identify each camshaft for location and position, then lift them out from the cylinder head cover **(see illustration)**. **Note:** The intake camshaft has a lug which is positioned over the hole for the Hall sender.

9 Obtain a suitable box with compartments for each of the roller/rocker arms and hydraulic tappets, so that they can be identified for their correct position. Remove the rocker arms and hydraulic tappets from the cylinder head and place them in the box **(see illustrations)**.

10 Clean the camshaft bearing surfaces in the cover and caps/housings.

Inspection

11 Visually inspect the camshafts for

7.4 Progressively unscrew the bolts . . .

7.5 . . . and remove the cylinder head cover complete with camshafts

7.7 Remove the camshaft bearing caps

7.8 Remove the camshafts from the cylinder head cover

7.9a Roller/rocker arms (arrowed)

7.9b Remove the roller/rocker arms and hydraulic tappets from the cylinder head . . .

7.9c . . . and place them in the box

7.17 Fitting the roller/rocker arms and hydraulic tappets

7.20 Camshaft bearing cap/housing bolt tightening sequence

7.21a Apply a bead of sealant as shown

evidence of wear on the surfaces of the lobes and journals. Normally their surfaces should be smooth and have a dull shine; look for scoring, erosion or pitting, and areas that appear highly polished, indicating excessive wear. Accelerated wear will occur once the hardened exterior of the camshafts has been damaged, so always renew worn items.

12 If the machined surfaces of the camshafts appear discoloured or blued, it is likely that they have been overheated at some point, probably due to inadequate lubrication.

13 To measure the camshaft endfloat, temporarily locate them on the cylinder head without the rockers and hydraulic tappets, and temporarily refit the caps. Anchor a DTI gauge to the end of the cylinder head and align the gauge probe with the camshaft axis. Push the camshaft to one end of the cylinder head as far as it will travel, then rest the DTI gauge probe on the end of the camshaft, and zero the gauge display. Push the camshaft as far as it will go to the other end of the cylinder head, and record the gauge reading. Verify the reading by pushing the camshaft back to its original position and checking that the gauge indicates zero again. Repeat the checking procedure for the remaining camshaft.

14 Check that the camshaft endfloat measurement is within the limit given in the

Specifications. Wear outside of this limit is unlikely to be confined to any one component, so renewal of the camshaft and cover must be considered.

15 Inspect the hydraulic tappets for obvious signs of wear or damage, and renew if necessary. Check that the oil holes in the tappets are free from obstructions.

Refitting

16 Remove the crankshaft TDC locking tool, then turn the engine anti-clockwise by 45° so that none of the pistons are at their TDC position.

7.21b Apply the sealant carefully to the cylinder head cover

17 Lubricate the roller/rocker arms and hydraulic tappets with engine oil and refit them to their correct positions on the cylinder head **(see illustration)**.

18 Apply a film of grease to the camshaft bearing surfaces in the caps/housings and cover.

19 Carefully locate the camshafts in their correct positions in the cover, noting that the lug on the intake camshaft must be positioned over the hole for the Hall sender.

20 Refit the bearing caps/housings and initially hand-tighten the retaining bolts. It is important that the caps are not tilted as the bolts are tightened. Tighten the bolts in sequence **(see illustration)** to the torque and angle given in the specifications.

21 Apply a 2.0 to 3.0 mm wide bead of sealant as shown **(see illustrations)** to the cylinder head cover. Make sure that the sealant is not allowed onto the camshaft bearing surfaces, and make sure that the bead runs around the inside of the bolt holes. **Note:** *The cylinder head cover must be refitted within 15 minutes of applying the sealant to the cylinder head.*

22 Check that the roller/rocker arms are correctly located on the valve stems and hydraulic tappets.

23 Lower the cover onto the cylinder head

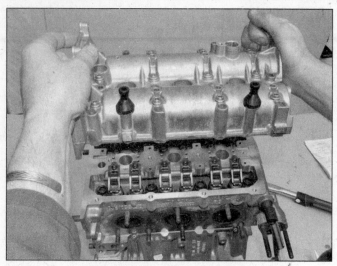

7.23 Refit the cylinder head cover

7.25 Cylinder head cover bolt tightening sequence

making sure that the location dowels enter their holes correctly (see illustration).

24 Insert new retaining bolts and initially hand-tighten all of them.

25 Tighten the retaining bolts to the specified torque and angle given in the Specifications, and in sequence (see illustration).

26 Refit the ignition coils and power output stage, followed by the pipe sections.

27 Refit the camshaft sprockets (Section 6) and timing cover (Section 5).

8 Cylinder head –
removal, inspection and refitting

Removal

1 Drain the cooling system as described in Chapter 1A.

2 Remove the timing cover as described in Section 5.

3 Remove the intake and exhaust manifolds as described in Chapter 4A and 4C respectively.

4 Remove the camshaft sprockets as described in Section 6.

5 Remove the cylinder head cover complete with camshafts, then remove the hydraulic tappets as described in Section 7. It is not necessary to remove the camshafts from the cover unless it is required to work on them.

6 Progressively slacken the cylinder head bolts in the reverse order to that given for tightening in paragraph 19. Remove the cylinder head bolts. Note: The bolts must not be re-used – obtain new ones.

7 With all the bolts removed, lift the cylinder head from the block (see illustration). If the cylinder head is stuck, tap it with a soft-faced mallet to break the joint. Do not insert a lever into the gasket joint.

8 Lift the cylinder head gasket from the block.

Inspection

9 Dismantling and inspection of the cylinder head is covered in Part D of this Chapter.

10 The mating faces of the cylinder head and block must be perfectly clean before refitting the head.

11 Use a scraper to remove all traces of gasket and carbon, also clean the tops of the pistons. Take particular care with the aluminium surfaces, as the soft metal is easily damaged.

12 Make sure that debris is not allowed to enter the oil and water passages – this is particularly important for the oil circuit, as carbon could block the oil supply to the camshaft and crankshaft bearings. Using adhesive tape and paper, seal the water, oil and bolt holes in the cylinder block. To prevent carbon entering the gap between the pistons and bores, smear a little grease in the gap. After cleaning a piston, rotate the crankshaft to that the piston moves down the bore, then wipe out the grease and carbon with a cloth rag. Clean the other piston crowns in the same way.

13 Check the head and block for nicks, deep scratches and other damage. If slight, they may be removed carefully with a file. More serious damage may be repaired by machining, but this is a specialist job. If warpage of the cylinder head is suspected, use a straight-edge to check it for distortion, as described in Part D of this Chapter.

Refitting

14 Ensure that the cylinder head bolt holes in the cylinder block are clean and free of oil. Syringe or soak up any oil left in the bolt holes. This is most important in order that the correct bolt tightening torque can be applied, and to prevent the possibility of the block being cracked by hydraulic pressure when the bolts are tightened.

15 Ensure that the crankshaft has been turned to position No 1 piston slightly down its bore from the TDC position (refer to timing chain refitting in Section 6). This will eliminate any risk of piston-to-valve contact as the cylinder head is refitted.

16 Ensure that the cylinder head locating dowels are in place in the cylinder block (see illustration), then fit a new cylinder head gasket over the dowels. Where applicable, the part number marking should be uppermost (see illustrations). Note that Seat recommend that the gasket is only removed from its packaging immediately prior to fitting.

17 Lower the cylinder head into position on the gasket, ensuring that it engages correctly over the dowels (see illustration).

18 Lightly oil the threads and heads of the

8.7 Remove the cylinder head from the block

8.16a Cylinder head locating dowel on the block (arrowed)

8.16b Fit a new cylinder head gasket

8.16c Typical cylinder head gasket markings

8.17 Lower the cylinder head onto the gasket

new cylinder head bolts, then insert them and screw in as far as possible by hand (see illustrations).

19 Working in sequence, tighten all the cylinder head bolts to the specified Stage 1 torque (see illustrations).

20 Again working in sequence, tighten all the cylinder head bolts through the specified Stage 2 angle (see illustration).

21 Finally, tighten all the cylinder head bolts, in sequence, through the specified Stage 3 angle.

22 Refit the hydraulic tappets, camshafts) and cylinder head cover with reference to Section 7.

23 Refit the camshaft sprockets as described in Section 6.

24 Refit the timing cover as described in Section 5.

25 Refit the manifolds as described in Chapter 4A.

26 The remainder of refitting is a reversal of removal, remembering to fill the cooling system as described in Chapter 1A.

9 Sump –
removal and refitting

Removal

1 Apply the handbrake, then jack up the front of the car and support securely on axle stands (see *Jacking and vehicle support*).

2 Remove the securing bolts and withdraw the engine undershield (see illustration 4.2).

3 Drain the engine oil as described in Chapter 1A.

4 Where fitted, disconnect the wiring connector from the oil level/temperature sender on the sump.

5 Unscrew and remove the bolts securing the sump to the cylinder block, then withdraw the sump (see illustrations). If necessary, release the sump by tapping with a soft-faced mallet.

Refitting

6 Commence refitting by thoroughly cleaning the mating faces of the sump and cylinder block. Ensure that all traces of old sealant are removed.

8.18a Lightly oil the threads and heads of the bolts . . .

8.18b . . . and screw them in as far as possible by hand

8.19a Cylinder head bolt tightening sequence

8.19b Tighten the bolts to the torque setting

8.20 Tighten the bolts through the specified angle

9.5a Unscrew the bolts . . .

9.5b . . . and withdraw the sump

9.7 Apply a bead of sealant to the sump

7 Ensure that the cylinder block mating face of the sump is free from all traces of old sealant, oil and grease, and then apply a 2.0 to 4.0 mm thick bead of silicone sealant (D 176404 A2 or equivalent) to the sump. Note that the sealant should be run around the inside of the bolt holes in the sump (see illustration). The sump must be fitted within 5 minutes of applying the sealant.

8 Offer the sump up to the cylinder block, then refit the retaining bolts, and progressively tighten them in diagonal sequence to the specified torque.

9 Reconnect the wiring to the oil level/temperature sender on the sump.

10 Refit the engine undershield and lower the car to the ground.

11 Allow at least 30 minutes from the time of refitting the sump for the sealant to dry, then refill the engine with oil, with reference to Chapter 1A.

10 Oil pump, drive chain and sprockets – removal, inspection and refitting

Removal

1 Remove the sump as described in Section 9. It is not necessary to remove the timing cover unless renewing the timing chain.

2 Unbolt the plastic cover from the oil pump, then hold the sprocket stationary and unscrew the retaining bolt (see illustrations). Discard the bolt as a new one must be used on refitting.

3 Swivel the chain tensioner outwards and release the sprocket from the oil pump. Leave the sprocket hanging in the chain.

4 Unscrew the mounting bolts and withdraw the oil pump from the dowels in the cylinder block (see illustrations).

5 If it is required to remove the oil pump chain and tensioner, first remove the timing cover as described in Section 6. Mark the chain and sprockets to ensure they are refitted the original way around. Slide the small sprocket from the end of the crankshaft, then remove both sprockets from the chain. Note: The sprocket is not keyed to the crankshaft. Unbolt and remove the tensioner (see illustrations).

Inspection

6 Thoroughly clean all components, then examine the oil pump drive chain for excessive wear. Also check the sprocket teeth for wear. If the engine has covered a high mileage, the chain and sprockets should be renewed as a matter of course.

7 The crankshaft pulley bolt must be renewed whenever removed.

10.2a Unbolt the plastic cover from the oil pump . . .

10.2b . . . then use a tool to hold the sprocket while the retaining bolt is loosened . . .

10.2c . . . then remove the bolt and sprocket

10.4a Unscrew the mounting bolts (arrowed) . . .

10.4b . . . and remove the oil pump

10.5a Remove the oil pump sprocket from the crankshaft

Refitting

8 If removed, refit the oil pump drive chain as follows. Refit the tensioner, then engage the small sprocket with the drive chain, then locate the sprocket on the end of the crankshaft making sure that it is the correct way around.
9 Locate the oil pump on the cylinder block dowels, insert the mounting bolts and tighten them to the specified torque.
10 Where removed, engage the oil pump sprocket in the chain. Swivel the chain tensioner outwards, then position the sprocket on the oil pump and screw on the new retaining bolt. Tighten the bolt to the specified torque and angle while holding the sprocket stationary.
11 Refit the oil pump plastic cover and tighten the bolts.
12 Refit the sump with reference to Section 9.

11 Oil pressure warning light switch – removal and refitting

Removal

1 The oil pressure warning light switch is located on the left-hand end of the cylinder head.
2 Disconnect the wiring connector and wipe clean the area around the switch.
3 Unscrew the switch from the cylinder head and remove it, along with its sealing washer. If the switch is to be left removed from the engine for any length of time, plug the cylinder head aperture.

12.3 Remove the old oil seal

12.5b . . . and use a suitable socket to tap it into position

10.5b Remove the oil pump chain and sprocket . . .

Refitting

4 Examine the sealing washer for signs of damage or deterioration and if necessary renew.
5 Refit the switch, complete with washer, and tighten it to the specified torque.
6 Securely reconnect the wiring connector then check and, if necessary, top-up the engine oil as described in *Weekly checks*.

12 Crankshaft oil seals – renewal

Right-hand oil seal

1 Remove the crankshaft pulley as described in Section 4, then note the fitted depth of the oil seal in the timing cover.

12.5a Locate the new oil seal in the timing cover . . .

12.6a Refit the O-ring seal . . .

10.5c . . . then unbolt and remove the tensioner

2 Slide the sleeve from the end of the crankshaft. **Note:** *This is necessary as the sleeve must be assembled onto the crankshaft through the oil seal.* If necessary, remove the sleeve-sealing O-ring from the crankshaft.
3 Carefully lever the old seal out of the timing cover using a suitable flat-bladed screwdriver **(see illustration)**, taking great care not to damage the cover or crankshaft. Alternatively, punch or drill two small holes opposite each other in the seal, then screw a self-tapping screw into each and pull on the screws with pliers to extract the seal.
4 Clean the seal housing, and polish off any burrs or raised edges on the crankshaft which may have caused the seal to fail in the first place.
5 Note that the new oil seal must not be oiled or greased, and the contact surfaces of the timing cover must be completely dry. New oil seals are provided with a fitting adapter. Locate the adapter and new seal over the crankshaft and onto the timing cover, and press it into position until it is at the fitted depth previously noted. If necessary, the seal can be tapped into position using a suitable tubular drift, such as a socket, which bears only on the hard outer edge of the seal **(see illustrations)**. Note that the sealing lips must face inwards.
6 If necessary, locate a new O-ring seal on the crankshaft, then carefully insert the sleeve through the new oil seal onto the crankshaft **(see illustrations)**.
7 Refit the crankshaft pulley as described in Section 4.

12.6b . . . and insert the sleeve

12.8 Note the fitted depth of the oil seal before removing it

12.9 Remove the crankshaft left-hand (flywheel end) oil seal

12.11a Locate the adapter and new oil seal over the crankshaft . . .

12.11b . . . and tap it into position

Left-hand oil seal

8 Remove the flywheel as described in Section 13, then note the fitted depth of the oil seal in the timing cover **(see illustration)**.
9 Carefully punch or drill two small holes

13.2 Home-made tool used to hold the flywheel stationary

13.3 Unscrew the flywheel retaining bolts

13.4 Remove the engine endplate

13.9 Fit the new flywheel retaining bolts

opposite each other in the seal. Screw a self-tapping screw into each hole, and pull on the screws with pliers to extract the seal **(see illustration)**.
10 Clean the cylinder block/crankcase, and

polish off any burrs or raised edges on the crankshaft which may have caused the seal to fail in the first place.
11 Note that the new oil seal must not be oiled or greased, and the contact surfaces of the housing and crankshaft must be completely dry. New oil seals are provided with a fitting adapter. Locate the adapter and new seal over the crankshaft and into the housing, and press it into position until it is at the fitted depth previously noted **(see illustrations)**. If necessary, the seal can be tapped into position using a suitable tubular drift, such as a socket, which bears only on the hard outer edge of the seal. Note that the sealing lips must face inwards.
12 Refit the flywheel as described in Section 13.

13 Flywheel – removal, inspection and refitting

Removal

1 Remove the transmission as described in Chapter 7A, then remove the clutch assembly as described in Chapter 6.
2 Prevent the flywheel from turning by locking the ring gear teeth **(see illustration)**, or by bolting a strap between the flywheel and the cylinder block/crankcase.
3 Unscrew and remove the flywheel retaining bolts **(see illustration)**; discard the bolts, as they must be renewed whenever they are disturbed.
4 Remove the flywheel, and if necessary remove the engine endplate **(see illustration)**. Do not drop the flywheel, as it is very heavy. **Note:** *The bolt holes are offset, so it is only possible to fit the flywheel in one position.*

Inspection

5 If the clutch mating surface of the flywheel is deeply scored, cracked or otherwise damaged, the flywheel must be renewed, unless it is possible to have it surface-ground. Seek the advice of a Seat dealer or engine reconditioning specialist.
6 If the ring gear teeth are badly worn, it must be renewed, but this job is best left to a Seat dealer or engine reconditioning specialist. The temperature to which the new ring gear must be heated for installation (150°C minimum) is critical and, if not done accurately, the hardness of the teeth will be destroyed.
7 If it is felt necessary, use the correct-size tap to clean the threads in the crankshaft of any old thread-locking fluid.

Refitting

8 Clean the mating surfaces of the flywheel and crankshaft, then refit the endplate and locate the flywheel on the crankshaft.
9 If the new flywheel retaining bolts are not supplied with their threads already pre-coated **(see illustration)**, apply a suitable thread-locking compound to the threads of each bolt. Fit the bolts, tightening them by hand only at this stage.

13.10a Tighten the bolts to the specified torque . . .

13.10b . . . and angle

14.9 Remove the engine right-hand mounting bracket

10 Lock the flywheel using the method employed on dismantling, and tighten the retaining bolts to the specified torque wrench and angle settings **(see illustrations)**.

11 Refit the clutch as described in Chapter 6, then remove the locking tool and refit the transmission as described in Chapter 7A.

14 Engine/transmission mountings – inspection and renewal

Inspection

1 If improved access is required, jack up the front of the car, and support it securely on axle stands (see *Jacking and vehicle support*). Remove the securing bolts and remove the engine undershields.

2 Check the mounting rubbers to see if they are cracked, hardened or separated from the metal at any point; renew the mounting if any such damage or deterioration is evident.

3 Check that all the mountings are securely tightened; use a torque wrench to check if possible.

4 Using a large screwdriver or a crowbar, check for wear in the mounting by carefully levering against it to check for free play. Where this is not possible, enlist the aid of an assistant to move the engine/transmission back-and-forth, or from side-to-side, whilst you observe the mounting. While some free play is to be expected, even from new components, excessive wear should be obvious. If excessive free play is found, check first that the fasteners are correctly secured, then renew any worn components as described in the following paragraphs.

Renewal

Right-hand mounting

5 Attach a hoist and lifting tackle to the engine lifting brackets on the cylinder head, and raise the hoist to just take the weight of the engine. Alternatively the engine can be supported on a trolley jack under the engine. Use a block of wood between the sump and the head of the jack, to prevent any damage to the sump.

6 Where necessary, unbolt the coolant reservoir and move it to one side, leaving the coolant hoses connected.

7 Where applicable, move any wiring harnesses, pipes or hoses to one side to enable removal of the engine mounting.

8 Unscrew the mounting centre nut securing the bracket to the flexible mounting.

9 Unscrew the three bolts securing the mounting bracket to the engine and remove the bracket **(see illustration)**.

10 Unbolt and remove the flexible mounting from the body.

11 Refitting is a reversal of removal, bearing in mind the following points:
a) *Use new securing bolts.*
b) *Tighten all fixings to the specified torque.*

Left-hand mounting

Note: *New mounting bolts will be required on refitting (there is no need to renew the smaller mounting-to-body bolts).*

12 Remove the engine top cover which also incorporates the air filter as described in Chapter 4A.

13 Attach a hoist and lifting tackle to the engine lifting brackets on the cylinder head, and raise the hoist to just take the weight of the engine and transmission. Alternatively the engine can be supported on a trolley jack under the transmission. Use a block of

wood between the transmission and the head of the jack, to prevent any damage to the transmission.

14 Remove the battery, as described in Chapter 5A, then disconnect the main starter motor feed cable from the positive battery terminal box.

15 Release any relevant wiring or hoses from the clips on the battery tray, then unscrew the four securing bolts and remove the battery tray.

16 Unscrew the bolts securing the mounting to the transmission, and the remaining bolts securing the mounting to the body, then lift the mounting from the engine compartment.

17 Refitting is a reversal of removal, bearing in mind the following points:
a) *Use new mounting bolts.*
b) *Tighten all fixings to the specified torque.*

Rear mounting (torque arm)

18 Apply the handbrake, then jack up the front of the car and support securely on axle stands (see *Jacking and vehicle support*). Remove the engine undershield(s) for access to the rear mounting (torque arm).

19 Support the rear of the transmission beneath the final drive housing. To do this, use a trolley jack and block of wood, or alternatively wedge a block of wood between the transmission and the subframe.

20 Working under the car, unscrew and remove the bolt securing the mounting to the subframe.

21 Unscrew the two bolts securing the mounting to the transmission, then withdraw the mounting from under the car.

22 Refitting is a reversal of removal, but use new mounting securing bolts, and tighten all fixings to the specified torque.

Notes

Chapter 2 Part B:
1.4 litre petrol engine in-car repair procedures

Contents

Degrees of difficulty

Easy, suitable for novice with little experience	**Fairly easy,** suitable for beginner with some experience	**Fairly difficult,** suitable for competent DIY mechanic	**Difficult,** suitable for experienced DIY mechanic	**Very difficult,** suitable for expert DIY or professional

Specifications

General

Type	Four-cylinder in-line, belt-driven double overhead camshaft (DOHC), four stroke, 16-valve, liquid-cooled
Cubic capacity	1390 cc
Engine codes*	AUB, BBY, BBZ, BKY and BXW
Power output:	
BBY and BKY	55 kW (74 bhp) @ 5000 rpm
BXW	63 kW (85 bhp) @ 5200 rpm
AUB and BBZ	74 kW (99 bhp) @ 6000 rpm
Torque output:	
BBY and BKY	126 Nm @ 3800 rpm
BXW	130 Nm @ 3800 rpm
AUB and BBZ	128 Nm @ 4400 rpm
Bore	76.5 mm
Stroke	75.6 mm
Compression ratio	10.5 : 1
Compression pressures:	
New engine	10 to 15 bar
Minimum compression pressure	7.0 bar
Maximum difference between cylinders	Approximately 3.0 bar
Firing order	1 – 3 – 4 – 2
No 1 cylinder location	Crankshaft pulley end
Direction of crankshaft rotation	Clockwise (when viewed from right-hand side of car)

* Note: See 'Vehicle identification' at the end of this manual for the location of engine code markings.

Camshafts

Camshaft endfloat (maximum)	0.15 mm
Camshaft bearing running clearance	No figure specified
Camshaft run-out	No figure specified

Lubrication system

Oil pump type	Gear type, driven directly from front of crankshaft
Oil pressure (oil temperature 80°C):	
At idle	1.0 bar
At 2000 rpm	2.0 bar

Torque wrench settings

	Nm	lbf ft
Alternator	20	15
Ancillary (alternator, etc) bracket mounting bolts	50	37
Auxiliary drivebelt tensioner securing bolt:		
M8 bolt:		
Stage 1	20	15
Stage 2	Angle-tighten a further 90°	
M10 bolt	45	33
Big-end bearing caps bolts:*		
Stage 1	30	22
Stage 2	Angle-tighten a further 90°	
Camshaft carrier bolts:*		
Stage 1	10	7
Stage 2	Angle-tighten a further 90°	
Camshaft left-hand endplate bolts	10	7
Camshaft sprocket bolts:*		
Stage 1	20	15
Stage 2	Angle-tighten a further 90°	
Clutch pressure plate mounting bolts:*		
Stage 1	60	44
Stage 2	Angle-tighten a further 90°	
Coolant pump bolts	20	15
Crankcase breather (oil separator) bolts	10	7
Crankshaft oil seal housing bolts	12	9
Crankshaft pulley/sprocket bolt:*		
Stage 1	90	66
Stage 2	Angle-tighten a further 90°	
Cylinder head bolts:*		
Stage 1	30	22
Stage 2	Angle-tighten a further 90°	
Stage 3	Angle-tighten a further 90°	
Engine/transmission left-hand mounting to transmission:*		
Stage 1	40	30
Stage 2	Angle-tighten a further 90°	
Engine/transmission left-hand mounting to body:*		
Stage 1	50	37
Stage 2	Angle-tighten a further 90°	
Engine/transmission rear mounting bracket to transmission:*		
Stage 1	30	22
Stage 2	Angle-tighten a further 90°	
Engine/transmission rear mounting link to subframe:*		
Stage 1	40	30
Stage 2	Angle-tighten a further 90°	
Engine/transmission right-hand mounting to engine:*		
Stage 1	20	15
Stage 2	Angle-tighten a further 90°	
Engine/transmission right-hand mounting to body:*		
Stage 1	30	22
Stage 2	Angle-tighten a further 90°	
Engine-to-automatic transmission bolts:		
M12 bolts	80	59
M10 cylinder block-to-transmission bolts	60	44
M10 sump-to-transmission bolts	25	18
Engine-to-manual transmission bolts	80	59
Engine-to-manual transmission cover plate bolts	10	7
Exhaust manifold nuts	25	18
Exhaust pipe-to-manifold nuts	40	30
Flywheel/driveplate bolts:*		
Stage 1	60	44
Stage 2	Angle-tighten a further 90°	
Knock sensor	20	15
Oil cooler securing nut	25	18
Oil drain plug	30	22
Oil level/temperature sensor-to-sump bolts	10	7
Oil pick-up pipe securing bolts	10	7
Oil pressure warning light switch	25	18
Oil pump securing bolts*	12	9
Roadwheel bolts	120	89

Torque wrench settings (continued)

	Nm	lbf ft
Sump:		
Sump-to-cylinder block bolts:		
Metal sump...	15	11
Aluminium sump...................................	13	10
Sump-to-transmission bolts....................................	45	33
Timing belt idler pulley bolt	50	37
Timing belt outer cover bolts:		
Small bolts	10	7
Large bolts	12	9
Timing belt rear cover bolts:		
Small bolts	10	7
Large bolt (coolant pump bolts)	20	15
Timing belt tensioners	20	15

Do not re-use

---

1 General information

Using this Chapter

This Part of Chapter 2 describes those repair procedures that can reasonably be carried out on the engine while it remains in the car. If the engine has been removed from the car and is being dismantled as described in Part D, any preliminary dismantling procedures can be ignored.

Note that while it may be possible physically to overhaul items such as the piston/connecting rod assemblies while the engine is in the car, such tasks are not usually carried out as separate operations, and usually require the execution of several additional procedures (not to mention the cleaning of components and of oilways); for this reason, all such tasks are classed as major overhaul procedures, and are described in Part D of this Chapter.

Caution: The crankshaft must not be removed on these engines. If the crankshaft or main bearing surfaces are worn or damaged, the complete crankshaft/cylinder block assembly must be renewed.

Part D describes the removal of the engine/transmission from the car and the full overhaul procedures that can then be carried out.

Engine description

The engine is a water-cooled, double overhead camshaft, in-line four-cylinder unit, with an aluminium-alloy cylinder block and cylinder head. It is mounted transversely at the front of the car, with the transmission bolted to the left-hand side of the engine.

The crankshaft is of five-bearing type, and thrustwashers are fitted to the centre main bearing to control crankshaft endfloat. The crankshaft and main bearings are matched to the alloy cylinder block, and it is not possible to reassemble the crankshaft and cylinder block once the components have been separated. If the crankshaft or bearings are worn, the complete cylinder block/crankshaft assembly must be renewed.

The intake camshaft is driven by a toothed belt from the crankshaft sprocket, and the exhaust camshaft is driven from the intake camshaft by a second toothed belt. The camshafts are located in a camshaft carrier, which is bolted to the top of the cylinder head.

The valves are closed by coil springs, and run in guides pressed into the cylinder head; the camshafts actuate the valves by roller rockers and hydraulic tappets. There are four valves per cylinder; two intake valves and two exhaust valves.

The oil pump is driven directly from the end of the crankshaft. Oil is drawn from the sump through a strainer, and then forced through an externally-mounted, renewable filter. From there, it is distributed to the cylinder head, where it lubricates the camshaft journals and hydraulic tappets, and also to the crankcase, where it lubricates the main bearings, connecting rod big-ends, gudgeon pins and cylinder bores. A coolant-fed oil cooler is fitted to certain engines.

On all engines, engine coolant is circulated by a pump, driven by the main timing belt. For details of the cooling system, refer to Chapter 3.

Repairs with engine in car

The following operations can be performed without removing the engine:

a) Compression pressure – testing.
b) Camshaft carrier – removal and refitting.
c) Crankshaft pulley – removal and refitting.
d) Timing belt covers – removal and refitting.
e) Timing belts – removal, refitting and adjustment.
f) Timing belt tensioner and sprockets – removal and refitting.
g) Camshaft oil seals – renewal.
h) Camshafts and hydraulic tappets – removal, inspection and refitting.
i) Cylinder head – removal and refitting*.
j) Sump – removal and refitting.
k) Oil pump – removal, overhaul and refitting.
l) Crankshaft oil seals – renewal.
m) Engine/transmission mountings – inspection and renewal.
n) Flywheel – removal, inspection and refitting.

Cylinder head dismantling procedures are detailed in Chapter 2D, with details of camshaft and hydraulic tappet removal.

Note: *It is possible to remove the pistons and connecting rods (after removing the cylinder head and sump) without removing the engine. However, this is not recommended. Work of this nature is more easily and thoroughly completed with the engine on the bench, as described in Chapter 2D.*

2 Compression test – description and interpretation

1 When engine performance is down, or if misfiring occurs which cannot be attributed to the ignition or fuel systems, a compression test can provide diagnostic clues as to the engine's condition. If the test is performed regularly, it can give warning of trouble before any other symptoms become apparent.

2 The engine must be fully warmed-up to normal operating temperature, the battery must be fully-charged and the spark plugs must be removed. The aid of an assistant will be required.

3 Disable the ignition system by disconnecting the wiring plug from the ignition module (engine code AUB) or ignition coils (engine codes BBY, BBZ, BKY and BXW).

4 Fit a compression tester to the No 1 cylinder spark plug hole. The type of tester that screws into the plug thread is preferred.

5 Remove the fuel injector fuse from the fusebox with reference to Chapter 12.

6 Have the assistant hold the throttle wide open and crank the engine for several seconds on the starter motor. **Note:** *The throttle will not operate until the ignition is switched on.* After one or two revolutions, the compression pressure should build-up to a maximum figure and then stabilise. Record the highest reading obtained.

7 Repeat the test on the remaining cylinders, recording the pressure in each.

8 All cylinders should produce very similar pressures. Any difference greater than that specified indicates the existence of a fault. Note that the compression should build-up quickly in a healthy engine. Low

3.4a Crankshaft pulley timing mark aligned with TDC mark on timing belt cover

3.4b Timing mark scribed on inner flange of pulley aligned with TDC mark on timing belt cover

3.5 Crankshaft sprocket tooth with chamfered edge aligns with cast arrow on oil pump

compression on the first stroke, followed by gradually increasing pressure on successive strokes, indicates worn piston rings. A low compression reading on the first stroke, which does not build-up during successive strokes, indicates leaking valves or a blown head gasket (a cracked head could also be the cause). Deposits on the undersides of the valve heads can also cause low compression.

9 If the pressure in any cylinder is reduced to the specified minimum or less, carry out the following test to isolate the cause. Introduce a teaspoonful of clean oil into that cylinder through its spark plug hole and repeat the test.

10 If the addition of oil temporarily improves the compression pressure, this indicates that bore or piston wear is responsible for the pressure loss. No improvement suggests that leaking or burnt valves, or a blown head gasket, may be to blame.

11 A low reading from two adjacent cylinders is almost certainly due to the head gasket having blown between them and the presence of coolant in the engine oil will confirm this.

12 If one cylinder is about 20 percent lower than the others and the engine has a slightly rough idle, a worn camshaft lobe could be the cause.

13 On completion of the test, refit the spark plugs, reconnect the ignition wiring and refit the fuel injector fuse.

3 Engine assembly and valve timing marks – general information and usage

General information

1 TDC is the highest point in the cylinder that each piston reaches as it travels up and down when the crankshaft turns. Each piston reaches TDC at the end of the compression stroke and again at the end of the exhaust stroke, but TDC generally refers to piston position on the compression stroke. No 1 piston is at the timing belt end of the engine.

2 Positioning No 1 piston at TDC is an essential part of many procedures, such as timing belt removal and camshaft removal.

3 The design of the engines covered in this Chapter is such that piston-to-valve contact may occur if the camshaft or crankshaft is turned with the timing belt removed. For this reason, it is important to ensure that the camshaft and crankshaft do not move in relation to each other once the timing belt has been removed from the engine.

4 The crankshaft pulley has a marking which, when aligned with a corresponding reference marking on the timing belt cover, indicates that No 1 piston (and hence also No 4 piston) is at TDC. Note that on some models, the crankshaft pulley timing mark is located on the outer flange of the pulley. In order to make alignment of the timing marks easier, it is advisable to remove the pulley (see Section 5) and, using a set-square, scribe a corresponding mark on the inner flange of the pulley (see illustrations).

5 Note that there is also a timing mark which can be used with the crankshaft sprocket – this is useful if the crankshaft pulley and timing belt have been removed. When No 1 piston is at TDC, the crankshaft sprocket tooth with the chamfered inner edge aligns with a cast arrow on the oil pump (see illustration).

6 The camshaft sprockets are equipped with TDC positioning holes. When the positioning holes are aligned with the corresponding holes in the camshaft carrier, No 1 piston is at TDC on the compression stroke (see illustration).

7 Additionally, on some models, the flywheel/ driveplate has a TDC marking, which can be observed by unscrewing a protective plastic cover from the transmission bellhousing. The mark takes the form of a notch in the edge of the flywheel on manual transmission models, or an O marking on automatic transmission models. Note that it is not possible to use these marks on all models due to the limited access available to view the marks.

3.6 Camshaft sprocket positioning holes (arrowed) aligned

Setting No 1 cylinder to TDC

Note: *Suitable locking pins will be required to lock the camshaft sprockets in position during this procedure. On some engines, it may be necessary to use a small mirror to view the timing marks from under the wheel arch.*

8 Before starting work, make sure that the ignition is switched off.

9 Remove the air cleaner assembly as described in Chapter 4A.

10 If desired, to make the engine easier to turn, remove all of the spark plugs as described in Chapter 1A.

11 Apply the handbrake, then jack up the front of the car and support on axle stands (see *Jacking and vehicle support*).

12 Remove the right-hand front roadwheel, then remove the securing bolts and/or clips, and remove the appropriate engine under-shields to enable access to the crankshaft pulley **(see illustration)**.

13 Remove the upper timing belt cover as described in Section 6.

14 Turn the engine clockwise, using a spanner on the crankshaft pulley bolt, until the TDC mark on the crankshaft pulley or flywheel/driveplate is aligned with the corresponding mark on the timing belt cover or transmission casing, and the locking pin holes in the camshaft sprockets are aligned with the corresponding holes in the camshaft carrier.

15 If necessary, to give sufficient clearance for the camshaft locking tool to be engaged with the camshaft sprockets, unbolt the air cleaner support bracket from the engine mounting. Similarly, if necessary, unbolt the power steering fluid reservoir and move it to one side, leaving the fluid hoses connected.

16 A suitable tool will now be required to lock the camshaft sprockets in the TDC position. A special Seat tool (T10016) is available for this purpose, but a suitable tool can be improvised using two M8 bolts and nuts, and a short length of steel bar. With the camshaft sprocket positioned as described in paragraph 14, measure the distance between the locking pin hole centres, and drill two corresponding 8 mm holes in the length of steel bar. Slide the M8 bolts through the holes in the bar, and secure them using the nuts.

17 Slide the tool into position in the holes in the camshaft sprockets, ensuring that the pins (or bolts) engage with the holes in the

3.12 Undo the bolts (arrowed) and remove the engine undershield

camshaft carrier **(see illustration)**. The engine is now locked in position, with No 1 piston at TDC on the compression stroke.

4 Auxiliary drivebelt – removal and refitting

General information

1 Depending on the vehicle specification, the auxiliary drivebelt, which is driven from a pulley mounted on the crankshaft, will provide drive for the alternator and, on models with air conditioning, the refrigerant compressor.

2 The ribbed auxiliary belt is fitted with an automatic tensioning device.

Removal

3 For improved access, apply the handbrake, then jack up the front of the car and support it on axle stands (see *Jacking and vehicle support*). Remove the right-hand front roadwheel, then remove the access panel from the inner wheel arch. Also remove the engine top cover and where necessary disconnect the ventilation hose.

4 Use a spanner to turn the tensioner central bolt clockwise to release the tension on the drivebelt **(see illustration)**.

5 Note how the drivebelt is routed, then remove it from the crankshaft pulley, alternator pulley and air conditioning compressor pulley (where applicable).

Refitting

6 Locate the new drivebelt on the pulleys,

3.17 Tool used to lock camshaft sprockets at TDC (engine and timing belt removed)

then release the tensioner. Check that the belt is located correctly in the multi-grooves in the pulleys.

7 Refit the access panel, roadwheel, and top cover, and lower the car to the ground.

5 Crankshaft pulley – removal and refitting

Removal

1 For improved access, jack up the front of the car, and support securely on axle stands (see *Jacking and vehicle support*). Remove the right-hand front roadwheel. Also remove the engine top cover and where necessary disconnect the ventilation hose.

2 Remove the securing bolts and/or release the clips, and withdraw the relevant engine undershield(s) to enable access to the crankshaft pulley **(see illustration 3.12)**.

3 If necessary (for any later work to be carried out), turn the crankshaft using a socket or spanner on the crankshaft pulley bolt, until the relevant timing marks align (see Section 3).

4 Remove the auxiliary drivebelt (see Section 4).

5 To prevent the crankshaft from turning as the pulley bolt is slackened, a tool similar to that shown can be used. Engage the tool with two of the slots in the pulley **(see illustration)**.

6 Counterhold the pulley, and slacken the pulley bolt (take care – the bolt is very tight) using a socket and a suitable extension.

7 Unscrew the bolt, and remove the pulley **(see illustration)**.

4.4 Rotate the central bolt clockwise to release the tension

5.5 Counterhold the crankshaft pulley using a tool similar to that shown

5.7 Remove the crankshaft pulley

6.2 Remove the upper outer timing belt cover

6.5a Release the two securing clips (arrowed) . . .

6.5b . . . then unscrew the two lower securing bolts (arrowed) . . .

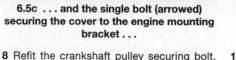

6.5c . . . and the single bolt (arrowed) securing the cover to the engine mounting bracket . . .

6.5d . . . then withdraw the lower timing belt cover

8 Refit the crankshaft pulley securing bolt, with a spacer washer positioned under its head, to retain the crankshaft sprocket.

Refitting

9 Unscrew the crankshaft pulley/sprocket bolt used to retain the sprocket, and remove the spacer washer, then refit the pulley to the sprocket. Ensure that the locating pin on the sprocket engages with the corresponding hole in the pulley.
10 Oil the threads of the new crankshaft pulley bolt. Prevent the crankshaft from turning as during removal, then fit the new pulley securing bolt, and tighten it to the specified torque, in the two stages given in the Specifications.
11 Refit the auxiliary drivebelt as described in Section 4.

12 Refit the engine undershield(s) and top cover.
13 Refit the roadwheel, lower the car to the ground, and tighten the roadwheel bolts to the specified torque.

---

6 Timing belt covers – removal and refitting

Upper outer cover

1 Remove the air cleaner assembly/engine top cover as described in Chapter 4A.
2 Release the two securing clips, and lift the timing belt outer, upper cover from the engine **(see illustration)**.
3 Refitting is a reversal of removal.

Lower outer cover

4 Remove the crankshaft pulley, as described in Section 5.
5 Release the two cover securing clips, located at the rear of the engine, then unscrew the two lower securing bolts, and the single bolt securing the cover to the engine mounting bracket. Withdraw the cover downwards from the engine **(see illustrations)**.
6 Refitting is a reversal of removal, but refit the crankshaft pulley with reference to Section 5.

Rear timing belt cover

Note: *As the rear timing belt cover securing bolts also secure the coolant pump, it is advisable to drain the cooling system (see Chapter 1A) before starting this procedure, and to renew the coolant pump seal/gasket (see Chapter 3) before refitting the cover. Refill the cooling system with reference to Chapter 1A.*
7 Remove the timing belt as described in Section 7.
8 Unbolt the timing belt idler pulley/bracket assembly **(see illustration)**.
9 Unscrew the rear timing belt cover securing bolt located next to the engine right-hand lifting eye **(see illustration)**.
10 Unscrew the two securing bolts, and remove the rear timing belt cover. Note that the bolts also secure the coolant pump **(see illustration)**.
11 Refitting is a reversal of removal, but tighten the timing belt idler pulley/bracket bolt to the specified torque, and refit the timing belt as described in Section 7.

6.8 Remove the idler pulley/bracket assembly (viewed with engine removed)

6.9 Unscrew the rear timing belt cover bolt next to engine right-hand lifting eye

6.10 Remove the rear timing belt cover (viewed with engine removed)

7 Timing belts – removal and refitting

Removal

1 These engines have two timing belts; the main timing belt drives the intake camshaft from the crankshaft, and the secondary timing belt drives the exhaust camshaft from the intake camshaft.

Main timing belt

2 Remove the air cleaner assembly as described in Chapter 4A.
3 Remove the upper and lower timing belt covers as described in Section 6.
4 Refit the crankshaft pulley securing bolt, with a spacer washer positioned under its head, to retain the crankshaft sprocket.
5 Turn the crankshaft to position No 1 piston at TDC on the compression stroke, and lock the camshaft sprockets in position, as described in Section 3.
6 Release the coolant reservoir and move it to one side. There is no need to disconnect the hoses.
7 Where applicable, on models with air conditioning, unscrew the securing bolt, and remove the auxiliary drivebelt idler pulley.
8 Attach a hoist and lifting tackle to the right-hand (timing belt end) engine lifting bracket, and raise the hoist to just take the weight of the engine.
9 Remove the complete engine right-hand mounting assembly, as described in Section 20.
10 Unscrew the four securing bolts, and remove the engine right-hand mounting bracket from the engine.
11 If either of the timing belts are to be refitted, mark their running directions to ensure correct refitting.
12 Engage a suitable Allen key with the hole in the main timing belt tensioner plate, then slacken the tensioner bolt, lever the tensioner anti-clockwise using the Allen key (to release the tension on the belt), and retighten the tensioner bolt **(see illustration)**.
13 Temporarily remove the camshaft sprocket locking tool, then slide the main timing belt from the sprockets, noting its routing **(see illustration)**. Refit the camshaft sprocket locking tool once the timing belt has been removed.
14 Turn the crankshaft a quarter-turn (90°) anti-clockwise to position Nos 1 and 4 pistons slightly down their bores from the TDC position. This will eliminate any risk of piston-to-valve contact if the crankshaft or camshaft is turned whilst the timing belt is removed.

Secondary timing belt

15 To remove the secondary timing belt, once the main timing belt has been removed, proceed as follows.
16 Engage a suitable Allen key with the hole in the secondary timing belt tensioner plate, then slacken the tensioner bolt, and lever

7.12 Slacken the tensioner bolt, lever the tensioner anti-clockwise, then retighten

the tensioner clockwise using the Allen key (to release the tension on the belt). Unscrew the securing bolt, and remove the secondary timing belt tensioner **(see illustrations)**.
17 Temporarily remove the camshaft sprocket locking tool, and slide the secondary timing belt from the sprockets **(see illustration)**. Refit the sprocket locking tool once the belt has been removed.

Refitting

Secondary timing belt

18 Check that the camshaft sprockets are still locked in position by the locking pins, then turn the crankshaft a quarter-turn (90°) clockwise to reposition Nos 1 and 4 pistons at TDC. Ensure that the crankshaft sprocket tooth with the chamfered inner edge is aligned with the corresponding mark on the oil pump housing **(see illustration)**.
19 Temporarily remove the camshaft

7.16a Slacken the tensioner bolt, and rotate the tensioner clockwise . . .

7.17 Remove the secondary timing belt

7.13 Remove the main timing belt

sprocket locking tool, and fit the secondary timing belt around the camshaft sprockets. Make sure that the belt is as tight as possible on its top run between the sprockets (but note that there will be some slack in the belt). If the original belt is being refitted, observe the running direction markings. Refit the camshaft sprocket locking tool once the belt has been fitted to the sprockets.
20 Check that the secondary timing belt tensioner pointer is positioned on the far left of the tensioner backplate. Remember that the terms 'left' and 'right' are in the sense of a person sat in the driver's seat, facing forwards.
21 Lift the lower run of the secondary timing belt using the tensioner, and fit the tensioner securing bolt (if necessary turn the tensioner with an Allen key until the bolt hole in the tensioner aligns with the bolt hole in the cylinder head). Make sure that the lug

7.16b . . . then unscrew the bolt and remove the tensioner

7.18 Crankshaft sprocket tooth with chamfered edge aligned with cast arrow on oil pump

7.21 Secondary timing belt tensioner pointer correctly positioned

7.22 Turn the tensioner anti-clockwise to align the tensioner pointer and the lug

29 Disconnect the hoist and lifting tackle from the engine lifting bracket.
30 Where applicable, refit the auxiliary drivebelt idler pulley.
31 Refit the lower outer timing belt cover, with reference to Section 6 if necessary.
32 Refit the crankshaft pulley as described in Section 5.
33 Refit the upper outer timing belt cover.
34 Refit the air cleaner assembly.

---

8 Timing belt tensioner and sprockets – removal, inspection and refitting

on the tensioner backplate engages with the core plug hole in the cylinder head **(see illustration)**.
22 Use the Allen key to turn the tensioner anti-clockwise until the tensioner pointer aligns with the lug on the tensioner backplate, with the lug positioned against the left-hand stop in the core plug hole **(see illustration)**. Tighten the tensioner bolt to the specified torque.

Main timing belt

23 Where applicable, ensure that the secondary drivebelt has been refitted and tensioned, then again temporarily remove the camshaft sprocket locking tool, and fit the main timing belt around the sprockets. If the original belt is being refitted, observe the running direction markings. Work in an anti-clockwise direction, starting at the coolant

8.3 Turn the tensioner anti-clockwise to position shown before fitting. Cut-out engages with bolt (A)

8.8a Remove the smaller . . .

pump sprocket, followed by the tensioner roller, crankshaft sprocket, idler pulley, intake camshaft sprocket and the second idler pulley. Once the belt has been refitted, refit the camshaft sprocket locking tool.
24 Ensure that the tensioner bolt is slack, then engage an Allen key with the hole in the tensioner plate, and turn the plate clockwise until the tension indicator pointer is aligned with the centre of the cut-out in the backplate. Tighten the tensioner securing bolt to the specified torque.
25 Remove the camshaft sprocket locking tool.
26 Using a spanner or socket on the crankshaft pulley bolt, turn the engine through two complete turns in the normal direction of rotation, until the crankshaft sprocket tooth with the chamfered inner edge is aligned with the corresponding mark on the oil pump housing **(refer to illustration 3.5)**. Check that the locking tool can again be fitted to lock the camshaft sprockets in position – if not, one or both of the timing belts may have been incorrectly fitted.
27 With the crankshaft timing marks aligned, and the camshaft sprockets locked in position, check the tension of the timing belts. The secondary and main belt tension indicators should be positioned as described in paragraphs 22 and 24 respectively – if not, repeat the appropriate tensioning procedure, then recheck the tension.
28 When the belt tension is correct, refit the engine right-hand mounting bracket, and tighten the securing bolts to the specified torque.

8.8b . . . and larger timing belt idler pulleys

Tensioner

Main timing belt

1 Remove the main timing belt as described in Section 7.
2 Unscrew the main timing belt tensioner bolt, and remove the tensioner from the engine.
3 Engage an Allen key with the hole in the tensioner plate, and turn the tensioner anti-clockwise to the position shown **(see illustration)**.
4 Refit the tensioner to the engine, ensuring that the cut-out in the tensioner backplate engages with the bolt on the cylinder block **(see illustration 8.3)**. Refit the tensioner securing bolt, and tighten by hand.
5 Refit and tension the main timing belt as described in Section 7.

Secondary timing belt

6 Removal and refitting of the tensioner is described as part of the timing belt removal procedure in Section 7.

Main timing belt idler pulleys

7 Remove the timing belt as described in Section 7.
8 Unscrew the securing bolt and remove the relevant idler pulley. Note that the smaller pulley (the idler pulley nearest the intake manifold side of the engine) can be removed complete with its mounting bracket (unbolt the mounting bracket bolt, leaving the pulley attached to the bracket) **(see illustrations)**.
9 Refit the relevant idler pulley and tighten the securing bolt to the specified torque. Note that if the smaller idler pulley has been removed complete with its bracket, ensure that the bracket locates over the rear timing belt cover bolt on refitting.
10 Refit and tension the main timing belt as described in Section 7.

Crankshaft sprocket

11 Remove the main timing belt as described in Section 7.
12 Unscrew the crankshaft pulley, and the washer used to retain the sprocket, and withdraw the sprocket from the crankshaft.
13 Commence refitting by positioning the sprocket on the end of the crankshaft, noting that the pulley locating pin must be outermost

8.13 Refit the crankshaft sprocket. Pulley locating pin (arrowed) must be outermost

(see illustration). Temporarily refit the pulley securing bolt and washer to retain the sprocket.

14 Refit the main timing belt as described in Section 7.

Camshaft sprockets

15 Remove the main and secondary timing belts as described in Section 7. Ensure that the crankshaft has been turned a quarter-turn (90°) anti-clockwise to position Nos 1 and 4 pistons slightly down their bores from the TDC position. This will eliminate any risk of piston-to-valve contact if the crankshaft or camshaft is turned whilst the timing belt is removed.

16 The relevant camshaft sprocket bolt must now be slackened. The camshaft must be prevented from turning as the sprocket bolt is unscrewed – do not rely solely on the sprocket locking tool for this. To hold the sprocket, make up a tool, and use it to hold the sprocket stationary by means of the holes in the sprocket (see illustration 8.19).

17 Unscrew the camshaft sprocket bolt, and withdraw the sprocket from the end of the camshaft, noting which way round it is fitted.

18 Commence refitting by offering the sprocket up to the camshaft, ensuring that lug on the sprocket engages with the notch in the end of the camshaft. If both camshaft sprockets have been removed, note that the double sprocket (for the main and secondary timing belts) should be fitted to the intake camshaft, and note that the exhaust camshaft sprocket must be fitted first (see illustration).

19 Fit a new sprocket securing bolt, then use the tool to hold the sprocket stationary,

9.3c . . . then remove the DIS module and HT leads

8.18 Ensure sprocket lug (1) engages with camshaft notch (2)

as during removal, and tighten the bolt to the specified torque, in the two stages given in the Specifications (see illustration).

20 Refit the secondary and main timing belts as described in Section 7.

Coolant pump sprocket

21 The coolant pump sprocket is integral with the coolant pump. Refer to Chapter 3 for details of coolant pump removal.

---

9 Camshaft carrier –
removal and refitting

Removal

1 Disconnect the battery negative lead as described in Chapter 5A.

2 Remove the main and secondary timing belts, as described in Section 7.

9.3a Use a hooked wire to pull off the plug connectors (AUB engines)

9.5 Disconnect the wiring connector from the intake camshaft position sensor

8.19 Tighten the sprocket securing bolt using a suitable tool to hold the sprocket stationary

3 On engine code AUB, disconnect the HT leads from the spark plugs. Use a hooked length of stout wire to pull the connectors from the spark plugs. Release the securing lug, and disconnect the wiring plug from the ignition module, then unscrew the securing bolts, and remove the module and HT leads as an assembly (see illustrations).

4 On engine codes BBY, BBZ, BKY and BXW, disconnect the wiring and remove the ignition coils from the spark plugs (see Chapter 5B), then remove the cable guide.

5 Disconnect the intake camshaft position sensor wiring connector (see illustration).

6 Unscrew the bolt securing the exhaust gas recirculation solenoid valve (where fitted) to the end of the camshaft carrier (see illustration). Move the valve to one side.

7 Disconnect the wiring plug from the oil pressure warning light switch, located at the front left-hand corner of the camshaft carrier.

9.3b Unscrew the DIS module securing bolts . . .

9.6 Unbolt the exhaust gas recirculation solenoid valve from the camshaft carrier

9.7a Disconnect the oil pressure warning light switch wiring plug . . .

9.7b . . . then release the wiring from the clip on the end of the camshaft carrier

9.8 Remove the timing belt rear cover bolt next to the engine right-hand lifting eye

9.9 Remove the camshaft carrier securing bolts

9.14 Spread sealant on the camshaft carrier's cylinder head mating face

9.17 Tighten the camshaft carrier bolts through the specified Stage 2 angle

Release the wiring harness from the clip on the end of the camshaft carrier, and move the wiring to one side (see illustrations).

8 Remove the rear timing belt cover securing bolt, located next to the engine right-hand lifting eye (see illustration).

9 Working progressively from the centre out, in a diagonal sequence, slacken and remove the camshaft carrier securing bolts (see illustration).

10 Carefully lift the camshaft carrier from the cylinder head. The camshafts can be removed from the carrier, as described in Section 10.

Refitting

11 Commence refitting by thoroughly cleaning all traces of old sealant, and all traces of oil and grease, from the mating faces of the cylinder head and camshaft carrier. Ensure that no debris enters the cylinder head or camshaft carrier.

12 Ensure that the crankshaft is still positioned a quarter-turn (90°) anti-clockwise from the TDC position, and that the camshafts are locked in position with the locking tool, as described in Section 3.

13 Check that the valve rockers are correctly located on the valves, and securely clipped into position on the hydraulic tappets.

14 Apply a thin, even coat of sealant (Seat AMV 188 003, or equivalent) to the cylinder head mating face of the camshaft carrier (see illustration). Do not apply the sealant too thickly, as excess sealant may enter and block the oilways, causing engine damage.

15 Carefully lower the camshaft carrier onto the cylinder head, until the camshafts rest on

the rockers. Note that the camshaft carrier locates on dowels in the cylinder head; if desired, to make fitting easier, two guide studs can be made up as follows:

a) Cut the heads off two M6 bolts, then cut slots in the top of each bolt to enable the bolt to be unscrewed using a flat-bladed screwdriver.

b) Screw one bolt into each of the camshaft carrier bolt locations at opposite corners of the cylinder head.

c) Lower the camshaft carrier over the bolts to guide it into position on the cylinder head.

16 Fit new camshaft carrier securing bolts, and tighten them progressively, working from the centre out, in a diagonal sequence (ie, tighten all bolts through one turn, then tighten all bolts through a further turn, and so on). Ensure that the camshaft carrier sits squarely on the cylinder head as the bolts are tightened,

10.3 Remove the intake camshaft position sensor

and make sure that the carrier engages with the cylinder head dowels. Where applicable, once the camshaft carrier contacts the surface of the cylinder head, unscrew the two guide studs, and fit the two remaining new camshaft carrier securing bolts in their place.

17 Tighten the camshaft carrier securing bolts to the specified torque, in the two stages given in the Specifications (see illustration).

18 Leave the camshaft carrier sealant to dry for approximately 30 minutes before carrying out any further work on the cylinder head or camshaft carrier.

19 The remainder of refitting is a reversal of removal.

10 Camshafts – removal, inspection and refitting

Removal

1 Remove the camshaft carrier as described in Section 9.

2 Remove the camshaft sprockets, with reference to Section 8 if necessary.

3 If the intake camshaft is to be removed, unscrew the securing bolt, and remove the intake camshaft position sensor (see illustration).

4 Remove the relevant camshaft carrier endplate (see illustration). Note that on engine code AUB the intake camshaft endplate is secured by the ignition module bolts, which have already been removed, and the exhaust camshaft endplate is secured by three bolts,

10.4 Remove the camshaft carrier endplate

10.5 Withdraw the camshaft from the endplate end of the camshaft carrier

10.10 Renew the camshaft carrier endplate O-ring

one of which also secures the exhaust gas recirculation solenoid valve.

5 Carefully withdraw the relevant camshaft from the endplate end of the camshaft carrier, taking care not to damage the bearing surfaces of the camshaft and housing as the camshaft is withdrawn **(see illustration)**.

Inspection

6 Visually inspect the camshafts for evidence of wear on the surfaces of the lobes and journals. Normally their surfaces should be smooth and have a dull shine; look for scoring, erosion or pitting and areas that appear highly polished, indicating excessive wear. Accelerated wear will occur once the hardened exterior of the camshaft has been damaged, so always renew worn items. **Note:** *If these symptoms are visible on the tips of the camshaft lobes, check the corresponding rocker, as it will probably be worn as well.*

7 If the machined surfaces of the camshaft appear discoloured or blued, it is likely that it has been overheated at some point, probably due to inadequate lubrication. This may have distorted the shaft, so check the run-out as follows: place the camshaft between two V-blocks and using a DTI gauge, measure the run-out at the centre journal. No maximum run-out figure is quoted by the manufacturers, but it should be obvious if the camshaft is excessively distorted.

8 To measure camshaft endfloat, temporarily refit the relevant camshaft to the camshaft carrier, and refit the camshaft sealing plate to the rear of the camshaft carrier. Anchor a DTI gauge to the timing belt end of the camshaft carrier and align the gauge probe with the camshaft axis. Push the camshaft to one end of the camshaft carrier as far as it will travel, then rest the DTI gauge probe on the end of the camshaft, and zero the gauge display. Push the camshaft as far as it will go to the other end of the camshaft carrier, and record the gauge reading. Verify the reading by pushing the camshaft back to its original position and checking that the gauge indicates zero again.

9 Check that the camshaft endfloat measurement is within the limit listed in the Specifications. Wear outside of this limit may be cured by renewing the relevant camshaft carrier endplate, although wear is unlikely to be confined to any one component, so

renewal of the camshafts and camshaft carrier must be considered.

Refitting

10 Refitting is a reversal of removal, bearing in mind the following points:

a) *Before refitting the camshaft, renew the camshaft right-hand oil seal, with reference to Section 12.*

b) *Lubricate the bearing surfaces in the camshaft carrier, and the camshaft lobes before refitting the camshaft(s).*

c) *Renew the sealing O-ring on each camshaft carrier endplate* **(see illustration).**

d) *Refit the camshaft sprocket(s) with reference to Section 8, noting that if both sprockets have been removed, the exhaust camshaft sprocket must be fitted first.*

e) *Refit the camshaft carrier as described in Section 9.*

11 Rockers and hydraulic tappets – removal, inspection and refitting

Removal

1 Remove the camshaft carrier, as described in Section 9.

2 As the components are removed, keep them in strict order, so that they can be refitted in their original locations.

3 Unclip the rockers from the hydraulic tappets, and lift them from the cylinder head **(see illustration)**.

11.3 Remove the rockers from above the hydraulic tappets (arrowed)

4 Carefully lift the hydraulic tappets from their bores in the cylinder head. It is advisable to store the tappets (in order) upright in an oil bath whilst they are removed from the engine.

Inspection

5 Check the tappet bores in the cylinder head for signs of scoring or damage. If significant scoring or damage is found, it may be necessary to renew the cylinder head and the complete set of tappets.

6 Inspect the hydraulic tappets for obvious signs of wear or damage, and renew if necessary. Check that the oil holes in the tappets are free from obstructions.

7 Check the valve, tappet, and camshaft contact faces of the rockers for wear or damage, and also check the rockers for any signs of cracking. Renew any worn or damaged rockers.

8 Inspect the camshaft lobes, as described in Section 10.

Refitting

9 Oil the tappet bores in the cylinder head, and the hydraulic tappets themselves, then carefully slide the tappets into their original bores **(see illustration)**.

10 Oil the rocker contact faces of the tappets, and the tops of the valve stems, then refit the rockers to their original locations, ensuring that the rockers are securely clipped onto the tappets.

11 Check the endfloat of each camshaft, as described in Section 10, then refit the camshaft carrier as described in Section 9.

11.9 Oil the tappets before fitting

12.12 Locate the new O-ring in the groove in the endplate

12 Camshaft oil seals – renewal

Right-hand oil seals

1 Remove the main and secondary timing belts as described in Section 7.

2 Remove the relevant camshaft sprocket as described in Section 8.

3 Drill two small holes into the existing oil seal, diagonally opposite each other. Take great care to avoid drilling through into the seal housing or camshaft sealing surface. Thread two self-tapping screws into the holes, and using a pair of pliers, pull on the heads of the screws to extract the oil seal.

4 Clean out the seal housing and the sealing

surface of the camshaft by wiping it with a lint-free cloth. Remove any swarf or burrs that may cause the seal to leak.

5 Lubricate the lip and outer edge of the new oil seal with clean engine oil, and push it over the camshaft until it is positioned above its housing. To prevent damage to the sealing lips, wrap some adhesive tape around the end of the camshaft.

6 Using a hammer and a socket of suitable diameter, drive the seal squarely into its housing. **Note:** *Select a socket that bears only on the hard outer surface of the seal, not the inner lip which can easily be damaged.*

7 Refit the relevant camshaft sprocket with reference to Section 8.

8 Refit and tension the secondary and main timing belts as described in Section 7.

Left-hand oil seals

9 The camshaft left-hand oil seals take the form of O-rings located in the grooves in the camshaft carrier endplates.

10 Unscrew the securing bolts, and remove the relevant camshaft endplate, noting that on engine code AUB the ignition module securing bolts secure the exhaust camshaft endplate.

11 Prise the old O-ring from the groove in the endplate.

12 Lightly oil the new O-ring, and carefully locate it in the groove in the endplate **(see illustration)**.

13 Refit the endplate (and the ignition module, where applicable), and tighten the securing bolts to the specified torque.

13 Cylinder head – removal, inspection and refitting

Note: *The cylinder head must be removed with the engine cold.*

Removal

1 Remove the battery as described in Chapter 5A, then undo the bolts and remove the battery tray.

2 Drain the cooling system as described in Chapter 1A.

3 Remove the main and secondary timing belts as described in Section 7.

4 As the engine is currently supported using a hoist attached to the engine lifting brackets bolted to the cylinder head, it is now necessary to attach a suitable bracket to the cylinder block, so that the engine can still be supported as the cylinder head is removed.

5 A suitable bracket can be bolted to the cylinder block using spacers, and a long bolt screwed into the hole located next to the coolant pump **(see illustration)**. Ideally, attach a second set of lifting tackle to the hoist, adjust the lifting tackle to support the engine using the bracket attached to the cylinder block, then disconnect the lifting tackle attached to the bracket on the cylinder head. Alternatively, temporarily support the engine under the sump using a jack and a block of wood, then transfer the lifting tackle from the bracket on the cylinder head to the bracket bolted to the cylinder block.

6 Release the hose clips, and disconnect the two radiator hoses from the coolant housing at the transmission end of the cylinder head **(see illustration)**. Similarly, release the hose clips and disconnect the remaining three small coolant hoses from the rear of the coolant housing.

7 Remove the air cleaner assembly, complete with the air trunking, as described in Chapter 4A.

8 Unscrew the bolt securing the oil level dipstick tube bracket to the cylinder head, then lift the dipstick tube, and turn it to one side, to clear the working area **(see illustration)**. Release the wiring harnesses from the clip on the dipstick tube bracket. Note that the dipstick tube bracket bolt also secures the intake manifold.

9 Unscrew the two securing bolts and disconnect the exhaust gas recirculation (EGR) pipe (where fitted) from the throttle body. Recover the gasket **(see illustration)**.

10 Unscrew the bolt securing the EGR pipe bracket to the coolant housing.

11 Unscrew the six securing bolts (three upper and three lower) and lift the intake manifold back from the engine **(see illustration)**. Ensure that the intake manifold is adequately supported in the engine compartment, and take care not to strain any wires, cables or hoses. Recover the O-rings if they are loose.

13.5 Home-made engine lifting bracket fitted next to the coolant pump

13.6 Disconnect the radiator hoses from the cylinder head coolant housing

13.8 Unscrew the dipstick tube bracket bolt from the cylinder head

13.9 Disconnect the EGR pipe from the throttle body and recover the gasket

13.11 Lift the intake manifold back from the engine

13.12 Unbolt the wiring bracket from the cylinder head right rear corner

13.13a Disconnect the coolant temperature sensor wiring plug . . .

12 Unbolt the wiring connector bracket from the right-hand rear corner of the cylinder head **(see illustration)**.

13 Disconnect the wiring plug from the coolant temperature sensor, located in the coolant housing at the transmission end of the cylinder head, then unclip the wiring harnesses from the coolant housing, and move them to one side **(see illustrations)**.

14 Disconnect the vacuum hose from the exhaust gas recirculation (EGR) valve **(see illustration)**.

15 Unclip the wiring from the bracket attached to the exhaust heat shield, then unscrew the securing bolts (two upper bolts and one lower bolt), and remove the heat shield **(see illustrations)**.

16 Disconnect the exhaust front section from the manifold with reference to Chapter 4C. If desired, the exhaust manifold can be removed as follows:

a) *Unscrew the union nut securing the EGR pipe to the exhaust manifold, and remove the EGR pipe.*

b) *Unscrew the exhaust manifold securing nuts, then lift off the manifold and recover the gasket.*

17 Remove the camshaft carrier, with reference to Section 9.

18 Pull out the metal clip securing the plastic coolant pipe to the coolant housing at the left-hand rear corner of the cylinder head **(see illustration)**.

19 Progressively slacken the cylinder head bolts in order, then unscrew and remove the bolts **(see illustration)**.

20 With all the bolts removed, lift the cylinder head from the block. If the cylinder head is stuck, tap it with a soft-faced mallet to break the joint. Do not insert a lever into the gasket joint. As the cylinder head is lifted off, release the coolant pump pipe from the thermostat housing on the cylinder head.

21 Lift the cylinder head gasket from the block.

Inspection

22 Dismantling and inspection of the cylinder head is covered in Part D of this Chapter. Additionally, check the condition of the coolant pump pipe-to-thermostat housing O-ring, and renew if necessary.

13.13b . . . then unclip the wiring harnesses and move them to one side

Refitting

23 The mating faces of the cylinder head and block must be perfectly clean before refitting the head. Use a scraper to remove all traces of gasket and carbon, also clean the

13.15a Unclip the wiring from the bracket on the exhaust heat shield . . .

13.18 Pull out the coolant pipe-to-housing metal clip (engine removed for clarity)

13.14 Disconnect the vacuum hose from the EGR valve

tops of the pistons. Take particular care with the aluminium surfaces, as the soft metal is easily damaged. Make sure that debris is not allowed to enter the oil and water passages – this is particularly important for the oil circuit,

13.15b . . . then remove the heat shield

13.19 Cylinder head bolt slackening sequence

13.28a Ensure that the dowels (arrowed) are in place in the cylinder block . . .

13.28b . . . and the gasket part number and OBEN/TOP markings are uppermost

13.31 Cylinder head bolt tightening sequence

as carbon could block the oil supply to the camshaft and crankshaft bearings. Using adhesive tape and paper, seal the water, oil and bolt holes in the cylinder block. To prevent carbon entering the gap between the pistons and bores, smear a little grease in the gap. After cleaning a piston, rotate the crankshaft to that the piston moves down the bore, then wipe out the grease and carbon with a cloth rag. Clean the other piston crowns in the same way.

24 Check the head and block for nicks, deep scratches and other damage. If slight, they may be removed carefully with a file. More serious damage may be repaired by machining, but this is a specialist job.

25 If warpage of the cylinder head is suspected, use a straight-edge to check it for distortion, as described in Part D of this Chapter.

26 Ensure that the cylinder head bolt holes in the crankcase are clean and free of oil. Syringe or soak up any oil left in the bolt holes. This is most important in order that the correct bolt tightening torque can be applied, and to prevent the possibility of the block being cracked by hydraulic pressure when the bolts are tightened.

27 Ensure that the crankshaft has been turned to position Nos 1 and 4 pistons slightly down their bores from the TDC position (see Section 7). This will eliminate any risk of piston-to-valve contact as the cylinder head is refitted. Also ensure that the camshaft sprockets are locked in the TDC position using the locking tool, as described in Section 3.

28 Ensure that the cylinder head locating dowels are in place in the cylinder block, then fit a new cylinder head gasket over the dowels, ensuring that the part number is uppermost. Where applicable, the OBEN/TOP marking should also be uppermost **(see illustrations)**. Note that Seat recommend that the gasket is only removed from its packaging immediately prior to fitting.

29 Lower the cylinder head into position on the gasket, ensuring that it engages correctly over the dowels. As the cylinder head is lowered into position, ensure that the coolant pump pipe engages with the thermostat housing (use a new O-ring if necessary).

30 Fit the new cylinder head bolts, and screw them in as far as possible by hand.

31 Working progressively, in sequence, tighten all the cylinder head bolts to the specified Stage 1 torque **(see illustration)**.

32 Again working progressively, in sequence, tighten all the cylinder head bolts through the specified Stage 2 angle.

33 Finally, tighten all the cylinder head bolts, in sequence, to the specified Stage 3 angle.

34 Reconnect the lifting tackle to the engine right-hand lifting bracket on the cylinder head, then adjust the lifting tackle to support the engine. Once the engine is adequately supported using the cylinder head bracket, disconnect the lifting tackle from the bracket bolted to the cylinder block, and unbolt the improvised engine lifting bracket from the cylinder block. Alternatively, remove the trolley jack and block of wood from under the sump.

35 Refit the clip securing the plastic coolant pipe to the coolant housing.

36 Refit the camshaft carrier as described in Section 9.

37 Further refitting is a reversal of removal, bearing in mind the following points:

a) *Refit the exhaust manifold and reconnect the EGR pipe, and/or reconnect the exhaust front section to the manifold, as described in Chapter 4.*

b) *Refit the intake manifold using new O-rings.*

c) *Reconnect the EGR pipe to the throttle body using a new gasket.*

d) *Refit the secondary and main timing belts as described in Section 7.*

e) *Ensure that all wires, pipes and hoses are correctly reconnected and routed, as noted before removal.*

f) *Tighten all fixings to the specified torque, where applicable.*

g) *On completion, refill the cooling system as described in Chapter 1A.*

14 Sump –
removal and refitting

Removal

1 Chock the rear wheels and apply the handbrake, then jack up the front of the car and support it on axle stands (see *Jacking and vehicle support*). Undo the fasteners

and remove the engine undershield **(see illustration 3.12)**.

2 Drain the engine oil, then clean and refit the engine oil drain plug, tightening it to the specified torque wrench setting. If the engine is nearing the service interval when the oil and filter are due for renewal, it is recommended that the filter is also removed and a new one fitted. After reassembly, the engine can then be replenished with fresh engine oil. Refer to Chapter 1A for further information.

3 Remove the exhaust front pipe with reference to Chapter 4C.

4 Disconnect the wiring from the oil level/temperature sender.

5 Unscrew the two bolts securing the sump rear flange to the transmission. On engine code BXW, undo the bolts and remove the cover plate from the transmission housing.

6 Progressively unscrew and remove the sump retaining bolts.

7 Break the joint by striking the sump with the palm of the hand, then lower the sump away from the engine and withdraw it.

8 While the sump is removed, take the opportunity to clean the oil pump pick-up/strainer pipe mesh using a suitable solvent. Inspect the strainer mesh for signs of clogging or splitting and renew if necessary, referring to Section 15 for further information.

Refitting

9 Thoroughly clean all traces of sealant and oil from the mating surfaces of the cylinder block/crankcase and sump, then use a clean rag to wipe out the sump and the engine's interior.

10 Apply a 2.0 to 3.0 mm diameter bead of sealant to the sump mating flange, making sure that the bead is around the inner edges of the bolt holes. The bead must not exceed 3.0 mm diameter. **Note:** *The sump must be refitted within 5 minutes of applying the sealant.*

11 When refitting the sump, to guide the sump into position on the cylinder block mating face, two guide studs can be improvised by cutting the heads off two M6 bolts, and cutting slots in the ends of the bolts so that they can later be unscrewed using a flat-bladed screwdriver. Screw the guide studs into two diagonally opposite sump securing bolt holes.

12 Offer the sump into position, then refit the

sump bolts and tighten them to the specified torque. Once the sump is held securely in position, unscrew the guide studs, and refit the remaining two sump securing bolts.

13 The remainder of refitting is a reversal of removal.

15.2 Crankshaft sprocket TDC timing mark (A)

15 Oil pump –
removal, inspection and refitting

Removal

1 Remove the main timing belt as described in Section 7.

2 Turn the crankshaft a quarter-turn (90°) clockwise to reposition Nos 1 and 4 pistons at TDC. Ensure that the crankshaft sprocket tooth with the chamfered inner edge is aligned with the corresponding mark on the oil pump housing **(see illustration)**.

3 Turn the crankshaft to move the crankshaft sprocket three teeth anti-clockwise away from the TDC position. The third tooth to the right of the tooth with the ground-down outer edge must align with the corresponding mark on the oil pump housing. This procedure positions the crankshaft correctly to enable oil pump refitting.

4 Remove the timing belt tensioner as described in Section 8.

5 Remove the sump as described in Section 14.

6 Unscrew the securing bolts and remove the oil pick-up pipe from the oil pump and cylinder block **(see illustration)**. Recover the gasket. **Note:** *As of 06/04 a plastic pipe*

is fitted without support brackets to manual transmission models.

7 Remove the crankshaft sprocket, noting which way round it is fitted.

8 Unscrew the securing bolts, noting their locations to ensure correct refitting, and remove the oil pump **(see illustration)**. Recover the gasket.

Inspection

9 No spare parts are available for the oil pump, and if worn or faulty the complete pump must be renewed.

10 To inspect the oil pump rotors, remove the securing bolts, and lift off the oil pump rear cover **(see illustration)**.

11 Note that the rotors fit with the punched dots on the edges of the rotors facing the oil pump cover **(see illustration)**.

12 Lift out the rotors, and inspect them. If there are any signs of wear or damage, the complete oil pump assembly must be renewed.

13 Lubricate the contact faces of the rotors with clean engine oil, then refit the rotors to the pump, ensuring that the punched dots on the edges of the rotors face the pump cover.

14 Refit the pump cover, and tighten the bolts securely.

15 Using a flat-bladed screwdriver, prise the crankshaft oil seal from the oil pump, and discard it **(see illustration)**.

16 Thoroughly clean the oil seal seat in the oil pump.

17 Press or drive a new oil seal into position in the oil pump, using a socket or tube of

suitable diameter **(see illustration)**. Ensure that the seal seats squarely in the oil pump. Ensure that the socket or tube bears only on the hard outer ring of the seal, and take care not to damage the seal lips. Press or drive the seal into position until it is seated on the shoulder in the housing. Make sure that the closed end of the seal is facing outwards.

Refitting

18 Commence refitting by cleaning all traces of old gasket and sealant from the mating faces of the cylinder block and oil pump.

19 Wind a length of tape around the end of

15.6 Remove the oil pick-up pipe

15.8 Remove the oil pump

15.10 Lift off the oil pump rear cover

15.11 Note that the rotors fit with the punched dots (arrowed) facing the oil pump cover

15.15 Prise the crankshaft oil seal from the oil pump

15.17 Drive a new oil seal into the oil pump using a socket

2B•16 1.4 litre petrol engine in-car repair procedures

15.20 Fit a new gasket over the dowels in the cylinder block

15.21 Align one of the rotor drive cut-outs (1) with the oil pump rear cover mark (2)

15.24 Slide the oil pump over the crankshaft. Note the tape used to protect the oil seal

15.25 Fit the new oil pump securing bolts to the locations (arrowed) noted before removal

15.27 Fit a new oil pick-up pipe gasket

the crankshaft to protect the oil seal lips as the oil pump is slid into position.

20 Fit a new oil pump gasket over the dowels in the cylinder block **(see illustration)**.

21 Turn the inner oil pump rotor to align one of the drive cut-outs in the edge of the inner rotor with the line mark on the oil pump rear cover **(see illustration)**.

22 Lightly oil the four tips of the oil pump drive cam on the end of the crankshaft.

23 Coat the lips of the crankshaft oil seal with a thin film of clean engine oil.

24 Slide the oil pump into position over the end of the crankshaft until it engages with the dowels, taking care not to damage the oil seal, and ensuring that the inner rotor engages

17.2 Disconnect the oil pressure switch wiring connector

with the drive cam on the crankshaft **(see illustration)**.

25 Fit new oil pump securing bolts to the locations noted before removal, and tighten them to the specified torque **(see illustration)**.

26 Remove the tape from the end of the crankshaft, then refit the crankshaft sprocket, noting that the pulley locating pin must be outermost. Temporarily refit the securing bolt and washer to retain the sprocket.

27 Refit the oil pick-up pipe, using a new gasket, and tighten the securing bolts to the specified torque **(see illustration)**.

28 Refit the sump as described in Section 14.

29 Refit the timing belt tensioner as described in Section 8.

30 Refit the main timing belt as described in Section 7.

16 Oil pressure relief valve –
removal, inspection
and refitting

The oil pressure relief valve is an integral part of the oil pump. The valve piston and spring are located to the side of the oil pump rotors and can be inspected once the oil pump has been removed from the engine and the rear cover has been removed (see Section 15). If any sign of wear or damage is found the oil pump assembly will have to be renewed; the

relief valve piston and spring are not available separately.

17 Oil pressure
warning light switch –
removal and refitting

Removal

1 The oil pressure warning light switch is fitted to the left-hand end of the cylinder head. To gain access to the switch, remove the air cleaner as described in Chapter 4A.

2 Disconnect the wiring connector and wipe clean the area around the switch **(see illustration)**.

3 Unscrew the switch from the cylinder head and remove it along with its sealing washer. If the switch is to be left removed from the engine for any length of time, plug the hole in the cylinder head.

Refitting

4 Examine the sealing washer for signs of damage or deterioration and if necessary renew.

5 Refit the switch, complete with washer, and tighten it to the specified torque.

6 Securely reconnect the wiring connector then refit the air cleaner. Check and, if necessary, top-up the engine oil as described in *Weekly checks*.

18 Crankshaft oil seals – renewal

Right-hand oil seal

1 Remove the main timing belt as described in Section 7, and the crankshaft sprocket with reference to Section 8.
2 To remove the seal without removing the oil pump, drill two small holes diagonally opposite each other, insert self-tapping screws, and pull on the heads of the screws with pliers.
3 Alternatively, the oil seal can be removed with the oil pump (see Section 15).
4 Thoroughly clean the oil seal seating in the oil pump.
5 Wind a length of tape around the end of the crankshaft to protect the oil seal lips as the seal is fitted.
6 Fit a new oil seal to the oil pump, pressing or driving it into position using a socket or tube of suitable diameter. Ensure that the socket or tube bears only on the hard outer ring of the seal, and take care not to damage the seal lips. Press or drive the seal into position until it is seated on the shoulder in the oil pump. Make sure that the closed end of the seal is facing outwards.
7 Refit the crankshaft sprocket with reference to Section 8, and the main timing belt as described in Section 7.

Left-hand oil seal

8 The crankshaft left-hand oil seal is integral with the housing, and must be renewed as an assembly, complete with the crankshaft speed/position sensor wheel. The sensor wheel is attached to the oil seal/housing assembly, and is a press-fit on the crankshaft flange. Seat special tool T10017 is required to fit this assembly and, in the workshop, we found that there is no means of accurately aligning the sensor wheel on the crankshaft without the tool (there is no locating key, and there are no alignment marks). If the sensor wheel is not precisely aligned on the crankshaft, the crankshaft speed/position sensor will send incorrect TDC signals to the engine management ECM, and the engine will not run correctly (the engine may not run at all). As the appropriate special tool is only available to Seat dealers, there is no alternative but to have the new assembly fitted by a Seat dealer.

19 Flywheel/driveplate – removal, inspection and refitting

Flywheel

Removal

1 Remove the manual transmission and clutch as described in Chapter 7A and Chapter 6.
2 Lock the flywheel in position using a

19.2 Flywheel locked in position with a home-made tool

home-made locking tool, fabricated from a piece of scrap metal (see illustration). Bolt it to one of the transmission bellhousing mounting holes. Mark the position of the flywheel with respect to the crankshaft using a dab of paint.
3 Slacken and withdraw the flywheel mounting bolts, then lift off the flywheel.
Caution: Get an assistant to help, as the flywheel is extremely heavy.

Inspection

4 If the flywheel's clutch mating surface is deeply scored, cracked or otherwise damaged, the flywheel must be renewed. However, it may be possible to have it surface-ground; seek the advice of a Seat dealer or engine reconditioning specialist.
5 If the ring gear is badly worn or has missing teeth, the flywheel must be renewed.

Refitting

6 Clean the mating surfaces of the flywheel and crankshaft. Remove any remaining locking compound from the threads of the crankshaft holes, using the correct-size tap, if available.

> **HAYNES HINT** *If a suitable tap is not available, cut two slots down the threads of one of the old flywheel bolts with a hacksaw, and use the bolt to remove the locking compound from the threads.*

7 If the new flywheel retaining bolts are not supplied with their threads pre-coated, apply a suitable thread-locking compound to the threads of each bolt (see illustration).

19.9 Tighten the flywheel bolts to the specified torque

19.7 Apply locking fluid to the new flywheel bolts, if necessary

8 Offer up the flywheel to the crankshaft, using the alignment marks made during removal, and fit the new retaining bolts.
9 Lock the flywheel using the method employed on dismantling, and tighten the retaining bolts to the specified torque and angle (see illustration).
10 Refit the clutch as described in Chapter 6. Remove the locking tool, and refit the transmission as described in Chapter 7A.

Driveplate

Removal

11 Remove the automatic transmission as described in Chapter 7B.
12 Lock the driveplate in position by bolting a piece of scrap metal between the driveplate and one of the transmission bellhousing mounting holes. Mark the position of the driveplate with respect to the crankshaft using a dab of paint.
13 Slacken and withdraw the driveplate mounting bolts, then lift off the driveplate. Recover the packing plate and the shim (where applicable).

Refitting

14 Refitting is a reversal of removal, using the alignment marks made during removal, but initially tighten the new mounting bolts to 30 Nm (22 lbf ft) only and check the distance between the cylinder block and flat face of the driveplate – not the outer lip (see illustration). Make the check at three points and calculate the average distance which should be between 19.7 and 21.3 mm. If the distance measured is outside the limits, fit a different shim and check again. With

19.14 The distance between cylinder block and driveplate should be 19.7 to 21.3 mm

the distance correct, fully tighten the mounting bolts to their specified torque and angle.

15 Remove the locking tool, and refit the transmission as described in Chapter 7B.

20 Engine/transmission mountings – inspection and renewal

Inspection

1 If improved access is required, jack up the front of the car, and support it securely on axle stands (see *Jacking and vehicle support*). Remove the securing bolts and remove the engine undershield **(see illustration 3.12)**.

2 Check the mounting rubbers to see if they are cracked, hardened or separated from the metal at any point; renew the mounting if any such damage or deterioration is evident.

3 Check that all the mounting fasteners are securely tightened; use a torque wrench to check if possible.

4 Using a large screwdriver or a crowbar, check for wear in the mounting by carefully levering against it to check for free play. Where this is not possible, enlist the aid of an assistant to move the engine/transmission back-and-forth, or from side-to-side, whilst you observe the mounting. While some free play is to be expected, even from new components, excessive wear should be obvious. If excessive free play is found, check first that the fasteners are correctly secured, then renew any worn components as described in the following paragraphs.

Renewal

Right-hand mounting

Note: *New mounting securing bolts/nut will be required on refitting.*

5 Attach a hoist and lifting tackle to the engine lifting brackets on the cylinder head, and raise the hoist to just take the weight of the engine. Alternatively the engine can be supported on a trolley jack under the engine. Use a block of wood between the sump and the head of the jack, to prevent any damage to the sump.

6 Unbolt the coolant reservoir and move it to one side, leaving the coolant hoses connected.

7 Unscrew the bolts securing the mounting to the bracket on the engine, and the bolts securing the mounting to the body, then lift the mounting from the engine compartment.

8 Unscrew the centre nut and separate the bracket from the mounting.

9 Refitting is a reversal of removal, but tighten the new bolts and nut to the specified torque.

Left-hand mounting

Note: *New mounting bolts will be required on refitting.*

10 Remove the engine undershield, then support the transmission with a trolley jack and block of wood.

11 Remove the battery, as described in Chapter 5A, then disconnect the main starter motor feed cable from the positive battery terminal box.

12 Release any relevant wiring or hoses from the clips on the battery tray, then unscrew the four securing bolts and remove the battery tray.

13 Where applicable, to improve access to the engine-transmission mounting, remove the air cleaner assembly as described in Chapter 4A.

14 Unscrew the bolts securing the mounting to the transmission, and the bolts securing the mounting to the body, then lift the mounting from the engine compartment.

15 Refitting is a reversal of removal, but tighten the new bolts to the specified torque.

Rear mounting

Note: *New mounting bolts will be required on refitting.*

16 Apply the handbrake, then jack up the front of the car and support securely on axle stands (see *Jacking and vehicle support*).

17 Remove the engine undershield, then support the transmission with a trolley jack and block of wood.

18 Working under the car, loosen the nut and bolt securing the rear mounting link to the transmission bracket.

19 Unscrew and remove the two bolts securing the mounting assembly to the transmission.

20 Unscrew the single bolt securing the mounting link to the subframe, then withdraw the assembly from under the car.

21 Unscrew the nut and bolt and separate the link from the bracket.

22 Refitting is a reversal of removal, but use new mounting bolts (except the link-to-bracket bolt), and tighten all fixings to the specified torque.

Chapter 2 Part C:
Diesel engine in-car repair procedures

Contents

Degrees of difficulty

Easy, suitable for novice with little experience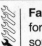

Fairly easy, suitable for beginner with some experience

Fairly difficult, suitable for competent DIY mechanic

Difficult, suitable for experienced DIY mechanic

Very difficult, suitable for expert DIY or professional

Specifications

General

Type	Three- or four-cylinder in-line, belt-driven single overhead camshaft (SOHC), four stroke, liquid-cooled
Manufacturer's engine codes:*	
1422 cc (1.4 litre), 3-cylinder	AMF, BMS, BNM and BNV
1896 cc (1.9 litre), 4-cylinder	ASZ, ATD, AXR, BLT and BMT
Maximum power output:	
Engine code AMF.	55kW at 4000 rpm
Engine code BMS.	59kW at 4000 rpm
Engine code BNM	51kW at 4000 rpm
Engine code BNV	58kW at 4000 rpm
Engine codes ASZ and BLT	96 kW at 4000 rpm
Engine codes ATD, AXR and BMT	74 kW at 4000 rpm
Maximum torque output:	
Engine codes AMF, BMS and BNV.	195 Nm at 2200 rpm
Engine code BNM	155 Nm at 2200 rpm
Engine codes ASZ and BLT	310 Nm at 1900 rpm
Engine codes ATD, AXR and BMT	240 Nm at 1800 to 2400 rpm
Bore	79.5 mm
Stroke.	95.5 mm
Compression ratio:	
Three-cylinder engines.	19.5 : 1
Four-cylinder engines.	19.0 : 1
Compression pressures:	
Minimum compression pressure	Approximately 19.0 bar
Maximum difference between cylinders.	Approximately 5.0 bar
Firing order:	
Three-cylinder engines.	1 – 2 – 3
Four-cylinder engines.	1 – 3 – 4 – 2
No 1 cylinder location.	Timing belt end

* Note: See 'Vehicle identification' at the end of this manual for the location of engine code markings.

Camshaft

Camshaft endfloat (maximum).	0.15 mm
Camshaft bearing running clearance (maximum).	0.11 mm
Camshaft run-out (maximum).	0.01 mm

Lubrication system

Oil pump type. . . . . Gear type, chain-driven from crankshaft
Oil pressure (oil temperature 80°C, at 2000 rpm). . . . . 2.0 bar

Torque wrench settings

	Nm	lbf ft
Ancillary (alternator, etc) bracket mounting bolts.	45	33
Auxiliary drivebelt tensioner securing bolt	25	18
Balancer shaft assembly to crankcase (3-cylinder engines)	20	15
Balancer shaft drive chain tensioner housing (3-cylinder engines):		
Stage 1	8	6
Stage 2	Angle-tighten a further 90°	
Balancer shaft weight/sprocket (3-cylinder engines):*		
Stage 1	100	74
Stage 2	Angle-tighten a further 90°	
Big-end bearing caps bolts:*		
Stage 1	30	22
Stage 2	Angle-tighten a further 90°	
Camshaft bearing cap bolts:*		
Stage 1	8	6
Stage 2	Angle-tighten a further 90°	
Camshaft cover nuts/bolts.	10	7
Camshaft sprocket hub centre bolt	100	74
Camshaft sprocket outer bolts:		
Stage 1	20	15
Stage 2	Angle-tighten a further 45°	
Coolant pump bolts	15	11
Crankshaft oil seal housing bolts	15	11
Crankshaft pulley-to-sprocket bolts:		
Stage 1	10	7
Stage 2	Angle-tighten a further 90°	
Crankshaft speed/position sensor wheel-to-crankshaft bolts:*		
Stage 1	10	7
Stage 2	Angle-tighten a further 90°	
Crankshaft sprocket bolt:*		
Stage 1	120	89
Stage 2	Angle-tighten a further 90°	
Cylinder head bolts:*		
Stage 1	40	30
Stage 2	60	44
Stage 3	Angle-tighten a further 90°	
Stage 4	Angle-tighten a further 90°	
Engine mountings:		
Right-hand mounting:*		
To engine:		
Stage 1	30	22
Stage 2	Angle-tighten a further 90°	
To body:		
Stage 1	20	15
Stage 2	Angle-tighten a further 90°	
Centre nut:		
Stage 1	40	30
Stage 2	Angle-tighten a further 90°	
Left-hand mounting:		
To transmission:*		
Stage 1	40	30
Stage 2	Angle-tighten a further 90°	
To body:		
Stage 1	50	37
Stage 2	Angle-tighten a further 90°	
Rear torque arm:*		
To subframe:		
Stage 1	40	30
Stage 2	Angle-tighten a further 90°	
To transmission:		
Stage 1	30	22
Stage 2	Angle-tighten a further 90°	
Exhaust manifold nuts	25	18
Exhaust pipe-to-manifold/turbocharger nuts.	25	18

Torque wrench settings (continued)

	Nm	lbf ft
Flywheel:		
Stage 1	60	44
Stage 2	Angle-tighten a further 90°	
Fuel injector pipe union nuts	25	18
Glow plugs	15	11
Guide pulley sprocket bolt (3-cylinder engines)	20	15
Injection pump sprocket bolts:		
Type 1:*		
Stage 1	20	15
Stage 2	Angle-tighten a further 90°	
Type 2 25	18	
Injector rocker shafts:*		
Stage 1	20	15
Stage 2	Angle-tighten a further 90°	
Main bearing cap bolts:*		
Stage 1	65	48
Stage 2	Angle-tighten a further 90°	
Oil cooler retaining cap	25	18
Oil drain plug	30	22
Oil filter housing-to-cylinder block bolts:*		
Stage 1	15	11
Stage 2	Angle-tighten a further 90°	
Oil filter cap	25	18
Oil level/temperature sensor-to-sump bolts	10	7
Oil pick-up pipe securing bolts	15	11
Oil pressure relief valve plug	40	30
Oil pressure warning light switch	20	15
Oil pump chain tensioner bolt	15	11
Oil pump securing bolts	15	11
Oil pump sprocket securing bolt/nut:		
3-cylinder engines:		
Stage 1	20	15
Stage 2	Angle-tighten a further 90°	
4-cylinder engines	25	18
Piston oil spray jet bolt	25	18
Pump injector rocker shaft:*		
Stage 1	20	15
Stage 2	Angle-tighten a further 90°	
Roadwheel bolts	120	89
Sump:		
Sump-to-cylinder block bolts	15	11
Sump-to-transmission bolts	45	33
Timing belt outer cover bolts	10	7
Timing belt rear cover-to-cylinder head bolt	10	7
Timing belt small idler pulley nut/bolt	20	15
Timing belt tensioner roller securing nut:		
Stage 1	20	15
Stage 2	Angle-tighten a further 45°	
Timing belt upper idler roller bolt	20	15
Turbocharger oil return pipe-to-cylinder block banjo bolt	40	30
Turbocharger oil supply pipe-to-oil filter housing:		
Banjo bolt	25	18
Union nut	22	16

Do not re-use

1 General information

Using this Chapter

This Part of Chapter 2 describes those repair procedures that can reasonably be carried out on the engine while it remains in the car. If the engine has been removed from the car and is being dismantled as described in Part D, any preliminary dismantling procedures can be ignored.

Note that while it may be possible physically to overhaul items such as the piston/connecting rod assemblies while the engine is in the car, such tasks are not usually carried out as separate operations, and usually require the execution of several additional procedures (not to mention the cleaning of components and of oilways); for this reason, all such tasks are classed as major overhaul procedures, and are described in Part D of this Chapter.

Part D describes the removal of the engine/transmission from the car and the full overhaul procedures that can then be carried out.

Engine description

The engines are water-cooled, single overhead camshaft, in-line three- or four-cylinder units, with cast-iron cylinder blocks and aluminium-alloy cylinder heads. All are mounted transversely at the front of the car, with the transmission bolted to the left-hand end of the engine.

2.3 Disconnect the injector solenoids wiring plug connector (arrowed)

On the 3-cylinder engine, the crankshaft is of four-bearing type, and thrustwashers are fitted to main bearing No 3 to control crankshaft endfloat. On 4-cylinder engines, the crankshaft is of five-bearing type, and thrustwashers are fitted to the centre main bearing.

The camshaft is driven by a toothed timing belt from the crankshaft. The camshaft is mounted at the top of the cylinder head, and is secured by bearing caps.

The valves are closed by coil springs, and run in guides pressed into the cylinder head. The camshaft actuates the valves directly, via hydraulic tappets. On the 3-cylinder engine there are six valves, one intake and one exhaust valve per cylinder. On the 4-cylinder engine there are eight valves, one intake and one exhaust valve per cylinder.

A chain-driven balancer shaft assembly is bolted to the bottom of the crankcase on the 3-cylinder engine. The balancer shaft counteracts vibrations within the engine to provide smooth running throughout the engine speed range.

On the 3-cylinder engine, an oil pump is located on the bottom of the balancer shaft assembly and is driven by chain from a sprocket on the crankshaft. The balancer shaft assembly and the oil pump are enclosed in a plastic cover which incorporates an oil strainer. On all 4-cylinder engines, the oil pump is chain-driven from the end of the crankshaft.

From the sump, the oil is forced through an externally-mounted, renewable filter. From there it is distributed to the cylinder head, where it lubricates the camshaft journals and hydraulic tappets, and also to the crankcase, where it lubricates the main bearings, connecting rod big-ends, gudgeon pins and cylinder bores. A coolant-fed oil cooler is fitted to the oil filter housing on all engines. Oil jets are fitted to the base of each cylinder – these spray oil onto the underside of the pistons, to improve cooling.

All engines are fitted with a brake servo vacuum pump driven by the camshaft on the transmission end of the cylinder head. On all engines, the pump is of tandem design, incorporating a vacuum pump and a fuel pump, driven by the camshaft.

On all engines, engine coolant is circulated by a pump, driven by the timing belt. For details of the cooling system, refer to Chapter 3.

Repairs with engine in car

The following operations can be performed without removing the engine:
a) *Compression pressure – testing.*
b) *Camshaft cover – removal and refitting.*
c) *Crankshaft pulley – removal and refitting.*
d) *Timing belt covers – removal and refitting.*
e) *Timing belt – removal, refitting and adjustment.*
f) *Timing belt tensioner and sprockets – removal and refitting.*
g) *Camshaft oil seals – renewal.*
h) *Camshaft and hydraulic tappets – removal, inspection and refitting.*
i) *Cylinder head – removal and refitting.*
j) *Cylinder head and pistons – decarbonising.*
k) *Sump – removal and refitting.*
l) *Oil pump (except 3-cylinder engines) – removal, overhaul and refitting.*
m) *Crankshaft oil seals – renewal.*
n) *Engine/transmission mountings – inspection and renewal.*
o) *Flywheel – removal, inspection and refitting.*

Note: *It is possible to remove the pistons and connecting rods (after removing the cylinder head and sump) without removing the engine. However, this is not recommended. Work of this nature is more easily and thoroughly completed with the engine on the bench, as described in Chapter 2D.*

2 Compression and leakdown tests – description and interpretation

Compression test

Note: *A compression tester suitable for use with diesel engines will be required for this test.*

1 When engine performance is down, or if misfiring occurs which cannot be attributed to the ignition or fuel systems, a compression test can provide diagnostic clues as to the engine's condition. If the test is performed regularly, it can give warning of trouble before any other symptoms become apparent.

2 The engine must be fully warmed-up to normal operating temperature, the battery must be fully-charged and you will require the aid of an assistant.

3 Disconnect the injector solenoids by unplugging the connector at the end of the cylinder head **(see illustration)**. **Note:** *As a result of the wiring being disconnected, faults will be stored in the ECM memory. These must be erased after the compression test.*

4 Remove the glow plugs as described in Chapter 5A, then fit a compression tester to the No 1 cylinder glow plug hole. The type of tester which screws into the plug thread is preferred.

5 Have your assistant crank the engine for several seconds on the starter motor. After one or two revolutions, the compression pressure should build-up to a maximum figure and then stabilise. Record the highest reading obtained.

6 Repeat the test on the remaining cylinders, recording the pressure in each.

7 The cause of poor compression is less easy to establish on a diesel engine than on a petrol engine. The effect of introducing oil into the cylinders (wet testing) is not conclusive, because there is a risk that the oil will sit in the recess on the piston crown, instead of passing to the rings. However, the following can be used as a rough guide to diagnosis.

8 All cylinders should produce very similar pressures. Any difference greater than that specified indicates the existence of a fault. Note that the compression should build-up quickly in a healthy engine. Low compression on the first stroke, followed by gradually increasing pressure on successive strokes, indicates worn piston rings. A low compression reading on the first stroke, which does not build-up during successive strokes, indicates leaking valves or a blown head gasket (a cracked head could also be the cause).

9 A low reading from two adjacent cylinders is almost certainly due to the head gasket having blown between them and the presence of coolant in the engine oil will confirm this.

10 On completion, remove the compression tester, and refit the glow plugs, with reference to Chapter 5A.

11 Reconnect the wiring.

Leakdown test

12 A leakdown test measures the rate at which compressed air fed into the cylinder is lost. It is an alternative to a compression test, and in many ways it is better, since the escaping air provides easy identification of where pressure loss is occurring (piston rings, valves or head gasket).

13 The equipment required for leakdown testing is unlikely to be available to the home mechanic. If poor compression is suspected, have the test performed by a suitably-equipped garage.

3 Engine assembly and valve timing marks – general information and usage

General information

1 TDC is the highest point in the cylinder that each piston reaches as it travels up-and-down when the crankshaft turns. Each piston reaches TDC at the end of the compression stroke and again at the end of the exhaust stroke, but TDC generally refers to piston position on the compression stroke. No 1 piston is at the timing belt end of the engine.

2 Positioning No 1 piston at TDC is an

3.4a Release the clips . . .

3.4b . . . and remove the upper outer timing belt cover

3.6 TDC locking pin (arrowed) inserted through the camshaft sprocket into the cylinder head

3.13a Position the crankshaft so the sprocket mark is almost vertical (arrowed) . . .

3.13b . . . then insert the tool T10050 . . .

3.13c . . . and align the marks (arrowed) on the tool and sprocket

essential part of many procedures, such as timing belt removal and camshaft removal.

3 The design of the engines covered in this Chapter is such that piston-to-valve contact may occur if the camshaft or crankshaft is turned with the timing belt removed. For

3.13d TDC setting tools

this reason, it is important to ensure that the camshaft and crankshaft do not move in relation to each other once the timing belt has been removed from the engine.

Setting TDC on No 1 cylinder

3-cylinder engines

4 Remove the timing belt covers as described in Section 6 (see illustrations).
5 Remove the glow plugs, as described in Chapter 5A, to allow the engine to turn more easily.
6 Turn the engine until the TDC hole in the camshaft sprocket is approximately at the 8 o'clock position and aligned with the TDC timing hole in the cylinder head; at this point a special Seat locking pin (T20102) may be inserted (see illustration). An improvised tool may be fabricated out of 6.0 mm diameter metal rod, but due to the exact measurements and machining involved, it is strongly recommended that the tool is either borrowed or hired from a Seat dealer, or purchased from a reputable tool manufacturer.
7 While in this position it should be possible to insert Seat tool T10050 to lock the crankshaft (see illustration 3.13b). Note: The mark on the crankshaft sprocket and the mark on the Seat tool T10050 must align, whilst at the same time the shaft of tool T10050 must engage in the drilling in the crankshaft oil seal housing.
8 The engine is now set to TDC on No 1 cylinder.

4-cylinder engines

Note: Seat special tool (T10050 for early models or T10100 for later models) is required

to lock the crankshaft sprocket in the TDC position.
9 Remove the auxiliary drivebelt(s) as described in Chapter 1B. Also, remove the auxiliary drivebelt tensioning unit.
10 Remove the crankshaft pulley/vibration damper as described in Section 5.
11 Remove the timing belt covers as described in Section 6.
12 Remove the glow plugs, as described in Chapter 5A, to allow the engine to turn more easily.
13 Using a spanner or socket on the crankshaft sprocket bolt, turn the crankshaft in the normal direction of rotation (clockwise) until the alignment mark on the face of the sprocket is almost vertical (see illustrations).
14 The arrow (marked 4Z) on the rear section of the upper timing belt upper cover aligns between the two lugs on the rear of the camshaft hub sender wheel (see illustration).

3.14 Alignment arrow on the rear of the timing belt cover (arrowed)

3.15 Insert a 6 mm drill bit (arrowed) to lock the camshaft

15 While in this position it should be possible to insert Seat tool T10050 or T10100 to lock the crankshaft, and a 6 mm diameter rod to lock the camshaft sprocket **(see illustration)**. **Note:** *The mark on the crankshaft sprocket and the mark on the Seat tool T10050 or T10100 must align, whilst at the same time the shaft of the tool must engage in the drilling in the crankshaft oil seal housing.*
16 The engine is now set to TDC on No 1 cylinder.

4 Camshaft cover – removal and refitting

Removal

3-cylinder engines

1 Remove the engine top cover (where fitted) by prising it upwards from the location pillars and disconnecting the vacuum pipes. Also remove the foam base.
2 Remove the intake air ducting from the rear of the cylinder head.
3 Release the clip and disconnect the crankcase ventilation hose from the camshaft cover.
4 Unclip the fuel lines from the front of the camshaft cover.
5 Remove the upper timing belt cover as described in Section 6.

4.13b Camshaft cover tightening sequence

6 Progressively unscrew and remove the camshaft cover retaining bolts and lift the cover away. If it sticks, do not attempt to lever it off – instead free it by working around the cover and tapping it lightly with a soft-faced mallet.
7 Recover the camshaft cover gasket. Inspect the gasket carefully, and renew it if damage or deterioration is evident.
8 Clean the mating surfaces of the cylinder head and camshaft cover thoroughly, removing all traces of oil and old gasket – take care to avoid damaging the surfaces as you do this.

4-cylinder engines

9 Remove the oil filler cap, then prise off and withdraw the engine top covers(s) (where fitted) from the supports. Where applicable, disconnect the breather hose from the camshaft cover.
10 Unscrew the camshaft cover retaining bolts and lift the cover away. If it sticks, do not attempt to lever it off – instead free it by working around the cover and tapping it lightly with a soft-faced mallet.
11 Recover the camshaft cover gasket **(see illustration)**. Inspect the gasket carefully, and renew it if damage or deterioration is evident.
12 Clean the mating surfaces of the cylinder head and camshaft cover thoroughly, removing all traces of oil and old gasket – take care to avoid damaging the surfaces as you do this.

Refitting

13 Refit the camshaft cover by following the removal procedure in reverse, noting the following points:

5.2 Remove the intercooler air duct for access to the crankshaft pulley

4.11 The camshaft cover gasket locates in a groove in the cover

4.13a Apply sealant to the points (arrowed) on the cylinder head

a) *Before refitting the camshaft cover, apply a small amount of sealant to the two points where the camshaft bearing caps contact the cylinder head (see illustration). Ensure that the gasket is correctly seated on the cylinder head, and take care to avoid displacing it as the camshaft cover is lowered into position.*
b) *Tighten the camshaft cover retaining nuts/bolts progressively to the specified torque in sequence (see illustration).*

5 Crankshaft pulley – removal and refitting

Removal

1 For improved access, raise the front right-hand side of the car, and support securely on axle stands (see *Jacking and vehicle support*). Remove the roadwheel.
2 Remove the securing Torx bolts and withdraw the engine undershield(s) and/or wheel arch liner panels. Unscrew the nut at the rear, and the washer-type fasteners further forward, then release the air hose clip and manipulate out the plastic air duct for the intercooler **(see illustration)**.
3 Remove the auxiliary drivebelt, as described in Chapter 1B.
4 Where applicable, prise the cover from the centre of the pulley to expose the securing bolts **(see illustration)**.
5 Slacken the bolts securing the crankshaft pulley to the sprocket **(see illustration)**. If

5.4 Prise out the crankshaft pulley centre cap

necessary, the pulley can be prevented from turning by counterholding with a spanner or socket on the crankshaft sprocket bolt.

6 Unscrew the bolts securing the pulley to the sprocket, and remove the pulley **(see illustration)**.

Refitting

7 Refit the pulley over the locating peg on the crankshaft sprocket, then refit the pulley securing bolts.

8 Prevent the crankshaft from turning as during removal, then fit the pulley securing bolts, and tighten to the specified torque.

9 Refit and tension the auxiliary drivebelt as described in Chapter 1B.

10 Refit the engine undershield(s), wheel arch liners and the intercooler air duct.

11 Refit the roadwheel, lower the car to the ground, and tighten the roadwheel bolts to the specified torque.

6 Timing belt covers – removal and refitting

Upper outer cover

1 Pull the plastic engine cover(s) upwards from its retaining clips.

2 Release the retaining clips and remove the air intake hose from across the top of the timing belt cover **(see illustration)**.

3 Release the uppermost part of the timing belt outer cover by prising open the metal spring clips, then withdraw the cover away from the engine **(see illustrations)**.

4 Refitting is a reversal of removal, noting that the lower edge of the upper cover engages with the centre cover.

Centre outer cover

5 Remove the auxiliary drivebelt as described in Chapter 1B.

6 Remove the crankshaft pulley as described in Section 5. It is assumed that, if the centre cover is being removed, the lower cover will be also – if not, simply remove the components described in Section 5 for access to the crankshaft pulley, and leave the pulley in position.

7 With the upper cover removed (paragraphs 1 to 3), unscrew and remove the retaining bolts from the centre cover. Withdraw the centre cover from the engine (noting how it fits over the lower cover, where applicable) **(see illustration)**.

8 Refitting is a reversal of removal.

Lower outer cover

9 Remove the upper and centre covers as described previously.

10 If not already done, remove the crankshaft pulley as described in Section 5.

11 Unscrew the remaining bolt(s) securing the lower cover, and lift it out.

12 Refitting is a reversal of removal; locate the centre cover in place before fitting the top two bolts.

5.5 Undo the four crankshaft pulley bolts (arrowed)

Rear cover

13 Remove the upper, centre and lower covers as described previously.

14 Remove the timing belt, tensioner and sprockets as described in Sections 7 and 8.

15 Slacken and withdraw the retaining bolts and lift the timing belt inner cover from the studs on the end of the engine, and remove it from the engine compartment.

16 Refitting is a reversal of removal.

7 Timing belt – removal, inspection and refitting

Removal

1 The primary function of the toothed timing belt is to drive the camshaft, but it also

6.2 Remove the air intake hose from across the top of the timing belt cover

6.3b . . . and withdraw the upper cover

5.6 Remove the crankshaft pulley

drives the coolant pump. Should the belt slip or break in service, the valve timing will be disturbed and piston-to-valve contact may occur, resulting in serious engine damage. For this reason, it is important that the timing belt is tensioned correctly, and inspected regularly for signs of wear or deterioration.

2 Remove the right-hand headlight as described in Chapter 12, and the intake manifold-to-intercooler air trunking as described in Chapter 4C.

3 Apply the handbrake, then jack up the front of the car and support securely on axle stands (see *Jacking and vehicle support*). Remove the right-hand front roadwheel.

4 Remove the securing bolts and withdraw the engine undershield(s) **(see illustration)**, and the right-hand wheel arch liner.

5 Using a hoist, support the weight of the engine/transmission, then remove the

6.3a Release the retaining clips (one arrowed) . . .

6.7 Remove the centre outer cover

7.4 Undo the bolts (arrowed) and remove the engine undershield

7.5a Use a trolley jack to support the weight of the engine/transmission

7.5b Remove the right-hand engine mounting . . .

7.5c . . . and bracket

7.6a Unscrew the bolts . . .

7.6b . . . and remove the auxiliary drivebelt tensioner

right-hand engine mounting and bracket, and the engine rear mounting/link as described in Chapter 2A **(see illustrations)**.

6 Remove the auxiliary drivebelt as described in Chapter 1B. On 3-cylinder engines, also unbolt the auxiliary drivebelt tensioner **(see illustrations)**.

7 Disconnect the fuel supply and return hoses from the fuel filter **(see illustration)**, referring to Chapter 1B if necessary. Label the hoses if necessary, to ensure correct refitting.

8 If required, to further improve working room, remove the windscreen washer reservoir (Chapter 12) and the coolant expansion reservoir **(see illustration)**, and place them to one side without disconnecting their hoses.

9 Remove the timing belt outer covers, as described in Section 6. This procedure includes removing the crankshaft pulley as described in Section 5. Where applicable, unbolt the lower inner cover **(see illustration)**.

3-cylinder engines

10 Remove the charge air pipe and hose located at the bottom right of the engine, also the intake pipe from the right-hand side of the engine compartment **(see illustrations)**.

11 Turn the crankshaft to position No 1 piston at TDC on its firing stroke (see Section 3) and lock the camshaft sprocket by inserting a

7.7 Fuel supply (A) and return (B) hoses at the fuel filter

7.8 Disconnect the wiring from the coolant expansion tank. Note the tank mounting nuts (arrowed)

7.9 Lower inner cover

7.10a Remove the charge air pipe from the bottom right of the engine

7.10b Remove the intake pipe from the engine compartment

7.11a Tool T10050 for locking the crankshaft sprocket in its TDC position

7.11b Use the special locking tool (arrowed) to retain the crankshaft sprocket in its TDC position

tight-fitting bolt through the TDC hole into the cylinder head. Seat technicians also use a tool (T10050) to lock the crankshaft sprocket in its TDC position (see illustrations).

12 If the original timing belt is to be refitted, mark the running direction of the belt, to ensure correct refitting (see illustration).

Caution: If the belt appears to be in good condition and can be re-used, it is essential that it is refitted the same way around, otherwise accelerated wear will result, leading to premature failure.

13 Slacken the timing belt tensioner nut, and allow the tensioner to relieve the tension on the timing belt (see illustration).

14 Unscrew the nut and remove the timing belt guide pulley (see illustration).

15 Slide the belt from the sprockets, taking care not to twist or kink the belt excessively if it is to be re-used (see illustration).

4-cylinder engines

16 Set the engine to TDC on No 1 cylinder as described in Section 3.

17 Relieve the tension on the timing belt by first slackening the tensioner mounting nut slightly. Turn the tensioner fully anti-clockwise by hand.

18 Undo the bolt and remove the idler roller (where fitted) (see illustration).

19 Examine the timing belt for manufacturer's

markings that indicate the direction of rotation. If none are present, make your own using typist's correction fluid or a dab of paint – do not cut or score the belt in any way.

Caution: If the belt appears to be in good condition and can be re-used, it is essential that it is refitted the same way around, otherwise accelerated wear will result, leading to premature failure.

20 Slide the belt off the sprockets, taking care to avoid twisting or kinking it excessively if it is to be re-used.

Inspection

21 Examine the belt for evidence of

7.12 Mark the running direction of the timing belt if it is to be re-used

contamination by coolant or lubricant. If this is the case, find the source of the contamination before progressing any further. Check the belt for signs of wear or damage, particularly around the leading edges of the belt teeth. Renew the belt if its condition is in doubt; the cost of belt renewal is negligible compared with potential cost of the engine repairs, should the belt fail in service. The belt must be renewed if it has covered the mileage given in Chapter 1B, however, if it has covered less, it is prudent to renew it regardless of condition as a precautionary measure.

22 If the timing belt is not going to be refitted for some time, it is a wise precaution to hang a

7.13 Slacken the timing belt tensioner nut

7.14 Timing belt guide pulley (arrowed)

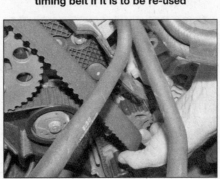

7.15 Remove the timing belt from the sprockets

7.18 Idler roller bolt (arrowed)

7.23 Hold the camshaft sprocket stationary while loosening the three bolts

7.26a Align the tensioner pointer in the baseplate cut-out (arrowed), then tighten the nut

7.26b The pointer must be in the middle of the cut-out

warning label on the steering wheel, to remind yourself (and others) not to attempt to start the engine.

Refitting

3-cylinder engines

23 If still fitted, remove the TDC pin from the camshaft sprocket, then hold the sprocket stationary with a suitable tool and loosen the three bolts securing it to the camshaft, so that it is free to turn within the three elongated slots **(see illustration)**. Turn the sprocket anti-clockwise so that the bolts are near the ends of the slots, then refit the TDC pin.

24 Fit the timing belt around the crankshaft sprocket, tensioner pulley, camshaft sprocket and coolant pump. Make sure that the tensioner pulley arm is correctly located in the rear timing cover hole. Check that the camshaft sprocket retaining bolts are positioned mid-way in their slots. If not, remove the timing belt and turn the sprocket slightly clockwise so that the belt can be located on the next tooth.

25 Refit the guide pulley and tighten the nut.

26 Using an Allen key in the hole provided, turn the tensioner anti-clockwise until the pointer is positioned in the middle of the cut-out of the baseplate. Hold the tensioner in this position, then tighten the retaining nut to the specified torque and angle **(see illustrations)**.

27 Tighten the bolts of the camshaft sprocket to their specified torque and angle while holding the sprocket stationary with a suitable tool inserted in two of the holes. The TDC

pin can remain in position, but the holding tool must take most of the torque pressure. Remove the tool after fully tightening the bolts.

28 With the TDC pins removed, turn the engine two complete turns clockwise, then re-insert the TDC pins to confirm the valve timing. Do not turn the engine anti-clockwise at any time to insert the pins.

29 The remaining procedure is a reversal of removal.

4-cylinder engines

30 Ensure that the crankshaft and camshaft are still set to TDC on No 1 cylinder, as described in Section 3.

31 Slacken the camshaft sprocket bolts by half a turn so that the sprocket is free to turn. Position the camshaft sprocket so that the securing bolts are in the centre part of the elongated holes **(see illustration)**.

32 Loop the timing belt loosely under the crankshaft sprocket. **Note:** *Observe any direction of rotation markings on the belt.*

33 Engage the timing belt teeth with the camshaft sprocket, then manoeuvre it into position around the tensioning roller, crankshaft sprocket, and finally around the coolant pump sprocket. Make sure that the belt teeth seat correctly on the sprockets. **Note:** *Slight adjustment to the position of the camshaft sprocket may be necessary to achieve this. Avoid bending the belt back on itself or twisting it excessively as you do this.*

34 Refit the idler roller and tighten the bolt to the specified torque **(see illustration)**.

35 Ensure that any slack in the belt is in the section of belt that passes over the tensioner roller.

36 Check that the arm on the tensioner rear plate is correctly located in the hole of the rear timing cover.

37 Loosen the tensioner mounting nut slightly, then use circlip pliers or Allen key (as applicable) to turn the tensioner clockwise until the pointer is located in the middle of the base plate gap. Hold the tensioner in this position and tighten the mounting nut to the specified torque and angle. Note that the pointer will turn a maximum of 5.0 mm to the right when the nut is tightened, however, this must not be corrected since the timing belt settles during the running-in period.

38 Tighten the camshaft sprocket bolts to the specified torque and angle, remove the sprocket locking pin and the crankshaft locking tool.

39 Using a spanner or wrench and socket on the crankshaft pulley centre bolt, rotate the crankshaft through two complete revolutions. Reset the engine to TDC on No 1 cylinder, with reference to Section 3 and check that the setting tools can be inserted. If not, repeat the refitting procedure.

40 Further refitting is a reversal of the removal procedure. When refitting the lower timing belt cover and the crankshaft pulley, note that the offset of the pulley mounting holes allows only one fitting position – tighten the bolts to the specified torque.

7.31 Camshaft sprocket bolts central in the elongated holes

7.34 Refit the idler roller

8 Timing belt tensioner and sprockets – removal and refitting

Timing belt tensioner

1 Remove the timing belt as described in Section 7.

2 Unscrew the timing belt tensioner nut, and remove the tensioner from the engine **(see illustration)**.

3 Refitting is a reversal of removal, with reference to Section 7 when refitting the timing belt. Make sure that the tensioner pulley arm is correctly located in the rear timing cover hole **(see illustration)**.

Idler pulleys

4 Remove the timing belt as described in Section 7.

5 Unscrew the relevant idler pulley securing bolt/nut, then withdraw the pulley.

6 Refit the pulley and tighten the securing bolt or nut to the specified torque.

7 Refit and tension the timing belt as described in Section 7.

Crankshaft sprocket

Note: *A new crankshaft sprocket securing bolt must be used on refitting.*

8 Remove the timing belt as described in Section 7.

9 The sprocket securing bolt must now be slackened, and the crankshaft must be prevented from turning as the sprocket bolt is unscrewed. To hold the sprocket, make up a suitable tool, and screw it to the sprocket using two bolts screwed into two of the crankshaft pulley bolt holes **(see illustration)**.

10 Hold the sprocket using the tool, then slacken the sprocket securing bolt. Take care, as the bolt is very tight. Do not allow the crankshaft to turn as the bolt is slackened.

11 Unscrew the bolt, and slide the sprocket from the end of the crankshaft, noting which way round the sprocket's raised boss is fitted.

12 Commence refitting by positioning the sprocket on the end of the crankshaft, with the raised boss fitted as noted on removal.

13 Fit a new sprocket securing bolt, then counterhold the sprocket using the method employed on removal, and tighten the bolt to the specified torque and angle given in the Specifications **(see illustration)**. Do not oil or grease the bolt threads.

14 Refit the timing belt as described in Section 7.

Camshaft sprocket

15 Remove the timing belt as described in Section 7.

16 The camshaft sprocket bolt(s) must now be slackened. Do not use the timing locking bar to hold the camshaft stationary; it must be removed before loosening the sprocket bolt. In order to eliminate any possibility of accidental piston-to-valve contact, turn the crankshaft 90° anti-clockwise so that all the pistons are halfway up the cylinder bore.

8.2 Timing belt tensioner nut (arrowed)

8.9 Use a home-made tool to hold the crankshaft sprocket while the bolt is loosened

17 Unscrew and remove the three retaining bolts and remove the camshaft sprocket from the camshaft hub.

18 Refit the sprocket, ensuring that it is fitted the correct way round, as noted before removal.

19 Refit the sprocket bolt(s), and tighten by hand only at this stage.

20 Refit and tension the timing belt as described in Section 7.

Camshaft hub

Note: *Seat technicians use special tool T10051 to counterhold the hub, however it is possible to fabricate a suitable alternative – see below.*

21 Remove the camshaft sprocket as described in this Section.

22 Engage special tool T10051 with the three locating holes in the face of the hub to prevent the hub from turning. If this tool is

8.3 Tensioner backplate lug engaged with the cut-out in the rear timing belt cover (arrowed)

8.13 Fit a new crankshaft sprocket securing bolt

not available, fabricate a suitable alternative. Whilst holding the tool, undo the central hub retaining bolt about two turns **(see illustration)**.

23 Leaving the central hub retaining bolt in place, attach Seat tool T10052 (or a similar three-legged puller) to the hub, and evenly tighten the puller until the hub is free of the camshaft taper **(see illustration)**.

24 Ensure that the camshaft taper and the hub centre is clean and dry, locate the hub on the taper, noting that the built-in key in the hub taper must align with the keyway in the camshaft taper **(see illustration)**.

25 Hold the hub in this position with tool T10051 (or similar home-made tool), and tighten the central bolt to the specified torque.

26 The remainder of refitting is a reversal of removal.

8.22 Use a fabricated tool to counterhold the camshaft hub

8.23 Use a three-legged puller to remove the hub from the camshaft

8.24 Align the hub key with the keyway in the camshaft taper (arrowed)

9.2 Starting with the outer bolts first, slacken the rocker shaft bolts (arrowed)

Coolant pump sprocket

27 The coolant pump sprocket is integral with the coolant pump. Refer to Chapter 3 for details of coolant pump removal.

9 Pump injector rocker shaft assembly – removal and refitting

Removal

1 Remove the camshaft cover as described in Section 4. In order to ensure that the rocker arms are refitted to their original locations, use a marker pen or paint and number the arms, with No 1 nearest the timing belt end of the engine. Note that if the arms are not fitted to their original locations, the injector basic clearance setting procedure must be carried out as described in Chapter 4B.

2 Starting with the outer bolts first, carefully and evenly unscrew the rocker shaft retaining bolts, half a turn at a time. Discard the rocker shaft bolts, new ones must be fitted **(see illustration)**.

Refitting

3 Carefully check the rocker shaft, rocker arms and camshaft bearing cap seating surface for any signs of excessive wear or damage.

4 Ensure that the shaft seating surface is clean and position the rocker shaft assembly in the camshaft bearing caps, making sure that, if re-using the original rocker arms, they are in their original locations.

10.6 Check the camshaft bearing caps (arrowed) for markings

5 Insert the new rocker shaft retaining bolts, and starting from the inner bolts, progressively tighten the bolts to the Stage 1 torque setting.

6 Again, starting with the inner retaining bolts, tighten the bolts to the Stage 2 angle as listed in this Chapter's Specifications.

7 Refit the camshaft cover as described in Section 4.

10 Camshaft and hydraulic tappets – removal, inspection and refitting

Removal

1 Turn the crankshaft to position No 1 piston at TDC on the firing stroke, and lock the camshaft and the fuel injection pump sprocket in position, as described in Section 3.

2 Remove the timing belt as described in Section 7.

3 Remove the camshaft sprocket and, where applicable, the hub, as described in Section 8.

4 Remove the brake vacuum/tandem pump as described in Chapter 9.

5 Remove the injector rocker shaft assembly as described in Section 9.

6 Check the camshaft bearing caps for identification markings **(see illustration)**. The bearing caps are normally stamped with their respective cylinder numbers. If no marks are present, make suitable marks using a scriber or punch, with No 1 at the timing belt end of the engine. Note on which side of the bearing caps the marks are made to ensure that they are refitted the correct way round.

7 The camshaft rotates in shell bearings. As the camshaft bearing caps are removed, recover the shell bearing halves from the camshaft. Number the back of the bearings with a felt pen to ensure that, if re-used, the bearings are fitted to their original locations. **Note:** *Fitted into the cylinder head, under each camshaft bearing cap, is a washer for each cylinder head bolt.*

8 On 3-cylinder engines, unscrew the securing nuts, and remove Nos 2 and 3 bearing caps. Working progressively in a diagonal sequence, slacken the nuts securing Nos 1 and 4 bearing caps. Note that as the nuts are slackened, the valve springs will push the camshaft up.

9 On 4-cylinder engines, unscrew the securing

10.11 Remove the camshaft oil seal

bolts, and remove Nos 1, 3 and 5 bearing caps. Working progressively, in a diagonal sequence, slacken the bolts securing Nos 2 and 4 bearing caps. Note that as the bolts are slackened, the valve springs will push the camshaft up.

10 Once the nuts/bolts have been fully slackened, lift off the bearing caps.

11 Carefully lift the camshaft from the cylinder head, keeping it level and supported at both ends as it is removed so that the journals and lobes are not damaged. Remove the oil seal from the end of the camshaft and discard it – a new one will be required for refitting **(see illustration)**.

12 Lift the hydraulic tappets from their bores in the cylinder head, and store them with the valve contact surfaces facing downwards, to prevent the oil from draining out. It is recommended that the tappets are kept immersed in oil for the period they are removed from the cylinder head. Make a note of the position of each tappet, as they must be refitted in their original locations on reassembly – accelerated wear leading to early failure will result if the tappets are interchanged.

13 Recover the lower shell bearing halves from the cylinder head; number the back of the shells with a felt pen to ensure that, if re-used, the bearings are fitted to their original locations.

Inspection

14 With the camshaft removed, examine the bearing caps and the bearing locations in the cylinder head for signs of obvious wear or pitting. If evident, a new cylinder head will probably be required. Also check that the oil supply holes in the cylinder head are free from obstructions.

15 Visually inspect the camshaft for evidence of wear on the surfaces of the lobes and journals. Normally their surfaces should be smooth and have a dull shine; look for scoring, erosion or pitting and areas that appear highly polished, indicating excessive wear. Accelerated wear will occur once the hardened exterior of the camshaft has been damaged, so always renew worn items. **Note:** *If these symptoms are visible on the tips of the camshaft lobes, check the corresponding tappet, as it will probably be worn as well.*

16 If the machined surfaces of the camshaft appear discoloured or blued, it is likely that it has been overheated at some point, probably due to inadequate lubrication. This may have distorted the shaft, so check the run-out as follows: place the camshaft between two V-blocks and using a DTI gauge, measure the run-out at the centre. If it exceeds the figure quoted in the Specifications at the start of this Chapter, renew the camshaft.

17 To measure the camshaft endfloat, temporarily refit the camshaft to the cylinder head, then fit Nos 1 and 4 (3-cylinder) or 1 and 5 (4-cylinder) bearing caps and tighten the retaining nuts to the specified torque setting. Anchor a DTI gauge to the timing belt end of the cylinder head **(see illustration)**. Push the camshaft to one end of the cylinder head as far as it will travel, then rest the DTI gauge probe on the end face of the camshaft, and zero the gauge. Push the camshaft as far as it will go to the other end of the cylinder head, and record the gauge reading. Verify the reading by pushing the camshaft back to its original position and checking that the gauge indicates zero again. **Note:** *The hydraulic tappets must not be fitted whilst this measurement is being taken.*

18 Check that the camshaft endfloat measurement is within the limit listed in the Specifications. If the measurement is outside the specified limit, wear is unlikely to be confined to any one component, so renewal of the camshaft, cylinder head and bearing caps must be considered.

19 The camshaft bearing running clearance should now be measured. This will be difficult to achieve without a range of micrometers or internal/external expanding calipers, measure the outside diameters of the camshaft bearing surfaces and the internal diameters formed by the bearing caps (and shell bearings where applicable) and the bearing locations in the cylinder head. The difference between these two measurements is the running clearance.

20 Compare the camshaft running clearance measurements with the figure given in the Specifications; if any are outside the specified tolerance, the camshaft, cylinder head and bearing caps (and shell bearings where applicable) should be renewed.

21 Inspect the hydraulic tappets for obvious signs of wear or damage, and renew if necessary. Check that the oil holes in the tappets are free from obstructions.

Refitting

22 Smear some clean engine oil onto the sides of the hydraulic tappets, and offer them into position in their original bores in the cylinder head. Push them down until they contact the valves, then lubricate the camshaft lobe contact surfaces.

23 Lubricate the camshaft and cylinder head bearing journals (and shell bearings where applicable) with clean engine oil.

24 Carefully lower the camshaft into position in the cylinder head making sure that the cam lobes for No 1 cylinder are pointing upwards.

25 Refit a new camshaft oil seal on the end of the camshaft. Make sure that the closed end of the seal faces the camshaft sprocket end of the camshaft, and take care not to damage the seal lip. Locate the seal against the seat in the cylinder head.

26 Oil the upper surfaces of the camshaft bearing journals (and shell bearings where applicable), then fit Nos 2 and 3 (3-cylinder) or 2 and 4 (4-cylinder) bearing caps. Ensure that they are fitted the right way round and in the correct locations, then progressively tighten the retaining nuts/bolts in a diagonal sequence to the specified torque. Note that as they are tightened, the camshaft will be forced down

10.17 Check camshaft endfloat using a DTI gauge

against the pressure of the valve springs.

27 Apply sealant to the outer shoulders of bearing caps 1 and 4 (3-cylinder) or 1 and 5 (4-cylinder), making sure that the lubrication slots remain clear **(see illustration)**.

28 Fit bearing caps 1 and 4 (3-cylinder) or 1, 3 and 5 (4-cylinder) over the camshaft and progressively tighten the nuts/bolts to the specified torque.

29 Refit the camshaft sprocket and, where applicable the hub, as described in Section 8.

30 Refit and tension the timing belt as described in Section 7.

31 Refit the brake vacuum/tandem pump as described in Chapter 9.

11 Hialulic tappets – testing

Warning: After fitting hydraulic tappets, wait a minimum of 30 minutes (or preferably, leave overnight) before starting the engine, to allow the tappets time to settle, otherwise the valve heads will strike the pistons.

1 The hydraulic tappets are self-adjusting, and require no attention whilst in service.

2 If the hydraulic tappets become excessively noisy, their operation can be checked as described below.

3 Start the engine, and run it until it reaches normal operating temperature, increase the engine speed to approximately 2500 rpm for 2 minutes.

11.8 Press down on the tappet using a wooden or plastic instrument

10.27 Apply sealant to shaded areas (1) – lubrication slots (arrowed) must remain clear

4 If any hydraulic tappets are heard to be noisy, carry out the following checks.

5 Remove the camshaft cover as described in Section 4.

6 Using a socket or spanner on the crankshaft sprocket bolt, turn the crankshaft until the tip of the camshaft lobe above the tappet to be checked is pointing vertically upwards.

7 Using feeler blades, check the clearance between the top of the tappet, and the cam lobe. If the play is in excess of 0.2 mm, renew the relevant tappet. If the play is less than 0.2 mm, or there is no play, proceed as follows.

8 Press down on the tappet using a wooden or plastic instrument **(see illustration)**. If free play in excess of 1.0 mm is present before the tappet contacts the valve stem, renew the relevant tappet.

9 On completion, refit the camshaft cover as described in Section 4.

12 Camshaft oil seals – renewal

Right-hand oil seal

1 Remove the timing belt as described in Section 7.

2 Remove the camshaft sprocket and, where applicable, the hub, as described in Section 8.

3 Drill two small holes into the existing oil seal, diagonally opposite each other. Take great care to avoid drilling through into the seal housing or camshaft sealing surface. Thread two self-tapping screws into the holes and, using a pair of pliers, pull on the heads of the screws to extract the oil seal.

4 Clean out the seal housing and the sealing surface of the camshaft by wiping it with a lint-free cloth. Remove any swarf or burrs that may cause the seal to leak.

5 Do not lubricate the lip and outer edge of the new oil seal, push it over the camshaft until it is positioned in place above its housing. To prevent damage to the sealing lips, wrap some adhesive tape around the end of the camshaft.

6 Using a hammer and a socket of suitable diameter, drive the seal squarely into its housing. **Note:** *Select a socket that bears only*

13.6a Where applicable, undo the bolt (arrowed) from the inner cover . . .

13.6b . . . and the one (arrowed) on the side of the cover

13.7 Use two nuts locked together to unscrew the tensioner mounting stud

on the hard outer surface of the seal, not the inner lip which can easily be damaged.

7 Refit the camshaft sprocket and, where applicable, the hub, as described in Section 8.

8 Refit and tension the timing belt as described in Section 7.

Left-hand oil seal

9 The left-hand camshaft oil seal is formed by the brake vacuum/tandem pump seal. Refer to Chapter 9 for details of brake vacuum pump removal and refitting.

13 Cylinder head –
removal, inspection and refitting

Note: *The cylinder head must be removed with the engine cold. New cylinder head bolts and a new cylinder head gasket will be required on refitting, and suitable studs will be required*

to guide the cylinder head into position – see text.

Removal

1 Disconnect the battery negative lead as described in Chapter 5A, and remove the engine top cover.

2 Drain the cooling system and engine oil as described in Chapter 1B.

3 Remove the camshaft cover as described in Section 4.

4 Remove the timing belt as described in Section 7.

5 Remove the camshaft sprocket and, where applicable, the hub, and timing belt tensioner as described in Section 8.

6 Where applicable, unscrew the bolt(s) securing the rear timing belt cover to the cylinder head **(see illustrations)**.

7 Using two suitable nuts locked together, unscrew the timing belt tensioner mounting

stud from the cylinder head **(see illustration)**.

8 If the engine is currently supported using a hoist and lifting tackle attached to the engine lifting brackets on the cylinder head, it is now necessary to attach a suitable bracket to the cylinder block, so that the engine can still be supported as the cylinder head is removed. Alternatively, the engine can be supported using a trolley jack and a block of wood positioned under the engine sump.

9 Remove the bolt securing the camshaft position sensor to the cylinder head. There is no need to disconnect the wiring at this stage **(see illustration)**.

10 Disconnect the charge air pipe from the intake manifold to the intercooler and place to one side.

11 Disconnect the central connector for the unit injectors **(see illustration)**. **Note:** *Unplugging the connector may cause a fault code to be logged by the engine management ECM. This code can only be erased by a Seat dealer or suitably-equipped specialist.*

12 Undo the two bolts securing the coolant junction to the end of the cylinder head **(see illustration)**. There is no need to disconnect the pipes or wiring plugs at this stage.

13 Unscrew the four retaining bolts and pull the tandem pump away from the cylinder head without disconnecting the fuel or vacuum hoses **(see illustration)**.

14 Disconnect and remove the hose connecting the upper coolant pipe to the pipe at the end of the cylinder head **(see illustration)**.

15 Remove the turbocharger as described in Chapter 4C.

13.9 Unscrew the bolt and remove the camshaft position sensor

13.11 Disconnect the central connector for the injectors

13.12 Coolant outlet bolts (arrowed) on the end of the cylinder head

13.13 Undo the four tandem pump retaining bolts (arrowed)

13.14 Disconnect the coolant hose from the end of the cylinder head

16 Slacken and remove the bolt securing the upper metal coolant pipe to the cylinder head.
17 Disconnect the wiring connectors from the glow plugs – if necessary, refer to Chapter 5A.
18 Disconnect the vacuum pipes from the EGR valve and the manifold flap actuator **(see illustration)**.
19 Using a multi-splined tool, undo the cylinder head bolts, working from the outside-in, evenly and gradually. Check that nothing remains connected, and lift the cylinder head from the engine block. Seek assistance if possible, as it is a heavy assembly, especially as it is being removed complete with the manifolds.
20 Remove the gasket from the top of the block, noting the locating dowels. If the dowels are a loose fit, remove them and store them with the head for safe-keeping. Do not discard the gasket yet – it will be needed for identification purposes.

Inspection

21 Dismantling and inspection of the cylinder head is covered in Chapter 2D.

Cylinder head gasket selection

22 Examine the old cylinder head gasket for manufacturer's identification markings **(see illustration)**. These will be in the form of holes or notches, and a part number on the edge of the gasket. Unless new pistons have been fitted, the new cylinder head gasket must be of the same type as the old one. In this case, purchase a new gasket, and proceed to paragraph 29.
23 If new piston assemblies have been fitted as part of an engine overhaul, or if a new short engine is to be fitted, the projection of the piston crowns above the cylinder head mating face of the cylinder block at TDC must be measured. This measurement is used to determine the thickness of the new cylinder head gasket required.
24 Anchor a dial test indicator (DTI) to the top face (cylinder head gasket mating face) of the cylinder block, and zero the gauge on the gasket mating face.
25 Rest the gauge probe on No 1 piston crown, and turn the crankshaft slowly by hand until the piston reaches TDC. Measure and record the maximum piston projection at TDC **(see illustration)**.
26 Repeat the measurement for the remaining pistons, and record the results.
27 If the measurements differ from piston-to-piston, take the highest figure, and use this to determine the thickness of the head gasket required as follows.

Piston projection	Gasket identification (number of holes/ notches)
0.91 to 1.00 mm	1
1.01 to 1.10 mm	2
1.11 to 1.20 mm	3

28 Purchase a new gasket according to the results of the measurements.

13.18 Disconnect the vacuum pipes (arrowed)

13.25 Measure the piston projection at TDC using a dial gauge

Refitting

Note: *If a Seat exchange cylinder head, complete with camshaft, is to be fitted, the manufacturers recommend the following:*
a) *Lubricate the contact surfaces between the tappets and the cam lobes before fitting the camshaft cover.*
b) *Do not remove the plastic protectors from the open valves until immediately before fitting the cylinder head.*
c) *Additionally, if a new cylinder head is fitted, Seat recommend that the coolant is renewed.*

29 The mating faces of the cylinder head and block must be perfectly clean before refitting the head. Use a scraper to remove all traces of gasket and carbon, also clean the tops of the pistons. Take particular care with the aluminium surfaces, as the soft metal is easily damaged.
30 Make sure that debris is not allowed to enter the oil and water passages – this is particularly important for the oil circuit, as carbon could block the oil supply to the camshaft and crankshaft bearings. Using adhesive tape and paper, seal the water, oil and bolt holes in the cylinder block.
31 To prevent carbon entering the gap between the pistons and bores, smear a little grease in the gap. After cleaning a piston, rotate the crankshaft to that the piston moves down the bore, then wipe out the grease and carbon with a cloth rag. Clean the other piston crowns in the same way.
32 Check the head and block for nicks, deep scratches and other damage. If slight,

13.22 The thickness of the cylinder head gasket can be identified by notches or holes

13.37 Two of the old head bolts (arrowed) can be used as cylinder head alignment guides

they may be removed carefully with a file. More serious damage may be repaired by machining, but this is a specialist job.
33 If warpage of the cylinder head is suspected, use a straight-edge to check it for distortion, as described in Chapter 2D.
34 Ensure that the cylinder head bolt holes in the crankcase are clean and free of oil. Syringe or soak up any oil left in the bolt holes. This is most important in order that the correct bolt tightening torque can be applied, and to prevent the possibility of the block being cracked by hydraulic pressure when the bolts are tightened.
35 Turn the crankshaft anti-clockwise until all the pistons at an equal height, approximately halfway down their bores from the TDC position (see Section 3). This will eliminate any risk of piston-to-valve contact as the cylinder head is refitted.
36 Where applicable, refit the manifolds with reference to Chapters 4B and/or 4C.
37 To guide the cylinder head into position, screw two long studs (or old cylinder head bolts with the heads cut off, and slots cut in the ends to enable the bolts to be unscrewed) into the cylinder block **(see illustration)**.
38 Ensure that the cylinder head locating dowels are in place in the cylinder block, then fit the new cylinder head gasket over the dowels, ensuring that the part number is uppermost. Where applicable, the OBEN/TOP marking should also be uppermost. Note that Seat recommend that the gasket is only removed from its packaging immediately prior to fitting.

13.42a Cylinder head bolt tightening sequence – 4-cylinder engines . . .

13.42b . . . and 3-cylinder engines

13.42c Use a torque wrench to tighten the cylinder head bolts

13.44 Angle-tighten the cylinder head bolts

14.4 Disconnect the wiring connector (arrowed) from the oil level/temperature sender

39 Lower the cylinder head into position on the gasket, ensuring that it engages correctly over the guide studs and dowels.

40 Fit the new cylinder head bolts to the remaining bolt locations, and screw them in as far as possible by hand.

41 Unscrew the two guide studs from the exhaust side of the cylinder block, then screw in the two remaining new cylinder head bolts as far as possible by hand.

42 Working progressively, in sequence, tighten all the cylinder head bolts to the specified Stage 1 torque **(see illustrations)**.

43 Again working progressively, in sequence, tighten all the cylinder head bolts to the specified Stage 2 torque.

44 Tighten all the cylinder head bolts, in sequence, through the specified Stage 3 angle **(see illustration)**.

45 Finally, tighten all the cylinder head bolts, in sequence, through the specified Stage 4 angle.

46 After finally tightening the cylinder head bolts, turn the camshaft so that the cam lobes for No 1 cylinder are pointing upwards.

47 Where applicable, reconnect the lifting tackle to the engine lifting brackets on the cylinder head, then adjust the lifting tackle to support the engine. Once the engine is adequately supported using the cylinder head brackets, disconnect the lifting tackle from the bracket bolted to the cylinder block, and unbolt the improvised engine lifting bracket from the cylinder block. Alternatively, remove the trolley jack and block of wood from under the sump.

48 The remainder of the refitting procedure is a reversal of the removal procedure, bearing in mind the following points.

a) *Refit the camshaft cover with reference to Section 4.*

b) *Use new sealing rings when reconnecting the turbocharger oil return pipe to the cylinder block.*

c) *Reconnect the exhaust front section*

to the turbocharger with reference to Chapter 4C.

d) *Refit the timing belt tensioner with reference to Section 8.*

e) *Refit the camshaft sprocket as described in Section 8, and refit the timing belt as described in Section 7.*

f) *Refill the cooling system and engine oil as described in Chapter 1B.*

14 Sump – removal and refitting

Note: *On 3-cylinder engines, the transmission must be removed first in order to remove the sump. This is for access to the sump retaining bolts at the flywheel end of the crankcase.*

Removal

1 Apply the handbrake, then jack up the front of the car and support securely on axle stands (see *Jacking and vehicle support*).

2 Remove the securing bolts and withdraw the engine undershield(s) **(see illustration 7.4)**.

3 Drain the engine oil as described in Chapter 1B.

4 Where fitted, disconnect the wiring connector from the oil level/temperature sender on the sump **(see illustration)**.

5 On 3-cylinder engines, the transmission must first be removed from the engine. Refer to Chapter 7A for the procedure. For additional working room, the exhaust front pipe may also be removed as described in Chapter 4C. Also on this engine, unscrew the bolts and remove the dipstick tube from the sump, then recover the O-ring seal **(see illustrations)**.

6 Unscrew and remove the bolts securing the sump to the cylinder block, then withdraw the sump **(see illustration)**. On 4-cylinder engines, access to the flywheel-end retaining bolts is limited, requiring the use of universal joint socket bar. If necessary, release the sump by tapping with a soft-faced mallet.

14.5a Unscrew the bolts . . .

14.5b . . . and remove the dipstick and O-ring seal

14.6 Remove the sump

Refitting

7 Commence refitting by thoroughly cleaning the mating faces of the sump and cylinder block/crankcase. Ensure that all traces of old sealant are removed.

8 Ensure that the mating face of the sump is free from all traces of old sealant, oil and grease, then apply a 2.0 to 3.0 mm thick bead of silicone sealant (D 176404 A2 or equivalent) to the sump. Note that the sealant must run around the inside of the bolt holes in the sump **(see illustration)**. The sump must be fitted within 5 minutes of applying the sealant.

9 Offer the sump up to the cylinder block, then refit the retaining bolts, and lightly tighten them by hand, working progressively in a diagonal sequence. On 4-cylinder engines, if the sump is being refitted with the engine on the bench, use a steel rule to align the rear face of the sump with that of the engine cylinder block. Fully tighten the bolts, again working in a diagonal sequence.

10 On 3-cylinder engines, refit the transmission with reference to Chapter 7A. Where removed, refit the exhaust front pipe.

11 Reconnect the wiring to the oil level/temperature sender on the sump.

12 Refit the engine undershield(s) and lower the car to the ground.

13 Allow at least 30 minutes from the time of refitting the sump for the sealant to dry, then refill the engine with oil, with reference to Chapter 1B.

15 Oil pump, drive chain and sprockets – removal, inspection and refitting

Oil pump, drive chain and sprockets – 3-cylinder engines

Note: The oil pump on 3-cylinder engines is driven by the balancer shaft drive chain; refer to Section 21 for more information. When removing the oil pump, the balancer shaft drive chain must first be removed, then realigned on refitting.

Removal

1 Remove the timing belt as described in Section 7.

2 Remove the crankshaft sprocket as described in Section 8.

3 Remove the sump as described in Section 14.

4 Unscrew the retaining bolts and remove the oil seal housing from the front right-hand side of the cylinder block. If it is stuck, release it by tapping with a soft-faced mallet. If the oil seal is to be re-used, wrap some tape around the end of the crankshaft to protect the oil seal lips.

5 Unscrew the mounting bolts and remove the plastic cover/strainer from the bottom of the crankcase. Recover the O-ring.

6 Apply inward pressure on the drive chain, then lock the chain tensioner by fitting and tightening a bolt through the tensioner into the tensioner body.

7 Unscrew the bolt and remove the sprocket from the guide pulley. Place the sprocket to one side.

8 Unbolt and remove the drive chain tensioner assembly. Discard the bolts and obtain new ones.

9 If the chain is to be re-used, mark it with paint to indicate its fitted position and rotational direction.

10 Remove the chain from the sprockets.

11 To remove the sprocket from the balancer shaft, refer to Section 21. If necessary, the oil pump sprocket may be removed at this stage by holding it stationary and loosening the retaining bolt. Discard the bolt and obtain a new one.

12 Unscrew the mounting bolts and remove the oil pump from the bottom of the balancer shaft assembly **(see illustration)**. Recover the two location dowels.

Inspection

13 Clean the pump and sprockets, and

15.12 Oil pump mounting bolts (arrowed)

14.8 Apply the sealant around the inside of the bolt holes

inspect them for signs of damage or wear. Renew them as necessary.

Refitting

14 Check that the two location dowels are in position, then refit the oil pump, insert the mounting bolts and tighten them to the specified torque.

15 Refit the sprocket to the oil pump and tighten the new bolt to the specified torque and angle. If removed, refit the sprocket to the balancer shaft with reference to Section 21.

16 Refit the chain tensioner assembly and tighten the new mounting bolts to the specified torque.

17 With the engine set at TDC, the mark on the crankshaft sprocket will be pointing upwards. The chain has two coloured links which are also notched; position one of these links on

15.17 The coloured links (arrowed) on the balance shaft chain must be positioned as shown

15.20 Apply sealant to the crankshaft oil seal housing

15.21 Use tin foil to protect the crankshaft oil seal when fitting the housing

the crankshaft sprocket mark, then feed the chain clockwise over the tensioner pad, around the oil pump sprocket and over the balancer shaft sprocket, making sure that the remaining coloured/notched link is aligned with the mark on the sprocket **(see illustration)**.

18 Locate the guide pulley sprocket in the chain, then refit the bolt and tighten it to the specified torque.

19 Unlock the tensioner by unscrewing the retaining bolt, then recheck that the coloured/notched links are still aligned with the marks on the sprockets.

20 Clean all traces of old sealant from the crankshaft oil seal housing and the cylinder block, then coat the cylinder block mating faces of the oil seal housing with a 2.0 to 3.0 mm thick bead of sealant (Seat D 176 404 A2, or

equivalent) **(see illustration)**. Note that the seal housing must be refitted within 5 minutes of applying the sealant.

Caution: DO NOT put excessive amounts of sealant onto the housing as it may get into the sump and block the oil pick-up pipe.

21 Refit the oil seal housing, taking care not to damage the seal and tighten the bolts progressively to the specified torque. If a new seal is to be fitted, refer to Section 17; if the oil seal is to be refitted, protect it with tin foil or plastic sheeting **(see illustration)**.

22 Refit the sump as described in Section 14.

23 Refit the crankshaft sprocket as described in Section 8.

24 Refit the timing belt as described in Section 7.

Oil pump – 4-cylinder engines

Removal

25 Remove the sump as described in Section 14.

26 Unbolt and remove the oil baffle from the crankcase, noting that on some models the baffle is retained by the oil pump rear left-hand mounting bolt.

27 Unscrew the mounting bolts, and release the oil pump from the dowels in the crankcase **(see illustration)**. Unhook the oil pump drive sprocket from the chain and withdraw the oil pump and oil pick-up pipe from the engine. Note that the tensioner will attempt to tighten the chain, and it may be necessary to use a screwdriver to hold it in its released position before releasing the oil pump sprocket from the chain.

28 If desired, unscrew the flange bolts and remove the pick-up pipe from the oil pump. Recover the O-ring seal. Unscrew the bolts and remove the cover from the oil pump. **Note:** *If the oil pick-up pipe is removed from the oil pump, a new O-ring will be required on refitting.*

Inspection

29 Clean the pump thoroughly, and inspect the gear teeth/rotors for signs of damage or wear. If evident, renew the oil pump.

30 To remove the sprocket from the oil pump, unscrew the retaining bolt and slide off the sprocket (note that the sprocket can only be fitted in one position).

Refitting

31 Prime the pump with oil by pouring oil into the pick-up pipe aperture while turning the driveshaft.

32 Refit the cover to the oil pump and tighten the bolts securely. Where removed, refit the pick-up pipe to the oil pump, using a new O-ring seal, and tighten the securing bolts.

33 Use a screwdriver to press the tensioner against its spring to provide sufficient slack in the chain to refit the oil pump. Engage the oil pump sprocket with the drive chain, then locate the oil pump on the dowels. Refit and tighten the three mounting bolts to the specified torque.

15.27 Sump and oil pump components

1 Oil pump	7 Drive chain tensioner	14 Oil baffle
2 Oil pump sprocket	8 Sump	15 Seal
3 Bolt	9 Seal	16 Oil level/temperature
4 Oil pump drive chain	10 Sump drain plug	sender
5 Crankshaft oil seal	11 Dowels	17 Bolt
housing	12 O-ring	18 Oil spray jet
6 Bolt	13 Oil pick-up pipe	19 Bolt

16.2 Flywheel locked in position with a home-made tool

16.7 Apply locking fluid to the new flywheel bolts, if necessary

16.9 Tighten the flywheel bolts to the specified torque

34 Refit the oil baffle, and tighten the securing bolts.
35 Refit the sump as described in Section 14.

Drive chain and sprockets – 4-cylinder engines

Note: *Seat sealant (D 176404 A2 or equivalent) will be required to seal the crankshaft oil seal housing on refitting, and it is advisable to fit a new crankshaft oil seal.*

Removal

36 Remove the sump as described in Section 14.
37 Unbolt and remove the oil baffle from the crankcase, noting that on some models the baffle is retained by the oil pump rear/left-hand mounting bolt.
38 To remove the oil pump sprocket, unscrew the securing bolt, then pull the sprocket from the pump shaft, and unhook it from the drive chain.
39 To remove the chain, remove the timing belt as described in Section 7, then unbolt the crankshaft oil seal housing from the cylinder block. Unbolt the chain tensioner from the cylinder block, then unhook the chain from the sprocket on the end of the crankshaft.
40 The oil pump drive sprocket is a press-fit on the crankshaft, and cannot easily be removed. Consult a Seat dealer for advice if the sprocket is worn or damaged.

Inspection

41 Examine the chain for wear and damage. Wear is usually indicated by excessive lateral play between the links, and excessive noise in operation. It is wise to renew the chain in any case if the engine is to be overhauled. Note that the rollers on a very badly worn chain may be slightly grooved. If there is any doubt as to the condition of the chain, renew it.
42 Examine the teeth on the sprockets for wear. Each tooth forms an inverted V. If worn, the side of each tooth under tension will be slightly concave in shape when compared with the other side of the tooth (ie, the teeth will have a hooked appearance). If the teeth appear worn, the sprocket should be renewed (consult a Seat dealer or engine reconditioning specialist for advice if the crankshaft sprocket is worn or damaged).

Refitting

43 Refit the chain tensioner to the cylinder

block, and tighten the securing bolt to the specified torque. Make sure that the tensioner spring is correctly positioned to pretension the tensioner arm.
44 Engage the oil pump sprocket with the chain, then engage the chain with the crankshaft sprocket. Use a screwdriver to press the tensioner against its spring to provide sufficient slack in the chain, then engage the sprocket with the oil pump. Note that the sprocket will only fit in one position.
45 Refit the oil pump sprocket bolt, and tighten to the specified torque.
46 Fit a new crankshaft oil seal to the housing, and refit the housing as described in Section 17.
47 Refit the oil baffle to the crankcase, and tighten the securing bolts.
48 Refit the sump as described in Section 14.

16 Flywheel – removal, inspection and refitting

Removal

1 Remove the manual transmission and clutch as described in Chapter 7A and Chapter 6.
2 Lock the flywheel in position using a home-made locking tool, fabricated from a piece of scrap metal **(see illustration)**. Bolt it to one of the transmission bellhousing mounting holes.
3 Remove the flywheel. Do not drop it, as it is very heavy. **Note:** *The bolt holes are offset, so it is only possible to fit the flywheel in one position.*

Inspection

4 If the flywheel's clutch mating surface is deeply scored, cracked or otherwise damaged, the flywheel must be renewed. However, it may be possible to have it surface-ground; seek the advice of a Seat dealer or engine reconditioning specialist.
5 If the ring gear is badly worn or has missing teeth, the flywheel must be renewed.

Refitting

6 Clean the mating surfaces of the flywheel and crankshaft. Remove any remaining locking compound from the threads of the crankshaft holes, using the correct-size tap, if available.

7 If the new flywheel retaining bolts are not supplied with their threads pre-coated, apply a suitable thread-locking compound to the threads of each bolt **(see illustration)**.
8 Offer up the flywheel to the crankshaft, and fit the new retaining bolts.
9 Lock the flywheel using the method employed on dismantling, and tighten the retaining bolts to the specified torque and angle **(see illustration)**.
10 Refit the clutch as described in Chapter 6. Remove the locking tool, and refit the transmission as described in Chapter 7A.

17 Crankshaft oil seals – renewal

Note 1: *The oil seals are a PTFE (Teflon) type and are fitted dry, without using any grease or oil. These have a wider sealing lip and have been introduced instead of the coil spring type oil seal.*
Note 2: *If the oil seal housing is removed, suitable sealant (Seat D 176 404 A2, or equivalent) will be required to seal the housing on refitting.*

Right-hand oil seal

1 Remove the timing belt as described in Section 7, and the crankshaft sprocket with reference to Section 8.
2 To remove the seal without removing the housing, drill two small holes diagonally opposite each other, insert self-tapping screws, and pull on the heads of the screws with pliers **(see illustrations)**.

17.2a Drill two small holes diagonally opposite each other . . .

17.2b . . . and use pliers to pull out the oil seal

17.3 Prise the oil seal from the crankshaft oil seal housing

17.5 Use a plastic cap to protect the oil seal during fitting

3 Alternatively, to remove the oil seal complete with its housing, proceed as follows.

a) *Remove the sump as described in Section 14. This is necessary to ensure a satisfactory seal between the sump and oil seal housing on refitting.*

b) *Unbolt and remove the oil seal housing.*

c) *Working on the bench, lever the oil seal from the housing using a suitable screwdriver. Take care not to damage the seal seating in the housing (see illustration).*

4 Thoroughly clean the oil seal seating in the housing.

5 Wind a length of tape around the end of the crankshaft to protect the oil seal lips as the seal (and housing, where applicable) is fitted. Alternatively, use a suitable plastic cap (**see illustration**).

6 Fit a new oil seal to the housing, pressing or driving it into position using a socket or tube

of suitable diameter. Ensure that the socket or tube bears only on the hard outer ring of the seal, and take care not to damage the seal lips. Press or drive the seal into position until it is seated on the shoulder in the housing. Make sure that the closed end of the seal is facing outwards.

7 If the oil seal housing has been removed, proceed as follows, otherwise proceed to paragraph 11.

8 Clean all traces of old sealant from the crankshaft oil seal housing and the cylinder block, then coat the cylinder block mating faces of the oil seal housing with a 2.0 to 3.0 mm thick bead of sealant (Seat D 176 404 A2, or equivalent). Note that the seal housing must be refitted within 5 minutes of applying the sealant. *Caution: DO NOT put excessive amounts of sealant onto the housing as it may get into the sump and block the oil pick-up pipe.*

9 Refit the oil seal housing, and tighten the

bolts progressively to the specified torque (**see illustration**).

10 Refit the sump as described in Section 14.

11 Refit the crankshaft sprocket with reference to Section 8, and the timing belt as described in Section 7.

Left-hand oil seal

12 Remove the flywheel as described in Section 16.

13 Remove the sump as described in Section 14. This is necessary to ensure a satisfactory seal between the sump and oil seal housing on refitting.

14 Unbolt and remove the oil seal housing, complete with the oil seal.

15 The new oil seal will be supplied ready-fitted to a new oil seal housing.

16 Thoroughly clean the oil seal housing mating face on the cylinder block.

17 New oil seal/housing assemblies are supplied with a fitting tool to prevent damage to the oil seal as it is being fitted. Locate the tool over the end of the crankshaft (**see illustration**).

18 If the original oil seal housing was fitted using sealant, apply a thin bead of suitable sealant (Seat D 176 404 A2, or equivalent) to the cylinder block mating face of the oil seal housing. Note that the seal housing must be refitted within 5 minutes of applying the sealant. *Caution: DO NOT put excessive amounts of sealant onto the housing as it may get into the sump and block the oil pick-up pipe.*

19 Carefully fit the oil seal/housing assembly over the end of the crankshaft, then refit the securing bolts and tighten the bolts progressively, in a diagonal sequence, to the specified torque (**see illustrations**).

20 Remove the oil seal protector tool from the end of the crankshaft.

21 Refit the sump as described in Section 14.

22 Refit the flywheel as described in Section 16.

17.9 Slide the oil seal housing over the end of the crankshaft

17.17 Locate the crankshaft oil seal fitting tool over the end of the crankshaft

18 Engine/transmission mountings – inspection and renewal

Inspection

1 If improved access is required, jack up the front of the car, and support it securely on axle stands (see *Jacking and vehicle support*).

17.19a Fit the oil seal/housing assembly over the end of the crankshaft . . .

17.19b . . . then tighten the securing bolts to the specified torque

Remove the securing bolts and remove the engine undershield(s).

2 Check the mounting rubbers to see if they are cracked, hardened or separated from the metal at any point; renew the mounting if any such damage or deterioration is evident.

3 Check that all the mountings are securely tightened; use a torque wrench to check if possible.

4 Using a large screwdriver or a crowbar, check for wear in the mounting by carefully levering against it to check for free play. Where this is not possible, enlist the aid of an assistant to move the engine/transmission back-and-forth, or from side-to-side, whilst you observe the mounting. While some free play is to be expected, even from new components, excessive wear should be obvious. If excessive free play is found, check first that the fasteners are correctly secured, then renew any worn components as described in the following paragraphs.

Renewal

Right-hand mounting

Note: *New mounting securing bolts will be required on refitting.*

5 Attach a hoist and lifting tackle to the engine lifting brackets on the cylinder head, and raise the hoist to just take the weight of the engine. Alternatively the engine can be supported on a trolley jack under the engine. Use a block of wood between the sump and the head of the jack, to prevent any damage to the sump.

6 Where necessary, unbolt the coolant reservoir and move it to one side, leaving the coolant hoses connected.

7 Where applicable, move any wiring harnesses, pipes or hoses to one side to enable removal of the engine mounting.

8 Unscrew the mounting centre nut securing the bracket to the flexible mounting.

9 Unscrew the three bolts securing the mounting bracket to the engine and remove the bracket.

10 Unbolt and remove the flexible mounting from the body.

11 Refitting is a reversal of removal, bearing in mind the following points.
  a) *Use new securing bolts.*
  b) *Tighten all fixings to the specified torque.*

Left-hand mounting

Note: *New mounting bolts will be required on refitting (there is no need to renew the smaller mounting-to-body bolts).*

12 Remove the engine top cover which also incorporates the air filter.

13 Attach a hoist and lifting tackle to the engine lifting brackets on the cylinder head, and raise the hoist to just take the weight of the engine and transmission. Alternatively the engine can be supported on a trolley jack under the transmission. Use a block of wood between the transmission and the head of the jack, to prevent any damage to the transmission.

14 Remove the battery, as described in

Chapter 5A, then disconnect the main starter motor feed cable from the positive battery terminal box.

15 Release any relevant wiring or hoses from the clips on the battery tray, then unscrew the four securing bolts and remove the battery tray.

16 Unscrew the bolts securing the mounting to the transmission, and the remaining bolts securing the mounting to the body, then lift the mounting from the engine compartment.

17 Refitting is a reversal of removal, bearing in mind the following points:
  a) *Use new mounting bolts.*
  b) *Tighten all fixings to the specified torque.*

Rear mounting (torque arm)

Note: *New mounting bolts will be required on refitting.*

18 Apply the handbrake, then jack up the front of the car and support securely on axle stands (see *Jacking and vehicle support*). Remove the engine undershield(s) for access to the rear mounting (torque arm).

19 Support the rear of the transmission beneath the final drive housing. To do this,

use a trolley jack and block of wood, or alternatively wedge a block of wood between the transmission and the subframe.

20 Working under the car, unscrew and remove the bolt securing the mounting to the subframe.

21 Unscrew the two bolts securing the mounting to the transmission, then withdraw the mounting from under the car.

22 Refitting is a reversal of removal, but use new mounting securing bolts, and tighten all fixings to the specified torque.

19 Engine oil cooler – removal and refitting

Note: *New sealing rings will be required on refitting.*

Removal

1 The oil cooler is mounted under the oil filter housing on the front of the cylinder block **(see illustration)**. **Note:** *The manufacturers*

19.1 Oil filter and oil cooler mounting details

1 Oil cooler retaining cap	7 Sealing plug	10 Oil pressure warning light switch	15 Oil supply pipe to turbo
2 O-ring	8 Oil pressure relief valve spring (early models only)	11 Gasket	16 Banjo bolt – turbo
3 Oil cooler	9 Oil pressure relief valve piston (early models only)	12 Mounting bolt	17 Oil filter cover
4 O-ring		13 Oil filter housing	18 O-ring
5 Washer		14 Seal	19 Oil filter
6 Sealing plug			

H31962

21.5 Oil seal housing (arrowed) on the front right-hand side of the cylinder block

21.6a Remove the plastic cover/strainer from the bottom of the crankcase . . .

21.6b . . . and recover the O-ring seal

21.7 Tensioner locking bolt (arrowed)

1 Guide sprocket
2 Tensioner assembly mounting bolts

recommend the oil cooler is renewed if considerable quantities of metal swarf have been found in the engine oil during servicing.

2 Position a container beneath the oil filter/cooler to catch escaping oil and coolant.

3 Clamp the oil cooler coolant hoses to minimise coolant spillage, then remove the clips, and disconnect the hoses from the oil cooler. Be prepared for coolant spillage.

4 Unscrew the oil cooler retaining cap from the bottom of the oil filter housing, then slide off the oil cooler. Recover the O-rings from the top and bottom of the oil cooler.

21.8 Guide sprocket (arrowed)

Refitting

5 Refitting is a reversal of removal, bearing in mind the following points:
a) Use new oil cooler O-rings.
b) Where applicable, press up the oil cooler retaining cap against the anti-twist lock before tightening it to the specified torque. Make sure the coolant hoses are positioned correctly clear of surrounding components.
c) On completion, check and if necessary top-up the oil and coolant levels.

20 Oil pressure warning light switch – removal and refitting

Removal

1 The oil pressure warning light switch is fitted to the oil filter housing. Remove the engine top cover(s) to gain access to the switch (see Section 4).

2 Disconnect the wiring connector and wipe clean the area around the switch.

3 Unscrew the switch from the filter housing and remove it, along with its sealing washer. If the switch is to be left removed from the engine for any length of time, plug the oil filter housing aperture.

Refitting

4 Examine the sealing washer for signs of damage or deterioration and if necessary renew.

21.9 Drive chain tensioner mounting bolts (arrowed)

5 Refit the switch, complete with washer, and tighten it to the specified torque.

6 Securely reconnect the wiring connector then check and, if necessary, top-up the engine oil as described in *Weekly checks*. On completion, refit the engine top cover(s).

21 Balancer shaft unit (3-cylinder engines) – removal and refitting

Removal

1 The 3-cylinder engine has a balancer unit bolted to the bottom of the crankcase/block. The unit consists of a single counter-rotating balancer shaft driven by the crankshaft.

2 Remove the timing belt as described in Section 7.

3 Remove the crankshaft sprocket as described in Section 8.

4 Remove the sump as described in Section 14.

5 Unscrew the retaining bolts and remove the oil seal housing from the front right-hand side of the cylinder block **(see illustration)**. If it is stuck, release it by tapping with a soft-faced mallet. If the oil seal is to be re-used, wrap some tape around the end of the crankshaft to protect the oil seal lips.

6 Unscrew the mounting bolts and remove the plastic cover/strainer from the bottom of the crankcase. Recover the O-ring **(see illustrations)**.

7 Apply inward pressure on the drive chain, then lock the chain tensioner by fitting and tightening a bolt through the tensioner into the tensioner body **(see illustration)**.

8 Unscrew the bolt and remove the guide sprocket **(see illustration)**. Place the sprocket to one side.

9 Unbolt and remove the drive chain tensioner assembly **(see illustration)**. Discard the bolts and obtain new ones.

10 If the chain is to be re-used, mark it with paint to indicate its fitted position and rotational direction.

11 Remove the chain from the sprockets.

12 Lock the balancer shaft by positioning a lever or long spanner between the eccentric weight at the flywheel end and the crankcase.

Loosen only the bolt securing the balancer weight at the timing end.

13 Unbolt the balancer shaft assembly from the crankcase **(see illustration)**. Recover the O-ring seal and the location dowel. Discard the seal and obtain a new one.

14 Fully unscrew the bolt and remove the balancer weight and sprocket from the balancer shaft. Mark the sprocket and weight to ensure correct refitting. Discard the bolt and obtain a new one.

15 Withdraw the balancer shaft from the housing.

Refitting

16 Thoroughly clean all the components and wipe dry. Lubricate the bearing surfaces of the balancer shaft and housing with fresh engine oil.

17 Insert the balancer shaft into the housing, then refit the sprocket and weight, noting that they can only be fitted in one position. Hand-tighten the new retaining bolt at this stage.

18 Make sure the location dowel is in place, then fit a new O-ring seal and offer the assembly to the crankcase. Insert the mounting bolts finger-tight, then check that the timing end of the assembly is correctly aligned with the cylinder block – no movement is possible near the location dowel, however some movement will be possible within the bolt holes by swivelling the assembly. With the assembly located correctly, fully tighten the mounting bolts to their specified torque.

19 Lock the balancer shaft as for removal, and tighten the new weight/sprocket bolt to the specified torque and angle.

21.13 Balance shaft assembly (arrowed)

20 Refit the drive chain tensioner housing and tighten the new mounting bolts to the specified torque and angle.

21 With the engine set at TDC, the mark on the crankshaft sprocket will be pointing upwards. The chain has two coloured links which are also notched; position one of these links on the crankshaft sprocket mark, then feed the chain clockwise over the tensioner pad, around the oil pump sprocket and over the balancer shaft sprocket, making sure that the remaining coloured/notched link is aligned with the mark on the sprocket **(see illustration)**.

22 Locate the guide pulley sprocket in the chain, then refit the bolt and tighten it to the specified torque.

23 Unlock the tensioner by unscrewing the retaining bolt, then recheck that the coloured/notched links are still aligned with the marks on the sprockets.

21.21 The coloured links (arrowed) on the balance shaft chain must be positioned as shown

24 Clean all traces of old sealant from the crankshaft oil seal housing and the cylinder block, then coat the cylinder block mating faces of the oil seal housing with a 2.0 to 3.0 mm thick bead of sealant (Seat D 176 404 A2, or equivalent). Note that the seal housing must be refitted within 5 minutes of applying the sealant. *Caution: DO NOT put excessive amounts of sealant onto the housing as it may get into the sump and block the oil pick-up pipe.*

25 Refit the oil seal housing, taking care not to damage the seal and tighten the bolts progressively to the specified torque. If a new seal is to be fitted, refer to Section 17.

26 Refit the sump as described in Section 14.

27 Refit the crankshaft sprocket as described in Section 8.

28 Refit the timing belt as described in Section 7.

Notes

Chapter 2 Part D:
Engine removal and overhaul procedures

Contents

Degrees of difficulty

Easy, suitable for novice with little experience	**Fairly easy,** suitable for beginner with some experience	**Fairly difficult,** suitable for competent DIY mechanic	**Difficult,** suitable for experienced DIY mechanic	**Very difficult,** suitable for expert DIY or professional

Specifications

Cylinder head

Minimum permissible dimension between top of valve stem and top surface of cylinder head:
  Petrol engines:
    1.2 litre:
      Engine code BXV .... N/A
      Engine codes AZQ and BME .... 7.6 mm
    1.4 litre:
      Intake valves....................................... 7.6 mm
      Exhaust valves .... 7.6 mm
  Diesel engines:
    1.4 litre .... N/A
    1.9 litre:
      Intake valves....................................... 43.4 mm
      Exhaust valves .... 43.2 mm
Minimum cylinder head height:
  Petrol engines:
    1.2 litre .... N/A
    1.4 litre .... 108.25 mm
  Diesel engines .... No reworking permitted
Maximum cylinder head gasket face distortion:
  Petrol engines... 0.05 mm
  Diesel engines .... 0.10 mm

Valves

	Intake	Exhaust
Valve stem diameter:		
Petrol engines:		
1.2 litre:		
Engine code BXV	N/A	N/A
Engine codes AZQ and BME	5.973 mm	5.953 mm
1.4 litre	5.973 mm	5.953 mm
Diesel engines:		
1.4 litre	6.980 mm	6.956 mm
1.9 litre	6.980 mm	6.956 mm
Valve head diameter:		
Petrol engines:		
1.2 litre:		
Engine code BXV	N/A	N/A
Engine codes AZQ and BME	29.5 mm	26.0 mm
1.4 litre	29.5 mm	26.0 mm
Diesel engines	35.95 mm	31.45 mm
Valve length:		
Petrol engines:		
1.2 litre:		
Engine code BXV	N/A	N/A
Engine codes AZQ and BME	100.9 mm	100.57 mm
1.4 litre	100.9 mm	100.5 mm
Diesel engines:		
1.4 litre	89.95 mm	89.95 mm
1.9 litre	89.95 mm	89.95 mm
Valve seat angle (all engines)	45°	45°

Piston and cylinder bore diameters

	Piston	Cylinder bore
Petrol engines:		
1.2 litre	See Note in Section 2	
1.4 litre:		
Standard	76.470 mm	76.510 mm
1st oversize	76.720 mm	76.760 mm
2nd oversize	76.970 mm	77.010 mm
Diesel engines:		
Standard	79.470 mm	79.510 mm
1st oversize	79.720 mm	79.760 mm
2nd oversize	79.970 mm	80.010 mm

Piston rings

	New	Wear limit
End gaps:		
Petrol engines:		
1.2 litre	See Note in Section 2	
1.4 litre:		
Top compression ring	0.20 to 0.50 mm	1.0 mm
Lower compression ring	0.40 to 0.70 mm	1.0 mm
Oil scraper ring	0.40 to 1.40 mm	N/A
Diesel engines:		
1.4 litre:		
Top compression ring	0.25 to 0.40 mm	1.0 mm
Lower compression ring	0.20 to 0.40 mm	1.0 mm
Oil scraper ring	0.25 to 0.50 mm	1.0 mm
1.9 litre:		
Compression rings	0.20 to 0.40 mm	1.0 mm
Oil scraper ring	0.25 to 0.50 mm	1.0 mm
Ring-to-groove clearance:		
Petrol engines:		
1.2 litre	See Note in Section 2	
1.4 litre:		
Compression rings	0.04 to 0.08 mm	0.15 mm
Oil scraper ring	N/A	N/A
Diesel engines:		
1st compression ring	0.06 to 0.09 mm	0.25 mm
2nd compression ring	0.05 to 0.08 mm	0.25 mm
Oil scraper ring	0.03 to 0.06 mm	0.15 mm

Pistons/connecting rods

	New	Wear limit
Connecting rod side-play on crankshaft journal:		
Petrol engines:		
1.2 litre	See Note in Section 2	
1.4 litre	0.10 to 0.35 mm	0.40 mm
Diesel engines	N/A	0.37 mm

Crankshaft

Petrol engines.	See Note in Section 2	
Diesel engines:		
Main journal diameter.	54.00 mm (nominal)	
Big-end journal diameter	47.80 mm (nominal)	
Endfloat:		
New.	0.07 to 0.17 mm	
Wear limit	0.37 mm	

Torque wrench settings

Refer to Chapter 2A, 2B or 2C as applicable.

1 General information

Included in this Part of Chapter 2 are details of removing the engine from the car and general overhaul procedures for the cylinder head, cylinder block and all other engine internal components.

The information given ranges from advice concerning preparation for an overhaul and the purchase of new parts, to detailed step-by-step procedures covering removal, inspection, renovation and refitting of engine internal components.

After Section 6, all instructions are based on the assumption that the engine has been removed from the car. For information concerning in-car engine repair, as well as the removal and refitting of those external components necessary for full overhaul, refer to the relevant in-car repair procedure section (Chapters 2A, 2B and 2C) and to Section 5 of this Chapter. Ignore any preliminary dismantling operations described in the relevant in-car repair sections that are no longer relevant once the engine has been removed from the car.

Apart from torque wrench settings, which are given at the beginning of the relevant in-car repair procedure in Chapters 2A, 2B or 2C, all specifications relating to engine overhaul are given at the beginning of this part of Chapter 2.

2 Engine overhaul – general information

Note 1: *On all petrol engines, the crankshaft must not be removed. Loosening the main bearing cap bolts will cause deformation of the cylinder block. If the crankshaft or main bearing surfaces are worn or damaged, the complete crankshaft/cylinder block assembly must be renewed.*
Note 2: *On 1.2 litre petrol engines, the pistons and connecting rods must not be removed.*

However, they can be removed on all other engines.

1 It is not always easy to determine when, or if, an engine should be completely overhauled, as a number of factors must be considered.

2 High mileage is not necessarily an indication that an overhaul is needed, while low mileage does not preclude the need for an overhaul. Frequency of servicing is probably the most important consideration. An engine which has had regular and frequent oil and filter changes, as well as other required maintenance, should give many thousands of miles of reliable service. Conversely, a neglected engine may require an overhaul very early in its life.

3 Excessive oil consumption is an indication that piston rings, valve seals and/or valve guides are in need of attention. Make sure that oil leaks are not responsible before deciding that the rings and/or guides are worn. Perform a compression (or leakdown) test, as described in Part A, B or C of this Chapter (as applicable), to determine the likely cause of the problem.

4 Check the oil pressure with a gauge fitted in place of the oil pressure switch, and compare it with that specified (see Specifications in Chapters 2A, 2B and 2C). If it is extremely low, the main and big-end bearings, and/or the oil pump, are probably worn.

5 Loss of power, rough running, knocking or metallic engine noises, excessive valve gear noise, and high fuel consumption may also point to the need for an overhaul, especially if they are all present at the same time. If a complete service does not remedy the situation, major mechanical work is the only solution.

6 An engine overhaul involves restoring all internal parts to the specification of a new engine. During an overhaul, the pistons and the piston rings are renewed. New main and big-end bearings are generally fitted (where possible); if necessary, the crankshaft may be renewed to restore the journals. The valves are also serviced as well, since they are usually in less-than-perfect condition at this point. While the engine is being overhauled, other components, such as the starter and

alternator, can be overhauled as well. The end result should be an as-new engine that will give many trouble-free miles. Critical cooling system components such as the hoses, thermostat and coolant pump should be renewed when an engine is overhauled. The radiator should be checked carefully, to ensure that it is not clogged or leaking. Also, it is a good idea to renew the oil pump whenever the engine is overhauled.

7 Before beginning the engine overhaul, read through the entire procedure, to familiarise yourself with the scope and requirements of the job. Overhauling an engine is not difficult if you follow carefully all of the instructions, have the necessary tools and equipment, and pay close attention to all specifications. It can, however, be time-consuming. Plan on the car being off the road for a minimum of two weeks, especially if parts must be taken to an engineering works for repair or reconditioning. Check on the availability of parts and make sure that any necessary special tools and equipment are obtained in advance. Most work can be done with typical hand tools, although a number of precision measuring tools are required for inspecting parts to determine if they must be renewed. Often an engineering works will handle the inspection of parts and offer advice concerning reconditioning and renewal. Always wait until the engine has been completely dismantled, and until all components (especially the cylinder block and the crankshaft) have been inspected, before deciding what service and repair operations must be performed by an engineering works. The condition of these components will be the major factor to consider when determining whether to overhaul the original engine, or to buy a reconditioned unit. Do not, therefore, purchase parts or have overhaul work done on other components until they have been thoroughly inspected. As a general rule, time is the primary cost of an overhaul, so it does not pay to fit worn or sub-standard parts.

8 As a final note, to ensure maximum life and minimum trouble from a reconditioned engine, everything must be assembled with care, in a spotlessly-clean environment.

4.5a Unscrew the four securing bolts . . .

4.5b . . . and remove the battery tray

4.8 Disconnect the radiator top hose from the thermostat housing

3 Engine/transmission removal – preparation and precautions

If you have decided that the engine must be removed for overhaul or major repair work, several preliminary steps should be taken.

Locating a suitable place to work is extremely important. Adequate work space, along with storage space for the vehicle, will be needed. If a workshop or garage is not available, at the very least a solid, level, clean work surface is required.

If possible, clear some shelving close to the work area and use it to store the engine components and ancillaries as they are removed and dismantled. In this manner, the components stand a better chance of staying clean and undamaged during the overhaul. Laying out components in groups, together with their fixings bolts, screws, etc, will save time and avoid confusion when the engine is refitted.

Clean the engine compartment and engine before beginning the removal procedure; this will help visibility and help to keep tools clean.

The help of an assistant is essential; there are certain instances when one person cannot safely perform all of the operations required to remove the engine from the vehicle. Safety is of primary importance, considering the potential hazards involved in this kind of operation. A second person should always be in attendance to offer help in an emergency. If this is the first time you have removed an engine, advice and aid from someone more experienced would also be beneficial.

Plan the operation ahead of time. Before starting work, obtain (or arrange for the hire of) all of the tools and equipment you will need. Access to the following items will allow the task of removing and refitting the engine to be completed safely and with relative ease: a hoist and lifting tackle – rated in excess of the weight of the engine, complete sets of spanners and sockets as described at the rear of this manual, wooden blocks, and plenty of rags and cleaning solvent for mopping-up spilled oil, coolant and fuel. A selection of different-sized plastic storage bins will

also prove useful for keeping dismantled components grouped together. If any of the equipment must be hired, make sure that you arrange for it in advance, and perform all of the operations possible without it beforehand; this may save you time and money.

Plan on the vehicle being out of use for quite a while, especially if you intend to carry out an engine overhaul. Read through the whole of this Section and work out a strategy based on your own experience, and the tools, time and workspace available to you. Some of the overhaul processes may have to be carried out by a Seat dealer or an engineering works – these establishments often have busy schedules, so it would be prudent to consult them before removing or dismantling the engine, to get an idea of the amount of time required to carry out the work.

When removing the engine from the vehicle, be methodical about the disconnection of external components. Labelling cables and hoses as they are removed will greatly assist the refitting process.

Always be extremely careful when lifting the engine from the engine compartment. Serious injury can result from careless actions. If help is required, it is better to wait until it is available rather than risk personal injury and/or damage to components by continuing alone. By planning ahead and taking your time, a job of this nature, although major, can be accomplished successfully and without incident.

4 Engine and transmission – removal and refitting

Removal

1 All engines are lifted together with the transmission from the front of the car after first moving the lock carrier assembly to one side, or removed completely on models without air conditioning.

2 Disconnect the battery negative lead as described in Chapter 5A.

3 Remove the engine top cover.

4 Remove the air cleaner and air ducting with reference to Chapter 4A or 4B.

5 Remove the battery as described in

Chapter 5A, then remove the battery tray **(see illustrations)**.

6 Drain the cooling system as described in Chapter 1A or 1B.

7 Apply the handbrake, then jack up the front of the vehicle and support securely on axle stands (see *Jacking and vehicle support*) and remove the engine undershield.

8 Disconnect all coolant hoses from the engine, making a note of their fitted positions **(see illustration)**.

9 Disconnect the wiring from the engine and transmission, noting its location and routing to aid refitting. Note that some of the wiring can remain attached to the engine.

10 On manual transmission models, disconnect the gearchange mechanism from the transmission (Chapter 7A), then unbolt the clutch slave cylinder and position it to one side.

11 On automatic transmission models, disconnect the selector cable from the transmission (Chapter 7B), then unbolt the bracket for the pressure line of the power steering.

12 On petrol models, depressurise the fuel system as described in Chapter 4A. Place a wad of clean cloth around the fuel supply and return hose connections on the right-hand side of the engine compartment, then depress the connector locking tabs, and disconnect the fuel line connectors. Be prepared for fuel spillage, and take adequate fire precautions.

13 On diesel models, disconnect the fuel hoses from the fuel filter. Be prepared for fuel spillage, and plug the open ends of the hoses and connections to prevent dirt entry and further fuel loss.

14 Disconnect the following vacuum hoses:
 a) *Charcoal canister solenoid valve (petrol models only).*
 b) *EGR valve.*
 c) *Brake servo hose on the intake manifold.*

15 On models without air conditioning, carry out the following:
 a) *Remove the front bumper and crossmember, and the bonnet lock, with reference to Chapter 11.*
 b) *Disconnect the headlight wiring.*
 c) *On models with headlight washers, disconnect the washer supply tubing at the T-piece.*
 d) *Unbolt the lock carrier and remove from the front of the car.*

e) *Remove the radiator with reference to Chapter 3.*

16 On models with air conditioning, carry out the following:

a) *Remove the front bumper and crossmember, and the bonnet lock, with reference to Chapter 11.*

b) *Disconnect the headlight wiring.*

c) *On models with headlight washers, disconnect the washer supply tubing at the T-piece.*

d) *Unbolt the lock carrier and swivel it out from the front of the car, leaving the air conditioning lines still attached. Support the assembly on axle stands or blocks of wood.*

e) *Remove the radiator and condenser with reference to Chapter 3.*

f) *Remove the auxiliary drivebelt as described in Chapter 1A or 1B.*

g) *Disconnect the wiring from the air conditioning compressor, then unbolt it and tie it to the lock carrier.* **Do not** *disconnect the refrigerant lines.*

17 Remove the rear engine mounting/link with reference to the relevant part of Chapter 2.

18 Remove the right-hand driveshaft as described in Chapter 8, and disconnect the left-hand driveshaft from the transmission.

19 Remove the exhaust front section as described in Chapter 4C.

20 Connect a hoist and lifting tackle to the engine lifting brackets on the cylinder head, and raise the hoist to just take the weight of the engine.

21 Remove the right-hand and left-hand engine/transmission mountings, with reference to the relevant part of Chapter 2.

22 Carefully lift the engine/transmission assembly from the engine compartment until it can be withdrawn from the front of the car **(see illustration)**.

Refitting

23 Refitting is a reversal of removal, bearing in mind the following points:

a) *Ensure that any brackets noted before removal are in place on the engine-to-transmission bolts.*

b) *Tighten all fixings to the specified torque, where given.*

c) *Refit the engine mountings with reference to Chapter 2A, 2B or 2C.*

d) *Reconnect the driveshafts to the transmission with reference to Chapter 8.*

e) *Check that all wiring, hoses and pipes are correctly reconnected and routed as noted before removal.*

f) *Ensure that the fuel lines are correctly reconnected.*

g) *On completion, refill the cooling system as described in Chapter 1A or 1B. On models with automatic transmission, check and if necessary top-up the automatic transmission fluid level as described in Chapter 1A.*

h) *Have the engine management system checked for fault codes by a Seat dealer.*

5 Engine overhaul – preliminary information

1 It is much easier to dismantle and work on the engine if it is mounted on a portable engine stand. These stands can often be hired from a tool hire shop. Before the engine is mounted on a stand, the flywheel should be removed, so that the stand bolts can be tightened into the end of the cylinder block/crankcase. **Note:** *Do not measure cylinder bore dimensions with the engine mounted on this type of stand.*

2 If a stand is not available, it is possible to dismantle the engine with it blocked up on a sturdy workbench, or on the floor. Be very careful not to tip or drop the engine when working without a stand.

3 If you intend to obtain a reconditioned engine, all ancillaries must be removed first, to be transferred to the new engine (just as they will if you are doing a complete engine overhaul yourself). These components include the following (it may be necessary to transfer additional components, such as the oil level dipstick/tube assembly, oil filter housing, etc, depending on which components are supplied with the reconditioned engine:

Petrol engines

a) *Alternator (including mounting brackets) and starter motor (Chapter 5A).*

b) *The ignition system components including all sensors and spark plugs (Chapters 1A and 5B).*

c) *The fuel injection system components (Chapter 4A).*

d) *All electrical switches, actuators and sensors, and the engine wiring harness (Chapters 3, 4A and 5B).*

e) *Intake and exhaust manifolds (Chapters 4A and 4C).*

f) *Engine mountings (Chapters 2A or 2B).*

g) *Clutch components (Chapter 6).*

h) *Oil separator (where applicable).*

Diesel engines

a) *Alternator (including mounting brackets) and starter motor (Chapter 5A).*

b) *The glow plug/preheating system components (Chapter 5A).*

c) *All fuel system components, fuel injectors, all sensors and actuators (Chapter 4B).*

d) *The brake vacuum/tandem pump (Chapter 9).*

e) *All electrical switches, actuators and sensors, and the engine wiring harness (Chapters 3, 4B and 5C).*

f) *Intake and exhaust manifolds, and turbocharger (Chapters 4B and 4C).*

g) *Engine mountings (Chapter 2C).*

h) *Clutch components (Chapter 6).*

All engines

Note: *When removing the external components from the engine, pay close attention to details that may be helpful during refitting. Note the*

4.22 Engine removal

fitted position of gaskets, seals, spacers, pins, washers, bolts, and other small components.

4 If you are obtaining a short engine (the engine cylinder block/crankcase, crankshaft, pistons and connecting rods, all fully assembled), then the cylinder head, sump, oil pump, timing belt(s) and chain (as applicable – together with tensioner(s) and covers), auxiliary drivebelt (together with its tensioner), coolant pump, thermostat housing, coolant outlet elbows, oil filter housing and where applicable oil cooler will also have to be removed.

5 If you are planning a full overhaul, the engine can be dismantled in the order given below:

a) *Intake and exhaust manifolds (see the relevant parts of Chapter 4).*

b) *Timing chain/belt(s), sprockets and tensioner(s) (see Chapter 2A, 2B or 2C).*

c) *Cylinder head (see Chapter 2A, 2B or 2C).*

d) *Flywheel/driveplate (see Chapter 2A, 2B or 2C).*

e) *Sump (see Chapter 2A, 2B or 2C).*

f) *Oil pump (see Chapter 2A, 2B or 2C).*

g) *Piston/connecting rod assemblies (see Section 9).*

h) *Crankshaft (see Section 10).*

6 Cylinder head – dismantling

Note: *A valve spring compressor tool will be required for this operation.*

Petrol engines

1 With the cylinder head removed as described in the relevant part of Chapter 2, proceed as follows.

2 Remove the intake and exhaust manifolds as described in Chapter 4A or 4C.

3 Remove the camshaft(s) and hydraulic tappets/roller rocker fingers as described in Chapter 2A or 2B.

4 If desired, unbolt the coolant housing from the rear of the cylinder head, and recover the seal.

5 Where applicable, remove the camshaft position sensor, with reference to Chapter 4A, Section 4.

6 Where applicable, unscrew the securing nut, and recover the washer, and remove the timing belt tensioner pulley from the stud on the cylinder head.

6.9a Compress the valve springs with a compressor tool

6.9b Removing the spring cap . . .

6.9c . . . and valve spring

7 Unbolt any remaining auxiliary brackets and/or engine lifting brackets from the cylinder head as necessary, noting their locations to aid refitting. Where applicable, unscrew the securing bolt and remove the secondary timing belt tensioner from the timing belt end of the cylinder head.

8 Turn the cylinder head over, and rest it on one side.

9 Using a valve spring compressor, compress each valve spring in turn, until the split collets can be removed. Release the compressor, and lift off the spring cap and spring. If, when the valve spring compressor is screwed down, the spring cap refuses to free and expose the split collets, gently tap the top of the tool, directly over the spring cap, with a light hammer. This will free the retainer (**see illustrations**).

10 Using a pair of pliers, or a removal tool, carefully extract the valve stem oil seal from the top of the valve guide (**see illustrations**).

11 Withdraw the valve from the gasket side of the cylinder head (**see illustration**).

12 It is essential that each valve is stored together with its collets, cap, spring and spring seat. The valves should be kept in their correct sequences, unless they are so badly worn that they are to be renewed.

HAYNES HINT *If they are going to be kept and used again, place each valve assembly in a labelled polythene bag or similar small container. Label each bag, noting that No 1 valve is nearest to the timing belt/chain end of the cylinder head.*

Diesel engines

13 With the cylinder head removed as described in Chapter 2C, proceed as follows.

14 Remove the intake and exhaust manifolds as described in Chapters 4B and 4C.

15 Remove the camshaft and hydraulic tappets, as described in Chapter 2C.

16 Remove the glow plugs, with reference to Chapter 5A.

17 Remove the fuel injectors, with reference to Chapter 4B.

18 Unscrew the nut and remove the timing belt tensioner pulley from the stud on the timing belt end of the cylinder head.

19 Unbolt any remaining auxiliary brackets and/or engine lifting brackets from the cylinder head as necessary, noting their locations to aid refitting.

20 Proceed as described in paragraphs 8 to 12.

7 Cylinder head and valves – cleaning and inspection

1 Thorough cleaning of the cylinder head and valve components, followed by a detailed inspection, will enable you to decide how much valve service work must be carried out during engine overhaul. **Note:** *If the engine has been severely overheated, it is best to assume that the cylinder head is warped – check carefully for signs of this.*

Cleaning

2 Using a suitable degreasing agent, remove all traces of oil deposits from the cylinder head,

paying particular attention to the camshaft bearing surfaces, hydraulic tappet bores, valve guides and oilways. Scrape off any traces of old gasket from the mating surfaces, taking care not to score or gouge them. If using emery paper, do not use a grade of less than 100. Turn the head over and, using a blunt blade, scrape any carbon deposits from the combustion chambers and ports. Finally, wash the entire head casting with a suitable solvent to remove the remaining debris.

3 Clean the valve heads and stems using a fine wire brush (or a power-operated wire brush). If the valve is covered with heavy carbon deposits, scrape off the majority of the deposits with a blunt blade first, then use the wire brush.

4 Thoroughly clean the remainder of the components using solvent and allow them to dry completely. Discard the oil seals, as new ones must be fitted when the cylinder head is reassembled.

Inspection

Cylinder head

Note: *If the valve seats are to be reground, ensure that the maximum permissible reworking dimension is not exceeded (the maximum dimension will only allow minimal reworking to produce a perfect seal between valve and seat). If the maximum dimension is exceeded, the function of the hydraulic tappets cannot be guaranteed, and the cylinder head must be renewed. Refer to paragraph 6 for details of how to calculate the maximum permissible reworking dimension.*

6.10a Use a removal tool . . .

6.10b . . . to remove the valve stem oil seals

6.11 Remove the valves

7.6 Distance (A) between top of valve stem and top surface of cylinder head

5 Examine the head casting closely to identify any damage or cracks that may have developed. Cracks can often be identified from evidence of coolant or oil leakage. Pay particular attention to the areas around the valve seats and spark plug/fuel injector holes. If cracking is discovered in this area, Seat state that, on diesel engines, the cylinder head may be re-used, provided the cracks are no larger than 0.5 mm wide. More serious damage will mean the renewal of the cylinder head casting.

6 Moderately pitted and scorched valve seats can be repaired by lapping the valves in during reassembly, as described later in this Chapter, however the maximum permissible reworking dimension must not be exceeded, which will only allow minimal reworking (see note at beginning of paragraph 5). To calculate the maximum permissible reworking dimension, proceed as follows **(see illustration)**:

a) *If a new valve is to be fitted, use the new valve for the following calculation.*
b) *Insert the valve into its guide in the cylinder head, and push the valve firmly on to its seat.*
c) *Measure the distance between the top face of the valve stem and the top surface of the cylinder head. Record the measurement obtained.*
d) *Consult the Specifications, and compare the measured distance with that given in the Specifications.*

7 Measure any distortion of the gasket surfaces using a straight-edge and a set of feeler blades. Take one measurement longitudinally on the manifold mating surface(s). Take several measurements across the head gasket surface, to assess the level of distortion in all planes **(see illustration)**. Compare the measurements with the figures in the Specifications.

8 On petrol engines, if the head is distorted beyond the specified limit, it may be possible to have it machined by an engineering works, provided that the minimum permissible cylinder head height is maintained.

9 On diesel engines, if the head is distorted beyond the specified limit, the head must be renewed.

7.7 Measure the distortion of the cylinder head gasket surface

7.13 Measure the free length of each valve spring

Valves and associated components

Note: *On all engines, the valve heads cannot be recut, although they may be lapped in.*

10 Examine each valve closely for signs of wear. Inspect the valve stems for wear ridges, scoring or variations in diameter; measure their diameters at several points along their lengths with a micrometer, and compare with the figures given in the Specifications **(see illustration)**.

11 The valve heads should not be cracked, badly pitted or charred. Note that light pitting of the valve head can be rectified by lapping-in the valves during reassembly, as described in Section 8.

12 Check that the valve stem end face is free from excessive pitting or indentation; this could be caused by defective hydraulic tappets.

13 Using vernier calipers, measure the free length of each of the valve springs. As a

8.2 Grinding-in a valve

7.10 Measure the diameter of the valve stems using a micrometer

7.14 Check the squareness of the valve springs

manufacturer's figure is not quoted, the only way to check the length of the springs is by comparison with a new component. Note that valve springs are usually renewed during a major engine overhaul **(see illustration)**.

14 Stand each spring on its end on a flat surface, against an engineer's square **(see illustration)**. Check the squareness of the spring visually, and renew it if it appears distorted.

15 Renew the valve stem oil seals regardless of their apparent condition.

8 Cylinder head – reassembly

Note: *A valve spring compressor tool will be required for this operation.*

1 To achieve a gas-tight seal between the valves and their seats, it will be necessary to lap-in (or grind-in) the valves. To complete this process you will need a quantity of fine/coarse grinding paste and a grinding tool – this can either be of the rubber sucker type, or the automatic type which is driven by a rotary power tool.

2 Smear a small quantity of fine grinding paste on the sealing face of the valve head. Turn the cylinder head over so that the combustion chambers are facing upwards and insert the valve into the correct guide. Attach the grinding tool to the valve head and using a backward/forward rotary action, grind the valve head into its seat. Periodically lift the valve and rotate it to redistribute the grinding paste **(see illustration)**.

8.8a Lubricate the valve stem with clean engine oil

8.8b Fit a protective sleeve over the valve stem before fitting the stem seal

8.9 Using a special installer to fit a valve stem oil seal

3 Continue this process until the contact between valve and seat produces an unbroken, matt grey ring of uniform width, on both faces. Repeat the operation on the remaining valves.

4 If the valves and seats are so badly pitted that coarse grinding paste must be used, bear in that there is a maximum permissible reworking dimension for the valves and seats. Refer to the Specifications at the beginning of this Chapter for the limits, and note that if exceeded due to excessive lapping-in, the hydraulic tappets may not operate correctly, and the cylinder head must be renewed.

5 Assuming the repair is feasible, work as described previously, but use coarse grinding paste initially, to achieve a dull finish on the valve face and seat. Wash off the coarse paste with solvent and repeat the process using fine grinding paste to obtain the correct finish.

6 When all the valves have been ground in,

remove all traces of grinding paste from the cylinder head and valves using solvent, and allow the head and valves to dry completely.

7 Turn the cylinder head on its side.

8 Working on one valve at a time, lubricate the valve stem with clean engine oil, and insert the valve into its guide. Fit one of the protective plastic sleeves supplied with the new valve stem oil seals over the end of the valve stem – this will protect the oil seal as it is being fitted **(see illustrations)**.

9 Dip a new valve stem seal in clean engine oil, and carefully push it over the valve stem and onto the top of the valve guide – take care not to damage the stem seal as it is fitted. Use a suitable long-reach socket or a suitable valve stem seal fitting tool to press the seal firmly into position **(see illustration)**. Remove the protective sleeve from the valve stem.

10 Locate the valve spring over the valve stem, ensuring that the lower end of the

spring seats correctly on the cylinder head **(see illustration)**.

11 Fit the upper spring seat over the top of the spring then, using a valve spring compressor, compress the spring until the upper seat is pushed beyond the collet grooves in the valve stem. Refit the split collets. Gradually release the spring compressor, checking that the collets remain correctly seated as the spring extends. When correctly seated, the upper spring seat should force the collets securely into the grooves in the end of the valve stem **(see illustrations)**.

> **HAYNES HiNT** *Use a little dab of grease to hold the collets in position on the valve stem while the spring compressor is released.*

12 Repeat this process for the remaining sets of valve components, ensuring that all components are refitted to their original locations. To settle the components after installation, strike the end of each valve stem with a mallet, using a block of wood to protect the stem from damage. Check before progressing any further that the split collets remain firmly seated in the grooves in the end of the valve stem.

Petrol engines

13 Refit the brackets previously removed, and also where applicable refit the secondary timing belt tensioner.

14 Where applicable, refit the timing belt tensioner pulley on the stud, and loosely refit the securing nut and washer.

15 Where applicable, refit the camshaft position sensor, with reference to Chapter 4A.

16 If removed, refit the coolant housing to the cylinder head, together with a new seal, and tighten the mounting bolts.

17 Refit the camshafts and hydraulic tappets/roller rocker fingers with reference to Chapter 2A or 2B.

18 Refit the intake and exhaust manifolds with reference to Chapter 4A and 4C.

Diesel engines

19 Refit the brackets previously removed, then refit the timing belt tensioner pulley on

8.10 Fit the valve spring

8.11a Fit the upper spring seat

8.11b Use grease to hold the split collets in the groove

8.11c Compress the valve spring using a compressor tool – 1.4 litre petrol engine

9.3 Mark the big-end caps and connecting rods with their cylinder numbers (arrowed)

9.6a Unscrew the big-end bearing cap bolts . . .

9.6b . . . and remove the cap

the stud, and loosely refit the securing nut and washer.

20 Refit the fuel injectors, with reference to Chapter 4B.

21 Refit the glow plugs, with reference to Chapter 5A.

22 Refit the camshaft and hydraulic tappets, with reference to Chapter 2C.

23 Refit the intake and exhaust manifolds (and turbocharger) with reference to Chapters 4B and 4C.

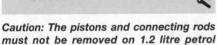

9 Piston/connecting rod assemblies – removal

Caution: The pistons and connecting rods must not be removed on 1.2 litre petrol engines.

1 Remove the cylinder head, sump, oil baffle and oil pump pick-up pipe with reference to Chapter 2B or 2C. On 3-cylinder diesel engines, also remove the balancer shaft assembly.

2 Inspect the tops of the cylinder bores for ridges at the point where the pistons reach top dead centre. These must be removed, otherwise the pistons may be damaged when they are pushed out of their bores. Use a scraper or ridge reamer to remove the ridges. Such a ridge indicates excessive wear of the cylinder bore.

3 Check the connecting rods and big-end caps for identification markings. Both connecting rods and caps should be marked with the cylinder number on one side of each assembly. Note that No 1 cylinder is at the timing belt end of the engine. If no marks are present, using a hammer and centre-punch, paint or similar, mark each connecting rod and big-end bearing cap with its respective cylinder number – note on which side of the connecting rods and caps the marks are made **(see illustration)**.

4 Similarly, check the piston crowns for direction markings. An arrow on each piston crown should point towards the timing belt end of the engine. On some engines, this mark may be obscured by carbon build-up, in which case the piston crown should be cleaned to check for a mark. In some cases, the direction arrow may have worn off, in which case a

suitable mark should be made on the piston crown using a scriber – do not deeply score the piston crown, but ensure that the mark is easily visible.

5 Turn the crankshaft to bring No 1 piston to bottom dead centre (on 4-cylinder engines, No 4 piston will also be at BDC).

6 Unscrew the bolts or nuts, as applicable, from No 1 piston big-end bearing cap. Lift off the cap, and recover the bottom half bearing shell. If the bearing shells are to be re-used, tape the cap and bearing shell together. Note that if the bearing shells are to be re-used, they must be fitted to the original connecting rod and cap **(see illustrations)**.

7 Where the bearing caps are secured with nuts, wrap the threaded ends of the bolts with insulating tape to prevent them scratching the crankpins and bores when the pistons are removed **(see illustration)**.

8 Using a hammer handle, push the piston

9.7 Wrap the threaded ends of the bolts (arrowed) with tape

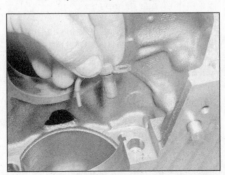

9.12b . . . and withdraw the piston cooling oil spray jets

up through the bore, and remove it from the top of the cylinder block. Where applicable, take care not to damage the piston cooling oil spray jets in the cylinder block as the piston/connecting rod assembly is removed. Recover the upper bearing shell, and tape it to the connecting rod for safe-keeping.

9 Loosely refit the big-end cap to the connecting rod, and secure with the bolts or nuts, as applicable – this will help to keep the components in their correct order.

10 On 4-cylinder engines, remove No 4 piston assembly in the same way.

11 Turn the crankshaft as necessary to bring No 2 piston to bottom dead centre, and remove them in the same way (on 4-cylinder engines, No 3 piston will also be at BDC).

12 Where applicable, remove the securing bolts, and withdraw the piston cooling oil spray jets from the bottom of the cylinder block **(see illustrations)**.

9.12a Remove the securing bolts . . .

9.12c Piston cooling spray jet and retainer

10.5 Slacken and remove the main bearing cap bolts

10.6 Lift the crankshaft from the cylinder block

10 Crankshaft (diesel engines) – removal

Caution: On petrol engines, the crankshaft must not be removed. Loosening the main bearing cap bolts will cause deformation of the cylinder block. On these engines, if the crankshaft or main bearing surfaces are worn or damaged, the complete crankshaft/cylinder block assembly must be renewed. The following procedure only applies to diesel engines.

Note: *If no work is to be done on the pistons and connecting rods, there is no need to remove the cylinder head and push the pistons out of the cylinder bores. The pistons should just be pushed far enough up the bores so that they are positioned clear of the crankshaft journals.*

1 Remove the timing belt and crankshaft sprocket, sump and oil baffle plate, oil pump and pick-up pipe, flywheel, and the crankshaft oil seal housings, as described in Chapter 2C.
2 Remove the pistons and connecting rods, or disconnect them from the crankshaft, as described in Section 9.
3 Check the crankshaft endfloat as described in Section 13, then proceed as follows.
4 The main bearing caps should be numbered 1 to 5 (4-cylinder) or 4 (3-cylinder) from the timing belt end of the engine. If the bearing caps are not marked, mark them accordingly using a centre-punch. Note the orientation of the markings to ensure correct refitting.
5 Slacken and remove the main bearing cap

11.7 To clean the cylinder block threads, run a correct-size tap into the holes

bolts, and lift off each cap. If the caps appear to be stuck, tap them with a soft-faced mallet to free them from the cylinder block **(see illustration)**. Recover the lower bearing shells, and tape them to their caps for safe-keeping.
6 Lift the crankshaft from the cylinder block **(see illustration)**. Take care, as the crankshaft is heavy. On engines with a crankshaft speed/position sensor fitted, lay the crankshaft on wooden blocks – do not rest the crankshaft on the sensor wheel.
7 Recover the upper bearing shells from the cylinder block, and tape them to their respective caps for safe-keeping. Similarly, recover the upper crankshaft endfloat control thrustwasher halves from either side of No 3 main bearing, noting their orientation.
8 On engines with a crankshaft speed/position sensor wheel fitted, unscrew the securing bolts, and remove the sensor wheel, noting which way round it is fitted.

11 Cylinder block/crankcase – cleaning and inspection

Cleaning

1 Remove all external components and electrical switches/sensors from the block, including mounting brackets, the coolant pump, the oil filter/cooler housing, etc. For complete cleaning, the core plugs should ideally be removed. Drill a small hole in the plugs, then insert a self-tapping screw into the hole. Extract the plugs by pulling on the screw with a pair of grips, or by using a slide hammer.
2 Scrape all traces of gasket and sealant from the cylinder block/crankcase, taking care not to damage the sealing surfaces.
3 Remove all oil gallery plugs (where fitted). The plugs are usually very tight – they may have to be drilled out, and the holes retapped. Use new plugs when the engine is reassembled.
4 If the casting is extremely dirty, it should be steam-cleaned. After this, clean all oil holes and galleries one more time. Flush all internal passages with warm water until the water runs clear. Dry thoroughly, and apply a light film of oil to all mating surfaces and cylinder bores,

to prevent rusting. If you have access to compressed air, use it to speed up the drying process, and to blow out all the oil holes and galleries.

 Warning: Wear eye protection when using compressed air.

5 If the castings are not very dirty, you can do an adequate cleaning job with hot, soapy water and a stiff brush. Take plenty of time, and do a thorough job. Regardless of the cleaning method used, be sure to clean all oil holes and galleries very thoroughly, and to dry all components well. Protect the cylinder bores as described above, to prevent rusting.
6 Where applicable, check the piston cooling oil spray jets for damage, and renew if necessary. Check the oil spray hole and the oil passages for blockage.
7 All threaded holes must be clean, to ensure accurate torque readings during reassembly. To clean the threads, run the correct-size tap into each of the holes to remove rust, corrosion, thread sealant or sludge, and to restore damaged threads **(see illustration)**. If possible, use compressed air to clear the holes free of debris produced by this operation. Take extra care to exclude all cleaning liquid from blind tapped holes, as the casting may be cracked by hydraulic action if a bolt is threaded into a hole containing liquid.

 A good alternative is to inject aerosol-applied water dispersant lubricant into each hole, using the long spout usually supplied.
 Warning: Wear eye protection when cleaning out these holes in this way.

8 After coating the mating surfaces of the new core plugs with suitable sealant, fit them to the cylinder block. Make sure that they are driven in straight and seated correctly, or leakage could result.

 A large socket with an outside diameter which will just fit into the core plug can be used to drive the core plug into position.

9 Apply suitable sealant to the new oil gallery plugs, and insert them into the holes in the block. Tighten them securely.
10 If the engine is not going to be reassembled immediately, cover it with a large plastic bag to keep it clean; protect all mating surfaces and the cylinder bores, to prevent rusting.

Inspection

11 Visually check the castings for cracks and corrosion. Look for stripped threads in the threaded holes. If there has been any history of internal coolant leakage, it may

be worthwhile having an engine overhaul specialist check the cylinder block/crankcase for cracks with special equipment. If defects are found, have them repaired, if possible, or renew the assembly.

12 Check each cylinder bore for scuffing and scoring.

13 If in any doubt as the condition of the cylinder block have the block/bores inspected and measured by an engine reconditioning specialist. They will be able to advise on whether the block is serviceable, whether a rebore is necessary, and supply the appropriate pistons and rings.

14 If the bores are in reasonably good condition and not excessively worn, then it may only be necessary to renew the piston rings.

15 If this is the case, the bores should be honed, to allow the new rings to bed-in correctly and provide the best possible seal. Consult an engine reconditioning specialist.

16 On diesel engines, if the oil filter/cooler housing was removed, it can be refitted at this stage if wished. Use a new gasket, and before fully tightening the bolts, align the housing faces with those of the engine block.

17 The cylinder block/crankcase should now be completely clean and dry, with all components checked for wear or damage, and repaired or overhauled as necessary.

18 Apply a light coating of engine oil to the mating surfaces and cylinder bores to prevent rust forming.

19 Refit as many ancillary components as possible, for safe-keeping. If reassembly is not to start immediately, cover the block with a large plastic bag to keep it clean, and protect the machined surfaces as described above to prevent rusting.

12 Piston/connecting rod assemblies – cleaning and inspection

Cleaning

1 Before the inspection process can begin, the piston/connecting rod assemblies must be cleaned, and the original piston rings removed from the pistons.

2 The rings should have smooth, polished working surfaces, with no dull or carbon-coated sections (showing that the ring is not sealing correctly against the bore wall, so allowing combustion gases to blow-by) and no traces of wear on their top and bottom surfaces. The end gaps should be clear of carbon, but not polished (indicating a too-small end gap), and all the rings (including the elements of the oil control ring) should be free to rotate in their grooves, but without excessive up-and-down movement. If the rings appear to be in good condition, they are probably fit for further use; check the end gaps (in an unworn part of the bore) as described in Section 16.

3 If any of the rings appears to be worn or damaged, or has an end gap significantly different from the specified value, the usual course of action is to renew all of them as a set. **Note:** *While it is usual to renew piston rings when an engine is overhauled, they may be re-used if in acceptable condition. If re-using the rings, make sure that each ring is marked during removal to ensure that it is refitted correctly.*

4 Carefully expand the old rings over the top of the pistons. The use of two or three old feeler blades will be helpful in preventing the rings dropping into empty grooves **(see illustration)**. Be careful not to scratch the piston with the ends of the ring. The rings are brittle, and will snap if they are spread too far. They are also very sharp – protect your hands and fingers. Note that the third ring incorporates an expander. Keep each set of rings with its piston if the old rings are to be re-used. Note which way up each ring is fitted to ensure correct refitting.

5 Scrape away all traces of carbon from the top of the piston. A hand-held wire brush (or a piece of fine emery cloth) can be used, once the majority of the deposits have been scraped away.

6 Remove the carbon from the ring grooves in the piston, using an old ring. Break the ring in half to do this (be careful not to cut your fingers – piston rings are sharp). Be careful to remove only the carbon deposits – do not remove any metal, and do not nick or scratch the sides of the ring grooves.

7 Once the deposits have been removed, clean the piston/connecting rod assembly with paraffin or a suitable solvent, and dry thoroughly. Make sure that the oil return holes in the ring grooves are clear.

Inspection

8 If the pistons and cylinder bores are not damaged or worn excessively, and if the cylinder block does not need to be rebored, the original pistons can be refitted.

9 Using a micrometer, measure the diameter of all four pistons at a point 10 mm from the bottom of the skirt, at right-angles to the gudgeon pin axis **(see illustration)**. Compare the measurements with those listed in the Specifications. Note that the piston size grades are stamped on the piston crowns.

10 If the piston diameter is incorrect for its particular size, then it must be renewed. If the cylinder block was rebored during a previous overhaul, oversize pistons may already have been fitted. Record all of the measurements and use them to check the piston clearances against the cylinder bore measurements made in Section 11.

11 Normal piston wear shows up as even vertical wear on the piston thrust surfaces, and slight looseness of the top ring in its groove. New piston rings should always be used when the engine is reassembled.

12 Carefully inspect each piston for cracks around the skirt, around the gudgeon pin

12.4 Old feeler blades can be used to prevent piston rings from dropping into empty grooves

holes, and at the piston ring 'lands' (between the ring grooves).

13 Look for scoring and scuffing on the piston skirt, holes in the piston crown, and burned areas at the edge of the crown. If the skirt is scored or scuffed, the engine may have been suffering from overheating, and/or abnormal combustion which caused excessively high operating temperatures. The cooling and lubrication systems should be checked thoroughly.

14 Scorch marks on the sides of the pistons show that blow-by has occurred.

15 A hole in the piston crown, or burned areas at the edge of the piston crown, indicates that abnormal combustion (pre-ignition, knocking, or detonation) has been occurring.

16 If any of the above problems exist, the causes must be investigated and corrected, or the damage will occur again. The causes may include incorrect ignition/injection pump timing, intake air leaks or incorrect air/fuel mixture (petrol engines), or a faulty fuel injector (diesel engines).

17 Corrosion of the piston, in the form of pitting, indicates that coolant has been leaking into the combustion chamber and/or the crankcase. Again, the cause must be corrected, or the problem may persist in the rebuilt engine.

18 Locate a new piston ring in the appropriate groove and measure the ring-to-groove clearance using a feeler blade **(see illustration)**. Note that the rings are of different widths, so use the correct ring for the groove. Compare the measurements with those listed; if the clearances are outside of

12.9 Use a micrometer to measure the diameter of a piston

12.18 Measure the piston ring-to-groove clearance using a feeler blade

12.22a Use a small flat-bladed screwdriver to prise out the circlip . . .

12.22b . . . then push out the gudgeon pin and separate the piston and connecting rod

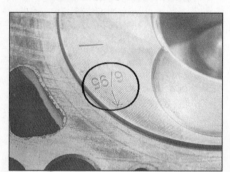

12.25a The piston crown arrow must point towards the timing belt end

12.25b The connecting rod and bearing cap recesses (arrowed) must face the timing belt end

with gudgeon pins and circlips. Circlips can also be purchased individually.

25 The orientation of the piston with respect to the connecting rod must be correct when the two are reassembled. The piston crown is marked with an arrow (which may be obscured by carbon deposits). The arrow must point towards the timing belt end of the engine when the piston is installed. The connecting rod and its bearing cap both have recesses machined into them on one side, close to their mating surfaces – these recesses must both face the same way as the arrow on the piston crown when correctly installed. Reassemble the two components to satisfy this requirement **(see illustrations)**.

26 Apply a smear of clean engine oil to the gudgeon pin. Slide it into the piston and through the connecting rod small-end. Check that the piston pivots freely on the rod, then secure the gudgeon pin in position with two new circlips. Ensure that each circlip is correctly located in its groove in the piston.

27 Repeat the cleaning and inspection process for the remaining pistons and connecting rods.

the tolerance band, then the piston must be renewed. Confirm this by checking the width of the piston ring with a micrometer.

19 New pistons can be purchased from a Seat dealer or engine reconditioning specialist.

20 Examine each connecting rod carefully for signs of damage, such as cracks around the big-end and small-end bearings. Check that the rod is not bent or distorted. Damage is highly unlikely, unless the engine has been seized or badly overheated. Detailed checking of the connecting rod assembly can only be carried out by a Seat dealer or engine repair specialist with the necessary equipment.

21 The gudgeon pins are of the floating type, secured in position by two circlips. The pistons and connecting rods can be separated as follows.

22 Using a small flat-bladed screwdriver, prise out the circlips, and push out the gudgeon

pin **(see illustrations)**. Hand pressure should be sufficient to remove the pin. Identify the piston and rod to ensure correct reassembly. Discard the circlips – new ones must be used on refitting. If the gudgeon pin proves difficult to remove, heat the piston to 60°C with hot water – the resulting expansion will then allow the two components to be separated.

23 Examine the gudgeon pin and connecting rod small-end bearing for signs of wear or damage. It should be possible to push the gudgeon pin through the connecting rod bush by hand, without noticeable play. Wear can be cured by renewing both the pin and bush. Bush renewal, however, is a specialist job – press facilities are required, and the new bush must be reamed accurately.

24 Examine all components, and obtain any new parts required. If new pistons are purchased, they will be supplied complete

13 Crankshaft (diesel engines) – checking endfloat and inspection

Checking endfloat

1 If the crankshaft endfloat is to be checked, this must be done when the crankshaft is still installed in the cylinder block/crankcase, but is free to move (see Section 10).

2 Check the endfloat using a dial gauge in contact with the end of the crankshaft. Push the crankshaft fully one way, and then zero the gauge. Push the crankshaft fully the other way, and check the endfloat. The result can be compared with the specified amount, and will give an indication as to whether new thrustwasher halves are required **(see illustration)**. Note that all thrustwashers must be of the same thickness.

3 If a dial gauge is not available, feeler blades can be used. First push the crankshaft fully towards the flywheel end of the engine, then use feeler blades to measure the gap between the web of No 3 crankpin and the thrustwasher halves **(see illustration)**.

13.2 Measure crankshaft endfloat using a dial gauge . . .

13.3 . . . or a set of feeler blades

Inspection

4 Clean the crankshaft using paraffin or a suitable solvent, and dry it, preferably with compressed air if available. Be sure to clean the oil holes with a pipe cleaner or similar probe, to ensure that they are not obstructed.

 Warning: Wear eye protection when using compressed air.

5 Have the crankshaft inspected by a Seat dealer or engine reconditioning specialist. They will have the measuring tools and the experience to accurately check the crankshaft, regrind the crankshaft (where possible), and supply the correct size of bearing shells.

6 Big-end bearing wear is accompanied by distinct metallic knocking when the engine is running (particularly noticeable when the engine is pulling from low speed) and some loss of oil pressure.

7 Main bearing wear is accompanied by severe engine vibration and rumble – getting progressively worse as engine speed increases – and again by loss of oil pressure.

14 Main and big-end bearings – inspection

Inspection

1 Even though the main and big-end bearings should be renewed during the engine overhaul, the old bearings should be retained for close examination, as they may reveal valuable information about the condition of the engine. The bearing shells are graded by thickness, the grade of each shell being indicated by the colour code marked on it.

2 Bearing failure can occur due to lack of lubrication, the presence of dirt or other foreign particles, overloading the engine, or corrosion **(see illustration)**. Regardless of the cause of bearing failure, the cause must be corrected (where applicable) before the engine is reassembled, to prevent it from happening again.

3 When examining the bearing shells, remove them from the cylinder block/crankcase, the connecting rods and the connecting rod big-end bearing caps. Lay them out on a clean surface in the same general position as their location in the engine. This will enable you to match any bearing problems with the corresponding crankshaft journal. *Do not* touch any shell's bearing surface with your fingers while checking it, or the delicate surface may be scratched.

4 Dirt and other foreign matter gets into the engine in a variety of ways. It may be left in the engine during assembly, or it may pass through filters or the crankcase ventilation system. It may get into the oil, and from there into the bearings. Metal chips from machining operations and normal engine wear are often present. Abrasives are sometimes left in engine components after reconditioning,

especially when parts are not thoroughly cleaned using the proper cleaning methods. Whatever the source, these foreign objects often end up embedded in the soft bearing material, and are easily recognised. Large particles will not embed in the bearing, and will score or gouge the bearing and journal. The best prevention for this cause of bearing failure is to clean all parts thoroughly, and keep everything spotlessly-clean during engine assembly. Frequent and regular engine oil and filter changes are also recommended.

5 Lack of lubrication (or lubrication breakdown) has a number of interrelated causes. Excessive heat (which thins the oil), overloading (which squeezes the oil from the bearing face) and oil leakage (from excessive bearing clearances, worn oil pump or high engine speeds) all contribute to lubrication breakdown. Blocked oil passages, which usually are the result of misaligned oil holes in a bearing shell, will also oil-starve a bearing, and destroy it. When lack of lubrication is the cause of bearing failure, the bearing material is wiped or extruded from the steel backing of the bearing. Temperatures may increase to the point where the steel backing turns blue from overheating.

6 Driving habits can have a definite effect on bearing life. Full-throttle, low-speed operation (labouring the engine) puts very high loads on bearings, tending to squeeze out the oil film. These loads cause the bearings to flex, which produces fine cracks in the bearing face (fatigue failure). Eventually, the bearing material will loosen in pieces, and tear away from the steel backing.

7 Short-distance driving leads to corrosion of bearings, because insufficient engine heat is produced to drive off the condensed water and corrosive gases. These products collect in the engine oil, forming acid and sludge. As the oil is carried to the engine bearings, the acid attacks and corrodes the bearing material.

8 Incorrect bearing installation during engine assembly will lead to bearing failure as well. Tight-fitting bearings leave insufficient bearing running clearance, and will result in oil starvation. Dirt or foreign particles trapped behind a bearing shell result in high spots on the bearing, which lead to failure.

9 *Do not* touch any shell's bearing surface with your fingers during reassembly; there is a risk of scratching the delicate surface, or of depositing particles of dirt on it.

10 As mentioned at the beginning of this Section, the bearing shells should be renewed as a matter of course during engine overhaul; to do otherwise is false economy.

15 Engine overhaul – reassembly sequence

1 Before reassembly begins, ensure that all new parts have been obtained, and that all necessary tools are available. Read through

the entire procedure to familiarise yourself with the work involved, and to ensure that all items necessary for reassembly of the engine are at hand. In addition to all normal tools and materials, thread-locking compound will be needed. A suitable tube of liquid sealant will also be required for the joint faces that are fitted without gaskets.

2 In order to save time and avoid problems, engine reassembly can be carried out in the following order, referring to Part A, B or C of this Chapter. Where applicable, use new gaskets and seals when refitting the various components.

a) Crankshaft (Section 17).
b) Piston/connecting rod assemblies (Section 18).
c) Oil pump.
d) Sump.
e) Flywheel/driveplate.
f) Cylinder head.
g) Timing chain/belt(s), tensioner and sprockets.
h) Intake and exhaust manifolds.
i) Engine external components.

3 At this stage, all engine components should be absolutely clean and dry, with all faults repaired. The components should be laid out (or in individual containers) on a completely clean work surface.

16 Piston rings – refitting

1 Before fitting new piston rings, the ring end gaps must be checked as follows.

2 Lay out the piston/connecting rod assemblies and the new piston ring sets, so that the ring sets will be matched with the same piston and cylinder during the end gap measurement and subsequent engine reassembly.

14.2 Typical bearing failures

16.4 Check the piston ring end gaps using a feeler blade

16.9 Piston ring TOP marking

3 Insert the top ring into the first cylinder, and push it down the bore using the top of the piston. This will ensure that the ring remains square with the cylinder walls. Position the ring approximately 15.0 mm the bottom of the cylinder bore, at the lower limit of ring travel. Note that the top and second compression rings are different.

4 Measure the end gap using feeler blades, and compare the measurements with the figures given in the Specifications **(see illustration)**.

5 If the gap is too small (unlikely if genuine Seat parts are used), it must be enlarged, or the ring ends may contact each other during engine operation, causing serious damage. Ideally, new piston rings providing the correct end gap should be fitted. As a last resort, the end gap can be increased by filing the ring

ends very carefully with a fine file. Mount the file in a vice equipped with soft jaws, slip the ring over the file with the ends contacting the file face, and slowly move the ring to remove material from the ends. Take care, as piston rings are sharp, and are easily broken.

6 With new piston rings, it is unlikely that the end gap will be too large. If the gaps are too large, check that you have the correct rings for your engine and for the particular cylinder bore size.

7 Repeat the checking procedure for each ring in the first cylinder, and then for the rings in the remaining cylinders. Remember to keep rings, pistons and cylinders matched up.

8 Once the ring end gaps have been checked and if necessary corrected, the rings can be fitted to the pistons.

9 Fit the piston rings using the same technique as for removal. Fit the bottom (oil control)

ring first, and work up. Note that a two- or three-section oil control ring may be fitted; where a two-section ring is fitted, first insert the wire expander, then fit the ring. Ensure that the rings are fitted the correct way up – the top surface of the rings is normally marked TOP **(see illustration)**. Offset the piston ring gaps by 120° from each other. Always follow any instructions supplied with the new piston ring sets – different manufacturers may specify different procedures. Do not mix up the top and second compression rings, as they have different cross-sections.

17 Crankshaft (diesel engines) – refitting

Selection of new bearing shells

1 Have the crankshaft inspected and measured by a Seat dealer or automotive engineering workshop. They will be able to carry out any regrinding/repairs, and supply suitable main and big-end bearing shells.

Crankshaft refitting

2 Where applicable, refit the speed/position sensor wheel to the crankshaft, and tighten the securing bolts to the specified torque. Make sure that the sensor wheel is correctly orientated as noted before removal.

3 Liberally coat the bearing shells in the crankcase with clean engine oil of the appropriate grade **(see illustrations)**. Make sure that the bearing shells are correctly seated in their locations.

4 Lower the crankshaft into position so that No 1 cylinder crankpin is at BDC, ready for fitting No 1 piston. Ensure that the crankshaft endfloat control thrustwasher halves, either side of the No 3 main bearing location, remain in position. Where applicable, take care not to damage the crankshaft speed/position sensor wheel as the crankshaft is lowered into position.

5 Lubricate the lower bearing shells in the main bearing caps with clean engine oil. Make sure that the crankshaft endfloat control thrustwasher halves are correctly seated either side of No 3 bearing cap **(see illustrations)**.

6 Fit the main bearing cap(s) in the correct location and orientation – where applicable, No 1 bearing cap must be at the timing end of the engine and the bearing shell tab locating recesses in the crankcase and bearing caps must be adjacent to each other **(see illustration)**. Insert new bearing cap bolts, and hand-tighten them only.

7 Working from the centre bearing cap outwards, tighten the bearing cap bolts to their specified torque. Tighten all bolts to the Stage 1 torque, then go round again, and tighten all bolts through the Stage 2 angle **(see illustrations)**.

8 Check that the crankshaft rotates freely by turning it by hand.

17.3a Bearing shell correctly refitted

A *Recess in cylinder block*
B *Lug on bearing shell*
C *Oil hole*

17.3b Lubricate the upper bearing shells

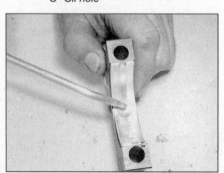

17.5a Lubricate the lower bearing shells . . .

17.5b . . . and make sure that the thrustwashers are correctly seated

17.6 Fit No 1 main bearing cap

17.7a Tighten the main bearing cap bolts to the specified torque . . .

17.7b . . . then through the specified angle

9 Check the crankshaft endfloat as described at the beginning of Section 13. If the thrust surfaces of the crankshaft have been checked and new thrustwashers have been fitted, then the endfloat should be within specification.

10 Refit the pistons and connecting rods or reconnect them to the crankshaft as described in Section 18.

11 Refit the crankshaft oil seal housings, flywheel, oil pump and pick-up pipe, sump and oil baffle plate, crankshaft sprocket and timing belt as described in Chapter 2C.

18 Piston/connecting rod assemblies – refitting and big-end bearing clearance check

Note: A piston ring compressor tool will be required for this operation.

Selection of bearing shells

1 There are a number of sizes of big-end bearing shell produced by Seat; a standard size for use with the standard crankshaft, and oversizes for use once the crankshaft journals have been reground.

2 Have the crankshaft inspected and measured by a Seat dealer or automotive engineering workshop. They will be able to carry out any regrinding/repairs, and supply suitable big-end bearing shells.

Piston/connecting rods refitting

3 Note that the following procedure assumes that the crankshaft main bearing caps are in place.

4 Where applicable, refit the piston cooling oil spray jets to the bottom of the cylinder block, and tighten the securing bolts to the specified torque.

5 On engines where the big-end bearing caps are secured by nuts, renew the bolts/ studs in the connecting rods. Tap the old bolts/studs out of the connecting rods using a soft-faced mallet, and tap the new bolts/studs into position. On engines where the caps are secured by bolts, renew the bolts.

6 Ensure that the bearing shells are correctly fitted. If new shells are being fitted, ensure that all traces of the protective grease are cleaned off using paraffin. Wipe dry the shells and connecting rods with a lint-free cloth.

7 Lubricate the cylinder bores, the pistons, piston rings and upper bearing shells with clean engine oil (see illustrations). Lay out each piston/connecting rod assembly in order on a clean work surface. Where the bearing caps are secured with nuts, pad the threaded ends of the bolts with insulating tape to prevent them scratching the crankpins and bores when the pistons are refitted.

8 Start with piston/connecting rod assembly No 1. Make sure that the piston rings are still spaced as described in Section 16, then clamp them in position with a piston ring compressor tool.

9 Insert the piston/connecting rod assembly into the top of No 1 cylinder. Lower the big-end in first, guiding it to protect the cylinder bores. Where oil jets are located at the bottoms of the bores, take particular care not to damage them when guiding the connecting rods onto the crankpins.

18.7a Lubricate the pistons . . .

18.7b . . . and big-end upper bearing shells with clean engine oil

18.10 Piston orientation and coding on diesel engines – for 3-cylinder engine use 1 to 3

10 Ensure that the orientation of the piston in its cylinder is correct – refer to Section 12 for details. On diesel engines, the piston crowns are specially shaped to improve the engine's combustion characteristics. Because of this, pistons 1 and 2 are different to pistons 3 and 4. When correctly fitted, the larger intake valve chambers on pistons 1 and 2 must face the flywheel end of the engine, and the larger intake valve chambers on the remaining pistons must face the timing belt end of the engine. Note that on the 3-cylinder engine, the pattern follows that of cylinders 1, 2 and 3. New pistons have number markings on their crowns to indicate their type – 1/2 denotes piston 1 or 2, 3/4 indicates piston 3 or 4 (see illustration).

11 Using a block of wood or hammer handle against the piston crown, tap the assembly into the cylinder until the piston crown is flush with the top of the cylinder (see illustration).

18.11 Use a hammer handle to tap the piston into its bore

18.15a Tighten the big-end bearing cap bolts/nuts to the specified torque . . .

18.15b . . . then through the specified angle

12 Ensure that the bearing shell is still correctly installed in the connecting rod, then liberally lubricate the crankpin and both bearing shells with clean engine oil.

13 Taking care not to mark the cylinder bores, tap the piston/connecting rod assembly down the bore and onto the crankpin. On engines where the big-end caps are secured by nuts, remove the insulating tape from the threaded ends of the connecting rod bolts. Oil the bolt threads, and on engines where the big-end caps are secured by bolts, oil the undersides of the bolt heads.

14 Fit the big-end bearing cap, tightening its new retaining nuts or bolts (as applicable) finger-tight at first. On diesel engines, the connecting rod and its bearing cap both have recesses machined into them on one side, close to their mating surfaces – these recesses must both face the same way as the arrow on the piston crown (ie, towards the timing belt end of the engine) when correctly installed. Reassemble the two components to satisfy this requirement.

15 Tighten the retaining bolts or nuts to the specified torque and angle as given in the Specifications **(see illustrations)**.

16 Refit the remaining piston/connecting rod assemblies in the same way.

17 Rotate the crankshaft by hand. Check that it turns freely; some stiffness is to be expected if new parts have been fitted, but there should be no binding or tight spots.

18 On diesel engines, if new pistons have been fitted, or if a new short engine has been fitted, the projection of the piston crowns above the cylinder head mating face of the cylinder block at TDC must be measured. This measurement is used to determine the

thickness of the new cylinder head gasket required. This procedure is described as part of the *Cylinder head – removal, inspection and refitting procedure* in Chapter 2C.

19 Proceed as follows according to engine type:

a) *On the 3-cylinder diesel engine, refit the balancer shaft assembly as described in Chapter 2C.*

b) *On the 1.4 litre petrol engine and all diesel engines, refit the oil pump pick-up pipe and oil baffle, the sump and the cylinder head as described in Chapters 2B or 2C.*

19 Engine – initial start-up after overhaul and reassembly

1 Refit the remainder of the engine components in the order listed in Section 5 of this Chapter. Refit the engine to the vehicle as described in Section 4 of this Chapter. Double-check the engine oil and coolant levels, and make a final check that everything has been reconnected. Make sure that there are no tools or rags left in the engine compartment.

2 Reconnect the battery negative lead as described in Chapter 5A.

Petrol models

3 Remove the spark plugs, referring to Chapter 1A for details.

4 The engine must be immobilised such that it can be turned over using the starter motor, without starting – refer to Section 2 of Chapter 2A or 2B.

Caution: To prevent damage to the catalytic converter, it is important to disable the fuel system.

5 Turn the engine using the starter motor until the oil pressure warning light goes out. If the light fails to extinguish after several seconds of cranking, check the engine oil level and oil filter security. Assuming these are correct, check the security of the oil pressure switch wiring – do not progress any further until you are satisfied that oil is being pumped around the engine at sufficient pressure.

6 Refit the spark plugs, and refit the fuses.

Diesel models

7 Disconnect the injector solenoids by disconnecting the connector at the end of the cylinder head. **Note:** *As a result of the wiring being disconnected, faults may be stored in the ECM memory. These must be erased after starting the engine.*

8 Turn the engine using the starter motor until the oil pressure warning light goes out.

9 If the light fails to extinguish after several seconds of cranking, check the engine oil level and oil filter security. Assuming these are correct, check the security of the oil pressure switch cabling – do not progress any further until you are satisfied that oil is being pumped around the engine at sufficient pressure.

10 Reconnect the wiring as applicable.

All models

11 Start the engine, but be aware that as fuel system components have been disturbed, the cranking time may be a little longer than usual.

12 While the engine is idling, check for fuel, water and oil leaks. Don't be alarmed if there are some odd smells and the occasional plume of smoke as components heat up and burn off oil deposits.

13 Assuming all is well, keep the engine idling until hot water is felt circulating through the top hose.

14 After a few minutes, stop the engine then recheck the oil and coolant levels, and top-up as necessary.

15 There is no need to retighten the cylinder head bolts once the engine has been run following reassembly.

16 If new pistons, rings or crankshaft bearings have been fitted, the engine must be treated as new, and run-in for the first 600 miles. *Do not operate the engine at full-throttle, or allow it to labour at low engine speeds in any gear.* It is recommended that the engine oil and filter are changed at the end of this period.

Chapter 3
Cooling, heating and ventilation systems

Contents

Degrees of difficulty

Easy, suitable for novice with little experience	**Fairly easy,** suitable for beginner with some experience	**Fairly difficult,** suitable for competent DIY mechanic	**Difficult,** suitable for experienced DIY mechanic	**Very difficult,** suitable for expert DIY or professional

Specifications

Cooling system pressure cap
Opening pressure . . . . 1.4 to 1.6 bar

Thermostat

Petrol engines
1.2 litre engines . . . . N/A
1.4 litre engines:
  Begins to open . . . . 84°C
  Fully open . . . . 98°C

Diesel engines
1.4 litre engines:
  Begins to open . . . . 85°C
  Fully open . . . . 105°C
1.9 litre engines . . . . N/A

Cooling fan
Fan speeds:
  1st speed cut-in . . . . 91 to 97°C
  1st speed cut-out . . . . 91 to 84°C
  2nd speed cut-in . . . . 99 to 105°C
  2nd speed cut-out . . . . 98 to 91°C

Coolant temperature sensor
Resistances:
  At 30°C . . . . 1500 to 2000 ohms
  At 80°C . . . . 275 to 375 ohms

Torque wrench settings

	Nm	lbf ft
Air conditioning condenser	5	4
Coolant pump:		
1.2 litre petrol engines	24	18
1.4 litre petrol engines	20	15
Diesel engines	15	11
Coolant pump pulley (1.2 litre petrol engines)	22	16
Distribution housing (diesel engines)	10	7
Radiator	5	4
Radiator cooling fan shroud bolts	10	7
Radiator cooling fan thermo-switch	35	26
Thermostat cover (diesel engines)	15	11
Thermostat/distribution housing:		
1.2 litre petrol engines	8	6
1.4 litre petrol engines	10	7
Timing belt guide pulley:		
1.4 litre petrol engines	50	37

1 General information and precautions

The cooling system comprises a centrifugal pump, crossflow radiator, electric cooling fan, thermostat and a heater matrix, as well as the interconnecting hoses. The system functions as follows. Cold coolant from the radiator passes through the bottom hose to the coolant pump where it is pumped around the cylinder block and head passages. After cooling the cylinder bores, combustion surfaces and valve seats, the coolant reaches the top of the engine and passes through the top hose to the radiator. The coolant also passes through the heater matrix where it heats incoming air to the inside of the car.

When the engine is cold the coolant circulation is restricted to the cylinder block, cylinder head, expansion tank, and heater by a thermostat positioned in the radiator circuit. On petrol engines the thermostat is located in the coolant distribution housing on the left-hand end of the cylinder head, however, on diesel engines it is located in the coolant return on the front of the cylinder block. When the coolant reaches a predetermined temperature, the wax-filled thermostat opens and the coolant passes through to the radiator.

2.4 Pull out the retaining clip

As the coolant circulates through the radiator it is cooled by the inrush of air when the car is in forward motion. Airflow is supplemented by the action of the electric cooling fan(s) when necessary. Upon leaving the radiator, the coolant has cooled and the cycle is repeated.

A thermostatic switch controls the electric cooling fan(s) mounted on the rear of the radiator. At a preset coolant temperature, the switch actuates the fan(s).

⚠️ *Warning: Do not attempt to remove the expansion tank filler cap or disturb any part of the cooling system while the engine is hot, as there is a high risk of scalding. If the expansion tank filler cap must be removed before the engine and radiator have fully cooled (even though this is not recommended) the pressure in the cooling system must first be relieved. Cover the cap with a thick layer of cloth, to avoid scalding, and slowly unscrew the filler cap until a hissing sound can be heard. When the hissing has stopped, indicating that the pressure has reduced, slowly unscrew the filler cap until it can be removed; if more hissing sounds are heard, wait until they have stopped before unscrewing the cap completely. At all times keep well away from the filler cap opening.*

• *Do not allow antifreeze to come into contact with skin or the car's painted surfaces. Rinse off spills immediately with plenty of water. Never leave antifreeze lying around in an open container or in a puddle in the driveway or on the garage floor. Children and pets are attracted by its sweet smell. Antifreeze can be fatal if ingested.*

• *If the engine is hot, the electric cooling fan may start rotating even if the engine is not running, so be careful to keep hands, hair and loose clothing well clear when working in the engine compartment.*

• *Refer to Section 8 for additional precautions to be observed when working on models with air conditioning.*

2 Cooling system hoses – disconnection and renewal

Note: *Refer to the warnings given in Section 1 of this Chapter before proceeding.*

1 If the checks described in the relevant part of Chapter 1 reveal a faulty hose, it must be renewed as follows.

2 First drain the cooling system as described in Chapter 1A or 1B. If the coolant is not due for renewal, it may be re-used if it is collected in a clean container.

3 To disconnect a hose, release its retaining clips, and then move them along the hose, clear of the relevant inlet/outlet union. Carefully work the hose free.

4 In order to disconnect the radiator inlet and outlet hoses, apply pressure to hold the hose on to the relevant union, pull out the spring clip and pull the hose from the union **(see illustration)**. Note that the radiator inlet and outlet unions are fragile; do not use excessive force when attempting to remove the hoses. If a hose proves to be difficult to remove, try to release it by rotating the hose ends before attempting to free it.

HAYNES HiNT *If all else fails, cut the hose with a sharp knife, then slit it so that it can be peeled off in two pieces. Although this may prove expensive if the hose is otherwise undamaged, it is preferable to buying a new radiator.*

5 When fitting a hose, first slide the clips onto the hose, then work the hose into position. If clamp type clips were originally fitted, it is a good idea to use screw-type clips when refitting the hose. If the hose is stiff, use a little soapy water as a lubricant, or soften the hose by soaking it in hot water.

6 Work the hose into position, checking that it is correctly routed, then slide each clip along the hose until it passes over the flared end of the relevant union, before securing it in position with the retaining clip.

7 Prior to refitting a radiator inlet or outlet hose, renew the connection O-ring regardless of condition. The connections are a push-fit over the radiator unions.

8 Refill the cooling system as described in Chapter 1A or 1B.

9 Check thoroughly for leaks as soon as possible after disturbing any part of the cooling system.

3 Radiator – removal, inspection and refitting

Removal

1 Disconnect the battery negative lead as described in Chapter 5A.

2 Drain the cooling system as described in the relevant part of Chapter 1.

3 Disconnect the wiring from the cooling fan thermo-switch and the cooling fan **(see illustration)**.

4 Disconnect the upper and lower hoses from the left-hand side of the radiator. To do so, pull out the spring clip, then ease the hoses from the stubs **(see illustration)**.

Models without air conditioning

5 Remove the front bumper and crossmember with reference to Chapter 11.

6 On diesel models, remove the intercooler as described in Chapter 4C, and disconnect the intake pipe from the lock carrier panel.

7 Undo the 2 bolts and detach the bonnet lock and cable from the lock carrier.

8 Remove both headlights as described in Chapter 12.

9 Unbolt the lock carrier and radiator and remove from the front of the car.

10 Unbolt the radiator from the lock carrier, then unbolt the cooling fan and shroud from the radiator.

Models with air conditioning

11 Disconnect the wiring from the air conditioning compressor, then unbolt it and tie it to the lock carrier. Do not disconnect the refrigerant lines.

12 Remove the front bumper and cross-member with reference to Chapter 11.

13 On diesel models, remove the intercooler as described in Chapter 4C, and disconnect the air intake pipe from the lock carrier panel.

14 Undo the 2 bolts and detach the bonnet lock and cable from the lock carrier.

15 Remove both headlights as described in Chapter 12.

16 Unbolt the lock carrier from the inner wing each side, and from the radiator **(see illustrations)**. Swivel the lock carrier panel out from the front of the car, leaving the condenser and radiator in place. Support the assembly on axle stands or blocks of wood.

17 Unbolt the condenser from the radiator,

3.3 Disconnect the thermo-switch wiring

3.4 Disconnect the top hose from the radiator

3.16a Undo the bolts (arrowed) each side retaining the lock carrier panel . . .

and the refrigerant pipe clips from the radiator, then lower the radiator to the floor and tie the condenser to the inner body with cable ties **(see illustration)**.

18 Unbolt the cooling fan and shroud from the radiator.

Inspection

19 If the radiator has been removed due to suspected blockage, reverse flush it as described in the relevant part of Chapter 1.

20 Clean dirt and debris from the radiator fins, using an airline (in which case, wear eye protection) or a soft brush. Be careful, as the fins are sharp and easily damaged.

21 If necessary, a radiator specialist can perform a 'flow test' on the radiator, to establish whether an internal blockage exists.

22 A leaking radiator must be referred to a specialist for permanent repair. Do not attempt

3.17 Undo the bolts (arrowed) each side securing the condenser to the radiator

3.16b . . . and the bolts (arrowed) securing the radiator to the lock carrier panel

to weld or solder a leaking radiator, as damage may result.

23 If the radiator is to be sent for repair or renewed, remove the cooling fan and thermo-switch.

Refitting

24 Refitting is a reversal of removal, but check the condition of the mounting rubbers and renew if necessary **(see illustration)**. On completion, refill the cooling system using the correct type of antifreeze as described in the relevant part of Chapter 1.

4 Thermostat – removal, testing and refitting

1 As the thermostat ages, it may become slower to react to changes in water temperature ('lazy'). Ultimately, the unit may

3.24 Check the radiator mounting rubbers each side

4.15 Remove the coolant distribution housing from the cylinder block

4.19 Disconnect the hose

4.20 Remove and discard the seal

stick in the open or closed position, and this causes problems. A thermostat which is stuck open will result in a very slow warm-up; a thermostat which is stuck shut will lead to rapid overheating.

2 Before assuming the thermostat is to blame for a cooling system problem, check the coolant level. If the system is draining due to a leak, or has not been properly filled, there may be an airlock in the system (refer to the coolant renewal procedure in Chapter 1A or 1B).

3 If the engine seems to be taking a long time to warm up (based on heater output), the thermostat could be stuck open. Don't necessarily believe the temperature gauge reading – some gauges never seem to register very high in normal driving.

4 A lengthy warm-up period might suggest that the thermostat is missing - it may have been removed or inadvertently omitted by a previous owner or mechanic. Don't drive the car without a thermostat – the engine management system's ECM will then stay in warm-up mode for longer than necessary, causing emissions and fuel economy to suffer.

5 If the engine runs hot, use your hand to check the temperature of the radiator top hose. If the hose isn't hot, but the engine clearly is, the thermostat is probably stuck closed, preventing the coolant inside the engine from escaping to the radiator – renew the thermostat. Again, this problem may also be due to an airlock (refer to the coolant renewal procedure in Chapter 1A or 1B).

6 If the radiator top hose is hot, it means that the coolant is flowing (at least as far as the

radiator) and the thermostat is open. Consult the *Fault diagnosis* section at the end of this manual to assist in tracing possible cooling system faults, but a lack of heater output would now definitely suggest an airlock or a blockage.

7 To gain a rough idea of whether the thermostat is working properly when the engine is warming up, without dismantling the system, proceed as follows.

8 With the engine completely cold, start the engine and let it idle, while checking the temperature of the radiator top hose. Periodically check the temperature indicated on the coolant temperature gauge – if overheating is indicated, switch the engine off immediately.

9 The top hose should feel cold for some time as the engine warms up, and should then get warm quite quickly as the thermostat opens.

10 The above is not a precise or definitive test of thermostat operation, but if the system does not perform as described, remove and test the thermostat as described below.

Removal

1.2 litre petrol engines

11 The thermostat is integral with the coolant distribution housing bolted to the left-hand end of the cylinder block. If it is faulty, the complete housing must be renewed.

12 Drain the cooling system as described in Chapter 1A.

13 To provide working room, remove the battery, air cleaner and ducting as described in Chapter 5A and 4A.

14 Loosen the clips and disconnect the hoses from the distribution housing.

15 Unscrew the mounting bolts and withdraw the housing from the distribution housing and intermediate coolant pipe on the rear of the engine **(see illustration)**. Recover the O-ring.

16 As the thermostat is integral with the distribution housing, it is not possible to test it by heating in water in the conventional way. Symptoms of a faulty thermostat will be overheating if it sticks in the closed position, or slow warm-up if it sticks in the open position.

1.4 litre petrol engines

17 The thermostat is located beneath a cover in a housing on the left-hand end of the cylinder head.

18 Drain the cooling system as described in Chapter 1A.

19 Release the retaining clip and disconnect the coolant radiator bottom hose from the thermostat cover **(see illustration)**.

20 Unscrew the retaining bolts and remove the thermostat housing cover and sealing ring from the engine. Discard the sealing ring; a new one must be used on refitting **(see illustration)**.

21 Remove the thermostat from the housing **(see illustration)**. Note that the thermostat is only available together with its spring housing.

Diesel engines

22 The thermostat is located beneath a cover on the front of the engine, in the coolant return from the bottom of the radiator.

23 Drain the cooling system as described in Chapter 1A.

24 Release the retaining clip and disconnect the coolant hose from the thermostat cover.

25 Unscrew the retaining bolts and remove the thermostat housing cover and sealing ring from the engine **(see illustrations)**. Discard the sealing ring; a new one must be used on refitting.

26 To remove the thermostat from the cover, twist the thermostat 90° anti-clockwise, and pull it from the cover.

Testing

Note: *Frankly, if there is any question about the operation of the thermostat, it's best to renew it – they are not expensive items. Testing involves heating in, or over, an open pan of boiling water, which carries with it the*

4.21 Remove the thermostat

4.25a Thermostat cover bolts (arrowed) . . .

4.25b . . . and thermostat – diesel engines

5.9 Remove the cooling fan and shroud from the radiator

risk of scalding. A thermostat which has seen more than five years' service may well be past its best already.

27 If the thermostat remains in the open position at room temperature, it is faulty, and must be renewed as a matter of course.

28 Check to see if there's an open temperature marking stamped on the thermostat.

29 Using a thermometer and container of water, heat the water until the temperature corresponds with the temperature marking stamped on the thermostat. If no marking is found, start the test with the water hot, and heat slowly until it boils.

30 Suspend the (closed) thermostat on a length of string in the water, and check that maximum opening occurs within two minutes, or before the water boils.

31 Remove the thermostat and allow it to cool down; check that it closes fully.

32 If the thermostat does not open and close as described, or if it sticks in either position, it must be renewed.

Refitting

Petrol engines

33 Refitting is a reversal of removal, noting the following points:

a) On 1.4 litre engines, use a new sealing ring.

b) Refill the cooling system with the correct type and quantity of coolant as described in Chapter 1A.

Diesel engines

34 Refitting is a reversal of removal, bearing in mind the following points:

a) Refit the thermostat using a new O-ring.

b) Insert the thermostat into the cover and twist 90° clockwise.

c) The thermostat should be fitted with the brace almost vertical.

d) Ensure that any brackets are in place on the thermostat cover bolts as noted before removal.

e) Refill the cooling system with the correct type and quantity of coolant as described in Chapter 1B.

---

5 Electric cooling fan –
testing, removal and refitting

Testing

1 One or two cooling fans may be fitted, depending on model. The cooling fan is supplied with current through the ignition switch, cooling fan control unit (where applicable), the relay(s) and fuses/fusible link (see Chapter 12). The circuit is completed by the cooling fan thermostatic switch, which is mounted in the left-hand end of the radiator. The cooling fan has two speed settings; the thermostatic switch actually contains two switches, one for the stage 1 fan speed setting and another for the stage 2 fan speed setting. Testing of the cooling fan circuit is as follows, noting that the following check should be carried out on both the stage 1 speed circuit and speed 2 circuit (see wiring diagrams at the end of Chapter 12).

2 If a fan does not appear to work, first check the fuses/fusible links. If they are good, run the engine until normal operating temperature is reached, then allow it to idle. If the fan does not cut in within a few minutes, switch off the ignition and disconnect the wiring plug from the cooling fan switch. Bridge the relevant two contacts in the wiring plug using a length of spare wire, and switch on the ignition. If the fan now operates, the switch is probably faulty and should be renewed.

3 If the switch appears to work, the motor can be checked by disconnecting the motor wiring connector and connecting a 12-volt supply directly to the motor terminals. If the motor is faulty, it must be renewed, as no spares are available.

4 If the fan still fails to operate, check the cooling fan circuit wiring (Chapter 12). Check each wire for continuity and ensure that all connections are clean and free of corrosion.

5 On models with a cooling fan control unit, if no fault can be found with the fuses/fusible

links, wiring, fan switch, or fan motor, then it is likely that the cooling fan control unit is faulty. Testing of the unit should be entrusted to a Seat dealer or specialist; if the unit is faulty it must be renewed.

Removal

6 Disconnect the battery negative lead as described in Chapter 5A.

7 Remove the engine top cover.

8 Disconnect the wiring plug from the cooling fan motor, and slide the connector from the retaining bracket.

9 Unscrew the bolts and remove the cooling fan and shroud from the radiator **(see illustration)**. Take care not to damage the radiator fins.

10 Undo the three Torx bolts securing the fan to the radiator shroud, and withdraw the fan.

Refitting

11 Refitting is a reversal of removal.

---

6 Cooling system electrical switches and sensors –
testing, removal and refitting

Cooling fan thermostatic switch

Testing

1 Testing of the switch is described in Section 5, as part of the electric cooling fan test procedure.

Removal

2 The thermo-switch is located in the left-hand side of the radiator. The engine and radiator must be cold before removing the switch.

3 Disconnect the battery negative lead as described in Chapter 5A. Where necessary, remove the engine top cover.

4 Either drain the radiator to below the level of the switch (as described in Chapter 1A or 1B), or have ready a suitable plug which can be used to plug the switch aperture in the radiator whilst the switch is removed. If a plug is used, take great care not to damage

6.6 Unscrew the thermo-switch

6.9 Coolant temperature sensor (arrowed) – diesel engine

the radiator, and do not use anything which will allow foreign matter to enter the radiator.
5 Disconnect the wiring plug from the thermo-switch.
6 Carefully unscrew the thermo-switch from the radiator (see illustration).

Refitting

7 Refitting is a reversal of removal, but apply a smear of suitable grease to the threads of the switch and tighten it to the specified torque. On completion, refill the cooling system with the correct type and quantity of coolant as described in Chapter 1A or 1B, or top-up as described in Weekly checks.
8 Start the engine and run it until it reaches normal operating temperature, then continue to run the engine and check that the cooling fan cuts in and functions correctly.

Coolant temperature sensor

Testing

9 The coolant temperature sensor is located on the coolant distribution housing on the left-hand end of the cylinder head. On petrol engines it is on the top or front of the housing, and on diesel engines it is on the rear of the housing (see illustration).
10 The sensor contains a thermistor, which consists of an electronic component whose electrical resistance decreases at a predetermined rate as its temperature rises. When the coolant is cold, the sensor resistance is high, current flow through the gauge is reduced, and the gauge needle points towards the 'cold' end of the scale. Typical resistances are given in the Specifications, however, the

sensor can also be checked by a Seat dealer or specialist using diagnostic equipment. If the sensor is faulty, it must be renewed.

Removal and refitting

11 Remove the engine top cover.
12 Disconnect the wiring plug from the sensor, located on the thermostat housing at the left-hand end of the cylinder head. Partially drain the cooling system to below the level of the sensor (as described in Chapter 1A or 1B).
13 Carefully withdraw the retaining clip and pull the sensor from the housing. Recover the O-ring.
14 Refitting is a reversal of removal, bearing in mind the following points:
   a) Refit the sensor with a new O-ring.
   b) Refill the cooling system as described in Chapter 1A or 1B, or top-up as described in 'Weekly checks'.

| 7 | Coolant pump – removal and refitting |

Note: New coolant pumps may be of a modified design, which do not require gaskets. Use a suitable sealer.

1.2 litre petrol engines

Removal

1 Drain the cooling system as described in Chapter 1A.
2 Before removing the auxiliary drivebelt, loosen the coolant pump pulley mounting bolts.

3 Remove the auxiliary drivebelt as described in Chapter 1A.
4 Fully unscrew the bolts and remove the pulley from the coolant pump (see illustration).
5 Unscrew the coolant pump retaining bolts, and withdraw the pump and gasket (if fitted) from the engine block. Identify the front retaining bolt, as it has sealant on its threads. If faulty, the pump must be renewed (see illustration).

Refitting

6 Refitting is a reversal of removal, bearing in mind the following points:
   a) Refit the pump using a new gasket (refer to note above).
   b) Apply suitable sealant to the threads of the front retaining bolt.
   c) Refill the cooling system as described in Chapter 1A.

1.4 litre petrol engines

Removal

7 Remove the main timing belt as described in Chapter 2B. If the belt is to be re-used, note the direction of rotation.
8 Remove the timing belt idler roller, and rear timing belt cover.
9 Unscrew the coolant pump retaining bolts, and withdraw the pump from the engine block. Note the gasket is integral with the pump and must not be removed. If faulty, the pump must be renewed (see illustration).

Refitting

10 Refitting is a reversal of removal, bearing in mind the following points:
   a) Clean the surface of the engine block before refitting the pump.
   b) Refill the cooling system as described in Chapter 1A.

Diesel engines

Removal

11 Drain the cooling system as described in Chapter 1B.
12 Remove the timing belt as described in Chapter 2C, noting the following points:
   a) The lower part of the timing belt guard need not be removed.
   b) The timing belt should be left in position on the crankshaft sprocket.

7.4 Undo the bolts and remove the coolant pump pulley – 1.2 litre engine

7.5 Remove the coolant pump – 1.2 litre petrol engine

7.9 Withdraw the coolant pump – 1.4 litre petrol engine

7.13a Coolant pump – 4-cylinder diesel engine

7.13b Coolant pump – 3-cylinder diesel engine

c) Cover the timing belt with a cloth to protect it from coolant.

13 Unscrew the coolant pump retaining bolts, and remove the pump and O-ring seal from the engine block. If the pump is faulty, it must be renewed (see illustrations).

Refitting

14 Refitting is a reversal of removal, bearing in mind the following points:
a) Fit the coolant pump with a new O-ring, lubricated with a little coolant.
b) Install the pump with the cast lug facing down.
c) Refill the cooling system as described in Chapter 1B.

8 Heating/air conditioning system – general information and precautions

Heating system

1 The heating/ventilation system consists of a four-speed blower motor (housed in the passenger compartment), face-level vents in the centre and at each end of the facia, and air ducts to the front and rear footwells.

2 The control unit is located in the facia, and the controls operate flap valves to deflect and mix the air flowing through the various parts of the heating/ventilation system. The flap valves are contained in the air distribution housing which acts as a central distribution unit, passing air to the various ducts and vents.

3 Cold air enters the system through the grille at the rear of the engine compartment. A pollen filter is fitted in the heater assembly to filter out dust, soot, pollen and spores from the air entering the car.

4 If warm air is required, the cold air is passed over the heater matrix, which is effectively a small radiator, with engine coolant flowing through it. Diesel models are fitted with an additional electric heating element below the matrix, to ensure quick heater output –

this heating element only operates when the coolant temperature is below 80°C.

5 The airflow, which can be boosted by the blower, then flows through the various ducts, according to the settings of the controls. Stale air is expelled through ducts below the rear window.

6 If necessary, the outside air supply can be closed off, allowing the air inside the car to be recirculated. This can be useful to prevent unpleasant odours entering from outside the car, but should only be used briefly as the recirculated air quality inside the car will soon deteriorate.

Air conditioning system

7 Air conditioning is fitted as standard to all but the most basic-specification UK models. It enables the temperature of incoming air to be lowered, and dehumidifies the air, which makes for rapid demisting and increased comfort. One of two systems may be fitted – the semi-automatic Climatic, or the optional fully-automatic Climatronic, which has an LCD display.

8 The cooling side of the system works in the same way as a domestic refrigerator. Refrigerant gas is drawn into a belt-driven compressor and passes into a condenser mounted in front of the radiator, where it loses heat and becomes liquid. The liquid passes through an expansion valve to an evaporator, where it changes from liquid under high pressure to gas under low pressure. This change is accompanied by a drop in temperature, which cools the evaporator. The refrigerant returns to the compressor and the cycle begins again.

9 Air blown through the evaporator passes to the air distribution unit, where it is mixed with hot air blown through the heater matrix (and heating element, where applicable) to achieve the desired temperature in the passenger compartment.

10 The heating side of the system works in the same way as on models without air conditioning.

11 The operation of the system is controlled electronically by coolant temperature switches, and pressure switches which are screwed into the compressor high-pressure line. Both the Climatic and Climatronic systems receive information on temperatures of the air outside, in the facia vents, and in the footwells, from various sensors. Electric motors are fitted to the main heater assembly to operate the air flaps which are cable-operated on non-air conditioned models, enabling the system to maintain the selected temperature. Any problems with the system should be referred to a Seat dealer or an air conditioning specialist (see illustration).

12 When an air conditioning system is fitted, it is necessary to observe special precautions whenever dealing with any part of the system, its associated components and any items which require disconnection of the system. If for any reason the system must be disconnected, entrust this task to your Seat dealer or an air conditioning specialist.

⚠ Warning: The refrigeration circuit contains a refrigerant, and it is therefore dangerous to disconnect any part of the system without specialised knowledge and equipment. The refrigerant is potentially dangerous and should only be handled by qualified persons. If it is splashed onto the skin it can cause

8.11 Refrigerant circuit service ports (arrowed)

9.2 Pull out the storage compartment below the radio/audio unit

9.3a Undo the bolt (arrowed) in the roof of the aperture . . .

9.3b . . . and the 2 (arrowed) each side

9.4 Pull the trim rearwards

9.5 Pull the control panel surround trim rearwards

Refitting

7 Refitting is a reversal of removal. Ensure that, where applicable, the control cables are refitted correctly (see illustration).

Heater unit

Removal

8 Disconnect the battery negative lead as described in Chapter 5A.

9 On models with air conditioning, have the refrigerant evacuated from the system by a Seat dealer or air conditioning specialist.

10 Unscrew the expansion tank cap (engine cold) to release any pressure present in the cooling system, then securely refit the cap.

11 Remove the engine cover. Clamp both heater hoses as close to the bulkhead as possible to minimise coolant loss. Alternatively, drain the cooling system as described in the relevant part of Chapter 1A or 1B. To ensure correct refitting, mark the hoses for position, as they differ according to model. On diesel models, to improve access to the hoses, release the clamps, unto the bolts, and remove the turbocharger intake ducting from the rear of the engine.

12 Release the clips and disconnect both hoses from the heater matrix outlets (see illustration). To prevent spillage of coolant when the heater is removed, use low air pressure to blow out the remaining coolant, then plug the outlets.

13 On models with air conditioning, unbolt the refrigerant lines from the evaporator expansion valve on the bulkhead in the

frostbite. It is not itself poisonous, but in the presence of a naked flame (including a cigarette) it forms a poisonous gas. Uncontrolled discharging of the refrigerant is dangerous and potentially damaging to the environment, and is illegal in most countries.

• Do not operate the air conditioning system if it is known to be short of refrigerant, as this may damage the compressor.

9	Heating/air conditioning system components – removal and refitting

Heater control panel

Removal

1 Remove the audio unit as described in

Chapter 12. Where a CD changer or satellite navigation unit is fitted in addition, or instead of, the radio unit, this should also be removed.

2 Where applicable, pull out the storage compartment below the radio unit location (see illustration).

3 Undo the 2 bolts each side in the aperture above the control panel, and the 1 bolt at the top of the aperture (see illustrations).

4 Pull the trim under the control panel rearwards to remove it (see illustration).

5 Carefully prise the control panel surround trim from place. Disconnect the switch wiring plugs as the trim is removed (see illustration).

6 Disconnect the wiring plugs and cable(s) from the control panel, then release the 2 clips each side and manoeuvre the panel rearwards from the facia (see illustrations).

9.6a Depress the clip (arrowed) to disconnect the cables

9.6b Press the clips (arrowed) to the centre and pull the panel from place

9.7 The end of the control cable locates over a 'master spline' (arrowed)

9.12 Disconnect the rubber heater hoses (arrowed) from the metal matrix outlet pipes

9.13 Undo the bolts (arrowed) and detach the refrigerant pipes

9.17 Heater matrix pipes adapter retaining bolt locations (arrowed) – shown removed for clarity

engine compartment, and recover the O-ring seals (see illustration). Plug the openings to prevent contamination.

14 Remove the centre console, facia assembly and crossmember as described in Chapter 11.

15 Where fitted, slide the convenience control unit upwards from the heater assembly and place to one side, then undo the bolts securing the right-hand support bracket to the heater assembly. The front bolts are easier to access as the assembly is withdrawn.

16 Where fitted, disconnect the wiring and earth cable for the auxiliary heating. Cut free any cable-ties securing wiring to the heater assembly.

17 Unbolt and remove the heater matrix pipes adapter from the bulkhead in the engine compartment. The retaining bolt is located between the two pipes at the engine compartment bulkhead (see illustration).

18 Place cloth rags in the passenger footwell, then carefully withdraw the heater/air conditioning assembly and remove from the car. Be prepared for some coolant spillage.

Refitting

19 Refitting is reversal of removal, noting the following points:
a) Check the condition of the foam gasket which fits between the heater assembly and the bulkhead, and renew if necessary (see illustration).
b) Make sure that all wiring is correctly reconnected and routed.
c) Make sure that the air ducts are securely clipped into position.
d) On completion, check the coolant level and top-up if necessary as described in 'Weekly checks'.

Heater matrix

Removal

20 Remove the heater unit as described earlier in this Section.

21 With the assembly on the bench, use a screwdriver to prise off the spring clips, then remove the heater matrix and cover from the bottom of the unit (see illustrations).

Refitting

22 Refitting is a reversal of removal.

Auxiliary heating element

Removal

23 Remove the heater matrix as described previously in this Section.

24 Lift out the heating element (where fitted), and disconnect its wiring.

Refitting

25 Refitting is a reversal of removal.

Heater blower motor

Removal

26 Remove the facia and crossmember as described in Chapter 11.

27 Disconnect the blower motor wiring plug.

28 Undo the bolts and withdraw the motor assembly from the housing (see illustration).

9.19 Renew the foam gasket if necessary

9.21b ... then lift the matrix from the cover

29 Depress the catches and remove the blower motor and fan wheel from the housing.

Refitting

30 Refitting is a reversal of removal.

Blower motor series resistor

Removal

31 Remove the facia as described in Chapter 11.

32 The resistor is located adjacent to the blower motor housing, on top of the heater assembly. Disconnect the wiring plug on top.

33 Turn the resistor anti-clockwise (see illustration). Remove the resistor through the top of the housing.

Refitting

34 Refitting is a reversal of removal, but

9.21a Release the spring clips and lift away the matrix and cover ...

9.28 Heater blower motor retaining bolts (arrowed)

9.33 Rotate the heater blower motor resistor anti-clockwise

9.39 Air conditioning compressor bolts (arrowed)

check the operation of the blower motor in all 4 speeds before refitting the glovebox.

Air conditioning compressor

⚠️ **Warning: Do not attempt to open the refrigerant circuit. Refer to the precautions given in Section 8.**

Removal

35 Have the refrigerant evacuated from the system by a Seat dealer or air conditioning specialist.
36 Remove the auxiliary drivebelt as described in Chapter 1A or 1B.
37 Disconnect the compressor wiring plug.
38 Undo the bolts and disconnect the refrigerant pipes from the compressor. Discard the O-ring seals – new ones must be fitted.
39 Undo the mounting bolts and lower the compressor from place **(see illustration)**.

Refitting

40 Refitting is a reversal of removal. Reconnect the refrigerant pipes using new O-ring seals.

Evaporator

Removal

41 Have the refrigerant evacuated from the system by a Seat dealer or air conditioning specialist.
42 Remove the heater assembly as previously described.
43 Remove the pollen filter as described in Chapter 1A or 1B.
44 Remove the heater blower motor as described earlier in this Section.
45 Undo the bolts and remove the heater distributor housing **(see illustrations)**.

46 Undo the bolts, release the spring clips and remove the flap housing **(see illustration)**.
47 In order to gain access to the evaporator, the housing must now be split into two halves. This involves removing the various spring clips, undoing the bolts around the expansion valve, and lifting the lower half from the upper half **(see illustrations)**.
48 Lift the evaporator from the housing **(see illustration)**.

Refitting

49 Refitting is a reversal of removal.

Condenser

Removal

50 Have the refrigerant evacuated from the system by a Seat dealer or air conditioning specialist.
51 Remove the front bumper and cross-member as described in Chapter 11.
52 On diesel models, unclip the intercooler ducting.
53 Undo the bolts securing the radiator to the lock carrier panel **(see illustration 3.16b)**.
54 Undo the bolts securing the lock carrier panel, and swivel it to one side, leaving the radiator and condenser in place.
55 Undo the bolts securing the refrigerant pipes to the condenser. Recover the O-ring seals – new seals must be fitted.
56 Undo the bolts securing the condenser to the radiator, and manoeuvre it from position **(see illustration 3.17)**.

9.45a Undo the bolts (arrowed) each side . . .

9.45b . . . and remove the distributor housing

9.46 Undo the bolts (arrowed) and remove the flap housing

9.47a Undo the bolts each side of the expansion valve (arrowed)

9.47b Lift the lower half of the housing

9.48 Lift the evaporator and expansion valve from the housing

9.59a Remove the rubber cap . . .

9.59b . . . and extract the circlip (arrowed)

9.64 Expansion valve retaining bolts
(arrowed)

Refitting

57 Refitting is a reversal of removal, using new O-ring seals when reconnecting the refrigerant pipes.

Receiver/drier

Removal

58 Remove the condenser as previously described.
59 Prise the rubber cap from the end of the condenser, the remove the circlip securing the receiver/drier **(see illustrations)**.

60 Pull the receiver/drier element from place. Discard the O-ring seals, new ones must be fitted.

Refitting

61 Refitting is a reversal of removal.

Expansion valve

62 Have the air conditioning system fully discharged by an air conditioning specialist.
63 Undo the bolts/nuts securing the refrigerant pipes to the connection at the engine compartment bulkhead. Plug/cover the

openings to prevent contamination/saturation. Recover and discard the O-ring seals – new ones must be fitted **(see illustration 9.13)**.

⚠ *Warning: Failure to seal the refrigerant pipe unions will result in the receiver/drier becoming saturated, necessitating its renewal.*

64 Undo the two bolts and remove the expansion valve **(see illustration)**. Recover and discard the O-ring seals – new ones must be fitted.

Refitting

65 Refitting is a reversal of removal.

Chapter 4 Part A:
Fuel systems – petrol engine

Contents

Degrees of difficulty

Easy, suitable for novice with little experience	**Fairly easy,** suitable for beginner with some experience	**Fairly difficult,** suitable for competent DIY mechanic	**Difficult,** suitable for experienced DIY mechanic	**Very difficult,** suitable for expert DIY or professional

Specifications

Engine codes*
1.2 litre . . .	AZQ, BME and BXV
1.4 litre:	
55 kW (74 bhp) . . .	BBY and BKY
63 kW (85 bhp) . . .	BXW
74 kW (99 bhp) . . .	AUB and BBZ

* **Note:** *The engine code may be found on the vehicle data sticker, by the spare wheel.*

System type
1.2 litre engines:	
Engine code AZQ . . .	Siemens Simos 3PE
Engine code BME . . .	Siemens Simos 3PG
Engine code BXV . . .	Siemens Simos 9.1
1.4 litre engines:	
Engine codes AUB, BBY and BBZ . . .	Magneti Marelli 4MV
Engine code BKY . . .	Magneti Marelli 4TV
Engine code BXW . . .	Magneti Marelli 4HV

Recommended fuel
Minimum octane rating. . .	95 RON unleaded (91 RON unleaded may be used, but with reduced performance)

Fuel system data
Fuel pump type . . .	Electric, immersed in fuel tank
Fuel pump delivery rate . . .	600 cc/30 secs (battery voltage of 12.5 V)
Regulated fuel pressure . . .	2.5 bar
Injector electrical resistance (typical) . . .	12 to 17 ohms

Torque wrench settings
	Nm	lbf ft
Camshaft position sensor	8	6
Fuel rail mounting bolts	10	7
Fuel tank	25	18
Intake air temperature/pressure sensor	2	1
Intake manifold	20	15
Knock sensor(s)	20	15
Oxygen sensor(s)	50	37
Throttle valve control unit:		
1.2 litre engines	8	6
1.4 litre engines	10	7

1 General information and precautions

General information

The systems described in this Chapter are all self-contained engine management systems, which control both the fuel injection and ignition. This Chapter deals with the fuel system components only – see Chapter 4C for information on the exhaust and emission control systems, and to Chapter 5B for details of the ignition system.

The fuel injection system comprises a fuel tank, an electric fuel pump/level sender unit, a fuel filter, fuel supply and return lines, a throttle valve control unit, a fuel rail, four electronic fuel injectors, and an Electronic Control Module (ECM) together with its associated sensors, actuators and wiring. All the fuel systems used operate in the same manner, but there are some detail differences. The electronic power control system (EPC) is completely electronic, and no accelerator cable is fitted. The position of the accelerator pedal is signalled from the pedal control unit by two variable resistors, and the throttle valve is then activated by an electric motor in the throttle valve control unit on the intake manifold. With the engine stopped, the position of the throttle valve is directly comparable to the position of the accelerator pedal, however, when the engine is running the engine control unit opens and closes the throttle valve independently according to the prevailing conditions. This may mean, for example, that the throttle valve may be fully open even though the accelerator pedal is only half open. The engine Electronic Control Module (ECM) determines the best position for the throttle valve in the interests of exhaust gas emission and fuel consumption. In the event of a fault in the system, the EPC warning light will illuminate on the instrument panel and the fault will be stored in the fault memory. The system then switches to its emergency settings and the engine speed is increased to allow the driver to take the car to a Seat dealer, however, the accelerator pedal position senders are no longer operational.

The fuel pump is immersed in the fuel inside the tank, and delivers a constant supply of fuel through a cartridge filter to the fuel rail. The pressure regulator is integral with the fuel filter located next to the fuel tank, and the return line is taken from the filter to the fuel tank. The fuel pressure regulator maintains a constant fuel pressure to the fuel injectors, and returns excess fuel to the tank through the return line. This constant flow system also helps to reduce fuel temperature, and prevents vaporisation.

The fuel injectors are opened and closed by the Electronic Control Module (ECM), which calculates the injection timing and duration according to engine speed, crankshaft/

camshaft position, throttle position and rate of opening, intake manifold depression, intake air temperature, coolant temperature and exhaust gas oxygen content information, received from sensors mounted on and around the engine.

Intake air is drawn into the engine through the air cleaner, which contains a renewable paper filter element. The air cleaner is integral with the engine top cover. On all engines, the intake air temperature is regulated by a valve mounted in the air cleaner intake trunking, which blends air at ambient temperature with hot air, drawn from over the exhaust manifold.

The temperature and pressure of the air entering the engine is measured by a sensor located on the intake manifold. This information is used by the ECM to fine-tune the fuelling requirements for different operating conditions.

Idle speed is determined by the ECM, and manual adjustment of the engine idle speed is not necessary or possible.

The exhaust gas oxygen content is constantly monitored by the ECM through two oxygen sensors (also known as lambda sensors). One is fitted before the catalytic converter, and the other after – this improves sensor response time and accuracy, and the ECM compares the signals from each sensor to confirm that the converter is working correctly. The ECM uses the information from the sensor(s) to modify the injection timing and duration to maintain the optimum air/fuel ratio – a result of this is that manual adjustment of the idle exhaust CO content is not necessary or possible. Refer to Chapter 4C for more information.

On all engines, the ECM controls the operation of the activated charcoal filter evaporative loss system – refer to Chapter 4C for further details.

It should be noted that fault diagnosis of all the engine management systems described in this Chapter is only possible with dedicated electronic test equipment. Problems with the systems operation should therefore be referred to a Seat dealer or suitably-equipped specialist for assessment. Once the fault has been identified, the removal/refitting sequences detailed in the following Sections will then allow the appropriate component(s) to be renewed as required.

2.1a Pull the engine cover/air filter housing upwards from the rubber mountings . . .

Precautions

Warning: Petrol is extremely flammable – great care must be taken when working on any part of the fuel system.

• *Do not smoke, or allow any naked flames or uncovered light bulbs near the work area. Note that gas-powered domestic appliances with pilot flames, such as heaters boilers and tumble-dryers, also present a fire hazard – bear this in mind if you are working in an area where such appliances are present. Always keep a suitable fire extinguisher close to the work area, and familiarise yourself with its operation before starting work. Wear eye protection when working on fuel systems, and wash off any fuel spilt on bare skin immediately with soap and water. Note that fuel vapour is just as dangerous as liquid fuel – possibly more so; a vessel that has been emptied of liquid fuel will still contain vapour, and can be potentially explosive.*

• *Many of the operations described in this Chapter involve the disconnection of fuel lines, which may cause an amount of fuel spillage. Before commencing work, refer to the above 'Warning' and the information in 'Safety first!' at the beginning of this manual.*

• *Residual fuel pressure always remains in the fuel system, long after the engine has been switched off. This pressure must be relieved in a controlled manner before work can commence on any component in the fuel system – refer to Section 8 for details.*

• *When working with fuel system components, pay particular attention to cleanliness – dirt entering the fuel system may cause blockages, which will lead to poor running.*

• *In the interests of personal safety and equipment protection, many of the procedures in this Chapter suggest that the negative lead be removed from the battery terminal. This firstly eliminates the possibility of accidental short-circuits being caused as the car is being worked upon, and secondly prevents damage to electronic components (eg, sensors, actuators, ECMs) which are particularly sensitive to the power surges caused by disconnection or reconnection of the wiring harness whilst they are still 'live'. Refer to Chapter 5A.*

2 Air cleaner and intake system – removal and refitting

Removal

1.2 litre engines

1 Pull the air cleaner/engine cover upwards from the rubber mountings, and pull the breather hose from the cylinder head cover **(see illustrations)**.

1.4 litre engines

2 The air filter is incorporated in the engine top cover.

3 Lift the cover and disconnect the hot-air hose from the control flap housing. Disconnect the breather hose as the cover is removed.

Refitting

4 Refitting is a reversal of removal, but check that the adapter ring is correctly located and ensure that all hoses are securely fitted.

---

3 Intake air temperature control system – general information

---

1 The intake air temperature control system consists of a temperature-controlled flap valve, mounted on the air cleaner housing, and a hose to the warm-air collector plate over the exhaust manifold.

2 The temperature sensor in the flap valve housing senses the temperature of the intake air, and opens the valve when a preset lower limit is reached. As the flap valve opens, warm air drawn from around the exhaust manifold blends with the intake air.

3 As the temperature of the intake air rises, the sensor closes the flap progressively, until the warm-air supply from the exhaust manifold is completely closed off, and only air at ambient temperature is admitted to the air cleaner.

4 With the warm-air hose removed from the temperature control flap valve housing, a hairdryer may be used to test the action of the sensor.

---

4 Fuel system components – removal and refitting

Note: *Observe the precautions in Section 1 before working on any component in the fuel system. Information on the engine management system sensors which are more directly related to the ignition system will be found in Chapter 5B. After fitting any of the components in this Section, have the engine management ECM's fault memory interrogated and any resident faults erased by a Seat dealer or suitably-equipped specialist.*

Throttle valve control unit

Caution: If the throttle valve control unit is renewed, it will be necessary to programme the new unit to the car before it can be used – this must be carried out by a Seat dealer or suitably-equipped specialist.

Removal

1 Remove the engine top cover as described in Section 2.

2 On 1.2 litre engines, unbolt the EGR valve pipe from the intermediate plate.

3 On 1.4 litre engines manufactured before

2.1b . . . and disconnect the breather hose

08/2003, unbolt the crankcase ventilation pipe from the intermediate plate located between the throttle valve control unit and intake manifold.

4 Disconnect the wiring plug from the throttle valve control unit **(see illustration)**.

5 Progressively unscrew the mounting bolts and lift the throttle valve control unit from the top of the intake manifold **(see illustration)**. Recover the O-ring or gasket (as applicable) and discard it, as a new one will be required on refitting.

6 Where applicable, remove the intermediate plate from the intake manifold and recover the O-ring. Discard the O-ring as a new one will be required on refitting.

7 Clean the contact faces of the control unit, intake manifold and intermediate plate as applicable.

4.4 Disconnect the wiring plug from the throttle valve control unit

4.10 Fuel injector wiring plug (arrowed) – 1.2 litre engine code BME

Refitting

8 Refitting is a reversal of removal, but use new O-rings/gaskets and progressively tighten the mounting bolts to the specified torque.

Fuel injectors and fuel rail

Note: *If a faulty injector is suspected, before removing the injectors, it is worth trying the effect of one of the proprietary injector-cleaning treatments. These can be added to the petrol in the tank, and are intended to clean the injectors as you drive.*

Removal

9 Remove the engine top cover as described in Section 2.

10 Unplug the injector harness connectors, labelling them to aid correct refitting later **(see illustration)**. Release the wiring harness clips from the top of the fuel rail, and lay the harness to one side.

11 Refer to Section 8 and depressurise the fuel system.

12 Squeeze the catch on the quick-release fitting, and disconnect the fuel supply hose from the bulkhead. Alternatively, release the spring clip securing the hose to the fuel rail.

13 Unscrew and remove the fuel rail mounting bolts, then carefully lift the rail away from the intake manifold, together with the injectors. Recover the injector lower O-ring seals as they emerge from the manifold **(see illustrations)**.

14 The injectors can be removed individually from the fuel rail by extracting the relevant

4.5 Throttle valve control unit mounting bolts (arrowed)

4.13a Unscrew the mounting bolts (arrowed) . . .

4.13b . . . and lift the fuel rail with injectors from the intake manifold . . .

4.13c . . . then recover the injector lower O-ring seals

4.14a Extract the metal clip . . .

4.14b . . . withdraw the injector from the fuel rail . . .

4.14c . . . and recover the injector upper O-ring seal

4.16 Apply a little engine oil to the O-ring seals to assist their refitting

metal clip and easing the injector out of the rail. Recover the injector upper O-ring seals **(see illustrations)**.

15 Check the electrical resistance of the injectors using a multimeter, and compare it with the Specifications.

Refitting

16 Refit the injectors and fuel rail by following the removal procedure in reverse, noting the following points:

a) *Renew the injector O-ring seals if they appear worn or damaged. Apply a little engine oil to the seals to assist their refitting* **(see illustration).**

b) *Ensure that the injector retaining clips are securely seated.*

c) *Check that all electrical connections are remade correctly.*

d) *Purge air from the fuel rail by loosening the vent valve and temporarily switching on the ignition in order to operate the fuel*

pump. Tighten the vent valve when the fuel is free of air bubbles.

e) *On completion, check for fuel leaks before bringing the car back into service.*

Fuel pressure regulator

17 The fuel pressure regulator is removed when changing the fuel filter, as described in Section 5.

Engine speed sensor

Removal

18 The engine speed sensor is mounted at the left-hand rear of the cylinder block, next to the transmission bellhousing, and access is very difficult. Remove the engine cover/air filter as described in Section 2. Where necessary, prise out the rubber bung for access to the sensor.

19 Trace the wiring back from the sensor, and unplug the harness connector.

20 Unscrew the retaining bolt and withdraw the sensor from the cylinder block/transmission **(see illustrations)**.

Refitting

21 Refitting is a reversal of removal.

Intake air temperature/pressure sensor

Removal

22 The combined intake air temperature and pressure sensor is located on the right-hand side of the intake manifold.

23 Remove the engine top cover (Section 2) and disconnect the wiring from the sensor.

24 Undo the two mounting bolts and remove the sensor from the intake manifold. Recover the O-ring seal(s). **Note:** *There are two O-ring seals and a guide plate on 1.4 litre engines – note how the guide plate is fitted.*

Refitting

25 Refitting is a reversal of removal, but renew the O-ring(s) and guide plate if necessary.

Knock sensor

Removal

26 The knock sensor is located on the rear of the cylinder block and is difficult to access **(see illustration)**.

27 Remove the engine top cover to gain access from above. Alternatively, firmly apply the handbrake then jack up the front of the car and support it on axle stands (see *Jacking and vehicle support*), then remove the engine undershield.

28 Disconnect the wiring connector from

4.20a Unscrew the bolt . . .

4.20b . . . and remove the engine speed sensor – 1.2 litre engine

4.26 The knock sensor is located on the rear of the cylinder block

4.33 Remove the camshaft position sensor

4.39a Oxygen (lambda) sensor (arrowed) on the exhaust manifold

4.39b Oxygen (lambda) sensor (arrowed) on the exhaust downpipe

4.39c Use a slotted socket to loosen the oxygen (lambda) sensor

4.39d Remove the oxygen (lambda) sensor from the exhaust manifold

the sensor or trace the wiring back from the sensor and disconnect its wiring connector.

29 Unscrew the mounting bolt and remove the sensor from the cylinder block.

Refitting

30 Refitting is the reverse of removal. Ensure the mating surfaces of the sensor and cylinder block are clean and dry, and ensure the mounting bolt is tightened to the specified torque to ensure correct operation.

Camshaft position sensor

Removal

31 The camshaft position sensor is located on the left-hand end of the cylinder head.

32 Remove the engine top cover, and disconnect the wiring from the sensor.

33 Unscrew the mounting bolt, and remove the sensor **(see illustration)**.

Refitting

34 Refitting is a reversal of removal.

Coolant temperature sensor

35 Refer to Chapter 3, Section 6.

Oxygen (lambda) sensors

Removal

36 One oxygen sensor is located upstream of the catalytic converter in the exhaust manifold, and a second sensor is located downstream of the catalytic converter in the exhaust front pipe. The upstream sensor is accessible after removing the engine top cover and the exhaust hot air cowl, however, it is difficult to access as it is hidden between the manifold and the

cylinder head. Access to the downstream sensor is possible after raising the front of the car and supporting on axle stands.

⚠️ **Warning: Working on the sensor(s) is only advisable with the engine (and therefore the exhaust system) completely cold. The catalytic converter in particular will be very hot for some time after the engine has been switched off.**

37 Working from the sensor, trace the wiring harness from the oxygen sensor back to the connector, and disconnect it.

38 Release the sensor wiring from any retaining clips, noting how it is routed.

39 Slacken and withdraw the sensor, taking care to avoid damaging the sensor probe as it is removed. As a flying lead remains connected to the sensor after it has been disconnected, if the correct-size spanner is not available, a slotted socket will be required to remove the sensor **(see illustrations)**.

4.42 Clutch pedal switch (arrowed)

Refitting

40 Apply a little high-temperature anti-seize grease to the sensor threads – avoid contaminating the probe tip.

41 Refit the sensor, tightening it to the correct torque. Restore the harness connection.

Clutch pedal switch

Removal

42 Fitted to all engines, the clutch switch is mounted on the clutch pedal bracket, and sends a signal to the ECM **(see illustration)**. The purpose of the switch is to avoid engine over-revving and load change jolts when the clutch is released. The switch also deactivates the cruise control system (where fitted) when the pedal is pressed.

43 To remove the switch, first remove the facia lower trim panel on the driver's side, as described in Chapter 11, Section 29.

44 Locate the switch wiring plug in front of the clutch pedal, and disconnect it.

45 Depress the clutch pedal, then rotate the switch 45° anti-clockwise and withdraw it from the pedal.

Refitting

46 When refitting the switch, hold the clutch pedal depressed, insert the switch and rotate it 45° clockwise. Further refitting is a reversal of removal.

Electronic control unit (ECM)

Caution: Always wait at least 30 seconds after switching off the ignition before disconnecting the wiring from the ECM.

4.47 The ECM is located on the left-hand side of the engine compartment bulkhead

4.50 Disconnect the wiring plugs and remove the ECM

5.2 Fuel filter location next to fuel tank – support collar retaining arm arrowed

When the wiring is disconnected, all the learned values are erased, although any contents of the fault memory are retained. After reconnecting the wiring, the basic settings must be reinstated by a Seat dealer using a special test instrument. Note also that if the ECM is renewed, the identification of the new ECM must be transferred to the immobiliser control unit by a Seat dealer or suitably-equipped specialist.

Removal

47 The ECM is located on the left-hand side of the engine compartment bulkhead (**see illustration**). First disconnect the battery negative lead as described in Chapter 5A.
48 Where necessary, remove the air cleaner assembly as described in Section 2.
49 Pull away the upper and lower retaining clips and, at the same time, slide the ECM outwards to release it.
50 Disconnect the wiring plug by releasing the catches (**see illustration**).

Refitting

51 Refitting is a reversal of removal. Press the unit to the left, once in position, to secure it. Bear in mind the comments made in the Caution above – the ECM will not work correctly until it has been electronically coded.

5 Fuel filter – renewal

Note: *Observe the precautions in Section 1 before working on any component in the fuel system.*

1 Depressurise the fuel system as described in Section 8. Remember, however, that this procedure merely relieves the fuel pressure, reducing the risk of fuel spraying when the connections are disturbed – fuel will still be spilt during filter renewal, so take precautions accordingly.
2 The fuel filter is located in front of the fuel tank, on the right-hand underside of the car (**see illustration**).
3 Jack up the right-hand rear of the car, and support it on an axle stand (see *Jacking and vehicle support*). When positioning the axle

stand, ensure that it will not inhibit access to the filter.
4 To further improve access, if necessary, unhook the handbrake cable from the adjacent wire clip.
5 Disconnect the fuel hoses at either end of the filter, noting their locations for refitting. At the tank end of the filter there are two hoses, a feed hose coloured black and a return hose coloured blue, and at the engine/fuel rail end of the filter there is just one hose coloured black. The connections are of quick-release type, disconnected by squeezing the catch on each. It may be necessary to release the hoses from the clips on the underside of the car to allow greater movement.
6 Before removing the filter, look for an arrow marking, which points in the direction of fuel flow – in this case, towards the front of the car. The new filter must be fitted the same way round.
7 The filter sits in a support collar – release the collar by carefully pulling the retaining arm off the peg on the filter body, and slide the filter out. Try to keep it as level as possible, to reduce fuel spillage. Dispose of the old filter carefully – even if the fuel inside is tipped out, the filter element will still be soaked in fuel, and will be highly flammable.
8 The fuel pressure regulator is secured to the filter by a large spring clip. Withdraw the clip, then carefully remove the regulator by pulling it from the fuel filter. Recover the O-rings – new ones should be used when refitting.
9 Fit new O-rings to the pressure regulator, then seat it fully into the new filter, and secure it using the spring clip.
10 Offer the new filter into position, ensuring

6.5 Prise up the rubber access hatch

that the direction-of-flow arrow is pointing towards the front of the car. Turn the filter so that the peg can be engaged with the retaining arm, and push the arm onto the peg to secure. Ensure that the filter is securely mounted on the car.
11 Connect the fuel hoses to each end of the filter, in the same positions as noted on removal. Push the hoses fully onto the filter stubs and, if necessary, clip them back to the underside of the car. Hook the handbrake cable back in place, if it was disturbed.
12 Switch on the ignition to activate the fuel pump. Check for signs of fuel leakage at both ends of the filter.
13 If all is well, lower the car to the ground, then start the engine. Check under the car for signs of fuel leaks from the filter.

6 Fuel pump and gauge sender unit – removal and refitting

Note: *Observe the precautions in Section 1 before working on any component in the fuel system.*

⚠ *Warning: Avoid direct skin contact with fuel – wear protective clothing and gloves when handling fuel system components. Ensure that the work area is well-ventilated to prevent the build-up of fuel vapour.*

General information

1 The fuel pump and gauge sender unit are combined in one assembly, which is mounted in the top of the fuel tank. Access is through a hatch provided in the load space floor.
Caution: Removal of the sender unit involves exposing the contents of the fuel tank to the atmosphere.

Removal

2 Depressurise the fuel system as described in Section 8.
3 Ensure that the car is parked on a level surface, then disconnect the battery negative lead as described in Chapter 5A.
4 Fold the rear seat cushion forwards, and lift the carpet section from the body panel.
5 Carefully prise the rubber hatch away from the floorpan (**see illustration**).

6.7 Depress the release catch and disconnect the hose(s)

6.8a Note the alignment marks . . .

6.8b . . . then unscrew the plastic securing ring. Home-made tool shown

6 Unplug the wiring harness connector from the pump/sender unit.

7 Pad the area around the supply and return fuel hoses with rags to absorb any spilt fuel, then squeeze the catch to release the hose clips and disconnect them from the ports at the sender unit (alternatively, use a screwdriver to depress the catch) **(see illustration)**. Observe the supply and return arrow markings on the ports – label the fuel hoses accordingly to ensure correct refitting later. The supply pipe is black, and may have white markings, while the return pipe is blue, or has blue markings.

8 Note the position of the alignment marks, then unscrew the plastic securing ring and remove it. Use a pair of water pump pliers or a suitable tool to grip and rotate the plastic securing ring, if necessary **(see illustrations)**.

9 Lift out the pump/sender unit, holding it above the level of the fuel in the tank until the excess fuel has drained out. Recover the flange seal with the sender/pump unit **(see illustrations)**.

10 Remove the pump/sender unit from the car, and lay it on an absorbent card or rag. Inspect the float at the end of the sender unit swinging arm for punctures and fuel ingress – renew the unit if it appears damaged. Temporarily refit the plastic securing ring to the fuel tank to prevent any distortion.

11 The fuel pick-up incorporated in the assembly is spring-loaded to ensure that it always draws fuel from the lowest part of the tank. Check that the pick-up is free to move under spring tension with respect to the sender unit body.

12 Inspect the rubber seal from the fuel tank aperture for signs of fatigue – renew it if necessary.

13 Inspect the sender unit wiper and track; clean off any dirt and debris that may have accumulated, and look for breaks in the track.

14 If required, the sender unit can be separated from the assembly, as follows. Disconnect the two small wires (note their positions), then release the clips and slide the unit downwards to remove **(see illustrations)**.

15 The unit top plate can be removed by releasing the plastic tags at either side; recover the large spring which fits onto a peg on the plate underside.

6.9a Lift out the pump/sender unit . . .

Refitting

16 Refit the pump/sender unit by following the removal procedure in reverse, noting the following points:

a) Take care not to bend the float arm as the unit is refitted.

b) Smear the outside of tank aperture rubber seal with clean fuel or lubricating spray, to ease fitting. Unless a new seal is required, the seal should be left on the pump unit before fitting. When the unit is almost fully in place, slide the seal down and locate it on the rim of the tank aperture, then slide the unit fully home.

c) The arrow markings on the sender unit body and the access aperture must be aligned.

d) Reconnect the fuel hoses to the correct ports – observe the direction-of-flow arrow markings, and refer to paragraph 7. The return port is marked R, while the supply

6.9b . . . and recover the flange seal

port is marked V; on some models, there may be arrow markings indicating fuel flow. Ensure that the fuel hose fittings click fully into place.

e) On completion, check that all associated pipes are securely clipped to the tank.

f) Before refitting the access hatch and rear seat, run the engine and check for fuel leaks.

7 Fuel tank – removal and refitting

Note: Observe the precautions in Section 1 before working on any component in the fuel system.

Removal

1 Before the tank can be removed, it must be drained of as much fuel as possible. As

6.14a Disconnect the wiring plugs (arrowed) . . .

6.14b . . . then release the clips (arrowed) and slide the sender unit downwards

no drain plug is provided, it is preferable to carry out this operation with the tank almost empty.

2 Open the fuel filler flap, and unscrew the fuel filler cap – leave the cap loosely in place.

3 Disconnect the battery negative lead as described in Chapter 5A. Using a hand pump or siphon, remove any remaining fuel from the bottom of the tank.

4 Loosen the right-hand rear wheel bolts, then jack up the rear of the car and remove the right-hand rear wheel.

5 Remove the right-hand rear wheel arch liner as described in Chapter 11, Section 25.

6 Gain access to the top of the fuel pump/ sender unit as described in Section 6, and disconnect the wiring harness from the top of the pump/sender unit at the multiplug connector.

7 Unscrew the fuel filler flap unit retaining bolt where fitted (on the side opposite the flap hinge), and ease the flap unit out of position. Recover the rubber seal which fits around the filler neck.

8 Undo the bolt securing the filler tube.

9 Fold the rear seat cushion forwards and lift the carpet section from the load space floor.

10 Slacken and withdraw the access hatch bolts, and lift the hatch away from the floorpan.

11 Unplug the wiring harness connector from the pump/sender unit.

12 Remove the activated charcoal (evaporative) filter from its location behind the filler tube as described in Chapter 4C.

13 The fuel tank is protected from below by one or more plastic covers. Undo the fasteners and remove the covers.

14 Referring to Chapter 4C if necessary, unbolt the exhaust rear silencer mounting, and carefully lower the rear section of the exhaust system. Given that the rear axle assembly has to be removed (or at least lowered) to allow the tank to be removed, it is preferable to remove the rear section of the exhaust system completely.

15 Refer to Chapter 10 and remove the rear axle assembly. Alternatively, it is possible to just lower the axle out of position, rather than completely removing it.

16 Depressurise the fuel system as described in Section 8.

17 Remove the fuel filter as described in Section 5, or alternatively disconnect the single outlet hose from the engine side of the filter.

18 Disconnect the activated charcoal (evaporative) filter just in front of the right-hand side of the fuel tank.

19 Unscrew and remove the retaining bolts and detach the tensioning strap from the tank.

20 Position a trolley jack under the centre of the tank. Insert a block of wood between the jack head and the tank to prevent damage to the tank surface. Raise the jack to support the weight of the tank.

21 Unscrew and remove the tank mounting bolts.

22 Lower the tank from the underside of the car. If necessary, detach the various pipes and hoses from the tank, and remove the fuel pump and gauge sender unit with reference to Section 6.

23 If the tank is contaminated with sediment or water, swill the tank out with clean fuel. The tank is injection-moulded from a synthetic material and, if damaged, should be renewed. However, in certain cases it may be possible to have small leaks or minor damage repaired. Seek the advice of a suitable specialist before attempting to repair the fuel tank.

Refitting

24 Refitting is the reverse of the removal procedure, noting the following points:

a) *When lifting the tank back into position, take care to ensure none of the hoses get trapped between the tank and vehicle body.*

b) *Ensure that all pipes and hoses are correctly routed, are not kinked, and are securely held in position with their retaining clips.*

c) *Tighten the tank strap retaining bolts to the specified torque.*

d) *On completion, refill the tank with fuel, and check for signs of leakage prior to taking the car out on the road.*

---

8 Fuel injection system – depressurisation

Note: *Observe the precautions in Section 1 before working on any component in the fuel system.*

⚠ **Warning: The following procedure will merely relieve the pressure in the fuel system – remember that fuel will still be present in the system components and take precautions accordingly before disconnecting any of them.**

1 The fuel system referred to in this Section is defined as the tank-mounted fuel pump, the fuel filter, the fuel injectors, and the metal

9.2 Coolant purge hose retaining clips (arrowed) on the top of the intake manifold

pipes and flexible hoses of the fuel lines between these components. All these contain fuel, which will be under pressure while the engine is running and/or while the ignition is switched on. The pressure will remain for some time after the ignition has been switched off, and must be relieved before any of these components are disturbed for servicing work. Ideally, the engine should be allowed to cool completely before work commences.

2 Place a suitable container beneath the relevant connection/union to be disconnected, then wrap clean cloth around it. Where a union connection is fitted, loosen it slightly before wrapping the cloth around.

3 Slowly open the connection to avoid a sudden release of pressure. Once the pressure has been released, disconnect the fuel line. Insert plugs to minimise fuel loss and prevent the entry of dirt into the fuel system.

---

9 Intake manifold – removal and refitting

Note: *Observe the precautions in Section 1 before working on any component in the fuel system.*

Removal

1 A one-piece intake manifold is fitted to the rear of the cylinder head on all models. First, disconnect the battery negative lead as described in Chapter 5A.

2 Remove the engine top cover. Where applicable, unclip the hose from the top of the intake manifold **(see illustration)**.

3 With reference to Section 4, remove the throttle valve control unit from the intake manifold.

4 Disconnect the vacuum hose for the brake vacuum servo noting how it is routed.

5 To allow the manifold to be removed completely, and to improve access to the manifold mounting bolts, remove the fuel rail and injectors as described in Section 4. However, if the manifold is being removed as part of another procedure (such as cylinder head or engine removal), the fuel rail can be left in place.

6 Disconnect the wiring plug from the intake air temperature/pressure sensor, referring if necessary to Section 4 for more details **(see illustration)**. Alternatively, remove it completely.

7 Progressively loosen the bolts and withdraw the manifold from the cylinder head. Recover the O-ring seals – all should be renewed when refitting the manifold **(see illustration)**.

Refitting

8 Refitting is a reversal of removal. Use a new gasket or seals, as applicable, and tighten the retaining bolts/nuts to the specified torque.

9.6 Intake manifold – 1.4 litre engine up to 08/2003

1 Throttle valve control unit	3 Gasket	6 Intake manifold bolt	8 Guide plate	11 Intake air temperature/ pressure sensor
2 Bolt	4 EGR pipe flange	7 Manifold seal	9 O-rings	12 Intake manifold
	5 Seal		10 Bolt	

10 Fuel injection system – testing and adjustment

1 If a fault appears in the fuel injection system, first ensure that all the system wiring connectors are securely connected and free of corrosion. Then ensure that the fault is not due to poor maintenance; ie, check that the air cleaner filter element is clean, the spark plugs are in good condition and correctly gapped, the cylinder compression pressures are correct, the ignition system wiring is in good condition and securely connected, and the engine breather hoses are clear and undamaged, referring to Chapter 1A, Chapter 2A or 2B and Chapter 5B.

2 If these checks fail to reveal the cause of the problem, the car should be taken to a suitably-equipped Seat dealer or specialist for testing. A diagnostic connector is incorporated in the engine management system wiring harness, into which dedicated electronic test equipment can be plugged (the purple-coloured connector is located under the facia, behind the driver's storage compartment) **(see illustration)**. The test equipment is capable of 'interrogating' the engine management system ECM electronically and accessing its internal fault log (reading fault codes).

3 Fault codes can only be extracted from the ECM using a dedicated fault code reader. A Seat dealer will obviously have such a reader, but they are also available from other suppliers. It is unlikely to be cost-effective for the private owner to purchase a fault code reader, but a well-equipped local garage or auto-electrical specialist will have one.

4 Using this equipment, faults can be pinpointed quickly and simply, even if their occurrence is intermittent. Testing all the system components individually in an attempt to locate the fault by elimination is a time-consuming operation that is unlikely to be fruitful (particularly if the fault occurs dynamically), and carries a high risk of damage to the ECM's internal components.

5 Experienced home mechanics equipped with an accurate tachometer and a carefully-calibrated exhaust gas analyser may be able to check the exhaust gas CO content and the engine idle speed; if these are found to be out of specification, then the car must be taken to a suitably-equipped Seat dealer or specialist for assessment. Neither the air/fuel mixture (exhaust gas CO content) nor the engine idle speed are manually adjustable.

9.7 Remove the inlet manifold – 1.2 litre engine

10.2 A diagnostic connector is located under the driver's side of the facia (arrowed)

11 Cruise control system – general information

1 Certain models may be equipped with a cruise control system, in which the driver can set a chosen speed, which the system will then try to maintain regardless of gradients, etc.

2 Once the desired speed has been set, the system is entirely under the control of the engine management ECM, which regulates the speed via the throttle valve control unit.

3 The system refers to signals from the engine speed sensor (see Section 4) and roadspeed sensor (on the transmission or supplied by the wheel speed sensors).

4 The system is deactivated if the clutch or brake pedals are pressed, signalled by the clutch pedal switch (Section 4) or the brake stop-light switch (Chapter 9).

5 The cruise control switch is part of the steering column combination switch assembly, which can be removed as described in Chapter 12, Section 4.

6 Any problems with the system which are not caused by wiring faults or failure of the components mentioned in this Section should be referred to a Seat dealer or suitably-equipped specialist. In the event of a problem occurring, it is advisable to first take the car to a suitably-equipped dealer or specialist for electronic fault diagnosis, using a fault code reader – refer to Section 10.

Air mass meter

Removal

20 With reference to Section 2, slacken the clips and disconnect the air ducting from the air mass meter, at the rear of the air cleaner housing.

21 Disconnect the wiring from the air mass meter, and the vacuum hose (see Section 2).

22 Remove the retaining bolts and extract the meter from the air cleaner housing. Recover the O-ring seal.

Caution: Handle the air mass meter carefully – its internal components are easily damaged.

Refitting

23 Refitting is a reversal of removal. Renew the O-ring seal if it appears damaged.

Absolute pressure (altitude) sensor

24 The absolute pressure sensor is an integral part of the ECM, and hence cannot be renewed separately.

Clutch and brake pedal switches

Removal

25 The clutch and brake pedal switches are clipped to mounting brackets directly above their respective pedals.

26 The brake pedal switch operates as a safety device, in the event of a problem with the accelerator position sensor. If the brake pedal switch is depressed while the accelerator pedal is held at a constant position, the engine speed will drop to idle. Thus, a faulty or incorrectly-adjusted brake pedal switch may result in a running problem.

27 The clutch pedal switch operation causes the injection pump to momentarily reduce its output while the clutch is disengaged, to permit smoother gearchanging.

28 To remove either switch, refer to Chapter 11, Section 29, and remove the trim panels from under the steering column area of the facia, to gain access to the pedal cluster.

29 The switches can be removed by unclipping them from their mountings and disconnecting the wiring plugs.

Refitting

30 Refitting is a reversal of removal. On completion, it may be necessary to have the switches reprogrammed by a Seat dealer or suitably-equipped specialist.

Camshaft position sensor

Removal

31 The camshaft position sensor is located behind the timing belt inner cover, on the right-hand end of the cylinder head.

32 Remove the upper timing cover as described in Chapter 2C.

33 Prise the rubber grommet from the timing belt inner cover.

34 Trace the wiring from the camshaft position sensor to the connector and disconnect.

4.4 Undo the adjustment bolt until the rocker arm lies against the plunger pin of the injector

35 Unscrew the mounting bolt and withdraw the sensor from the engine.

Refitting

36 Refitting is a reversal of removal.

Electronic control module (ECM)

Caution: Always wait at least 30 seconds after switching off the ignition before disconnecting the wiring from the ECM. When the wiring is disconnected, all the learned values are erased, however any contents of the fault memory are retained. After reconnecting the wiring, the basic settings must be reinstated by a Seat dealer or suitably-equipped specialist using a special test instrument. Note also that if the ECM is renewed, the identification of the new ECM must be transferred to the immobiliser control unit by a Seat dealer or suitably-equipped specialist.

Removal

37 The ECM is located on the left-hand side of the engine compartment bulkhead. First disconnect the battery negative lead as described in Chapter 5A.

38 Remove the air cleaner assembly as described in Section 2.

39 Pull away the upper and lower retaining clips and, at the same time, slide the ECM outwards to release it.

40 Disconnect the wiring plug by releasing the catches.

Refitting

41 Refitting is a reversal of removal. Press the unit to the left, once in position, to secure it. Bear in mind the comments made in the Caution above – the ECM will not work correctly until it has been electronically coded.

4 Injectors –
general information,
removal and refitting

⚠ *Warning: Exercise extreme caution when working on the fuel injectors. Never expose the hands or any part of the body to injector spray, as the high working pressure can cause the fuel to penetrate the skin, with possibly*

4.7 Remove the clamping block securing bolt (arrowed)

fatal results. You are strongly advised to have any work which involves testing the injectors under pressure carried out by a dealer or fuel injection specialist. Refer to the precautions given in Section 1 of this Chapter before proceeding.

General information

1 Injectors do deteriorate with prolonged use, and it is reasonable to expect them to need reconditioning or renewal after 60 000 miles or so. Accurate testing, overhaul and calibration of the injectors must be left to a specialist.

Removal

Note: *Take care not to allow dirt into the injectors or fuel pipes during this procedure. Do not drop the injectors or allow the needles at their tips to become damaged. The injectors are precision-made to fine limits, and must not be handled roughly.*

1.4 litre engines

2 With reference to Chapter 2C, remove the upper timing belt cover and camshaft cover.

3 A single rocker arm shaft is fitted. Using a spanner or socket, turn the crankshaft pulley until the crankshaft is positioned at TDC (No 1 cylinder) as described in Chapter 2C. Adjust the position of the crankshaft so that the injector operating arms are all pointing upwards evenly, ie, the injector plunger springs are under the least amount of tension.

4 Working on each of the injectors in turn, slacken the locknut of the adjustment screw on the end of the rocker arm, and undo the adjustment screw until the rocker arm lies against the plunger pin of the injector **(see illustration)**.

5 Starting at the outside and working in, progressively slacken and remove the rocker shaft retaining bolts. Lift the rocker shaft from the camshaft bearing caps. Check the contact face of each adjustment screw, and renew any that show signs of wear.

6 Position the engine so that the exhaust lobe of No 1 cylinder (nearest camshaft sprocket) is pointing upwards. In this position, all three injector clamping pads can be removed.

7 Working on the first injector, undo the clamping block securing bolt and remove the block from the side of the injector **(see illustration)**.

4.9a Unit injector removal tool

a = 5 mm
b = 15 mm
c = 25 mm

d   Weld/braze the rod to
     the angle-iron
e   Threaded rod

f   Cylindrical weight
g   Locknut

4.9b Seat the slide hammer/tool in the slot on the side on the injector, and pull the injector out

4.11a Undo the two nuts at the back of the head and slide the injector loom/rail out

4.11b The injector connectors will slide into the loom/rail to prevent them from being damaged

8 Using a small screwdriver, carefully prise the wiring connector from the injector.

9 Seat technicians use a slide hammer (tool No T10055) to pull the injector from the cylinder head. This is a slide hammer which engages in the side of the injector. If this tool is not available, it is possible to fabricate an equivalent using a short section of angle-iron, a length of threaded rod, a cylindrical weight, and two locknuts. Weld/braze the rod to the

4.17 Set No 2 cylinder exhaust lobe as shown for access to all four injector clamping pads

angle-iron, slide the weight over the rod, and lock the two nuts together at the end of the rod to provide the stop for the weight **(see illustration)**. Seat the slide hammer/tool in the slot on the side on the injector, and pull the injector out using a few gently taps. Recover circlip, the heat shield and O-rings and discard. New ones must be used for refitting **(see illustration)**. **Note:** *Seat recommend that each injector is identified to ensure refitting in its original location.*

10 Remove the remaining injectors using the procedure described in paragraphs 7 to 9.

11 If required, the injector wiring loom/rail can be removed from the cylinder head by undoing the two retaining nuts/bolts. To prevent the wiring connectors fouling the cylinder head casting as the assembly is withdrawn, insert the connectors into the storage slots in the plastic wiring rail. Carefully push the assembly to the rear, and out of the casting **(see illustrations)**.

1.9 litre engines

12 With reference to Chapter 2C, remove the upper timing belt cover and camshaft cover.
13 Two rocker arm shafts are fitted, each one operating a pair of injectors. Using a spanner or socket, turn the crankshaft pulley until the rocker arms for injectors 1 and 2 are both pointing upwards, ie, the injector plunger springs are under the least amount of tension.
14 Working on each of the two injectors in turn, slacken the locknut of the adjustment

screw on the end of the rocker arm, and undo the adjustment screw until the rocker arm lies against the plunger pin of the injector.
15 Starting at the outside and working in, progressively slacken and remove the rocker shaft retaining bolts. Lift off the rocker shaft. Check the contact face of each adjustment screw, and renew any that show signs of wear.
16 Turn the engine one complete turn and remove the injector rocker shaft for cylinders 3 and 4, using the procedure described in paragraphs 14 and 15.
17 Position the engine so that the exhaust lobe of No 2 cylinder is pointing upwards in-line with the rear edge of the rocker shaft lower bearing support **(see illustration)**. In this position, all four injector clamping pads can be removed.
18 Follow the procedure described in paragraphs 7 to 11.

Refitting

19 Prior to refitting the injectors, the three O-rings, heat insulation washer and clip must be renewed. Due to the high injection pressures, it is essential that the O-rings are fitted without being twisted. Seat recommend the use of three special assembly sleeves to install the O-rings squarely. It may be prudent to entrust O-ring renewal to a Seat dealer or suitably-equipped injection specialist, rather than risk subsequent leaks **(see illustration)**.

4.19 Care must be used to ensure that the injector O-rings are fitted without being twisted

20 After renewing the O-rings, fit the heat shield and secure it in place with the circlip **(see illustration)**.

21 Smear clean engine oil onto the O-rings, and push the injector evenly down into the cylinder head onto its stop. Make sure that the injectors are refitted in their previously-noted locations.

22 Fit the clamping block alongside the injector, but only hand-tighten the new retaining bolt at this stage.

23 It is essential that the injectors are fitted at right-angles to the clamping block. In order to achieve this, measure the distance from the left-hand end face of the cylinder head to the rounded section of the solenoid valve nut, but note that there are two different types of nut fitted **(see illustrations)**. The dimensions (a) are as follows:

1.4 litre engines

Old solenoid valve nut
Cylinder 1 = 244.2 ± 0.8 mm
Cylinder 2 = 156.2 ± 0.8 mm
Cylinder 3 = 64.8 ± 0.8 mm

New solenoid valve nut
Cylinder 1 = 245.0 ± 0.8 mm
Cylinder 2 = 157.0 ± 0.8 mm
Cylinder 3 = 65.6 ± 0.8 mm

1.9 litre engines

Old solenoid valve nut
Cylinder 1 = 332.2 ± 0.8 mm
Cylinder 2 = 244.2 ± 0.8 mm
Cylinder 3 = 152.8 ± 0.8 mm
Cylinder 4 = 64.8 ± 0.8 mm

New solenoid valve nut
Cylinder 1 = 333.0 ± 0.8 mm
Cylinder 2 = 245.0 ± 0.8 mm
Cylinder 3 = 153.6 ± 0.8 mm
Cylinder 4 = 65.6 ± 0.8 mm

24 Once the injectors are aligned correctly, tighten the clamping bolt to the specified Stage one torque setting followed by the Stage two angle tightening setting. **Note:** *If an injector has been renewed, it is essential that the adjustment screw, locknut of the corresponding rocker and ball-pin are renewed at the same time. The ball-pins simply pull out of the injector spring cap. There is an O-ring*

4.20 Unit injector (1.9 litre engine shown)

1	Bolt	3	Cylinder	5	Rocker arm	8	Unit injector	11	O-ring
2	Clamping		head	6	Nut	9	O-ring	12	Heat shield
	block	4	Bolt	7	Adjuster	10	O-ring	13	Circlip

in each spring cap to stop the ball-pins from falling out.

25 If removed, refit the injector wiring loom/ rail to the cylinder head and tighten the two retaining nuts/bolts. Reconnect the wiring to each injector.

26 Smear some grease (Seat No G000 100) onto the contact face of each rocker arm adjustment screw, and refit the rocker shaft assembly to the camshaft bearing caps,

tightening the retaining bolts as follows. Starting from the inside out, hand-tighten the bolts. Again, from the inside out, tighten the bolts to the Stage one torque setting. Finally, from the inside out, tighten the bolts to the Stage two angle tightening setting.

27 The following procedure is only necessary if an injector has been renewed. Attach a DTI (Dial Test Indicator) gauge to the cylinder head upper surface, and position the DTI

4.23a Distance (a) from end of cylinder head to rounded section of injector (see text)

A Injector with early nut
B Injector with late nut

4.23b Use a set square against the edge of the injector . . .

4.23c . . . and measure the distance to the end of the cylinder head

4.27 Set up a DTI probe against the top of the adjustment bolt

probe against the top of the adjustment screw **(see illustration)**. Turn the crankshaft until the rocker arm roller is on the highest point of its corresponding camshaft lobe, and the adjustment screw is at its lowest. Once this position has been established, remove the DTI gauge, screw the adjustment screw in until firm resistance is felt, and the injector spring cannot be compressed further. Turn the adjustment screw anti-clockwise 225°, and tighten the locknut to the specified torque.

28 Refit the camshaft cover and upper timing belt cover, as described in Chapter 2C.
29 Start the engine and check that it runs correctly.

5 Intake manifold – removal and refitting

1.4 litre engines

Removal

1 Remove the engine top cover.
2 Remove the air intake ducting from the air cleaner to the turbocharger with reference to Section 2.
3 Remove the flap housing and EGR valve from the intake manifold as described in Section 9. Note that the engine rear lifting eye is bolted to the valve housing.
4 Unscrew and remove the mounting nuts

8.2b Fuel tandem pump securing bolts (arrowed)

1 *Brake servo hose*	3 *Fuel return hose*
2 *Fuel supply hose*	4 *Tandem pump*

8.2a Fuel tandem pump (arrowed)

and withdraw the intake manifold from the rear of the cylinder head. Remove the gaskets and discard them as new ones must be used on refitting.

Refitting

5 Refitting is a reversal of removal. Ensure that the mating surfaces are clean. Use new gaskets and tighten the manifold bolts to the specified torque.

1.9 litre engines

Removal

6 Remove the engine top cover.
7 Remove the air intake ducting from the air cleaner to the turbocharger with reference to Section 2.
8 Remove the flap housing and EGR valve from the intake manifold as described in Section 9. Note that the engine rear lifting eye is bolted to the valve housing.
9 Unscrew the nuts and withdraw the intake manifold from the studs on the cylinder head. Remove the gasket and discard it as a new one must be used on refitting.

Refitting

10 Refitting is a reversal of removal, using new manifold, EGR pipe and manifold flap assembly gaskets.

6 Fuel gauge sender/pump unit – removal and refitting

Note: *Observe the precautions in Section 1 before working on any component in the fuel system.*

> ⚠ **Warning: Avoid direct skin contact with fuel – wear protective clothing and gloves when handling fuel system components. Ensure that the work area is well-ventilated to prevent the build-up of fuel vapour.**

1 The fuel gauge sender unit is mounted on the top of the fuel tank. Access is through a hatch provided in the load space floor. The unit protrudes into the fuel tank, and its removal involves exposing the contents of the tank to the atmosphere.
2 Refer to the procedures in Chapter 4A for removal and refitting.

7 Fuel tank – removal and refitting

Note: *Observe the precautions in Section 1 before working on any component in the fuel system.*

1 Refer to the procedures in Chapter 4A. There is no activated charcoal breather pipe to disconnect at the front of the tank – instead, the fuel supply pipe (coloured black) should be disconnected.

8 Tandem fuel pump – removal and refitting

Removal

1 Remove the engine top cover.
2 Disconnect the brake servo vacuum pipe from the tandem fuel pump **(see illustrations)**.
3 Position a container beneath the fuel filter in the front right-hand corner of the engine compartment, then disconnect the supply (white) and return (blue) hoses from the filter. Drain the fuel into the container.
4 Disconnect the supply (white) hose from the tandem fuel pump.
5 Unscrew the four mounting bolts and withdraw the pump from the cylinder head. Pull the pump upwards and disconnect the return (blue) hose, then remove the pump. Note how the drive pinion locates in the end of the camshaft. Be prepared for fuel spillage. There are no serviceable parts within the tandem pump. If the pump is faulty, it must be renewed.

Refitting

6 Reconnect the fuel return hose to the pump and refit the pump to the cylinder head, using new rubber seals, and ensuring that the pump pinion engages correctly with the drive slot in the camshaft **(see illustration)**.
7 Insert the pump retaining bolts, and tighten them to the specified torque.
8 Reconnect the fuel supply hose and brake servo hose to the pump.

8.6 Ensure that the tandem pump pinion engages correctly with the drive slot in the camshaft

9 Reconnect the supply (white) hose to the fuel filter.

10 Connect a hand vacuum pump to the fuel filter return hose (marked blue). Operate the vacuum pump until fuel comes out of the return hose. This primes the tandem pump. Reconnect the return hose to the fuel filter.

11 Refit the engine top cover.

9 Intake manifold flap and valve – removal and refitting

Flap housing and vacuum control element/electric motor

1 As diesel engines have a very high compression ratio, when the engine is turned off, the pistons still compress a large quantity of air for a few revolutions and cause the engine unit to shudder. The intake manifold changeover flap is built into the EGR valve, and the flap is operated by a vacuum element, or the flap is electrically-operated, with a motor attached to the housing, and a separate EGR valve. When the ignition switch is turned to the 'off' position, the engine management ECM-controlled valve actuates the flap, which shuts off the air supply to the cylinders. This allows the pistons to compress very little air, and the engine runs softly to a halt. The flap must open again approximately 3 seconds after switching off the ignition switch. On vacuum-operated flaps, the EGR (Exhaust Gas Recirculation) valve is also incorporated into the flap housing.

Vacuum-operated

2 Removal and refitting of the flap housing is identical to that for the EGR valve in Chapter 4C. Once removed, the flap control element can be removed by disconnecting the arm from the flap and unbolting the mounting bracket.

9.8 Unclip the intake manifold flap solenoid valve . . .

Electrically-operated

3 Release the clamps and disconnect the air intake ducting from the flap housing.

4 Disconnect the flap housing wiring plug.

5 Undo the retaining bolts and detach the flap housing from the EGR valve. Renew the O-ring seal.

6 Refitting is a reversal of removal.

Changeover valve

Vacuum-operated only

7 The changeover valve controls the supply of vacuum to the changeover flap. The electrical supply to the valve is controlled by the engine management ECM. When the ignition key is turned to the 'off' position, the ECM signals the valve, which allows vacuum to pull the flap shut. Approximately three seconds later, the power supply to the valve is cut, the vacuum to the actuator collapses, and the flap opens.

8 The valve is located on the top of the air filter housing. Note the fitted positions and disconnect the vacuum pipes from the valve (see illustration).

9 Disconnect the wiring plug from the valve (see illustration).

9.9 . . . and disconnect the wiring plug

10 Undo the retaining bolt and remove the valve.

11 Refitting is a reversal of removal.

10 Fuel cooler – removal and refitting

Removal

1 On some models, a fuel cooler is fitted in the return line to the fuel tank. It is attached to the underbody. First, chock the front wheels, then jack up the rear of the car and support it on axle stands (see *Jacking and vehicle support*).

2 Unbolt the cover from the fuel cooler.

3 Place cloth rags around the cooler to soak up spilt fuel, then disconnect the supply and return lines from it.

4 Unscrew the mounting nuts and remove the fuel cooler from under the car.

Refitting

5 Refitting is a reversal of removal, but tighten the mounting nuts to the specified torque.

Notes

Chapter 4 Part C:
Emission control and exhaust systems

Contents

Degrees of difficulty

Easy, suitable for novice with little experience	**Fairly easy,** suitable for beginner with some experience	**Fairly difficult,** suitable for competent DIY mechanic	**Difficult,** suitable for experienced DIY mechanic	**Very difficult,** suitable for expert DIY or professional

Specifications

Petrol engines
System type . . . .   Single catalytic converter on 1.2 litre engines, two converters on 1.4 litre engines. Twin oxygen sensors. EGR system fitted to all except 1.2 litre engine code BME from 11/2005 and 1.4 litre engine code BXW

Diesel engines
System type . . . .   Single catalytic converter, EGR system. Turbocharger and intercooler fitted to all engines. Particulate filter fitted to 1.9 litre engine code BMT and 1.4 litre engine code BMS

Torque wrench settings

	Nm	lbf ft
Petrol engines		
EGR adapter to cylinder head	20	15
EGR connecting pipe to intermediate plate or intake manifold	10	7
EGR valve	20	15
Exhaust clamp nuts	25	18
Exhaust manifold nuts*	25	18
Exhaust manifold support bracket to engine (1.4 litre engines)	40	30
Exhaust mounting bracket bolts	25	18
Oxygen sensors	50	37
Diesel engines		
EGR pipe nuts/bolts	25	18
EGR valve/flap housing-to-intake manifold	10	7
Exhaust clamp nuts	40	30
Exhaust manifold nuts*	25	18
Exhaust manifold/turbocharger-to-downpipe nuts*	25	18
Intercooler mounting bolts	8	6
Turbocharger oil feed union adapter	30	22
Turbocharger oil feed union nut	22	16
Turbocharger oil return pipe flange bolts	15	11
Turbocharger oil return union bolt	30	22
Turbocharger vacuum union bolt (1.4 litre engines)	15	11
Turbocharger-to-manifold bolts (1.4 litre engines)*	30	22

* Do not re-use

1 General information

Petrol engine systems

All petrol models are designed to use unleaded petrol, and are controlled by engine management systems that are programmed to give the best compromise between driveability, fuel consumption and exhaust emission production. In addition, a number of systems are fitted that help to minimise other harmful emissions. A crankcase emission control system is fitted, which reduces the release of pollutants from the engine's lubrication system, and one or two catalytic converters are fitted to reduce exhaust gas pollutant. An evaporative loss emission control system is fitted which reduces the release of gaseous hydrocarbons from the fuel tank.

Crankcase emission control

To reduce the emission of unburned hydrocarbons from the crankcase into the atmosphere, the engine is sealed and the blow-by gases and oil vapour are drawn from inside the crankcase, through a wire-mesh oil separator, into the intake tract to be burned by the engine during normal combustion.

Under conditions of high manifold depression, the gases will be sucked positively out of the crankcase. Under conditions of low manifold depression, the gases are forced out of the crankcase by the (relatively) higher crankcase pressure. If the engine is worn, the raised crankcase pressure (due to increased blow-by) will cause some of the flow to return under all manifold conditions. 1.2 litre engines and 1.4 litre engine codes BBY, BBZ and BKY are fitted with a PCV valve which supplies fresh air to the crankcase under certain conditions.

Exhaust emission control

To minimise the amount of pollutants which escape into the atmosphere, all petrol models are fitted with one or two catalytic converters in the exhaust system. The fuelling system is of the closed-loop type, in which two oxygen (lambda) sensors in the exhaust system provide the engine management system ECM with constant feedback, enabling the ECM to adjust the air/fuel mixture to optimise combustion.

1.2 litre models have one catalytic converter built into the exhaust manifold. 1.4 litre models have two catalytic converters, one located in the exhaust manifold and the other in the rear of the exhaust front pipe.

All engines have one oxygen sensor before and one after the catalytic converter(s) – this enables more efficient monitoring of the exhaust gas, allowing a faster response time. The overall efficiency of the converter itself can also be checked. Details of the oxygen sensor removal and refitting are given in Chapter 4A.

The oxygen sensor has a built-in heating element, controlled by the ECM through the oxygen sensor relay, to quickly bring the sensor's tip to its optimum operating temperature. The sensor's tip is sensitive to oxygen, and sends a voltage signal to the ECM that varies according on the amount of oxygen in the exhaust gas. If the intake air/fuel mixture is too rich, the exhaust gases are low in oxygen so the sensor sends a low-voltage signal, the voltage rising as the mixture weakens and the amount of oxygen rises in the exhaust gases. Peak conversion efficiency of all major pollutants occurs if the intake air/fuel mixture is maintained at the chemically-correct ratio for the complete combustion of petrol of 14.7 parts (by weight) of air to 1 part of fuel (the stoichiometric ratio). The sensor output voltage alters in a large step at this point, the ECM using the signal change as a reference point and correcting the intake air/fuel mixture accordingly by altering the fuel injector pulse width.

An Exhaust Gas Recirculation (EGR) system is also fitted to most models (see Specifications). This reduces the level of nitrogen oxides produced during combustion by introducing a proportion of the inert exhaust gas back into the intake manifold, under certain engine operating conditions, through a plunger valve. The system is controlled electronically by the engine management ECM.

Evaporative emission control

To minimise the escape of unburned hydrocarbons into the atmosphere, an evaporative loss emission control system is fitted to all petrol models. The fuel tank filler cap is sealed and a charcoal canister is mounted underneath the right-hand rear wheel arch to collect the petrol vapours released from the fuel contained in the fuel tank. It stores them until they can be drawn from the canister (under the control of the fuel injection/ignition system ECM) through the purge valve(s) into the intake tract, where they are then burned by the engine during normal combustion.

To ensure that the engine runs correctly when it is cold and/or idling and to protect the catalytic converter from the effects of an over-rich mixture, the purge control valve(s) are not opened by the ECM until the engine has warmed-up, and the engine is under load; the valve solenoid is then modulated on and off to allow the stored vapour to pass into the intake tract.

Exhaust systems

The exhaust system comprises the exhaust manifold, front pipe, intermediate pipe and silencer, and tailpipe and silencer. When new, the intermediate and tailpipe sections are one, however, service replacement sections are available separately.

The system is supported by various metal brackets attached to the underbody, with rubber vibration dampers fitted to suppress noise.

Diesel engine systems

All diesel-engined models have a crankcase emission control system and, in addition, are fitted with a catalytic converter. All diesel engines are also fitted with an Exhaust Gas Recirculation (EGR) system to reduce exhaust emissions.

Crankcase emission control

To reduce the emission of unburned hydrocarbons from the crankcase into the atmosphere, the engine is sealed and the blow-by gases and oil vapour are taken from inside the crankcase, through a wire mesh oil separator, into the intake tract to be burned by the engine during normal combustion.

The gases are forced out of the crankcase by the relatively higher crankcase pressure. All diesel engines have a pressure-regulating valve on the camshaft cover, to control the flow of gases from the crankcase.

Exhaust emission control

An oxidation catalyst (catalytic converter) is fitted in the exhaust system of all diesel-engined models. This has the effect of removing a large proportion of the gaseous hydrocarbons, carbon monoxide and particulates present in the exhaust gas. On 1.9 litre engine code BMT and 1.4 litre engine code BMS, a particulate filter is fitted to the exhaust system instead of the catalyst.

An Exhaust Gas Recirculation (EGR) system is fitted to all diesel-engined models. This reduces the level of nitrogen oxides produced during combustion by introducing a proportion of the exhaust gas back into the intake manifold, under certain engine operating conditions, through a plunger valve. The system is controlled electronically by the diesel engine management ECM.

Exhaust systems

The exhaust system comprises the exhaust manifold, front pipe with catalytic converter or particulate filter, intermediate pipe (and silencer according to model), and tailpipe and silencer. The turbocharger is either bolted to, or integral with, the exhaust manifold, and is driven by the exhaust gases.

The system is supported by various metal brackets attached to the underbody, with rubber vibration dampers fitted to suppress noise.

2 Evaporative loss emission control system – information and component renewal

Note: *This system is only fitted to petrol engine models.*

1 The evaporative loss emission control system consists of the purge valve, the activated charcoal filter canister and connecting vacuum hoses.

2 The purge (or solenoid) valve is located in the right-hand rear corner of the engine

compartment, and the canister is located near the fuel tank behind the right-hand rear wheel arch liner.

3 To remove the purge valve, check that the ignition is switched off, then disconnect the wiring plug and the two hoses.

4 To remove the canister, chock the front wheels, then jack up the rear of the car and support it on axle stands (see *Jacking and vehicle support*). Remove the right-hand rear roadwheel and the wheel arch liner. Disconnect the hose leading to the solenoid valve from the top of the adapter, then disconnect the hose from the fuel tank from the side of the adapter. Unscrew the mounting bolt and lower the canister from the body.

5 Refitting is a reversal of removal.

3 Crankcase emission system – general information

1 The crankcase emission control system consists of hoses connecting the crankcase to the air cleaner or intake manifold.

2 On some petrol engines, an oil separator unit is fitted to the rear of the engine.

3 On diesel engines, a pressure-regulating valve is fitted to the camshaft cover.

4 The system requires no attention other than to check at regular intervals that the hoses, valve and oil separator (as applicable) are free of blockages and in good condition.

4 Exhaust Gas Recirculation (EGR) system – component removal

Petrol engines

EGR valve

1 The EGR system consists of a combined EGR valve and potentiometer (solenoid) valve, together with a series of connecting vacuum hoses. The EGR valve is mounted on an adapter located on the front, left-hand end of the cylinder head. It is connected by a metal pipe to a flange joint on the intermediate plate at the throttle valve control unit on engine codes AUB, and pre-09/2003 engine code BBY, or directly to the intake manifold on 09/2003-on engine code BBY, and engine codes BKY, AZQ, BBZ and BME. A vacuum hose is connected between the EGR valve and the air filter.

2 To remove the EGR valve/potentiometer, first remove the engine top cover.

3 Disconnect the wiring plug and vacuum hose.

4 Unbolt the connecting tube from the throttle valve control unit or intake manifold as applicable **(see illustration)**. Remove and discard the gasket, as a new one must be used on refitting. Also, unscrew the tube support bolt.

4.4 EGR valve connecting tube on the intake manifold

4.5b and gasket . . .

5 Unscrew the mounting nuts/bolts securing the EGR valve to the adapter flange on the cylinder head and recover the gasket(s). The nuts/bolts also secure the connecting tube to the valve **(see illustrations)**. Remove and discard the gaskets, as new ones must be used on refitting.

6 If necessary, unbolt the adapter from the cylinder head and discard the gasket.

7 Refitting is a reversal of removal. Use new gaskets, and tighten the mounting nuts/bolts to the specified torque.

4.5a Unscrew the nuts and remove the connecting pipe . . .

4.5c . . . then remove the EGR valve from the adapter (engine code BME)

Diesel engines

Vacuum-operated EGR valve

8 The EGR system consists of the EGR (mechanical) valve, the modulator (solenoid) valve and a series of connecting vacuum hoses.

9 The EGR valve is part of the intake manifold flap housing, and cannot be removed separately.

10 If required, the pipe from the housing to the exhaust manifold can be removed, after unscrewing the flange nuts and bolts. Recover the gasket from each end of the pipe **(see illustration)**.

4.10 EGR pipe mounting details – diesel engine
1 Intake manifold
2 O-ring
3 Intake manifold flap housing
4 EGR valve
5 Mounting bolt
6 From intercooler
7 Gasket
8 Flange nut/bolt
9 Exhaust manifold
10 EGR pipe

H32049

5.4 Turbocharger intake hose

5.5 Connecting tube (arrowed) from the exhaust manifold to the flap/EGR valve housing

11 Refitting the pipe is a reversal of removal. Use new gaskets, and tighten the flange nuts and bolts to the specified torque.

Electrically-operated EGR valve

12 On these engines, the EGR valve is positioned by an electric servo motor integral with the valve housing. The EGR valve housing is separate from the flap housing.

13 The valve housing is secured to the intake manifold by the same bolts that retain the intake manifold flap housing. Remove the flap housing as described in Chapter 4B.

14 Disconnect the motor wiring plug.

15 Detach the EGR pipe from the valve housing, and withdraw it from position.

16 Refitting is a reversal of removal, using new O-ring seals.

EGR solenoid valve/valve block

17 The solenoid valve is mounted on the bulkhead at the right-hand rear of the engine compartment. It is combined into one valve block which includes the flap valve and turbocharge pressure control valve; the valve block can only renewed as one unit.

18 Disconnect the wiring plug.

19 Identify their locations, then disconnect the vacuum hoses.

20 Remove the retaining bolt, and withdraw the valve from the bulkhead.

21 Refitting is a reversal of removal. Ensure that the hoses and wiring plug are reconnected securely and correctly.

> **5 Turbocharger** – general information, precautions, removal and refitting

General information

The turbocharger is fitted to all diesel engines. On 1.4 litre engines except engine code BMS, it is bolted to the bottom of the exhaust manifold, and on 1.9 litre engines and engine code BMS, it is integral with the manifold.

The turbocharger increases engine efficiency by raising the pressure in the intake manifold above atmospheric pressure. Instead of the air simply being sucked into the cylinders, it is forced in. Additional fuel is supplied by the

injection pump, in proportion to the increased amount of air.

Energy for the operation of the turbocharger comes from the exhaust gas. The gas flows through a specially-shaped housing (the turbine housing) and in so doing spins the turbine wheel. The turbine wheel is attached to a shaft, at the end of which is another vaned wheel, known as the compressor wheel. The compressor wheel spins in its own housing, and compresses the inducted air on the way to the intake manifold.

Between the turbocharger and the intake manifold, the compressed air passes through an intercooler. The purpose of the intercooler is to remove from the inducted air some of the heat gained by being compressed. Because cooler air is denser, removal of this heat further increases engine efficiency.

Boost pressure (the pressure in the intake manifold) is limited by a wastegate, which diverts the exhaust gas away from the turbine wheel in response to a pressure-sensitive actuator.

The turbo shaft is pressure-lubricated by an oil feed pipe from the engine oil filter mounting. The shaft 'floats' on a cushion of oil. Oil is returned to the sump through a return pipe that connects to the sump.

Some engines have a so-called 'adjustable' turbocharger, which further boosts the engine's power output compared with a normal turbo installation. At low engine speeds, vanes are used to restrict the exhaust gas supply pathway before the gases hit the turbine wheel – this has the effect of increasing the gas flow

5.6 Turbocharger oil feed pipe (arrowed)

through the restriction, and the wheel reaches optimum speed faster (reducing turbo 'lag'). At higher engine speeds, the vanes open up the supply pathway, which lowers the exhaust back-pressure and reduces fuel consumption.

Precautions

The turbocharger operates at extremely high speeds and temperatures. Certain precautions must be observed to avoid premature failure of the turbo, or injury to the operator.

• *Do not operate the turbo with any parts exposed. Foreign objects falling onto the rotating vanes could cause excessive damage and (if ejected) personal injury.*

• *Cover the turbocharger air intake ducts to prevent debris entering, and clean using lint-free cloths only.*

• *Do not race the engine immediately after start-up, especially if it is cold. Give the oil a few seconds to circulate.*

• *Always allow the engine to return to idle speed before switching it off – do not blip the throttle and switch off, as this will leave the turbo spinning without lubrication.*

• *Allow the engine to idle for several minutes before switching off after a high-speed run.*

• *Observe the recommended intervals for oil and filter changing, and use a reputable oil of the specified quality. Neglect of oil changing, or use of inferior oil, can cause carbon formation on the turbo shaft and subsequent failure. Thoroughly clean the area around all oil pipe unions before disconnecting them, to prevent the ingress of dirt. Store dismantled components in a sealed container to prevent contamination.*

1.4 litre engines

Except engine code BMS

1 Apply the handbrake, then jack up the front of the car and support it on axle stands (see *Jacking and vehicle support*). Remove the engine compartment undershield.

2 Remove the engine top cover.

3 Loosen the clips and remove the charge air pipe leading from the intercooler to the flap/EGR housing on the intake manifold. Also disconnect the charge air pipe from the air cleaner to the rear tube.

4 Loosen the clip and disconnect the hose from the turbocharger intake **(see illustration)**, then unbolt and remove the rear tube.

5 Unscrew the nuts and remove the connecting tube leading from the exhaust manifold to the flap/EGR valve housing. Recover the gaskets **(see illustration)**.

6 Unscrew the union nuts connecting the oil feed pipe to the turbocharger and engine **(see illustration)**, then unscrew the nut from the support bracket. Remove the oil feed pipe.

7 Unscrew the two bolts securing the turbocharger to the bottom of the exhaust manifold. Do not remove the mounting nut at this stage.

8 Remove the right-hand driveshaft as described in Chapter 8. Also, unbolt the driveshaft heat shield from the cylinder block.

9 Release the clip and disconnect the outlet air hose from the bottom of the turbocharger.

10 Identify then disconnect the wastegate and valve block vacuum hoses from the turbocharger.

11 Working beneath the car, unscrew the union nut connecting the oil return line from the turbocharger to the cylinder block **(see illustration)**. Unscrew the bolts and detach the return line flange from the turbocharger. Recover the gasket.

12 Refer to Section 9 and remove the exhaust front pipe and catalytic converter. Recover the gasket from the studs on the turbocharger **(see illustration)**.

13 Support the turbocharger, then unscrew the remaining mounting nut from the manifold stud. Lower the turbocharger and remove from under the car. No gasket is fitted between the turbocharger and exhaust manifold.

14 Refit the turbocharger by following the removal procedure in reverse, noting the following points:

a) *Renew all gaskets, sealing washers and O-rings.*

b) *Renew the turbocharger mounting bolts and nut, and before fitting them, coat their threads and heads with anti-seize compound.*

c) *Before reconnecting the oil supply pipe, fill the turbocharger with fresh oil using an oil can.*

d) *Tighten all nuts and bolts to the specified torque, where given.*

e) *Ensure that the air hose clips are securely tightened, to prevent air leaks.*

5.11 Oil return line and turbocharger outlet hose (arrowed)

f) *When the engine is started after refitting, allow it to idle for approximately one minute to give the oil time to circulate around the turbine shaft bearings. Check for signs of oil or coolant leakage from the relevant unions.*

Engine code BMS

15 Pull the inner and outer engine cover upwards from their rubber mountings.

16 Release the clamps and remove the air hose and duct from the intercooler to the intake manifold. Disconnect the air pressure sensor wiring plug as the ducting is removed.

17 Remove the electrically-operated EGR valve as described in the previous Section.

18 Note their fitted positions and the harness routing, then disconnect the oxygen sensor and exhaust temperature sensor wiring plugs.

19 Unscrew the oxygen sensor and temperature sensor from the exhaust manifold **(see illustration)**.

20 Undo the bolts and remove the heat shield from the particulate filter.

5.12 Exhaust front pipe-to-turbocharger gasket (arrowed)

21 Release the clamp securing the particulate filter to the turbocharger.

22 Raise the front of the vehicle and support it securely on axle stands (see *Jacking and vehicle support*). Undo the fasteners and remove the engine undershield.

23 Undo the unions and detach the pressure sensor hose and temperature sensor from the base of the particulate filter.

24 Disconnect the wiring plug, undo the retaining bolts and remove the exhaust pressure sensor along with the hoses.

25 Slacken the clamp securing the front section of the exhaust pipe to the intermediate section.

26 Working underneath the vehicle, undo the four nuts and remove the brace beneath the exhaust system.

27 Undo the bolts and remove the support bracket from the base of the particulate filter and the engine block. Lower the particulate filter/exhaust pipe and allow it to rest on the steering rack **(see illustration)**.

5.19 Particulate filter details – engine code BMS

1 *Turbocharger*	5 *Heat shield*
2 *Pressure take-off union*	6 *Pressure tube*
3 *Pressure take-off union*	7 *Oxygen sensor*
4 *Filter-to-turbocharger clamp*	8 *Exhaust gas temperature sensor*

5.27 Undo the bolts (arrowed) securing the support bracket to the particulate filter

5.28 Turbocharger details – engine code BMS

1	Turbocharger oil return pipe	4	Turbocharger lower mounting bolt
2	EGR pipe	5	Intake hose clamp
3	EGR cooler	6	Outlet hose clamp

6.3 Vacuum hose connections

1	Valve block	7	Vacuum unit for intake manifold flap valve
2	Vacuum connector strip	8	Connectors
3	Connector	9	Vacuum reservoir
4	Tandem vacuum pump	10	Charge pressure control vacuum unit
5	Brake vacuum servo unit	11	To air cleaner
6	Mechanical EGR valve		

28 Release the clamp and remove the air intake hose and outlet hoses from the turbocharger **(see illustration)**.

29 Undo the bolts securing the EGR pipe to the exhaust manifold.

30 Undo the union bolt and nuts, then manoeuvre the turbocharger oil return pipe from position.

31 Undo the nuts and remove the heat shield from the exhaust manifold.

32 Undo the union nuts, release the pipe support bracket and disconnect the oil supply pipe from the oil filter housing and turbocharger.

33 Undo the retaining nuts, and lower the exhaust manifold/turbocharger assembly onto the steering rack.

34 Remove the intake manifold as described in Chapter 4B, then manoeuvre the exhaust manifold/turbocharger upwards from the engine compartment.

35 Refit the turbocharger by following the removal procedure in reverse, noting the following points:

a) Renew all gaskets, sealing washers and O-rings.

b) Renew the exhaust manifold mounting nuts, and before fitting them, coat their threads and heads with anti-seize compound.

c) Before reconnecting the oil supply pipe, fill the turbocharger with fresh oil using an oil can.

d) Tighten all nuts and bolts to the specified torque, where given.

e) Ensure that the air hose clips are securely tightened, to prevent air leaks.

f) When the engine is started after refitting, allow it to idle for approximately one minute to give the oil time to circulate

around the turbine shaft bearings. Check for signs of oil or coolant leakage from the relevant unions.

1.9 litre engines

Except engine code BMT

36 Apply the handbrake, then jack up the front of the car and support it on axle stands (see *Jacking and vehicle support*). Remove the engine compartment undershield.

37 Remove the engine top cover.

38 Remove the right-hand driveshaft as described in Chapter 8. Also unbolt the driveshaft heat shield from the cylinder block.

39 Release the clips and disconnect the air hose and connecting tube leading from the bottom of the intercooler to the turbocharger outlet hose by the crankshaft pulley, then disconnect both charge air hoses from the turbocharger. Also disconnect the charge air pipe from the air cleaner.

40 Unscrew the union nut and detach the oil return line from the cylinder block.

41 Unbolt and remove the turbocharger lower support bracket.

42 Disconnect the vacuum hose from the wastegate control on the turbocharger.

43 Refer to Section 9 and remove the exhaust front pipe and catalytic converter from the turbocharger. Recover the gasket from the studs.

44 Unscrew the nuts and remove the connecting tube leading from the exhaust manifold to the flap/EGR valve housing. Recover the gaskets.

45 Unscrew the union nuts connecting the oil feed pipe to the turbocharger and engine, then unscrew the nut/bolt from the support bracket. Remove the oil feed pipe.

46 Progressively unscrew the nuts and bolts securing the exhaust manifold/turbocharger to

the cylinder head, then withdraw the assembly and recover the gasket. Discard the gasket as a new one must be used for refitting.

47 Refit the turbocharger by following the removal procedure in reverse, noting the following points:

a) Renew all gaskets, sealing washers and O-rings.

b) Before reconnecting the oil supply pipe, fill the turbocharger with fresh oil using an oil can.

c) Tighten all nuts and bolts to the specified torque, where given.

d) Ensure that the air hose clips are securely tightened, to prevent air leaks.

e) When the engine is started after refitting, allow it to idle for approximately one minute to give the oil time to circulate around the turbine shaft bearings. Check for signs of oil or coolant leakage from the relevant unions.

Engine code BMT

48 Removal and refitting of the turbocharger/ exhaust manifold for this engine is identical to that described for the 1.4 litre engine code BMS previously in this Section.

6 Turbocharger boost pressure solenoid valve – removal and refitting

Removal

1 The boost pressure solenoid valve is incorporated into a valve block on the right-hand side of the bulkhead.

2 Disconnect the wiring plug.

3 Identify their locations, then disconnect the vacuum hoses **(see illustration)**.

4 Remove the retaining bolt and withdraw the valve from the bulkhead.

Refitting

5 Refitting is a reversal of removal. Ensure that the hoses and wiring plug are reconnected securely and correctly.

---

7 Intercooler – general information, removal and refitting

General information

1 The intercooler is effectively an 'air radiator', used to cool the pressurised intake air before it enters the engine. When the turbocharger compresses the intake air, one side-effect is that the air is heated, causing the air to expand. If the intake air can be cooled, a greater effective volume of air will be inducted, and the engine will produce more power.

2 The compressed air from the turbocharger, which would normally be fed straight into the intake manifold, is instead ducted around the engine to the base of the intercooler. The intercooler is mounted behind the wheel arch liner beneath the right-hand front wing, in the airflow. The heated air entering the base of the unit rises upwards, and is cooled by the airflow over the intercooler fins, much as with the radiator. When it reaches the top of the intercooler, the cooled air is then ducted into the intake manifold.

Removal

All except engine codes ASZ and BLT

3 To gain access to the intercooler, remove the front bumper as described in Chapter 11, and the right-hand headlight as described in Chapter 12, Section 7. Also, remove the right-hand front wheel arch liner, and the intercooler air ducting (see illustration).

4 Disconnect the wiring from the intake manifold pressure/temperature sender located on the top of the intercooler.

5 Release the outlet hose/ducting from its supports, then use grips to release the spring clip and disconnect the hose from the top of the intercooler. **Note:** *Some models have quick-release fittings; pull out the clip to release it.*

6 Release the spring clip and disconnect the intake hose from the bottom of the intercooler.

7 Unscrew the mounting bolts and withdraw the intercooler from the engine compartment (see illustration).

8 Examine the intercooler for any damage, and check the air hoses for splits. The charge pressure/temperature sender may be removed from the top of the intercooler by unscrewing the two mounting bolts – recover the O-ring seal and examine it for condition.

Engine codes ASZ and BLT

9 Remove the front bumper and mounting bar as described in Chapter 11.

7.3 Remove the intercooler air ducting

10 Release the clamps securing the intake and outlet hoses to the intercooler.

11 Undo the bolts and remove the intercooler.

Refitting

12 Refitting is a reversal of removal. Ensure that the hose clips are securely tightened, to prevent air leaks, and fit a new O-ring seal to the charge pressure/temperature sender (where applicable).

---

8 Exhaust manifold – removal and refitting

Petrol engines

Removal

1 All engines have a catalytic converter

8.1 Exhaust manifold and catalytic converter on engine code BME (arrowed)

8.5b ... and lower mounting bolts

7.7 The intercooler is located beneath the right-hand front wheel arch

integrated into the exhaust manifold (see illustration).

2 Remove the engine top cover.

3 Apply the handbrake, then jack up the front of the car and support it on axle stands (see *Jacking and vehicle support*). Remove the engine undershield. If necessary for additional working room, remove the electric cooling fan and shroud from the rear of the radiator as described in Chapter 3.

4 Pull the warm-air hose (for the air cleaner) from the heat shield over the manifold, and place the hose end to one side.

5 Unscrew the bolts and remove the heat shield from the manifold. Note that on some models, additional extended shields are fitted, including some bolted to the cylinder block (see illustrations).

6 Trace the wiring from the oxygen sensor in the manifold to the connector plug. Disconnect the wiring plug, and free the wiring from any

8.5a Heat shield upper mounting bolts (arrowed) . . .

8.5c Remove the heat shield from the exhaust manifold

8.5d Cylinder block heat shield (arrowed) on engine code BME (exhaust manifold removed)

8.10a . . . remove the exhaust manifold . . .

9.4 Front pipe and catalytic converter on engine code BBY

8.9 Unscrew the retaining nuts . . .

8.10b . . . and recover the gasket

retaining clips or ties. Unscrew and remove the sensor, alternatively, leave it in position until after the manifold has been removed.

7 Where fitted, unbolt and remove the manifold support bracket.

8 Unscrew the nuts and detach the exhaust front pipe from the bottom of the exhaust manifold. On some models, it may be necessary to completely remove the front pipe with reference to Section 9. Discard the gasket, and obtain a new one for refitting.

9 Unscrew and remove the manifold retaining nuts, noting that some manifold studs may come out with the nuts **(see illustration)**.

10 Remove the washers, then withdraw the manifold from the cylinder head, and recover the gasket(s) from the studs **(see illustrations)**.

11 Where any studs have unscrewed, grip them in a vice and unscrew the nuts. Apply locking fluid to the threads before refitting and

tightening the studs into the cylinder head again. Use two nuts tightened against each other to tighten the studs.

Refitting

12 Refitting is a reversal of the removal procedure, noting the following points:
   a) *Always fit new gaskets.*
   b) *If any studs were broken when removing, drill out the remains of the stud, and fit new studs and nuts.*
   c) *Tighten all nuts and bolts to the specified torque where given.*

Diesel engines

Note: *Removal and refitting of the exhaust manifold/turbocharger on 1.9 litre engines and 1.4 litre engine code BMS, is covered in Section 5. This sub-section covers removal on the remaining 1.4 litre engines only.*

Removal

13 The turbocharger is bolted to the underside of the exhaust manifold.

14 Remove the engine top cover.

15 Apply the handbrake, then jack up the front of the car and support it on axle stands (see *Jacking and vehicle support*). Remove the engine undershield.

16 Access to the exhaust manifold is greatly improved if the intake manifold is removed first, as described in Part B of this Chapter.

17 Remove the turbocharger as described in Section 5.

18 Referring to Section 4, remove the EGR connecting pipe from the exhaust manifold.

19 Unscrew the retaining nuts, and separate the exhaust downpipe from the manifold

or turbocharger. There should be sufficient movement in the pipe to free it from the studs – if not, loosen the bolts securing the exhaust front mounting.

20 Support the manifold, then unscrew and remove the manifold retaining nuts and recover the washers. Withdraw the exhaust manifold from the cylinder head studs and withdraw from under the car. Recover the manifold gasket from the cylinder head studs, and discard them.

Refitting

21 Refitting is a reversal of the removal procedure, but fit new gaskets, and tighten all nuts and bolts to the specified torque where given.

9 Exhaust system – component renewal

Warning: Allow ample time for the exhaust system to cool before starting work. In particular, note that the catalytic converter runs at very high temperatures. If there is any chance that the system may still be hot, wear suitable gloves.

Removal

1 The original Seat system fitted in the factory is in two sections. The front section can be removed separately. The original rear section cannot be removed in one piece, as it passes over the rear axle – the pipe must be cut through between the centre and rear silencers, at the point marked on the pipe. There are three markings, and the pipe must be cut on the centre mark.

2 To remove part of the system, first jack up the front or rear of the car and support it on axle stands (see *Jacking and vehicle support*). Alternatively, position the car over an inspection pit or on car ramps.

3 On diesel models equipped with a particulate filter (codes BMS and BMT), in order to remove the filter, numerous special tools are needed and the front subframe must be lowered. Once renewed, the adaption values stored in the engine management ECM must be reset using dedicated diagnostic equipment. Consequently, we recommend that filter renewal is entrusted to a Seat dealer or suitably-equipped specialist.

Front pipe (with catalytic converter)

Note: *Handle the flexible, braided section of the front pipe carefully, and do not bend it excessively.*

4 On petrol models, carry out the following:
   a) *Before removing the front section of the exhaust, check if any oxygen sensors are fitted (see illustration). Trace the wiring back from the sensors, and disconnect the wiring connector. On some models, the sensor wiring disappears behind an access panel behind the right-hand*

9.5 Remove the clamp securing the exhaust front pipe to the rear pipe

driveshaft, and it will be necessary to remove the cover fitted over the right-hand inner CV joint (or even the complete driveshaft, as described in Chapter 8) for access.

b) Unclip the oxygen sensor wiring from any clips or brackets, noting how it is routed for refitting.

c) If a new front section is being fitted, unscrew the oxygen sensor(s) from the pipe where applicable. If two sensors are fitted, note which fits where, as they must not be interchanged.

5 Loosen the two nuts on the clamp at the rear of the front pipe, and free the clamp so

H31995

9.6c Exhaust front pipe – diesel models

1 From turbocharger	4 Catalytic converter
2 Front pipe gasket	5 To exhaust rear section
3 Mounting nut/ bolt	6 Front mounting

9.6a Exhaust front flange (arrowed) on the manifold

that it can be moved relative to the front and rear pipes **(see illustration)**.

6 Unscrew and remove the nuts securing the front flange to the exhaust manifold or turbocharger. On some models, the shield over the right-hand driveshaft inner CV joint must be removed to improve access, and additionally on some models, the front pipe is supported by a metal rod **(see illustrations)**. Separate the front joint, and move the front pipe down sufficiently to clear the mounting studs. Recover and discard the gasket.

7 Release the rubber mountings from the metal pegs and support the front of the pipe **(see illustration)**.

8 Slide the clamp behind the catalyst either forwards or backwards to separate the joint. Twist the front pipe slightly from side-to-side, while pulling towards the front to release it from the rear section. When the pipe is free, lower it to the ground and remove it from under the car.

Rear pipe and silencer(s)

9 If the factory-fitted Seat rear section is being worked on, examine the pipe for three pairs of punch marks, or three line markings. The centre marking indicates the point at which to cut the pipe, while the outer marks indicate the position for the ends of the new clamp required when refitting. Cut through the pipe using the centre mark as a guide, making the cut as square to the pipe as possible if either resulting section is to be re-used.

10 If the factory-fitted rear section has already been renewed, loosen the nuts securing the clamp between the two sections so that the clamp can be moved.

Centre silencer

11 To remove the centre silencer, loosen the nuts on the front and rear clamps.

12 Slide the clamps at either end of the silencer section to release the pipe ends, withdraw the support peg from the rubber mounting, and withdraw the silencer from under the car.

Rear silencer

13 The rear silencer is supported in front and behind by rubber mountings attached to the underside of the car. Loosen the nuts on the clamp securing the rear silencer to the centre silencer.

9.6b Front exhaust pipe support rod (arrowed) on engine code BME

14 Ease the rear silencer from the clamp, withdraw the support pegs from the rubber mountings and withdraw the silencer from under the car.

Refitting

15 Each section is refitted by a reversal of the removal sequence, noting the following points:

a) Ensure that all traces of corrosion have been removed from the flanges or pipe ends, and renew the downpipe gasket where removed.

b) The design of the clamps used between the exhaust sections means that they play a greater role in ensuring a gas-tight seal – fit new clamps if they are in less than perfect condition.

c) When fitting the clamps, use the markings on the pipes as a guide to the clamp's correct fitted position.

d) Inspect the mountings for signs of damage or deterioration, and renew as necessary.

e) If using exhaust assembly paste, make sure this is only applied to joints downstream of the catalyst.

f) Prior to tightening the exhaust system mountings and clamps, ensure that all rubber mountings are correctly located and that there is adequate clearance between the exhaust system and vehicle underbody. Try to ensure that no unnecessary twisting stresses are applied to the pipes – move the pipes relative to each other at the clamps to relieve this.

g) If the particulate filter on diesel engines

9.7 Using a special tool to remove the exhaust rubber mountings

has be renewed, the adaption values stored in the engine management ECM must be reset using special diagnostic equipment. Entrust this task to a SEAT dealer or suitably-equipped diesel specialist.

10 Catalytic converter – general information and precautions

The catalytic converter is a reliable and simple device which needs no maintenance in itself, but there are some facts of which an owner should be aware if the converter is to function properly for its full service life:

a) DO NOT use leaded or lead-replacement petrol in a car equipped with a catalytic converter – the lead (or other additives) will coat the precious metals, reducing their converting efficiency and will eventually destroy the converter.

b) Always keep the ignition/fuel systems well-maintained in accordance with the manufacturer's schedule.

c) If the engine develops a misfire, do not drive the car at all (or at least as little as possible) until the fault is cured.

d) DO NOT use fuel or engine oil additives – these may contain substances harmful to the catalytic converter.

e) DO NOT continue to use the car if the engine burns oil to the extent of leaving a visible trail of blue smoke.

f) Remember that the catalytic converter operates at very high temperatures. DO NOT, therefore, park the car in dry undergrowth, over long grass or piles of dead leaves after a long run.

g) Remember that the catalytic converter is FRAGILE – do not strike it with tools during servicing work, and take care handling it when removing it from the car for any reason.

h) In some cases, a sulphurous smell (like that of rotten eggs) may be noticed from the exhaust. This is common to many catalytic converter-equipped cars, and has more to do with the sulphur content of the brand of fuel being used than the converter itself.

i) The catalytic converter, used on a well-maintained and well-driven car, should last for between 50 000 and 100 000 miles – if the converter is no longer effective, it must be renewed.

Chapter 5 Part A:
Starting and charging systems

Contents

Degrees of difficulty

Easy, suitable for novice with little experience	**Fairly easy,** suitable for beginner with some experience	**Fairly difficult,** suitable for competent DIY mechanic	**Difficult,** suitable for experienced DIY mechanic	**Very difficult,** suitable for expert DIY or professional

Specifications

General

System type . . . . 12 volt, negative-earth

Starter motor

Rating:
    Petrol engines . . . . 12V, 1.1 kW
    Diesel engines . . . . 12V, 2.0 kW

Battery

Ratings . . . . 36 to 72 Ah (depending on model and market)

Alternator

Rating . . . . 55, 60, 70 or 90 amp
Minimum brush length . . . . 5.0 mm

Glow plugs

Electrical resistance (typical – no value quoted by Seat) . . . . 1.5 ohms
Current consumption (typical – no value quoted by Seat) . . . . 8 amps (per plug)

Torque wrench settings

	Nm	lbf ft
Alternator mounting bolts:		
Petrol engines:		
1.2 litre	23	17
1.4 litre	20	15
Diesel engines	25	18
Battery clamping plate bolt	22	16
Battery tray.	20	15
Glow plug to cylinder head	15	11
Starter motor mounting bolts.	65	48

1 General information and precautions

General information

The engine electrical system consists mainly of the charging and starting systems. Because of their engine-related functions, these are covered separately from the body electrical devices such as the lights, instruments, etc (which are covered in Chapter 12). On petrol engine models refer to Part B of this Chapter for information on the ignition system.

The electrical system is of the 12 volt negative-earth type.

The battery may of the low-maintenance or maintenance-free (sealed for life) type and is charged by the alternator, which is belt-driven from the crankshaft pulley.

The starter motor is of the pre-engaged type, with an integral solenoid. On starting, the solenoid moves the drive pinion into engagement with the flywheel ring gear before the starter motor is energised. Once the engine has started, a one-way clutch prevents the motor armature being driven by the engine until the pinion disengages from the flywheel.

Further details of the various systems are given in the relevant Sections of this Chapter. While some repair procedures are given, the usual course of action is to renew the component concerned.

Precautions

⚠ **Warning: It is necessary to take extra care when working on the electrical system to avoid damage to semi-conductor devices (diodes and transistors), and to avoid the risk of personal injury. In addition to the precautions given in 'Safety first!', observe the following when working on the system:**

• Always remove rings, watches, etc, before working on the electrical system. Even with the battery disconnected, capacitive discharge could occur if a component's live terminal is earthed through a metal object. This could cause a shock or nasty burn.

• Do not reverse the battery connections. Components such as the alternator, electronic control modules, or any other components having semi-conductor circuitry could be irreparably damaged.

• Never disconnect the battery terminals, the alternator, any electrical wiring or any test instruments when the engine is running.

• Do not allow the engine to turn the alternator when the alternator is not connected.

• Never test for alternator output by flashing the output lead to earth.

• Always ensure that the battery negative lead is disconnected when working on the electrical system.

• If the engine is being started using jump leads and a slave battery, connect the batteries positive-to-positive and negative-to-negative

(see Jump starting at the beginning of the manual). This also applies when connecting a battery charger.

• Before using electric-arc welding equipment on the car, disconnect the battery, alternator and components such as the electronic control units (where applicable) to protect them from the risk of damage.

Caution: Certain radios fitted as standard equipment by Seat have a built-in security code to deter thieves. If the power source to the unit is cut, the anti-theft system will activate. Even if the power source is immediately reconnected, the radio will not function until the correct security code has been entered. Therefore, if you do not know the correct security code for the radio do not disconnect the battery negative terminal or remove the audio unit from the car. Refer to your Seat dealer for further information on whether the unit fitted to your car has a security code.

2 Battery – testing and charging

Testing

Standard and low-maintenance battery

1 If the car covers a small annual mileage, it is worthwhile checking the specific gravity of the electrolyte every three months to determine the state of charge of the battery. Remove the battery (see Section 3) then remove the cell caps/cover (as applicable) and use a hydrometer to make the check, comparing the results with the following table. Note that the specific gravity readings assume an electrolyte temperature of 15°C; for every 10°C below 15°C subtract 0.007. For every 10°C above 15°C add 0.007. If the electrolyte level of any cell is low, top it up to the MAX level mark with distilled water.

	Above 25°C	Below 25°C
Fully-charged	1.210 to 1.230	1.270 to 1.290
70% charged	1.170 to 1.190	1.230 to 1.250
Discharged	1.050 to 1.070	1.110 to 1.130

2 If the battery condition is suspect, first check the specific gravity of electrolyte in each cell. A variation of 0.040 or more between any cells indicates loss of electrolyte or deterioration of the internal plates.

3 If the specific gravity variation is 0.040 or more, the battery should be renewed. If the cell variation is satisfactory but the battery is discharged, it should be charged as described later in this Section.

Maintenance-free battery

4 In cases where a sealed for life maintenance-free battery is fitted, topping-up and testing of the electrolyte in each cell is not possible. The condition of the battery can therefore only be tested using a battery condition indicator or a voltmeter.

5 Certain models may be fitted with a maintenance-free battery with a built-in charge condition indicator. The indicator is located in the top of the battery casing, and indicates the condition of the battery from its colour. If the indicator shows green, then the battery is in good condition and charged up. If the indicator turns darker, eventually to black, then the battery requires charging, as described later in this Section. If the indicator shows clear/yellow, then the electrolyte is low and in a critical condition, and should be topped-up with distilled water. If charging the battery does not return the eye to green, the battery should be scrapped.

All battery types

6 If testing the battery using a voltmeter, connect the voltmeter across the battery and note the voltage. The test is only accurate if the battery has not been subjected to any kind of charge for the previous six hours. If this is not the case, switch on the headlights for 30 seconds, then wait four to five minutes before testing the battery after switching off the headlights. All other electrical circuits must be switched off, so check that the doors and tailgate are fully shut when making the test.

7 If the voltage reading is less than 12.2 volts, then the battery is discharged, whilst a reading of 12.2 to 12.4 volts indicates a partially-discharged condition.

8 If the battery is to be charged, remove it from the car and charge it as described later in this Section.

Charging

Note: *The following is intended as a guide only. Always refer to the manufacturer's recommendations (often printed on a label attached to the battery) before charging a battery.*

Standard and low-maintenance battery

9 Charge the battery at a rate equivalent to 10% of the battery capacity (eg, for a 45 Ah battery, charge at 4.5 A) and continue to charge the battery at this rate until no further rise in specific gravity is noted over a four-hour period.

10 Alternatively, a trickle charger charging at the rate of 1.5 amps can safely be used overnight.

11 Specially rapid boost charges which are claimed to restore the power of the battery in 1 to 2 hours are not recommended, as they can cause serious damage to the battery plates through overheating.

12 While charging the battery, note that the temperature of the electrolyte should never exceed 38°C.

Maintenance-free battery

13 This battery type takes considerably longer to fully recharge than the standard type, the time taken being dependent on the extent of discharge, but it can take anything up to three days.

3.3a Release the clip and fold open the cover . . .

3.3b . . . then slacken the nut (arrowed) and disconnect the positive terminal

6 Using a long, flat-bladed screwdriver, release the clip each side, and the one at the rear, and lift up/move to one side the fuse holder assembly **(see illustrations)**.
7 Lift the battery 'box' from place **(see illustration)**.
8 Unscrew the bolt and remove the battery mounting clamp **(see illustration)**. The battery can then be lifted out of position.

Refitting

9 Refit the battery by following the removal procedure in reverse. Tighten the mounting clamp bolt to the correct torque. Tighten the terminal clamp nuts securely, but do not overtighten them to the point where the clamps are distorted.
10 Reconnect the battery as described previously in this Section.

4 Alternator/charging system – testing in car

Note: *Refer to Section 1 of this Chapter before starting work.*
1 If the charge warning light fails to illuminate when the ignition is switched on, first check the alternator wiring connections for security. If the light still fails to illuminate, check the continuity of the warning light feed wire from the alternator to the bulbholder. If all is satisfactory, the alternator is at fault and should be renewed or taken to an auto-electrician for testing and repair.
2 Similarly, if the charge warning light comes on with the ignition, but is then slow to go out when the engine is started, this may indicate an impending alternator problem. Check all

rrowed) and
terminal

ger is required,
9 to 14.9 volts
amps. Using
d be useable
ge reading of
ly-discharged
charging can

from a fully-
ng less than
y your local
charge rate
sion during

disconnection, removal and refitting

Note: *If the car has a security-coded radio, make sure that you have the code number before disconnecting the battery. If necessary, a 'code-saver' or 'memory-saver' can be used to preserve the radio code and any other relevant memory values whilst the battery is disconnected.*

Disconnection

1 The battery is located in the front, left-hand corner of the engine compartment.
2 Loosen the clamp nut and disconnect the battery negative (-) lead from the terminal **(see illustration)**.
3 Depress the clip and open the cover over the positive terminal. Loosen the clamp nut and disconnect the positive (+) lead from the battery terminal **(see illustrations)**.
4 Reconnection is a reversal of removal. The following operations must be performed after battery reconnection:
  a) *Turn the ignition switch on, off and on again.*
  b) *Completely open and close all electric windows. Hold the switch in the closed position for at least 5 seconds, then lower the window fully and hold the button in the closed position for at least 5 seconds to reinitialise the windows positions.*

Removal

5 Disconnect the battery as described previously in this Section.

3.6a Release the clip each side . . .

3.6b . . . and lift the fuse holder/cover assembly upwards

3.7 Lift the battery 'box'

3.8 Undo the battery clamp bolt (arrowed)

5.3 Unplug the 2-pin connector

5.4 Disconnect the positive lead (arrowed)

5.8 Unscrew the mounting bolts (arrowed)

the items listed in the preceding paragraph, and refer to an auto-electrical specialist if no obvious faults are found.

3 If the charge warning light illuminates when the engine is running, stop the engine and check that the auxiliary drivebelt is intact and correctly tensioned, and that the alternator connections are secure. If all is so far satisfactory, check the alternator brushes and slip-rings as described in Section 6. If the fault persists, the alternator should be renewed, or taken to an auto-electrician for testing and repair.

4 If the alternator output is suspect even though the warning light functions correctly, the regulated voltage may be checked as follows.

5 Connect a voltmeter across the battery terminals, and start the engine.

6 Increase the engine speed until the voltmeter reading remains steady; the reading should be approximately 12 to 13 volts, and no more than 14 volts.

7 Switch on as many electrical accessories (eg, the headlights, heated rear window and heater blower) as possible, and check that the alternator maintains the regulated voltage at around 13 to 14 volts.

8 If the regulated voltage is not as stated, this may be due to worn brushes, weak brush springs, a faulty voltage regulator, a faulty diode, a severed phase winding or worn or damaged slip-rings. The brushes and slip-rings may be checked as described in Section 6, but if the fault persists, the alternator should be renewed or taken to an auto-electrician.

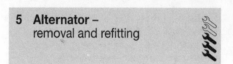

5 Alternator – removal and refitting

Removal

1 Disconnect the battery negative lead as described in Section 3, then remove the engine cover.

2 Remove the auxiliary drivebelt from the alternator pulley (see Chapter 1A or 1B). Mark the drivebelt for direction of rotation to ensure it is refitted correctly.

3 Pull the 2-pin push-in connector from the alternator (see illustration).

4 Remove the protective cap (where fitted), unscrew and remove the nut and washers, then disconnect the battery positive cable from the alternator terminal. Where applicable, unscrew the nut and remove the cable guide (see illustration).

5 On 1.2 litre petrol models, undo the central bolt and remove the auxiliary belt tensioner assembly.

6 On 1.4 litre diesel models from 04/05, undo the 3 bolts and remove the auxiliary belt tensioner assembly.

7 On 1.9 litre diesel models, release the clamps, and remove the section of the air intake ducting to the right-hand side of the alternator.

8 Unscrew and remove the lower and upper bolts, then lift the alternator away from its bracket (see illustration).

Refitting

9 The alternator mounting bushes are self-

centralising and should be carefully tapped back approximately 1.0 mm before refitting.

10 Refitting is a reversal of removal. Refer to Chapter 1A or 1B as applicable for details of refitting the auxiliary drivebelt. Tighten the alternator mounting bolts to the specified torque.

6 Alternator – brush holder/ regulator module renewal

1 Remove the alternator, as described in Section 5.

2 Place the alternator on a clean work surface, with the pulley facing down.

Bosch alternator

3 Undo the bolt and the two retaining nuts, and lift away the outer plastic cover (see illustration).

4 Undo the 3 bolts, and remove the voltage regulator (see illustrations).

Valeo alternator

5 Remove the suppressor rings, and remove the protective cap from the rear of the alternator.

6 Undo the 3 bolts and remove the voltage regulator/brush holder.

All alternators

7 Measure the free length of the brush contacts (see illustration). Check the measurement with the Specifications; renew the module if the brushes are worn below the minimum limit.

6.3 Remove the outer cover

6.4a Undo the three bolts . . .

6.4b . . . and remove the brush holder regulator

8 Clean and inspect the surfaces of the slip-rings, at the end of the alternator shaft **(see illustration)**. If they are excessively worn, or damaged, the alternator must be renewed.

9 Before refitting the module, depress the brushes in their released position, and hold them there by pulling out the cap – with the module in position, press the cap to release the brushes. The remaining reassembly is a reversal of the dismantling procedure. On completion, refer to Section 5 and refit the alternator.

7 Starting system – testing

Note: *Refer to Section 1 of this Chapter before starting work.*

1 If the starter motor fails to operate when the ignition key is turned to the appropriate position, the following faults may be the cause:

  a) *The battery is faulty.*
  b) *The electrical connections between the switch, solenoid, battery and starter motor are somewhere failing to pass the necessary current from the battery through the starter to earth.*
  c) *The solenoid is faulty.*
  d) *The starter motor is mechanically or electrically defective.*

2 To check the battery, switch on the headlights. If they dim after a few seconds, this indicates that the battery is discharged – recharge (see Section 2) or renew the battery. If the headlights glow brightly, operate the ignition switch and

8.3 Solenoid trigger wire

8.5a Remove the earth cable (arrowed) . . .

6.7 Measure the brush length

observe the lights. If they dim, then this indicates that current is reaching the starter motor, therefore the fault must lie in the starter motor. If the lights continue to glow brightly (and no clicking sound can be heard from the starter motor solenoid), this indicates that there is a fault in the circuit or solenoid – see following paragraphs. If the starter motor turns slowly when operated, but the battery is in good condition, then this indicates that either the starter motor is faulty, or there is considerable resistance somewhere in the circuit.

3 If a fault in the circuit is suspected, disconnect the battery leads (including the earth connection to the body), the starter/solenoid wiring and the engine/transmission earth strap. **Note:** *Before disconnecting the battery, refer to Section 3 of this Chapter.* Thoroughly clean the connections, and reconnect the leads and wiring, then use a voltmeter or test light to check that full battery voltage is available at the battery positive lead

8.4 Battery positive cable (arrowed) on the starter solenoid terminal

8.5b . . . then unscrew the starter top bolt

6.8 Clean and inspect the surfaces of the slip-rings (arrowed)

connection to the solenoid, and that the earth is sound.

4 If the battery and all connections are in good condition, check the circuit by disconnecting the wire from the solenoid blade terminal. Connect a voltmeter or test light between the wire end and a good earth (such as the battery negative terminal), and check that the wire is live when the ignition switch is turned to the start position. If it is, then the circuit is sound, if not, the circuit wiring can be checked as described in Chapter 12.

5 The solenoid contacts can be checked by connecting a voltmeter or test light between the battery positive feed connection on the starter side of the solenoid, and earth. When the ignition switch is turned to the start position, there should be a reading or lighted bulb, as applicable. If there is no reading or lighted bulb, the solenoid is faulty and should be renewed.

6 If the circuit and solenoid are proved sound, the fault must lie in the starter motor. It may be possible to have the starter motor overhauled by a specialist, but check on the availability and cost of spares before proceeding, as it may prove more economical to obtain a new or exchange motor.

8 Starter motor – removal and refitting

Removal

1 Disconnect the battery negative lead as described in Section 3. Remove the engine top cover.

2 Where necessary for improved access, remove the battery with reference to Section 3, then unbolt and remove the battery mounting bracket.

3 Disconnect the trigger wiring from the solenoid **(see illustration)**.

4 Remove the cap (if fitted), then unscrew the nut and disconnect the battery positive cable from the solenoid terminal **(see illustration)**.

5 Unscrew the upper starter motor mounting bolts, noting that one of the bolts is facing inwards and the other outwards. On most models, an earth cable is located on the bolt facing outwards **(see illustrations)**.

11.9 Test the glow plugs using a multimeter

11.12 Wiring loom for the glow plugs – 1.9 litre engine shown

6 In order to gain access to the underside of the car, apply the handbrake, then jack up the front of the car and support it on axle stands (see *Jacking and vehicle support*). Remove the engine undershield.

7 Unscrew the remaining lower mounting bolt, withdraw the starter motor and lift it from the engine.

Refitting

8 Refit the starter motor by following the removal procedure in reverse. Tighten the mounting bolts to the specified torque.

9 Starter motor – testing and overhaul

If the starter motor is thought to be defective, it should be removed from the car and taken to an auto-electrician for assessment. In the majority of cases, new starter motor brushes can be fitted at a reasonable cost. However, check the cost of repairs first as it may prove more economical to purchase a new or exchange motor.

10 Diesel preheating system – general information

To assist cold starting, diesel models are fitted with a preheating system, which comprises one glow plug per cylinder, a glow plug control unit (incorporated in the ECM), a facia-mounted warning light and the associated electrical wiring.

The glow plugs are miniature electric heating elements, encapsulated in a metal case with a probe at one end and electrical connection at the other. Each combustion chamber has a glow plug threaded into it, which is positioned directly in line with the incoming spray of fuel. When the glow plug is energised, the fuel passing over it is heated, allowing its optimum combustion temperature to be achieved more quickly.

The duration of the preheating period is governed by the glow plug control unit (in the ECM), which monitors the temperature of the engine via the coolant temperature sensor and alters the preheating time to suit the conditions.

A facia-mounted warning light informs the driver that preheating is taking place. The light extinguishes when sufficient preheating has taken place to allow the engine to be started, but power will still be supplied to the glow plugs for a further period until the engine is started. If no attempt is made to start the engine, the power supply to the glow plugs is switched off to prevent battery drain and glow plug burn-out. Note that if a fault occurs in the engine management system while the car is moving, the glow plug warning lamp will start flashing and the system will then switch to fail-safe mode. Should this occur, the car must be taken to a Seat dealer or suitably equipped specialist for fault diagnosis.

After the engine has been started, the glow plugs continue to operate for a further period of time. This helps to improve fuel combustion whilst the engine is warming-up, resulting in quieter, smoother running and reduced exhaust emissions.

11 Glow plugs – testing, removal and refitting

⚠️ *Warning: A correctly-functioning glow plug will become red-hot in a very short time. This fact should also be borne in mind when removing the glow plugs if they have recently been in use.*

Testing

1 If the engine is difficult to start, one or more of the glow plugs may be faulty or the preheating system circuit may not be operating correctly. Some preliminary checks may be made as described in the following paragraphs.

2 Before testing the system, check that the battery voltage is at least 11.5 volts, using a multimeter. Switch off the ignition.

3 Remove the engine top cover.

4 Disconnect the wiring plug from the coolant temperature sender at the left-hand end of the engine (as seen from the driver's seat) with reference to Chapter 3. Disconnecting the sender in this way simulates a cold engine, which is a requirement for the glow plug system to activate.

5 Disconnect the wiring connector from the most convenient glow plug, and connect a suitable voltmeter between the wiring connector and a good earth.

6 Have an assistant switch on the ignition for approximately 20 seconds.

7 Battery voltage should be displayed – note that the voltage will drop to zero when the preheating period ends.

8 If no supply voltage can be detected at the glow plug, then either the glow plug relay (where applicable) or the supply wiring must be faulty. Also check that the glow plug fuse or fusible link (usually located on top of the battery) has not blown – if it has, this may indicate a faulty glow plug or serious wiring fault; consult a Seat dealer or specialist for advice.

9 To locate a faulty glow plug, make sure that the ignition is switched off, then disconnect the wiring plug from the glow plug terminal. Measure the electrical resistance between the glow plug terminal and the engine earth **(see illustration)**. At the time of writing, this information is not available – as a guide, a resistance of more than a few ohms indicates that the plug is defective.

10 If a suitable ammeter is available, connect it between the glow plug and its wiring connector, and measure the steady-state current consumption (ignore the initial current surge, which will be about 50% higher). As a guide, high current consumption (or no current draw at all) indicates a faulty glow plug.

11 As a final check, remove the glow plugs and inspect them visually, as described in the next sub-Section.

Removal

Note: *Refer to the Warning at the start of this Section before proceeding.*

12 Make sure the ignition is switched off, then disconnect the wiring connectors/rail from the glow plugs, where necessary label the wiring to make refitting easier **(see illustration)**.

13 Unscrew and remove the glow plugs.

14 Inspect the glow plug stems for signs of damage. A badly burned or charred stem may be an indication of a faulty fuel injector.

Refitting

15 Refitting is a reversal of removal, but tighten the glow plug to the specified torque.

Chapter 5 Part B:
Ignition system – petrol engines

Contents

Degrees of difficulty

Easy, suitable for novice with little experience	Fairly easy, suitable for beginner with some experience	Fairly difficult, suitable for competent DIY mechanic	Difficult, suitable for experienced DIY mechanic	Very difficult, suitable for expert DIY or professional

Specifications

Engine codes*
1.2 litre . . . . AZQ, BME and BXV
1.4 litre:
    55 kW (74 bhp) . . . . BBY and BKY
    63 kW (85 bhp) . . . . BXW
    74 kW (99 bhp) . . . . AUB and BBZ
Note: *See 'Vehicle identification' at the end of this manual for the location of engine code markings.*

System type
1.2 litre engines:
    Engine code AZQ . . . . Siemens Simos 3PE
    Engine code BME. . . . . Siemens Simos 3PG
    Engine code BXV . . . . Siemens Simos 9.1
1.4 litre engines:
    Engine codes AUB, BBY and BBZ. . . . . Magneti Marelli 4MV
    Engine code BKY . . . . Magneti Marelli 4TV
    Engine code BXW. . . . . Magneti Marelli 4HV

Ignition coil
Type:
    1.2 litre engines . . . . Individual coil per cylinder (no HT leads), camshaft position sensor (in cylinder head), knock sensor

    1.4 litre engines:
        Engine code AUB . . . . Single remote DIS coil with four HT leads, camshaft position sensor (in cylinder head), knock sensor
        Engines codes BBY, BBZ, BKY and BXW . . . . Individual coil per cylinder (no HT leads), camshaft position sensor (in cylinder head), knock sensor
Primary winding resistance . . . . N/A
Secondary resistance:
    Single DIS coil (four HT lead outputs) . . . . 4000 to 6000 ohms

Spark plugs
See Chapter 1A Specifications

Torque wrench settings

	Nm	lbf ft
Ignition coil mounting bolts (single DIS coil)	10	7
Knock sensor mounting bolt	20	15
Spark plugs	30	22

1 General information

The Siemens and Magneti-Marelli ignition systems described in this Chapter are part of the self-contained engine management systems which control both the fuel injection and ignition. This Chapter deals with the ignition system components only – refer to Chapter 4A for details of the fuel system components.

The ignition system comprises the spark plugs, High Tension (HT) leads where fitted (1.4 litre engine code AUB), ignition coil(s), and the Electronic Control Module (ECM) together with its associated sensors, actuators and wiring. The component layout varies from system to system but the basic operation is the same for all models.

The ECM supplies a voltage to the input stage of the ignition coil which causes the primary windings in the coil to be energised. The supply voltage is periodically interrupted by the ECM and this results in the collapse of the primary magnetic field, which then induces a much larger voltage (called the HT voltage) in the secondary coil. This voltage is directed to the spark plug in the cylinder where the piston is currently at the end of its compression stroke. The spark plug electrodes form a gap small enough for the HT voltage to arc across, and the resulting spark ignites the fuel/air mixture in the cylinder. The timing of this sequence of events is critical and is regulated solely by the ECM.

1.4 litre engine code AUB is fitted with a single DIS (Distributorless Ignition System) ignition coil, which operates on the 'wasted spark' principle. The coil unit in fact contains two separate coils – one for cylinders 1 and 4, the other for cylinders 2 and 3. Each of the two coils produces an HT voltage at both outputs every time its primary coil voltage is interrupted – ie, cylinders 1 and 4 always 'fire' together, then 2 and 3 'fire' together. When this happens, one of the two cylinders concerned will be on its compression stroke (and will ignite the fuel/air mixture), while the other one is on the exhaust stroke. Because the spark on the exhaust stroke has no effect, it is effectively wasted, hence the term 'wasted spark'.

On 1.2 litre engines and 1.4 litre engine codes BBY, BBZ, BKY and BXW, each spark plug has its own dedicated 'plug-top' HT coil which fits directly onto the spark plug. Unlike the 'wasted spark' system, on these models a spark is only generated at each plug once every engine cycle.

The ECM calculates and controls the ignition timing primarily according to engine speed, crankshaft/camshaft position, throttle position and intake air temperature, received from sensors mounted on and around the engine. Other parameters that affect ignition timing are coolant temperature and engine knock, these being monitored by sensors mounted on the engine.

The knock sensor is mounted on the cylinder block in order to detect engine pre-ignition (or 'pinking'). If pre-ignition occurs, the ECM retards the ignition timing in steps until the pre-ignition ceases. The ECM then advances the ignition timing in steps until it is restored to normal, or until pre-ignition occurs again.

Idle speed control is achieved partly by the electronic throttle valve positioning module, and partly by the ignition system, which gives fine control of the idle speed by altering the ignition timing. Manual adjustment of the engine idle speed or ignition timing is not necessary or possible.

It should be noted that comprehensive fault diagnosis of all the engine management systems described in this Chapter is only possible with dedicated electronic test equipment. Problems with the system's operation that cannot be pinpointed by following the basic guidelines in Section 2 should therefore be referred to a Seat dealer or suitably-equipped specialist for assessment. Once the fault has been identified, the removal/refitting sequences detailed in the following Sections will then allow the appropriate components to be renewed as required.

2 Ignition system – testing

Warning: Extreme care must be taken when working on the system with the ignition switched on; it is possible to get a substantial electric shock from a vehicle's ignition system. Persons with cardiac pacemaker devices should keep well clear of the ignition circuits, components and test equipment. Always switch off the ignition before disconnecting or connecting any component and when using a multimeter to check resistances.

Engine code AUB

1 Refer to the information given in paragraphs 7 to 9. The only other likely cause of ignition trouble is the HT leads, linking the HT coil to the spark plugs. Check the leads as follows; never disconnect more than one HT lead at a time to avoid possible confusion.

2 Pull the first lead from the plug by gripping the end fitting, not the lead, otherwise the lead connection may be fractured. Check inside the end fitting for signs of corrosion, which will look like a white crusty powder. Push the end fitting back onto the spark plug, ensuring that it is a tight fit on the plug. If not, remove the lead again and use pliers to carefully crimp the metal connector inside the end fitting until it fits securely on the end of the spark plug.

3 Using a clean rag, wipe the entire length of the lead to remove any built-up dirt and grease. Once the lead is clean, check for burns, cracks and other damage. Do not bend the lead excessively, nor pull the lead lengthwise – the conductor inside is quite fragile, and might break.

4 Disconnect the other end of the lead from the HT coil. Again, pull only on the end fitting. Check for corrosion and a tight fit in the same manner as the spark plug end.

5 If an ohmmeter is available, check for continuity between each end of the HT lead. If there is no continuity the lead is faulty and must be renewed (as a guide, the resistance of each lead should be in the region of 4 to 8 kohms).

6 Refit the lead securely on completion of the check then check the remaining leads one at a time, in the same way. If there is any doubt about the condition of any HT leads, renew them as a complete set.

All other engines

7 If a fault appears in the engine management (fuel injection/ignition) system which is thought to be ignition related, first ensure that the fault is not due to a poor electrical connection or poor maintenance; ie, check that the air cleaner filter element is clean, the spark plugs are in good condition and correctly gapped, that the engine breather hoses are clear and undamaged, referring to Chapter 1A for further information. If the engine is running very roughly, check the compression pressures as described in Chapter 2A or 2B.

8 If these checks fail to reveal the cause of the problem the vehicle should be taken to a Seat dealer or suitably-equipped specialist for testing. A diagnostic connector is incorporated in the engine management circuit into which a special electronic diagnostic tester can be plugged (see Chapter 4A). The tester will locate the fault quickly and simply, alleviating the need to test all the system components individually which is a time consuming operation that carries a high risk of damaging the ECM.

9 The only ignition system checks which can be carried out by the home mechanic are those described in Chapter 1A, relating to the spark plugs. If necessary, the system wiring and wiring connectors can be checked as described in Chapter 12 ensuring that the ECM wiring connector has first been disconnected.

3 HT coil – removal and refitting

Removal

Engine code AUB

1 The ignition coil unit is mounted on the top left-hand end of the engine (see illustration).

2 Make sure the ignition is switched off, then remove the engine top cover.

3 Unplug the main wiring plug (LT connector) from the ignition coil (see illustration).

4 The original HT leads should be marked from 1 to 4, corresponding to the cylinder/spark

3.1 On engine code AUB, the coil is mounted on the left-hand end of the cylinder head

3.3 Disconnect the LT wiring plug from the ignition coil

3.5a Note their positions, then disconnect the HT leads . . .

3.5b . . . unscrew the 3 Allen bolts, and remove the coil

3.6 Plug top ignition coils (arrowed)

5.1 The knock sensor is located on the rear of the cylinder block

plug they serve (No 1 is at the timing end of the engine). Some leads are also marked from A to D, and corresponding markings are found on the ignition coil HT terminals – in this case, cylinder A corresponds to No 1, B to No 2, and so on. If there are no markings present, label the HT leads before disconnecting, and either paint a marking on the ignition coil terminals or make a sketch of the lead positions for use when reconnecting.

5 Disconnect the HT leads from the ignition coil terminals, then unscrew the three mounting bolts and remove the coil unit from the engine **(see illustrations)**.

All other engine codes

6 Removal of the ignition coils is covered in the spark plug renewal procedure in Chapter 1A, since the coils must be removed for access to the plugs **(see illustration)**.

Refitting

7 Refitting is a reversal of the relevant removal procedure.

| 4 | Ignition timing – checking and adjusting | |

The ignition timing is under the control of the engine management system ECM and is not manually adjustable without access to dedicated electronic test equipment. A basic setting cannot be quoted because the ignition timing is constantly being altered to control engine idle speed (see Section 1 for details).

The vehicle must be taken to a Seat dealer or suitably-equipped specialist if the timing requires checking or adjustment.

| 5 | Knock sensor – removal and refitting |

Removal

1 The knock sensor is located on the rear of

the cylinder block, beneath the intake manifold **(see illustration)**.

2 Remove the engine top cover to gain access to the sensor from above. Alternatively for access from below, apply the handbrake, then jack up the front of the vehicle and support it on axle stands (see *Jacking and vehicle support*). Access to the knock sensor is very awkward, and can only be improved by removing the intake manifold (see Chapter 4A).

3 Disconnect the wiring from the sensor or trace the wiring back from the sensor and disconnect its wiring connector.

4 Unscrew the mounting bolt and remove the sensor from the cylinder block.

Refitting

5 Refitting is the reverse of removal. Ensure the mating surfaces of the sensor and cylinder block are clean and dry and ensure the mounting bolt is tightened to the specified torque to ensure correct operation.

Chapter 6
Clutch

Contents

Degrees of difficulty

Easy, suitable for novice with little experience	Fairly easy, suitable for beginner with some experience	Fairly difficult, suitable for competent DIY mechanic	Difficult, suitable for experienced DIY mechanic	Very difficult, suitable for expert DIY or professional

Specifications

General

Type	Single dry plate, diaphragm spring
Operation	Hydraulic with master and slave cylinders
Application:	
Petrol models	5-speed transmission code 02T
Diesel models:	
1.4 litre engines:	
Engine code BNM.	5-speed transmission code 02T
Engine codes AMF, BMS and BNV	5-speed transmission code 02R
1.9 litre engines:	
Engine codes ATD, AXR and BMT	5-speed transmission code 02R
Engine codes ASZ and BLT	6-speed transmission code 0A8
Friction disc diameter:	
5-speed transmission:	
Code 02T	200 mm
Code 02R	228 mm
6-speed transmission.	N/A

Torque wrench settings

	Nm	lbf ft
Clutch master cylinder mounting nuts*	28	21
Clutch pedal mounting bracket nuts*	28	21
Clutch pedal pivot nut*	25	18
Clutch pressure plate-to-flywheel bolts	20	15
Clutch slave cylinder mounting bolts:		
5-speed transmission.	20	15
6-speed transmission:		
Metal slave cylinder*	12	9
Plastic slave cylinder*	15	11
Guide tube-to-transmission bolts	9	7

* Use new bolts/nuts.

1 General information

The clutch is of single dry plate type, incorporating a diaphragm spring pressure plate, and is hydraulically-operated.

The pressure plate is bolted to the rear face of the flywheel, and the friction disc is located between the pressure plate and the flywheel friction surface. The friction disc hub is splined to the transmission input shaft and is free to slide along the splines. Friction lining material is riveted to each side of the disc, and the disc hub incorporates cushioning springs to absorb transmission shocks and ensure a smooth take-up of drive.

When the clutch pedal is depressed, the slave cylinder pushrod moves the top of the release lever towards the engine, and the lower end of the lever pivots on a ball-stud located in the transmission bellhousing. The release bearing is forced onto the pressure plate diaphragm spring fingers. As the centre of the diaphragm spring is pushed in, the outer part of the spring moves out and releases the pressure plate from the friction disc. Drive then ceases to be transmitted to the transmission.

When the clutch pedal is released, the diaphragm spring forces the pressure plate into contact with the linings on the friction disc, and at the same time pushes the disc slightly forward along the input shaft splines into engagement with the flywheel. The friction disc is now firmly sandwiched between the pressure plate and flywheel. This causes drive to be taken up.

As the linings wear on the friction disc, the pressure plate rest position moves closer to the flywheel resulting in the 'rest' position of the diaphragm spring fingers being raised. The hydraulic system requires no adjustment since the quantity of hydraulic fluid in the circuit automatically compensates for wear every time the clutch pedal is operated.

2 Hydraulic system – bleeding

⚠️ **Warning: Hydraulic fluid is poisonous; thoroughly wash off spills from bare skin without delay. Seek immediate medical advice if any fluid is swallowed or gets into the eyes. Certain types of hydraulic fluid are inflammable and may ignite when brought into contact with hot components. Hydraulic fluid is also an effective paint stripper. If spillage occurs onto painted bodywork or fittings, it should be washed off immediately, using copious quantities of cold water. It is also hygroscopic (it absorbs moisture from the air) therefore old fluid should never be re-used.**

1 The correct operation of any hydraulic system is only possible after removing all air from the components and circuit; this is achieved by bleeding the system.

2 During the bleeding procedure, add only clean, unused hydraulic fluid of the recommended type; never re-use fluid that has already been bled from the system. Ensure that sufficient fluid is available before starting work.

3 If there is any possibility of incorrect fluid being already in the system, the hydraulic circuit must be flushed completely with uncontaminated, correct fluid.

4 If hydraulic fluid has been lost from the system, or air has entered because of a leak, ensure that the fault is cured before continuing further.

5 The bleed screw is located on the slave cylinder located on the left-hand upper side of the transmission. As access to the bleed screw is limited it will be necessary to jack up the front of the vehicle and support it on axle stands so that the screw can be reached from below.

6 Check that all pipes and hoses are secure, unions tight and the bleed screw is closed. Clean any dirt from around the bleed screw.

7 Unscrew the master cylinder fluid reservoir cap (the clutch shares the same fluid reservoir as the braking system), and top the master cylinder reservoir up to the upper (MAX) level line. Refit the cap loosely, and remember to maintain the fluid level at least above the lower (MIN) level line throughout the procedure, or there is a risk of further air entering the system.

8 There are a number of one-man, do-it-yourself bleeding kits currently available from motor accessory shops. It is recommended that one of these kits is used whenever possible, as they greatly simplify the bleeding operation, and reduce the risk of expelled air and fluid being drawn back into the system. If such a kit is not available, the basic (two-man) method must be used, which is described in detail below.

9 If a kit is to be used, prepare the vehicle as described previously, and follow the kit manufacturer's instructions, as the procedure may vary slightly according to the type being used; generally, they are as outlined below in the relevant sub-section.

Bleeding

Basic (two-man) method

10 Collect a clean glass jar, a suitable length of plastic or rubber tubing which is a tight fit over the bleed screw, and a ring spanner to fit the screw. The help of an assistant will also be required.

11 Remove the dust cap from the bleed screw. Fit the spanner and tube to the screw, place the other end of the tube in the jar, and pour in sufficient fluid to cover the end of the tube.

12 Ensure that the fluid level is maintained at least above the lower level line in the reservoir throughout the procedure.

13 Have the assistant fully depress the clutch pedal several times to build-up pressure, then maintain it on the final downstroke.

14 While pedal pressure is maintained, unscrew the bleed screw (approximately one turn) and allow the compressed fluid and air to flow into the jar. The assistant should maintain pedal pressure and should not release it until instructed to do so. When the flow stops, tighten the bleed screw again, have the assistant release the pedal slowly, and recheck the reservoir fluid level.

15 Repeat the steps given in paragraphs 13 and 14 until the fluid emerging from the bleed screw is free from air bubbles. If the master cylinder has been drained and refilled allow approximately five seconds between cycles for the master cylinder passages to refill.

16 When no more air bubbles appear, tighten the bleed screw securely, remove the tube and spanner, and refit the dust cap. Do not overtighten the bleed screw.

Using a one-way valve kit

17 As their name implies, these kits consist of a length of tubing with a one-way valve fitted, to prevent expelled air and fluid being drawn back into the system; some kits include a translucent container, which can be positioned so that the air bubbles can be more easily seen flowing from the end of the tube.

18 The kit is connected to the bleed screw, which is then opened. The user returns to the driver's seat, depresses the clutch pedal with a smooth, steady stroke, and slowly releases it; this is repeated until the expelled fluid is clear of air bubbles.

19 Note that these kits simplify work so much that it is easy to forget the fluid reservoir level; ensure that this is maintained at least above the lower level line at all times.

Using a pressure-bleeding kit

20 These kits are usually operated by the reservoir of pressurised air contained in the spare tyre. However, note that it will probably be necessary to reduce the pressure to a lower level than normal; refer to the instructions supplied with the kit.

21 By connecting a pressurised, fluid-filled container to the fluid reservoir, bleeding can be carried out simply by opening the bleed screw and allowing the fluid to flow out until no more air bubbles can be seen in the expelled fluid.

22 This method has the advantage that the large reservoir of fluid provides an additional safeguard against air being drawn into the system during bleeding.

All methods

23 When bleeding is complete, and correct pedal feel is restored, tighten the bleed screw securely and wash off any spilt fluid. Refit the dust cap to the bleed screw.

24 Check the hydraulic fluid level in the master cylinder reservoir, and top-up if necessary (see *Weekly checks*).

25 Discard any hydraulic fluid that has been bled from the system; it will not be fit for re-use.

26 Check the operation of the clutch pedal. If the clutch is still not operating correctly, air must still be present in the system, and further bleeding is required. Failure to bleed satisfactorily after a reasonable repetition of the bleeding procedure may be due to worn master cylinder/release cylinder seals.

3 Clutch pedal – removal and refitting

Removal

1 Remove the driver's side lower facia trim panel, with reference to Chapter 11, Section 29.
2 Where fitted, remove the clutch pedal switch from the pedal bracket by turning it 90° anti-clockwise.
3 The over-centre spring must now be disconnected from the pedal and removed. On RHD models, position a screwdriver between the clutch pedal and the spring, then depress the pedal and unhook the spring. On LHD models, make up a tool from a length of metal bar which just fits over the spring, to 'catch' as many of the spring coils as possible. Press it into position over the spring to hold the clutch pedal over-centre spring in the compressed position – depress the pedal to unhook the spring. If necessary, this method can also be used on RHD models (see illustrations). Alternatively, thread through a couple of strong cable-ties to hold the spring compressed as this is done.
4 With the over-centre spring removed, remove the spring seat from the pedal bracket. The seat must be renewed whenever removed.
5 The master cylinder pushrod is attached to the clutch pedal by a plastic clip. Ideally, a scissor-type caliper tool should be used to compress the ends of the clip through the access holes in the pedal, however, two screwdrivers can be used instead.
6 With the pedal disconnected from the pushrod, if necessary, remove the plastic retaining clip from the pushrod using pliers.
7 Unscrew the nut from the pedal pivot bolt.
8 Pull out the pivot bolt until the pedal can be removed from the bracket assembly into the driver's footwell.
9 If necessary, remove the spacer bushes and centre sleeve from the pedal.

Refitting

10 Examine the pedal components for wear, and renew as necessary.
11 Refitting is a reversal of removal, noting the following points:
  a) Fit a new over-centre spring seat in the pedal bracket, making sure that the tab is locked in the master cylinder recess.
  b) Use a new pedal pivot bolt nut, and tighten it to the specified torque.
  c) Make sure that the pedal-to-master cylinder pushrod retaining clip is fitted

3.3a Use a screwdriver to disconnect the over-centre spring

to the master cylinder pushrod before attempting to reconnect the pushrod to the pedal.
  d) Push the pedal onto the pushrod to engage the retaining clip. Make sure that the clip is securely engaged.
  e) On completion, check the brake/clutch fluid level, and top-up if necessary.

4 Master cylinder – removal, overhaul and refitting

Note: Refer to the warning at the beginning of Section 2.

Removal

1 The clutch master cylinder is located inside the car on the clutch and brake pedal mounting bracket (see illustration). Hydraulic fluid for the unit is supplied from the brake master cylinder reservoir.
2 Remove the air cleaner assembly as described in Chapter 4A or 4B.
3 Before proceeding, place cloth rags on the carpet inside the car to prevent damage from spilt hydraulic fluid.
4 Working in the engine compartment, clamp the hydraulic fluid hose leading from the brake fluid reservoir to the clutch master cylinder using a brake hose clamp.
5 Similarly, clamp the rubber section of the hydraulic hose leading from the master cylinder to the slave cylinder using a brake hose clamp, to prevent loss of hydraulic fluid.

3.3b Over-centre spring retaining tool (typical) – dimensions will vary according to model

6 Position a suitable container, or some cloth rags, beneath the master cylinder to catch escaping hydraulic fluid.
7 Release the clamp and pull the hydraulic supply hose from the clutch master cylinder on the bulkhead.
8 Pull the fluid outlet hose retaining clip from the union on the master cylinder, then pull the pipe from the union. Again, be prepared for fluid spillage.
9 Remove the driver's side lower facia trim panel, with reference to Chapter 11, Section 29.
10 Where fitted, remove the clutch pedal switch from the pedal bracket by turning it 90° anti-clockwise.
11 The pedal must now be disconnected from the master cylinder pushrod by squeezing together the tabs of the retaining clip (see Section 3), and moving the pushrod away from the pedal.
12 Twist the clutch pedal stop anti-clockwise, and remove it from the bulkhead.
13 Unscrew the three nuts securing the clutch pedal mounting bracket to the bulkhead, then remove the mounting bracket complete with pedal from the bulkhead (see illustration).
14 With the mounting bracket on the bench, the over-centre spring must be disconnected and removed from the pedal – see Section 3, paragraph 3.
15 With the over-centre spring removed, remove the spring seat from the pedal bracket. The seat must be renewed whenever removed.
16 Remove the master cylinder from the bracket.

4.1 Clutch master cylinder (arrowed)

4.13 Undo the pedal bracket nuts (arrowed)

5.9 Remove the clutch slave cylinder

Overhaul

17 No spare parts are available from Seat for the master cylinder. If the master cylinder is faulty or worn, the complete assembly must be renewed.

Refitting

18 Refitting is a reversal of removal, bearing in mind the following points:
a) Ensure that the pedal-to-master cylinder pushrod retaining clip is fitted to the master cylinder pushrod before attempting to reconnect the pushrod to the pedal.
b) Push the pedal onto the pushrod to engage the retaining clip. Make sure that the clip is securely engaged.
c) On completion, bleed the clutch hydraulic system as described in Section 2.

5 Slave cylinder –
removal, overhaul and refitting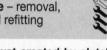

Note: *Refer to the warning at the beginning of Section 2 regarding the hazards of working with hydraulic fluid.*

Removal

5-speed transmission

1 The slave cylinder is located on the top of the transmission casing. First remove the engine top cover.
2 Remove the battery as described in Chapter 5A, then unbolt and remove the battery tray.

3 Where necessary, remove the air cleaner and air ducting with reference to Chapter 4A or 4B.
4 Unscrew the nut and remove the gearchange lever from the top of the transmission.
5 Extract the circlip and disconnect the selector cable from the relay lever.
6 Unscrew the three bolts and tie the support bracket to one side.
7 Clamp the rubber section of the hydraulic hose leading from the master cylinder to the slave cylinder using a brake hose clamp, to prevent loss of hydraulic fluid. Place a wad of clean rag beneath the fluid line connection on the slave cylinder to catch escaping fluid.
8 Pull the fluid pipe retaining clip from the union on the slave cylinder, then disconnect the pipe from the union. Release the fluid line from the bracket, and position it clear of the slave cylinder. Be prepared for fluid spillage.
9 Unscrew the two bolts securing the slave cylinder to the transmission casing, and withdraw the slave cylinder (see illustration).

6-speed transmission

10 The slave cylinder is inside the transmission housing, and is only accessible once the transmission is removed, as described in Chapter 7A.
11 With the transmission separated from the engine, unscrew the three slave cylinder mounting bolts and withdraw the cylinder and release bearing from the transmission input shaft. The slave cylinder mounting bolts should not be re-used. Recover the O-ring seal from the slave cylinder hydraulic connection – a new one should be used when refitting.

Overhaul

12 No spare parts are available from Seat for the slave cylinder. If the slave cylinder is faulty or worn, the complete assembly must be renewed.

Refitting

5-speed transmission

13 Refitting is a reversal of removal, bearing in mind the following points:
a) Apply a little molybdenum sulphide-based grease to the end of the slave cylinder plunger.

b) Tighten the slave cylinder securing bolts to the specified torque.
c) On completion, bleed the clutch hydraulic system as described in Section 2.

6-speed transmission

14 Refitting is a reversal of removal, bearing in mind the following points:
a) Use new slave cylinder securing bolts, and tighten them gradually to the specified torque – particularly on the plastic-bodied slave cylinder, there is a risk of fracturing the bolt holes if the bolts are not evenly tightened.
b) Refit the transmission as described in Chapter 7A.

6 Clutch friction disc and pressure plate – removal, inspection and refitting

⚠ **Warning: Dust created by clutch wear and deposited on the clutch components may contain asbestos, which is a health hazard. DO NOT blow it out with compressed air or inhale any of it. DO NOT use petrol or petroleum-based solvents to clean off the dust. Brake system cleaner or methylated spirit should be used to flush the dust into a suitable receptacle. After the clutch components are wiped clean with clean rags, dispose of the contaminated rags and cleaner in a sealed container.**

Removal

1 Access to the clutch is obtained by removing the transmission as described in Chapter 7A.
2 Mark the clutch pressure plate and flywheel in relation to each other (see illustration).
3 Hold the flywheel stationary, then unscrew the clutch pressure plate bolts progressively in diagonal sequence (see illustration). With the bolts unscrewed two or three turns, check that the pressure plate is not binding on the dowel pins. If necessary, use a screwdriver to release the pressure plate.
4 Remove all the bolts, then lift the clutch pressure plate and friction disc from the flywheel (see illustration).

6.2 Mark the clutch pressure plate and flywheel in relation to each other

6.3 Unscrew the pressure plate bolts (arrowed) . . .

6.4 . . . then lift the pressure plate and friction disc away from the flywheel

6.11 Locate the friction disc on the flywheel using a centring tool

6.12 Locate the clutch pressure plate over the friction disc

6.13 Insert the bolts finger-tight initially

Inspection

5 Clean the pressure plate, disc and flywheel. Do not inhale the dust, as it may contain asbestos which is dangerous to health.

6 Examine the fingers of the diaphragm spring for wear or scoring. If the depth of wear exceeds half the thickness of the fingers, a new pressure plate assembly must be fitted. Given the amount of work involved in accessing the clutch, it is standard practice to renew the clutch pressure plate and friction disc together, almost regardless of their condition.

7 Examine the pressure plate for scoring, cracking and discoloration. Light scoring is acceptable, but if excessive, a new pressure plate assembly must be fitted.

8 Examine the friction disc linings for wear and cracking, and for contamination with oil or grease. The linings are worn excessively if they are worn down to, or near, the rivets. Check the disc hub and splines for wear, by temporarily fitting it on the transmission input shaft. Renew the friction disc as necessary.

9 Examine the flywheel friction surface for scoring, cracking and discoloration (caused by overheating). If excessive, it may be possible to have the flywheel machined by an engineering works, otherwise it should be renewed.

10 Ensure that all parts are clean, and free of oil or grease, before reassembling. Apply just a small amount of high melting-point grease to the splines of the friction disc hub. Note that new pressure plates may be coated with protective grease. It is only permissible to clean the grease away from the friction lining

contact area. Removal of the grease from other areas will shorten the service life of the clutch.

Refitting

11 Commence reassembly by locating the friction disc on the flywheel, with the raised, torsion spring side of the hub facing outwards. If necessary, the centralising tool (see paragraph 14) may be used to hold the disc on the flywheel at this stage **(see illustration)**.

12 Locate the clutch pressure plate on the disc, and fit it onto the location dowels **(see illustration)**. If refitting the original pressure plate, make sure that the previously-made marks are aligned.

13 Insert the bolts finger-tight to hold the pressure plate in position **(see illustration)**.

14 The friction disc must now be centralised, to ensure correct alignment of the transmission input shaft with the spigot bearing in the crankshaft. To do this, a proprietary tool may be used, or alternatively, use a wooden mandrel made to fit inside the friction disc and flywheel spigot bearing. Insert the tool through the friction disc into the spigot bearing, and make sure that it is central.

15 Tighten the pressure plate bolts progressively and in diagonal sequence, until the specified torque setting is achieved, then remove the centralising tool.

16 Check the release bearing in the transmission bellhousing for smooth operation, and if necessary renew it with reference to Section 7.

17 Refit the transmission with reference to Chapter 7A.

7 Release bearing and lever – removal, inspection and refitting

5-speed transmission code 02T

Removal

1 The release bearing and lever are removed together with the guide tube, then separated on the bench. First, remove the transmission as described in Chapter 7A.

2 Unscrew and remove the two retaining bolts **(see illustration)**, then prise the release lever from the ball-stud on the transmission housing. To do this, press the retaining spring through the release lever.

3 Slide the guide tube, together with the release lever and bearing, over the transmission input shaft.

4 Turn the guide tube 90° to align the tabs with the slots in the release bearing, and withdraw the tube **(see illustration)**.

5 Using a screwdriver, depress the clips and remove the bearing from the release lever **(see illustrations)**.

Inspection

6 Spin the release bearing by hand, and check it for smooth running. Any tendency to seize or run rough will necessitate renewal of the bearing. If the bearing is to be re-used, wipe it clean with a dry cloth; the bearing should not be washed in a liquid solvent, as this will remove the internal grease.

7 Clean the release lever, ball-stud and guide sleeve.

7.2 Unscrew the retaining bolts

7.4 Remove the guide tube from the release bearing. Note the tab and slot (arrowed)

7.5a Depress the clips (arrowed) . . .

7.5b . . . and remove the bearing from the release lever

7.8 Lubricate the ball-stud with molybdenum disulphide-based grease

7.9a Hook the spring over the end of the lever . . .

7.9b . . . and press the other end into the hole

7.12 Locate the release lever and spring onto the ball-stud

Refitting

8 Lubricate the ball-stud in the transmission bellhousing with molybdenum disulphide-based grease **(see illustration)**. Also smear a little grease on the release bearing surface which contacts the diaphragm spring fingers in the clutch cover.

9 Refit the ball-stud spring to the release lever **(see illustrations)**.

10 Locate the bearing on the lever, and press until the clips engage.

11 Locate the guide tube on the bearing, align the tabs with the slots, then insert and turn through 90°.

12 Locate the release lever on the ball-stud, and press until the retaining spring holds it in position **(see illustration)**.

13 Slide the guide tube with bearing and lever over the input shaft, then insert the retaining bolts and tighten to the specified torque.

14 Refit the transmission as described in Chapter 7A.

5-speed transmission code 02R

Removal

15 Remove the transmission as described in Chapter 7A.

16 Unhook the spring from the lower part of the release lever, and prise the release lever from the ball-stud.

17 Depress the retaining clip each side, and slide the release socket from the release lever.

Inspection

18 Inspection is described in paragraphs 6 and 7.

Refitting

19 Lubricate the ball stud with a little molybdenum disulphide-based grease.

20 Press the release socket into the lever until the clips engage.

21 Slide the assembly into place and hook the return spring into the lever.

22 Press the lever over the ball-stud.

6-speed transmission

23 The release bearing is integral with the slave cylinder, and is removed as described in Section 5. Once removed, the bearing can be checked as described in paragraph 6 – however, given the amount of work necessary to access it, it is good practice to renew it regardless.

Chapter 7 Part A:
Manual transmission

Contents

Degrees of difficulty

Easy, suitable for novice with little experience 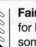	Fairly easy, suitable for beginner with some experience	Fairly difficult, suitable for competent DIY mechanic	Difficult, suitable for experienced DIY mechanic	Very difficult, suitable for expert DIY or professional

Specifications

General

Type	Transversely-mounted, front-wheel-drive layout with integral transaxle differential/final drive. Five or six forward speeds, one reverse.
Application:	
Petrol models	5-speed transmission code 02T
Diesel models:	
1.4 litre engines	5-speed transmission code 02R
1.9 litre engines:	
Engine codes ATD, AXR and BMT	5-speed transmission code 02R
Engine codes ASZ and BLT	6-speed transmission code 0A8

Torque wrench settings

	Nm	lbf ft
Engine mounting to transmission:		
Stage 1	40	30
Stage 2	Angle-tighten a further 90°	
Reversing light switch:		
Transmission code 02T	25	18
Transmission codes 02R and 0A8	20	15
Transmission to engine:		
M12 bolts	80	59
M10 bolts	45	33

1 General information

The manual transmission is bolted directly to the left-hand end of the engine. This layout has the advantage of providing the shortest possible drive path to the front wheels, as well as locating the transmission in the airflow through the engine bay, optimising cooling. The unit is cased in aluminium alloy.

Drive from the crankshaft is transmitted by the clutch to the gearbox input shaft, which is splined to accept the clutch friction disc.

All forward gears are fitted with synchromesh. The floor-mounted gear lever is connected to the gearbox by selector and shift cables **(see illustration)**. This actuates selector forks inside the gearbox which are slotted onto the synchromesh sleeves. The sleeves, which are locked to the gearbox shafts but can slide axially by means of splined hubs, press baulk rings into contact with the respective gear/pinion. The coned surfaces between the baulk rings and the pinion/gear act as a friction clutch, that progressively matches the speed of the synchromesh sleeve (and hence the gearbox shaft) with that of the gear/pinion. This allows gearchanges to be carried out smoothly.

Drive is transmitted to the differential

1.3 Gearchange cable components

1 Shift cable	5 Shift housing	8 Relay lever	12 Shift lever with	15 Grommet
2 Selector cable	6 Pivot	9 Bushes	weight	16 Spacer
3 Press-stud	7 Selector cable	10 Circlip	13 Shift cable lock	17 Circlip
4 Circlip	lock	11 Sliding shoe	14 Nut	18 Bolt

H45885

crownwheel, which rotates the differential case and planetary gears, thus driving the sun gears and driveshafts. The rotation of the differential planetary gears on their shaft allows the inner roadwheel to rotate at a slower speed than the outer roadwheel during cornering.

2 Gearchange cables – checking and adjustment

Note: *Seat locking pin T10027, or a suitable alternative, will be required for this operation.*

Checking

5-speed transmissions

1 The following check will enable you to decide whether adjustment is necessary. First, engage neutral so that the shift lever is in the gate of 3rd/4th.
2 Start the engine and allow it to idle, then depress the clutch pedal. Allow 3 to 6 seconds for the input shaft to stop rotating, then move the gear lever through all the gears, checking in particular that reverse gear engages smoothly.
3 If any gear is difficult to engage, have an assistant observe the shift lever on the top of the gearbox while you engage 1st gear and temporarily move the gear lever to the left. The shift lever should make a stroke of approximately 1.0 mm. If not, carry out the adjustment below.

6-speed transmissions

4 Position the gear lever in neutral in the gate for 3rd/4th gear.
5 Start the engine and allow it to idle, then depress the clutch pedal. Allow 3 to 6 seconds for the input shaft to stop rotating, then move the gear lever through all the gears, checking in particular that reverse gear engages smoothly.
6 If, following repeated operation, the gears 1, 2, 5 or 6 are difficult to engage, proceed as follows.

Adjustment

7 Where necessary for access to the top of the transmission, remove the air cleaner assembly and ducting as described in Chapter 4A or 4B.
8 With the gearchange set in the neutral position, push the two locking collars (one on each cable) forwards to compress the springs, then turn them clockwise (looking from the driver's seat) to lock them **(see illustration)**.

5-speed transmissions

9 Press down on the selector shaft on the top of the transmission and, at the same time, turn the angle lever on the side of the transmission clockwise **(see illustration)**.
10 Working inside the car, carefully unclip the gear lever gaiter from the centre console. Still in the neutral position, move the gear lever as far to the left as possible so that it is in the

2.8 Push the collar down and lock in position

gate of the 1st/2nd gear, and insert the locking pin (T10027 – or drill bit) through the hole in the base of the gear lever and into the hole in the housing **(see illustration)**.
11 Working back in the engine bay, turn the two locking collars on the cables anti-clockwise to release them **(see illustration)**.
12 With the cable adjustment set, the angle lever can now be turned anti-clockwise to its original position.
13 Inside the car, remove the locking pin/drill bit from the gear lever, then check the operation of the selector mechanism as described in paragraphs 1 to 3. When the gear lever is at rest in neutral, it should be central in the gate of the 3rd/4th gear. The gear lever gaiter can now be refitted to the centre console.

6-speed transmissions

14 Press down the selector shaft on the transmission and at the same time press the retention pin into the housing **(see illustration 2.9)**. The pin will hold the shaft in this position.
15 Working inside the car, carefully unclip the gear lever gaiter from the centre console. Still in the neutral position, move the gear lever and insert the locking pin (T10027 – or drill bit) through the hole in the base of the gear lever and into the hole in the housing **(see illustration 2.10)**.
16 Working back in the engine bay, turn the two locking collars on the cables anti-clockwise to lock them.
17 Pull the retention pin outwards to release the selector shaft.
18 Refit the gear lever gaiter.

2.10 Lock the gear lever in position with a drill bit (arrowed)

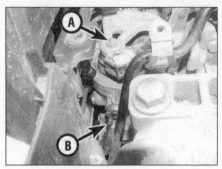

2.9 Press down on (A), then turn the angle lever (B)

All transmissions

19 Where applicable, refit the air cleaner assembly and ducting with reference to Chapter 4A or 4B.

3 Manual transmission – removal and refitting

Removal

1 Select a solid, level surface to park the car on. Give yourself enough space to move around it easily. Apply the handbrake and chock the rear wheels.
2 Raise the front of the car and support it securely on axle stands (see *Jacking and vehicle support*).
3 Remove the engine top cover and engine/transmission undershield.
4 Remove the left-hand front roadwheel and wheel arch liner.
5 Position a suitable container beneath the transmission, then unscrew the drain plug and drain the transmission oil.
6 On models with a remotely-mounted air cleaner (ie, one not incorporated in the engine top cover), remove the air cleaner assembly and ducting as described in Chapter 4A or 4B.
7 Remove the battery and battery tray with reference to Chapter 5A. On some models, it may also be necessary to disconnect the battery positive lead from the starter motor solenoid.
8 Unscrew the three bolts securing the gearchange cable bracket to the top of the transmission.

2.11 Release the two locking collars (arrowed)

3.9a Slide off the clips, disconnect the cables . . .

3.9b . . . and unbolt the bracket

3.10 Gate selector cable (B) and balance weight (A)

9 Detach the relay/reversing lever together with the selector and shift cables from the top of the transmission, by extracting the circlip and pulling out the pivot. Recover the bushes. Alternatively, disconnect the cables and unbolt the bracket **(see illustrations)**.

10 Unscrew the nut and remove the gearchange lever with the balance weight **(see illustration)**. Note that the lever will only engage with the shaft in one position. Tie the cable assembly to one side.

11 Remove the starter motor as described in Chapter 5A.

12 Disconnect the wiring from the reversing light switch.

13 On 5-speed transmissions, unbolt the clutch slave cylinder and support bracket from the transmission, and tie to one side **(see illustration)**. On 6-speed transmissions, clamp the slave cylinder hydraulic hose, then pull out the connector's spring clip to its stop, and disconnect the hose from the top of the transmission.

Caution: Do not depress the clutch pedal with the slave cylinder removed or disconnected.

14 Remove the exhaust front pipe as described in Chapter 4C.

15 Release the oxygen sensors wiring from the clip on the underbody, to enable lowering the exhaust without straining the wiring.

16 Unbolt the earth cable from the front of the transmission.

17 Unscrew the nut and move aside the wiring support bracket.

18 With reference to Chapter 8, unbolt the driveshafts from the gearbox drive flanges.

On transmission code 02R, remove the shield for the right-hand steering inner joint boot. Also on this transmission, we found it an advantage to temporarily unbolt the left-hand drive flange from the transmission, to allow the transmission bellhousing extra clearance during removal **(see illustration)**.

19 Refer to Chapter 10 and mark the position of the bolts securing the left-hand swivel hub to the front suspension lower arm, then unscrew and remove the bolts. Unscrew the nut and disconnect the end of the anti-roll bar link from the left-hand strut.

20 Turn the steering fully to the left-hand lock, then use string or wire to tie up the driveshafts as high as possible away from the gearbox. Do not damage the surrounding bodywork. For additional working room, remove the left-hand driveshaft completely.

21 Working under the rear of the engine, unscrew the single nut from the transmission-to-engine mounting stud. On transmission code 02R, unbolt the small cover plate for the flywheel, located behind the right-hand drive flange.

22 Unbolt and remove the engine rear mounting/link from the transmission and subframe.

23 Using a suitable hoist, support the weight of the engine.

24 On transmission code 02R only, remove the right-hand engine mounting top section, by first positioning the coolant expansion tank to one side, and then removing the nut and bolts securing the section to the bracket on the engine.

25 Slightly raise the hoist, and unscrew

the bolts securing the left-hand engine/transmission mounting to the body. Now slightly lower the hoist and unscrew the mounting lower bolts from the transmission. Remove the mounting.

26 Unscrew and remove the upper and lower transmission-to-engine mounting bolts.

27 Position a trolley jack beneath the transmission so that it can be withdrawn from the left-hand side of the car.

28 Carefully pull the transmission directly away from the engine, taking care not to allow its weight to rest on the clutch friction disc hub. It may be necessary to push the engine forwards slightly during the separation.

> ⚠ **Warning: Support the transmission to ensure that it remains steady on the jack head. Keep the transmission level until the input shaft is fully withdrawn from the clutch friction disc.**

29 When the transmission is clear of the locating dowels and clutch components, lower the transmission to the ground and withdraw from under the car.

Refitting

30 Refitting the transmission is a reversal of the removal procedure, but note the following points:
a) Apply a smear of high melting-point grease to the clutch friction disc hub splines, taking care to avoid contamination of the friction surfaces.
b) Check that the location dowels are correctly fitted to the cylinder block.
c) Tighten all bolts to the specified torque where given, with reference to the relevant Chapters.
d) Refer to Section 2 and check the gearchange cable adjustment.
e) Refill the transmission with the correct grade and quantity of oil. Refer to 'Lubricants and fluids' and Chapter 1A or 1B, as appropriate.

3.13 Unbolt the clutch slave cylinder and bracket and tie to one side

3.18 On transmission code 02R, temporarily remove the left-hand drive flange

4	**Manual transmission overhaul –** general information

The overhaul of the manual transmission is a complex and often expensive task for the DIY home mechanic to undertake, which requires access to specialist equipment. It involves dismantling and reassembly of many small components, measuring clearances precisely and, if necessary, adjusting them by selecting shims and spacers. Internal transmission components are also often difficult to obtain and in many instances, extremely expensive. Because of this, if the transmission develops a fault or becomes noisy, the best course of action is to have the unit overhauled by a specialist repairer or to obtain an exchange reconditioned unit.

Nevertheless, it is not impossible for the more experienced mechanic to overhaul the transmission if the special tools are available and the job is carried out in a deliberate step-by-step manner, to ensure nothing is overlooked.

The tools necessary for an overhaul include internal and external circlip pliers, bearing pullers, a slide hammer, a set of pin punches, a dial test indicator and possibly a hydraulic press. In addition, a large, sturdy workbench and a vice will be required.

During dismantling of the transmission,

make careful notes of how each component is fitted to make reassembly easier and accurate.

Before dismantling the transmission, it will help if you have some idea of where the problem lies. Certain problems can be closely related to specific areas in the transmission, which can make component examination and renewal easier. Refer to the *Fault finding* Section in this manual for more information.

5 Reversing light switch – testing, removal and refitting

Testing

1 Ensure that the ignition switch is turned to the 'off' position.
2 Disconnect the wiring from the reversing light switch. The switch is screwed into the front of the casing on 02T and 0A8 transmissions, and into the shift cover on the top of the 02R transmission.
3 Connect the probes of a continuity tester, or multimeter set to the resistance measurement

function, across the terminals of the reversing light switch.
4 The switch contacts are open when any gear other than reverse is selected; the tester/meter should indicate an open circuit or infinite resistance. When reverse gear is selected, the switch contacts should close, causing the tester/meter to indicate continuity or zero resistance.
5 If the switch does not operate correctly, it should be renewed.

Removal

6 Ensure that the ignition switch is turned to the 'off' position.
7 Disconnect the wiring from the reversing light switch.
8 Unscrew and remove the switch. On the 02T and 0A8 transmissions, recover the sealing ring.

Refitting

9 Refitting is a reversal of removal, but tighten the switch to the specified torque. On the 02T and 0A8 transmissions, renew the sealing ring. On the 02R transmission, apply some molybdenum disulphide grease to the peg.

Notes

Chapter 7 Part B:
Automatic transmission

Contents

Degrees of difficulty

Easy, suitable for novice with little experience	**Fairly easy,** suitable for beginner with some experience	**Fairly difficult,** suitable for competent DIY mechanic	**Difficult,** suitable for experienced DIY mechanic	**Very difficult,** suitable for expert DIY or professional

Specifications

General

Transmission type number	001
Application	1.4 litre petrol engine models
Description	4-speed electro-hydraulically-controlled planetary gearbox. Hydrokinetic torque converter, with lock-up clutch on 3rd and 4th speeds. ECM control of driving modes and shift points

Ratios

1st.	2.875:1
2nd	1.510:1
3rd	1.000:1
4th	0.726:1
Reverse	2.656:1
Final drive	4.050:1

Torque wrench settings

	Nm	lbf ft
Roadspeed sensor mounting bolt	6	4
Sump to transmission shield	45	33
Torque converter-to-driveplate nuts.	85	63
Transmission bellhousing-to-engine bolts:		
Upper M12 bolts.	80	59
Rear M12 bolt	80	59
Front lower M12 bolt	45	33
Transmission speed sensor mounting bolt.	6	4

1 General information

Automatic transmission is available as an option on 1.4 litre petrol engine models only.

The automatic transmission (see illustration) has four forward speeds (and one reverse). The automatic gearchanges are electronically-controlled, rather than hydraulically as with previous conventional types. The advantage of electronic management is to provide a faster gearchange response. The separate transmission ECM (located behind the battery) employs 'Fuzzy logic' to determine the gear shift points. Instead of having predetermined points for up-shift and down-shift, the ECM takes into account several influencing factors before deciding to shift. These factors include engine speed, driving 'resistance' (engine load), brake pedal position, throttle position, and the rate at which the throttle pedal position is changed. This results in an almost infinite number of shift points, which the ECM can tailor to match the driving style, be that sporty or economic. A kickdown facility is also provided, to enable a faster acceleration response when required.

The transmission consists of three main assemblies, these being the torque converter, which is directly coupled to the engine; the final drive unit, which incorporates the differential unit; and the planetary gearbox, with its multi-disc clutches and brake bands. The transmission is lubricated with automatic transmission fluid (ATF), and is regarded by the manufacturers as being 'filled for life', with no requirement for the fluid to be changed at regular intervals. No provision is made for easy DIY checking of the fluid level, either – this must be carried out by a Seat dealer, using special equipment capable of monitoring the fluid temperature (see Chapter 1A).

The torque converter incorporates an automatic lock-up feature, which eliminates converter slip in 3rd and 4th gears; this aids performance and economy. In addition to the normal alternative of manual change, two further modes are available – Sport and Economy mode. In Sport mode, upshifts are delayed longer and downshifts occur at higher engine speeds, to make full use of engine power, whereas in Economy mode, upshifts are taken sooner and downshifts are delayed as late as possible, to permit optimum economy. The decision as to which operating mode to use is determined by the ECM, based on the driving style of the driver; a moderate style will invoke the economy mode, and a faster style will invoke the sport mode.

Another feature of this transmission is the automatic selector lever lock when the ignition is on with P or N selected, and the car is stationary or moving at less than 5 km/h. In order to move the selector lever, the brake pedal must first be depressed and the Shiftlock button pressed at the same time.

The kickdown function of the transmission, which acts to select a lower gear (where possible) on full-throttle acceleration, is operated by the throttle pedal position sensor (see Chapter 4A for details).

A starter inhibitor relay is fitted, to prevent starter motor operation unless the transmission is in P or N. The relay is located on the relay carrier behind the storage area on the driver's side, and is marked with the number 53.

Some models also feature a security/safety device which locks the transmission in P when the ignition key is removed.

The transmission is fitted with an electronic roadspeed sensor. This device measures the rotational speed of the transmission final drive, and converts the information into a vehicle speed signal, which is then sent to the speedometer module in the instrument panel – this despite the fitment of ABS to all Ibiza models, which normally provides this information. The signal is also used as an input by the engine management system ECM.

A fault diagnosis system is integrated into the control module, but analysis can only be undertaken with specialised equipment. If a malfunction should occur in the transmission electrical system, control will switch to one of two emergency programmes; either the transmission still switches automatically but the changes are not smooth, or the transmission does not change automatically and only manual selection of 3rd and reverse gears is possible. When the transmission enters emergency mode, it is important that any fault be identified and rectified at the earliest possible opportunity. Delay in doing so will only cause further problems. A Seat dealer can 'interrogate' the ECM fault memory for stored fault codes, enabling him to pinpoint the fault quickly. Once the fault has been corrected and any fault codes have been cleared, normal transmission operation should be restored.

Because of the need for special test equipment, the complexity of some of the parts, and the need for scrupulous cleanliness when servicing automatic transmissions, the amount of work which the owner can do is

H45363

1.2 External components on the automatic transmission

1 Bolt	6 Bolt	10 Multifunction
2 Series resistance	7 Transmission speed sender	switch
3 Wiring harness	8 Transmission	11 Bolt
4 Roadspeed sensor	9 Solenoid valve wiring	12 Selector shaft lever
5 Bolt	harness	13 Nut

limited. Repairs to the final drive differential are also not recommended. Major repairs and overhaul operations should be left to a Seat dealer, who will be equipped with the necessary equipment for fault diagnosis and repair. The information in this Chapter is therefore limited to a description of the removal and refitting of the transmission as a complete unit. The removal, refitting and adjustment of the selector cable is also described.

In the event of a transmission problem occurring, consult a Seat dealer or transmission specialist before removing the transmission from the car, since the majority of fault diagnosis is carried out with the transmission *in situ*.

2 Automatic transmission – removal and refitting

Removal

1 Select a solid, level surface to park the car on. Give yourself enough space to move around it easily. Apply the handbrake and chock the rear wheels.
2 Loosen the front wheel bolts, and the left-hand driveshaft hub nut, then raise the front of the car and support it securely on axle stands (see *Jacking and vehicle support*). Remove the front wheels, the left-hand front wheel arch liner and the engine undershield. Allow a suitable working clearance underneath for the eventual withdrawal of the transmission.
3 If necessary for the hoist or lifting bar being used, remove the bonnet with reference to Chapter 11.
4 Remove the engine top cover.
5 Remove the battery and battery tray with reference to Chapter 5A.
6 Pull out the retaining clip and detach the selector lever control cable from the support bracket on the front of the transmission.
7 Using a 13 mm open-ended spanner, lever the control cable end fitting from the gearchange lever/shaft.
8 Clamp off the automatic transmission fluid cooler hoses with brake hose type clamps. Release the retaining clips and detach the hoses from the cooler. Tape over or plug the cooler stubs to prevent entry of dust and dirt.
9 Unbolt and remove the control cable support bracket.
10 Disconnect all wiring and connectors from the transmission, noting the location to ensure correct refitting **(see illustration)**.
11 Unbolt and remove the wiring support bracket, noting that an earth cable is located beneath one of the bolts.
12 Release the plastic wiring conduit from the transmission lifting eye and from the special transmission-to-engine bolt.
13 Unscrew and remove the upper transmission-to-engine bolts.
14 Refer to Chapter 5A and remove the starter motor.

15 Remove the left-hand driveshaft as described in Chapter 8.
16 Remove the exhaust front pipe as described in Chapter 4C.
17 Unbolt the right-hand driveshaft from the transmission flange with reference to Chapter 8, then tie it to one side.
18 Unclip the blanking cap, located next to the right-hand transmission flange, and turn the engine to locate one of the torque converter-to-driveplate nuts in the opening. Unscrew and remove the nut whilst preventing the engine from turning by using a wide-bladed screwdriver engaged with the ring gear teeth on the driveplate visible through the starter aperture. Unscrew the remaining two nuts, turning the engine a third of a turn at a time to locate them.
19 Unbolt the engine rear mounting link and bracket from the transmission and subframe. Also remove the transmission oil pan guard.
20 Unbolt the cover plate from the bottom of the transmission bellhousing.
21 Working under the rear of the engine, unscrew the single nut from the transmission-to-engine mounting stud.
22 Support the engine with a hoist, or with a support bar located on the front wing inner channels. Depending on the engine, temporarily remove components as necessary to attach the hoist.
23 Remove the right-hand engine mounting completely, by first positioning the coolant expansion tank to one side, and then removing the bolts securing the mounting sections to the body and engine. There is no need to separate the two sections.
24 Position a trolley jack underneath the transmission, and raise it to just take the weight of the unit.
25 Undo and remove the two bolts securing the left-hand gearbox mounting to the triangular mounting spacer. By controlling both the engine hoist/support bar and the trolley jack, lower the transmission approximately 60 mm. Unscrew the two remaining bolts and one nut, and remove the transmission mounting spacer.
26 Unscrew and remove the lower bolts securing the transmission bellhousing to the engine, noting the bolt locations, as they are of different sizes and lengths.
27 Check that all the fixings and attachments are clear of the transmission. Enlist the aid of an assistant to help in guiding and supporting the transmission during its removal.
28 The transmission is located on two dowels, and it may be necessary to prise the transmission from them. Once the transmission is disconnected from the location dowels, swivel the unit out and lower it out of the car.

⚠ **Warning: Support the transmission to ensure that it remains steady on the jack head. Ensure that the torque converter remains in position on its shaft in the torque converter housing.**

29 With the transmission removed, bolt a suitable bar and spacer across the front face of the torque converter housing, to retain the torque converter in position.

Refitting

30 Refitting is a reversal of the removal procedure, but note the following special points:
a) *When reconnecting the transmission to the engine, ensure that the location dowels are in position, and that the transmission is correctly aligned with them before pushing it fully into engagement with the engine. As the torque converter is refitted, ensure that the drive pins at the centre of the torque converter hub engage with the recesses in the automatic transmission fluid pump inner wheel.*
b) *Tighten all retaining bolts to their specified torque.*
c) *Reconnect and adjust the selector cable, as described in Section 4.*
d) *On completion, check the transmission fluid level (see Chapter 1A).*
e) *If a new transmission unit has been fitted, it may be necessary to have the transmission ECM 'matched' to the engine management ECM electronically, to ensure correct operation – seek the advice of your Seat dealer.*

3 Automatic transmission overhaul – general information

In the event of a fault occurring, it will be necessary to establish whether the fault is electrical, mechanical or hydraulic in nature, before repair work can be contemplated. Diagnosis requires detailed knowledge of the transmission's operation and construction, as well as access to specialised test equipment, and so is deemed to be beyond the scope

2.10 Gearbox electrical connections

1 *Solenoid valves*
2 *Roadspeed sensor*
3 *Multifunction switch*
4 *Gearbox speed sensor*

of this manual. It is therefore essential that problems with the automatic transmission are referred to a Seat dealer for assessment.

Note that a faulty transmission should not be removed before the car has been assessed by a dealer, as fault diagnosis is carried out with the transmission *in situ*.

4 Selector cable –
removal, refitting and adjustment

Removal

1 Disconnect the battery negative lead as described in Chapter 5A.
2 Apply the handbrake, then jack up the front of the car and support it on axle stands (see *Jacking and vehicle support*). Allow a suitable working clearance underneath the car. Remove the engine undershield and engine top cover as applicable.
3 Move the selector lever to the P position.
4 Pull out the retaining clip and detach the selector lever control cable from the support bracket on the front of the transmission **(see illustration)**.
5 Using a 13 mm open-ended spanner, lever the control cable end fitting from the gearchange lever/shaft. Also release the cable from its supports.
6 Working beneath the car, unbolt the underbody crossmember from under the exhaust system.
7 Separate the exhaust downpipe from the intermediate pipe with reference to Chapter 4C.
8 Release the exhaust intermediate pipe mounting rubber, and lower the rear exhaust system as far as possible. Remove the exhaust heat shield from the underbody tunnel.
9 Undo the bolts and remove the cover from the bottom of the selector lever housing.
10 Using a screwdriver, prise the selector cable end fitting from the lever, then pull out the clip and remove the selector cable from the housing. Recover the seal.
11 Withdraw the selector cable from the engine compartment.

Refitting

12 Refit the selector cable by reversing the removal procedure, noting the following points:
  a) *Lightly grease the cable end fittings before refitting the cable.*
  b) *Ensure that the cable is correctly routed, as noted on removal, and that it is securely held by its retaining clips.*

4.4 Selector cable

| 1 Selector cable | 3 Circlip |
| 2 Nut | 4 Selector lever |

  c) *Check and if necessary renew the cable and housing cover seals.*
  d) *Take care not to bend or kink the cable.*
  e) *Carry out the cable adjustment procedure described below.*

Adjustment

13 Inside the car, check that the selector lever is still in the P position.
14 At the front of the transmission, slacken the cable adjustment locking bolt at the ball socket.
15 Check that the selector lever on the transmission is in the P position. It must not be possible to simultaneously rotate both front roadwheels in the same direction.
16 Tighten the cable adjustment locking bolt securely.
17 Verify the operation of the selector lever by shifting through all gear positions and checking that every gear can be selected smoothly and without delay.
18 Lower the car to the ground.

5 Selector lever housing –
removal and refitting

Removal

1 Disconnect the battery negative lead as described in Chapter 5A.
2 Apply the handbrake, then jack up the front of the car and support it on axle stands (see *Jacking and vehicle support*). Remove the engine undershield.
3 Inside the car, move the selector lever to position 2, then push down the sleeve beneath

the lever grip, and pull off the grip upwards **(see illustration)**.
4 Move the selector lever to the P position.
5 Remove the centre console as described in Chapter 11.
6 Remove the selector lever cover and position indicator, by pulling upwards from the housing, and at the same time disconnect the wiring at the front.
7 Disconnect the wiring for the selector lever lock solenoid.
8 Working beneath the car, unbolt the underbody crossmember from under the exhaust system.
9 Separate the exhaust downpipe from the intermediate pipe with reference to Chapter 4C.
10 Release the exhaust intermediate pipe mounting rubber, and lower the rear exhaust system as far as possible. Remove the exhaust heatshield from the underbody tunnel.
11 Undo the bolts and remove the cover from the bottom of the selector lever housing.
12 Using a screwdriver, prise the selector cable end fitting from the lever, then pull out the clip and remove the selector cable from the housing. Recover the seal.
13 Support the housing from below, then unscrew the mounting nuts from inside the car. Withdraw the housing from under the car.

Refitting

14 Refitting is a reversal of removal, but check and if necessary renew the cable and housing cover seals. Finally, check and adjust the cable as described in Section 4.

6 Electronic control module –
removal and refitting

Note: *If the electronic control module is renewed, the new module must be initialised by a Seat dealer or suitably-equipped specialist.*

Removal

1 The transmission electronic control module (ECM) is located behind the battery on the battery tray.
2 With the ignition switched off, unlock and disconnect the wiring plug from the ECM.
3 Undo the two retaining bolts and withdraw the ECM from the engine compartment.

Refitting

4 Refitting is a reversal of removal.

5.3 Selector lever assembly

1 Selector lever handle	7 Frame	14 Roller	22 Gasket	30 Steering lock	38 Nut
2 Sleeve	8 Bolt	15 Circlip	23 Cover	31 Bolt	39 Locking cable
3 Cover	9 Shim	16 Lever housing	24 Bolt	32 Lock solenoid	40 Circlip
4 Cover strip	10 Locking segment	17 Pivot pin	25 O-ring	33 Cable tie	41 Gasket
5 Lever position display	11 Plate	18 Bolt	26 Bolt	34 Spring	42 Selector cable
6 Retaining clip	12 Locating spring with roller	19 Locking lever	27 Contact spring	35 Locking pin	43 Lever
	13 Selector lever	20 Washer	28 Bolt	36 Nut	44 Support bracket
		21 Bolt	29 Clip	37 Washer	45 Circlip

H32008

Chapter 8
Driveshafts

Contents

Degrees of difficulty

Easy, suitable for novice with little experience	Fairly easy, suitable for beginner with some experience	Fairly difficult, suitable for competent DIY mechanic	Difficult, suitable for experienced DIY mechanic	Very difficult, suitable for expert DIY or professional

Specifications

Lubrication

Type of grease	G-052 13 A2 (inner joint), G-052 738 A0 (outer joint)

Quantity of grease per joint:
Outer joint:

Joint diameter 90 mm.	80 g (40 in joint, 40 in gaiter)
Joint diameter 100 mm.	100 g (60 in joint, 40 in gaiter)

Inner joint:
Tripod type CV joint:

Joint diameter 100 mm.	110 g (55 in joint, 55 in gaiter)
Joint diameter 108 mm.	120 g (60 in joint, 60 in gaiter)

Ball-and-cage type CV joint:

Joint diameter 90 mm.	80 g (40 in joint, 40 in gaiter)
Joint diameter 100 mm.	120 g (50 in joint, 70 in gaiter)

Torque wrench settings

	Nm	lbf ft
Driveshaft shield.	35	26
Driveshaft-to-transmission flange bolts:*		
M8:		
Stage 1	20	15
Stage 2	Angle-tighten a further 90°	
M10:		
Stage 1	50	37
Stage 2	Angle-tighten a further 45°	
Hub nut:*		
Stage 1	50	37
Stage 2	Angle-tighten a further 45°	
Lower arm-to-balljoint nuts:*		
Stage 1	20	15
Stage 2	Angle-tighten a further 90°	

* Use new nut/bolt

1 General information

Drive is transmitted from the differential to the front wheels by means of two steel driveshafts of either solid or hollow construction (depending on model). Both driveshafts are splined at their outer ends, to accept the wheel hubs, and are secured to the hub by a large nut. The inner end of each driveshaft is bolted to the transmission drive flange.

Constant velocity (CV) joints are fitted to each end of the driveshafts, to ensure the smooth and efficient transmission of drive at all the angles possible as the roadwheels move up-and-down with the suspension, and as they turn from side-to-side under steering. On all models with manual transmission, both inner and outer constant velocity joints are of the ball-and-cage type. On all models with automatic transmission, the outer joint is of the ball-and-cage type, but the inner joint is of the tripod type.

Rubber or plastic gaiters are secured over both CV joints with steel clips. The gaiters contain the grease which lubricates the joints, and also protect the joints from the entry of dirt and debris.

2 Driveshaft – removal and refitting

Note: A new hub nut will be required on refitting. On automatic transmission models, in order to gain the necessary clearance required to withdraw the left-hand driveshaft, it may be necessary to unbolt the rear engine transmission mounting from the subframe, and lift the engine slightly.

Removal

1 Remove the wheel trim/hub cap (as

2.1 Home-made tool for holding the front hub while loosening the hub nut

2.3 Remove the heat shield (arrowed)

applicable) then have an assistant depress the footbrake, and partially slacken the hub/driveshaft nut with the vehicle resting on its wheels – note that the nut is very tight, and a suitable extension bar will probably be required to aid slackening. Alternatively, the hub nut may be loosened later using a home-made tool consisting of two lengths of metal bar **(see illustration)**. Also slacken the roadwheel securing bolts.

2 Apply the handbrake, then jack up the front of the vehicle and support it on axle stands (see *Jacking and vehicle support*). Remove the appropriate front roadwheel.

3 Remove the retaining bolts and/or clips, and remove the undershields from beneath the engine/transmission unit to gain access to the driveshafts. Where necessary, also unbolt the heat shield from the transmission housing to improve access to the driveshaft inner joint **(see illustration)**.

4 Mark the inner driveshaft joint and drive flange in relation to each other, then, using a multi-splined tool, unscrew and remove the bolts and, where applicable, recover the retaining plates from underneath the bolts. Place a plastic bag over the joint to prevent entry of dust and dirt **(see illustrations)**.

Caution: Support the driveshaft by suspending it with wire or string – do not allow it to hang under its own weight, or the joint may be damaged.

5 Using a suitable marker pen or scriber, draw around the outline of the end of the suspension lower arm on the lower arm balljoint, marking the correct fitted position of the balljoint.

6 Unscrew the lower arm balljoint securing nuts, and push the lower arm downwards to detach it from the balljoint assembly.

7 Unscrew and remove the hub/driveshaft nut, and discard it as a new one is required for refitting **(see illustration)**.

8 Carefully pull the hub carrier outwards, and withdraw the driveshaft outer constant velocity joint from the hub. The joint may be a very tight fit in the hub; tap the joint out of the hub using a soft-faced mallet (refit the hub nut to the end of the driveshaft to protect the threads). If this fails to free the driveshaft from the hub, the joint will have to be pressed out using a suitable tool bolted to the hub.

9 Manoeuvre the driveshaft out from underneath the vehicle and (where fitted) recover the gasket from the end of the inner constant velocity joint. Discard the gasket – a new one should be used on refitting.

Caution: Do not allow the vehicle to rest on its wheels with one or both driveshaft(s) removed, as damage to the wheel bearings may result.

10 If moving the vehicle is unavoidable, temporarily insert the outer end of the driveshaft in the hub, and tighten the driveshaft retaining nut; in this case, the inner end of the driveshaft must be supported, for example by suspending with string from the vehicle underbody.

Refitting

11 Ensure that the transmission flange and inner joint mating surfaces are clean and dry. Where necessary, fit a new gasket to the joint by peeling off its backing foil and sticking it in position.

12 Ensure that the outer joint and hub splines are clean and dry. Coat the splines of the outer constant velocity joint, the threads on the end of the outer joint, the splines in the hub, and the contact face of the hub nut with a little grease.

13 Manoeuvre the driveshaft into position, and engage the outer joint with the hub. Fit the new hub/driveshaft nut and use it to draw the joint fully into position.

14 Align the suspension lower arm balljoint, lower arm, and retaining plate/hub assembly, then fit new lower arm balljoint securing nuts, and tighten them to the specified torque setting, using the marks made on removal to ensure that the balljoint is correctly positioned.

15 Align the driveshaft inner joint with the transmission flange, and refit the retaining bolts and (where necessary) plates. Tighten the retaining bolts to the specified torque.

16 Where applicable (see Note at the beginning of this Section), fit new rear engine/transmission mounting-to-subframe bolts, and tighten the bolts to the specified torque (see relevant part of Chapter 2).

17 Ensure that the outer joint is drawn fully into position, then refit the roadwheel and lower the vehicle to the ground.

18 Tighten the driveshaft nut to the torque given in the Specifications.

19 Once the driveshaft nut is correctly tightened, tighten the wheel bolts to the specified torque (see relevant part of Chapter 1) and refit the wheel trim/hub cap.

2.4a Mark the driveshaft joint and flange in relation to each other . . .

2.4b . . . then unscrew and remove the bolts and retaining plates (arrowed)

2.4c Place plastic bags over the joint and flange to protect them

2.7 Remove the hub/driveshaft nut

3.1a Driveshaft with inner CV joint components

1 12-point hub/ driveshaft nut
2 Thrower ring
3 Outer CV joint
4 Circlip
5 Thrust ring
6 Dished washer
7 Gaiter securing clip
8 Outer joint gaiter
9 Gaiter securing clip
10 Left-hand driveshaft (solid)

11 Right-hand driveshaft (tubular)
12 Driveshaft-to-transmission flange bolts
13 Retaining plate
14 Gaiter securing clip
15 Inner joint gaiter
16 Dished washer
17 Inner CV joint
18 Gasket
19 Circlip

3 Driveshaft rubber gaiters – renewal

1 Remove the driveshaft from the car, as described in Section 2. Continue as described under the relevant sub-heading. Driveshafts with a tripod type inner joint can be identified by the shape of the inner CV joint; the driveshaft retaining bolt holes are in cast extensions, giving it a six-pointed star-shaped exterior, in contrast to the smooth, circular shape of the ball-and-cage joint (see illustrations).

Outer CV joint gaiter

2 Secure the driveshaft in a vice equipped with soft jaws, and release the two outer joint gaiter retaining clips. If necessary, the retaining clips can be cut to release them.
3 Slide the rubber gaiter down the shaft to expose the constant velocity joint, and scoop out excess grease.
4 Using a soft-faced mallet, tap the joint off the end of the driveshaft.
5 Remove the circlip from the driveshaft groove, and slide off the thrustwasher and dished washer, noting which way around it is fitted.
6 Slide the rubber gaiter off the driveshaft and discard it.
7 Thoroughly clean the constant velocity joint(s) using paraffin, or a suitable solvent, and dry thoroughly. Carry out a visual inspection as follows.

3.1b Inner tripod joint components

1 Metal cover
2 Gaiter securing clip
3 Inner joint gaiter
4 Driveshaft-to-transmission flange bolts
5 Inner joint
6 Tripod/roller assembly (chamfer arrowed faces towards driveshaft)
7 Circlip
8 Seal

8 Move the inner splined driving member from side-to-side to expose each ball in turn at the top of its track. Examine the balls for cracks, flat spots or signs of surface pitting.
9 Inspect the ball tracks on the inner and outer members. If the tracks have widened, the balls will no longer be a tight fit. At the same time, check the ball cage windows for wear or cracking between the windows.
10 If on inspection any of the constant velocity joint components are found to be worn or damaged, it will be necessary to renew the complete joint assembly. If the joint is in satisfactory condition, obtain a new gaiter and retaining clips, a constant velocity joint circlip and the correct type of grease. Grease is often supplied with the joint repair kit – if not, use a good-quality molybdenum disulphide grease.
11 Tape over the splines on the end of the driveshaft, to protect the new gaiter as it is slid into place (see illustration).
12 Slide the new gaiter onto the end of the driveshaft, then remove the protective tape from the driveshaft splines.

3.11 Tape over the driveshaft splines, then slide the new gaiter along the shaft

3.13a Slide on the dished washer, with its convex side innermost . . .

3.13b . . . then slide on the thrustwasher

3.14a Fit the new circlip to the driveshaft groove . . .

3.14b . . . then locate the joint on the driveshaft splines . . .

3.14c . . . and tap the joint onto the driveshaft

13 Slide on the dished washer, making sure its convex side is innermost, followed by the thrustwasher **(see illustrations)**.

14 Fit a new circlip to the driveshaft, then tap the joint onto the driveshaft until the circlip engages in its groove **(see illustrations)**. Make sure that the joint is securely retained by the circlip.

15 Pack the joint with the specified type of grease. Work the grease well into the bearing tracks whilst twisting the joint, and fill the rubber gaiter with any excess.

16 Ease the gaiter over the joint, and ensure that the gaiter lips are correctly located on both the driveshaft and constant velocity joint. Lift the outer sealing lip of the gaiter to equalise air pressure within the gaiter **(see illustration)**.

17 Fit the large metal retaining clip to the gaiter. Pull the clip as tight as possible, and locate the hooks on the clip in their slots. Remove any slack in the gaiter retaining clip by carefully compressing the raised section of the clip. In the absence of the special tool, a pair of side-cutters may be used, taking care not to cut the clip **(see illustrations)**. Secure the small retaining clip using the same procedure.

18 Check the constant velocity joint moves freely in all directions, then refit the driveshaft to the vehicle, as described in Section 2.

Tripod inner CV joint gaiter

19 Secure the driveshaft in a vice equipped with soft jaws, with the inner joint uppermost, and release the two inner joint gaiter retaining clips. If necessary, the retaining clips can be cut to release them. Slide the rubber gaiter down the shaft, away from the joint housing.

20 Using a screwdriver, prise up the tabs of the metal cap over the inner end of the joint. Lever off the cover.

21 Scoop out excess grease from the joint, then remove the O-ring from the groove in the joint housing.

22 Using a suitable marker pen or a scriber, make alignment marks between the end of the driveshaft, the tripod roller assembly, and the housing.

23 Slide the joint housing down the driveshaft, away from the joint.

24 Remove the circlip from the end of the driveshaft.

25 Press or drive the driveshaft from the tripod, taking great care not to damage the rollers.

26 Slide the housing and the rubber gaiter from the end of the driveshaft.

3.16 Lift the inner lip to equalise the air pressure

3.17a Compress the clip and engage the hook into the furthest possible hole of the gaiter securing clip . . .

3.17b . . . then use special pliers to squeeze together the sides, and compress the raised section of the clip

3.28 Check the tripod rollers and outer member for signs of wear

3.30a Tape over the driveshaft splines to protect the new gaiter . . .

3.30b . . . then lever the gaiter carefully over the ridge on the driveshaft

3.34 Work the grease into the joint outer member

3.36 Lift the gaiter outer end to equalise the air pressure

27 Thoroughly clean the joint components using paraffin, or a suitable solvent, and dry thoroughly. Carry out a visual inspection as follows.

28 Inspect the tripod rollers and the joint outer housing for signs of wear, pitting or scuffing on their mating surfaces. Check that the joint rollers rotate smoothly, with no traces of roughness **(see illustration)**.

29 If the rollers or outer housing shown signs of wear or damage, it will be necessary to renew the complete driveshaft, since the joint is not available separately. If the joint is in satisfactory condition, obtain a repair kit, consisting of a new gaiter, retaining clips, circlip, and the correct type and quantity of grease.

30 Tape over the splines on the end of the driveshaft, to protect the new gaiter as it is slid into place, then slide the new gaiter and securing clips, and the joint housing over the end of the driveshaft **(see illustrations)**. Remove the protective tape from the driveshaft splines.

31 Press or drive the tripod onto the end of the driveshaft until it contacts the stop, ensuring that the marks made on the end of the driveshaft and the tripod before dismantling are aligned. Note that the chamfered edge of the internal splines on the tripod should face towards the driveshaft. Take care not to damage the rollers as the tripod is refitted.

32 Fit the new circlip to retain the tripod on the end of the driveshaft.

33 Work half of the grease supplied with the repair kit into the inner end of the joint housing, then slide the housing over the tripod, ensuring that the marks made during dismantling are aligned, and clamp the housing in the vice.

34 Work the rest of the grease supplied with the repair kit into the outer end of the joint housing **(see illustration)**.

35 Slide the rubber gaiter up the driveshaft onto the joint housing, ensuring that the end of the gaiter seats in the groove in the joint housing, and secure with the large clip as described in paragraph 17.

36 Lift the gaiter outer end to equalise the air pressure in the gaiter, then secure the outer gaiter securing clip in position using the same method used previously **(see illustration)**.

37 Check that the grease in the joint outer housing is evenly distributed around the tripod rollers.

38 Wipe any excess grease from the inner face of the joint housing, then fit the O-ring provided in the repair kit into the groove.

39 Fit the new cover supplied in the repair kit to the inner end of the joint housing, ensuring that the bolt holes in the housing and cover are aligned.

40 Secure the cover by bending the securing tabs around the edge of the outer housing flange.

41 Check the driveshaft joint moves freely in all directions, then refit the driveshaft to the vehicle, as described in Section 2. To prevent the tripod joint from being pushed back down the driveshaft during refitting, temporarily stick adhesive tape over the open end of the joint outer member **(see illustration)**. Remove the tape just before reconnecting the inner end of the driveshaft to the transmission.

Ball-and-cage inner CV joint

42 Secure the driveshaft in a vice equipped with soft jaws, then release the gaiter outer securing clip, securing the gaiter to the driveshaft. If necessary, the clip can be cut to release it.

43 Using a hammer and a small drift, carefully drive the inner end of the gaiter from the joint housing.

44 Slide the gaiter down the driveshaft to expose the constant velocity joint, and scoop out excess grease.

45 Remove the circlip from the end of the driveshaft.

46 Press or drive the driveshaft from the joint, taking great care not to damage the joint.

Recover the dished washer fitted between the constant velocity joint and the gaiter.

47 Slide the gaiter from the end of the driveshaft.

48 Proceed as described previously in paragraphs 7 to 12.

49 Slide the dished washer onto the driveshaft, making sure its convex side is innermost.

50 Fit the joint to the end of the driveshaft, noting that the chamfered edge of the internal splines on the joint should face towards the driveshaft. Drive or press the joint into position until it contacts the shoulder on the driveshaft.

3.41 Tape over the end of the driveshaft joint

51 Fit a new circlip to retain the joint on the end of the driveshaft.

52 If the left-hand driveshaft is being worked on, mark the final installation position of the gaiter outboard end on the driveshaft using tape or paint – do not scratch the surface of the driveshaft **(see illustration)**.

53 Pack the joint with the recommended quantity of grease (see Specifications), then pack the gaiter with the recommended quantity of grease.

54 Slide the gaiter up the driveshaft, and push or drive the inner end of the gaiter onto the joint housing.

55 If the left-hand driveshaft is being worked on, slide the outboard end of the gaiter into position using the mark made previously (see paragraph 52), then secure the outer gaiter securing clip in position as described in paragraph 17.

56 If the right-hand driveshaft is being worked on, slide the outboard end of the gaiter into position, and secure the outer gaiter securing clip in position as described in paragraph 17 **(see illustration)**.

57 Check the driveshaft joint moves freely in all directions, then refit the driveshaft to the vehicle, as described in Section 2.

4 Driveshaft overhaul – general information

If any of the checks described in Chapter 1A or 1B reveal wear in any driveshaft joint, first remove the roadwheel trim or centre cap (as applicable) and check that the hub nut is tight. If the nut is loose, obtain a new nut, and tighten it to the specified torque (see Section 2). If the nut is tight, refit the centre cap/trim, and repeat the check on the other hub nut.

Road test the vehicle, and listen for a metallic clicking from the front of the vehicle as the vehicle is driven slowly in a circle on full-lock. If a clicking noise is heard, this indicates wear in the outer constant velocity joint; this means that the joint must be renewed.

If vibration consistent with roadspeed is felt through the car when accelerating, there is a possibility of wear in the inner constant velocity joints.

To check the joints for wear, remove the driveshafts, then dismantle them as described in Section 3. If any wear or free play is found, the affected joint must be renewed. Refer to a Seat dealer or parts specialist for information on the availability of driveshaft components.

3.52 Installation position of inner joint gaiter on left-hand driveshaft

A = 17.0 mm

3.56 Installation position of inner joint gaiter on right-hand driveshaft

A Vent chamber in gaiter   B Vent hole

Chapter 9
Braking system

Contents

Degrees of difficulty

Easy, suitable for novice with little experience | **Fairly easy,** suitable for beginner with some experience | **Fairly difficult,** suitable for competent DIY mechanic | **Difficult,** suitable for experienced DIY mechanic | **Very difficult,** suitable for expert DIY or professional

Specifications

Front brakes

Caliper types:
  1.9 litre diesel engine codes ASZ and BLT.................... C54-ll or FN-3
  All other engines....................................... FSIII
Disc diameter:
  1.9 litre diesel engine codes ASZ and BLT.................... 288 mm
  All other engines....................................... 256 mm
Disc thickness:
  New:
    1.9 litre diesel engine codes ASZ and BLT.................. 25.0 mm
    All other engines..................................... 22.0 mm
  Minimum permissible thickness:
    1.9 litre diesel engine codes ASZ and BLT.................. 22.0 mm
    All other engines..................................... 19.0 mm
Maximum disc run-out..................................... 0.1 mm
Brake pad thickness:
  Minimum (including backing plate)......................... 7.0 mm
  Minimum (friction lining only)*........................... 2.0 mm
* The pad wear warning light illuminates when the pads are 2 to 3 mm thick.

Rear drum brakes

Drum diameter:
  New .... 200 mm
  Maximum diameter....................................... 201 mm (stamped on inner surface of drum)
Brake shoe friction material thickness:
  New .... 5.4 mm
  Minimum... 1.5 mm

Rear disc brakes

Disc diameter:
Ibiza FR models	256 mm
All other models	232 mm

Disc thickness:

New:
FR models	22.0 mm
All other models	9.0 mm

Minimum thickness:
FR models	19.0 mm
All other models	7.0 mm
Maximum disc run-out	0.1 mm

Brake pad thickness:
Minimum (including backing plate)	7.6 mm
Minimum (friction lining only)	2.0 mm

Torque wrench settings

	Nm	lbf ft
ABS control module bracket-to-wing nuts	20	15
ABS control module retaining bolts	8	6
ABS wheel sensor retaining bolts	8	6
Brake pedal pivot shaft nut	25	18
Brake pressure sensor (models with brake assist)	20	15
Front brake caliper:		
Guide pins (FSIII and FN-3)	28	21
Guide pin bolts (C54-II)*	30	22
Mounting bracket bolts (C54-II and FN-3)	125	92
Front brake disc shield	10	7
Handbrake lever bracket:		
Stage 1	20	15
Stage 2	Angle-tighten a further 90°	
Master cylinder mounting nuts	20	15
Pedal bracket	28	21
Rear brake caliper (disc brakes):		
Guide pin bolts*	35	26
Mounting bracket bolts:		
Stage 1	30	22
Stage 2	Angle-tighten a further 30°	
Rear wheel cylinder (drum brakes)	8	6
Roadwheel bolts	120	89
Servo unit mechanical vacuum pump (diesel models)	20	15
Servo unit mounting nuts	28	21

Use new bolts

1 General information and precautions

General information

The braking system is of servo-assisted, diagonal dual-circuit hydraulic type. The arrangement of the hydraulic system is such that each circuit operates one front and one rear brake from a tandem master cylinder. Under normal circumstances, both circuits operate in unison. However, if there is hydraulic failure in one circuit, full braking force will still be available at two wheels.

All models covered by this manual are equipped with disc brakes at the front. Either rear drum brakes or rear disc brakes may be fitted. An Anti-lock Braking System (ABS) is fitted to all models.

The front disc brakes are actuated by single-piston sliding type calipers, which ensure that equal pressure is applied to each disc pad.

On models with rear drum brakes, the rear brakes incorporate leading and trailing shoes, which are actuated by twin-piston wheel cylinders. A self-adjust mechanism is incorporated, to compensate for brake shoe wear. The handbrake lever operates the rear shoes by two cables.

On models with rear disc brakes, the brakes are actuated by single-piston sliding calipers which incorporate mechanical handbrake mechanisms.

Precautions

The car's braking system is one of its most important safety features. When working on the brakes, there are a number of points to be aware of, to ensure that your health (or even your life) is not being put at risk.

⚠️ **Warning: Brake fluid is poisonous. Take care to keep it off bare skin, and in particular not to get splashes in your eyes. The fluid also attacks paintwork and plastics – wash off spillages immediately with cold water. Finally, brake fluid is highly inflammable, and should be handled with the same care as petrol.**

• Make sure the ignition is off (take out the key) before disconnecting any braking system hydraulic union, and do not switch it on until after the hydraulic system has been bled. Failure to do this could lead to air entering the ABS hydraulic unit. If air enters the hydraulic unit pump, it will prove very difficult (in some cases impossible) to bleed the unit.

• When servicing any part of the system, work carefully and methodically – do not take short-cuts; also observe scrupulous cleanliness when overhauling any part of the hydraulic system.

• Always renew components in axle sets, where applicable – this means replacing brake pads on BOTH sides, even if only one set of pads is worn, or one wheel cylinder is leaking (for example). In the instance of uneven brake wear, the cause should be investigated and fixed (on disc brakes, sticking caliper pistons is a likely problem).

• Use only genuine Seat parts, or at least those of known good quality.

• Although genuine Seat brake pads are asbestos-free, the dust created by wear of non-genuine parts may contain asbestos,

which is a health hazard. Never blow it out with compressed air, and don't inhale any of it.
• DO NOT use petroleum-based solvents to clean brake parts; use brake cleaner or methylated spirit only.
• DO NOT allow any brake fluid, oil or grease to contact the brake pads or disc.

2 Hydraulic system – bleeding

⚠️ *Warning: Hydraulic fluid is poisonous; wash off immediately and thoroughly in the case of skin contact, and seek immediate medical advice if any fluid is swallowed or gets into the eyes. Certain types of hydraulic fluid are flammable, and may ignite when allowed into contact with hot components; when servicing any hydraulic system, it is safest to assume that the fluid is flammable, and to take precautions against the risk of fire as though it is petrol that is being handled. Hydraulic fluid is also an effective paint stripper, and will attack plastics; if any is spilt, it should be washed off immediately, using copious quantities of fresh water. Finally, it is hygroscopic (it absorbs moisture from the air) – old fluid may be contaminated and unfit for further use. When topping-up or renewing the fluid, always use the recommended type, and ensure that it comes from a freshly-opened sealed container.*

Note: *It is recommended that at least 0.25 litre of brake fluid is expelled from each caliper.*

General

1 The correct operation of any hydraulic system is only possible after removing all air from the components and circuit; this is achieved by bleeding the system. Since the clutch hydraulic system also uses fluid from the brake system reservoir, it should also be bled at the same time by referring to Chapter 6, Section 2.
2 During the bleeding procedure, add only clean, unused hydraulic fluid of the recommended type; never re-use fluid that has already been bled from the system. Ensure that sufficient fluid is available before starting work.
3 If there is any possibility of incorrect fluid being already in the system, the brake components and circuit must be flushed completely with uncontaminated, correct fluid, and new seals should be fitted to the various components.
4 If hydraulic fluid has been lost from the system, or air has entered because of a leak, ensure that the fault is cured before continuing further.
5 Park the car on level ground, then chock the wheels and release the handbrake.
6 Check that all pipes and hoses are secure, unions tight and bleed screws closed. Clean any dirt from around the bleed screws.

7 Unscrew the master cylinder reservoir cap, and top the reservoir up to the MAX level line; refit the cap loosely, and remember to maintain the fluid level at least above the MIN level line throughout the procedure, or there is a risk of further air entering the system.
8 There is a number of one-man, do-it-yourself brake bleeding kits currently available from motor accessory shops. It is recommended that one of these kits is used whenever possible, as they greatly simplify the bleeding operation, and reduce the risk of expelled air and fluid being drawn back into the system. If such a kit is not available, the basic (two-man) method must be used, which is described in detail below.
9 If a kit is to be used, prepare the car as described previously, and follow the kit manufacturer's instructions, as the procedure may vary slightly according to the type being used; generally, they are as outlined below in the relevant sub-section.
10 Whichever method is used, the same sequence must be followed (paragraph 12) to ensure the removal of all air from the system.

Bleeding sequence

11 If the system has been only partially disconnected, and suitable precautions were taken to minimise fluid loss, it should be necessary only to bleed that part of the system.
12 If the complete system is to be bled, then it should be done working in the following sequence:

Left-hand drive models

   a) *Right-hand rear brake.*
   b) *Left-hand rear brake.*
   c) *Right-hand front brake.*
   d) *Left-hand front brake.*

Right-hand drive models

   a) *Left-hand rear brake.*
   b) *Right-hand rear brake.*
   c) *Left-hand front brake.*
   d) *Right-hand front brake.*

Bleeding

Basic (two-man) method

13 Collect together a clean glass jar of reasonable size, a suitable length of plastic or rubber tubing which is a tight fit over the bleed

screw, and a ring spanner to fit the screw. The help of an assistant will also be required.
14 Remove the dust cap from the first screw in the sequence **(see illustration)**. Fit the spanner and tube to the screw, place the other end of the tube in the jar, and pour in sufficient fluid to cover the end of the tube.
15 Ensure that the master cylinder reservoir fluid level is maintained at least above the MIN level line throughout the procedure.
16 Have the assistant fully depress the brake pedal several times to build-up pressure, then maintain it on the final downstroke.
17 While pedal pressure is maintained, unscrew the bleed screw (approximately half a turn) and allow the compressed fluid and air to flow into the jar. The assistant should maintain pedal pressure, following it down to the floor if necessary, and should not release it until instructed to do so. When the flow stops, tighten the bleed screw again, have the assistant release the pedal slowly, and recheck the reservoir fluid level.
18 Repeat the steps given in paragraphs 16 and 17 until the fluid emerging from the bleed screw is free from air bubbles. If the master cylinder has been drained and refilled, and air is being bled from the first screw in the sequence, allow approximately five seconds between cycles for the master cylinder passages to refill.
19 When no more air bubbles appear, tighten the bleed screw securely, remove the tube and spanner, and refit the dust cap. Do not overtighten the bleed screw.
20 Repeat the procedure on the remaining screws in the sequence, until all air is removed from the system and the brake pedal feels firm.

Using a one-way valve kit

21 As their name implies, these kits consist of a length of tubing with a one-way valve fitted, to prevent expelled air and fluid being drawn back into the system; some kits include a translucent container, which can be positioned so that the air bubbles can be more easily seen flowing from the end of the tube.
22 The kit is connected to the bleed screw, which is then opened. The user returns to the driver's seat, depresses the brake pedal with a smooth, steady stroke, and slowly releases it; this is repeated until the expelled fluid is clear of air bubbles **(see illustration)**.
23 Note that these kits simplify work so

2.14 Remove the dust cap (arrowed) from the first screw in the sequence

2.22 Bleeding a brake using a one-way valve kit

much that it is easy to forget the master cylinder reservoir fluid level; ensure that this is maintained at least above the MIN level line at all times.

Using a pressure-bleeding kit

24 These kits are usually operated by the reservoir of pressurised air contained in the spare tyre. However, note that it will be probably necessary to reduce the pressure to less than 1.0 bar (14.5 psi); refer to the instructions supplied with the kit.

25 By connecting a pressurised, fluid-filled container to the master cylinder reservoir, bleeding can be carried out simply by opening each screw in turn (in the specified sequence), and allowing the fluid to flow out until no more air bubbles can be seen in the expelled fluid.

26 This method has the advantage that the large reservoir of fluid provides an additional safeguard against air being drawn into the system during bleeding.

27 Pressure-bleeding is particularly effective when bleeding 'difficult' systems, or when bleeding the complete system at the time of routine fluid renewal.

All methods

28 When bleeding is complete, and firm pedal feel is restored, wash off any spilt fluid, tighten the bleed screws securely, and refit their dust caps.

29 Check the hydraulic fluid level in the master cylinder reservoir, and top-up if necessary (see *Weekly checks*).

30 Discard any hydraulic fluid that has been bled from the system; it will not be fit for re-use.

4.2a Prise out the rubber caps from the guide pins (arrowed) . . .

4.2c Use a screwdriver to push the inner pad away from the disc a little . . .

31 Check the feel of the brake pedal. If it feels at all spongy, air must still be present in the system, and further bleeding is required. Failure to bleed satisfactorily after a reasonable repetition of the bleeding procedure may be due to worn master cylinder seals.

3 Hydraulic pipes and hoses – renewal

Note: *Refer to the note in Section 2 concerning the dangers of hydraulic fluid.*

1 If any pipe or hose is to be renewed, minimise fluid loss by first removing the master cylinder reservoir cap, then tightening it down onto a piece of polythene to obtain an airtight seal. Alternatively, flexible hoses can be sealed, if required, using a proprietary brake hose clamp; metal brake pipe unions can be plugged (if care is taken not to allow dirt into the system) or capped immediately they are disconnected. Place a wad of rag under any union that is to be disconnected, to catch any spilt fluid.

2 If a flexible hose is to be disconnected, where applicable unscrew the brake pipe union nut before removing the spring clip which secures the hose to its mounting bracket.

3 To unscrew the union nuts, it is preferable to obtain a brake pipe spanner of the correct size; these are available from most large motor accessory shops. Failing this, a close-fitting open-ended spanner will be required, though if the nuts are tight or corroded, their flats may be rounded-off if the spanner slips. In such a case, a self-locking wrench is often the only

4.2b . . . then unscrew and remove the guide pins

4.2d . . . then pull the caliper and pads from place

way to unscrew a stubborn union, but it follows that the pipe and the damaged nuts must be renewed on reassembly. Always clean a union and surrounding area before disconnecting it. If disconnecting a component with more than one union, make a careful note of the connections before disturbing any of them.

4 If a brake pipe is to be renewed, it can be obtained, cut to length and with the union nuts and end flares in place, from Seat dealers. All that is then necessary is to bend it to shape, following the line of the original, before fitting it to the car. Alternatively, most motor accessory shops can make up brake pipes from kits, but this requires very careful measurement of the original, to ensure that the new pipe is of the correct length. The safest answer is usually to take the original to the shop as a pattern.

5 On refitting, do not overtighten the union nuts. It is not necessary to exercise brute force to obtain a sound joint.

6 Ensure that the pipes and hoses are correctly routed, with no kinks, and that they are secured in the clips or brackets provided. After fitting, remove the polythene from the reservoir, and bleed the hydraulic system as described in Section 2. Wash off any spilt fluid, and check carefully for fluid leaks.

4 Front brake pads – renewal

⚠️ *Warning: Renew both sets of brake pads at the same time -- never renew the pads on only one wheel, as uneven braking may result. Note that the dust created by wear of the pads may contain asbestos, which is a health hazard. Never blow it out with compressed air, and do not inhale any of it. An approved filtering mask should be worn when working on the brakes. DO NOT use petrol or petroleum-based solvents to clean brake parts; use brake cleaner or methylated spirit only.*

Renewal

1 Apply the handbrake, then slacken the front roadwheel bolts. Jack up the front of the vehicle and support it on axle stands (see *Jacking and vehicle support*). Remove both front roadwheels.

FSIII calipers

2 Follow the accompanying photos (**illustrations 4.2a to 4.2q**) for the pad renewal procedure. Be sure to stay in order and read the caption under each illustration, and note the following points:

a) *New pads may have an adhesive foil on the backplates. Remove this foil prior to installation.*

b) *Thoroughly clean the caliper guide surfaces, and apply a little brake assembly (Copperslip) grease.*

c) *When pushing the caliper piston back to accommodate new pads, keep a close eye on the fluid level in the reservoir.*

4.2e Unclip the pad from the piston . . .

4.2f . . . and from the caliper body

4.2g Suspend the caliper from the suspension spring – don't strain the rubber hose

4.2h Measure the thickness of the pad's friction material

4.2i If new pads are to be fitted, the piston must be pushed back into the caliper body using a piston retraction tool. Keep an eye on the fluid level in the reservoir

4.2j Ensure the mounting surface of the caliper is clean (arrowed)

4.2k Clip the inner pad into the caliper piston . . .

4.2l . . . and slide the outer pad down into the caliper body

4.2m Slide the assembly over the disc and into place . . .

4.2n . . . ensuring the lower edges of the caliper and pads engage correctly

4.2o Insert the guide pins . . .

4.2p . . . and tighten them to the specified torque

4.2q Refit the rubber caps

C54-II calipers

3 Slacken and remove the lower guide pin bolt, using a slim open-ended spanner to prevent the guide pin itself from rotating. Discard the guide pin bolt – a new one must be fitted.

4 With the lower guide pin bolt removed, pivot the caliper upwards until it is clear of the brake pads and mounting bracket. If it is loose, recover the heat shield from the caliper piston.

5 Withdraw the two brake pads from the caliper mounting bracket.

6 First measure the thickness of the lining on each brake pad. If either pad is worn at any point to the specified minimum thickness or less, all four pads must be renewed. Also, the pads should be renewed if any are fouled with oil or grease; there is no satisfactory way of degreasing friction material, once contaminated. If any of the brake pads are worn unevenly, or are fouled with oil or grease, trace and rectify the cause before reassembly.

New brake pad kits are available from Seat dealers.

7 If the brake pads are still serviceable, carefully clean them using a clean, fine wire brush or similar, paying particular attention to the sides and back of the metal backing. Clean out the grooves in the friction material (where applicable), and pick out any large embedded particles of dirt or debris. Carefully clean the pad locations in the caliper body.

8 Prior to fitting the pads, check that the guide pins are free to slide easily in the caliper body bushes, and are a reasonably tight fit. Brush the dust and dirt from the caliper and piston, but do not inhale it, as it is injurious to health. Inspect the dust seal around the piston for damage, and the piston for evidence of fluid leaks, corrosion or damage. If attention to any of these components is necessary, refer to Section 5.

9 Clean and examine the pad retaining springs in the mounting bracket. If they are damaged or distorted, renew them.

10 If new pads are to be fitted, use a piston retraction tool to push the piston back into the caliper body. Keep an eye on the fluid level in the reservoir – the level will rise as the piston is pushed back.

11 Install the pads in the caliper mounting bracket, ensuring that the friction material of each pad is against the brake disc. Note the pad with the wear sensor wiring should be installed as the inner pad.

12 If removed, refit the heat shield to the caliper piston. **Note:** *A new heat shield is supplied with genuine Seat pads.* Pivot the caliper

down into position, and pass the pad warning sensor wiring through the caliper aperture. If the threads of the new guide pin bolt are not already precoated with locking compound, apply a suitable thread-locking compound to them. Install the lower guide pin bolt, tightening it to the specified torque setting while retaining the guide pin with an open-ended spanner.

FN-3 calipers

13 Trace the brake pad wear sensor wiring (where fitted) back from the pads, and disconnect it from the wiring connector. Note the routing of the wiring, and free it from any relevant retaining clips.

14 Using a flat-bladed screwdriver, prise the ends of the retaining spring from the holes in the caliper body, and remove the spring **(see illustration)**.

15 Remove the two protective rubber caps and, using a suitable hexagon key, loosen and remove the two caliper guide pins from the caliper, then lift the caliper together with the pads away from the hub carrier **(see illustrations)**.

16 Inspect the pads and caliper as described in paragraphs 6 to 8 of this Section.

17 If new pads are to be fitted, use a piston retraction tool to push the piston back into the caliper body. Keep an eye on the fluid level in the reservoir – the level will rise as the piston is pushed back.

18 Remove the protective plastic cover from the back of the outer pad. Note that the inner pads are particular to the left- or right-hand caliper **(see illustration)**. The arrow on the backplate **must** point downwards.

19 Press the inner pad into the piston, and fit

4.14 Pull the ends of the retaining spring from the caliper

4.15a Remove the rubber end caps . . .

4.15b . . . then slacken . . .

4.15c . . . and remove the caliper guide pins . . .

4.15d . . . slide the caliper from place

4.18 The arrow on the backplate must point downwards

the outer pad to the caliper mounting bracket. Note the pad with the wear sensor wiring should be installed as the inner pad.

20 Slide the caliper into place, then insert both guide pins and tighten them to the specified torque. Refit the rubber caps.

21 Manoeuvre the retaining spring into position. Insert one end of the spring into the hole in the caliper body, then use a screwdriver to lever the other end of the spring into place.

All calipers

22 Depress the brake pedal repeatedly, until the pads are pressed into firm contact with the brake disc, and normal (non-assisted) pedal pressure is restored.

23 Repeat the above procedure on the remaining front brake caliper.

24 Before refitting the roadwheels, use a wire brush or mildly abrasive cloth (Scotchbrite, etc) to clean the mating surfaces of the hub and wheel. Apply a little anti-seize grease (Copperslip) to the hub and wheel surface prior to refitting **(see illustration)**.

25 Refit the roadwheels, then lower the vehicle to the ground and tighten the roadwheel bolts to the specified torque.

26 Check the hydraulic fluid level as described in *Weekly checks*.

Caution: New pads will not give full braking efficiency until they have bedded-in. Be prepared for this, and avoid hard braking as far as possible for the first hundred miles or so after pad renewal.

5 Front brake caliper –
removal, overhaul and refitting

Note: *Before starting work, refer to the note at the beginning of Section 2 concerning the dangers of hydraulic fluid, and to the warning at the beginning of Section 4 concerning the dangers of asbestos dust.*

Removal

1 Apply the handbrake, then jack up the front of the car and support it on axle stands (see *Jacking and vehicle support*). Remove the appropriate roadwheel.

2 Minimise fluid loss by first removing the master cylinder reservoir cap, and then tightening it down onto a piece of polythene, to obtain an airtight seal. Alternatively, use a brake hose clamp, a G-clamp or a similar tool to clamp the flexible hose.

3 Clean the area around the union, then loosen the brake hose union nut.

4 Remove the brake pads as described in Section 4, but on the C54-II caliper, unscrew the upper guide pin bolt.

5 Unscrew the caliper from the end of the brake hose and remove it from the car.

Overhaul

6 With the caliper on the bench, wipe away all traces of dust and dirt, *but avoid inhaling the dust, as it may be injurious to health.*

4.24 Apply anti-seize grease to the wheel mounting surface of the hub

7 Withdraw the partially-ejected piston from the caliper body, and remove the dust seal.

 HAYNES HiNT *If the piston cannot be withdrawn by hand, it can be pushed out by applying compressed air to the brake hose union hole. Only low pressure should be required, such as is generated by a foot pump. As the piston is expelled, take great care not to trap your fingers between the piston and caliper.*

8 Using a small screwdriver, extract the piston hydraulic seal, taking great care not to damage the caliper bore **(see illustration)**.

9 Thoroughly clean all components, using only methylated spirit, isopropyl alcohol or clean hydraulic fluid as a cleaning medium. Never use mineral-based solvents such as petrol or paraffin, as they will attack the hydraulic system rubber components. Dry the components immediately, using compressed air or a clean, lint-free cloth. Use compressed air to blow clear the fluid passages.

10 Check all components, and renew any that are worn or damaged. Check particularly the cylinder bore and piston; these should be renewed if they are scratched, worn or corroded in any way (note that this means the renewal of the complete caliper body assembly). Similarly check the condition of the guide pins and their bushes; both pins should be undamaged and a reasonably tight sliding fit in their bores. If there is any doubt about the condition of any component, renew it.

5.8 Use a small screwdriver to extract the caliper piston hydraulic seal

11 If the assembly is fit for further use, obtain the appropriate repair kit; the components are available from Seat dealers in various combinations.

12 Renew all rubber seals, dust covers and caps disturbed on dismantling as a matter of course; these should never be re-used.

13 On reassembly, ensure that all components are clean and dry.

14 Thinly coat the piston and piston seal with brake fitting paste (Seat part no G 052 150 A2). This should be included in the Seat caliper overhaul/repair kit.

15 Fit the new piston (fluid) seal, using only your fingers (no tools) to manipulate it into the cylinder bore groove. Fit the new dust seal to the piston, and refit the piston to the cylinder bore using a twisting motion; ensure that the piston enters squarely into the bore. Press the piston fully into the bore, then press the dust seal into the caliper body.

Refitting

16 Screw the caliper fully onto the flexible hose union.

17 Refit the brake pads as described in Section 4. On the C54-II caliper, also tighten the upper guide pin bolt.

18 Securely tighten the brake hose union nut.

19 Remove the brake hose clamp or polythene, as applicable, and bleed the hydraulic system as described in Section 2. Note that, providing the precautions described were taken to minimise brake fluid loss, it should only be necessary to bleed the relevant front brake.

20 Refit the roadwheel, then lower the car to the ground and tighten the roadwheel bolts to the specified torque.

6 Brake disc –
inspection, removal and refitting

Note: *Before starting work, refer to the note at the beginning of Section 4 concerning the dangers of asbestos dust. If either disc requires renewal, BOTH should be renewed at the same time, to ensure even and consistent braking. New brake pads should also be fitted.*

Front brake disc

Inspection

1 Apply the handbrake, then jack up the front of the car and support it on axle stands (see *Jacking and vehicle support*). Remove the appropriate front roadwheel.

2 Slowly rotate the brake disc so that the full area of both sides can be checked; remove the brake pads if better access is required to the inboard surface. Light scoring is normal in the area swept by the brake pads, but if heavy scoring or cracks are found, the disc must be renewed.

3 It is normal to find a lip of rust and brake dust around the perimeter of the disc; this can be scraped off if required. If, however, a lip has formed due to excessive wear of the

6.4 Use a DTI gauge to measure disc run-out

6.9 Undo the disc retaining screw

6.14 Lift away the disc

brake pad swept area, then the disc thickness must be measured using a micrometer. Take measurements at several places around the disc, at the inside and outside of the pad swept area; if the disc has worn at any point to the specified minimum thickness or less, the disc must be renewed.

4 If the disc is thought to be warped, it can be checked for run-out. Either use a dial gauge mounted on any convenient fixed point, while the disc is slowly rotated, or use feeler blades to measure (at several points all around the disc) the clearance between the disc and a fixed point, such as the caliper mounting bracket. If the measurements obtained are at the specified maximum or beyond, the disc is excessively warped, and must be renewed; however, it is worth checking first that the hub bearing is in good condition (Chapter 1A or 1B, as appropriate). If the run-out is excessive, the disc must be renewed **(see illustration)**.

5 Check the disc for cracks, especially around the wheel bolt holes, and any other wear or damage, and renew if necessary.

Removal

6 Remove the brake pads as described in Section 4.

7 On models with the C54-II caliper, unscrew and remove the caliper upper guide pin bolt, then use a piece of wire or string to tie the caliper to the front suspension coil spring, to avoid placing any strain on the brake hose.

8 On models with C54-II or FN-3 calipers, unscrew the two bolts securing the brake caliper mounting bracket to the hub carrier, and remove the bracket.

9 Use paint to mark the relationship of the disc to the hub, then remove the screw securing the brake disc to the hub, and remove the disc **(see illustration)**. If it is tight, apply penetrating fluid, and tap its rear face with a hide or plastic mallet, but bear in mind that the use of excessive force could damage the disc.

Refitting

10 Refitting is the reverse of the removal procedure, noting the following points:
 a) Ensure that the mating surfaces of the disc and hub are clean.
 b) Align the marks made on removal, and securely tighten the disc retaining screw.
 c) If a new disc has been fitted, use a

suitable solvent to wipe any preservative coating from the disc, before refitting the caliper.
 d) On models with the C54-II or FN-3 brake calipers, tighten the bracket mounting bolts to the specified torque.
 e) Fit the pads as described in Section 4.
 f) Refit the roadwheel, then lower the car to the ground and tighten the roadwheel bolts to the specified torque. On completion, repeatedly depress the brake pedal until normal (non-assisted) pedal pressure returns.

Rear brake disc

Inspection

11 Firmly chock the front wheels, then jack up the rear of the car and support it on axle stands. Remove the appropriate rear roadwheel.

12 Inspect the disc as described in paragraphs 2 to 5.

Removal

13 Unscrew the two bolts securing the brake caliper mounting bracket in position, then slide the caliper assembly off the disc. Using a piece of wire or string, tie the caliper to the rear suspension coil spring, to avoid placing any strain on the hydraulic brake hose.

14 Use paint to mark the relationship of the disc to the hub, then remove the screw securing the brake disc to the hub, and remove the disc **(see illustration)**. If it is tight, apply penetrating fluid, and tap its rear face gently with a hide or plastic mallet. The use of excessive force could cause the disc to be damaged.

Refitting

15 Refitting is a reversal of the removal procedure, noting the following points:
 a) Ensure that the mating surfaces of the disc and hub are clean and flat.
 b) Align (if applicable) the marks made on removal, and securely tighten the disc retaining screw.
 c) If a new disc has been fitted, use a suitable solvent to wipe any preservative coating from the disc, before refitting the caliper.
 d) Slide the caliper into position over the disc, making sure the pads pass either side of the disc. Tighten the caliper bracket mounting bolts to the specified

torque. If new discs have been fitted and there is insufficient clearance between the pads to accommodate the new, thicker disc, it may be necessary to push the piston back into the caliper body as described in Section 8.
 e) Refit the roadwheel, then lower the car to the ground and tighten the roadwheel bolts to the specified torque. On completion, repeatedly depress the brake pedal until normal (non-assisted) pedal pressure returns.

7 Front brake disc shield – removal and refitting

Removal

1 Remove the brake disc as described in Section 6.

2 Unscrew the securing bolts, and remove the brake disc shield.

Refitting

3 Refitting is a reversal of removal. Tighten the shield retaining bolts to the specified torque. Refit the brake disc with reference to Section 6.

8 Rear brake pads – renewal

Note: Before starting work, refer to the note at the beginning of Section 4 concerning the dangers of asbestos dust. New caliper guide pin bolts will be required on refitting.

1 Apply the handbrake, then slacken the rear roadwheel bolts. Jack up the rear of the vehicle and support it on axle stands (see Jacking and vehicle support). Remove both rear roadwheels.

2 Follow the accompanying photos **(illustrations 8.2a to 8.2x)** for the pad renewal procedure. Be sure to stay in order and read the caption under each illustration, and note the following points:
 a) New pads may have an adhesive foil on the backplates. Remove this foil prior to installation.
 b) Thoroughly clean the caliper guide

8.2a Prise out the handbrake outer cable retaining clip (arrowed)

8.2b Use a pair of pliers to pull the inner cable fitting upwards and out from the caliper lever . . .

8.2c . . . then pull the cable down through the bracket

8.2d Unscrew the caliper guide pin bolts (arrowed). Use a second spanner to counterhold the bolts. Note that the bolts must be renewed

8.2e Slide the caliper rearwards from place. Don't let it hang on the rubber hose, place it on top of the wheel hub

8.2f Remove the inner brake pad . . .

8.2g . . . and the outer brake pad

8.2h Remove the lower . . .

8.2i . . . and upper brake pad shim from the caliper mounting bracket

8.2j Use a wire brush to clean the pad mounting surfaces on the caliper bracket

8.2k Measure the thickness of the pad friction material, and inspect the disc as described in Section 6

8.2l Refit the lower . . .

8.2m . . . and upper pad shims

8.2n Apply a thin smear of copper anti-seize grease to the mounting edges of the brake pads. Take care not to get any grease on the friction material

8.2o If the pads are not being renewed, apply a thin smear of copper anti-seize grease to the pad backing plate

8.2p Fit the inner brake pad . . .

8.2q . . . and the outer brake pad. Ensure the friction material is against the brake disc

8.2r If new pads are being fitted, to make room for the increased thickness of the pads, the caliper piston must be screwed back into the caliper body using a retraction tool . . .

8.2s . . . a pair of long-nosed pliers . . .

8.2t . . . or a tool that locates in the cut-outs in the piston face. Press the piston into the body, and rotate clockwise at the same time

8.2u Slide the caliper into place over the pads . . .

8.2v . . . then fit the new guide pin bolts and tighten them to the specified torque

8.2w Refit the handbrake cable and secure it with the retaining clip

8.2x Use pliers to refit the inner cable end fitting into place in the caliper lever

surfaces, and apply a little brake assembly (Copperslip) grease.
c) When pushing the caliper piston back to accommodate new pads, keep a close eye on the fluid level in the reservoir.
d) Renew the rear caliper guide pin bolts.

3 Depress the brake pedal repeatedly, until the pads are pressed into firm contact with the brake disc, and normal (non-assisted) pedal pressure is restored.
4 Repeat the above procedure on the remaining rear brake caliper.
5 Refit the roadwheels (see Section 4), then lower the vehicle to the ground and tighten the roadwheel bolts to the specified torque.
6 Check the hydraulic fluid level as described in *Weekly checks*.
7 Check, and if necessary, adjust the handbrake as described in Section 17.
Caution: New pads will not give full braking efficiency until they have bedded-in. Be prepared for this, and avoid hard braking as far as possible for the first hundred miles or so after pad renewal.

9 Rear brake caliper – removal, overhaul and refitting

Note: *Before starting work, refer to the note at the beginning of Section 2 concerning the dangers of hydraulic fluid, and to the warning at the beginning of Section 4 concerning the dangers of asbestos dust.*

Removal

1 Chock the front wheels, then jack up the rear of the car and support on axle stands (see *Jacking and vehicle support*). Remove the relevant rear wheel.
2 Minimise fluid loss by first removing the master cylinder reservoir cap, and then tightening it down onto a piece of polythene, to obtain an airtight seal. Alternatively, use a brake hose clamp, a G-clamp or a similar tool to clamp the flexible hose.
3 Clean the area around the union on the caliper, then unscrew the brake hose union bolt.
4 Remove the brake pads as described in Section 8.
5 Withdraw the caliper and remove it from the car.

Overhaul

Note: *It is not possible to overhaul the brake caliper handbrake mechanism. If the mechanism is faulty, or fluid is leaking from the handbrake lever seal, the caliper assembly must be renewed.*

6 With the caliper on the bench, wipe away all traces of dust and dirt, but avoid inhaling the dust, as it is injurious to health.
7 Using a small screwdriver, carefully prise out the dust seal from the caliper, taking care not to damage the piston.
8 Remove the piston from the caliper bore

by rotating it in an anti-clockwise direction. This can be achieved using a suitable pair of circlip pliers engaged in the caliper piston slots. Once the piston turns freely but does not come out any further, the piston can be withdrawn by hand.

 If the piston cannot be withdrawn by hand, it can be pushed out by applying compressed air to the brake hose union hole. Only low pressure should be required, such as is generated by a foot pump. As the piston is expelled, take care not to trap your fingers between the piston and caliper.

9 Using a small screwdriver, extract the piston hydraulic seal, taking care not to damage the caliper bore.
10 Withdraw the guide pins from the caliper, and remove the guide sleeve gaiters.
11 Thoroughly clean all components, using only methylated spirit, isopropyl alcohol or clean hydraulic fluid as a cleaning medium. Never use mineral-based solvents such as petrol or paraffin, as they will attack the hydraulic system rubber components. Dry the components immediately, using compressed air or a clean, lint-free cloth. Use compressed air to blow clear the fluid passages.
12 Check all components, and renew any that are worn or damaged. Check particularly the cylinder bore and piston; these should be renewed (note that this means the renewal of the complete caliper body assembly) if they are scratched, worn or corroded in any way. Similarly check the condition of the guide pins and their bores; both pins should be undamaged and a reasonably tight sliding fit in their bores. If there is any doubt about the condition of any component, renew it.
13 If the assembly is fit for further use, obtain the appropriate repair kit; the components are available from Seat dealers in various combinations.
14 Renew all rubber seals, dust covers and caps disturbed on dismantling as a matter of course; these should never be re-used.
15 On reassembly, ensure that all components are clean and dry.

10.3a Rear brake drum securing screw (arrowed)

16 Smear a thin coat of brake fitting paste (Seat part no G 052 150 A2) on the piston, seal and caliper bore. This should be included in the overhaul/repair kit. Fit the new piston (fluid) seal, using only the fingers (no tools) to manipulate into the cylinder bore groove.
17 Fit the new dust seal to the piston groove, then refit the piston assembly. Turn the piston in a clockwise direction, using the method employed on dismantling, until it is fully retracted into the caliper bore.
18 Press the dust seal into position in the caliper housing.
19 Apply the grease supplied in the repair kit, or a copper-based brake grease or anti-seize compound, to the guide pins. Fit the new gaiters to the guide pins and fit the pins to the caliper ensuring that the gaiters are correctly located in the grooves on both the pins and caliper.
20 Prior to refitting, fill the caliper with fresh hydraulic fluid by slackening the bleed screw and pumping the fluid through the caliper until bubble-free fluid is expelled from the union hole.

Refitting

21 Refit the brake pads as described in Section 8.
22 Refit the brake hose union bolt and tighten it.
23 Remove the brake hose clamp or remove the polythene from the fluid reservoir, as applicable, and bleed the hydraulic system as described in Section 2. Note that, providing the precautions described were taken to minimise brake fluid loss, it should only be necessary to bleed the relevant rear brake.
24 Adjust the handbrake as described in Section 17.
25 Refit the roadwheel, then lower the car to the ground and tighten the roadwheel bolts to the specified torque. On completion, check the hydraulic fluid level as described in *Weekly checks*.

10 Rear brake drum – removal, inspection and refitting

Note: *Before starting work, refer to the warning at the beginning of Section 4 concerning the dangers of asbestos dust.*

Removal

1 Remove the wheel trim (where applicable), then loosen the rear roadwheel bolts and chock the front wheels. Jack up the rear of the car, and support on axle stands positioned under the body sidemembers (see *Jacking and vehicle support*). Remove the roadwheel.
2 Fully release the handbrake.
3 Extract the drum securing screw and remove the drum. The drum may be tight due to the brake shoes binding on the inner circumference of the drum. If this is the case, insert a screwdriver through one of the wheel

10.3b If the drum is tight, insert a screwdriver in through one of the wheel bolt holes . . .

10.3d Remove the rear brake drum

10.3c . . . and lever up on the wedge key (arrowed) to retract the brake shoes (drum removed for clarity)

10.6 The maximum diameter of the drum is stamped on its inner surface

4 Brush the dust and dirt from the drum, taking care not to inhale it.
5 Examine the internal friction surface of the drum. If deeply scored, or so worn that the drum has become ridged to the width of the shoes, then both drums must be renewed.
6 Regrinding of the friction surface may be possible provided the maximum diameter given in the Specifications and on the drum itself is not exceeded (see illustration).

Refitting

7 If a new brake drum is to be fitted, use a suitable solvent to remove any preservative coating that may have been applied to its interior. Prior to refitting the drum, fully retract the brake shoes by lifting up the wedge key.
8 Refit the brake drum and tighten the securing screw.
9 Adjust the brakes by operating the footbrake a number of times. A clicking noise will be heard at the drum as the automatic adjuster operates. When the clicking stops, adjustment is complete.
10 Refit the roadwheel and lower the car to the ground.
11 Repeat the above procedure on the remaining rear brake assembly, then check and, if necessary, adjust the handbrake cable (see Section 17).
12 On completion, refit the roadwheels, then lower the car to the ground and tighten the wheel bolts to the specified torque.

bolt holes in the brake drum and hub, and lever up the wedge key in order to allow the brake shoes to retract fully. The wedge key is located beneath the front of the wheel cylinder (see illustrations). The brake drum can now be withdrawn.

Inspection

Note: *If either drum requires renewal, BOTH should be renewed at the same time, to ensure even and consistent braking. New brake shoes should also be fitted.*

11.5 Note the position of the brake shoes before dismantling them

11.8a Ease the shoes out from the lower pivot point . . .

11.7 Remove the shoe retainer spring cup, spring and retainer pin

11.8b . . . and detach the lower return spring

11 Rear brake shoes –
removal, inspection and refitting

Note: *Refer to the warning at the start of Section 4 before starting work.*
1 Remove the brake drum (see Section 10), then carefully remove all traces of brake dust from the brake drum, backplate and shoes.
2 Measure the thickness of the friction material of each brake shoe at several points; if either shoe is worn at any point to the specified minimum thickness or less, all four shoes must be renewed as a set. The shoes should also be renewed if any are fouled with oil or grease; there is no way of degreasing friction material, once contaminated.
3 If any of the brake shoes are worn unevenly, or fouled with oil or grease, trace and rectify the cause before reassembly.
4 To renew the brake shoes, continue as follows. If all is well, refit the brake drum as described in Section 10.
5 Note the position of the brake shoes and springs, and mark the webs of the shoes, if necessary, to aid refitting (see illustration).
6 To facilitate easy removal and refitting of the brake shoes, we found it necessary to remove the hub first (see Chapter 10), although this may not be necessary on some models.
7 Using a pair of pliers, remove the shoe retainer spring cups by depressing and turning them through 90°. With the cups removed, lift

11.9a Ease the upper ends of the shoes from their wheel cylinder locations . . .

11.9b . . . then disconnect the handbrake cable and remove the shoe assembly

11.9c Use a cable-tie or elastic band to retain the wheel cylinder pistons

11.10 Unhook the adjuster wedge key spring and remove it

11.11a Use a length of bent welding rod to unhook the upper return spring

11.11b Remove the trailing shoe from the leading shoe and strut

off the springs and withdraw the retainer pins **(see illustration)**.

8 Ease the shoes out one at a time from the lower pivot point, to release the tension of the return spring, then disconnect the lower return spring from both shoes **(see illustrations)**.

9 Ease the upper end of both shoes out from their wheel cylinder locations, taking care not to damage the wheel cylinder seals, and disconnect the handbrake cable from the trailing shoe. The brake shoe assembly can then be manoeuvred out of position and away from the backplate. Do not depress the brake pedal until the brakes are reassembled; wrap a strong elastic band or fit a cable-tie around the wheel cylinder pistons to retain them **(see illustrations)**.

10 Make a note of the correct fitted positions of all components, then unhook the upper return spring, and disengage the wedge key spring **(see illustration)**.

11 Unhook the upper return spring and remove the trailing shoe from the leading shoe and strut. A length of bent welding rod may be used to unhook the spring **(see illustrations)**.

12 Withdraw the wedge key, noting which way around it is fitted, then ease the strut out from the leading shoe and detach the tensioning spring. If necessary, mount the strut in a vice, and use the length of bent welding rod to remove the spring **(see illustrations)**.

13 Examine all components for signs of wear or damage, and renew as necessary.

14 Peel back the rubber protective caps, and check the wheel cylinder for fluid leaks or other damage; check that both cylinder pistons are free to move easily. Refer to Section 12, if

necessary, for information on wheel cylinder overhaul.

15 Apply a little brake grease to the contact areas of the pushrod and handbrake lever.

16 Hook the tensioning spring into the leading shoe. Engage the strut with the opposite end

11.12a Mount the strut in a vice, and use welding rod to unhook the tensioning spring

11.12c . . . then separate the strut from the leading shoe

of the spring, and pivot the strut into position into the leading shoe slot.

17 Insert the wedge key between the leading shoe and pushrod, making sure it is fitted the correct way around **(see illustration)**.

18 Fit the upper return spring to the leading

11.12b Remove the wedge key and unhook the spring . . .

11.17 Insert the wedge key, ensuring its peg is facing away from the shoe

11.18 Refit the upper return spring

11.20 Apply high-temperature brake grease to the shoe contact areas on the backplate

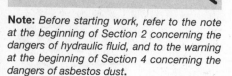

shoe and engage the spring in its hole in the trailing shoe **(see illustration)**. Ensure the spring is correctly fitted then pivot the trailing shoe into position making sure both the shoe and handbrake lever are correctly engaged with the strut.

19 Fit the spring to the wedge key, and hook it onto the trailing shoe.

20 Prior to installation, clean the backplate, and apply a thin smear of high-temperature brake grease or anti-seize compound to the shoe contact areas **(see illustration)**, and to the wheel cylinder pistons and lower pivot point. Do not allow the lubricant to foul the friction material.

21 Remove the elastic band or cable-tie fitted to the wheel cylinder, and offer up the shoe assembly.

22 Connect the handbrake cable to the handbrake lever, and locate the top of the shoes in the wheel cylinder piston slots.

23 Fit the lower return spring to the shoes, then lever the bottom of the shoes onto the bottom anchor.

24 Tap the shoes to centralise them with the backplate, then refit the shoe retainer pins and springs, and secure them in position with the spring cups.

25 Refit the hub and brake drum as described in Section 10.

26 Repeat the above procedure on the remaining rear brake.

27 Once both sets of rear shoes have been renewed, adjust the lining-to-drum clearance by repeatedly depressing the brake pedal until normally (non-assisted) pedal pressure returns.

28 Check and, if necessary, adjust the handbrake as described in Section 17.

29 On completion, check the hydraulic fluid level as described in *Weekly checks*.

> **HAYNES HINT** *New shoes will not give full braking efficiency until they have bedded-in. Be prepared for this, and avoid hard braking as far as possible for the first hundred miles or so after shoe renewal.*

12 Rear wheel cylinder – removal, overhaul and refitting

Note: *Before starting work, refer to the note at the beginning of Section 2 concerning the dangers of hydraulic fluid, and to the warning at the beginning of Section 4 concerning the dangers of asbestos dust.*

Removal

1 Remove the brake drum (see Section 10).

2 Using pliers, carefully unhook the upper brake shoe return spring, and remove it from both brake shoes. Pull the upper ends of the shoes away from the wheel cylinder to disengage them from the pistons.

3 Minimise fluid loss by first removing the master cylinder reservoir cap, and then tightening it down onto a piece of polythene, to obtain an airtight seal. Alternatively, use a brake hose clamp, a G-clamp or a similar tool to clamp the flexible hose at the nearest convenient point to the wheel cylinder.

4 Wipe away all traces of dirt around the brake pipe union at the rear of the wheel cylinder, and unscrew the union nut. Carefully ease the pipe out of the wheel cylinder, and plug or tape over its end to prevent dirt entry. Wipe off any spilt fluid immediately.

5 Unscrew the two wheel cylinder retaining bolts from the rear of the backplate, and remove the cylinder, taking great care not to allow surplus hydraulic fluid to contaminate the brake shoe linings.

Overhaul

6 Brush the dirt and dust from the wheel cylinder, but take care not to inhale it.

7 Pull the rubber dust seals from the ends of the cylinder body **(see illustration)**.

8 The pistons will normally be ejected by the pressure of the coil spring, but if they are not, tap the end of the cylinder body on a piece of wood, or apply low air pressure – eg, from a foot pump – to the hydraulic fluid union hole to eject the pistons from their bores.

9 Inspect the surfaces of the pistons and their bores in the cylinder body for scoring, or evidence of metal-to-metal contact. If evident, renew the complete wheel cylinder assembly.

10 If the pistons and bores are in good condition, discard the seals and obtain a repair kit, which will contain all the necessary renewable items.

11 Remove the seals from the pistons noting their correct fitted orientation. Lubricate the new piston seals with clean brake fluid, and fit them onto the pistons with their larger diameters innermost.

12 Dip the pistons in clean brake fluid, then fit the spring to the cylinder.

13 Insert the pistons into the cylinder bores using a twisting motion.

14 Fit the dust seals, and check that the pistons can move freely in their bores.

H31035

12.7 Exploded view of a rear wheel cylinder

| 1 *Dust seal* | 2 *Piston* | 3 *Coil spring* | 4 *Fluid seal* |

13.5a Tool made from an exhaust clamp to release the brake pedal from the servo pushrod

13.5b Using the tool to release the brake pedal from the servo pushrod

13.5c Plastic lugs (arrowed) securing pedal to servo pushrod

Refitting

15 Ensure that the backplate and wheel cylinder mating surfaces are clean, then spread the brake shoes and manoeuvre the wheel cylinder into position. Engage the brake pipe, and screw in the union nut two or three turns to ensure that the thread has started.

16 Insert the two wheel cylinder retaining bolts, and tighten them to the specified torque. Now fully tighten the brake pipe union nut.

17 Remove the clamp from the flexible brake hose, or the polythene from the master cylinder reservoir (as applicable).

18 Ensure that the brake shoes are correctly located in the cylinder pistons, then refit the brake shoe upper return spring, using a screwdriver to stretch the spring into position.

19 Refit the brake drum (see Section 10).

20 Bleed the brake hydraulic system as described in Section 2. Providing suitable precautions were taken to minimise loss of fluid, it should only be necessary to bleed the relevant rear brake.

13 Brake pedal –
removal and refitting

Removal

1 Disconnect the battery negative lead as described in Chapter 5A.

2 With reference to Chapter 11, Section 29, remove the driver's side lower facia trim panel.

3 Where fitted, remove the convenience system central control unit from its location above the accelerator pedal with reference to Chapter 12.

4 Remove the brake light switch as described in Section 21, then disconnect the wiring from the pedal position sender.

5 It is now necessary to release the brake pedal from the ball on the vacuum servo pushrod. To do this, a Seat special tool is available, but a suitable alternative can be improvised. Note that the plastic lugs in the pedal are very stiff, and it will not be possible to release them by hand. Using the tool, release the securing lugs, and pull the pedal from the servo pushrod (see illustrations).

6 If removing the pedal bracket support,

undo and remove the retaining nut (see illustration).

7 Where necessary, unscrew the nuts securing the pedal support bracket to the bulkhead/ servo sufficiently to allow the bracket some movement. Do not remove the nuts completely (see illustration).

8 Undo the pivot shaft nut and slide the pivot shaft to the right, until the pedal is free. Remove the pedal and recover the pivot bush (see illustration).

9 Carefully clean all components, and renew any that are worn or damaged.

Refitting

10 Prior to refitting, apply a smear of multi-purpose grease to the pivot shaft and pedal bearing surfaces.

11 Using a screwdriver, lever the pedal bracket away from the bulkhead (see illustration).

12 Pull the servo unit pushrod down, and

at the same time manoeuvre the pedal into position, ensuring that the pivot bush is correctly located.

13 Tighten the pedal bracket retaining nuts securely, and refit the bracket support retaining nut.

14 Hold the servo unit pushrod, and push the pedal back onto the pushrod ball. Make sure the pedal is securely fastened to the pushrod.

15 Insert the pedal pivot bolt and tighten the retaining nut to the specified torque.

16 Reconnect the wiring to the pedal position sender, then refit the brake light switch as described in Section 21.

17 Where fitted, refit the convenience system central control unit.

18 Refit the facia trim panel as described in Chapter 11, Section 29.

19 Reconnect the battery negative lead as described in Chapter 5A.

13.6 Undo the support bracket nut

13.7 Slacken the five securing nuts (arrowed)

13.8 Recover the pivot bush

13.11 Lever the bracket away from the bulkhead

14.8 Brake cylinder nuts (A), and clutch cylinder supply hose (B)

14 Master cylinder –
removal, overhaul and refitting

Note: *Before starting work, refer to the warning at the beginning of Section 2 concerning the dangers of hydraulic fluid. A new master cylinder O-ring will be required on refitting.*

Removal

1 Remove the engine top cover, then remove the air inlet ducts as necessary from the rear of the engine compartment (refer to the relevant part of Chapter 4).

2 Remove the battery and battery tray as described in Chapter 5A.

3 Remove the master cylinder reservoir cap (disconnect the wiring plug from the brake fluid level sender unit), and siphon the hydraulic fluid from the reservoir. **Note:** *Do not siphon the fluid by mouth, as it is poisonous; use a syringe or an old poultry baster.*

4 Release the vacuum hose from the clip on the brake fluid reservoir.

5 Wipe clean the area around the brake pipe unions on the side of the master cylinder, and place absorbent rags beneath the pipe unions to catch any leaking fluid. Make a note of the correct fitted positions of the unions, then unscrew the union nuts and carefully withdraw the pipes. Plug or tape over the pipe ends and master cylinder orifices, to minimise the loss of brake fluid, and to prevent the entry of dirt into the system. Wash off any spilt fluid immediately with cold water.

6 Disconnect and plug the clutch master

15.11 Brake servo unit mounting nuts (arrowed)

cylinder supply hose from the brake fluid reservoir.

7 On models equipped with ESP (Electronic Stability Program – see Section 22 and Chapter 10), disconnect the two pressure sensors from the underside of the master cylinder.

8 Unscrew and remove the two nuts and washers securing the master cylinder to the vacuum servo unit, remove the heat shield (where fitted), then withdraw the unit from the engine compartment **(see illustration)**. Remove the O-ring from the rear of the master cylinder, and discard it.

Overhaul

9 If the master cylinder is faulty, it must be renewed. Repair kits are not available from Seat dealers, so the cylinder must be considered a sealed unit.

10 The only items which can be renewed are the mounting seals for the fluid reservoir; if these show signs of deterioration, withdraw the retaining pin, pull off the reservoir and remove the old seals. Lubricate the new seals with clean brake fluid, and press them into the master cylinder ports. Ease the fluid reservoir into position, push it fully home, and insert the retaining pin.

Refitting

11 Clean the master cylinder and servo unit mating surfaces, and fit a new O-ring to the groove on the master cylinder body.

12 Fit the master cylinder to the servo unit, ensuring that the servo unit pushrod enters the master cylinder bore centrally. Refit the heat shield (where applicable), and the master cylinder mounting nuts and washers, and tighten them to the specified torque.

13 Wipe clean the brake pipes and unions, then refit them to the master cylinder ports and tighten them securely.

14 On models equipped with ESP, reconnect the pressure sensors on the underside of the master cylinder.

15 Reconnect the clutch master cylinder supply hose to the reservoir.

16 Secure the vacuum hose to the clip on the brake fluid reservoir.

17 Refit the battery and battery tray (Chapter 5A), air inlet ducts (Chapter 4A or 4B) and engine top cover.

18 Refill the master cylinder reservoir with new fluid, and bleed the complete hydraulic system as described in Section 2. Also bleed the clutch hydraulic system.

15 Servo unit –
testing, removal and refitting

Testing

1 To test the operation of the servo unit, depress the footbrake several times to exhaust the vacuum, then start the engine whilst keeping the pedal firmly depressed. As

the engine starts, there should be a noticeable 'give' in the brake pedal as the vacuum builds-up. Allow the engine to run for at least two minutes, then switch it off. If the brake pedal is now depressed, it should feel normal, but further applications should result in the pedal feeling firmer, with the pedal stroke decreasing with each application.

2 If the servo does not operate as described, first inspect the servo unit non-return valve as described in Section 16. On diesel models, also check the operation of the vacuum pump as described in Section 24.

3 If the servo unit still fails to operate satisfactorily, the fault lies within the unit itself. Repairs to the unit are not possible – if faulty, the servo unit must be renewed.

Removal

Note: *A new servo unit gasket will be required on refitting.*

4 Remove the master cylinder as described in Section 14.

5 With reference to Chapter 11, Section 29, remove the driver's side lower facia trim panel.

6 Remove the heating/air conditioning air duct from the driver's footwell.

7 Where fitted, remove the convenience system central control unit from its location above the accelerator pedal with reference to Chapter 12.

8 Where applicable remove the heat shield from the servo, then carefully ease the vacuum hose out from the sealing grommet in the front of the servo.

9 Remove the brake light switch as described in Section 21.

10 It is now necessary to release the brake pedal from the ball on the vacuum servo pushrod. To do this, a Seat special tool is available, but a suitable alternative can be improvised **(see illustrations 13.5a, 13.5b and 13.5c)**. Note that the plastic lugs in the pedal are very stiff, and it will not be possible to release them by hand. Using the tool, release the securing lugs, and pull the pedal from the servo pushrod.

11 Again working in the footwell, undo the nuts securing the servo unit to the bulkhead **(see illustration)**, then return to the engine compartment and manoeuvre the servo unit out of position, noting the gasket which is fitted to the rear of the unit.

Refitting

12 Check the servo unit vacuum hose sealing grommet for signs of damage or deterioration, and renew if necessary.

13 Fit a new gasket to the rear of the servo unit, and reposition the unit in the engine compartment.

14 From inside the car, ensure that the servo unit pushrod is correctly engaged with the brake pedal, and push the pedal onto the pushrod ball. Check the pushrod ball is securely engaged, then refit the servo unit mounting nuts and tighten them to the specified torque.

15 With reference to Section 21, refit the brake light switch.
16 Refit the facia trim panels.
17 Carefully ease the vacuum hose back into position in the servo, taking great care not to displace the sealing grommet. As applicable, refit the heat shield to the servo, and reconnect the vacuum sensor wiring plug.
18 Where fitted, refit the convenience system central control unit with reference to Chapter 12.
19 Refit the heating/air conditioning air duct to the driver's footwell.
20 Refit the master cylinder as described in Section 14 of this Chapter.
21 On completion, start the engine and check the operation of the braking system.

16 Servo non-return valve – testing, removal and refitting

1 The non-return valve is located in the vacuum hose from the intake manifold to the brake servo. If the valve is to be renewed, the complete hose/valve assembly should be renewed.

Removal

2 Ease the vacuum hose out of the servo unit, taking care not to displace the grommet.
3 Loosen the retaining clip and disconnect the opposite end of the hose assembly from the manifold/pump hose, and remove it from the car.

Testing

4 Examine the check valve and vacuum hose for signs of damage, and renew if necessary.
5 The valve may be tested by blowing through it in both directions, air should flow through the valve in one direction only; when blown through from the servo unit end of the valve. Renew the valve if this is not the case.
6 Examine the servo unit rubber sealing grommet for signs of damage or deterioration, and renew as necessary.

Refitting

7 Ensure that the sealing grommet is correctly fitted to the servo unit.
8 Ease the hose union into position in the servo unit, taking great care not to displace or damage the grommet.
9 Connect the hose to the inlet manifold/pump hose, and ensure that the hose is secured in the retaining clips.
10 On completion, start the engine and check the operation of the braking system.

17 Handbrake – adjustment

1 To check the handbrake adjustment, first apply the footbrake firmly several times to establish correct shoe-to-drum/pad-to-disc

17.3 Prise the rear cup holder upwards from the console

clearance, then apply and release the handbrake three times.
2 Applying normal moderate pressure, pull the handbrake lever to the fully-applied position, counting the number of clicks emitted from the handbrake ratchet mechanism. If adjustment is correct, there should be approximately 4 clicks before the handbrake is fully applied. If there are more clicks, adjust as follows.
3 Remove the centre console as described in Chapter 11 to gain access to the handbrake lever. Note that on some models with a rear cup holder, it's possible to access the adjustment nut by simply prising the cup holder from place **(see illustration)**.
4 Chock the front wheels, then jack up the rear of the car and support it on axle stands. Continue as described under the relevant sub-heading.

Rear drum brake models

5 With the handbrake set on the 1st notch of the ratchet mechanism, turn the adjustment nut until it is just difficult to turn both rear wheels. Now release the handbrake lever, and check that the wheels rotate freely; if not, back off the adjustment nut. Apply the handbrake fully, and check that the handbrake is fully applied on the 4th notch.
6 Once adjustment is correct, refit the centre console as described in Chapter 11, or cup holder as applicable.

Rear disc brake models

7 With the handbrake fully released, slacken the adjustment nut until both the rear caliper handbrake levers are back against their stops.

18.2 Remove the handbrake lever cover sleeve

17.8 The gap (A) between caliper handbrake levers and end stops should be 1.0 to 1.5 mm

8 Tighten the adjustment nut until both handbrake levers just move off the caliper stops. The nut is contoured to prevent it coming loose, and it is important that the adjustment is checked with the nut fully seated in the equaliser bar. The gap between each caliper handbrake lever and its stop must be between 1.0 and 1.5 mm **(see illustration)**.
9 Fully apply the handbrake lever three times, then release it and check that both wheels still rotate freely. Check the adjustment by applying the handbrake fully, counting the clicks emitted from the handbrake ratchet. The handbrake must be fully applied on the 4th notch.
10 Once adjustment is correct, refit the centre console upper rear section as described in Chapter 11, or cup holder.

18 Handbrake lever – removal and refitting

Removal

1 Remove the centre console as described in Chapter 11.
2 If desired, remove the handbrake lever cover sleeve by depressing the locating tag with a screwdriver, then sliding the sleeve from the lever **(see illustration)**.
3 Disconnect the wiring plug from the handbrake 'on' warning light switch.
4 Loosen the handbrake cable adjuster nut sufficiently to allow the ends of the cables to be disengaged from the equaliser plate **(see illustration)**.

18.4 Handbrake cable adjusting nut (arrowed)

18.5 Handbrake lever mounting nuts (arrowed)

19.4a Handbrake cable fixing (arrowed) on the rear trailing arm

19.4b Handbrake cable clip (arrowed) on the front of the rear trailing arm

19.6 Release the inner cable from its lever and withdraw the cable from the caliper

5 Unscrew the retaining nuts, and withdraw the lever **(see illustration)**.

Refitting

6 Refitting is a reversal of removal, bearing in mind the following points.
  a) *Before refitting the handbrake lever cover, adjust the handbrake as described in Section 17.*
  b) *Check the operation of the handbrake 'on' warning switch before refitting the centre console.*

19 Handbrake cables – removal and refitting

Removal

1 Remove the centre console as described in

Chapter 11, to gain access to the handbrake lever. The handbrake cable consists of a right- and a left-hand section, which are linked to the handbrake lever by an equaliser plate. Each section can be removed individually.
2 Loosen the handbrake cable adjuster nut sufficiently to allow the ends of the cables to be disengaged from the equaliser plate.
3 Chock the front wheels, then jack up the rear of the car and support it on axle stands (see *Jacking and vehicle support*).
4 Work back along the length of the cable, noting its correct routing, and free it from all the relevant guides and retaining clips **(see illustrations)**.
5 On rear drum brake models, remove the brake shoes as described in Section 11, then release the cable from the backplate.
6 On rear disc brake models, disengage the inner cable from the caliper handbrake lever, then remove the outer cable retaining clip

and detach the cable from the caliper **(see illustration)**.
7 Withdraw the cable from beneath the car.

Refitting

8 Refitting is a reversal of removal, but adjust the handbrake as described in Section 17 before refitting the centre console.

20 Handbrake 'on' warning light switch – removal and refitting

Removal

1 Remove the centre console as described in Chapter 11.
2 Disconnect the wiring from the switch **(see illustration)**.
3 Squeeze the securing lugs, and withdraw the switch from the handbrake lever assembly **(see illustration)**.

Refitting

4 Refitting is a reversal of removal.

21 Brake light switch – removal and refitting

Removal

1 The brake light switch is located on the pedal bracket beneath the facia. Remove the driver's lower facia panel as described in Chapter 11, Section 29.
2 Reach up behind the facia and disconnect the wiring connector from the switch **(see illustration)**.
3 Twist the switch anti-clockwise through 45°, and release it from the mounting bracket.

Refitting

4 Fully extend the brake light switch plunger. Do not depress the brake pedal, but simply insert the switch into the bracket and twist it clockwise through 45° **(see illustration)**. The switch will automatically set itself.
5 Reconnect the wiring, and check the operation of the brake lights. The brake lights should illuminate after the brake pedal has

20.2 Handbrake 'on' warning switch

20.3 Remove the handbrake 'on' warning switch

21.2 Disconnect the brake switch wiring plug (arrowed)

travelled approximately 5 mm. If the switch is not functioning correctly, it is faulty and must be renewed.

6 Finally, refit the lower facia panel with reference to Chapter 11.

22 Anti-lock braking system (ABS) – general information and precautions

ABS is fitted as standard on all models covered by this manual; the system may also be referred to as including EBD (Electronic Brake Distribution), which means it adjusts the front and rear braking forces according to the weight being carried. Two types of ABS are fitted – the standard system, and one with 'extras' such as TCS, ESP and BAS. On models equipped with traction control (TCS), the ABS unit has a dual function, controlling both the anti-lock braking system (ABS) and the electronic differential locking (EDL) system. On models with ESP (Electronic Stability Programme), the system recognises critical driving conditions and stabilises the car by individual wheel braking and by intervention in the engine control, which occurs independently of the position of the brake and accelerator pedals. Models with ESP are also equipped with a Brake Assist System (BAS) which recognises an emergency braking situation, and applies the brakes harder than most people would normally do, to shorten the stopping distance.

The system comprises a hydraulic unit which contains the hydraulic solenoid valves and accumulators, the electrically-driven fluid return pump, four roadwheel sensors (one fitted for each wheel), and the electronic control module (ECM). The purpose of the system is to prevent wheels locking during heavy braking. This is achieved by automatic release of the brake on the relevant wheel, followed by re-application of the brake.

The solenoids are controlled by the ECM, which itself receives signals from the four wheel sensors, which monitor the speed of rotation of each wheel. By comparing these speed signals, the ECM can determine the speed at which the car is travelling. It can then use this speed to determine when a wheel is decelerating at an abnormal rate, compared to the speed of the car, and therefore predicts when a wheel is about to lock. During normal operation, the system functions in the same way as a non-ABS braking system.

If the ECM senses that a wheel is about to lock, it operates the relevant solenoid valve in the hydraulic unit, which then isolates the brake caliper on the wheel which is about to lock from the master cylinder, effectively sealing-in the hydraulic pressure.

If the speed of rotation of the wheel continues to decrease at an abnormal rate, the ECM switches on the electrically-driven return pump, which pumps the hydraulic fluid back into the master cylinder, releasing pressure on the brake caliper so that the brake is released.

21.4 Align the shaped lug with the corresponding cut-out in the bracket

Once the speed of rotation of the wheel returns to an acceptable rate, the pump stops and the solenoid valve opens, allowing the hydraulic master cylinder pressure to return to the caliper, which then re-applies the brake. This cycle can be carried out at 10 times a second.

The action of the solenoid valves and return pump creates pulses in the hydraulic circuit. When the ABS system is functioning, these pulses can be felt through the brake pedal.

The operation of the ABS system is entirely dependent on electrical signals. To prevent the system responding to any inaccurate signals, a built-in safety circuit monitors all signals received by the ECM. If an inaccurate signal or low battery voltage is detected, the ABS system is automatically shut down, and the warning light on the instrument panel is illuminated, to inform the driver that the ABS system is not operational. Normal braking should still be available, however.

If a fault does develop in the ABS system, the car must be taken to a Seat dealer or suitably-equipped specialist for fault diagnosis and repair.

23 Anti-lock braking system (ABS) components – removal and refitting

Hydraulic unit

1 Removal and refitting of the hydraulic unit is best entrusted to a Seat dealer or specialist, as a fault diagnosis check must be performed on completion using specialist equipment **(see illustration)**.

Electronic control module (ECM)

2 The ECM is mounted next to the hydraulic unit. Although it can be separated from the hydraulic unit, due to the delicacy of the components and the need for absolute cleanliness, it is recommended that the work be entrusted to a Seat dealer or specialist.

Front wheel sensor

Removal

3 Chock the rear wheels, then firmly apply the handbrake, jack up the front of the car

23.1 The ABS hydraulic unit (arrowed) is located on the left-hand side of the engine compartment

and support on axle stands (see *Jacking and vehicle support*). Remove the appropriate front roadwheel.

4 Disconnect the electrical connector from the sensor by carefully lifting up the retaining tag, and pulling the connector from the sensor **(see illustration)**.

5 Slacken and remove the hexagon socket-head bolt securing the sensor to the hub carrier, and remove the sensor.

Refitting

6 Ensure that the sensor and hub carrier sealing faces are clean.

7 Apply a little anti-seize grease to the mounting hole inner surface, then fit the sensor to the hub carrier. Refit the retaining bolt and tighten it to the specified torque.

8 Ensure that the sensor wiring is correctly routed and retained by all the necessary clips, and reconnect the wiring connector.

9 Refit the roadwheel, then lower the car to the ground and tighten the roadwheel bolts to the specified torque.

Rear wheel sensor

Removal

10 The sensor is located to the inner face of the rear stub axle, and is secured with a single hexagon socket-head bolt.

11 Chock the front wheels, then jack up the rear of the car and support it on axle stands (see *Jacking and vehicle support*). Remove the appropriate roadwheel.

12 Remove the sensor as described in paragraphs 4 and 5.

23.4 Wheel speed sensor

24.1 Brake vacuum pump (arrowed)

Refitting

13 Refit the sensor as described above in paragraphs 6 to 9.

Wheel sensor rings

14 The sensor rings are integral with and built into the inner ends of the wheel hubs. Unlike the earlier type of reluctor with teeth, the sensor rings have alternating magnetic cores within the continuous rings. Examine the rings for any damage. If renewal is necessary, the complete hub assembly must be renewed together with the bearings as described in Chapter 10.

Steering angle sender

Note: *When removing or installing the steering angle sender, use tape to ensure that the coil connector remains in its central position.*

Removal

15 The steering angle sender is located beneath the steering wheel, on the steering column, and is incorporated into the airbag wiring slip-ring (see Chapter 12). Do not attempt to separate the steering angle sender from the airbag slip-ring. First, turn the front wheels to their straight-ahead position.
16 Disconnect the battery negative lead as described in Chapter 5A.
17 Refer to Chapter 10 and remove the steering wheel.
18 Remove the steering column shrouds with reference to Chapter 11, Section 29.
19 Check that with the front wheels straight-ahead, a yellow dot is visible through the small hole in the top right-hand corner of the sender. The markings in the bottom right-hand corner of the sender must also be aligned with each other. Use tape to hold the inner hub of the sender to the outer housing while the sender is removed.
20 Disconnect the wiring plug on the underside on the unit. Release the locking lugs, and pull the unit with the slip-ring from the column.

Refitting

21 Refitting is a reversal of removal, but remove the temporary tape before refitting the steering wheel. As a safety precaution, ensure

that no-one is inside the car as the wiring plug is reconnected.

Lateral acceleration/yaw rate sender

Removal

22 The lateral acceleration sender is located beneath the left-hand front seat, just in front of the crossmember. First, disconnect the battery negative lead as described in Chapter 5A.
23 Remove the left-hand front seat as described in Chapter 11.
24 Note that the wiring plug is located on the rear of the sender, then disconnect it.
25 Unscrew the mounting nuts and remove the sender.

Refitting

26 Refitting is a reversal of removal.

Brake pressure sensor

Removal

27 Remove the engine top cover. On models where the air cleaner is separate (not part of the top cover), remove the air cleaner as described in Chapter 4A or 4B.
28 Clean the area around the brake line connections on top of the hydraulic unit thoroughly, and allow any solvents used to dry before proceeding. It is essential that no dirt is allowed to enter the hydraulic unit.
29 Mark the fitted positions of the hydraulic unit brake pipes by wrapping a label around each one. Place clean cloth around each union, then loosen it and disconnect each pipe in turn. Tape over or plug the open unions to prevent the entry of dirt.
30 Disconnect the wiring plug from the pressure sensor, which is at the front of the hydraulic unit. Unscrew and remove the sensor.

Refitting

31 Refitting is a reversal of removal. Tighten the brake pipe unions securely, and the sensor to the specified torque.

24 Servo unit vacuum pump (diesel models) – testing, removal and refitting

Testing

1 A vacuum pump is fitted to diesel engine models to provide vacuum for the brake servo unit **(see illustration)**. The pump includes a fuel lift pump for the injection system. The operation of the braking system vacuum pump can be checked using a vacuum gauge.
2 Remove the engine top cover, then disconnect the vacuum hose from the pump, and connect the gauge to the pump union using a suitable length of hose.
3 Start the engine and allow it to idle, then

24.6 Fuel inlet and outlet hoses (arrowed)

measure the vacuum created by the pump. As a guide, after one minute, a minimum of approximately 500 mm Hg should be recorded. If the vacuum registered is significantly less than this, it is likely that the pump is faulty. However, seek the advice of a Seat dealer before condemning the pump.
4 Reconnect the vacuum hose. Overhaul of the vacuum pump is not possible, since no major components are available separately for it. If faulty, the complete pump assembly must be renewed.

Removal

Note: *A new pump O-ring will be required on refitting.*
5 Loosen the clip, and disconnect the brake servo vacuum hose from the top of the pump.
6 Position a container beneath the fuel filter in the front right-hand corner of the engine compartment, then disconnect the supply (white) and return (blue) hoses from the filter. Drain the fuel into the container, then disconnect the hoses from the pump **(see illustration)**.
7 Unscrew the mounting bolts and withdraw the pump from the cylinder head. Recover the gasket/ring and discard it, as a new one must be used for refitting. Note how the drive pinion locates in the end of the camshaft. Be prepared for fuel spillage. There are no serviceable parts within the pump. If the pump is faulty, it must be renewed.

Refitting

8 Reconnect the fuel hoses to the pump.
9 Refit the pump to the cylinder head, using a new gasket/ring, and ensuring that the pump pinion engages correctly with the drive slot in the camshaft.
10 Insert the pump retaining bolts, and tighten them to the specified torque.
11 Reconnect the fuel and vacuum hoses as applicable, however, connect a hand vacuum pump to the fuel filter return hose (marked blue). Operate the vacuum pump until fuel comes out of the return hose. This primes the tandem pump. Reconnect the return hose to the fuel filter.
12 Refit the engine top cover.

Chapter 10
Suspension and steering

Contents

Degrees of difficulty

Easy, suitable for novice with little experience	**Fairly easy,** suitable for beginner with some experience	**Fairly difficult,** suitable for competent DIY mechanic	**Difficult,** suitable for experienced DIY mechanic	**Very difficult,** suitable for expert DIY or professional

Specifications

Front suspension
Type . . . . Independent, with MacPherson struts incorporating coil springs and telescopic shock absorbers. Anti-roll bar fitted to all models

Rear suspension
Type . . . . Transverse torsion beam axle with trailing arms. Separate gas-filled telescopic shock absorbers and coil springs. Anti-roll bar fitted to all models

Steering
Type . . . . Rack-and-pinion. Power assistance standard

Wheel alignment and steering angles*
Front wheel:
  Camber angle:
    Standard suspension . . . . -39' ± 30'
    Heavy duty suspension . . . . -15' ± 30'
    Maximum difference between sides (all models) . . . . 30'
  Castor angle:
    Standard suspension . . . . 4° 42' ± 30'
    Heavy duty suspension . . . . 4° 14' ± 30'
    Maximum difference between sides (all models) . . . . 30'
  Toe setting . . . . +10' ± 10'
  Toe-out on turns (20° left or right):
    Standard suspension . . . . 1° 32' ± 20'
    Heavy duty suspension . . . . 0° 53' ± 20'
Rear wheel:
  Camber angle. . . . . -1°30' ± 10'
  Maximum difference between sides. . . . . 20'
  Toe setting:
    Standard suspension . . . . +26' ± 10'
    Heavy duty suspension . . . . +16' ± 10'

Refer to a Seat dealer for the latest recommendations.

Torque wrench settings

	Nm	lbf ft
Front suspension		
Anti-roll bar:		
Links	40	30
Mounting clamp:		
Stage 1	20	15
Stage 2	Angle-tighten a further 90°	
Engine rear mounting link:*		
To transmission:		
Stage 1	30	22
Stage 2	Angle-tighten a further 90°	
To subframe:		
Stage 1	40	30
Stage 2	Angle-tighten a further 90°	
Hub nut*	See Chapter 8	
Lower arm:		
Front pivot bolt:*		
Stage 1	70	52
Stage 2	Angle-tighten a further 90°	
Rear pivot bolt:		
Stage 1	70	52
Stage 2	Angle-tighten a further 90°	
Lower arm mounting bracket rear plate:		
Small bolts:		
Stage 1	20	15
Stage 2	Angle-tighten a further 90°	
Large bolt:		
Stage 1	70	52
Stage 2	Angle-tighten a further 90°	
Balljoint-to-lower arm nuts/bolts:*		
Stage 1	20	15
Stage 2	Angle-tighten a further 90°	
Balljoint nut:*		
Stage 1	20	15
Stage 2	Angle-tighten a further 90°	
Mounting bracket to subframe:		
Stage 1	50	37
Stage 2	Angle-tighten a further 90°	
Splash plate to wheel housing	10	7
Subframe-to-underbody bolts:*		
Stage 1	50	37
Stage 2	Angle-tighten a further 90°	
Suspension strut:		
Bottom clamp bolt nut:*		
Stage 1	60	44
Stage 2	Angle-tighten a further 90°	
Piston rod nut*	60	44
Upper mounting-to-body:*		
Stage 1	15	11
Stage 2	Angle-tighten a further 90°	
Rear suspension		
Axle mounting bolts and nuts:*		
Stage 1	45	33
Stage 2	Angle-tighten a further 90°	
Hub nut (12-point)*	175	129
Shock absorber:		
Lower mounting bolt and nut:*		
Stage 1	40	30
Stage 2	Angle-tighten a further 90°	
Upper mounting bracket-to-body bolts:*		
Stage 1	30	22
Stage 2	Angle-tighten a further 90°	
Upper mounting nut to bracket*	25	18
Stub axle bolts:*		
Stage 1	30	22
Stage 2	Angle-tighten a further 90°	
Vehicle level sender:		
Sender to underbody (pop-rivet screw)	8	6
Sender link to lower arm	6	4

Torque wrench settings (continued)

	Nm	lbf ft
Steering		
Power steering hose union to electric pump	30	22
Power steering hose union to steering gear:		
Supply.	35	26
Return.	30	22
Steering column:		
Upper mounting bolts to bracket	23	17
Lower mounting bolt.	19	14
Steering column mounting bracket to cross bar	23	17
Steering column universal joint clamp bolt:*		
Stage 1	20	15
Stage 2	Angle-tighten a further 90°	
Steering gear mounting bolts:*		
Stage 1	50	37
Stage 2	Angle-tighten a further 90°	
Steering wheel bolt.	50	37
Track rod balljoint locknut	50	37
Track rod balljoint nut:*		
Stage 1	20	15
Stage 2	Angle-tighten a further 90°	
Track rod inner balljoint to steering rack	80	59
Roadwheels		
Roadwheel bolts.	120	89

Renew the nut/bolt every time it is removed

1 General information

The independent front suspension is of the MacPherson strut type, incorporating coil springs and integral telescopic shock absorbers. The struts are located by transverse lower suspension arms, which use rubber inner mounting bushes, and incorporate a balljoint at the outer ends. The front wheel bearing housings, which carry the wheel bearings, brake calipers and the hub/disc assemblies, are attached to the MacPherson struts by clamp bolts, and connected to the lower arms through the balljoints. A front anti-roll bar is fitted to all models. The anti-roll bar is rubber-mounted, and is connected to both lower suspension arms by short links.

The rear suspension consists of a torsion beam axle with telescopic shock absorbers and coil springs. An anti-roll bar is incorporated into the rear axle beam. One of three different rear axles may be fitted, according to which engine is fitted – each axle has different geometry and rigidity characteristics.

The safety steering column incorporates an intermediate shaft at its lower end. The intermediate shaft is connected to both the steering column and steering gear by universal joints, although the shaft is supplied as part of the column assembly and cannot be separated. Both the inner steering column and intermediate shaft have splined sections which collapse during a major frontal impact. The outer column is also telescopic with two sections, to facilitate reach adjustment.

The steering gear is mounted onto the front subframe, and is connected by two track rods with balljoints at their inner and outer ends to the steering arms projecting rearwards from the wheel bearing housings. The track rod ends are threaded to the track rods in order to allow adjustment of the front wheel toe setting.

Electrically Powered Hydraulic Steering (EPHS) is fitted as standard on all UK models. The system's electric pump and hydraulic fluid reservoir are located behind the front bumper, on the left-hand side.

All UK models are fitted with an Anti-lock Brake System (ABS), and most models can also be fitted with a Traction Control System (TCS), an Electronic Differential Lock (EDL) system and an Electronic Stability Program (ESP). The ABS may also be referred to as including EBD (Electronic Brake Distribution) which means it adjusts the front and rear braking forces according to the weight being carried, and the TCS may also be referred to as ASR (Anti Slip Regulation).

The TCS system prevents the front wheels from losing traction during acceleration by reducing the engine output. The system is switched on automatically when the engine is started, and it utilises the ABS system sensors to monitor the rotational speeds of the front wheels.

The ESP system extends the ABS, TCS and EDL functions to reduce wheel spin in difficult driving conditions. It does this by using highly-sensitive sensors which monitor the speed of the car, lateral movement of the car, the brake pressure, and the steering angle of the front wheels. If, for example, the car is tending to oversteer, the brake will be applied to the front outer wheel to correct the situation. If the car is tending to understeer, the brake will be applied to the rear inside wheel. The steering angle of the front wheels is monitored by an angle sensor on the top of the steering column.

The TCS/ESP systems are switched on automatically each time the engine is started, and should be left on except when driving with snow chains, driving in snow or driving on loose surfaces, when some wheel spin may be advantageous. The ESP switch is located in the centre of the facia.

Some models are also fitted with an Electronic Differential Lock (EDL) which reduces unequal traction from the front wheels. If one front wheel spins 100 rpm or more faster than the other, the faster wheel is slowed down by applying the brake to that wheel. The system is not the same as the traditional differential lock, where the actual differential gears are locked. Because the system applies a front brake, in the event of a brake disc overheating the system will shut down until the disc has cooled. No warning light is displayed if the system shuts down. As is the case with the TCS system, the EDL system uses the ABS sensors to monitor front wheel speeds.

2 Front wheel bearing housing – removal and refitting

Note: *All self-locking nuts and bolts disturbed on removal must be renewed as a matter of course.*

Removal

1 Remove the wheel trim/hub cap (as applicable) and loosen the driveshaft retaining nut with the car resting on its wheels. Also loosen the wheel bolts.

2.3 Remove the 12-point driveshaft retaining nut

2.9a Unscrew the bolts . . .

2.9b . . . and remove the retaining plate from the top of the lower arm

2.9c On some models, the balljoint is secured by nuts from below (arrowed)

2.9d Pull out the hub carrier and release the driveshaft from the hub

2 Apply the handbrake, then jack up the front of the car and support it on axle stands (see *Jacking and vehicle support*). Remove the front roadwheel and also remove the engine compartment undershield.

3 Unscrew and remove the driveshaft retaining nut **(see illustration)**.

4 Unscrew the nut securing the link to the anti-roll bar, and separate the link.

5 Remove the ABS wheel sensor as described in Chapter 9.

6 Remove the brake disc as described in Chapter 9. This procedure includes removing the brake caliper, however do not disconnect the hydraulic brake hose from the caliper. Using a piece of wire or string, tie the caliper to the front suspension coil spring, to avoid placing any strain on the hydraulic brake hose.

7 Unbolt the splash plate from the wheel bearing housing (where fitted).

8 Loosen the nut securing the steering track rod balljoint to the wheel bearing housing. To do this, fit a ring spanner to the nut, then, where applicable, hold the balljoint pin stationary using an Allen key. With the nut removed, it may be possible to release the balljoint from the wheel bearing housing by turning the balljoint pin with an Allen key. If not, leave the nut on by a few turns to protect the threads, then use a universal balljoint separator to release the balljoint. Remove the nut completely once the taper has been released.

9 Unscrew the front suspension lower balljoint-to-lower arm retaining nuts/bolts, and push the front suspension lower arm downwards to detach it from the balljoint assembly, or pull the bearing housing outwards to detach the arm from the balljoint. Where applicable, recover the retaining plate from above the arm. Now use a soft-faced mallet to tap the driveshaft from the hub splines while pulling out the bottom end of the wheel bearing housing. If the driveshaft is tight on the splines, it may be necessary to use a puller bolted to the hub to remove it **(see illustrations)**.

10 Note which way round it is fitted, then unscrew the nut and remove the clamp bolt securing the wheel bearing housing to the bottom of the strut.

11 The wheel bearing housing must now be released from the strut. To do this, Seat technicians insert a special tool into the split wheel bearing housing, and turn it through 90° to open up the clamp. A similar tool can be made out of an old screwdriver, or alternatively a suitable cold chisel can be driven into the split as a wedge. Slightly press inwards the top of the wheel bearing housing, then push it downwards from the bottom of the strut **(see illustrations)**.

12 Unscrew the nut and remove the balljoint from the bottom of the wheel bearing housing. If it is tight, use a puller.

Refitting

13 Note that all self-locking nuts and bolts disturbed on removal must be renewed as a matter of course.

2.11a Tool used by Seat technicians to open up the split wheel bearing housing

2.11b Using a cold chisel to open up the wheel bearing housing

14 Refit the balljoint to the wheel bearing housing and tighten the nut to the specified torque.

15 Ensure that the driveshaft outer joint and hub splines are clean and dry, then lubricate the splines with fresh engine oil. Also lubricate the threads and contact surface of the hub nut with oil.

16 Lift the wheel bearing assembly into position, and engage the hub with the splines on the outer end of the driveshaft. Fit the new hub nut, tightening it by hand only at this stage.

17 Engage the wheel bearing housing with the bottom of the suspension strut, making sure that the hole in the side plate aligns with the holes in the split housing. Remove the tool used to open the split.

18 Insert the strut-to-wheel bearing housing clamp bolt from the front, and fit the new retaining nut. Tighten the nut to the specified torque.

19 Refit the lower arm balljoint, refit the retaining plate (where applicable) and tighten the nuts/bolts to the specified torque.

20 Refit the track rod balljoint to the wheel bearing housing, then fit a new retaining nut and tighten it to the specified torque. If necessary, hold the balljoint pin with an Allen key while tightening the nut.

21 Refit the splash plate (where fitted) and tighten the bolts.

22 Refit the brake disc and caliper with reference to Chapter 9.

23 Refit the ABS wheel sensor as described in Chapter 9.

24 Refit the link to the anti-roll bar and tighten the nut to the specified torque.

25 Ensure that the outer joint is drawn fully into the hub, then refit the roadwheel and engine compartment undershield. Lower the car to the ground, and tighten the roadwheel bolts.

26 Tighten the driveshaft retaining nut in the stages given in the Specifications. It is recommended that an angle gauge is used to ensure the correct tightening angle.

3 Front hub and bearings – renewal

Note: *The front hub is supplied complete with bearings, and it is not possible to renew the bearings separately. Note that the hub and bearing assembly must be assembled to the hub carrier in one single operation, by applying force to the bearing and not the hub. Seat technicians use special tools T20149/1 which locate only on the bearing, however, it is possible to fabricate spacers to insert between the hub flange and the bearing, making it possible to apply pressure to the hub itself. If these tools cannot be obtained or fabricated, it is recommended that the work be carried out by a Seat dealer or suitably-equipped specialist.*

1 Remove the wheel bearing housing as described in Section 2.

2.11c Withdraw the wheel bearing housing from the bottom of the suspension strut

2 A press will be required to remove the hub and bearing, however, if such a tool is not available, a large bench vice and spacers (such as large sockets) will serve as an adequate substitute. As a last resort, it is possible to use a lump hammer to drive out the hub and bearing **(see illustration)**.

3 Support the wheel bearing housing securely on blocks or in a vice. Using a metal tube which bears on the inner end of the hub, press the hub and bearing out of the housing **(see illustration)**. Note that the internal circlip, retaining the bearing in the housing, will be destroyed during the removal operation.

4 Thoroughly clean the wheel bearing housing, removing all traces of dirt and grease, and polish away any burrs or raised edges which might hinder reassembly. Check for cracks or any other signs of wear or damage, and renew if necessary. Note that the new hub and bearing is supplied with a new circlip, which

3.2 Driving out the hub and bearing with a lump hammer

3.7a Press the hub and bearing into the wheel bearing housing

2.11d Wheel bearing housing

locates automatically if the special Seat tool is used.

5 On reassembly, apply a light coating of molybdenum disulphide grease to the bearing outer race and bearing surface of the wheel bearing housing.

6 If using the special Seat tools, fit it to the bearing, then draw the assembly into the hub carrier until the circlip is heard to click into position. The tools include grippers and spacers which cannot be fabricated easily. Check that the hub rotates freely, and wipe off any excess oil or grease.

7 If not using the special tools, make up suitable spacers to fit firmly between the hub flange and the bearing, then press the hub with bearing fully into the wheel bearing housing. Using this method, it may be necessary to tap the circlip into its groove **(see illustrations)**.

8 Refit the wheel bearing housing as described in Section 2.

3.3 Using a press to remove the hub and bearing from the wheel bearing housing

3.7b Make sure the circlip (arrowed) is fully entered in its groove

4.12a Unscrew the upper mounting bolts (arrowed) . . .

4.12b . . . and lower the strut from the wheel arch

4.13 Fit the coil spring compressor

4 Front suspension strut – removal, overhaul and refitting

Note: *All self-locking nuts and bolts disturbed on removal must be renewed as a matter of course.*

Removal

1 Remove the wheel trim/hub cap (as applicable) and loosen the driveshaft retaining nut with the car resting on its wheels. Also loosen the wheel bolts.

2 Apply the handbrake, then jack up the front of the car and support it on axle stands (see *Jacking and vehicle support*). Remove the front roadwheel and also remove the engine compartment undershield.

3 Unscrew and remove the driveshaft retaining nut. A new nut will be required.

4 Unscrew the nut securing the anti-roll bar link to the strut.

5 Using a suitable marker pen or scriber, draw around the outline of the end of the suspension lower arm on the lower arm balljoint, marking the correct fitted position of the balljoint.

6 Unscrew the front suspension balljoint-to-lower arm retaining nuts/bolts, then push the lower arm downwards to detach it from the balljoint assembly or pull the bearing housing outwards to detach the arm from the balljoint. Recover the retaining plate where applicable. This is necessary to provide additional room in order to lower the wheel bearing housing from the strut.

7 Disconnect the wiring from the ABS wheel sensor, and remove the wiring from the strut support.

8 Loosen the nut securing the steering track rod balljoint to the wheel bearing housing. To do this, fit a ring spanner to the nut, then, where applicable, hold the balljoint pin stationary using an Allen key. With the nut removed, it

may be possible to release the balljoint from the wheel bearing housing by turning the balljoint pin with an Allen key. If not, leave the nut on by a few turns to protect the threads, then use a universal balljoint separator to release the balljoint. Remove the nut completely once the taper has been released.

9 Pull the front hub and carrier from the driveshaft, then tie the driveshaft to one side. Support the weight of the hub carrier on a trolley jack.

10 Note which way round it is fitted, then unscrew the nut and remove the clamp bolt securing the wheel bearing housing to the bottom of the strut.

11 Release the wheel bearing housing from the strut by slightly opening the split housing with reference to Section 2, then slightly pressing inwards the top of the wheel bearing housing, and lowering it from the bottom of the strut.

12 Support the strut, then unscrew and remove the upper mounting bolts. Lower the strut and manoeuvre it out from underneath the wheel arch **(see illustrations)**. Discard the upper mounting bolts, as new ones must be used on refitting.

Overhaul

⚠️ **Warning: Before attempting to dismantle the suspension strut, a suitable tool to hold the coil spring in compression must be obtained. Adjustable coil spring compressors are readily available, and are recommended for this operation. Any attempt to dismantle the strut without such a tool is likely to result in damage or personal injury.**

13 Support the lower end of the strut in a vice, then fit the coil spring compressor into position, and check that it is securely located **(see illustration)**.

14 Compress the spring until the upper spring seat is free of tension, then remove the nut from the top of the piston rod. Hold the piston rod with an Allen key while the nut is unscrewed **(see illustrations)**. The need to hold the piston rod means that an ordinary deep socket cannot readily be used; in the workshop, we used a deep angled ring spanner (a short box spanner together with an open-ended spanner would also work). The nut is especially tight – don't expect to use makeshift means to loosen it safely.

4.14a Hold the piston rod with an Allen key while the nut is loosened . . .

4.14b . . . then remove the nut

4.15a Remove the strut mounting . . .

4.15b . . . and bellows

4.16 Remove the bump stop . . .

4.17 . . . and coil spring

4.20 The ends of the coil springs must locate correctly in the seatings (arrowed)

15 Remove the strut mounting, followed by the bellows **(see illustrations)**. Note the fitted order and orientation of all components, for use when refitting.

16 Withdraw the bump stop from the piston rod **(see illustration)**.

17 Lift the coil spring from the strut with the compressor still in position **(see illustration)**. Mark the top of the spring for reference.

18 Move the shock absorber piston rod up-and-down through its complete stroke, and check that the resistance is even and smooth. If there are any signs or seizing or lack of resistance, or if fluid has been leaking excessively, the shock absorber should be renewed.

19 The coil springs are normally colour-coded, and if the springs are to be renewed (it is advisable to renew both at the same time), be sure to get the correct type with an identical colour code.

20 Reassembly is a reversal of disassembly, but make sure that the ends of the coil spring are correctly located in the seatings **(see illustration)**. On completion, secure it all with the shock absorber piston rod nut, tightened to the specified torque.

Refitting

21 Manoeuvre the strut into position under the wheel arch, then fit the new upper mounting bolts and tighten them to the specified torque.

22 Engage the wheel bearing housing with the bottom of the suspension strut, making sure that the hole in the side plate aligns with the holes in the split housing. Remove the tool used to open the split.

23 Insert the new strut-to-wheel bearing housing clamp bolt from the front, and fit the new retaining nut. Tighten the nut to the specified torque.

24 Manoeuvre the driveshaft into position, and engage the outer joint with the hub. Fit the new hub nut and use it to draw the joint fully into position.

25 Align the suspension lower arm balljoint with the lower arm, then fit the new retaining nuts/bolts and retaining plate (where applicable), and tighten them to the specified torque and angle setting, using the marks made on removal to ensure that the balljoint is correctly positioned.

26 Refit the steering track rod balljoint to the

wheel bearing housing and tighten the nut to the specified torque.

27 Reconnect the wiring to the ABS wheel sensor, and attach the wiring to the strut support.

28 Refit the anti-roll bar link and tighten the nuts to the specified torque.

29 Ensure that the outer joint is drawn fully into position, then refit the roadwheel and engine compartment undershield, and lower the car to the ground.

30 Tighten the driveshaft nut in the Stages given in the Specifications.

31 Once the driveshaft nut is correctly tightened, tighten the wheel bolts to the specified torque and refit the wheel trim/hub cap.

---

5 Front suspension lower arm and bracket – removal, overhaul and refitting

Note: *All self-locking nuts and bolts disturbed on removal must be renewed as a matter of course.*

Removal

1 Apply the handbrake, then jack up the front of the car and support it on axle stands (see *Jacking and vehicle support*). Remove the appropriate front roadwheel and the engine compartment undershield.

2 Mark their position, then unscrew the front suspension lower balljoint-to-lower arm retaining nuts/bolts, and push the arm downwards to detach it from the balljoint assembly or pull the bearing housing outwards as applicable. **Note:** *On early models, the camber setting is adjusted by the position of the balljoint on the lower arm.*

3 Unscrew and remove the lower arm front pivot bolt.

Models with a rear pivot pin

4 Swivel out the front of the lower arm, and withdraw it forwards to release the rear pin from the rubber mounting. Only swivel out the arm sufficiently to clear the mounting bracket, and if necessary use a slide hammer to force the rear pin from the rubber mounting.

5 If it is required to renew the rear mounting rubber, unbolt the mounting bracket from the subframe.

Models with a rear pivot bolt

6 Undo the rear pivot bolt/nut and manoeuvre the arm from position.

Overhaul

7 Thoroughly clean the lower arm and bracket, then check carefully for cracks or any other signs of wear or damage, paying particular attention to the pivot and rear mounting rubber bushes. If either bush requires renewal, the lower arm and bracket should be taken to a Seat dealer or suitably-equipped garage. A hydraulic press and suitable spacers are required to press out the bushes and install the new ones. When fitting a new mounting bush, make sure that it is correctly aligned with the markings.

Refitting

Models with a rear pivot pin

8 Refit the mounting bracket to the subframe and tighten the bolts to the specified torque.

9 Locate the lower arm rear pin in the rubber mounting making sure that the hexagon profile aligns correctly **(see illustration)**.

5.9 The surfaces (A) on the lower arm rear pin, must align with the surfaces (B) in the rubber mounting

1 Lower arm	3 Rubber
2 Bracket	mounting

6.2a The front suspension lower balljoint on the wheel bearing housing

10 Insert the front pivot bolt and tighten to the specified torque.

11 Refit the balljoint and retaining plate to the lower arm using new bolts, align it with the markings previously-made, then tighten the bolts to the specified torque and angle.

12 Refit the roadwheel and undershield then lower the car to the ground.

Models with a rear pivot bolt

13 Manoeuvre the arm into position, then fit the new bolts/nuts, only finger-tighten them at this stage.

14 Engage the balljoint bolts with the lower arm, and tighten the new nuts to the specified torque.

15 Refit the roadwheel, and lower the vehicle to the ground. Now tighten the front and rear pivot bolts to the specified torque.

6 Front suspension lower arm balljoint – removal, inspection and refitting

Note: All self-locking nuts and bolts disturbed on removal must be renewed as a matter of course.

Removal

Method 1

1 Remove the wheel bearing housing as described in Section 2.

2 Unscrew and remove the balljoint retaining nut, then release the balljoint from the wheel bearing housing using a universal balljoint separator **(see illustrations)**. Withdraw the balljoint.

Method 2

3 Remove the wheel trim/hub cap (as applicable) and loosen the driveshaft retaining nut with the car resting on its wheels. Also loosen the wheel bolts.

4 Apply the handbrake, then jack up the front of the car and support it on axle stands (see *Jacking and vehicle support*). Remove the front roadwheel and also remove the engine compartment undershield.

5 Unscrew and remove the driveshaft retaining nut.

6 Unscrew the nut securing the anti-roll bar link to the strut.

7 Using a suitable marker pen or scriber, draw

6.2b Use a universal balljoint separator tool to remove the lower balljoint

around the outline of the end of the suspension lower arm on the lower arm balljoint, marking the correct fitted position of the balljoint.

8 Unscrew the front suspension balljoint-to-lower arm retaining bolts/nuts, and remove the retaining plate (where applicable) from the top of the lower arm.

9 Disconnect the wiring from the ABS wheel sensor, and remove the wiring from the strut support.

10 Loosen the nut securing the steering track rod balljoint to the wheel bearing housing. To do this, fit a ring spanner to the nut, then, where applicable, hold the balljoint pin stationary using an Allen key. With the nut removed, it may be possible to release the balljoint from the wheel bearing housing by turning the balljoint pin with an Allen key. If not, leave the nut on by a few turns to protect the threads, then use a universal balljoint separator to release the balljoint. Remove the nut completely once the taper has been released.

11 Pull the front hub and carrier from the driveshaft, then tie the driveshaft to one side. Retain the wheel bearing housing away from the lower arm by inserting a block of wood between the strut and the inner body panel.

12 Unscrew and remove the balljoint retaining nut, then release the balljoint from the wheel bearing housing using a universal balljoint separator. Withdraw the balljoint.

Inspection

13 With the balljoint removed, check that it moves freely, without any sign of roughness. Check also that the balljoint rubber gaiter shows no sign of deterioration, and is free from cracks and splits. Renew as necessary.

Refitting

Method 1

14 Fit the balljoint to the wheel bearing housing and fit the new retaining nut. Tighten the nut to the specified torque setting, noting that the balljoint shank can be retained with an Allen key if necessary to prevent it from rotating.

15 Refit the wheel bearing housing with reference to Section 2.

Method 2

16 Fit the balljoint to the wheel bearing housing and fit the new retaining nut. Tighten the nut

to the specified torque setting, noting that the balljoint shank can be retained with an Allen key if necessary to prevent it from rotating.

17 Remove the wooden block and move the strut inwards, at the same time inserting the driveshaft into the hub splines.

18 Refit the balljoint and retaining plate (where applicable) to the lower arm using new bolts/nuts, and tighten them to the specified torque and angle.

19 Fit the new hub nut and use it to draw the joint fully into position.

20 Refit the steering track rod balljoint to the wheel bearing housing and secure with a new nut tightened to the specified torque.

21 Reconnect the ABS wiring and attach to the strut support.

22 Refit the anti-roll bar link to the strut and tighten the nut to the specified torque.

23 Ensure that the outer joint is drawn fully into position, then refit the roadwheel and engine compartment undershield, and lower the car to the ground.

24 Tighten the driveshaft nut in the Stages given in the Specifications.

25 Once the driveshaft nut is correctly tightened, tighten the wheel bolts to the specified torque and refit the wheel trim/hub cap.

7 Front anti-roll bar – removal and refitting

Note: All self-locking nuts and bolts disturbed on removal must be renewed as a matter of course.

Removal

1 Apply the handbrake, then jack up the front of the car and support it on axle stands (see *Jacking and vehicle support*). Remove both front roadwheels and the engine compartment undershield.

2 Unscrew the bolts securing the engine rear mounting link to the bottom of the transmission.

3 Unscrew the bolts securing the anti-roll bar clamps to the rear of the lower arm brackets. Note that the lower right-hand bolt cannot be completely removed at this stage.

4 Unscrew the nuts and disconnect the side connecting links from the anti-roll bar.

5 Unscrew the steering gear mounting bolts from the bottom of the subframe. Tie the steering gear to the underbody.

6 Mark the position of the subframe on the underbody to retain the wheel alignment. Also, mark the anti-roll bar to indicate which way round it is fitted, and the position of the rubber mounting bushes. This will aid refitting.

7 Support the subframe on a trolley jack, then unscrew the mounting bolts and lower the subframe approximately 4 cm.

8 Remove the clamp, then turn the anti-roll bar upwards and withdraw towards the rear of the car. Remove the rubber mounting bushes from the bar.

9 Carefully examine the anti-roll bar components for signs of wear, damage or deterioration, paying particular attention to the rubber mounting bushes. Renew worn components as necessary.

Refitting

10 Fit the rubber mounting bushes to the anti-roll bar, aligning them with the marks made prior to removal.

11 Manoeuvre the anti-roll bar into position, then refit the mounting clamps and insert the retaining bolts. Ensure that the bush markings are still aligned with the marks on the bars, then tighten the mounting clamp retaining bolts to the specified torque.

12 Raise the subframe and align with the previously-made marks. Insert the mounting bolts and tighten to the specified torque and angle.

13 Untie the steering gear, then secure it to the subframe with the bolts tightened to the specified torque.

14 Refit the anti-roll bar side connecting links and tighten the nuts to the specified torque.

15 Refit the engine rear mounting link bolts, then push the transmission forwards as far as possible and tighten the bolts to the specified torque.

16 Refit the roadwheels and engine compartment undershield, then lower the car to the ground and tighten the wheel bolts to the specified torque.

8 Front anti-roll bar connecting link – removal and refitting

Note: *All self-locking nuts and bolts disturbed on removal must be renewed as a matter of course.*

Removal

1 Apply the handbrake, then jack up the front of the car and support it on axle stands (see *Jacking and vehicle support*). Remove the relevant front roadwheel.

2 Unscrew the nuts securing the anti-roll bar link to the front suspension strut and anti-roll bar and remove it.

3 Inspect the link rubbers for signs of damage or deterioration. If evident, renew the link complete.

Refitting

4 Refitting is a reversal of removal, but delay fully tightening the link bolts until the weight of the car is on the front suspension.

9 Rear hub assembly – removal and refitting

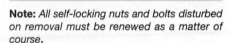

Note: *The rear wheel bearings cannot be renewed independently of the rear hub, because the outer races are formed in the hub itself. If excessive wear is evident, the rear hub*

9.3 Use a chisel or screwdriver to remove the rear hub dust cap

must be renewed complete. The rear hub nut must always be renewed after removal.

Removal

1 Chock the front roadwheels, then jack up the rear of the car and support on axle stands (see *Jacking and vehicle support*). Release the handbrake and remove the relevant rear roadwheel.

2 Remove the rear brake drum or disc (as applicable) with reference to Chapter 9.

3 Remove the dust cap from the centre of the hub using a screwdriver or cold chisel (see illustration).

4 Unscrew and remove the self-locking 12-point hub nut. Note that it is tightened to a high torque and a socket extension bar may be required to loosen it (see illustration). It is recommended that the nut is renewed whenever removed.

5 Using a suitable puller if necessary, pull the hub and bearings from the stub axle (see illustration). Take care not to damage the ABS sensor ring on the inside of the hub.

6 Examine the hub and bearings for wear, pitting and damage. If all the bearing surfaces and balls appear to be in good order upon inspection, the hub may be re-used.

Refitting

7 Wipe clean the stub axle, then check that the bearing races are adequately lubricated with suitable grease.

8 Locate the hub as far as possible onto the stub axle. Seat technicians use a special drift to drive the inner race onto the stub, however,

9.5 . . . and remove the hub and bearings from the stub axle

9.4 Unscrew the self-locking 12-point hub nut . . .

a suitable metal tube or deep socket will do the same (see illustration). Make sure that the tube is only located on the inner race.

9 Screw on the new self-locking nut and tighten it to the specified torque.

10 Check the dust cap for damage and renew it if necessary. Use a hammer to carefully tap the cap into the hub. **Note:** *A badly fitting dust cap will allow moisture to enter the bearing, reducing its service life.*

11 Refit the brake drum or disc (as applicable) with reference to Chapter 9.

12 Refit the roadwheel and lower the car to the ground.

10 Rear stub axle – removal and refitting

Note: *All self-locking nuts and bolts disturbed on removal must be renewed as a matter of course.*

Removal

1 Chock the front roadwheels, then jack up the rear of the car and support on axle stands (see *Jacking and vehicle support*). Release the handbrake and remove the relevant roadwheel.

2 Remove the rear hub as described in Section 9.

3 Disconnect the wiring, then unscrew the bolt and remove the ABS speed sensor from the rear axle trailing arm (see illustration).

4 Unscrew the mounting bolts securing the

9.8 Use a socket to drive the hub onto the stub axle

10.3 ABS rear wheel speed sensor (arrowed)

stub axle and backplate to the rear axle trailing arm. Carefully withdraw the backplate and stub axle, taking care not to bend the brake line excessively. If necessary, remove the rear wheel cylinder or rear caliper as applicable with reference to Chapter 9.

5 Inspect the stub axle for signs of damage and renew if necessary. Do not attempt to straighten the stub axle.

Refitting

6 Ensure the mating surfaces of the axle, stub axle and backplate are clean and dry. Check the backplate for signs of damage.

7 Refit the stub axle together with the backplate, then insert the new bolts and progressively tighten to the specified torque.

8 If removed, refit the rear wheel cylinder or rear caliper as applicable with reference to Chapter 9.

11.3 Position the trolley jack and block of wood beneath the trailing arm

11.5b . . . and withdraw the shock absorber from the trailing arm

9 Refit the speed sensor, tighten the bolt, and reconnect the wiring.

10 Refit the rear hub with reference to Section 9.

11 Refit the roadwheel and lower the car to the ground.

---

11 Rear suspension shock absorber and coil spring – removal, inspection and refitting

Note: *All self-locking nuts and bolts disturbed on removal must be renewed as a matter of course.*

Shock absorber

Removal

1 Before removing the shock absorber, an idea of how effective it is can be gained by depressing the rear corner of the car. If the shock absorber is in good condition, the body should rise then settle in its normal position. If the body oscillates more than this, the shock absorber is defective. **Note:** *The rear shock absorbers should only be renewed as a pair.*

2 Chock the front roadwheels, then jack up the rear of the car and support on axle stands (see *Jacking and vehicle support*). Remove the relevant rear roadwheel.

3 Position a trolley jack and block of wood beneath the coil spring position on the trailing arm, and raise the arm so that the shock absorber is slightly compressed **(see illustration)**. Note that on some models, it may be necessary to remove the stone protection guard first.

11.5a Remove the lower mounting bolt . . .

11.6a Unscrew the upper mounting bolts (arrowed) . . .

4 On models with gas-discharge (xenon) headlights, disconnect the tension rod for the rear sender.

5 Unscrew and remove the shock absorber lower mounting nut and bolt, and lever the bottom of the shock absorber from the trailing arm **(see illustrations)**.

6 Support the shock absorber, then unscrew the upper mounting bolts located in the rear wheel arch. Lower the shock absorber and withdraw from under the wheel arch **(see illustrations)**.

7 With the shock absorber on the bench, prise off the cover, then unscrew the nut from the top of the piston rod and remove the upper mounting bracket. The piston rod can be held stationary with a pair of grips on the raised peg on the top of the rod. Remove the rubber stop and protectors from the top of the rod.

Inspection

8 If necessary, the action of the shock absorber can be checked by mounting it upright in a vice. Fully depress the rod, then pull it up fully. The piston rod must move smoothly over its complete length.

Refitting

9 Locate the rubber stop and protectors on the piston rod followed by the upper mounting bracket. Fit the new nut and tighten to the specified torque while holding the piston rod as for removal, then refit the cover.

10 Locate the shock absorber in the rear wheel arch, then insert the upper mounting bolts and tighten to the specified torque.

11 Locate the bottom of the shock absorber in the trailing arm, insert the bolt from the outside, then screw on the nut. Raise the trailing arm with the jack to take the weight of the rear suspension, then tighten the lower mounting bolt to the specified torque.

12 Lower the jack, and where necessary refit the stone protection guard.

13 On models with gas-discharge (xenon) headlights, reconnect the tension rod and adjust it so that the lever points towards the rear and not upwards when the rear suspension is flexed.

14 Refit the roadwheel and lower the car to the ground.

Coil spring

Note: *It is possible to remove the rear*

11.6b . . . and withdraw the rear shock absorber from under the wheel arch

11.20 Release the handbrake cable from the bracket on the trailing arm

11.21a Lever down the trailing arm . . .

11.21b . . . then release the coil spring from its lower seat . . .

coil spring without the use of a coil spring compressor; both methods are described in the following paragraphs.

 Warning: Adjustable coil spring compressors are readily available, and are recommended for this operation.

15 Chock the front roadwheels, then jack up the rear of the car and support on axle stands (see *Jacking and vehicle support*). Remove the relevant rear roadwheel.

16 If removing the left-hand rear coil spring, first remove the exhaust tail pipe and silencer as described in Chapter 4C.

With a spring compressor

17 Support the trailing arm with a trolley jack, then fit the tool to the coil spring and compress it until it can be removed from the trailing arm and underbody. With the coil spring on the bench, carefully release the tension of the tool and remove it.

Without a spring compressor

18 Position a trolley jack and block of wood beneath the coil spring position on the trailing arm, and raise the arm so that the shock absorber is slightly compressed. Note on some models, it may be necessary to remove the stone protection guard first.

19 Unscrew and remove the shock absorber lower mounting nut and bolt, and lever the bottom of the shock absorber from the trailing arm.

20 Release the handbrake cable from the bracket on the trailing arm **(see illustration)**.

21 Lower the trolley jack and remove it from under the trailing arm, then carefully lever the arm down until the coil spring can be removed. Lever against a block of wood to prevent damage to the underbody. Make sure that the car is adequately supported on the axle stands **(see illustrations)**.

Inspection

22 With the coil spring removed, recover the upper and lower spring seats and check them for damage **(see illustration)**. Obtain new ones if necessary. Also clean the spring locations on the underbody and trailing arm.

Refitting

23 Refitting is a reversal of removal, but make sure that the upper spring seat is located

11.21c . . . and underbody seat

correctly on the top of the coil spring, with the spring end abutting the shoulder on the seat. The lower seat is circular and locates only in the centre of the spring. Before tightening the shock absorber lower mounting bolt to the specified torque, raise the trailing arm to its normal running position.

12 Rear anti-roll bar – removal and refitting

The rear anti-roll bar runs along the length of the rear axle beam. It is an integral part of the axle assembly, and cannot be removed. If the anti-roll bar is damaged, which is unlikely, the complete axle assembly must be renewed.

13 Rear axle assembly – removal and refitting

Note: *All self-locking nuts and bolts disturbed on removal must be renewed as a matter of course.*

Removal

1 Chock the front roadwheels, then jack up the rear of the car and support on axle stands positioned beneath the underbody (see *Jacking and vehicle support*). Remove both rear roadwheels. Fully release the handbrake.

2 Working on each side at a time, slightly raise the trailing arm so that the shock absorber is not fully extended, then unscrew and remove the shock absorber upper mounting bolts from

11.22 Recover the upper and lower spring seats

inside the rear wheel arch. Carefully lower the trailing arm to relieve the tension in the coil spring.

3 On models fitted with gas-discharge (xenon) headlights, disconnect the tension rod at the rear of the vehicle level sensor. If necessary, disconnect the wiring and unbolt the sensor.

4 With both shock absorber upper mountings detached, lower the trailing arms until the coil springs and seats can be removed.

5 Remove the stone protection plates from the trailing arms where fitted, then unscrew the lower mounting bolts and remove the shock absorbers from the rear axle.

6 Release the handbrake cable from the supports/clips on the rear axle and underbody.

7 Pull out the clips and disconnect the flexible brake hoses from the supports on the rear axle and underbody bracket on both sides **(see illustration)**. Do not disconnect the rigid brake lines from the hoses.

13.7 Flexible brake hose on the rear axle and underbody

13.9 Rear axle front mounting bolt (arrowed)

14.9a Fitting position of the rear axle rubber mounting (except GT models)

The cut-out (1) must align with the point indicated by the arrow on the trailing arm (2)

14.9b Fitting position of the rear axle rubber mounting (GT models)

The axis (1) must align with the point indicated by the arrow on the trailing arm (2)

8 Refer to Section 10 and remove the rear stub axles from the rear trailing arms. Release the rigid pipes from their clips and place the rear wheel cylinders or calipers (as applicable) to one side, together with the handbrake cables. Where fitted, also unbolt the rear brake load regulator.

9 Support the rear axle with a trolley jack, then unscrew and remove the rear axle front mounting bolts from the underbody brackets **(see illustration)**.

10 Manoeuvre the rear axle down from the underbody brackets and withdraw from under the car. The help of an assistant is recommended.

11 Inspect the rear axle mountings for signs of damage or deterioration, and refer to Section 14 if renewal is necessary.

Refitting

12 Apply a little brake grease or soapy water to the kidney-shaped cavity in the front mounting rubbers, then manoeuvre the rear axle into the underbody brackets and insert the mounting bolts from the outside. Screw on the nuts finger-tight at this stage. **Note:** *Make sure that the bolts are inserted through the centres of the rubber mountings and are not located in one of the three off-centre cut-outs.* If the bolts are not correctly centred, the rear wheel alignment will be incorrect causing excessive tyre wear.

13 Refit the rear stub axles as described in Section 10. Secure the brake lines to their clips, and where applicable refit the rear brake load regulator.

14 Refit the flexible brake hoses to the supports and secure with the clips.

15 Refit the handbrake cables and locate them in the supports/clips.

16 Locate the shock absorbers on the trailing arms and insert the lower mounting bolts loosely.

17 On models with gas-discharge (xenon) headlights, refit the vehicle level sensor if removed, then reconnect the wiring and tension rod.

18 Carefully locate the coil springs and seats on the rear axle with reference to Section 11.

19 Working on each side at a time, raise the trailing arm until the shock absorber upper mounting bolts can be inserted. Tighten the bolts to the specified torque.

20 Working on each side at a time, raise the trailing arm with a trolley jack until the weight of the car is taken on the coil spring. Fully tighten the front mounting bolts to the specified torque, then tighten the shock absorber mounting bolts to the specified torque.

21 Refit the stone protection plates under the trailing arms.

22 Check and if necessary adjust the handbrake as described in Chapter 9.

23 Refit the roadwheels and lower the car to the ground.

14 Rear axle rubber mountings – renewal

Note: *It is recommended that the rubber mountings are renewed on both sides at the same time to ensure correct rear wheel alignment.*

1 Most models covered by this manual are fitted with hydraulic type rubber mountings to the rear axle when new, although early 1.4 litre models may have the solid rubber type. In the event of leakage or excessive wear of the hydraulic type, both sides MUST be renewed with the solid rubber type. The following paragraphs describe renewal of the solid rubber type mountings, however the procedure for removing the hydraulic type is the same.

2 Chock the front roadwheels, then jack up the rear of the car and support on axle stands positioned beneath the underbody (see *Jacking and vehicle support*). Remove both rear roadwheels.

3 Release the handbrake cables from the supports/clips on the rear axle and underbody.

4 Pull out the clips and disconnect the flexible brake hoses from the supports on the rear axle and underbody brackets.

5 Unscrew and remove both rear axle front mounting bolts from the underbody brackets.

6 Working on one side at a time, pull the front end of the trailing arm down from the underbody bracket and retain it in this position by placing a block of wood between the arm and underbody.

7 Note the fitted position of the rubber mounting to aid refitting.

8 Seat technicians use a slide hammer tool to remove the rubber mounting from the rear axle. If a similar tool is not available, use a long bolt with suitable-sized metal tubing and washers to force out the mounting.

9 The new mounting must be located correctly in the rear axle **(see illustrations)**.

15.3 Undo the steering wheel retaining bolt with a multi-spline tool

15.4 Make alignment marks between the steering wheel and the end of the column shaft (arrowed)

15.5 Pull the steering wheel from the column shaft

Using a suitable tool, pull the mounting into the rear axle until it is positioned as noted on removal.

10 Renew the mounting on the other side using the same procedure described in paragraphs 6 to 9 inclusive.

11 Apply a little brake grease or soapy water to the kidney-shaped cavity in the front mounting rubbers, then locate the rear axle in the underbody brackets. Insert the mounting bolts from the outside, hand-tight at this stage.

12 Refit the flexible brake hoses and hand-brake cables, and secure with the clips.

13 Working on one side at a time, raise the trailing arm with a trolley jack until the weight of the car is taken on the coil spring, then fully tighten the front mounting bolt to the specified torque.

14 Refit the roadwheels and lower the car to the ground.

15 Steering wheel – removal and refitting

Removal

1 Set the front wheels in the straight-ahead position, and release the steering lock by inserting the ignition key.

2 Remove the driver's airbag as described in Chapter 12.

3 Using a multi-spline tool, unscrew and remove the retaining bolt, while holding the steering wheel stationary – do not use the steering lock to hold the wheel, as it may be damaged **(see illustration)**. **Note:** *The steering wheel retaining bolt can be re-used up to 5 times, after which it must be renewed. It is recommended that the nut is marked with a centre punch to indicate the number of times it has been unscrewed.*

4 The wheel should have a punch mark already, to indicate its correct fitted position. If necessary, use a centre-punch or dab of paint to mark the steering wheel in relation to the column in order to aid refitting **(see illustration)**.

5 Ease the steering wheel from the column splines by firmly rocking it side-to-side **(see illustration)**.

6 Secure the airbag rotary contact unit in place using adhesive tape. The contact unit must not be allowed to rotate.

Refitting

7 Remove the tape from the contact unit.

8 Locate the steering wheel on the column splines making sure that the previously-made marks are correctly aligned.

9 Apply suitable locking compound to the threads of the bolt, then screw it on and tighten to the specified torque while holding the steering wheel stationary.

10 Refit the driver's airbag as described in Chapter 12.

16 Steering column – removal, inspection and refitting

Removal

1 Remove the steering wheel as described in Section 15.

2 Remove the steering column shrouds with reference to Chapter 11, Section 29.

3 Note that on models equipped with ESP (electronic stability program) and TCS (traction control system), the airbag slip-ring is different to models without ESP/TCS, and incorporates a steering wheel angle sensor. To remove this type, make sure that the front wheels are still pointing straight-ahead, then check that a yellow spot is visible through the hole in the top, right-hand corner of the slip-ring housing. If necessary, temporarily refit the steering wheel and move the column until the spot is visible.

4 Slacken the combination switch clamp ring bolt, and slide the assembly upwards over the end of the column shaft **(see illustrations)**. Slide up the locking catch and disconnect the wiring plugs as the assembly is withdrawn.

5 Disconnect the wiring from the ignition switch and immobiliser reading coil, then unscrew the nut and disconnect the earth cable.

6 Beneath the pedal bracket, undo the plastic nuts and remove the cover for access to the steering column lower universal joint **(see illustration)**.

16.4a Slacken the clamp ring bolt (arrowed)

16.4b Slide up the locking catch (arrowed) and disconnect the wiring plug

16.6 Remove the plastic cover from the steering column lower universal joint

16.7a Steering column lower universal joint

16.7b Remove the clamp bolt

16.7c Splined pinion shaft on the steering gear

16.7d The splined universal joint, showing the flat to ensure fitting in one position only

7 Unscrew and remove the clamp bolt and free the steering column universal joint from the steering gear pinion (the shaft is telescopic to enable it to be easily disconnected). Discard the clamp bolt as a new one should be used

on refitting. Note that the pinion shaft has a cut-out to enable fitting of the clamp bolt, and the splined pinion shaft incorporates a flat, making it impossible to assemble the joint to the shaft in the wrong position (see

illustrations). Some models may have a clamp ring securing the universal joint to the inner column.

8 Unclip the wiring guides and release the wiring cable ties from the steering column.

9 Note that the inner and outer columns, and the intermediate shaft, are telescopic to facilitate the reach adjustment. It is important to keep the splined sections of the inner steering column engaged with each other while the steering column is removed. If they become detached due to the outer column sections being separated, especially on a car which has completed a high mileage, it is possible that rattling noises may occur. Seat technicians use a special plastic clip to hold the outer column sections together, although a retainer can be made out of a tapered wooden dowel, or the plastic end of a ballpoint pen can be put to good use. First, release the reach adjustment handle and position the outer column tubes so that the transportation holes are in alignment. Insert the dowel or plug to hold the sections of the column together during removal (see illustration).

10 Unscrew and remove the lower mounting bolt, then support the steering column and unscrew the upper mounting bolts. Withdraw the steering column from inside the car (see illustrations).

11 If necessary, remove the ignition switch/ steering column lock with reference to Section 17.

Inspection

12 The steering column is designed to

16.9 Insert a dowel or plug (arrowed) to hold the steering column together during removal

16.10a Loosen the nut . . .

16.10b . . . and remove the steering column lower mounting bolt

16.10c Unscrew the upper mounting bolts . . .

16.10d . . . and withdraw the steering column from inside the vehicle

16.10e The steering column removed from the car

16.12 Measure the distance between the upper mounting brackets

a = 37.0 mm min   *1   Mounting bolt*

16.14 The intermediate shaft is permanently attached to the inner steering column

collapse in the event of a front-end crash to prevent the steering wheel injuring the driver. Before refitting the steering column, examine the column and mountings for signs of damage and deformation. Using vernier calipers, measure the distance between the upper mounting brackets **(see illustration)**. The distance must be a minimum of 37.0 mm. If it is less than this, the steering column is damaged and should be renewed.

13 Check the inner column sections for signs of free play in the column bushes. If any damage or wear is found on the steering column bushes, the column must be renewed as an assembly.

14 The intermediate shaft is permanently attached to the inner column and cannot be renewed separately **(see illustration)**. Inspect the universal joints for excessive wear. If evident, the complete steering column must be renewed.

Refitting

15 If a new steering column is being fitted, the roller bracket must be removed from the old outer column and secured to the new one **(see illustration)**.

16 Refit the ignition switch/steering column lock with reference to Section 17.

17 Apply a little locking fluid to the threads of the mounting bolts. Offer the steering column onto its mounting bracket and insert all of the mounting bolts loosely. Tighten the lower mounting bolt to the specified torque, then tighten the upper bolts to the specified torque.

18 Remove the clip or retainer securing the telescopic tube sections, and remove the retainer/wire from the inner column.

19 Locate the universal joint onto the steering gear pinion shaft so that the cut-out is aligned with the bolt holes. Insert the new clamp bolt and tighten to the specified torque.

20 Refit the plastic cover beneath the pedal bracket and secure with the plastic nuts.

21 Refit the earth cable and tighten the nut, then reconnect the wiring to the ignition switch and immobiliser reading coil.

22 Refit the combination switch/contact slip-ring to the top of the steering column, and tighten the clamp bolt. Reconnect the wiring plugs.

23 On models with EPS/TCS, make sure that the yellow spot is visible (see paragraph 3), then refit the steering wheel angle sensor in its central position **(see illustration)**. **Note:** *The basic setting of the sensor should be checked by a Seat dealer whenever it is removed or whenever the steering wheel is repositioned.*

24 Temporarily locate the steering wheel on the column splines and check that the clearance between the steering wheel and the clock spring housing is approximately 2.5 mm.

16.15 The roller bracket is secured to the steering column with a single shear-head bolt

16.23 Steering wheel angle sensor on models with ESP and TCS

The yellow spot must be visible through the hole (1) with the steering angle sensor in its central position (arrowed)

17.4 Disconnect the ignition switch wiring plug

If not, loosen the combination switch clamp bolt and reposition it, then retighten the bolt. Remove the steering wheel.

25 The remainder of refitting is a reversal of removal.

17 Ignition switch and steering column lock – removal and refitting

Ignition switch

Removal

1 Remove the steering wheel as described in Section 15.
2 Remove the steering column shrouds as described in Chapter 11, Section 29.
3 Remove the steering column combination switch as described in Chapter 12.
4 Carefully pull the wiring plug from the ignition switch (see illustration).
5 Remove the locking paint from the switch retaining screw heads, then loosen them slightly and pull out the switch from the steering lock housing.

Refitting

6 Insert the ignition key and turn it to the 'on' position. Also turn the switch in the same position.
7 Carefully insert the switch into the housing, then insert the screws and tighten securely. Lock the screws by applying some paint over their heads and onto the housing.
8 Reconnect the wiring plug to the ignition switch.

17.20 Remove the ignition switch lock cylinder from the housing

9 The remainder of refitting is a reversal of removal.

Steering column lock

Removal

10 Remove the ignition switch as previously described.
11 The lock is secured to the outer column by shear-head bolts (see illustration), and the heads are broken off in the tightening procedure. To remove the old bolts, either drill them out, or use a sharp cold chisel to cut off their heads or turn them anti-clockwise. Withdraw the lock from the steering column.

Refitting

12 If removed, refit the lock cylinder with the ignition key in the 'on' position, then remove the wire. Make sure that the immobiliser coil connection is located correctly in the guide when inserting the lock cylinder.
13 Locate the lock on the outer column and insert the new shear-head bolts. Tighten the bolts until their heads break off.
14 The remainder of refitting is a reversal of removal.

Ignition switch lock cylinder

Removal

15 Remove the steering wheel as described in Section 15.
16 Adjust the steering column to the lowest position.
17 Remove the upper and lower column shrouds with reference to Chapter 11, Section 29.
18 Disconnect the wiring from the ignition key immobiliser sensor/reader coil.
19 Insert the ignition key and turn it to position 'ignition on'.
20 Insert a 1.5 mm diameter wire or drill fully into the hole in the lock cylinder located next to the key, then withdraw the key, lock cylinder and sensor from the housing (see illustration).

Refitting

21 Refitting is a reversal of removal.

18 Steering gear assembly (EPHS) – removal, overhaul and refitting

Note: *New subframe mounting bolts, track rod balljoint nuts, steering gear retaining bolts, and an intermediate shaft universal joint clamp bolt will be required on refitting.*

Removal

1 Apply the handbrake, then jack up the front of the car and support it on axle stands positioned on the underbody, leaving the subframe free (see *Jacking and vehicle support*). Position the steering straight-ahead, then remove both front roadwheels. Also remove the engine compartment undershield. As a precaution against the steering wheel

17.11 The steering column lock is secured to the outer column by shear-head bolts (arrowed)

turning and damaging the airbag contact spring, use adhesive tape to secure it to the facia or steering column.
2 Beneath the pedal bracket, undo the plastic nuts and remove the cover for access to the steering column lower universal joint.
3 Unscrew and remove the clamp bolt and free the steering column universal joint from the steering gear pinion (the shaft is telescopic to enable it to be easily disconnected). Discard the clamp bolt as a new one should be used on refitting. Note that the pinion shaft has a cut-out to enable fitting of the clamp bolt, and the splined pinion shaft incorporates a flat making it impossible to assemble the joint to the shaft in the wrong position. Some models may have a clamp ring securing the universal joint to the inner column.
4 Remove the battery and battery tray as described in Chapter 5A.
5 Remove the air filter and air ducting from the engine compartment with reference to the relevant part of Chapter 4.
6 Release the power-assisted steering sensor wiring from the holder on the inner panel above the left-hand driveshaft.
7 On models where the front exhaust pipe runs beneath the front subframe, remove it with reference to Chapter 4C.
8 Unscrew the two bolts securing the rear engine/transmission mounting link to the underside of the transmission unit. Discard both bolts, new ones must be used on refitting, and leave the mounting attached to the subframe.
9 Unscrew the nuts and disconnect the links from the anti-roll bar on each side.
10 Working on each side at a time, unscrew the nuts from the track rod ends, then use a balljoint separator tool to release the ends from the steering arms on the front wheel bearing housings.
11 Unscrew the filler cap from the top of the hydraulic fluid reservoir on top of the electric power steering pump, then siphon all the fluid into a suitable container. Note that there will still be fluid in the system lines. Discard the removed fluid. **Note:** *Seat specifically state that a hose clamp must not be fitted to the hydraulic fluid line.*
12 Support the weight of the subframe with a trolley jack, then mark the position of the bolts securing the subframe to the underbody, and

unscrew them. There are four bolts on each side of the subframe.

13 Position a suitable container beneath the steering gear to catch spilt fluid.

14 Lower the subframe approximately 4 cm, at the same time guiding the pinion shaft from the rubber grommet in the floor, and making sure that the hydraulic lines are not damaged.

15 Unscrew the union nut and disconnect the supply line and return lines from the steering gear, then recover the copper sealing washers. Tape over or plug the ends of the lines and the apertures in the steering gear to prevent entry of dust and dirt into the hydraulic system. The line ends can be wrapped in a plastic bag if preferred.

16 Unscrew the bolts and remove the power-assisted steering sensor from the steering gear pinion housing. Be prepared for some loss of fluid.

17 Unscrew the mounting bolts and withdraw the steering gear from the subframe to the rear. Note that the mounting on the passenger side of the gear incorporates a clamp and rubber mounting. Examine the mounting for wear and damage, and renew it if necessary. Discard the steering gear mounting bolts, new ones should be used on refitting.

Overhaul

18 Examine the steering gear assembly for signs of wear or damage, and check that the rack moves freely throughout the full length of its travel, with no signs of roughness or excessive free play between the steering gear pinion and rack. It is not possible to overhaul the steering gear assembly housing components, and if it is faulty the assembly must be renewed. The only components which can be renewed individually are the steering gear gaiters, the track rod end balljoints and the track rods, as described later in this Chapter.

Refitting

19 Locate the steering gear on the subframe, and insert the new mounting bolts. Make sure that the location dowel is correctly fitted. Tighten the bolts to the specified torque and Stage 2 angle.

20 Refit the power-assisted steering sensor together with a new seal to the steering gear pinion housing, and tighten the bolts.

21 Refit the hydraulic supply and return lines to the steering gear together with new copper washers, and tighten to the specified torque.

22 Raise the subframe and at the same time guide the steering gear pinion shaft through the rubber grommet in the floor. Align the subframe with the previously-made marks, then insert the new mounting bolts and tighten them to the specified torque and angle.

23 Align the engine/transmission rear mounting with the transmission unit and fit the new mounting bolts. Tighten the bolts to the specified torque and angle.

24 Refit the track rod ends to the steering arms, screw on the new nuts, and tighten them to the specified torque.

25 Refit the links to the anti-roll bar and tighten the nuts to the specified torque.

26 Where applicable, refit the exhaust front pipe with reference to Chapter 4C.

27 Secure the power-assisted steering sensor to the holder on the inner panel.

28 Refit the air filter and ducting with reference to Chapter 4A or 4B.

29 Refit the battery and battery tray with reference to Chapter 5A. **Note:** *On some models access to the hydraulic fluid reservoir is restricted by the battery, therefore delay refitting the battery until the hydraulic system has been bled.*

30 Working inside the car, locate the steering column universal joint on the pinion shaft, making sure that the cut-out is aligned with the bolt holes. Insert the new bolt and tighten to the specified torque.

31 Check that the rubber grommet is located correctly in the floor, then refit the plastic cover and secure with the screws.

32 Refit the engine compartment undershield and roadwheels, then lower the car to the ground. On completion check and, if necessary, adjust the front wheel alignment as described in Section 23.

33 Refill and bleed the hydraulic system as described in Section 20.

34 Have the system checked for fault codes by a Seat dealer or suitably-equipped specialist at the earliest opportunity.

19 Steering gear rubber gaiters and track rods – renewal

Steering gear rubber gaiters

1 Remove the track rod end balljoint as described in Section 22.

2 Note the fitted position of the gaiter on the track rod, then release the retaining clips and slide the gaiter off the steering gear housing and track rod.

3 Wipe clean the track rod and the steering gear housing, then apply a film of suitable grease to the surface of the rack. To do this, turn the steering wheel as necessary to fully extend the rack from the housing, then reposition it in its central position.

4 Carefully slide the new gaiter onto the track rod, and locate it on the steering gear housing. Position the gaiter as previously noted on removal, making sure that it is not twisted, then lift the outer sealing lip of the gaiter to equalise air pressure within the gaiter.

5 Secure the gaiter in position with new retaining clips. Where crimped-type clips are used, pull the clip as tight as possible, and locate the hooks in their slots. Remove any slack in the clip by carefully compressing the raised section. In the absence of the special crimping tool, a pair of side-cutters may be used, taking care not to cut the clip.

6 Refit the track rod end balljoint as described in Section 22.

Track rods

7 Remove the relevant steering gear rubber gaiter as described earlier. If there is insufficient working room with the steering gear mounted in the car, remove it as described in Section 18 and hold it in a vice while renewing the track rod.

8 Hold the steering rack stationary with one spanner on the flats provided, then loosen the balljoint nut with another spanner. Fully unscrew the nut and remove the track rod from the rack.

9 Locate the new track rod on the end of the steering rack and screw on the nut. Hold the rack stationary with one spanner and tighten the balljoint nut to the specified torque. A crow's foot adapter may be required since the track rod prevents access with a socket, and care must be taken to apply the correct torque in this situation.

10 Refit the steering gear or rubber gaiter with reference to the earlier paragraphs or Section 18. On completion check and, if necessary, adjust the front wheel alignment as described in Section 23.

20 Power steering system – bleeding

1 Apply the handbrake, then jack up the front of the car and support it on axle stands (see *Jacking and vehicle support*). Turn the front roadwheels to their straight-ahead position.

2 Unscrew the filler cap from the electric power steering hydraulic fluid reservoir and top-up the level to the MAX mark.

3 With the engine switched off, turn the steering from lock-to-lock ten times, then check and top-up the level again.

4 Screw on the filler cap loosely, then start the engine and allow it to idle for approximately 10 seconds.

5 Switch off the engine and top-up the fluid level.

6 Screw on the filler cap loosely, start the engine, and turn the steering from lock-to-lock ten times.

7 Switch off the engine and top-up the fluid level.

8 Repeat the procedure in paragraphs 6 and 7 until the fluid level no longer requires topping-up.

9 Refit and tighten the filler cap.

21 Electric power steering pump – removal and refitting

Removal

1 On models where access to the electric power steering hydraulic fluid reservoir is restricted by the battery, remove the battery and battery tray as described in Chapter 5A.

21.1 Electric power steering pump (arrowed) viewed with the front bumper removed

For improved access, remove the front bumper as described in Chapter 11 **(see illustration)**.

2 Unscrew the filler cap from the top of the hydraulic fluid reservoir on top of the electric power steering pump, then siphon all the fluid into a suitable container. Note that there will still be fluid in the system lines. Discard the removed fluid. **Note:** *Seat specifically state that a hose clamp must not be fitted to the hydraulic fluid line.*

3 Apply the handbrake, then jack up the front of the car and support it on axle stands (see *Jacking and vehicle support*). Remove the left-hand front roadwheel. Remove the engine undershield.

4 Remove the left-hand front wheel arch liner with reference to Chapter 11, Section 25.

5 On models with a radiator fan control unit, disconnect the wiring and unscrew the mounting nuts, then remove the radiator fan control unit from the car.

6 Release the support clip and remove the supply and return hydraulic lines from the inner body.

7 Locate a suitable container beneath the electric power steering pump to catch spilled hydraulic fluid.

8 Note their location, then disconnect the three wiring plugs from the electric power steering pump **(see illustration)**. The plugs are for the Data BUS and terminal 15, earth plug and terminal 30, and power steering sensor.

9 Unscrew the union nut and disconnect the pressure line from the pump. Recover the O-ring seal, then loosen the clip and disconnect the return line from the pump

22.4a Use an Allen key to hold the balljoint shank while loosening the nut

21.8 Wiring plugs (arrowed) on the electric power steering pump

reservoir. Tape over or plug the ends of the lines and the apertures in the steering gear to prevent entry of dust and dirt into the hydraulic system. The line ends can be wrapped in a plastic bag if preferred.

10 Unscrew the mounting bolts and lower the electric power steering pump and bracket from the underbody.

11 Unscrew the nuts/bolts and remove the mounting bracket from the pump. Where applicable, unscrew the rubber mountings from the pump.

Caution: The power steering control unit and the electric motor must not be separated.

Refitting

12 Refitting is a reversal of removal, but finally bleed the system as described in Section 20. At the earliest opportunity, have a Seat dealer or suitably-equipped specialist perform a system self-diagnosis and erase any fault codes.

---

22 Track rod end – removal and refitting

Note: *A new balljoint retaining nut will be required on refitting.*

Removal

1 Apply the handbrake, then jack up the front of the car and support it on axle stands (see *Jacking and vehicle support*). Remove the relevant roadwheel.

22.4b Use a balljoint separator to release the track rod balljoint

2 If the track rod end is to be re-used, mark its position in relation to the track rod to facilitate refitting.

3 Unscrew the track rod end locknut by a quarter of a turn. Do not move the locknut from this position, as it will serve as a handy reference mark on refitting.

4 Loosen and remove the nut securing the track rod end balljoint to the wheel bearing housing, and release the balljoint tapered shank using a universal balljoint separator. Note that the balljoint shank has a hexagon hole – hold the shank with an Allen key while loosening the nut **(see illustrations)**.

5 Counting the exact number of turns necessary to do so, unscrew the track rod end from the track rod **(see illustration)**.

6 Carefully clean the balljoint and the threads. Renew the balljoint if its movement is sloppy or too stiff, if excessively worn, or if damaged in any way; carefully check the stud taper and threads. If the balljoint gaiter is damaged, the complete balljoint assembly must be renewed; it is not possible to obtain the gaiter separately.

Refitting

7 Screw the track rod end onto the track rod by the number of turns noted on removal. This should bring the track rod end to within a quarter of a turn of the locknut, with the alignment marks that were made on removal (if applicable) lined up. Tighten the locknut.

8 Refit the balljoint shank to the steering arm on the wheel bearing housing, then fit a new retaining nut and tighten it to the specified torque. Hold the shank with an Allen key if necessary.

9 Refit the roadwheel, then lower the car to the ground and tighten the roadwheel bolts to the specified torque.

10 Check and, if necessary, adjust the front wheel toe setting as described in Section 23.

---

23 Wheel alignment and steering angles – general information

Definitions

1 A car's steering and suspension geometry

22.5 Unscrew the track rod end from the track rod

is defined in three basic settings – all angles are expressed in degrees; the steering axis is defined as an imaginary line drawn through the axis of the suspension strut, extended where necessary to contact the ground **(see illustration)**.

2 Camber is the angle between each roadwheel and a vertical line drawn through its centre and tyre contact patch, when viewed from the front or rear of the car. Positive camber is when the roadwheels are tilted outwards from the vertical at the top; negative camber is when they are tilted inwards.

3 Camber angle is only adjustable by loosening the front suspension subframe mounting bolts and moving it slightly to one side. This also alters the Castor angle. The camber angle can be checked using a camber checking gauge.

4 Castor is the angle between the steering axis and a vertical line drawn through each roadwheel's centre and tyre contact patch, when viewed from the side of the car. Positive castor is when the steering axis is tilted so that it contacts the ground ahead of the vertical; negative castor is when it contacts the ground behind the vertical. Slight castor angle adjustment is possible by loosening the front suspension subframe bolts and moving it slightly to one side. This also alters the Camber angle.

5 Castor is not easily adjustable, and is given for reference only; while it can be checked using a castor checking gauge, if the figure obtained is significantly different from that specified, the car must be taken for careful checking by a professional, as the fault can only be caused by wear or damage to the body or suspension components.

6 Toe is the difference, viewed from above, between lines drawn through the roadwheel centres and the car's centre-line. Toe-in is when the roadwheels point inwards, towards each other at the front, while toe-out is when they splay outwards from each other at the front.

7 The front wheel toe setting is adjusted by screwing the track rod(s) in/out of the outer balljoint(s) to alter the effective length of the track rod assembly.

8 Rear wheel toe setting is not adjustable, and is given for reference only. While it can be checked, if the figure obtained is significantly different from that specified, the car must be taken for careful checking by a professional, as the fault can only be caused by wear or damage to the body or suspension components.

Checking and adjustment

9 Due to the special measuring equipment necessary to check the wheel alignment, and the skill required to use it properly, the checking and adjustment of these settings is best left to a Seat dealer or similar expert. Note that most tyre-fitting centres now possess sophisticated checking equipment.

23.1 Steering geometry

Chapter 11
Bodywork and fittings

Contents

Degrees of difficulty

Easy, suitable for novice with little experience | **Fairly easy,** suitable for beginner with some experience | **Fairly difficult,** suitable for competent DIY mechanic | **Difficult,** suitable for experienced DIY mechanic | **Very difficult,** suitable for expert DIY or professional

Specifications

Torque wrench settings	Nm	lbf ft
Bonnet hinge bolts	23	17
Bonnet lock	10	7
Door lock retaining bolts	20	15
Door striker	20	15
Front bumper crossmember	30	22
Front door upper hinge nut*	14	10
Front door lower hinge bolts:*		
Stage 1	20	15
Stage 2	Angle-tighten a further 90°	
Front seat mounting retaining bolts	24	18
Rear bumper crossmember	30	22
Seat belt components:		
Front:		
Anchor rail (3-door):		
Front bolt	40	30
Rear bolt	23	17
Height adjuster bolts	23	17
Inertia reel lower mounting bolt	40	30
Inertia reel upper mounting bolt	8	6
Lower anchor bolt (5-door)	40	30
Stalk mounting bolt	40	30
Upper anchor bolt	40	30
Rear:		
All bolts except centre belt guide bolts	40	30
Centre belt guide bolts	23	17
Centre belt inertia reel mounting nut	40	30
Tailgate hinge	22	16
Tailgate lock mounting bolts	23	17
Tailgate lock striker bolts	22	16

* Do not re-use

1 General information

The body shell is made of pressed-steel sections, and is available in three- and five-door Hatchback versions. Most components are welded together, though double-skinned panels such as the bonnet and tailgate are created by press-fitting the metal sheet together with a mould and plunger – a process known as clinching. The front wings are bolted on, as is the front structure, for easier accident repair.

The body is fully galvanised, with high-strength steel used in the sills, front floorpans and the B-pillars. Laser welding is used on the roof where it joins the body side panels, instead of seam sealing after spot welding. Similarly, the doors are made from metal with a thin coating of epoxy resin, which means the edges self-seal during production.

Extensive use is made of plastic materials, mainly in the interior, but also in exterior components. The front and rear bumpers, and front grille are injection-moulded from a synthetic material that is very strong and yet light. Plastic components such as wheel arch liners are fitted to the underside of the car to improve the body's resistance to corrosion.

2 Maintenance – bodywork and underframe

The general condition of a car's bodywork is the one thing that significantly affects its value. Maintenance is easy, but needs to be regular. Neglect, particularly after minor damage, can lead quickly to further deterioration and costly repair bills. It is important also to keep watch on those parts of the car not immediately visible, for instance the underside, inside all the wheel arches, and the lower part of the engine compartment.

The basic maintenance routine for the bodywork is washing – preferably with a lot of water, from a hose. This will remove all the loose solids which may have stuck to the car. It is important to flush these off in such a way as to prevent grit from scratching the finish. The wheel arches and underside need washing in the same way, to remove any accumulated mud which will retain moisture and tend to encourage rust. Strange as it sounds, the best time to clean the underside and wheel arches is in wet weather, when the mud is thoroughly wet and soft. In very wet weather, the underside is usually cleaned of large accumulations automatically, and this is a good time for inspection.

Periodically, except on cars with a wax-based underbody protective coating, it is a good idea to have the whole of the underframe of the car steam-cleaned, engine compartment included, so that a thorough inspection can be carried out to see what minor repairs and renovations are necessary. Steam-cleaning is available at many garages, and is necessary for the removal of the accumulation of oily grime, which sometimes is allowed to become thick in certain areas. If steam-cleaning facilities are not available, grease solvents are available, which can be brush-applied; the dirt can then be simply hosed off. Note that these methods should not be used on cars with wax-based underbody protective coating, or the coating will be removed. Such cars should be inspected annually, preferably just prior to Winter, when the underbody should be washed down, and any damage to the wax coating repaired. Ideally, a completely fresh coat should be applied. It would also be worth considering the use of such wax-based protection for injection into door panels, sills, box sections, etc, as an additional safeguard against rust damage, where such protection is not provided by the car manufacturer.

After washing the paintwork, wipe off with a chamois leather to give an unspotted clear finish. A coat of clear protective wax polish will give added protection against chemical pollutants in the air. If the paintwork sheen has dulled or oxidised, use a cleaner/polisher combination to restore the brilliance of the shine. This requires a little effort, but such dulling is usually caused because regular washing has been neglected. Care needs to be taken with metallic paintwork, as special non-abrasive cleaner/polisher is required to avoid damage to the lacquer finish – also note that many 'solid' colours are in fact lacquered ('clear over base') these days. Always check that the door and ventilator opening drain holes and pipes are completely clear, so that water can be drained out. Brightwork should be treated in the same way as paintwork. Windscreens and windows can be kept clear of the smeary film which often appears, by the use of proprietary glass cleaner. Never use wax polish on the windscreen.

3 Maintenance – upholstery and carpets

Mats and carpets should be brushed or vacuum-cleaned regularly, to keep them free of grit. If they are badly stained, remove them from the car for scrubbing or sponging, and make quite sure they are dry before refitting.

Cloth or velour seats and interior trim panels can be kept clean by wiping with a damp cloth. If they do become stained (which can be more apparent on light-coloured cloth or velour upholstery), use a little liquid detergent and a soft nail brush to scour the grime out of the grain of the material. Keep the headlining clean in the same way as the upholstery.

In the case of leather upholstery, a whole range of different products exist to clean, feed and generally restore the leather, and it is recommended that these are used exclusively. Ordinary detergents should be avoided, as they will prematurely dry out leather, causing it to crack and split.

When using liquid cleaners inside the car, do not over-wet the surfaces being cleaned. Excessive damp could get into the seams and padded interior, causing stains, offensive odours or even rot. If the inside of the car gets wet accidentally, it is worthwhile taking some trouble to dry it out properly, particularly where carpets are involved. *Do not leave oil or electric heaters inside the car for this purpose.*

4 Minor body damage – repair

Minor scratches

If the scratch is very superficial, and does not penetrate to the metal of the bodywork, repair is very simple. Lightly rub the area of the scratch with a paintwork renovator, or a very fine cutting paste, to remove loose paint from the scratch, and to clear the surrounding bodywork of wax polish. Rinse the area with clean water.

In the case of metallic paint, the most commonly-found scratches are not in the paint, but in the lacquer top coat, and appear white. If care is taken, these can sometimes be rendered less obvious by very careful use of paintwork renovator (which would otherwise not be used on metallic paintwork); otherwise, repair of these scratches can be achieved by applying lacquer with a fine brush. Also note that damage to the lacquer coat will show up worse if (white) polish residue collects in the chip or scratch – clean any suspected area thoroughly.

Apply touch-up paint to the scratch using a fine paint brush; continue to apply fine layers of paint (allowing each one time to dry) until the surface of the paint in the scratch is level with the surrounding paintwork. Allow the new paint at least two weeks to harden, then blend it into the surrounding paintwork by rubbing the scratch area with a paintwork renovator or a very fine cutting paste. Finally, apply wax polish.

Where the scratch has penetrated right through to the metal of the bodywork, causing the metal to rust, a different repair technique is required. Remove any loose rust from the bottom of the scratch with a penknife, then apply rust-inhibiting paint, to prevent the formation of rust in the future. Using a rubber or nylon applicator, fill the scratch with bodystopper paste. If required, this paste can be mixed with cellulose thinners, to provide a very thin paste which is ideal for filling narrow scratches. Before the stopper-paste in the scratch hardens, wrap a piece of smooth cotton rag around the top of a finger. Dip the finger in cellulose thinners, and quickly sweep it across the surface of the stopper-paste in the scratch; this will ensure that the surface of the stopper-paste is slightly hollowed. The scratch can now be painted over as described earlier in this Section.

Dents

If the dent is shallow, and the paint has not been broken, it may be possible to have the dent repaired professionally, by one of the specialist mobile dent repair companies.

When deep denting of the car's bodywork has taken place, the first task is to pull the dent out, until the affected bodywork almost attains its original shape. There is little point in trying to restore the original shape completely, as the metal in the damaged area will have stretched on impact, and cannot be reshaped fully to its original contour. It is better to bring the level of the dent up to a point which is about 3 mm below the level of the surrounding bodywork. In cases where the dent is very shallow anyway, it is not worth trying to pull it out at all. If the underside of the dent is accessible, it can be hammered out gently from behind, using a mallet with a wooden or plastic head. Whilst doing this, hold a block of wood firmly against the outside of the panel, to absorb the impact from the hammer blows and thus prevent a large area of the bodywork from being 'belled-out'.

Should the dent be in a section of the bodywork which has a double skin, or some other factor making it inaccessible from behind, a different technique is called for. Drill several small holes through the metal inside the area – particularly in the deeper section. Then screw long self-tapping screws into the holes, just sufficiently for them to gain a good purchase in the metal. Now the dent can be pulled out by pulling on the protruding heads of the screws with a pair of pliers.

The next stage of the repair is the removal of the paint from the damaged area, and from an inch or so of the surrounding 'sound' bodywork. This is accomplished most easily by using a wire brush or abrasive pad on a power drill, although it can be done just as effectively by hand, using sheets of abrasive paper. To complete the preparation for filling, score the surface of the bare metal with a screwdriver or the tang of a file, or alternatively, drill small holes in the affected area. This will provide a really good 'key' for the filler paste.

To complete the repair, see the Section on filling and respraying.

Rust holes or gashes

Remove all paint from the affected area, and from an inch or so of the surrounding 'sound' bodywork, using an abrasive pad or a wire brush on a power drill. If these are not available, a few sheets of abrasive paper will do the job most effectively. With the paint removed, you will be able to judge the severity of the corrosion, and therefore decide whether to renew the whole panel (if this is possible) or to repair the affected area. New body panels are not as expensive as most people think, and it is often quicker and more satisfactory to

fit a new panel than to attempt to repair large areas of corrosion.

Remove all fittings from the affected area, except those which will act as a guide to the original shape of the damaged bodywork (e.g. light units). Then, using tin snips or a hacksaw blade, remove all loose metal and any other metal badly affected by corrosion. Hammer the edges of the hole inwards, in order to create a slight depression for the filler paste.

Wire-brush the affected area to remove the powdery rust from the surface of the remaining metal. Paint the affected area with rust-inhibiting paint; if the back of the rusted area is accessible, treat this also.

Before filling can take place, it will be necessary to block the hole in some way. This can be achieved by the use of aluminium or plastic mesh, or aluminium tape.

Aluminium or plastic mesh, or glass-fibre matting is probably the best material to use for a large hole. Cut a piece to the approximate size and shape of the hole to be filled, then position it in the hole so that its edges are below the level of the surrounding bodywork. It can be retained in position by several blobs of filler paste around its periphery.

Aluminium tape should be used for small or very narrow holes. Pull a piece off the roll, trim it to the approximate size and shape required, then pull off the backing paper (if used) and stick the tape over the hole; it can be overlapped if the thickness of one piece is insufficient. Burnish down the edges of the tape with the handle of a screwdriver or similar, to ensure that the tape is securely attached to the metal underneath.

Filling and respraying

Before using this Section, see the Sections on dent, deep scratch, rust holes and gash repairs.

Many types of bodyfiller are available, but generally speaking, those proprietary kits which contain a tin of filler paste and a tube of resin hardener are best for this type of repair. A wide, flexible plastic or nylon applicator will be found invaluable for imparting a smooth and well-contoured finish to the surface of the filler.

Mix up a little filler on a clean piece of card or board – measure the hardener carefully (follow the maker's instructions on the pack), otherwise the filler will set too rapidly or too slowly. Using the applicator, apply the filler paste to the prepared area; draw the applicator across the surface of the filler to achieve the correct contour and to level the surface. As soon as a contour that approximates to the correct one is achieved, stop working the paste – if you carry on too long, the paste will become sticky and begin to 'pick-up' on the applicator. Continue to add thin layers of filler paste at 20-minute intervals, until the level of the filler is just proud of the surrounding bodywork.

Once the filler has hardened, the excess can be removed using a metal plane or file.

From then on, progressively-finer grades of abrasive paper should be used, starting with a 40-grade production paper, and finishing with a 400-grade wet-and-dry paper. Always wrap the abrasive paper around a flat rubber, cork, or wooden block – otherwise the surface of the filler will not be completely flat. During the smoothing of the filler surface, the wet-and-dry paper should be periodically rinsed in water. This will ensure that a very smooth finish is imparted to the filler at the final stage.

At this stage, the 'dent' should be surrounded by a ring of bare metal, which in turn should be encircled by the finely 'feathered' edge of the good paintwork. Rinse the repair area with clean water, until all of the dust produced by the rubbing-down operation has gone.

Spray the whole area with a light coat of primer – this will show up any imperfections in the surface of the filler. Repair these imperfections with fresh filler paste or bodystopper, and once more smooth the surface with abrasive paper. If bodystopper is used, it can be mixed with cellulose thinners, to form a really thin paste which is ideal for filling small holes. Repeat this spray-and-repair procedure until you are satisfied that the surface of the filler, and the feathered edge of the paintwork, are perfect. Clean the repair area with clean water, and allow to dry fully.

The repair area is now ready for final spraying. Paint spraying must be carried out in a warm, dry, windless and dust-free atmosphere. This condition can be created artificially if you have access to a large indoor working area, but if you are forced to work in the open, you will have to pick your day very carefully. If you are working indoors, dousing the floor in the work area with water will help to settle the dust which would otherwise be in the atmosphere. If the repair area is confined to one body panel, mask off the surrounding panels; this will help to minimise the effects of a slight mis-match in paint colours. Bodywork fittings (e.g. chrome strips, door handles etc) will also need to be masked off. Use genuine masking tape, and several thicknesses of newspaper, for the masking operations.

Before commencing to spray, agitate the aerosol can thoroughly, then spray a test area (an old tin, or similar) until the technique is mastered. Cover the repair area with a thick coat of primer; the thickness should be built up using several thin layers of paint, rather than one thick one. Using 400-grade wet-and-dry paper, rub down the surface of the primer until it is really smooth. While doing this, the work area should be thoroughly doused with water, and the wet-and-dry paper periodically rinsed in water. Allow to dry before spraying on more paint.

Spray on the top coat, again building up the thickness by using several thin layers of paint. Start spraying at the top of the repair area, and then, using a side-to-side motion, work downwards until the whole repair area and about 2 inches of the surrounding original

6.1 Undo the bolts at the top of the bumper (arrowed) . . .

6.2 . . . and the ones at the rear ends of the bumper in the wheel arch each side (arrowed)

6.3 Undo the bolts (arrowed) each side under the bumper . . .

paintwork is covered. Remove all masking material 10 to 15 minutes after spraying on the final coat of paint.

Allow the new paint at least two weeks to harden, then, using a paintwork renovator or a very fine cutting paste, blend the edges of the paint into the existing paintwork. Finally, apply wax polish.

Plastic components

With the use of more and more plastic body components by the car manufacturers (e.g. bumpers, spoilers, and in some cases major body panels), rectification of more serious damage to such items has become a matter of either entrusting repair work to a specialist in this field, or renewing complete components. Repair of such damage by the DIY owner is not really feasible, owing to the cost of the equipment and materials required for effecting such repairs. The basic technique involves making a groove along the line of the crack in the plastic, using a rotary burr in a power drill. The damaged part is then welded back together, using a hot-air gun to heat up and fuse a plastic filler rod into the groove. Any excess plastic is then removed, and the area rubbed down to a smooth finish. It is important that a filler rod of the correct plastic is used, as body components can be made of a variety of different types (e.g. polycarbonate, ABS, polypropylene).

Damage of a less serious nature (abrasions, minor cracks etc) can be repaired by the DIY owner using a two-part epoxy filler repair. Once mixed in equal, this is used in similar

fashion to the bodywork filler used on metal panels. The filler is usually cured in twenty to thirty minutes, ready for sanding and painting.

If the owner is renewing a complete component himself, or if he has repaired it with epoxy filler, he will be left with the problem of finding a suitable paint for finishing which is compatible with the type of plastic used. At one time, the use of a universal paint was not possible, owing to the complex range of plastics encountered in body component applications. Standard paints, generally speaking, will not bond to plastic or rubber satisfactorily, but suitable paints to match any plastic or rubber finish, can be obtained from dealers. However, it is now possible to obtain a plastic body parts finishing kit which consists of a pre-primer treatment, a primer and coloured top coat. Full instructions are normally supplied with a kit, but basically, the method of use is to first apply the pre-primer to the component concerned, and allow it to dry for up to 30 minutes. Then the primer is applied, and left to dry for about an hour before finally applying the special-coloured top coat. The result is a correctly-coloured component, where the paint will flex with the plastic or rubber, a property that standard paint does not normally possess.

5 Major body damage – repair

Where serious damage has occurred, or large

areas need renewal due to neglect, it means that complete new panels will need welding-in, and this is best left to professionals. If the damage is due to impact, it will also be necessary to check completely the alignment of the body shell, and this can only be carried out accurately by a Seat dealer using special jigs. If the body is left misaligned, it is primarily dangerous, as the car will not handle properly, and secondly, uneven stresses will be imposed on the steering, suspension and possibly transmission, causing abnormal wear, or complete failure, particularly to such items as the tyres.

6 Front bumper – removal and refitting

Removal

Models up to 02/2006

1 Undo the 4 bolts at the top of the bumper (see illustration).
2 Working in the wheel arch either side, undo the 5 retaining bolts located on the rear ends of the bumper (see illustration).
3 Undo the 3 bolts each side at the lower edge of the bumper (see illustration).
4 Remove the 2 bolts at the front of the bumper (see illustration).
5 With the help of an assistant, carefully ease the rear ends of the bumper from the guides, and withdraw from the front of the car.
6 Disconnect the foglight wiring plugs (where fitted) and the headlight washer tubing (where fitted) as the bumper is withdrawn.
7 If required, unbolt the guides and cross-member from the front of the car.

Models from 03/2006

8 Undo the 4 bolts at the top of the bumper (see illustration).
9 Working in the wheel arch either side, undo the 5 retaining bolts located on the rear ends of the front bumper (see illustration).
10 Undo the 2 bolts each side at the lower edge of the bumper (see illustration).
11 Undo the 2 bolts at the centre, lower part of the bumper (see illustration).
12 With the help of an assistant, carefully ease the rear ends of the bumper from the

6.4 . . . and the bolt (arrowed) each side at the front of the bumper

6.8 Undo the bolts at the top of the bumper (arrowed)

guides, and withdraw from the front of the car **(see illustration)**. Disconnect the foglight wiring plugs (where fitted) and the headlight washer tubing (where fitted) as the bumper is withdrawn.

13 If required, unbolt the guides and cross-member from the front of the car.

Refitting

14 Refitting is a reversal of removal.

7 Rear bumper –
removal and refitting

Removal

1 Remove both body-mounted rear light units as described in Chapter 12.

2 Remove the 3 bumper mounting bolts below each rear light unit location **(see illustration)**.

3 Working in the rear wheel arches, undo the 4 mounting bolts from the ends of the rear bumper **(see illustration)**.

4 Remove the 3 mounting bolts each side underneath the bumper **(see illustration)**.

5 Lift the top edge of the bumper each side over the lugs, then with the help of an assistant, carefully pull the bumper rearwards, and withdraw it from the rear of the car with a sharp tug each side **(see illustration)**.

6 Disconnect the number plate light wiring plugs (release the retaining clips with a small screwdriver), and remove the bumper.

7 If required, unbolt the guides and cross-member from the rear of the car.

6.9 Remove the bolts (arrowed) each side in the wheel arch

6.11 . . . and the 2 in the centre (right-hand bolt arrowed)

Refitting

8 Refitting is a reversal of removal. Remember to reconnect the number plate light wiring before offering the bumper into place, and take care that the sides engage properly on

6.10 Undo the bolts (arrowed) each side . . .

6.12 Pull the rear ends of the bumper from the guides

the guides (press the ends in sideways as the bumper slides into place).

8 Radiator grille –
removal and refitting

Removal

1 The radiator grille must be cut from the bumper using a sharp craft knife, and when refitted the holding mounts must be melted using a hot air gun or similar. Begin by removing the front bumper as described in the previous Section.

2 Cut through the holding mounts with a sharp knife, and remove the grilles.

Refitting

3 Position the new grilles, then melt the holding mounts with a hot air gun.

9 Bonnet –
removal, refitting and adjustment

Removal

1 Open the bonnet, unclip the grommet, then trace the windscreen washer tubing up to the connector, and disconnect it. On certain models, it may be necessary to unclip the bonnet sound-deadening material for access. Similarly, where applicable, disconnect the heated washer jet wiring at the connector.

2 Using a pencil or felt tip pen, mark the

7.2 Undo the bolts (arrowed) in the lights aperture each side

7.3 Remove the bolts each side (arrowed) in the wheel arch . . .

7.4 . . . and the bolts (arrowed) each side underneath

7.5 Lift the bumper edges over the lugs (arrowed)

10.1a Use a small screwdriver . . .

10.1b . . . to prise out the handle retaining clip

10.4 Bonnet lock retaining bolts (arrowed)

10.5 Depress the clip (arrowed) and slide the outer cable from place

screwdriver, release the clip and pull the lever from position (see illustrations).

2 Remove the footwell trim panel on the driver's side as described in Section 29.

3 Pull the outer cable from place, and disconnect the inner cable end fitting from the operating lever mechanism.

4 Undo the 2 mounting bolts and lift the bonnet lock upwards a little (see illustration). Disconnect the wiring plug from the lock.

5 Unclip the outer cable, then disconnect the inner cable end fitting from the bonnet lock (see illustration).

6 Unclip the cable outer from the plastic bracket, then trace the cable back round the engine compartment, releasing it from the various clips.

7 Tie a length of string (approximately 1.0 m long) to the end of the cable inside the car, then withdraw the cable through into the engine compartment.

8 Once the cable is free, untie the string and leave it in position in the car; the string can then be used to draw the new cable back into position.

Refitting

9 Tie the inner end of the string to the end of the cable, then use the string to draw the bonnet release cable back from the engine compartment. Once the cable is through, untie the string.

10 The remaining refitting procedure is a reversal of removal. Ensure the cable is correctly routed and secured to all the relevant retaining clips. Before closing the bonnet, check the operation of the release lever and cable.

11 Bonnet lock – removal and refitting

Bonnet lock removal is described in Section 10.

12 Door – removal, refitting and adjustment

Note: The hinge bolts/nuts must always be renewed if loosened.

Removal

Front door

1 With the front door open, prise the wiring protector rubber boot from the A-pillar, then disconnect the door wiring.

2 Have an assistant support the front door, then unscrew the nut from the base of the top hinge pin (see illustration).

3 Unscrew the lower of the two splined socket-head bolts securing the lower hinge to the door (see illustration). Access to this bolt is not easy, and it is also tight – be sure to use good-quality tools, otherwise the bolt head may strip.

outline of each bonnet hinge relative to the bonnet, to use as a guide on refitting.

3 Have an assistant support the bonnet in its open position.

4 Unscrew the bonnet retaining bolts and carefully lift the bonnet clear. Store the bonnet out of the way in a safe place. If necessary, the grille and brackets can be unbolted from the bonnet.

5 Inspect the bonnet hinges for signs of wear and free play at the pivots, and if necessary renew them. Each hinge is secured to the body by two bolts; mark the position of the hinge on the body then undo the retaining bolts and remove it from the car.

Refitting and adjustment

6 Where removed, refit the bonnet hinges, and align them with the previously-made marks. Tighten the bolts securely.

7 With the aid of an assistant, offer up the

12.2 Unscrew the nut (arrowed) from the base of the top hinge pin

bonnet and loosely fit the retaining bolts. Align the hinges with the marks made on removal, then tighten the retaining bolts securely.

8 Close the bonnet, and check for alignment with the adjacent panels. If necessary, slacken the hinge bolts and re-align the bonnet. Adjust the height of the bonnet so that it is level with the surrounding front wings, by turning the rubber buffer at each front corner of the bonnet. Once the bonnet is correctly aligned, tighten the hinge bolts. Check that the bonnet fastens and releases satisfactorily.

10 Bonnet release cable – removal and refitting

Removal

1 Pull the bonnet release lever rearwards approximately 2 cm, then using a flat-bladed

12.3 Unscrew the lower of the two lower hinge bolts (arrowed)

12.13 Door lock striker bolts (arrowed)

4 Carefully lift the front door upwards from the hinges, and remove from the car.
5 Examine the hinges for signs of wear or damage. If renewal is necessary, mark the position of the hinge, then unscrew the retaining bolts and remove the hinge from the car. If there is a requirement to remove the top hinge from the front pillar, then the facia panel must be removed as described in Section 31. Fit the new hinge, aligning it with the marks made before removal, then tighten the retaining bolts to the specified torque.

Rear door

6 Remove the B-pillar trim panels as described in Section 29.
7 With the rear door open, prise the wiring protector rubber boot from the B-pillar, then disconnect the door wiring.
8 Have an assistant support the front door, then unscrew the nut from the base of the top hinge pin.

9 Unscrew the lower of the two splined socket-head bolts securing the lower hinge to the door. Access to this bolt is not easy, and it is also tight – be sure to use good-quality tools, otherwise the bolt head may strip.
10 Carefully lift the rear door upwards from the hinges, and remove from the car.
11 Examine the hinges for signs of wear or damage. If renewal is necessary, mark the position of the hinge, then unscrew the retaining bolts and remove the hinge from the car. Fit the new hinge, aligning it with the marks made before removal, then tighten the retaining bolts securely.

Refitting

12 Refitting is a reversal of removal. When refitting the hinges to the A- and B-pillars, align them with the previously-made marks before tightening the bolts. Check the door alignment and if necessary adjust as described in the following paragraph. If the paintwork around the hinges has been damaged, paint the area with a suitable touch-in brush to prevent corrosion.

Adjustment

13 To adjust the door to compensate for general wear in the hinges, this is best done by adjusting the position of the lock striker **(see illustration)**.
14 If adjusting the door after removal, close the door and check that the gap between the door and surrounding bodywork is equal around the complete perimeter. If necessary, slight adjustment of the door position can be made by slackening the hinge retaining

bolts and repositioning the hinge/door as necessary. If there is a requirement to loosen the top hinge on the door pillar (front doors only), then the facia panel must be removed as described in Section 31. Once the door is correctly positioned, tighten the hinge bolts. Check that the door striker engages centrally with the lock, and if necessary, adjust the position of the striker.

13 Door trim panel – removal and refitting

Note: *On models with electric windows, disconnect the battery as described in Chapter 5A.*

Removal

Front door

1 Carefully prise the trim panel from the side of the door pull handle location. Slide the switch panel upwards (driver's door), and undo the exposed bolts **(see illustrations)**.
2 Undo the 2 Torx bolts at the base of the door trim panel **(see illustration)**.
3 Carefully prise the door trim panel from the door, releasing the 6 retaining clips **(see illustration)**.
4 As the panel is withdrawn, unhook the cable from the interior release handle, and disconnect the various wiring plugs **(see illustration)**. On models with manually adjustable mirrors, undo the 3 Torx bolts and detach the remote control from the door trim as it's withdrawn **(see illustration)**.

13.1a Prise the trim panel from the driver's door pull handle . . .

13.1b . . . and slide up the switch panel

13.1c Undo the bolts in the handle recess (arrowed) – driver's side . . .

13.1d . . . and passenger's side (arrowed)

13.2 Undo the bolts (arrowed) at the base of the door trim

13.3 Pull the trim panel from the door to release the clips

13.4a Disconnect the various wiring plugs as the panel is removed

13.4b Disconnect the release handle cable

13.4c Undo the bolts (arrowed) and detach the mirror remote control

13.5 Slide the spacer ring (arrowed) across to release the spring

13.6 Prise the door handle cover from place

13.7 Undo the bolts (arrowed) in the handle recess

Rear door

5 On manual window models, with the window fully closed, note the position of the window crank, to ensure correct refitting. Slide the spacer ring (fitted between the handle and the door trim) 'across' or 'along' the handle to release the internal spring, then withdraw the crank handle from the splines on the regulator **(see illustration)**. The spacer ring will only move in one direction – not always the same one – and some trial-and-error may be needed to release it.

6 Remove the door pull handle cover by carefully prising it from place using a flat-bladed blunt tool **(see illustration)**.

7 Remove the two bolts now exposed by removing the door pull handle cover **(see illustration)**.

8 Starting at the bottom of the door, release the trim panel securing clips along the bottom and rear edges of the door.

Caution: Where applicable, take care when releasing the trim panel near the rear tweeter speaker, as the speaker wire is quite short, and can easily be snapped off – do not pull the panel away too far.

9 Lift the trim panel out of the window channel at the top of the door.

10 As the trim panel comes free, reach in behind and unhook the door lock operating cable from the handle, and disconnect the various wiring plugs.

Refitting

11 Refitting is a reversal of removal, noting the following points:

a) *The trim panel clips often get 'left behind' in the door, and should be transferred back to the panel before refitting it.*

b) *Once the trim panel wiring has been reconnected, check the operation of the door electrical equipment as applicable, before clipping the panel back in place.*

Also check the operation of the interior lock handle, once the operating cable has been reconnected.

14 Door handle and lock components – removal and refitting

Removal

Interior door handle

1 Remove the door trim panel as described in Section 13.

2 Unclip the optical connector and lamp (where fitted) from the handle.

3 Undo the 2 Torx bolts, and unclip the handle from the panel **(see illustration)**.

Front door handle and lock cylinder

4 With the front door open, prise out the rubber grommet on the door rear edge, nearest to the exterior door handle **(see illustration)**.

5 Fully pull out the exterior door handle, and hold it in this position, while at the same time unscrewing the lock cylinder locking bolt until it comes to a stop (approx 15 turns) with a multi-splined key.

6 Pull out the lock cylinder **(see illustration)**. If the lock cylinder is tight, use a small screwdriver to lever it out, but take care not to damage the paintwork. **Note:** *The passenger exterior door handle is fitted with a cover instead of a lock cylinder, but the cover is removed the same way. On older cars, the cylinder may be corroded into the door aperture, making it difficult to remove.*

14.3 Undo the bolts (arrowed) and remove the interior handle assembly

14.4 Prise out the rubber grommet, and undo the locking bolt (arrowed) approximately 15 turns . . .

14.6 . . . then pull out the lock cylinder

14.7a Disconnect the lock release cable . . .

14.7b . . . and swivel the exterior handle from the door

14.10 Undo the bolt approximately 6 turns . . .

14.11 and pull out the cap/housing

14.15a Release the clip on the rear of the lock . . .

7 Working through the lock cylinder aperture, disconnect the lock release cable from the handle, then manoeuvre the handle out from the door by swivelling it outwards **(see illustrations)**. Recover the gasket where fitted.
8 To remove the exterior door handle housing from the inside of the door, it is necessary to first remove the door lock and regulator assembly as described later, then undo the retaining bolts and withdraw the housing.

Rear door handle

9 With the rear door open, prise out the rubber grommet on the door rear edge.
10 Fully pull out the exterior door handle, and hold it in this position, while at the same time unscrewing the lock cylinder locking bolt approximately 6 turns with a multi-splined key **(see illustration)**. Do not undo the bolt further, as it may fall into the bottom of the door, requiring removal of the door lock and regulator assembly.
11 Pull out the housing and cap and remove it **(see illustration)**. If the housing is tight, use a small screwdriver to lever it out, but take care not to damage the paintwork.
12 Working through the aperture, disconnect the lock release cable from the handle then manoeuvre the handle out from the door by swivelling it outwards. Recover the gasket, where fitted **(see illustrations 14.7a and 14.7b)**.
13 To remove the exterior door handle housing from the inside of the door, it is necessary to first remove the door lock and regulator assembly as described later, then undo the retaining bolts and withdraw the housing.

14.15b . . . and the front (arrowed) . . .

Front and rear door locks

14 Remove the door window regulator and lock assembly as described in Section 15.
15 Unclip the lock from the bracket, then disconnect the cable **(see illustrations)**.

15.2 Lock securing bolts at the edge of the door

14.15c . . . then disconnect the cable

16 The door lock cannot be dismantled, and must be renewed complete if faulty.

Refitting

17 Refitting is a reversal of removal.

15 Window regulator and lock carrier – removal and refitting

Note: *The window regulator mechanism is part of the carrier, and cannot be obtained individually.*

Removal

1 Remove the door inner trim panel as described in Section 13.
2 Remove the exterior door handle as described in Section 14, then undo the multi-spline bolts securing the door lock to the rear edge of the door **(see illustration)**.

15.3 Prise open the rubber grommet(s)

15.4a Window glass retaining clamp bolt (front door)

15.4b Window glass retaining roll-pin (rear door)

15.6 Use suitable bolts to remove the inner and outer roll-pins (rear door)

15.7 Retain the window glass with adhesive tape

15.8 Window regulator/lock carrier retaining bolts (arrowed)

3 Prise the rubber grommet(s) from the hole(s) in the carrier, for access to the window glass retaining bolts or roll-pin. The front door has two holes for access to the retaining clamp bolts, and the rear door has one hole for access to the single roll-pin (see illustration).
4 Lower the window glass until the bolts or plastic retaining roll-pin are visible in the hole (see illustrations). On models with electric windows, temporarily reconnect the battery and control switch to operate the glass, then disconnect the battery again. If the electric motor is not functioning correctly, unbolt the motor from the carrier to allow the window to be lowered.
5 On the front door, slacken the two clamp bolts.
6 On the rear door, screw an M5 bolt approximately 70 mm long into the inner roll-pin, then use pliers to pull it out of the

outer section. Similarly, screw an M8 bolt approximately 80 mm long into the outer roll-pin, and use the pliers to pull it out (see illustration). This will disconnect the window glass from the regulator.
7 Lift the window glass to the top of the door and use adhesive tape to retain it in this position (see illustration).
8 Undo the bolts securing the carrier to the door frame (see illustration).
9 Carefully withdraw the carrier and disconnect the wiring plugs. Also, release the wiring harness from the cable-ties. Remove the carrier from the door (see illustration).

Refitting

10 To ensure correct adjustment of the door lock cable on the exterior door handle, the door lock must be set as follows. Pull out the control lever and use a screwdriver to hook

the spring onto the lever (see illustration). When the exterior door handle is refitted and operated, the spring will be released.
11 Before refitting the rear carrier, refit and centralise the plastic retaining roll-pins to the window glass so that the glass can be tapped down to engage the regulator (see illustration). Although it is possible to refit the pins with the carrier in position, it is far easier to centralise the pins with the carrier removed. In practice, we removed the glass completely from the door to fit the pins (see Section 16). Note that on models with electric windows, the pins must be aligned with the lug.
12 With the glass retained with the adhesive tape, refit the carrier and reconnect the wiring. At this stage retain the carrier with only two bolts, so that the operation of the lock can be checked before fitting the remainder.
13 Remove the tape and lower the glass

15.9 Pull the front edge inwards, then slide the carrier forwards and manoeuvre it from the door

15.10 Hook the spring onto the control lever

15.11 On the rear door, refit and centralise the plastic retaining roll-pins to the window glass

onto the regulator. Tighten the bolts on the front door. On the rear door, gently tap the top edge of the glass until the retaining pin is heard to engage the clip on the regulator (see illustration). Refit the rubber grommet(s).
14 Refit the exterior door handle with reference to Section 14, then refit and tighten the door lock mounting bolts.
15 Before shutting the door for the first time, operate the lock with a screwdriver and check that it is functioning correctly.
16 Fit the remaining carrier bolts.
17 Refit the door inner trim panel with reference to Section 13.

16 Door window glass – removal and refitting

Removal

Front door window
1 Remove the door inner trim panel as described in Section 13.
2 Prise the rubber grommet(s) from the hole(s) in the carrier, for access to the window glass retaining bolts or roll-pin. The front door has two holes for access to the retaining clamp bolts.
3 Lower the window glass until the bolts are visible in the hole. On models with electric windows, temporarily reconnect the battery and control switch to operate the glass, then disconnect the battery again. If the electric motor is not functioning correctly, unbolt the motor from the carrier to allow the window to be lowered.
4 Slacken the two clamp bolts.
5 Lift the window glass to the top of the door and use adhesive tape to retain it in this position. Fully lower the regulator, then tilt the glass and withdraw it from the outside of the door.

Rear door window
6 Remove the window regulator and lock carrier as described in the previous Section.
7 Pull the triangular trim panel forwards, undo the bolt now exposed, remove the outer trim and the bolt securing the window riser guide.
8 Pull the inner rear window trim strip up from the base of the window aperture, and carefully prise out the window rubber seal from the window aperture. Manoeuvre the window upwards from the door.

Refitting
9 Refitting is a reversal of removal.

17 Tailgate and support struts – removal and refitting

Tailgate
Removal
1 Open the tailgate, then prise out the panels behind the tailgate lights and the lock surround panel.
2 Remove the 5 bolts securing the tailgate trim panel (see illustrations).
3 Pull the panel away from the tailgate to release the retaining clips.
4 Disconnect all wiring connectors from inside the tailgate, and disconnect the washer hose from the rear wiper motor (see Chapter 12). Also, prise all wiring grommets from the tailgate.
Note: On later models, a wiring multiconnector is provided near the left-hand support strut, which can be disconnected instead of removing the wiring.
5 Tie a piece of string to each end of the wiring then, noting the correct routing of the wiring harness, release the harness rubber grommets from the tailgate and withdraw the wiring. When the end of the wiring appears, untie the string and leave it in position in the tailgate; it can then be used on refitting to draw the wiring into position.
6 Using a suitable marker pen, draw around the outline of each hinge, marking its correct position on the tailgate (see illustration).
7 With the help of an assistant to support the tailgate, remove the support struts as described below.
8 Unscrew and remove the bolts securing the hinges to the tailgate. Protect the surrounding paintwork with adhesive tape. Where necessary, recover the gaskets which are fitted between the hinge and body.
9 Inspect the hinges for signs of wear or damage and renew if necessary.

15.13 On the rear door, gently tap the glass until the retaining pin engages

Refitting
10 Refitting is a reversal of removal, but tighten the tailgate mounting bolts to the specified torque. Check the tailgate alignment with the surrounding panels. If necessary, slight adjustment can be made by slackening the retaining bolts and repositioning the tailgate on its hinges.

Support struts

⚠️ **Warning: The support struts are filled with gas, and must be disposed of safely.**

Removal
11 With the help of an assistant, support the tailgate in the open position.
12 Using a small screwdriver, lift the locking clip and pull the gas support strut off its balljoint mounting on the tailgate (see

17.2a Undo the bolt (arrowed) in each light access aperture . . .

17.2b . . . one each side of the lock (arrowed) . . .

17.2c . . . and one in the handle recess (arrowed)

17.6 Tailgate hinge bolts

17.12 Prise out the locking clips

illustration). Repeat the procedure on the lower strut mounting and remove the strut from the body. **Note:** *If the gas strut is to be re-used, the locking clip must not be taken all the way out, or the clip will be damaged.*

18.2a Disconnect the operating rod (arrowed)

18.10 Prise the rod from the lock

18.11b . . . and remove the outer handle . . .

Refitting

13 Refitting is a reversal of removal.

18 Tailgate lock components – removal and refitting

Lock

1 Remove the tailgate trim panel as described in the previous Section.
2 Disconnect the wiring plug, then unclip the lock operating rod. Remove the 2 bolts and withdraw the lock from the tailgate **(see illustrations)**.
3 Refitting is a reversal of removal.

Lock striker

4 Remove the tailgate aperture trim panel as described in Section 29.

18.2b Lock retaining bolts (arrowed)

18.11a Undo the 3 nuts (arrowed) . . .

18.11c . . . followed by the lock cylinder assembly

5 Mark around the striker with paint (such as typist's correction fluid) to ensure it is accurately refitted.
6 Unscrew the two mounting bolts, and withdraw the striker from the tailgate aperture.
7 Refitting is a reversal of removal. Align the striker with the previously-made marks, and tighten the bolts to the specified torque.

Lock cylinder assembly

8 Remove the tailgate trim panel as described in the previous Section.
9 Disconnect the wiring plug from the lock motor.
10 Unclip and disconnect the lock operating rod **(see illustration)**.
11 Undo the 3 nuts and manoeuvre the outer handle, lock cylinder assembly/motor from place **(see illustrations)**.
12 Undo the 2 bolts and remove the lock motor **(see illustration)**.
13 The lock cylinder is not available separately from the bracket, etc. If defective, the complete assembly must be renewed. Consult a Seat dealer.
14 Refitting is a reversal of removal.

Tailgate handle

15 Remove the tailgate trim panel as described in the previous Section.
16 Undo the 3 retaining nuts, and withdraw the handle from the tailgate **(see illustration 18.11a and 18.11b)**.
17 Refitting is a reversal of removal.

Lock motor

18 Removal of the motor is described within the lock cylinder assembly removal as described earlier in this Section.

19 Central locking components – general

The operation of the central locking is integrated into the door locks, and is controlled by the comfort system central module, located above the driver's pedals under the facia. Removal is described in Chapter 12. If a fault

18.12 Lock motor bolts (arrowed)

occurs in the system, the car should be taken to a Seat dealer or specialist who will have the special diagnostic equipment necessary to find the fault quickly. The control unit also operates the alarm, sunroof, electric windows and exterior mirrors.

20 Electric window components – removal and refitting

Window switch

1 Refer to Chapter 12.

Window winder motor

Removal

2 Remove the door inner trim panel as described in Section 13.
3 Disconnect the wiring from the motor.
4 Undo the mounting bolts and withdraw the motor from the regulator carrier (see illustration).

Refitting

5 Refitting is a reversal of removal. On completion, switch the ignition on and off, then switch it on again. Close the window and continue to press the switch for approximately 5 seconds, then fully lower the window and continue to press the switch for at least 5 seconds in order to complete the basic setting and activate the 'one-touch' function. Finally, switch off the ignition.

21 Exterior mirrors and associated components – removal and refitting

Mirror assembly

1 Remove the door inner trim panel as described in Section 13 – this is necessary to gain access to the mirror wiring plug.
2 Unclip and remove the mirror inner trim panel (see illustration).
3 Pull out the mirror wiring, and disconnect the plug.
4 Support the mirror, then unscrew the mounting bolt and withdraw the mirror from the outside of the door (see illustration).
5 Refitting is a reversal of removal.

20.4 Window winder motor mounting bolts (arrowed)

Mirror glass

6 Push the glass fully into the housing at the top, so that the lower edge is sticking out. Insert a wide, flat-bladed tool (wrapped with tape to protect the housing) into the gap between the glass and mirror housing, and unclip the lower edge. If necessary, pull out the glass at the top, and repeat this process to unclip the upper edge (see illustrations).
7 Disconnect the wiring connectors from the mirror heating element (where fitted), and remove the glass.
8 Refitting is a reversal of removal. Press the glass firmly at the centre, using a wad of cloth and taking care not to use excessive force, as the glass is easily broken.

Mirror front housing

9 Remove the mirror glass as previously described.
10 Release the 4 retaining clips and pull the

21.2 Pull the mirror inner trim panel from the door frame

21.6a Gently lever away the lower edge of the mirror glass . . .

21.6b . . . to release the clips

mirror housing forwards from position (see illustration).
11 Refitting is a reversal of removal.

Mirror switch

12 Refer to Chapter 12.

Mirror motor

13 Remove the mirror glass as described above.
14 Undo the retaining bolts and remove the motor, disconnecting its wiring connector as it becomes accessible.
15 Refitting is a reversal of removal.

22 Hinged rear side window (3-door) – removal, refitting and adjustment

Removal

1 Open the window, and have an assistant support it. Alternatively, tape it securely to the car.
2 Carefully unclip the trim strip from the front edge of the window, and pull it forwards.
3 Remove the single vertical pivot bolt from the rear hinge/catch.
4 Unscrew the two hinge bolts at the front, and withdraw the window from the car.

Refitting

5 Refitting is a reversal of removal. Renew the exterior trim adhesive strip. Check the operation of the window, and if necessary adjust it as described below.

21.4 Mirror mounting bolt (arrowed)

21.10 Squeeze together the clips (arrowed) to remove the housing

Adjustment

6 Remove the C-pillar trim panel as described in Section 29.

7 Refit the hinge/catch pivot bolt, which will have been removed during removal of the C-pillar trim panel.

8 Loosen the single bolt which secures the hinge/catch to the glass by two turns.

9 Similarly, loosen the two bolts securing the hinge/catch to the body.

10 Close the window (if not already done), then have an assistant press the glass firmly closed against the rubber seal. While this is being done, tighten the three loosened bolts securely.

11 Once the adjustment is complete, remove only the pivot bolt from the hinge/catch to refit the C-pillar trim panel.

23 Windscreen, tailgate and fixed rear quarter window glass – general information

These areas of glass are bonded in position with a special adhesive. Renewal of such fixed glass is a difficult, messy and time-consuming task, which is beyond the scope of the home mechanic. It is difficult, unless one has plenty of practice, to obtain a secure, waterproof fit. In view of this, owners are strongly advised to have this work carried out by one of the many specialist windscreen fitters.

24 Sunroof – general information

Due to the complexity of the sunroof mechanism, considerable expertise is needed to repair, renew or adjust the sunroof components successfully. Removal of the roof first requires the headlining to be removed, which is a complex and tedious operation, and not a task to be undertaken lightly. Therefore, any problems with the sunroof should be referred to a Seat dealer. On models with an electric sunroof, if the sunroof motor fails to operate, first check the relevant fuse. If the fault cannot be traced and rectified, the sunroof can be opened and closed manually using an

25.1 Wheel arch liner retaining bolts (arrowed)

Allen key to turn the motor spindle (a suitable key is supplied with the car, and should be clipped onto the inside of the sunroof motor trim). To gain access to the motor, unclip the rear of the trim cover to open. Unclip the Allen key, then insert it fully into the motor opening (against spring pressure). Rotate the key to move the sunroof to the required position.

25 Body exterior fittings – removal and refitting

Wheel arch liners and body under-panels

1 The various plastic covers fitted to the underside of the car are secured in position by a mixture of bolts, nuts and retaining clips, and removal will be fairly obvious on inspection **(see illustration)**. Work methodically around the panel removing its retaining bolts and releasing its retaining clips until the panel is free and can be removed from the underside of the car. Most clips used on the car are simply prised out of position. Remove the wheels to ease the removal of the wheel arch liners.

2 On refitting, renew any retaining clips that may have been broken on removal, and ensure that the panel is securely retained by all the relevant clips and bolts.

Body trim strips and badges

3 The various body trim strips and badges (including the door entrance plates on certain

models) are held in position with a special adhesive tape and locating lugs. Removal requires the trim/badge to be heated to soften the adhesive, and then carefully lifted away from the surface. Due to the high risk of damage to the paintwork during this operation, it is recommended that this task should be entrusted to a Seat dealer.

26 Seats – removal and refitting

Note: *Refer to the warnings in Chapter 12 if side airbags are fitted.*

Removal

Front seats

1 On models with side airbags, disconnect the battery negative lead as described in Chapter 5A.

2 Slide the seat fully forwards, then unscrew the rear mounting bolts securing the sliding rail to the floor, using a multi-spline key **(see illustration)**.

3 Slide the seat fully rearwards, and unscrew the front mounting bolts **(see illustration)**.

4 Tilt the seat backwards and disconnect the wiring plugs for the side airbag, seat heating and seat belt buckle signalling, as applicable.

5 Carefully remove the seat from inside the car, taking care not to damage the surrounding trim panels. The help of an assistant may be necessary, as the seat is heavy.

Rear seat cushion

6 Pull up the front of the rear seat cushion, then lift the rear and fold the cushion forwards.

7 Push the hooks from the pivot brackets and remove the cushion from the car **(see illustration)**.

Rear seat backrest

8 Fold the rear seat cushion forwards.

9 Where an inertia reel centre seat belt is fitted in the backrest, unscrew the anchorage bolt from the floor.

10 Pull up the locking handle to release the relevant backrest section, and fold it forwards.

26.2 Front seat rear mounting bolts (arrowed)

26.3 Front seat front mounting bolts (arrowed)

26.7 Push the hooks (arrowed) towards each other and remove the seat cushion

26.11 Depress the catch hook with a screwdriver

11 Using a screwdriver, depress the catch hook and pull the backrest pivot pin from the side bracket **(see illustration)**.

12 Slide the backrest from the pivot pin on the centre bracket and remove it from the car **(see illustration)**. If necessary, remove the plastic cap from the bracket.

Rear seat armrest

13 Pull up the locking handle to release the backrest section, and fold it forwards.

14 Unlock the armrest housing and remove it together with the armrest from the backrest.

Refitting

15 Refitting is a reversal of removal.

---

27 Front seat belt tensioning mechanism – general information

The front seat belt inertia reels are fitted with integral automatic belt tensioners (the rear seat belt inertia reels are not fitted with tensioners). The system is designed to instantaneously take up any slack in the seat belt in the case of a sudden frontal impact, therefore reducing the possibility of injury to the front seat occupants.

The seat belt tensioner is triggered by a frontal impact above a predetermined force. Lesser impacts, including impacts from behind, will not trigger the system. If the impact is sufficient to trigger the airbags, the seat belt tensioners will also be deployed.

When the system is triggered, the explosive gas in the tensioner mechanism retracts and locks the seat belt through a cable which acts on the inertia reel. This prevents the seat belt moving and keeps the occupant firmly in position in the seat. Once the tensioner has been triggered, the seat belt will be permanently locked and the assembly must be renewed.

Note the following warnings before contemplating any work on the front seat belts.

⚠ *Warning: Do not expose the tensioner mechanism to temperatures in excess of 100°C.*
• *If the tensioner mechanism is dropped, it must be renewed, even it has suffered no apparent damage.*

• *Do not allow any solvents to come into contact with the tensioner mechanism.*
• *Do not attempt to open the tensioner mechanism as it contains explosive gas.*
• *Tensioners must be discharged before they are disposed of, but this task should be entrusted to a Seat dealer.*
• *If the battery is to be disconnected, refer to Chapter 5A.*

28 Seat belt components – removal and refitting

Front seat belt

⚠ *Warning: The seat belt inertia reel incorporates a pyrotechnic automatic tensioner; do not subject the unit to temperatures in excess of 100°C, or allow any solvents or cleaning agents to contact the unit. The unit is sensitive to impact; if it is dropped or damaged, it should be renewed.*

1 Disconnect the battery negative lead as described in Chapter 5A.

2 Remove the door sill trim panel as described in Section 29.

3-door models

3 Remove the B-pillar upper trim panel as described in Section 29.

4 Remove the large front and smaller rear bolt from the belt anchor rail, collecting the washer fitted to the front bolt **(see illustration)**. Slide the looped end of the belt

---

26.12 Slide the backrest from the pivot pin

off the rail, and feed it through the B-pillar trim panel.

5 Unscrew the seat belt upper anchor bolt, and separate the anchor plate from the height adjuster **(see illustration)**.

6 Unbolt the seat belt guide (where fitted) from the B-pillar.

7 Disconnect the wiring plug for the seat belt tensioner from the inertia reel. Remove the upper and lower mounting bolts, and withdraw the inertia reel assembly from the base of the B-pillar **(see illustrations)**. Remove the seat belt from the car.

8 Refitting is a reversal of removal. Tighten all bolts to the specified torque, where given.

5-door models

9 Remove both B-pillar trim panels as described in Section 29.

10 Fold back the carpet and remove the seat belt lower anchor bolt, and remove the anchor

---

28.4 Seat belt anchor rail retaining bolts (arrowed)

28.5 Undo the seat belt upper anchor bolt (arrowed)

28.7a Prise out the locking clip (arrowed) and disconnect the wiring plug

28.7b Inertia reel lower mounting bolt (arrowed)

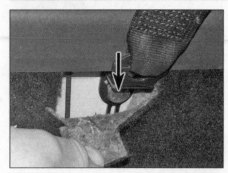

28.10 Front seat belt lower anchorage bolt (arrowed)

28.12 Front seat belt upper anchorage bolt (arrowed)

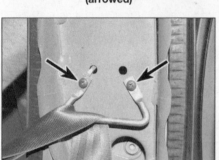

28.13 Seat belt guide bolts (arrowed)

28.14 Seat belt inertia reel mounting bolt and nut (arrowed)

28.20 Seat belt height adjuster bolts (arrowed)

28.29 Seat belt lower anchorage bolt (arrowed)

28.32 Rear side belt inertia reel bolt (arrowed)

28.35 Use a small screwdriver to push in the clip and remove the headrest guide tubes

plate from the floor mounting, noting how it fits over its locating pin (see illustration).
11 Feed the end of the belt and the anchor plate through the B-pillar trim panel.
12 Unscrew the seat belt upper anchor bolt,

and separate the anchor plate from the height adjuster (see illustration).
13 Unbolt the seat belt guide from the B-pillar (see illustration).
14 Disconnect the wiring plug for the seat

belt tensioner from the inertia reel. Remove the mounting bolt and nut, then withdraw the inertia reel assembly from the base of the B-pillar (see illustration). Remove the seat belt from the car.
15 Refitting is a reversal of removal. Tighten all bolts to the specified torque, where given.

Front height adjuster

16 Remove the door sill trim panel as described in Section 29.
17 On 3-door models, remove the B-pillar upper trim panel and the rear side trim panel as described in Section 29.
18 On 5-door models, remove both B-pillar trim panels as described in Section 29.
19 Unscrew the seat belt upper anchor bolt, and separate the anchor plate from the height adjuster.
20 Unscrew the height adjuster upper and lower mounting bolts, and remove the adjuster from the B-pillar (see illustration).
21 Refitting is a reversal of removal. Tighten all bolts to the specified torque.

Front belt stalk

22 Remove the front seat assembly as described in Section 26.
23 Where necessary, undo the bolts and remove the plastic cover from the inner side of the seat.
24 Disconnect the wiring from the seat occupancy monitor and stalk buckle indicator (where applicable), and unclip the wiring from under the seat.
25 Unscrew the stalk mounting bolt and remove the stalk from the seat.
26 Refitting is a reversal of removal. Tighten the mounting bolt to the specified torque.

Rear side belt

27 Fold the rear seat cushion forwards.
28 Remove the parcel shelf support panel, as described in Section 29. On 5-door models, also remove the C-pillar trim panel, and the rear door aperture trim panel.
29 Unscrew and remove the rear belt lower anchor bolt from the floor (see illustration). Feed the end of the belt through the trim panel.
30 Fold down the rear seat backrest.
31 Unscrew the bolt, and remove the belt upper anchor plate (where fitted), noting the spacer and washer fitted behind it.
32 Unscrew the inertia reel mounting bolt, and remove the seat belt from the car (see illustration).
33 Refitting is a reversal of removal. Tighten all bolts to the specified torque.

Rear centre belt

34 Remove the rear seat backrest as described in Section 26.
35 With the backrest on the bench, remove the headrests, then remove the headrest guides using a small screwdriver to depress the locking tabs (see illustration).
36 Prise out the plastic covers from the top of the backrest (see illustrations).

28.36a Remove the rear . . .

28.36b . . . and front cover from around the seat belt

28.37 Pull out the beading to remove the cover from the rear of the backrest

37 Pull out the beading and remove the cover from the rear of the backrest **(see illustration)**.

38 Unscrew the mounting nut and remove the reel from the backrest **(see illustration)**.

39 A cable-operated safety mechanism is fitted to the backrest, to ensure that the backrest is fully locked in position before allowing the seat belt buckle to be inserted. To remove the mechanism, release the clip from the locking lever **(see illustration)**.

40 Refitting is a reversal of removal.

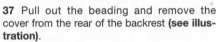

29 Interior trim and fittings – removal and refitting

28.38 Rear seat centre belt inertia reel mounting nut (arrowed)

28.39 Cable-operated safety mechanism to ensure the backrest is locked before using the seat belt

General

1 The interior trim panels are secured by a combination of clips and bolts, with metal and plastic clips featuring heavily – these clips often get 'left behind' in the bodywork when the panels are removed, and should be prised out for refitting to the panels. Removal and refitting is generally self-explanatory, noting that it may be necessary to remove or loosen surrounding panels to allow a particular panel to be removed. The following paragraphs describe the removal and refitting of the major panels in more detail.

Door inner trim panels

2 Refer to Section 13.

Steering column shrouds

3 To remove the upper shroud completely requires the instrument panel to be removed first, as described in Chapter 12. In most cases, however, complete removal will not be necessary.

4 Remove the steering wheel as described in Chapter 10.

5 Use a small screwdriver to release the clip on either side securing the upper shroud to the lower shroud **(see illustrations)**. Fold the upper shroud upwards without straining it.

6 Working from above, remove the upper bolt on either side securing the lower shroud **(see illustration)**.

7 From underneath the steering column, remove the third bolt from the lower shroud,

located just in front of the column height adjuster lever **(see illustration)**.

8 Remove the lower shroud, manoeuvring it out past the column height adjuster lever, and over the ignition switch.

9 Refitting is a reversal of removal.

29.5a Depress the clip (arrowed) each side . . .

29.5b . . . and lift the upper shroud

29.6 Undo the bolt (arrowed) each side . . .

29.7 . . . and one (arrowed) underneath

29.12 Depress the clips (arrowed) and pull the diagnostic socket from the panel

29.18a Pull out the hinge pin each side . . .

29.18b . . . and remove the glovebox lid

29.19 Glovebox retaining bolts (arrowed)

29.22 Starting at the top, pull the pillar trim inwards to release the clips

Lower facia trim panel

Driver's side

10 Undo the 3 bolts at the rear edge securing the panel to the facia.
11 Pull the panel rearwards to release the 2 retaining clips.
12 Unclip the diagnostic socket as the panel is withdrawn (see illustration).
13 Refitting is a reversal of removal.

Passenger's side

14 Undo the 4 bolts and remove the lower facia trim panel.
15 Pull the panel rearwards to release the front clip, and remove it.
16 Refitting is a reversal of removal.

Glovebox

17 Remove the passenger's lower facia trim panel as described previously in this Section.
18 Carefully prise the panel from the end of the

facia, then pull out the hinge pin at each end, and remove the glovebox lid (see illustrations).
19 Undo the 3 bolts and remove the glovebox from the facia (see illustration). Disconnect the airbag switch plug as the glovebox is removed.
20 Refitting is a reversal of removal.

A-pillar trim panels

21 On models with head airbags, prise out the airbag emblem, and remove the bolt exposed.
22 The A-pillar trim panels are held in place by three clips along their length. Start at the top of the panel, and pull the panel towards the facia to release the clips (see illustration). Lift the panel to free the lugs at the base from the facia, and remove it.
23 Refitting is a reversal of removal. Transfer any clips back onto the panel as necessary before refitting.

Sill trim panels

3-door models

24 Remove the rear side panel as described in this Section.
25 Starting at one end, carefully prise up the sill trim panel to release the row of 7 clips securing it to the door sill, then prise out the rear clip and pull the panel inwards to release the 3 rear side clips (see illustration). The clips are quite stiff to release, and some effort will be required.
26 Refitting is a reversal of removal. Transfer any clips back onto the panel as necessary before refitting, and fold the rubber weatherstrip over the panel edges.

5-door models

27 Note that, in many cases, it will not be necessary to remove the complete panel, which runs in one piece across both doors. Use the information here as required.
28 To remove the panel completely, fold forward the rear seat cushion. Also partially unclip the rear wheel arch trim panel at the base.
29 At the rear of the panel, prise out the rearmost securing clip.
30 Working at each end in turn, prise up the panel to release the clips, working towards the B-pillar in the centre (see illustration). The clips are quite stiff to release, and some effort will be required.
31 Unclip the sill trim panel from the base of the B-pillar trim panel, and the front sill, then remove it from the car.
32 Refitting is a reversal of removal. Transfer any clips back onto the panel as necessary before refitting, and fold the rubber weatherstrip over the panel edges.

Footwell side trim panels

33 Unclip the front part of the sill trim panel – it should not be necessary to remove the sill trim completely.
34 If working on the driver's side, use a screwdriver to carefully unclip the bonnet release handle – insert the blade at the top, from the front side of the handle (see illustrations 10.1a and 10.1b).
35 Pull the panel into the footwell to release the clips, and remove it (see illustration).
36 Refitting is a reversal of removal. Transfer

29.25 Prise out the clip at the rear of the sill trim panel

29.30 Pull the sill trim panel upwards to release the clips

29.35 Pull the footwell panel inwards to release the clips

29.39 Undo the bolts (arrowed) at the base of the B-pillar trim panel

29.40 Pull the panel gently downwards to disengage the clips

29.42 Pull the top of the lower B-pillar trim panel inwards to release the clips

29.45 Undo the bolts (arrowed) at the lower edge of the panel

29.46 Pull the trim panel downwards to disengage the clips (arrowed)

any clips back onto the panel as necessary before refitting.

B-pillar trim panels

37 Detach the rubber weatherstrip from the B-pillar as necessary to free the edges of the trim panel.

3-door models

38 Remove the rear side trim panel as described in this Section.
39 Undo the 2 bolts at the base of the pillar trim panel **(see illustration)**.
40 On models with a head airbag, carefully prise out the airbag emblem at the top of the trim, undo the bolt exposed. On all models, pull the panel downwards to remove it **(see illustration)**. If required, undo the seat belt anchor as described in Section 28, and feed the belt through the trim panel.
41 Refitting is a reversal of removal. Tighten

the front seat belt anchor rail bolts to the specified torques (where applicable).

5-door models – lower panel

42 Starting at the top, pull the trim panel into the car to release the clips **(see illustration)**. Slide the panel upwards from the sill panel.
43 Refitting is a reversal of removal.

5-door models – upper panel

44 Remove the lower panel as previously described in this Section.
45 Undo the 2 bolts at the lower edge of the panel **(see illustration)**.
46 Carefully prise out the airbag emblem at the top of the trim, undo the bolt exposed (only on models with headlining airbag), then pull the panel downwards to remove it **(see illustration)**.
47 Using the information in Section 28, unbolt the front seat belt anchor plate from

the floor. Feed the end of the seat belt through the panel, and it can be removed completely.
48 Refitting is a reversal of removal. Tighten the front seat belt lower anchor bolt to the specified torque.

Rear trim panels

C-pillar trim panel – 3-door models

49 Remove the rear side trim panel as described in this Section.
50 Carefully prise down the trim strip from the rear of the headlining **(see illustration)**.
51 Carefully prise up the tailgate sill trim panel, and sill side trims **(see illustrations)**.
52 Using the information in Section 28, unbolt the rear side seat belt anchor plate from the floor – this is so that the rear seat belt can be fed through the panel if complete removal is required.

29.50 Pull down the trim panel at the rear of the headlining

29.51a Pull up the tailgate sill trim panel . . .

29.51b . . . then pull the sill side trim inwards to release the clips

29.53a Undo the bolts (arrowed) at the rear of the parcel shelf support . . .

29.53b . . . and the one (arrowed) at the front

29.54a Remove the bolts (arrowed) at the base of the C-pillar trim panel . . .

C-pillar trim panel – 5-door models

56 Remove the rear seat backrest as described in Section 26.
57 Undo the 2 plastic nuts, and pull the lower C-pillar trim panel inwards to release the clips **(see illustrations)**.
58 Carefully prise down the trim strip from the rear of the headlining **(see illustration 29.50)**.
59 Carefully prise up the tailgate sill trim panel, and sill side trims **(see illustrations 29.51a and 29.51b)**.
60 Undo the 3 bolts and remove the parcel shelf support bracket **(see illustration)**.
61 Undo the 4 bolts and pull the pillar trim panel inwards to release the clips **(see illustrations)**.

29.54b . . . the one (arrowed) at the top . . .

29.54c . . . then pull the panel inwards

53 Undo the 3 bolts and remove the parcel shelf support bracket **(see illustrations)**.
54 Undo the 3 bolts and remove the C-pillar trim panel **(see illustrations)**.
55 Refitting is a reversal of removal, noting

the following points:
a) Transfer any clips back onto the panel as necessary before refitting.
b) Tighten the rear seat belt lower anchor bolt to the specified torque.

Rear side trim panel – 3-door models

62 Remove the rear seat as described in Section 26.
63 Unscrew the 2 retaining clips at the rear of the panel **(see illustration)**.

29.57a Unscrew the plastic nuts (arrowed) . . .

29.57b . . . and pull the panel inwards to release the clips (arrowed)

29.60 Undo the bolts (arrowed) and remove the parcel shelf support

29.61a Undo the bolts (arrowed) at the base of the C-pillar trim panel . . .

29.61b . . . and the bolt (arrowed) at the top

29.63 Unscrew the clips (arrowed) at the rear of the panel

64 Pull the panel inwards to release the retaining clips. Disconnect any wiring plugs as the panel is withdrawn.

65 Refitting is a reversal of removal, noting the following points:

a) Refit the surround to the bass speaker, if it came loose or was removed with the panel.

b) Transfer any clips back onto the panel as necessary before refitting.

Luggage area trim panels

Parcel shelf support panel

66 Partially unclip the tailgate aperture trim panel, where it meets the back of the parcel shelf support. Fold away the carpet from the side of the luggage area. Disconnect the wiring plugs for the power socket and boot light, where applicable **(see illustrations 29.51a and 29.51b)**.

67 Remove the three bolts securing the parcel shelf support panel to the side and rear of the car **(see illustrations 29.53a and 29.53b)**.

68 Unclip the panel by pulling it into the car **(see illustration)**. If the panel is to be completely removed, undo the seat belt lower anchorage bolt as described in Section 28.

69 Refitting is a reversal of removal.

Luggage area side trim panel

70 Remove the tailgate aperture trim panel as described later in this Section.

71 Fold the rear seat cushion and backrest forwards, and lift out the boot floor covering.

72 On 3-door models, remove the rear side trim panel as described in this Section.

73 On all models, remove the parcel shelf support panel as previously described.

74 Prise out the 2 clips and pull the panel into the car.

75 Refitting is a reversal of removal.

Tailgate aperture trim panel

76 Fold the rear seat backrest forwards, and lift up the boot floor covering.

77 Lift the sill trim panel upwards to free it from the tailgate seal, and remove it **(see illustration 29.51a)**.

78 Working on each side panel in turn, unclip the tops of the panel towards each other. Pull the panels upwards to release the lower clip **(see illustration 29.51b)**.

79 Refitting is a reversal of removal. Transfer any clips back onto the panel as necessary before refitting, and fold the rubber weatherstrip over the panel edges.

Tailgate trim panel

80 Open the tailgate, then prise out the panels behind the tailgate lights and the lock surround panel.

81 Remove the 5 bolts securing the tailgate trim panel **(see illustrations 17.2a, 17.2b and 17.2c)**.

82 Pull the panel away from the tailgate to release the retaining clips. Note that it's quite likely the clips will be damaged during removal. Obtain replacements for refitting.

83 The tailgate window surround panel (where fitted) is secured by clips along its

29.68 Pull the parcel shelf support panel inwards

length – two at each side, and five along the top. Starting at one end, carefully prise the panel with a wide-bladed screwdriver and progressively release all the clips.

84 Refitting is a reversal of removal.

Carpets

85 The passenger compartment floor carpet is in several pieces, and is secured along the edges by various types of clips.

86 Carpet removal and refitting is reasonably straightforward, but time-consuming, due to the fact that all adjoining trim panels must be released, and the seats and centre console must be removed.

Grab handles

87 Fold the grab handle down, away from the roof, then carefully prise down the bolt covers using a small screwdriver **(see illustration)**.

88 Unscrew and remove the single bolt at each end of the handle, and remove it from the roof.

89 Refitting is a reversal of removal.

Sun visors

Side visors

90 Unclip the visor from the inner support, then move it for the best access to the outer mounting.

91 Carefully prise out the bolt cap from the outer mounting, then remove the bolt and withdraw the mounting and sun visor from the roof **(see illustration)**. Where applicable, disconnect the wiring plug for the vanity mirror illumination.

92 To remove the inner support, carefully prise off the cover, then remove the two

29.91 Remove the sun visor mounting bolt (arrowed)

29.87 Prise down the grab handle bolt covers (arrowed)

bolts and withdraw the mounting from the headlining **(see illustration)**.

93 Refitting is a reversal of removal.

Centre visor

94 Fold the centre visor (where fitted) down towards the windscreen, to access the single securing bolt.

95 Remove the bolt, and withdraw the centre visor from the headlining.

96 Refitting is a reversal of removal.

Headlining

97 The headlining is clipped to the roof, and can be withdrawn only once all fittings such as the grab handles, sun visors, sunroof, A-, B- and C-pillar trim panels, and associated components have been removed. The door, tailgate and sunroof aperture weatherseals will also have to be prised clear.

98 Note that headlining removal requires considerable skill and experience if it is to be carried out without damage, and is therefore best entrusted to an expert.

99 On models equipped with side curtain airbags, note that the curtain airbag units are contained within the headlining, and it may therefore be dangerous to proceed with removing the headlining unless the battery is first disconnected (see Chapter 5A).

Interior mirror

With rain sensor

100 On models with rain-sensitive wipers, carefully unclip the left and right halves of the mirror trim, then disconnect the wiring plug inside.

29.92 Prise off the sun visor inner support cover to access the bolts (arrowed)

29.103 Rotate the mirror base 90° anti-clockwise

29.104 Offer the mirror at 90° to the base and twist it on

101 According to Seat, the mirror is removed by sliding it downwards to release the spring clip in the base. It seems quite likely that this will un-bond the bonded mirror base from the windscreen – if this happens on a model with a rain sensor, the base will have to be refitted by a Seat dealer, or the sensor will not work properly.

102 Refitting is a reversal of removal.

Without rain sensor

103 Rotate the mirror base 90° anti-clockwise to release it from the mounting base (see illustration).

104 Refitting is a reversal of removal. Offer the mirror up to the base, twisted round

approximately 90° anti-clockwise. Engage the mirror onto the base, then twist it 90° clockwise to secure (see illustration).

30 Centre console – removal and refitting

Removal

Manual transmission

1 Starting at the front edge, carefully prise up and remove the gear lever surround gaiter and trim (see illustration).

Automatic transmission

2 Pull the selector lever sleeve surround downwards, and pull the knob upwards to remove it (see illustration).

3 Carefully prise up the lever surround trim panel, and remove it. Disconnect any wiring plugs as the panel is withdrawn.

All models

4 Carefully prise up and remove the trim panel beneath the handbrake lever (see illustration).

5 Open the rear ashtray, and lift it from place. On models without a rear ashtray, prise up and remove the rear cup holder (see illustration).

6 Fully apply the handbrake, then insert a flat-bladed screwdriver into the underside of the handbrake lever, and pivot the screwdriver forwards to release the lever grip (see illustration).

7 Undo the 2 bolts at the front of the gear/selector lever aperture, and the 2 bolts in the rear ashtray/cup holder aperture (see illustrations).

8 At the front of the console, the 'legs' either side tuck under the facia, and are attached to it by Velcro strips. Gently pull the facia panels sideways to detach them.

9 Press the front of the console down slightly, to release the pegs on the driver's and passenger's lower facia panels, and slide the console back slightly. Lift the console upwards

30.1 Starting at the front edge, prise up the gear lever surround

30.2 Pull the sleeve (2) down, then pull the knob (1) upwards. Prise at the points arrowed to remove the lever surround trim panel

30.4 Remove the trim beneath the handbrake lever

30.5 Prise up and remove the rear cup holder

30.6 Insert a screwdriver, and pivot it forwards to release the lever grip

30.7a Undo the bolts in the gear lever/ selector aperture (arrowed) . . .

to clear the handbrake lever, and remove it from the car **(see illustration)**. Disconnect any wiring plugs as the console is withdrawn. If the console will not clear the handbrake lever, even when it is fully applied, it may be necessary to loosen the handbrake adjuster (behind the lever) by a few turns, so the lever will go higher.

Refitting

10 Refitting is a reversal of removal. If necessary, re-adjust the handbrake as described in Chapter 9.

31 Facia panel assembly – removal and refitting

Note: *This is a difficult procedure, carried out in two stages – removing the plastic facia panel, and then the large metal crossmember underneath it. Both facia sections have to be removed, for example, to gain access to the heater assembly. It is strongly recommended that this Section is read through thoroughly before starting the procedure.*

⚠️ **Warning: Remove the ignition key, disconnect both battery leads, negative first (see Chapter 5A). If this precaution is not observed, there is danger of activating the airbags and seat belt tensioners.**

Removal

Facia panel

1 Disconnect the battery negative lead (refer to Chapter 5A).

30.7b . . . and the bolts at the rear (arrowed)

2 Remove the steering wheel as described in Chapter 10.
3 Remove the steering column switches, lighting switch, instrument panel and radio unit as described in Chapter 12.
4 Remove the centre console as described in Section 30.
5 Remove the A-pillar trim panels, driver's and passenger's lower facia trim panel, and the glovebox, as described in Section 29.
6 Remove the passenger's airbag unit as described in Chapter 12.
7 Undo the 2 bolts securing the facia bracket to the crossmember in front of the passenger's airbag location.
8 Open the front doors, then carefully prise off the facia end panels using a flat-bladed screwdriver **(see illustration)**.
9 Remove the two bolts securing the fusebox to the driver's end of the facia panel, and move it clear **(see illustration)**.

31.8 Prise the end covers from the facia

31.11 Undo the bolts (arrowed) in the glovebox aperture

31.12 Undo the bolts (arrowed) in the centre aperture

30.9 Lift the rear of the console and manoeuvre it over the handbrake lever

10 Remove the heater or climate control panel (as applicable) as described in Chapter 3.
11 Undo the 3 bolts in the glovebox aperture **(see illustration)**.
12 Undo the 5 bolts in the centre facia aperture **(see illustration)**.
13 Remove the 5 bolts at each end of the facia **(see illustration)**. Note that one bolt is set vertically.
14 Prise up the cover from the solar sensor from the centre of the facia top, undo the retaining bolt, lift the sensor and disconnect the wiring plug.
15 Check that all wiring and retaining bolts have been removed, then, with the help of an assistant, withdraw the facia from the bulkhead and remove from one side of the car. Disconnect any remaining wiring plugs as the facia is withdrawn. The front of the facia may be tight on the front guides located just behind the windscreen.

31.9 Remove the fusebox retaining bolts (arrowed)

31.13 Undo the bolts (arrowed) at each end of the facia

31.18 Windscreen vent retaining bolts (arrowed)

31.19 Remove the duct over the driver's footwell

31.22 Undo the bolts (arrowed) securing the right-hand support bracket to the crossmember

31.23 Crossmember retaining bolts (arrowed) on the driver's side

Crossmember

16 Remove the facia panel as described previously in this Section.

17 Referring to Chapter 10 if necessary, remove the bolts securing the steering column to the crossmember, and lower the column into the footwell.

18 Remove the windscreen ventilation duct by removing the 2 central bolts (see illustration).

19 Remove the bolt securing the ventilation duct over the driver's footwell, and release the duct from the crossmember (see illustration).

20 Reach down in front of the crossmember and remove the three bolts securing the relay box at the right-hand end – move the box clear of the crossmember.

21 Release the facia panel wiring harness from the crossmember at the central supports, noting how it is routed.

22 Remove three bolts from the crossmember's central side support, two more bolts from the two central support legs near the floor, and two adjacent to the heater blower motor (see illustration).

23 The crossmember is now held by three main bolts – two on the driver's side, one on the passenger's (see illustration). Remove the bolts, and with the help of an assistant, withdraw the crossmember into the car. Note that the crossmember is removed leaving the right-hand support bracket attached to the heater assembly.

Refitting

24 Refitting is a reversal of the removal procedure, noting the following points:

a) Make sure the wiring is correctly routed and connected, and secure where necessary with cable-ties. Refit all the facia fasteners, and tighten them securely.

b) On completion, check that all the electrical components and switches function correctly. As a precaution against the airbags being activated, make sure no one is sitting in the car as the battery is being reconnected.

Body electrical systems

Chapter 12
Body electrical systems

Contents

Degrees of difficulty

Easy, suitable for novice with little experience	**Fairly easy,** suitable for beginner with some experience	**Fairly difficult,** suitable for competent DIY mechanic	**Difficult,** suitable for experienced DIY mechanic	**Very difficult,** suitable for expert DIY or professional

Specifications

System type................................ 12 volt negative-earth

Fuses................................ See *Wiring diagrams* commencing on page 12•17

Bulbs	Wattage	Type
Direction indicators	21	PY Bayonet
Door warning light	5	Festoon
Foglight:		
Front	55	H3 Halogen
Rear	21	Bayonet
Glovebox light	3	Wedge
Headlight:		
Single reflector (main/dipped beam)	60/55	H4 Halogen
Double reflector:		
Main beam	55	H3 Halogen
Dipped beam	55	H7 Halogen
High-level stop-light	N/A	LED
Interior light	10	Festoon
Luggage compartment light	5	Wedge
Number plate light	5	Wedge
Reading light	5	Festoon
Reversing light	21	Bayonet
Sidelight	5	Wedge
Stop/tail light (body-mounted)	21/5	Bayonet
Tail light (tailgate-mounted)	5	Wedge

Torque wrench setting	Nm	lbf ft
Airbag (passenger)	10	7

1 General information and precautions

⚠️ *Warning: Before carrying out any work on the electrical system, read through the precautions given in Safety first! at the beginning of this manual, and in Chapter 5A.*

The electrical system is of 12 volt negative-earth type. Power for the lights and all electrical accessories is supplied by a lead-acid type battery, which is charged by the alternator.

This Chapter covers repair and service procedures for the various electrical components not associated with the engine. Information on the battery, alternator and starter motor can be found in Chapter 5A.

It should be noted that prior to working on any component in the electrical system, the ignition and all electrical consumers must be switched off. Additionally, where stated, the battery negative lead must be disconnected, however, note the information given in Chapter 5A, as special procedures have to be carried out when reconnecting the battery.

2 Electrical fault finding – general information

Note: *Refer to the precautions given in Safety first! and in Chapter 5A before starting work. The following tests relate to testing of the main electrical circuits, and should not be used to test delicate electronic circuits (such as anti-lock braking systems), particularly where an electronic control module is used.*

General

1 A typical electrical circuit consists of an electrical component, any switches, relays, motors, fuses, fusible links or circuit breakers related to that component, and the wiring and connectors which link the component to both the battery and the chassis. To help to pinpoint a problem in an electrical circuit, wiring diagrams are included at the end of this Chapter.

2 Before attempting to diagnose an electrical fault, first study the appropriate wiring diagram to obtain a complete understanding

2.20a Battery negative lead earth connection (arrowed)

of the components included in the particular circuit concerned. The possible sources of a fault can be narrowed down by noting if other components related to the circuit are operating properly. If several components or circuits fail at one time, the problem is likely to be related to a shared fuse or earth connection.

3 Electrical problems usually stem from simple causes, such as loose or corroded connections, a faulty earth connection, a blown fuse, a melted fusible link, or a faulty relay (refer to Section 3 for details of testing relays). Visually inspect the condition of all fuses, wires and connections in a problem circuit before testing the components. Use the wiring diagrams to determine which terminal connections will need to be checked in order to pinpoint the trouble spot.

4 The basic tools required for electrical fault finding include a circuit tester or voltmeter (a 12 volt bulb with a set of test leads can also be used for certain tests); a self-powered test light (sometimes known as a continuity tester); an ohmmeter (to measure resistance); a battery and set of test leads; and a jumper wire, preferably with a circuit breaker or fuse incorporated, which can be used to bypass suspect wires or electrical components. Before attempting to locate a problem with test instruments, use the wiring diagram to determine where to make the connections.

5 To find the source of an intermittent wiring fault (usually due to a poor or dirty connection, or damaged wiring insulation), a wiggle test can be performed on the wiring. This involves wiggling the wiring by hand to see if the fault occurs as the wiring is moved. It should be possible to narrow down the source of the fault to a particular section of wiring. This method of testing can be used in conjunction with any of the tests described in the following sub-Sections.

6 Apart from problems due to poor connections, two basic types of fault can occur in an electrical circuit – open-circuit, or short-circuit.

7 Open-circuit faults are caused by a break somewhere in the circuit, which prevents current from flowing. An open-circuit fault will prevent a component from working, but will not cause the relevant circuit fuse to blow.

8 Short-circuit faults are caused by a short somewhere in the circuit, which allows the current flowing in the circuit to escape along an alternative route, usually to earth. Short-circuit faults are normally caused by a breakdown in wiring insulation, which allows a feed wire to touch either another wire, or an earthed component such as the bodyshell. A short-circuit fault will normally cause the relevant circuit fuse to blow.

Finding an open-circuit

9 To check for an open-circuit, connect one lead of a circuit tester or voltmeter to either the negative battery terminal or a known good earth.

10 Connect the other lead to a connector in the circuit being tested, preferably nearest to the battery or fuse.

11 Switch on the circuit, bearing in mind that

some circuits are live only when the ignition switch is moved to a particular position.

12 If voltage is present (indicated either by the tester bulb lighting or a voltmeter reading, as applicable), this means that the section of the circuit between the relevant connector and the battery is problem-free.

13 Continue to check the remainder of the circuit in the same fashion.

14 When a point is reached at which no voltage is present, the problem must lie between that point and the previous test point with voltage. Most problems can be traced to a broken, corroded or loose connection.

Finding a short-circuit

15 To check for a short-circuit, first disconnect the load(s) from the circuit (loads are the components which draw current from a circuit, such as bulbs, motors, heating elements, etc).

16 Remove the relevant fuse from the circuit, and connect a circuit tester or voltmeter to the fuse connections.

17 Switch on the circuit, bearing in mind that some circuits are live only when the ignition switch is moved to a particular position.

18 If voltage is present (indicated either by the tester bulb lighting or a voltmeter reading, as applicable), this means that there is a short circuit.

19 If no voltage is present, but the fuse still blows with the load(s) connected, this indicates an internal fault in the load(s).

Finding an earth fault

20 The battery negative terminal is connected to earth – the metal of the engine/transmission and the car body – and most systems are wired so that they only receive a positive feed, the current returning through the metal of the car body. This means that the component mounting and the body form part of that circuit. Loose or corroded mountings can therefore cause a range of electrical faults, ranging from total failure of a circuit, to a puzzling partial fault. In particular, lights may shine dimly (especially when another circuit sharing the same earth point is in operation), motors (eg, wiper motors or the radiator cooling fan motor) may run slowly, and the operation of one circuit may have an apparently unrelated effect on another. Note that on many cars, earth straps are used between certain components, such as the engine/transmission and the body, usually where there is no metal-to-metal contact between components due to flexible rubber mountings, etc **(see illustrations)**.

21 To check whether a component is properly earthed, disconnect the battery (refer to the warnings given in the Reference section at the rear of the manual) and connect one lead of an ohmmeter to a known good earth point. Connect the other lead to the wire or earth connection being tested. The resistance reading should be zero; if not, check the connection as follows.

22 If an earth connection is thought to be faulty, dismantle the connection and clean back to bare metal both the bodyshell and the wire terminal or the component earth connection mating surface. Be careful to remove all traces of dirt and corrosion, then use a knife to trim away any paint, so that a clean metal-to-metal joint is made. On reassembly, tighten the joint fasteners securely; if a wire terminal is being refitted, use serrated washers between the terminal and the bodyshell to ensure a clean and secure connection. When the connection is remade, prevent the onset of corrosion in the future by applying a coat of petroleum jelly or silicone-based grease or by spraying on (at regular intervals) a proprietary ignition sealer or a water dispersant lubricant.

3 Fuses and relays – general information

Fuses and fusible links

1 Fuses are designed to break a circuit when a predetermined current is reached, in order to protect the components and wiring which could be damaged by excessive current flow. Any excessive current flow will be due to a fault in the circuit, usually a short-circuit (see Section 2).

2 The main fuses are located in the fusebox on the driver's side of the facia. Open the driver's door and prise out the fusebox cover from the end of the facia to gain access to the fuses (see illustration). The fuse locations are marked onto the inside of the fusebox cover.

3 To remove a fuse, first switch off the circuit concerned (or the ignition), then pull the fuse out of its terminals (see illustration).

4 The wire within the fuse should be visible; if the fuse has blown it will be broken or melted.

5 Always renew a fuse with one of the correct rating, never use a fuse with a different rating from that specified.

6 Refer to the wiring diagrams for details of the fuse ratings and the circuits protected. The fuse rating is stamped on the top of the fuse, the fuses are also colour-coded as follows.

Colour	Rating
Light brown	5A
Dark brown	7.5A
Red	10A
Blue	15A
Yellow	20A
White	25A
Green	30A

7 Never renew a fuse more than once without tracing the source of the trouble. If the new fuse blows immediately, find the cause before renewing it again; a short to earth as a result of faulty insulation is most likely. Where a fuse protects more than one circuit, try to isolate the fault by switching on each circuit in turn (where possible) until the fuse blows again. Always carry a supply of spare fuses of each relevant rating on the car.

8 Additional heavy-duty fusible links are located in the fuse holder which is fitted to the

2.20b Earth connection on the left-hand front suspension turret (arrowed) . . .

top of the battery. Unclip and open the fuse holder cover to gain access to these links (see illustration).

9 To renew a fusible link, first disconnect the battery negative terminal. Unscrew the retaining nuts then remove the blown link from the holder. Fit the new link to its terminals and reconnect the lead. Ensure the link and lead are correctly seated then refit the retaining nuts and tighten securely. Clip the cover back into position then reconnect the battery.

Relays

10 A relay is an electrically-operated switch, which is used for the following reasons:

a) A relay can switch a heavy current remotely from the circuit in which the current is flowing, allowing the use of lighter-gauge wiring and switch contacts.

b) A relay can receive more than one control input, unlike a mechanical switch.

3.2 Prise the fusebox cover from the end of the facia

3.8 Open the cover on the top of the battery to access the fusible links

2.20c . . . beneath the heater assembly (arrowed) . . .

2.20d . . . and on the steering column (arrowed)

c) A relay can have a timer function – for example, the intermittent wiper relay.

11 Most of the relays are located on the relay plate behind the driver's side facia. Remove the driver's side storage compartment to access the relays (see illustration).

3.3 Pull the fuse from its terminals

3.11 Fold down the driver's storage compartment and disengage the hinges

4.4a Slacken the switch clamp bolt (arrowed)

4.4b Slide up the locking element (arrowed) and pull the wiring plug from the switch

4.5 Depress the tab and release the clips (arrowed)

4.7 Turn the switch to position 0 and pull it from the facia

12 If greater access to the relays is required, unclip the panel from the driver's end face of the facia, and undo the 2 bolts securing the fusebox, and move it to one side.

13 If a circuit or system controlled by a relay develops a fault, and the relay is suspect, operate the system. If the relay is functioning, it should be possible to hear it click as it is energised. If this is the case, the fault lies with the components or wiring of the system. If the relay is not being energised, then either the relay is not receiving a main supply or a switching voltage, or the relay itself is faulty. Testing is by the substitution of a known good unit, but be careful – while some relays are identical in appearance and in operation, others look similar but perform different functions.

14 To remove a relay, first ensure that the relevant circuit is switched off. The relay can then simply be pulled out from the socket, and pushed back into position.

4 Switches – removal and refitting

Ignition switch/steering lock

1 Refer to Chapter 10.

Steering column switches

2 Remove the steering wheel as described in Chapter 10 – this involves first removing the driver's airbag, as described in Section 22.

3 Remove the steering column shrouds as described in Chapter 11, Section 29, then apply adhesive tape to the airbag contact unit slip-ring to prevent accidental rotation.

4 Loosen the switch clamp bolt on top, disconnect the wiring plug on the side by sliding the locking element upwards, and pull the switch assembly from the column (see illustrations).

5 If necessary, depress the release tabs and separate the airbag contact unit from the switch assembly (see illustration).

6 Refitting is a reversal of removal.

Lighting switch

7 With the light switch in position 0, press the switch centre inwards and turn it slightly to the right. Hold this position and pull the switch from the facia (see illustration).

8 As the switch is withdrawn from the facia, disconnect the wiring plug.

9 Refitting is a reversal of removal. Insert the switch into the facia until it is heard to lock in place. Check the switch for correct operation.

Headlight range control

10 Remove the lighting switch as previously described.

11 Lift the securing tabs and remove the switch from the panel.

12 Refitting is a reversal of removal.

Instrument lighting dimmer

13 Proceed as described previously in this Section for the headlight range control switch.

Sliding roof/interior light switch

14 Carefully prise out the interior light lens (see illustration 6.2).

15 Undo the 2 bolts, then release the clips at the front of the light unit. Note that the switch is only available with the rest of the light and switch assembly.

16 Refitting is a reversal of removal.

Electric mirror switch

17 Remove the door trim panel as described in Chapter 11.

18 Press-in the retaining clips each side and remove the switch.

19 Refitting is a reversal of removal.

Central locking switch

20 The switch is located on the same panel as the interior door handle, and must be removed from behind, with the door trim panel removed as described in Chapter 11. Do not try to prise the switch out from the front.

21 With the door trim panel removed, use a very slim screwdriver to free the retaining tabs on each side of the switch, and withdraw it from the back of the panel (see illustration).

22 Refitting is a reversal of removal.

Electric window switches

Driver's side

23 Using a wide-bladed tool and starting at the front, carefully prise the door pull handle trim from place (see illustration).

24 Slide the switch panel upwards from the door trim panel, and disconnect the wiring plug(s) (see illustration).

25 The switch assemblies can be removed from the panel after releasing their locating tabs (see illustrations).

26 Refitting is a reversal of removal. Ensure

4.21 Release the 2 clips (arrowed) and remove the central locking switch

4.23 Prise away the door pull handle vtrim ...

4.24 . . . and slide up the switch panel

4.25a Release the tabs . . .

4.25b . . . and remove the window switch

4.29a Undo the bolt in the roof of the audio unit aperture (arrowed) . . .

4.29b . . . and the 2 each side (arrowed) . . .

4.29c . . . then pull the panel from the facia

that the switches are securely located in their holders.

Passenger's side

27 Carefully prise the switch from the door trim. Disconnect the wiring plug as the switch is removed.

Facia panel switches

28 Remove the audio unit as described in Section 17.
29 Undo the 5 bolts and remove the facia central panel (see illustrations). Disconnect the wiring plugs as the panel is withdrawn.
30 Undo the 2 bolts, remove the cup holder/ switch frame, and remove the switches (see illustration).
31 Refitting is a reversal of removal.

Brake light switch

32 Refer to Chapter 9.

Handbrake warning light switch

33 Refer to Chapter 9.

Reversing light switch

34 Refer to Chapter 7A.

Courtesy light switches

35 The courtesy light switch is integrated into the door lock mechanism, and cannot be renewed independently. If the switch is faulty, renew the door lock mechanism as described in Chapter 11.

Luggage area light switch

36 The luggage area light switch is integrated into the tailgate lock mechanism, and cannot

be renewed independently. If the switch is faulty, renew the tailgate lock mechanism as described in Chapter 11.

Glovebox light switch

37 Switch off the ignition and all electrical consumers.
38 Carefully prise the end panel from the facia.
39 Disconnect the wiring plug, then prise the switch from the bracket.
40 Refitting is a reversal of removal.

5 Bulbs (exterior lights) – renewal

General

1 Whenever a bulb is renewed, note the following points:
 a) Disconnect the battery negative lead, or

4.30 Undo the bolts (arrowed) and remove the cup holder/switch frame

at least make sure that the lighting circuit is switched off before starting work.
 b) Remember that if the light has recently been in use, the bulb may be extremely hot.
 c) Always check the bulb contacts and/or holder (as applicable). Ensure that there is clean metal-to-metal contact between the bulb contacts and the contacts in the holder, and/or the holder and the wiring plug. Clean off any corrosion or dirt before fitting a new bulb.
 d) Ensure that the new bulb is of the correct rating and that it is completely clean before fitting; this applies particularly to headlight bulbs.

Headlight

2 Pull the retaining clips outwards, and remove the plastic cover from the rear of the headlight (see illustration).
3 Disconnect the bulb's wiring plug. Unhook

5.2 Press the clips (arrowed) outwards and remove the plastic cover

5.3a Press the main beam bulb retaining clip to the right (arrowed)

5.3b Press the dipped beam bulb retaining clip to the right (arrowed)

5.3c Note the cut-outs for the main beam bulb (arrowed) . . .

5.3d . . . and the dipped beam (arrowed)

5.8 Release the foglight cover retaining clip

5.9 Press the ends of the clip (arrowed) towards each other

and release the ends of the bulb retaining clip from the light unit, then withdraw the bulb (see illustrations).

4 When handling the new bulb, use a tissue or clean cloth to avoid touching the glass with the fingers; moisture and grease from the skin can cause blackening and rapid failure of this type of bulb. If the glass is accidentally touched, wipe it clean using methylated spirit.

5 Install the new bulb, ensuring that its locating tabs are correctly located in the light cut-outs, and secure it in position with the retaining clip.

6 Refit the headlight cover, making sure it is secure.

Front foglight

7 Remove the foglight as described in Section 7.

8 Release the retaining clip and remove the cover from the rear of the foglight (see illustration).

9 Disconnect the wiring plug from the inside of the cover, then unhook and release the ends of the bulb retaining clip from the light unit, and withdraw the bulb (see illustration).

10 When handling the new bulb, use a tissue or clean cloth to avoid touching the glass with the fingers; moisture and grease from the skin can cause blackening and rapid failure of this type of bulb. If the glass is accidentally touched, wipe it clean using methylated spirit.

11 Install the new bulb, ensuring that its locating tabs are correctly located in the light cut-outs, and secure it in position with the retaining clip.

12 Reconnect the wiring plug and refit the foglight cover, making sure that it is secure.

Sidelight

13 Release the retaining clip and remove the outer cover from the rear of the headlight (see illustration).

14 Pull the bulbholder from the light, then pull out the wedge-base bulb (see illustration).

15 Push the new bulb into place, and refit the bulbholder.

Direction indicator

16 Release the retaining clip and remove the outer cover from the rear of the headlight (see illustration 5.13).

17 Rotate the bulbholder anti-clockwise and pull it from the headlight (see illustration).

18 Press the bulb in a little, twist it anti-clockwise and remove it.

19 Refitting is a reversal of removal.

5.13 Release the clip and remove the triangular cover

5.14 Pull the sidelight from the headlight

5.17 Rotate the indicator bulbholder anti-clockwise

5.20 Push the side repeater forwards or rearwards to compress the clip (arrowed)

5.21 Pull the bulbholder from the side repeater . . .

5.22 . . . and pull the wedge type bulb from the holder

5.24 Undo the light unit retaining bolts (arrowed)

5.25 Bulbholder retaining bolt (arrowed)

5.26 Depress and twist the bulb anti-clockwise to remove it

Direction indicator side repeater

20 Using your fingers only, push the side repeater light forwards or rearwards to compress the plastic clip, and at the same time unhook the front or rear edge to release it from the wing. Take care as the light may be fitted either way around. Push gently to determine at which end the compressible clip is fitted (see illustration).
21 Withdraw the side repeater from the front wing, and pull out the bulbholder from the back (see illustration).
22 Pull out the wedge-type bulb (see illustration).
23 Fit the new bulb using a reversal of the removal procedure. Press the light fully into the front wing until the clip engages.

Rear light cluster

Body-mounted lights

24 Open the tailgate, prise out the caps then undo the 2 light unit mounting bolts (see illustration). Pull the light unit rearwards and disconnect the wiring plug.
25 Undo the retaining bolt and withdraw the bulbholder from the light unit (see illustration). Recover the rubber seal.
26 Depress the relevant bulb and twist anti-clockwise to remove it (see illustration).
27 Fit the new bulb using a reversal of the removal procedure. When refitting the bulbholder, check the condition of the seal, and fit a new one if necessary.
28 Refitting is a reverse of removal. Note the lugs at the outer edges of the light units engage with the slots in the body (see illustration).

Tailgate-mounted lights

29 Open the tailgate, prise out the cover behind the lights, and the caps at the tailgate edge.
30 Undo the 3 bolts and remove the light unit (see illustration). Disconnect the wiring plug as the unit is withdrawn.
31 Undo the 2 retaining bolts and detach the bulbholder assembly from the light unit (see illustration).
32 The large bulbs are bayonet fitting – press-in and rotate anti-clockwise. The small bulbs are wedge type, and simply pull from place.
33 Refitting is a reversal of removal.

High-level stop-light

34 The high-level brake light is illuminated by LEDs (light emitting diodes). It is not possible

5.28 The lugs must engage with the slots (arrowed)

5.30 Undo the bolts (arrowed) and remove the tailgate-mounted light unit

5.31 Bulbholder retaining bolts (arrowed)

5.35 Depress the clip (arrowed) at the edge of the number plate light lens

to renew them separately. If defective the complete light unit should be renewed as described in Section 7.

Number plate light

35 Using a small screwdriver, release the clip and remove the light lens (see illustration).
36 Pull the festoon-type bulb from the spring contacts and fit the new bulb (see illustration). Make sure that the spring contacts are clean and sufficiently tensioned to hold the bulb firmly.
37 Refit the lens.

6 Bulbs (interior lights) – renewal

General

1 Whenever a bulb is renewed, note the following points:

6.2 Starting at the front edge, prise down the light lens . . .

6.13 Lever the luggage compartment light unit from place

5.36 Prise the festoon bulb from the contacts

a) Switch off the ignition and all electrical consumers before commencing work.
b) Remember that if the light has just been in use the bulb may be extremely hot.
c) Always check the bulb contacts and holder, ensuring that there is clean metal-to-metal contact between the bulb and its live(s) and earth. Clean off any corrosion or dirt before fitting a new bulb.
d) Wherever bayonet-type bulbs are fitted ensure that the live contact(s) bear firmly against the bulb contact.
e) Always ensure that the new bulb is of the correct rating and that it is completely clean before fitting it.

Front interior light

2 Using a small screwdriver, carefully prise down the lens and remove it (see illustration).
3 Remove the festoon-type bulb from the spring contacts (see illustration).

6.3 . . . and remove the festoon bulb from the contacts

7.2a Undo the bolts above the headlight (arrowed) . . .

4 Fit the new bulb using a reversal of the removal procedure, but make sure that the spring contacts hold the bulb firmly in position, and if necessary tension them before fitting the bulb.

Door edge lights

5 Taking care to protect the door trim panel, prise out the light unit from the door.
6 Squeeze the two lugs together, and disconnect the wiring plug from the light.
7 Pull the bulbholder out of the light, then pull out the wedge-base bulb.
8 Press the new bulb into the holder, then refit the holder to the light.
9 Refitting is a reversal of removal.

Glovebox illumination light

10 Working at the outer edge, carefully prise the light unit from place.
11 Remove the festoon-type bulb from the spring contacts.
12 Fit the new bulb using a reversal of the removal procedure, but make sure that the spring contacts hold the bulb firmly in position, and if necessary tension them before fitting the bulb.

Luggage compartment light

13 Carefully lever the light from place, using the slot provided (see illustration).
14 Pull the festoon bulb from the holder.
15 Fit the new bulb using a reversal of the removal procedure.

Instrument panel lights

16 All warning/illumination lights in the instrument panel are non-renewable LEDs, therefore, if any are faulty, it is necessary to renew the complete instrument panel. Note, however, that a new instrument panel must be reprogrammed by a Seat dealer using special equipment. The dealer will also transfer the mileage from the old unit onto the new one.

Heater control panel lights

17 The control panel is illuminated by LEDs built into the panel. Consequently, if a fault develops, renewal of the panel is necessary.

Switch illumination

18 The switch illumination bulbs are integral with the switches. If a bulb fails, the complete switch must be renewed.

7 Exterior light units – removal and refitting

Headlight

1 Remove the front bumper as described in Chapter 11.
2 Unscrew the four mounting bolts (two above, two underneath) and withdraw the headlight forwards from the front of the car (see illustrations).

7.2b . . . and the ones below (arrowed)

7.8 Prise out the grommet and disconnect the brake light wiring plug

7.9a Undo the bolts (arrowed) . . .

7.9b . . . then pull the spoiler rearwards to release the clips

7.10 Brake light retaining bolts (arrowed)

7.12 Depress the clip and prise the number plate light from place

3 Reach in behind the headlight and disconnect the wiring multiplug, then the headlight can be removed completely.
4 Refitting is a reversal of removal, noting the following points:
  a) *Set the headlight in position relative to the bodywork before tightening the mounting bolts. Where applicable, re-align the marks made before removal.*
  b) *On completion, it may be advisable to have the headlight alignment checked.*

Direction indicator side repeater

5 The procedure is described as part of the bulb renewal procedure in Section 5.

Rear light cluster

6 The procedure is described as part of the bulb renewal procedure in Section 5.

High-level stop-light

7 Open the tailgate, and prise out the caps (where fitted) over the spoiler retaining bolts.
8 Prise out the grommet in the centre of the tailgate and disconnect the brake light wiring plug **(see illustration)**.
9 Undo the 4 retaining bolts and pull the spoiler away to release the 4 retaining clips. Note that it's quite likely the clips will break on removal. Obtain replacements for refitting **(see illustrations)**.
10 Undo the 2 bolts and detach the brake light from the spoiler **(see illustration)**.
11 Refitting is a reversal of removal.

Number plate light

12 Using a small, flat-bladed screwdriver,

press the retaining clip towards the centre, and pull the light unit from place **(see illustration)**. Disconnect the wiring plug as the unit is withdrawn.
13 Refitting is a reversal of removal.

7.14a Undo the retaining bolt (arrowed)

7.14c . . . note the locating lugs at the outside edge (arrowed)

Front foglight

14 Undo the retaining bolt, and carefully prise the foglight surround trim from the bumper, starting at the inside edge **(see illustrations)**.
15 Undo the 3 bolts and pull the foglight

7.14b Carefully prise out the inside edge . . .

7.15 Foglight retaining bolts (arrowed)

7.16 Foglight adjustment bolt (arrowed)

9.2 Headlight aim adjustment bolts (arrowed)

forwards **(see illustration)**. Disconnect the wiring plug.
16 Refitting is a reversal of removal. If required, the aim of the foglight can be adjusted by rotating the alignment bolt **(see illustration)**.

8 Headlight beam adjustment components – removal and refitting

Range control switch

1 Removal and refitting is covered in Section 4.

Range control motor

2 Remove the headlight as described in Section 7.
3 Press the clips outwards and remove the cover from the rear of the headlight.
4 Disconnect the wiring plug, then rotate the

motor anti-clockwise (right-hand motor) or clockwise (left-hand motor) and detach the shaft spherical head from the reflector.
5 Refitting is a reversal of removal.

9 Headlight beam alignment – general information

1 Accurate adjustment of the headlight beam is only possible using optical beam-setting equipment, and this work should therefore be carried out by a Seat dealer or suitably-equipped workshop.
2 For reference, the headlights can be adjusted using the two bolts accessed through the top of each light unit. The innermost bolt controls vertical adjustment, and the outer one controls horizontal adjustment **(see illustration)**.

Note: *If the instrument panel is to be renewed, the new unit must be programmed with the current service information by a Seat dealer or suitably-equipped specialist.*

Removal

1 Release the steering wheel adjustment lock, pull the wheel out as far as possible, and set it in the lowest position.
2 Carefully pull the steering column upper shroud upwards to release the retaining clips. Refer to Chapter 11 if necessary.
3 Undo the 4 bolts and remove the instrument cluster surround trim **(see illustrations)**.
4 Remove the 4 instrument panel retaining bolts – 2 at the base, 2 at the top, and lift the panel out of the facia sufficiently to allow the wiring plugs on the rear of the unit to be disconnected **(see illustrations)**.

Refitting

5 Refitting is a reversal of removal, making sure that the wiring plugs are securely reconnected.

11 Instrument panel components – removal and refitting

It is not possible to dismantle the instrument panel. If any of the gauges or displays are faulty, the complete instrument panel must be renewed.

12 Horn – removal and refitting

10.3a Undo the bolts (arrowed) . . .

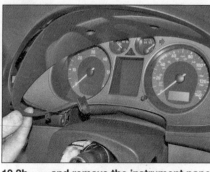

10.3b . . . and remove the instrument panel surround trim

Removal

1 Ensure that the ignition is switched off (take out the key).
2 The horn is located behind the left-hand side of the front bumper (left as seen from the driver's seat) – unclip the left-hand lower grille from the bumper for access.

10.4a Undo the instrument panel upper bolts (arrowed) . . .

10.4b . . . and lower bolts (arrowed) . . .

10.4c . . . then pull the panel rearwards

3 Unscrew the horn unit mounting bolt, and withdraw the unit **(see illustration)**. Disconnect the wiring plug (or two plugs, on dual-tone horns) and remove the unit completely.

Refitting

4 Refitting is a reversal of removal. Take care that the horn trumpet(s) do not contact the surrounding components when refitted, as their sound will be adversely affected.

13 Wiper arms – removal and refitting

Removal

1 Operate the wiper motor, then switch off so that the wiper arm(s) return to the at-rest position.
2 Stick a piece of masking tape to the glass along the edge of the wiper blade to use as an alignment aid on refitting **(see illustration)**.

Front wiper arm

3 With the bonnet open, prise off the cap, then unscrew and remove the spindle nut, but do not remove it completely **(see illustrations)**.
4 Lift the blade off the glass and pull the wiper arm from side-to-side until it releases from the spindle splines – if it is tight, use a puller **(see illustration)**. Remove the spindle nut. **Note:** *If both windscreen wiper arms are to be removed at the same time mark them for identification; the arms are not interchangeable.*

12.3 Horn mounting bolt (arrowed)

Rear wiper arm

5 Pull up the wiper arm spindle nut cover, then unscrew the spindle nut, but do not remove it completely **(see illustrations)**.
6 Lift the blade off the glass and pull the wiper arm from side-to-side until it releases from the spindle – if it is tight, use a puller. Remove the spindle nut **(see illustration)**.

Refitting

7 Ensure that the wiper arm and spindle splines are clean and dry, then refit the arm to the spindle, aligning the wiper blade with the tape fitted on removal. Refit the spindle nut, tightening it securely, and refit the cover. **Note:** *If the windscreen has been renewed or the wiper position lost, position the front arms so the ends of the blades are 20 mm above the base of the windscreen trim.*

13.2 Stick some masking tape to the screen to re-align the blade

14 Windscreen wiper motor and linkage – removal and refitting

Removal

1 Remove the wiper arms as described in Section 13.
2 Pull off the rubber weatherseal, then starting at one end, unclip and lift off remove the plenum chamber cover from in front of the windscreen **(see illustrations)**.
3 On right-hand-drive models, unbolt and remove the engine compartment rear panel from the bulkhead **(see illustrations)**, as there is insufficient room to remove the wiper motor and linkage with the panel in position. It will be necessary to remove the engine management ECM at the same time.

13.3a Prise off the cap . . .

13.3b . . . and slacken the nut beneath (arrowed)

13.4 If necessary, use a puller to remove the wiper arm

13.5a Pull up the spindle cover . . .

13.5b . . . and slacken the spindle nut

13.6 If necessary, use a puller to remove the tailgate wiper arm

14.2a Pull off the rubber weatherstrip . . .

14.2b . . . then starting at one end, unclip . . .

14.2c . . . and remove the plenum chamber cover

14.3a Unscrew the bolts . . .

4 Unscrew the two mounting bolts, then carefully manoeuvre the windscreen wiper motor and linkage out from the scuttle and disconnect the wiring plug **(see illustrations)**.
5 Recover the washers and spacers from the motor mounting rubbers, noting their locations, then inspect the rubbers for signs of damage or deterioration, and renew if necessary.
6 To separate the motor from the linkage, proceed as follows.
  a) *Make alignment marks between the motor*

spindle and the linkage to ensure correct alignment on refitting, and note the orientation of the linkage.
  b) *Unscrew the nut securing the linkage to the motor spindle* **(see illustration)**.
  c) *Undo the three bolts securing the motor to the mounting plate, then withdraw the motor* **(see illustration)**.

Refitting

7 Refitting is a reversal of removal, bearing in mind the following points:
  a) *If the motor has been separated from the linkage, ensure that the marks made on the motor spindle and linkage before removal are aligned, and ensure that the linkage is orientated as noted before removal.*
  b) *Ensure that the washers and spacers are fitted to the motor mounting rubbers as noted before removal.*
  c) *Refit the wiper arms as described in Section 13.*

15 Rear wiper motor –
removal and refitting

Removal

1 Remove the wiper arm as described in Section 13.
2 Open the tailgate, then remove the tailgate trim panel with reference to Chapter 11.
3 Unplug the wiring connector from the motor.

14.3b . . . and remove the engine compartment rear panel from the bulkhead

14.4a Unscrew the mounting bolts . . .

14.4b . . . manoeuvre out the wiper motor and linkage, and disconnect the wiring plug

14.4c Windscreen wiper motor and linkage removed from the car

14.6a Unscrew the nut (arrowed) and disconnect the linkage . . .

14.6b . . . then undo the bolts (arrowed) securing the motor to the plate

4 Disconnect the washer fluid hose from the washer nozzle connector on the motor assembly.
5 Unscrew the three nuts securing the motor, then withdraw the assembly **(see illustration)**.
6 Remove the wiper motor shaft sealing ring from the tailgate.

Refitting

7 Refitting is a reversal of removal, but ensure that the motor shaft rubber sealing ring is correctly refitted to prevent water leaks, and refit the wiper arm with reference to Section 13.

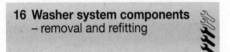

16 Washer system components – removal and refitting

Washer fluid reservoir

1 Switch off the ignition and all electrical consumers.
2 The washer fluid reservoir is located behind the left-hand side of the front bumper. First, remove the front bumper as described in Chapter 11.
3 Disconnect the wiring from the washer pump(s).
4 Disconnect and plug the washer hoses.
5 Unscrew the upper and lower mounting nuts and withdraw the fluid reservoir to the front **(see illustration)**.
6 Refitting is a reversal of removal.

Washer fluid pumps

7 Switch off the ignition and all electrical consumers.
8 Remove the washer fluid reservoir as described previously in this Section.
9 Carefully pull the pump from its grommet in the reservoir **(see illustration)**. Disconnect the washer fluid hose(s) and the wiring plug from the pump.
10 Refitting is a reversal of removal, but take care not to push the pump grommet into the reservoir. Use a little soapy water to ease the pump into the grommet.

Windscreen washer jets

11 The washer jets are located on the rear edge of the bonnet, and access is gained from inside.

16.12 Release the clip at the front of the jet

15.5 Undo the tailgate wiper motor retaining nuts (arrowed)

12 Open the bonnet, release the clip at the front of the jet, then withdraw it from the bonnet **(see illustration)**.
13 Carefully pull off the washer supply tube from the jet, and remove it **(see illustration)**. Disconnect the wiring plug from the jet (where applicable).
14 Refitting is a reversal of removal. Note that the jets are preset by the manufacturer, and their aim cannot be adjusted.

Tailgate washer jet

15 The tailgate washer jet is located within the tailgate wiper spindle, beneath the wiper arm cover. To remove it, lift the cover, then use a pair of pliers to extract the jet from the spindle **(see illustration)**.
16 Refitting is a reversal of removal, but check the operation of the jet. The jet should be aimed to spray at the centre of the screen, using a pin.

16.5 Washer fluid reservoir upper mounting nut (arrowed)

16.13 Disconnect the washer supply tube, and remove the jet

Headlight washer jets

17 It is not necessary to remove the front bumper in order to remove the headlight washer jets. Lift and hold the spray nozzle holder.
18 Slightly raise the securing clip using a screwdriver, then pull out the spray nozzle holder and disconnect the hose.
19 Refitting is a reversal of removal, but adjust the nozzle to direct the spray to the centre of the headlight.

Headlight washer jet lift cylinder

20 Remove the front bumper as described in Chapter 11.
21 Remove the relevant headlight as described in Section 7, and the washer jets as described in the previous sub-Section.
22 Undo the 3 retaining bolts, and withdraw the cylinder.
23 Clamp the hose, squeeze the retaining clip, and disconnect the hose.
24 Refitting is a reversal of removal.

17 Audio unit – removal and refitting

Note: *This Section only applies to standard-fit audio equipment.*

Radio/cassette/CD player

1 The radio is fitted with special side-mounting spring clips, requiring the use of special removal tools, which may be supplied with

16.9 Washer fluid pump location

16.15 Pull the jet from the centre of the spindle using pliers

17.3a Insert the removal tools into the slots at the base of the audio unit ...

17.3b ... and pull the unit from the facia

the car, or can be obtained from an in-car entertainment specialist. The Seat tool number is T20076 – suitable tools should be provided with the car from new, and will typically be found with the handbook in the glovebox.

2 Switch off the ignition and all electrical consumers.

3 Insert the keys and push them in until they engage with the side retaining spring clips. Using the rings on the tools, pull the unit straight out (don't push the tools to the sides), and disconnect the wiring and aerial **(see illustrations)**. Once the unit has been removed, the removal tools can be released by pressing the lugs on the sides of the unit.

4 Reconnect the wiring connectors and aerial lead, then push the unit into the facia until the retaining lugs click into place.

CD changer

5 Remove the passenger's glovebox and lower facia panel as described in Chapter 11.

6 Undo the Torx bolts securing the changer bracket and manoeuvre it from position. Disconnect the wiring plug as the unit is withdrawn. If required, the bracket can be detached from the changer.

7 Refitting is a reversal of removal.

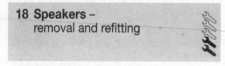

18 Speakers –
removal and refitting

Front tweeter speaker

1 Carefully prise the triangular trim panel from

18.4 Drill out the rivets (arrowed) and remove the door speaker

the front of the door, then prise the speaker from place. Disconnect the wiring plug as the speaker is withdrawn.

2 Refitting is a reversal of removal.

Front bass speaker

3 Remove the door trim panel as described in Chapter 11. Recover the rubber trim ring fitted around the speaker.

4 Carefully drill out the four retaining rivets (screws may be fitted where the speakers have previously been removed), and withdraw the speaker from the front door **(see illustration)**. If not already done, disconnect the speaker wiring.

5 Refitting is a reversal of removal, noting the following points:
   a) Clean away the swarf inside the door, and make good any damaged paint, otherwise there is a risk of corrosion.
   b) Either secure the speaker using new rivets, or use appropriate self-tapping screws – note that, if these are too long, they may interfere with the window glass opening.
   c) Refit the rubber trim ring to the speaker before refitting the door trim panel as described in Chapter 11.

Rear tweeter speaker

6 Where fitted, the rear tweeter speaker is attached to the inside of the rear door trim panel (or rear side trim panel on 3-door models).

7 On 3-door models, carefully prise the speaker from the side panel. Disconnect the wiring plug as the speaker is withdrawn.

18.12 Drill out the rivets (arrowed) and remove the rear speaker

8 On 5-door models, remove the rear door trim panel as described in Chapter 11, Section 13, then release the clips and prise the speaker from place. Disconnect the wiring plug as the speaker is withdrawn.

Rear bass speaker

9 On 3-door models, remove the rear side trim panel as described in Chapter 11, Section 29.

10 On 5-door models, remove the rear door trim panel as described in Chapter 11, Section 13.

11 Recover the rubber surround panel around the speaker (where fitted).

12 Carefully drill out the four retaining rivets (screws may be fitted where the speakers have previously been removed), and withdraw the speaker **(see illustration)**. If not already done, disconnect the speaker wiring.

13 Refitting is a reversal of removal, noting the following points:
   a) Clean away the swarf inside the door, and make good any damaged paint, otherwise there is a risk of corrosion.
   b) Either secure the speaker using new rivets, or use appropriate self-tapping screws. On 5-door models, if these are too long, they may interfere with the window glass opening.
   c) Refit the rubber surround panel to the speaker before refitting the trim panel as described in Chapter 11.

19 Radio aerial –
removal and refitting

Removal

1 The aerial mast can be unscrewed from the base by twisting anti-clockwise.

2 If the aerial base is to be removed, the rear of the headlining must be lowered for access. This requires unclipping the trim panel which runs across the rear of the headlining, and removing the C-pillar trim panels as described in Chapter 11, Section 29.

3 With the rear of the headlining lowered slightly for access, peel back the foam covering on the aerial leads, and disconnect the connectors inside – typically, there will be two leads.

4 Hold the aerial base to stop it rotating and scratching the roof panel, then unscrew the aerial mounting nut with its serrated washer – note how the aerial leads sit in the nut's slot. Withdraw the aerial, and recover the rubber spacer.

Refitting

5 Refitting is a reversal of removal, noting the following points:
   a) Ensure the aerial leads are fitted into the nut's slot as noted on removal.
   b) Before tightening the nut, apply a little 'contact grease' (copper brake grease will probably suffice) to the area inside

the roof where the nut will make contact – this is necessary to ensure a good earth connection.
c) Tighten the nut securely.
d) Refit the removed trim panels as described in Chapter 11, Section 29.

20 Anti-theft alarm system and engine immobiliser – general information

Note: *This information is applicable only to the anti-theft alarm system fitted by Seat as standard equipment.*

Some models in the range are fitted with an anti-theft alarm system as standard equipment. The alarm has switches on all the doors (including the tailgate), the bonnet and the ignition switch. If the tailgate, bonnet or any of the doors are opened, or the ignition switch is switched on whilst the alarm is set, the alarm horn will sound and the hazard warning lights will flash. Some models are also equipped with an internal monitoring system, which will activate the alarm system if any movement in the cabin is detected.

The alarm is set using the key in the driver's front door lock, or by the central locking remote control transmitter. The alarm system will then start to monitor its various switches approximately 30 seconds later.

The alarm is switched off if the car is unlocked using the remote control transmitter, or if you switch on the ignition, however, if unlocked with the remote control, it is automatically reset if the door is not opened within 30 seconds. If the driver's door is manually unlocked with the ignition key, the key must be inserted in the ignition switch within 15 seconds to deactivate the alarm.

All models are fitted with an immobiliser system, which is activated by the ignition switch. A module incorporated in the ignition switch reads a code contained within the ignition key. The module sends a signal to the engine management electronic control module (ECM) which allows the engine to start if the code is correct. If an incorrect ignition key is used, the engine will not start.

If a fault is suspected with the alarm or immobiliser systems, the car should be taken to a Seat dealer for examination. They will have access to a special diagnostic tester which will quickly trace any fault present in the system.

21 Airbag system – general information and precautions

⚠️ **Warning: Before carrying out any operations on the airbag system, disconnect the battery negative terminal (refer to Chapter 5A). When operations are complete, make sure no one is inside the car when the battery is reconnected.**

• *Note that the airbag(s) must not be subjected to temperatures in excess of 100°C. When the airbag is removed, ensure that it is stored the with the pad upwards to prevent possible inflation.*
• *Do not allow any solvents or cleaning agents to contact the airbag assemblies. They must be cleaned using only a damp cloth.*
• *The airbags and control module are both sensitive to impact. If either is dropped or damaged they should be renewed.*
• *Remove the airbag units prior to using arc-welding equipment on the car.*

Driver's and passenger's airbags, and front seat side airbags are fitted as standard equipment. Later models may also be fitted with side curtain airbags, which deploy from the headlining. The airbag system comprises of the airbag unit (complete with gas generator) which is fitted to the steering wheel (driver's side), facia (passenger's side) and front seats, an impact sensor, the control unit and a warning light in the instrument panel. The front passenger airbag may be switched off when there is no one seated in the passenger seat.

The airbag system is triggered in the event of a heavy frontal or side impact above a predetermined force; depending on the point of impact. The airbag is inflated within milliseconds and forms a safety cushion between the driver and the steering wheel, the passenger and the facia, and in the case of side impact, between front seat occupants and the sides of the cabin. This prevents contact between the upper body and cabin interior, and therefore greatly reduces the risk of injury. The airbag then deflates almost immediately.

The front seat belt tensioners described in Chapter 11 are linked to the airbag system, and are designed to be deployed if the impact is sufficient to trigger the airbags.

Every time the ignition is switched on, the airbag control unit performs a self-test. The self-test takes approximately 3 seconds, and during this time the airbag warning light on the facia is illuminated. After the self-test has been completed, the warning light should go out. If the warning light fails to come on, remains illuminated after the initial 3-second period, or

comes on at any time when the car is being driven, there is a fault in the airbag system. The car should then be taken to a Seat dealer or suitably-equipped specialist for examination at the earliest possible opportunity.

22 Airbag system components – removal and refitting

Note: *Refer to the warnings in Section 21 before carrying out the following operations.*
1 Disconnect the battery negative terminal as described in Chapter 5A. Unlike earlier systems, there is, according to Seat, no requirement to wait for a few minutes once the battery has been disconnected, before proceeding with airbag disconnection. However, it may be prudent to err on the side of caution and wait 5 minutes before proceeding.

Driver's airbag

2 Set the front wheels in the straight-ahead position, and release the steering lock by inserting the ignition key.
3 Adjust the steering column to its lowest position by releasing the adjustment handle, then pull out the column and lower it as far as possible. Lock the column in this position by returning the adjustment handle. Turn the steering wheel so the spokes are vertical (90° from the straight-ahead).
4 Insert a screwdriver approximately 5 mm wide into the hole in the upper rear of the steering wheel hub, then move the screwdriver handle upwards to release the clip and free the airbag locking lug **(see illustrations)**. As this is done, the airbag unit should rise slightly out of the steering wheel. Now turn the steering wheel through 180° and release the remaining airbag locking lug on the opposite side.
5 Turn the steering wheel to its central, straight-ahead position.
6 Carefully withdraw the airbag module and disconnect the wiring **(see illustration)**. Note that the airbag module must not be knocked or dropped, and should be stored the correct way up with its active surface uppermost.
7 On refitting, reconnect the wiring connector and locate the airbag unit in the steering wheel, making sure that the wire does not become trapped, and that the unit engages

22.4a Insert a screwdriver and lift the handle . . .

22.4b . . . to release the locking clip (arrowed)

22.6 Depress the locking clip and disconnect the airbag wiring plug

22.11 Undo the bolts each side securing the passenger's airbag (arrowed)

22.12 Depress the locking catch and disconnect the wiring plug

22.18 Airbag control unit retaining nuts (arrowed)

23.2 Push the convenience system control unit (arrowed) upwards from the bracket

on both sides. Reconnect the battery negative lead, ensuring that no-one is inside the car as the lead is connected.

Passenger's airbag

Note: *The facia panel must be renewed in the event of the passenger airbag being deployed.*

8 With reference to Chapter 11, remove the passenger's glovebox and lower facia panel.
9 Remove the passenger's airbag de-activation switch as described in this Section.
10 Where fitted, remove the CD changer as described in this Chapter.
11 Undo the bolts securing the airbag to the facia crossmember brackets, and the bolts securing the airbag to the facia **(see illustration)**.
12 Carefully withdraw the airbag unit and bracket from the facia, and disconnect the wiring connector **(see illustration)**. Note that the airbag module must not be knocked or dropped, and should be stored with its active surface uppermost.
13 Refitting is a reversal of removal. Reconnect the battery negative lead as described in Chapter 5A, ensuring that no-one is inside the car as the lead is connected.

Front side airbags

14 The side impact airbags are integral with the seats. As seat upholstery removal requires

considerable skill and experience, if it is to be carried out without damage, it is best entrusted to an expert.

Side curtain airbags

15 The side curtain airbags, where fitted, are mounted above the headlining. As headlining removal requires considerable skill and experience, if it is to be carried out without damage, it is best entrusted to an expert.

Airbag control unit

Removal

16 Remove the centre console as described in Chapter 11.
17 Reach under the facia, depress the locking catch, and disconnect the control unit wiring plug.
18 Unscrew the three mounting nuts, then withdraw the control unit **(see illustration)**.
19 Refitting is the reverse of removal, making sure the wiring connector is securely reconnected. Reconnect the battery negative lead, ensuring that no-one is inside the car as the lead is connected.

Front passenger airbag switch

20 Where fitted, the front passenger airbag switch is located within the glovebox.

21 With the glovebox lid open, insert the ignition key in the airbag switch to its middle position, then carefully pull out the switch.
22 Disconnect the wiring plug.
23 Refitting is a reversal of removal. Ensure that the switch is completely refitted and reconnected before reconnecting the battery.

Airbag wiring contact (slip-ring)

24 Remove the driver's airbag as described previously in this Section, then remove the steering wheel as described in Chapter 10, and finally the steering column switch as described in Section 4. Removal of the contact unit is described as part of the switch removal.

23 Convenience system – general information

1 The convenience system controls the operation of the central locking, electric windows, alarm system and electric exterior mirrors. It also monitors the operation of the interior lights in the interests of battery discharge protection. The system uses CAN databus cabling which effectively reduces the amount of wiring required for operating the system, by sending different frequency signals down the same wiring rather than using several different wires. A fault memory is incorporated which allows diagnostic equipment to determine the location of faults easily.
2 The convenience system control unit is located below the driver's side of the facia panel, above the accelerator pedal position. To remove it, first remove the facia as described in Chapter 11. Push the control unit upwards from the bracket and disconnect the wiring plug **(see illustration)**. Refitting is a reversal of removal.

Seat Ibiza wiring diagrams

Diagram 1

 WARNING: *This vehicle is fitted with a supplemental restraint system (SRS) consisting of a combination of driver (and passenger) airbag(s), side impact protection airbags and seatbelt pre-tensioners. The use of electrical test equipment on any SRS wiring systems may cause the seatbelt pre-tensioners to abruptly retract and airbags to explosively deploy, resulting in potentially severe personal injury. Extreme care should be taken to correctly identify any circuits to be tested to avoid choosing any of the SRS wiring in error.*

For further information see airbag system precautions in body electrical systems chapter.

Note: The SRS wiring harness can normally be identified by yellow and/or orange harness or harness connectors.

Key to symbols

Solenoid actuator	Bulb	Wire splice, soldered joint, or unspecified connector
Earth point and location	Switch	Connecting wires
Wire colour (red with black tracer) — Ro/Sw —	Fuse/Fusible link **F26**	Diode
	Resistor	Light-emitting diode
Dashed outline denotes part of a larger item, containing in this case an electronic or solid state device (pins 1 and 3 of a single connector designated 6y).	Variable resistor	Item number **12**
	Variable resistor	Motor/pump
		Heating element

Engine fusebox ④

(up to November 2005)

F1	175A	Alternator/starter
F2	110A	Interior
F3	50A	Power steering
F4	40A	Glow plugs (Diesel only)
F5	40A	Engine cooling fan
F6	40A	ABS
F7	25A	ABS
F8	30A	Engine cooling fan
F9	10A	ABS
F10	5A	On-board supply control unit
F11	5A	Engine cooling fan control unit
F12	-	Spare
F13	5A	Automatic gearbox control unit
F14	-	Spare
F15	-	Spare
F16	-	Spare

Engine fusebox ④

(from November 2005)

F1	175A	Alternator/starter
F2	110A	Interior
F3	40A	Engine cooling fan
F4	40A	ABS
F5	50A	Power steering pump
F6	50A	Secondary air pump (petrol) Glow plugs (Diesel)
F7	25A	ABS
F8	30A	Engine cooling fan
F9	5A	Engine cooling fan control unit
F10	15A	ABS
F11	5A	On-board supply control unit
F12	5A	Diesel engine management control unit, automatic gearbox control unit

H47054

Seat Ibiza wiring diagrams

Diagram 2

Passenger fusebox ⑦

F1	15A	Spare (up to November 2005), coolant pump (from November 2005)
F2	10A	ABS/ESP
F3	-	Spare
F4	5A	Stop light, clutch switch
F5	5A	Engine management control unit (petrol)
F6	5A	RH sidelight
F7	5A	LH sidelight
F8	5A	On-board power supply control unit, heated mirrors
F9	10A	Oxygen sensor
F10	5A	On-board supply control unit, audio system
F11	5A	Spare (up to May 2005), folding mirrors (from May 2005)
F12	5A	Headlight levelling
F13	5A	Power steering, engine management, additional heating
F14	10A	Additional heater, engine management
F15	10A	Automatic gearbox control unit
F16	15A	Heated seats
F17	5A	Engine management
F18	10A	Instrument cluster, air conditioning, headlight leveling
F19	10A	Reversing lights, heated washer jets
F20	10A	Washer pump
F21	10A	RH main beam
F22	10A	LH main beam
F23	5A	Number plate light, side light indicator
F24	10A	Rear wiper
F25	10A	Engine management
F26	10A	Stop light switch, ESP steering angle sensor
F27	5A	Instrument cluster, diagnostic connector
F28	10A	On-board power supply control unit, glovebox light, luggage compartment light, interior light
F29	5A	Climate control
F30	5A	On-board power supply control unit, rain sensor
F31	25A	LH front electric window
F32	15A	Spare (up to May 2006), cigar lighter (from May 2006)
F33	15A	Alarm
F34	15A	Engine management
F35	20A	Sunroof
F36	25A	Heater blower
F37	20A	Headlight washer
F38	15A	Front/rear foglight
F39	15A	Engine management (Petrol)
F40	30A	Engine management (Diesel)
F41	15A	Fuel gauge
F42	15A	Engine management
F43	15A	RH dip beam
F44	25A	LH rear electric window
F45	25A	RH front electric window
F46	20A	Front wiper
F47	20A	Heated rear window
F48	15A	Direction indicators
F49	15A	Cigar lighter (up to May 2006), spare (from May 2006)
F50	15A	Central locking
F51	20A	Audio, navigation, telephone
F52	20A	Horn
F53	15A	LH dip beam
F54	25A	RH rear electric window

Earth locations

E1	Earth strap - battery to body
E2	Earth strap - engine to body
E3	Front LH side member
E4	LH strut tower, behind battery
E5	On top of steering column
E6	In front of gearstick
E7	Front LH side member
E8	Front RH side member
E9	Next to ABS control unit
E10	On engine block
E11	In front of gearstick
E12	In front of gearstick
E13	In front of gearstick
E14	LH side luggage compartment
E15	RH side luggage compartment

H47055

Colour codes

Ws	White	Or	Orange
Bl	Blue	Ro	Red
Gr	Grey	Rs	Pink
Ge	Yellow	Gn	Green
Br	Brown	Li	Purple
Sw	Black		

Key to items

Diagram 3

1 Battery
2 Starter motor
3 Alternator
4 Engine fusebox
5 Ignition switch
6 On-board power supply control unit
7 Passenger fusebox
8 Engine cooling fan control unit
9 LH cooling fan
10 RH cooling fan
11 Engine cooling fan thermal switch
12 Light switch
  a = side/headlight switch
13 Combination switch
  a = indicator/parking light
14 LH headlight
  a = sidelight
15 RH headlight
  a = sidelight
16 LH body mounted light unit
  a = tail light
  b = stop light
17 LH tailgate mounter light unit
  a = tail light
  b = reversing light
18 RH body mounted light unit
  a = tail light
  b = stop light
19 RH tailgate mounted light unit
  a = tail light
  b = reversing light
20 Number plate light
21 High level brake light
22 Stop light switch
23 Reversing light switch

H47056

Typical starting & charging

Typical engine cooling fan

Typical stop, reversing, side, tail & number plate lights

Colour codes

Ws	White	Or	Orange
Bl	Blue	Ro	Red
Gr	Grey	Rs	Pink
Ge	Yellow	Gn	Green
Br	Brown	Li	Purple
Sw	Black		

Key to items

1 Battery
4 Engine fusebox
5 Ignition switch
6 On-board power supply control unit
7 Passenger fusebox
12 Light switch
    a = side/headlight switch
    b = rear/front foglight
13 Combination switch
    b = main/dip/flash
14 LH headlight
    b = dip beam
    c = main beam
    d = direction indicator

15 RH headlight
    b = dip beam
    c = main beam
    d = direction indicator
16 LH tailgate mounted light unit
    c = foglight
    d = direction indicator
18 RH tailgate mounted light unit
    d = direction indicator
25 LH front foglight
26 RH front foglight
27 LH indicator side repeater
28 RH indicator side repeater
29 'X' contact relay

30 Hazard warning light switch
31 Headlight levelling adjuster
32 LH headlight levelling motor
33 RH headlight levelling motor

Diagram 4

H47057

Typical headlights & foglights

See diagram 4
Headlight
levelling

See diagram 5
Instrument cluster
(main beam
warning light)

Typical direction indicators & hazard warning lights

Typical headlight levelling

See diagram 4
Headlights
& foglights

Colour codes

Ws	White	**Or**	Orange
Bl	Blue	**Ro**	Red
Gr	Grey	**Rs**	Pink
Ge	Yellow	**Gn**	Green
Br	Brown	**Li**	Purple
Sw	Black		

Key to items

1 Battery
4 Engine fusebox
5 Ignition switch
6 On-board power supply control unit
7 Passenger fusebox
12 Light switch
   a = side/headlight switch
35 Immobilizer reader coil
36 Vehicle speed sensor
37 Handbrake switch
38 Driver's seatbelt switch
39 Wiper switch
   a = trip computer function
   b = trip computer reset
40 Low brake fluid switch
41 Oil pressure switch

42 Fuel gauge sender
43 Outside air temperature sensor
44 Instrument cluster
   a = immobilizer control unit
   b = instrument cluster control unit
   c = multifunction display
   d = speedometer
   e = LH direction indicator
   f = RH direction indicator
   g = servotronic indicator
   h = low washer fluid indicator
   i = coolant temp/level indicator
   j = engine fault indicator
   k = low brake fluid/handbrake indicator
   l = TCS indicator
   m = ABS indicator

n = fuel gauge
o = dip beam indicator
p = main beam indicator
q = odometer
r = coolant temperature gauge
s = tachometer
t = lights on buzzer
u = immobilizer indicator
v = alternator indicator
w = power steering fault indicator
x = SRS indicator
y = seatbelt indicator
z = emission control fault indicator

Diagram 5

H47058

Typical instrument cluster

Colour codes

Ws	White	Or	Orange
Bl	Blue	Ro	Red
Gr	Grey	Rs	Pink
Ge	Yellow	Gn	Green
Br	Brown	Li	Purple
Sw	Black		

Key to items

1 Battery
4 Engine fusebox
5 Ignition switch
6 On-board power supply control unit
7 Passenger fusebox
29 'X' contact relay
47 Interior light
   a = reading light
   b = interior light
48 Luggage compartment light

49 Luggage compartment light switch
50 Glovebox light
51 Glovebox light switch
52 Driver's door switch
53 Passenger's door switch
54 LH rear door switch
55 RH rear door switch
56 Heated rear window switch
57 Heated rear window
58 A/C control unit

59 Heater blower resistors
60 Heater blower motor
61 High pressure switch
62 Compressor clutch
63 Centre vent temperature sensor
64 Footwell temperature sensor
65 Evaporator temperature sensor
66 Air recirc. flap motor/potentiometer
67 Temp. flap control motor/potentiometer

Diagram 6

H47059

Typical interior lighting

Typical air conditioning

Typical heated rear window

Colour codes

Ws	White	Or	Orange
Bl	Blue	Ro	Red
Gr	Grey	Rs	Pink
Ge	Yellow	Gn	Green
Br	Brown	Li	Purple
Sw	Black		

Key to items

1 Battery
4 Engine fusebox
5 Ignition switch
6 On-board power supply control unit
7 Passenger fusebox
39 Wash/wipe switch
   c = intermittent wiper rheostat
   d = front wash/wipe
   e = rear wash/wipe
70 Front/rear washer pump
71 Front wiper motor

72 Rear wiper motor
73 Audio unit
74 Aerial amplifier
75 LH front bass speaker
76 LH front mid range/tweeter
77 RH front bass speaker
78 RH front mid range/tweeter
79 LH rear bass speaker
80 RH rear bass speaker
81 CD player

Diagram 7

*   2 door models
** 4 door models

H47060

Typical wash/wipe

Typical audio system

Colour codes

Ws	White	**Or**	Orange
Bl	Blue	**Ro**	Red
Gr	Grey	**Rs**	Pink
Ge	Yellow	**Gn**	Green
Br	Brown	**Li**	Purple
Sw	Black		

Key to items

1 Battery
4 Engine fusebox
5 Ignition switch
6 On-board power supply control unit
7 Passenger fusebox
12 Light switch
   a = side/headlight switch
85 Cigar lighter
86 Horn
87 Horn switch
88 Steering wheel clock springs
89 LH heated washer jet
90 RH heated washer jet
91 Headlight washer relay
92 Headlight washer pump
93 Driver's door control unit
94 Mirror control switch
   a = mirror adjustment
   b = mirror retraction
   c = mirror heating
95 Driver's mirror asembly
   a = mirror adjustment
   b = mirror retraction
   c = mirror heating
96 Passenger's mirror asembly
   a = mirror adjustment
   b = mirror retraction
   c = mirror heating
97 Passenger's door control unit

Diagram 8

H47061

Typical horn & cigar lighter

Typical electric mirrors

Typical headlight washer

Typical heated washer jets

Colour codes

Ws	White	**Or**	Orange
Bl	Blue	**Ro**	Red
Gr	Grey	**Rs**	Pink
Ge	Yellow	**Gn**	Green
Br	Brown	**Li**	Purple
Sw	Black		

Key to items

1 Battery
4 Engine fusebox
5 Ignition switch
6 On-board power supply control unit
7 Passenger fusebox
93 Driver's door control unit
97 Passenger's door control unit
100 LH rear door control unit
101 RH rear door control unit

102 Driver's door front window switch
103 Driver's door rear window switch
104 Rear window isolation switch
105 Passenger's door front window switch
106 LH rear door window switch
107 RH rear door window switch

Diagram 9

H47062

Typical electric windows

Colour codes

Ws	White	Or	Orange
Bl	Blue	Ro	Red
Gr	Grey	Rs	Pink
Ge	Yellow	Gn	Green
Br	Brown	Li	Purple
Sw	Black		

Key to items

1   Battery
4   Engine fusebox
6   On-board power supply control unit
7   Passenger fusebox
110 Convenience system control unit
111 Driver's door lock assembly
112 Passenger's door lock assembly
113 LH rear door lock assembly

114 RH rear door lock assembly
115 Driver's interior locking switch
116 Tailgate lock motor
117 'SAFE' indicator

Diagram 10

H47063

Typical central locking

Dimensions and weights

Note: *All figures and dimensions are approximate and may vary according to model. Refer to manufacturer's data for exact figures.*

Dimensions

Overall length	3953 mm
Overall width:	
Excluding mirrors	1698 mm
Including mirrors	1890 mm
Overall height (unladen)	1441 mm
Wheelbase	2460 mm
Turning circle	10.6 m

Weights

Kerb weight (including driver)*	1102 to 1252 kg
Maximum gross vehicle weight*	1537 to 1693 kg
Maximum roof rack load	75 kg
Maximum towing weights:	
Unbraked trailer	500 kg
Braked trailer*	700 to 1200 kg

* Exact weights depend upon model and specification.

Fuel economy

Although depreciation is still the biggest part of the cost of motoring for most car owners, the cost of fuel is more immediately noticeable. These pages give some tips on how to get the best fuel economy.

Working it out

Manufacturer's figures

Car manufacturers are required by law to provide fuel consumption information on all new vehicles sold. These 'official' figures are obtained by simulating various driving conditions on a rolling road or a test track. Real life conditions are different, so the fuel consumption actually achieved may not bear much resemblance to the quoted figures.

How to calculate it

Many cars now have trip computers which will

display fuel consumption, both instantaneous and average. Refer to the owner's handbook for details of how to use these.

To calculate consumption yourself (and maybe to check that the trip computer is accurate), proceed as follows.

1. Fill up with fuel and note the mileage, or zero the trip recorder.
2. Drive as usual until you need to fill up again.
3. Note the amount of fuel required to refill the tank, and the mileage covered since the previous fill-up.
4. Divide the mileage by the amount of fuel used to obtain the consumption figure.

For example:

    Mileage at first fill-up (a) = 27,903
    Mileage at second fill-up (b) = 28,346
    Mileage covered (b - a) = 443
    Fuel required at second fill-up = 48.6 litres

The half-completed changeover to metric units in the UK means that we buy our fuel

in litres, measure distances in miles and talk about fuel consumption in miles per gallon. There are two ways round this: the first is to convert the litres to gallons before doing the calculation (by dividing by 4.546, or see Table 1). So in the example:

    48.6 litres ÷ 4.546 = 10.69 gallons
    443 miles ÷ 10.69 gallons = 41.4 mpg

The second way is to calculate the consumption in miles per litre, then multiply that figure by 4.546 (or see Table 2).

So in the example, fuel consumption is:

    443 miles ÷ 48.6 litres = 9.1 mpl
    9.1 mpl x 4.546 = 41.4 mpg

The rest of Europe expresses fuel consumption in litres of fuel required to travel 100 km (l/100 km). For interest, the conversions are given in Table 3. In practice it doesn't matter what units you use, provided you know what your normal consumption is and can spot if it's getting better or worse.

Table 1: conversion of litres to Imperial gallons

litres	1	2	3	4	5	10	20	30	40	50	60	70
gallons	0.22	0.44	0.66	0.88	1.10	2.24	4.49	6.73	8.98	11.22	13.47	15.71

Table 2: conversion of miles per litre to miles per gallon

miles per litre	5	6	7	8	9	10	11	12	13	14
miles per gallon	23	27	32	36	41	46	50	55	59	64

Table 3: conversion of litres per 100 km to miles per gallon

litres per 100 km	4	4.5	5	5.5	6	6.5	7	8	9	10
miles per gallon	71	63	56	51	47	43	40	35	31	28

Maintenance

A well-maintained car uses less fuel and creates less pollution. In particular:

Filters

Change air and fuel filters at the specified intervals.

Oil

Use a good quality oil of the lowest viscosity specified by the vehicle manufacturer (see *Lubricants and fluids*). Check the level often and be careful not to overfill.

Spark plugs

When applicable, renew at the specified intervals.

Tyres

Check tyre pressures regularly. Under-inflated tyres have an increased rolling resistance. It is generally safe to use the higher pressures specified for full load conditions even when not fully laden, but keep an eye on the centre band of tread for signs of wear due to over-inflation.

When buying new tyres, consider the 'fuel saving' models which most manufacturers include in their ranges.

Driving style

Acceleration

Acceleration uses more fuel than driving at a steady speed. The best technique with modern cars is to accelerate reasonably briskly to the desired speed, changing up through the gears as soon as possible without making the engine labour.

Air conditioning

Air conditioning absorbs quite a bit of energy from the engine – typically 3 kW (4 hp) or so. The effect on fuel consumption is at its worst in slow traffic. Switch it off when not required.

Anticipation

Drive smoothly and try to read the traffic flow so as to avoid unnecessary acceleration and braking.

Automatic transmission

When accelerating in an automatic, avoid depressing the throttle so far as to make the transmission hold onto lower gears at higher speeds. Don't use the 'Sport' setting, if applicable.

When stationary with the engine running, select 'N' or 'P'. When moving, keep your left foot away from the brake.

Braking

Braking converts the car's energy of motion into heat – essentially, it is wasted. Obviously some braking is always going to be necessary, but with good anticipation it is surprising how much can be avoided, especially on routes that you know well.

Carshare

Consider sharing lifts to work or to the shops. Even once a week will make a difference.

Electrical loads

Electricity is 'fuel' too; the alternator which charges the battery does so by converting some of the engine's energy of motion into electrical energy. The more electrical accessories are in use, the greater the load on the alternator. Switch off big consumers like the heated rear window when not required.

Freewheeling

Freewheeling (coasting) in neutral with the engine switched off is dangerous. The effort required to operate power-assisted brakes and steering increases when the engine is not running, with a potential lack of control in emergency situations.

In any case, modern fuel injection systems automatically cut off the engine's fuel supply on the overrun (moving and in gear, but with the accelerator pedal released).

Gadgets

Bolt-on devices claiming to save fuel have been around for nearly as long as the motor car itself. Those which worked were rapidly adopted as standard equipment by the vehicle manufacturers. Others worked only in certain situations, or saved fuel only at the expense of unacceptable effects on performance, driveability or the life of engine components.

The most effective fuel saving gadget is the driver's right foot.

Journey planning

Combine (eg) a trip to the supermarket with a visit to the recycling centre and the DIY store, rather than making separate journeys.

When possible choose a travelling time outside rush hours.

Load

The more heavily a car is laden, the greater the energy required to accelerate it to a given speed. Remove heavy items which you don't need to carry.

One load which is often overlooked is the contents of the fuel tank. A tankful of fuel (55 litres / 12 gallons) weighs 45 kg (100 lb) or so. Just half filling it may be worthwhile.

Lost?

At the risk of stating the obvious, if you're going somewhere new, have details of the route to hand. There's not much point in achieving record mpg if you also go miles out of your way.

Parking

If possible, carry out any reversing or turning manoeuvres when you arrive at a parking space so that you can drive straight out when you leave. Manoeuvering when the engine is cold uses a lot more fuel.

Driving around looking for free on-street parking may cost more in fuel than buying a car park ticket.

Premium fuel

Most major oil companies (and some supermarkets) have premium grades of fuel which are several pence a litre dearer than the standard grades. Reports vary, but the consensus seems to be that if these fuels improve economy at all, they do not do so by enough to justify their extra cost.

Roof rack

When loading a roof rack, try to produce a wedge shape with the narrow end at the front. Any cover should be securely fastened – if it flaps it's creating turbulence and absorbing energy.

Remove roof racks and boxes when not in use – they increase air resistance and can create a surprising amount of noise.

Short journeys

The engine is at its least efficient, and wear is highest, during the first few miles after a cold start. Consider walking, cycling or using public transport.

Speed

The engine is at its most efficient when running at a steady speed and load at the rpm where it develops maximum torque. (You can find this figure in the car's handbook.) For most cars this corresponds to between 55 and 65 mph in top gear.

Above the optimum cruising speed, fuel consumption starts to rise quite sharply. A car travelling at 80 mph will typically be using 30% more fuel than at 60 mph.

Supermarket fuel

It may be cheap but is it any good? In the UK all supermarket fuel must meet the relevant British Standard. The major oil companies will say that their branded fuels have better additive packages which may stop carbon and other deposits building up. A reasonable compromise might be to use one tank of branded fuel to three or four from the supermarket.

Switch off when stationary

Switch off the engine if you look like being stationary for more than 30 seconds or so. This is good for the environment as well as for your pocket. Be aware though that frequent restarts are hard on the battery and the starter motor.

Windows

Driving with the windows open increases air turbulence around the vehicle. Closing the windows promotes smooth airflow and

reduced resistance. The faster you go, the more significant this is.

And finally . . .

Driving techniques associated with good fuel economy tend to involve moderate acceleration and low top speeds. Be considerate to the needs of other road users who may need to make brisker progress; even if you do not agree with them this is not an excuse to be obstructive.

Safety must always take precedence over economy, whether it is a question of accelerating hard to complete an overtaking manoeuvre, killing your speed when confronted with a potential hazard or switching the lights on when it starts to get dark.

Conversion factors

Length (distance)

Inches (in)	x 25.4	= Millimetres (mm)	x 0.0394 =	Inches (in)
Feet (ft)	x 0.305	= Metres (m)	x 3.281 =	Feet (ft)
Miles	x 1.609	= Kilometres (km)	x 0.621 =	Miles

Volume (capacity)

Cubic inches (cu in; in³)	x 16.387	= Cubic centimetres (cc; cm³)	x 0.061 =	Cubic inches (cu in; in³)
Imperial pints (Imp pt)	x 0.568	= Litres (l)	x 1.76 =	Imperial pints (Imp pt)
Imperial quarts (Imp qt)	x 1.137	= Litres (l)	x 0.88 =	Imperial quarts (Imp qt)
Imperial quarts (Imp qt)	x 1.201	= US quarts (US qt)	x 0.833 =	Imperial quarts (Imp qt)
US quarts (US qt)	x 0.946	= Litres (l)	x 1.057 =	US quarts (US qt)
Imperial gallons (Imp gal)	x 4.546	= Litres (l)	x 0.22 =	Imperial gallons (Imp gal)
Imperial gallons (Imp gal)	x 1.201	= US gallons (US gal)	x 0.833 =	Imperial gallons (Imp gal)
US gallons (US gal)	x 3.785	= Litres (l)	x 0.264 =	US gallons (US gal)

Mass (weight)

Ounces (oz)	x 28.35	= Grams (g)	x 0.035 =	Ounces (oz)
Pounds (lb)	x 0.454	= Kilograms (kg)	x 2.205 =	Pounds (lb)

Force

Ounces-force (ozf; oz)	x 0.278	= Newtons (N)	x 3.6 =	Ounces-force (ozf; oz)
Pounds-force (lbf; lb)	x 4.448	= Newtons (N)	x 0.225 =	Pounds-force (lbf; lb)
Newtons (N)	x 0.1	= Kilograms-force (kgf; kg)	x 9.81 =	Newtons (N)

Pressure

Pounds-force per square inch (psi; lbf/in²; lb/in²)	x 0.070	= Kilograms-force per square centimetre (kgf/cm²; kg/cm²)	x 14.223 =	Pounds-force per square inch (psi; lbf/in²; lb/in²)
Pounds-force per square inch (psi; lbf/in²; lb/in²)	x 0.068	= Atmospheres (atm)	x 14.696 =	Pounds-force per square inch (psi; lbf/in²; lb/in²)
Pounds-force per square inch (psi; lbf/in²; lb/in²)	x 0.069	= Bars	x 14.5 =	Pounds-force per square inch (psi; lbf/in²; lb/in²)
Pounds-force per square inch (psi; lbf/in²; lb/in²)	x 6.895	= Kilopascals (kPa)	x 0.145 =	Pounds-force per square inch (psi; lbf/in²; lb/in²)
Kilopascals (kPa)	x 0.01	= Kilograms-force per square centimetre (kgf/cm²; kg/cm²)	x 98.1 =	Kilopascals (kPa)
Millibar (mbar)	x 100	= Pascals (Pa)	x 0.01 =	Millibar (mbar)
Millibar (mbar)	x 0.0145	= Pounds-force per square inch (psi; lbf/in²; lb/in²)	x 68.947 =	Millibar (mbar)
Millibar (mbar)	x 0.75	= Millimetres of mercury (mmHg)	x 1.333 =	Millibar (mbar)
Millibar (mbar)	x 0.401	= Inches of water (inH₂O)	x 2.491 =	Millibar (mbar)
Millimetres of mercury (mmHg)	x 0.535	= Inches of water (inH₂O)	x 1.868 =	Millimetres of mercury (mmHg)
Inches of water (inH₂O)	x 0.036	= Pounds-force per square inch (psi; lbf/in²; lb/in²)	x 27.68 =	Inches of water (inH₂O)

Torque (moment of force)

Pounds-force inches (lbf in; lb in)	x 1.152	= Kilograms-force centimetre (kgf cm; kg cm)	x 0.868 =	Pounds-force inches (lbf in; lb in)
Pounds-force inches (lbf in; lb in)	x 0.113	= Newton metres (Nm)	x 8.85 =	Pounds-force inches (lbf in; lb in)
Pounds-force inches (lbf in; lb in)	x 0.083	= Pounds-force feet (lbf ft; lb ft)	x 12 =	Pounds-force inches (lbf in; lb in)
Pounds-force feet (lbf ft; lb ft)	x 0.138	= Kilograms-force metres (kgf m; kg m)	x 7.233 =	Pounds-force feet (lbf ft; lb ft)
Pounds-force feet (lbf ft; lb ft)	x 1.356	= Newton metres (Nm)	x 0.738 =	Pounds-force feet (lbf ft; lb ft)
Newton metres (Nm)	x 0.102	= Kilograms-force metres (kgf m; kg m)	x 9.804 =	Newton metres (Nm)

Power

Horsepower (hp)	x 745.7	= Watts (W)	x 0.0013 =	Horsepower (hp)

Velocity (speed)

Miles per hour (miles/hr; mph)	x 1.609	= Kilometres per hour (km/hr; kph)	x 0.621 =	Miles per hour (miles/hr; mph)

Fuel consumption*

Miles per gallon, Imperial (mpg)	x 0.354	= Kilometres per litre (km/l)	x 2.825 =	Miles per gallon, Imperial (mpg)
Miles per gallon, US (mpg)	x 0.425	= Kilometres per litre (km/l)	x 2.352 =	Miles per gallon, US (mpg)

Temperature

Degrees Fahrenheit = (°C x 1.8) + 32   Degrees Celsius (Degrees Centigrade; °C) = (°F - 32) x 0.56

It is common practice to convert from miles per gallon (mpg) to litres/100 kilometres (l/100km), where mpg x l/100 km = 282

Spare parts are available from many sources, including maker's appointed garages, accessory shops, and motor factors. To be sure of obtaining the correct parts, it will sometimes be necessary to quote the vehicle identification number. If possible, it can also be useful to take the old parts along for positive identification. Items such as starter motors and alternators may be available under a service exchange scheme – any parts returned should be clean.

Our advice regarding spare parts is as follows.

Officially appointed garages

This is the best source of parts which are peculiar to your car, and which are not otherwise generally available (eg, badges, interior trim, certain body panels, etc). It is also the only place at which you should buy parts if the car is still under warranty.

Accessory shops

These are very good places to buy materials and components needed for the maintenance of your car (oil, air and fuel filters, light bulbs, drivebelts, greases, brake pads, touch-up paint, etc). Components of this nature sold by a reputable shop are usually of the same standard as those used by the car manufacturer.

Besides components, these shops also sell tools and general accessories, usually have convenient opening hours, charge lower prices, and can often be found close to home. Some accessory shops have parts counters where components needed for almost any repair job can be purchased or ordered.

Motor factors

Good factors will stock all the more important components which wear out comparatively quickly, and can sometimes supply individual components needed for the overhaul of a larger assembly (eg, brake seals and hydraulic parts, bearing shells, pistons, valves). They may also handle work such as cylinder block reboring, crankshaft regrinding, etc.

Tyre and exhaust specialists

These outlets may be independent, or members of a local or national chain. They frequently offer competitive prices when compared with a main dealer or local garage, but it will pay to obtain several quotes before making a decision. When researching prices, also ask what extras may be added – for instance fitting a new valve and balancing the wheel are both commonly charged on top of the price of a new tyre.

Other sources

Beware of parts or materials obtained from market stalls, car boot sales or similar outlets. Such items are not invariably sub-standard, but there is little chance of compensation if they do prove unsatisfactory. In the case of safety-critical components such as brake pads, there is the risk not only of financial loss, but also of an accident causing injury or death.

Second-hand components or assemblies obtained from a car breaker can be a good buy in some circumstances, but this sort of purchase is best made by the experienced DIY mechanic.

Vehicle identification numbers

Modifications are a continuing and unpublicised process in vehicle manufacture, quite apart from major model changes. Spare parts manuals and lists are compiled upon a numerical basis, the individual vehicle identification numbers being essential to correct identification of the component concerned.

When ordering spare parts, always give as much information as possible. Quote the car model, year of manufacture and registration, chassis and engine numbers as appropriate.

The *Vehicle Identification Number* (or chassis number) is located in the engine compartment, on a plate on the left-hand side suspension turret (left as seen from the driver's seat) – on some models, it may also be stamped into the right-hand suspension turret. The VIN is also visible through the bottom left-hand corner of the windscreen **(see illustrations)**.

The *Vehicle Data Sticker* is located in the spare wheel well, under the boot floor – one of the most useful pieces of information on it is the engine code **(see illustration)**.

The *engine number* is stamped into the left-hand end of the cylinder block and, in addition, a sticker may be attached to the timing cover/engine mounting which shows the engine code above the barcode **(see illustrations)**.

Vehicle identification number (VIN) located on the left-hand suspension turret

VIN stamped into the vehicle body on the right-hand suspension turret

The VIN is visible through the windscreen

The vehicle data sticker is adjacent to the spare wheel well

Engine number located on the left-hand end of the cylinder block

Engine code sticker located on the timing cover

Whenever servicing, repair or overhaul work is carried out on the car or its components, observe the following procedures and instructions. This will assist in carrying out the operation efficiently and to a professional standard of workmanship.

Joint mating faces and gaskets

When separating components at their mating faces, never insert screwdrivers or similar implements into the joint between the faces in order to prise them apart. This can cause severe damage which results in oil leaks, coolant leaks, etc upon reassembly. Separation is usually achieved by tapping along the joint with a soft-faced hammer in order to break the seal. However, note that this method may not be suitable where dowels are used for component location.

Where a gasket is used between the mating faces of two components, a new one must be fitted on reassembly; fit it dry unless otherwise stated in the repair procedure. Make sure that the mating faces are clean and dry, with all traces of old gasket removed. When cleaning a joint face, use a tool which is unlikely to score or damage the face, and remove any burrs or nicks with an oilstone or fine file.

Make sure that tapped holes are cleaned with a pipe cleaner, and keep them free of jointing compound, if this is being used, unless specifically instructed otherwise.

Ensure that all orifices, channels or pipes are clear, and blow through them, preferably using compressed air.

Oil seals

Oil seals can be removed by levering them out with a wide flat-bladed screwdriver or similar implement. Alternatively, a number of self-tapping screws may be screwed into the seal, and these used as a purchase for pliers or some similar device in order to pull the seal free.

Whenever an oil seal is removed from its working location, either individually or as part of an assembly, it should be renewed.

The very fine sealing lip of the seal is easily damaged, and will not seal if the surface it contacts is not completely clean and free from scratches, nicks or grooves. If the original sealing surface of the component cannot be restored, and the manufacturer has not made provision for slight relocation of the seal relative to the sealing surface, the component should be renewed.

Protect the lips of the seal from any surface which may damage them in the course of fitting. Use tape or a conical sleeve where possible. Lubricate the seal lips with oil before fitting and, on dual-lipped seals, fill the space between the lips with grease.

Unless otherwise stated, oil seals must be fitted with their sealing lips toward the lubricant to be sealed.

Use a tubular drift or block of wood of the appropriate size to install the seal and, if the seal housing is shouldered, drive the seal down to the shoulder. If the seal housing is unshouldered, the seal should be fitted with its face flush with the housing top face (unless otherwise instructed).

Screw threads and fastenings

Seized nuts, bolts and screws are quite a common occurrence where corrosion has set in, and the use of penetrating oil or releasing fluid will often overcome this problem if the offending item is soaked for a while before attempting to release it. The use of an impact driver may also provide a means of releasing such stubborn fastening devices, when used in conjunction with the appropriate screwdriver bit or socket. If none of these methods works, it may be necessary to resort to the careful application of heat, or the use of a hacksaw or nut splitter device.

Studs are usually removed by locking two nuts together on the threaded part, and then using a spanner on the lower nut to unscrew the stud. Studs or bolts which have broken off below the surface of the component in which they are mounted can sometimes be removed using a stud extractor. Always ensure that a blind tapped hole is completely free from oil, grease, water or other fluid before installing the bolt or stud. Failure to do this could cause the housing to crack due to the hydraulic action of the bolt or stud as it is screwed in.

When tightening a castellated nut to accept a split pin, tighten the nut to the specified torque, where applicable, and then tighten further to the next split pin hole. Never slacken the nut to align the split pin hole, unless stated in the repair procedure.

When checking or retightening a nut or bolt to a specified torque setting, slacken the nut or bolt by a quarter of a turn, and then retighten to the specified setting. However, this should not be attempted where angular tightening has been used.

For some screw fastenings, notably cylinder head bolts or nuts, torque wrench settings are no longer specified for the latter stages of tightening, "angle-tightening" being called up instead. Typically, a fairly low torque wrench setting will be applied to the bolts/nuts in the correct sequence, followed by one or more stages of tightening through specified angles.

Locknuts, locktabs and washers

Any fastening which will rotate against a component or housing during tightening should always have a washer between it and the relevant component or housing.

Spring or split washers should always be renewed when they are used to lock a critical component such as a big-end bearing retaining bolt or nut. Locktabs which are folded over to retain a nut or bolt should always be renewed.

Self-locking nuts can be re-used in non-critical areas, providing resistance can be felt when the locking portion passes over the bolt or stud thread. However, it should be noted that self-locking stiffnuts tend to lose their effectiveness after long periods of use, and should then be renewed as a matter of course.

Split pins must always be replaced with new ones of the correct size for the hole.

When thread-locking compound is found on the threads of a fastener which is to be re-used, it should be cleaned off with a wire brush and solvent, and fresh compound applied on reassembly.

Special tools

Some repair procedures in this manual entail the use of special tools such as a press, two or three-legged pullers, spring compressors, etc. Wherever possible, suitable readily-available alternatives to the manufacturer's special tools are described, and are shown in use. In some instances, where no alternative is possible, it has been necessary to resort to the use of a manufacturer's tool, and this has been done for reasons of safety as well as the efficient completion of the repair operation. Unless you are highly-skilled and have a thorough understanding of the procedures described, never attempt to bypass the use of any special tool when the procedure described specifies its use. Not only is there a very great risk of personal injury, but expensive damage could be caused to the components involved.

Environmental considerations

When disposing of used engine oil, brake fluid, antifreeze, etc, give due consideration to any detrimental environmental effects. Do not, for instance, pour any of the above liquids down drains into the general sewage system, or onto the ground to soak away. Many local council refuse tips provide a facility for waste oil disposal, as do some garages. If none of these facilities are available, consult your local Environmental Health Department, or the National Rivers Authority, for further advice.

With the universal tightening-up of legislation regarding the emission of environmentally-harmful substances from motor vehicles, most vehicles have tamperproof devices fitted to the main adjustment points of the fuel system. These devices are primarily designed to prevent unqualified persons from adjusting the fuel/air mixture, with the chance of a consequent increase in toxic emissions. If such devices are found during servicing or overhaul, they should, wherever possible, be renewed or refitted in accordance with the manufacturer's requirements or current legislation.

OIL CARE

FOLLOW THE CODE

OIL BANK LINE
0800 66 33 66
www.oilbankline.org.uk

Note: It is antisocial and illegal to dump oil down the drain. To find the location of your local oil recycling bank, call this number free.

The jack supplied with the vehicle tool kit should only be used for changing the roadwheels – see *Wheel changing* at the front of this book. When carrying out any other kind of work, raise the car using a hydraulic (or 'trolley') jack, and always supplement the jack with axle stands positioned under the vehicle jacking points.

When using a hydraulic jack or axle stands, always position the jack head or axle stand head under one of the relevant jacking points.

To raise the front and/or rear of the car, use the jacking/support points at the front and rear ends of the door sills, indicated by the triangular depressions in the sill panel **(see illustration)**. Position a block of wood with a groove cut in it on the jack head to prevent the vehicle weight resting on the sill edge; align the sill edge with the groove in the wood so that the vehicle weight is spread evenly over the surface of the block. Supplement the jack with axle stands (also with slotted blocks of

wood) positioned as close as possible to the jacking points **(see illustrations)**.

Do not jack the car under any other part of the sill, sump, floor pan, or any of the steering or suspension components. With the car raised, an axle stand should be positioned beneath the jack location point on the sill.

Warning: Never work under, around, or near a raised car, unless it is adequately supported in at least two places.

Front and rear jacking points (arrowed)

H31271

The jacking points are indicated by an arrow on the sill

Use an axle stand with a suitable block of wood

Introduction

A selection of good tools is a fundamental requirement for anyone contemplating the maintenance and repair of a motor vehicle. For the owner who does not possess any, their purchase will prove a considerable expense, offsetting some of the savings made by doing-it-yourself. However, provided that the tools purchased meet the relevant national safety standards and are of good quality, they will last for many years and prove an extremely worthwhile investment.

To help the average owner to decide which tools are needed to carry out the various tasks detailed in this manual, we have compiled three lists of tools under the following headings: *Maintenance and minor repair*, *Repair and overhaul*, and *Special*. Newcomers to practical mechanics should start off with the *Maintenance and minor repair* tool kit, and confine themselves to the simpler jobs around the vehicle. Then, as confidence and experience grow, more difficult tasks can be undertaken, with extra tools being purchased as, and when, they are needed. In this way, a *Maintenance and minor repair* tool kit can be built up into a *Repair and overhaul* tool kit over a considerable period of time, without any major cash outlays. The experienced do-it-yourselfer will have a tool kit good enough for most repair and overhaul procedures, and will add tools from the *Special* category when it is felt that the expense is justified by the amount of use to which these tools will be put.

Maintenance and minor repair tool kit

The tools given in this list should be considered as a minimum requirement if routine maintenance, servicing and minor repair operations are to be undertaken. We recommend the purchase of combination spanners (ring one end, open-ended the other); although more expensive than open-ended ones, they do give the advantages of both types of spanner.

☐ *Combination spanners:*
  Metric - 8 to 19 mm inclusive
☐ *Adjustable spanner - 35 mm jaw (approx.)*
☐ *Spark plug spanner (with rubber insert) - petrol models*
☐ *Spark plug gap adjustment tool - petrol models*
☐ *Set of feeler gauges*
☐ *Brake bleed nipple spanner*
☐ *Screwdrivers:*
  Flat blade - 100 mm long x 6 mm dia
  Cross blade - 100 mm long x 6 mm dia
  Torx - various sizes (not all vehicles)
☐ *Combination pliers*
☐ *Hacksaw (junior)*
☐ *Tyre pump*
☐ *Tyre pressure gauge*
☐ *Oil can*
☐ *Oil filter removal tool*
☐ *Fine emery cloth*
☐ *Wire brush (small)*
☐ *Funnel (medium size)*
☐ *Sump drain plug key (not all vehicles)*

Repair and overhaul tool kit

These tools are virtually essential for anyone undertaking any major repairs to a motor vehicle, and are additional to those given in the *Maintenance and minor repair* list. Included in this list is a comprehensive set of sockets. Although these are expensive, they will be found invaluable as they are so versatile - particularly if various drives are included in the set. We recommend the half-inch square-drive type, as this can be used with most proprietary torque wrenches.

The tools in this list will sometimes need to be supplemented by tools from the *Special* list:

☐ *Sockets (or box spanners) to cover range in previous list (including Torx sockets)*
☐ *Reversible ratchet drive (for use with sockets)*
☐ *Extension piece, 250 mm (for use with sockets)*
☐ *Universal joint (for use with sockets)*
☐ *Flexible handle or sliding T "breaker bar" (for use with sockets)*
☐ *Torque wrench (for use with sockets)*
☐ *Self-locking grips*
☐ *Ball pein hammer*
☐ *Soft-faced mallet (plastic or rubber)*
☐ *Screwdrivers:*
  Flat blade - long & sturdy, short (chubby), and narrow (electrician's) types
  Cross blade – long & sturdy, and short (chubby) types
☐ *Pliers:*
  Long-nosed
  Side cutters (electrician's)
  Circlip (internal and external)
☐ *Cold chisel - 25 mm*
☐ *Scriber*
☐ *Scraper*
☐ *Centre-punch*
☐ *Pin punch*
☐ *Hacksaw*
☐ *Brake hose clamp*
☐ *Brake/clutch bleeding kit*
☐ *Selection of twist drills*
☐ *Steel rule/straight-edge*
☐ *Allen keys (inc. splined/Torx type)*
☐ *Selection of files*
☐ *Wire brush*
☐ *Axle stands*
☐ *Jack (strong trolley or hydraulic type)*
☐ *Light with extension lead*
☐ *Universal electrical multi-meter*

Sockets and reversible ratchet drive

Brake bleeding kit

Torx key, socket and bit

Hose clamp

Angular-tightening gauge

Special tools

The tools in this list are those which are not used regularly, are expensive to buy, or which need to be used in accordance with their manufacturers' instructions. Unless relatively difficult mechanical jobs are undertaken frequently, it will not be economic to buy many of these tools. Where this is the case, you could consider clubbing together with friends (or joining a motorists' club) to make a joint purchase, or borrowing the tools against a deposit from a local garage or tool hire specialist. It is worth noting that many of the larger DIY superstores now carry a large range of special tools for hire at modest rates.

The following list contains only those tools and instruments freely available to the public, and not those special tools produced by the vehicle manufacturer specifically for its dealer network. You will find occasional references to these manufacturers' special tools in the text of this manual. Generally, an alternative method of doing the job without the vehicle manufacturers' special tool is given. However, sometimes there is no alternative to using them. Where this is the case and the relevant tool cannot be bought or borrowed, you will have to entrust the work to a dealer.

- [ ] Angular-tightening gauge
- [ ] Valve spring compressor
- [ ] Valve grinding tool
- [ ] Piston ring compressor
- [ ] Piston ring removal/installation tool
- [ ] Cylinder bore hone
- [ ] Balljoint separator
- [ ] Coil spring compressors (where applicable)
- [ ] Two/three-legged hub and bearing puller
- [ ] Impact screwdriver
- [ ] Micrometer and/or vernier calipers
- [ ] Dial gauge
- [ ] Stroboscopic timing light
- [ ] Dwell angle meter/tachometer
- [ ] Fault code reader
- [ ] Cylinder compression gauge
- [ ] Hand-operated vacuum pump and gauge
- [ ] Clutch plate alignment set
- [ ] Brake shoe steady spring cup removal tool
- [ ] Bush and bearing removal/installation set
- [ ] Stud extractors
- [ ] Tap and die set
- [ ] Lifting tackle
- [ ] Trolley jack

Buying tools

Reputable motor accessory shops and superstores often offer excellent quality tools at discount prices, so it pays to shop around.

Remember, you don't have to buy the most expensive items on the shelf, but it is always advisable to steer clear of the very cheap tools. Beware of 'bargains' offered on market stalls or at car boot sales. There are plenty of good tools around at reasonable prices, but always aim to purchase items which meet the relevant national safety standards. If in doubt, ask the proprietor or manager of the shop for advice before making a purchase.

Care and maintenance of tools

Having purchased a reasonable tool kit, it is necessary to keep the tools in a clean and serviceable condition. After use, always wipe off any dirt, grease and metal particles using a clean, dry cloth, before putting the tools away. Never leave them lying around after they have been used. A simple tool rack on the garage or workshop wall for items such as screwdrivers and pliers is a good idea. Store all normal spanners and sockets in a metal box. Any measuring instruments, gauges, meters, etc, must be carefully stored where they cannot be damaged or become rusty.

Take a little care when tools are used. Hammer heads inevitably become marked, and screwdrivers lose the keen edge on their blades from time to time. A little timely attention with emery cloth or a file will soon restore items like this to a good finish.

Working facilities

Not to be forgotten when discussing tools is the workshop itself. If anything more than routine maintenance is to be carried out, a suitable working area becomes essential.

It is appreciated that many an owner-mechanic is forced by circumstances to remove an engine or similar item without the benefit of a garage or workshop. Having done this, any repairs should always be done under the cover of a roof.

Wherever possible, any dismantling should be done on a clean, flat workbench or table at a suitable working height.

Any workbench needs a vice; one with a jaw opening of 100 mm is suitable for most jobs. As mentioned previously, some clean dry storage space is also required for tools, as well as for any lubricants, cleaning fluids, touch-up paints etc, which become necessary.

Another item which may be required, and which has a much more general usage, is an electric drill with a chuck capacity of at least 8 mm. This, together with a good range of twist drills, is virtually essential for fitting accessories.

Last, but not least, always keep a supply of old newspapers and clean, lint-free rags available, and try to keep any working area as clean as possible.

Micrometers

Dial test indicator ("dial gauge")

Strap wrench

Compression tester

Fault code reader

This is a guide to getting your vehicle through the MOT test. Obviously it will not be possible to examine the vehicle to the same standard as the professional MOT tester. However, working through the following checks will enable you to identify any problem areas before submitting the vehicle for the test.

It has only been possible to summarise the test requirements here, based on the regulations in force at the time of printing. Test standards are becoming increasingly stringent, although there are some exemptions for older vehicles.

An assistant will be needed to help carry out some of these checks.

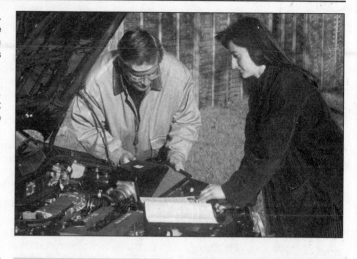

The checks have been sub-divided into four categories, as follows:

1 Checks carried out **FROM THE DRIVER'S SEAT**

2 Checks carried out **WITH THE VEHICLE ON THE GROUND**

3 Checks carried out **WITH THE VEHICLE RAISED AND THE WHEELS FREE TO TURN**

4 Checks carried out on **YOUR VEHICLE'S EXHAUST EMISSION SYSTEM**

---

1 Checks carried out **FROM THE DRIVER'S SEAT**

Handbrake

☐ Test the operation of the handbrake. Excessive travel (too many clicks) indicates incorrect brake or cable adjustment.
☐ Check that the handbrake cannot be released by tapping the lever sideways. Check the security of the lever mountings.

Footbrake

☐ Depress the brake pedal and check that it does not creep down to the floor, indicating a master cylinder fault. Release the pedal, wait a few seconds, then depress it again. If the pedal travels nearly to the floor before firm resistance is felt, brake adjustment or repair is necessary. If the pedal feels spongy, there is air in the hydraulic system which must be removed by bleeding.

☐ Check that the brake pedal is secure and in good condition. Check also for signs of fluid leaks on the pedal, floor or carpets, which would indicate failed seals in the brake master cylinder.
☐ Check the servo unit (when applicable) by operating the brake pedal several times, then keeping the pedal depressed and starting the engine. As the engine starts, the pedal will move down slightly. If not, the vacuum hose or the servo itself may be faulty.

Steering wheel and column

☐ Examine the steering wheel for fractures or looseness of the hub, spokes or rim.
☐ Move the steering wheel from side to side and then up and down. Check that the steering wheel is not loose on the column, indicating wear or a loose retaining nut. Continue moving the steering wheel as before, but also turn it slightly from left to right.
☐ Check that the steering wheel is not loose on the column, and that there is no abnormal

movement of the steering wheel, indicating wear in the column support bearings or couplings.

Windscreen, mirrors and sunvisor

☐ The windscreen must be free of cracks or other significant damage within the driver's field of view. (Small stone chips are acceptable.) Rear view mirrors must be secure, intact, and capable of being adjusted.

290mm

☐ The driver's sunvisor must be capable of being stored in the "up" position.

Seat belts and seats

Note: *The following checks are applicable to all seat belts, front and rear.*

☐ Examine the webbing of all the belts (including rear belts if fitted) for cuts, serious fraying or deterioration. Fasten and unfasten each belt to check the buckles. If applicable, check the retracting mechanism. Check the security of all seat belt mountings accessible from inside the vehicle.

☐ Seat belts with pre-tensioners, once activated, have a "flag" or similar showing on the seat belt stalk. This, in itself, is not a reason for test failure.

☐ The front seats themselves must be securely attached and the backrests must lock in the upright position.

Doors

☐ Both front doors must be able to be opened and closed from outside and inside, and must latch securely when closed.

2 Checks carried out **WITH THE VEHICLE ON THE GROUND**

Vehicle identification

☐ Number plates must be in good condition, secure and legible, with letters and numbers correctly spaced – spacing at (A) should be at least twice that at (B).

☐ The VIN plate and/or homologation plate must be legible.

Electrical equipment

☐ Switch on the ignition and check the operation of the horn.

☐ Check the windscreen washers and wipers, examining the wiper blades; renew damaged or perished blades. Also check the operation of the stop-lights.

☐ Check the operation of the sidelights and number plate lights. The lenses and reflectors must be secure, clean and undamaged.

☐ Check the operation and alignment of the headlights. The headlight reflectors must not be tarnished and the lenses must be undamaged.

☐ Switch on the ignition and check the operation of the direction indicators (including the instrument panel tell-tale) and the hazard warning lights. Operation of the sidelights and stop-lights must not affect the indicators - if it does, the cause is usually a bad earth at the rear light cluster.

☐ Check the operation of the rear foglight(s), including the warning light on the instrument panel or in the switch.

☐ The ABS warning light must illuminate in accordance with the manufacturers' design. For most vehicles, the ABS warning light should illuminate when the ignition is switched on, and (if the system is operating properly) extinguish after a few seconds. Refer to the owner's handbook.

Footbrake

☐ Examine the master cylinder, brake pipes and servo unit for leaks, loose mountings, corrosion or other damage.

☐ The fluid reservoir must be secure and the fluid level must be between the upper (**A**) and lower (**B**) markings.

☐ Inspect both front brake flexible hoses for cracks or deterioration of the rubber. Turn the steering from lock to lock, and ensure that the hoses do not contact the wheel, tyre, or any part of the steering or suspension mechanism. With the brake pedal firmly depressed, check the hoses for bulges or leaks under pressure.

Steering and suspension

☐ Have your assistant turn the steering wheel from side to side slightly, up to the point where the steering gear just begins to transmit this movement to the roadwheels. Check for excessive free play between the steering wheel and the steering gear, indicating wear or insecurity of the steering column joints, the column-to-steering gear coupling, or the steering gear itself.

☐ Have your assistant turn the steering wheel more vigorously in each direction, so that the roadwheels just begin to turn. As this is done, examine all the steering joints, linkages, fittings and attachments. Renew any component that shows signs of wear or damage. On vehicles with power steering, check the security and condition of the steering pump, drivebelt and hoses.

☐ Check that the vehicle is standing level, and at approximately the correct ride height.

Shock absorbers

☐ Depress each corner of the vehicle in turn, then release it. The vehicle should rise and then settle in its normal position. If the vehicle continues to rise and fall, the shock absorber is defective. A shock absorber which has seized will also cause the vehicle to fail.

Exhaust system

☐ Start the engine. With your assistant holding a rag over the tailpipe, check the entire system for leaks. Repair or renew leaking sections.

3 Checks carried out **WITH THE VEHICLE RAISED AND THE WHEELS FREE TO TURN**

Jack up the front and rear of the vehicle, and securely support it on axle stands. Position the stands clear of the suspension assemblies. Ensure that the wheels are clear of the ground and that the steering can be turned from lock to lock.

Steering mechanism

☐ Have your assistant turn the steering from lock to lock. Check that the steering turns smoothly, and that no part of the steering mechanism, including a wheel or tyre, fouls any brake hose or pipe or any part of the body structure.

☐ Examine the steering rack rubber gaiters for damage or insecurity of the retaining clips. If power steering is fitted, check for signs of damage or leakage of the fluid hoses, pipes or connections. Also check for excessive stiffness or binding of the steering, a missing split pin or locking device, or severe corrosion of the body structure within 30 cm of any steering component attachment point.

Front and rear suspension and wheel bearings

☐ Starting at the front right-hand side, grasp the roadwheel at the 3 o'clock and 9 o'clock positions and rock gently but firmly. Check for free play or insecurity at the wheel bearings, suspension balljoints, or suspension mountings, pivots and attachments.

☐ Now grasp the wheel at the 12 o'clock and 6 o'clock positions and repeat the previous inspection. Spin the wheel, and check for roughness or tightness of the front wheel bearing.

☐ If excess free play is suspected at a component pivot point, this can be confirmed by using a large screwdriver or similar tool and levering between the mounting and the component attachment. This will confirm whether the wear is in the pivot bush, its retaining bolt, or in the mounting itself (the bolt holes can often become elongated).

☐ Carry out all the above checks at the other front wheel, and then at both rear wheels.

Springs and shock absorbers

☐ Examine the suspension struts (when applicable) for serious fluid leakage, corrosion, or damage to the casing. Also check the security of the mounting points.

☐ If coil springs are fitted, check that the spring ends locate in their seats, and that the spring is not corroded, cracked or broken.

☐ If leaf springs are fitted, check that all leaves are intact, that the axle is securely attached to each spring, and that there is no deterioration of the spring eye mountings, bushes, and shackles.

☐ The same general checks apply to vehicles fitted with other suspension types, such as torsion bars, hydraulic displacer units, etc. Ensure that all mountings and attachments are secure, that there are no signs of excessive wear, corrosion or damage, and (on hydraulic types) that there are no fluid leaks or damaged pipes.

☐ Inspect the shock absorbers for signs of serious fluid leakage. Check for wear of the mounting bushes or attachments, or damage to the body of the unit.

Driveshafts
(fwd vehicles only)

☐ Rotate each front wheel in turn and inspect the constant velocity joint gaiters for splits or damage. Also check that each driveshaft is straight and undamaged.

Braking system

☐ If possible without dismantling, check brake pad wear and disc condition. Ensure that the friction lining material has not worn excessively, (A) and that the discs are not fractured, pitted, scored or badly worn (B).

☐ Examine all the rigid brake pipes underneath the vehicle, and the flexible hose(s) at the rear. Look for corrosion, chafing or insecurity of the pipes, and for signs of bulging under pressure, chafing, splits or deterioration of the flexible hoses.

☐ Look for signs of fluid leaks at the brake calipers or on the brake backplates. Repair or renew leaking components.

☐ Slowly spin each wheel, while your assistant depresses and releases the footbrake. Ensure that each brake is operating and does not bind when the pedal is released.

☐ Examine the handbrake mechanism, checking for frayed or broken cables, excessive corrosion, or wear or insecurity of the linkage. Check that the mechanism works on each relevant wheel, and releases fully, without binding.

☐ It is not possible to test brake efficiency without special equipment, but a road test can be carried out later to check that the vehicle pulls up in a straight line.

Fuel and exhaust systems

☐ Inspect the fuel tank (including the filler cap), fuel pipes, hoses and unions. All components must be secure and free from leaks.

☐ Examine the exhaust system over its entire length, checking for any damaged, broken or missing mountings, security of the retaining clamps and rust or corrosion.

Wheels and tyres

☐ Examine the sidewalls and tread area of each tyre in turn. Check for cuts, tears, lumps, bulges, separation of the tread, and exposure of the ply or cord due to wear or damage. Check that the tyre bead is correctly seated on the wheel rim, that the valve is sound and properly seated, and that the wheel is not distorted or damaged.

☐ Check that the tyres are of the correct size for the vehicle, that they are of the same size

and type on each axle, and that the pressures are correct.

☐ Check the tyre tread depth. The legal minimum at the time of writing is 1.6 mm over at least three-quarters of the tread width. Abnormal tread wear may indicate incorrect front wheel alignment.

Body corrosion

☐ Check the condition of the entire vehicle structure for signs of corrosion in load-bearing areas. (These include chassis box sections, side sills, cross-members, pillars, and all suspension, steering, braking system and seat belt mountings and anchorages.) Any corrosion which has seriously reduced the thickness of a load-bearing area is likely to cause the vehicle to fail. In this case professional repairs are likely to be needed.

☐ Damage or corrosion which causes sharp or otherwise dangerous edges to be exposed will also cause the vehicle to fail.

4 Checks carried out on YOUR VEHICLE'S EXHAUST EMISSION SYSTEM

Petrol models

☐ The engine should be warmed up, and running well (ignition system in good order, air filter element clean, etc).

☐ Before testing, run the engine at around 2500 rpm for 20 seconds. Let the engine drop to idle, and watch for smoke from the exhaust. If the idle speed is too high, or if dense blue or black smoke emerges for more than 5 seconds, the vehicle will fail. Typically, blue smoke signifies oil burning (engine wear); black smoke means unburnt fuel (dirty air cleaner element, or other fuel system fault).

☐ An exhaust gas analyser for measuring carbon monoxide (CO) and hydrocarbons (HC) is now needed. If one cannot be hired or borrowed, have a local garage perform the check.

CO emissions (mixture)

☐ The MOT tester has access to the CO limits for all vehicles. The CO level is measured at idle speed, and at 'fast idle' (2500 to 3000 rpm). The following limits are given as a general guide:
  At idle speed – Less than 0.5% CO
  At 'fast idle' – Less than 0.3% CO
  Lambda reading – 0.97 to 1.03
☐ If the CO level is too high, this may point to poor maintenance, a fuel injection system problem, faulty lambda (oxygen) sensor or catalytic converter. Try an injector cleaning treatment, and check the vehicle's ECU for fault codes.

HC emissions

☐ The MOT tester has access to HC limits for all vehicles. The HC level is measured at 'fast idle' (2500 to 3000 rpm). The following limits are given as a general guide:
  At 'fast idle' – Less then 200 ppm
☐ Excessive HC emissions are typically caused by oil being burnt (worn engine), or by a blocked crankcase ventilation system ('breather'). If the engine oil is old and thin, an oil change may help. If the engine is running badly, check the vehicle's ECU for fault codes.

Diesel models

☐ The only emission test for diesel engines is measuring exhaust smoke density, using a calibrated smoke meter. The test involves accelerating the engine at least 3 times to its maximum unloaded speed.

Note: *On engines with a timing belt, it is VITAL that the belt is in good condition before the test is carried out.*

☐ With the engine warmed up, it is first purged by running at around 2500 rpm for 20 seconds. A governor check is then carried out, by slowly accelerating the engine to its maximum speed. After this, the smoke meter is connected, and the engine is accelerated quickly to maximum speed three times. If the smoke density is less than the limits given below, the vehicle will pass:
  Non-turbo vehicles: 2.5m-1
  Turbocharged vehicles: 3.0m-1
☐ If excess smoke is produced, try fitting a new air cleaner element, or using an injector cleaning treatment. If the engine is running badly, where applicable, check the vehicle's ECU for fault codes. Also check the vehicle's EGR system, where applicable. At high mileages, the injectors may require professional attention.

Engine

- [ ] Engine fails to rotate when attempting to start
- [ ] Engine rotates, but will not start
- [ ] Engine difficult to start when cold
- [ ] Engine difficult to start when hot
- [ ] Starter motor noisy or excessively-rough in engagement
- [ ] Engine starts, but stops immediately
- [ ] Engine idles erratically
- [ ] Engine misfires at idle speed
- [ ] Engine misfires throughout the driving speed range
- [ ] Engine hesitates on acceleration
- [ ] Engine stalls
- [ ] Engine lacks power
- [ ] Engine backfires
- [ ] Oil pressure warning light illuminated with engine running
- [ ] Engine runs-on after switching off
- [ ] Engine noises

Cooling system

- [ ] Overheating
- [ ] Overcooling
- [ ] External coolant leakage
- [ ] Internal coolant leakage
- [ ] Corrosion

Fuel and exhaust systems

- [ ] Excessive fuel consumption
- [ ] Fuel leakage and/or fuel odour

Clutch

- [ ] Pedal travels to floor – no pressure or very little resistance
- [ ] Clutch fails to disengage (unable to select gears)
- [ ] Clutch slips (engine speed increases, with no increase in vehicle speed)
- [ ] Judder as clutch is engaged
- [ ] Noise when depressing or releasing clutch pedal

Manual transmission

- [ ] Noisy in neutral with engine running
- [ ] Noisy in one particular gear
- [ ] Difficulty engaging gears
- [ ] Vibration
- [ ] Jumps out of gear
- [ ] Lubricant leaks

Automatic transmission

- [ ] Fluid leakage
- [ ] General gear selection problems
- [ ] Transmission fluid brown, or has burned smell
- [ ] Transmission will not downshift (kickdown) with accelerator fully depressed
- [ ] Engine will not start in any gear, or starts in gears other than Park or Neutral
- [ ] Transmission slips, shifts roughly, is noisy, or has no drive in forward or reverse gears

Braking system

- [ ] Car pulls to one side under braking
- [ ] Noise (grinding or high-pitched squeal) when brakes applied
- [ ] Brakes binding
- [ ] Excessive brake pedal travel
- [ ] Brake pedal feels spongy when depressed
- [ ] Excessive brake pedal effort required to stop car
- [ ] Judder felt through brake pedal or steering wheel when braking
- [ ] Rear wheels locking under normal braking

Driveshafts

- [ ] Clicking or knocking noise on turns (at slow speed on full-lock)

Suspension and steering

- [ ] Car pulls to one side
- [ ] Excessive pitching and/or rolling around corners, or during braking
- [ ] Lack of power assistance
- [ ] Wandering or general instability
- [ ] Excessively-stiff steering
- [ ] Excessive play in steering
- [ ] Wheel wobble and vibration
- [ ] Tyre wear excessive

Electrical system

- [ ] Battery will not hold a charge for more than a few days
- [ ] Ignition/no-charge warning light remains illuminated with engine running
- [ ] Ignition/no-charge warning light fails to come on
- [ ] Lights inoperative
- [ ] Instrument readings inaccurate or erratic
- [ ] Horn inoperative, or unsatisfactory in operation
- [ ] Windscreen wipers inoperative, or unsatisfactory in operation
- [ ] Windscreen washers inoperative, or unsatisfactory in operation
- [ ] Electric windows inoperative, or unsatisfactory in operation
- [ ] Central locking system inoperative, or unsatisfactory in operation

Introduction

The car owner who does his or her own maintenance according to the recommended service schedules should not have to use this section of the manual very often. Modern component reliability is such that, provided those items subject to wear or deterioration are inspected or renewed at the specified intervals, sudden failure is comparatively rare. Faults do not usually just happen as a result of sudden failure, but develop over a period of time. Major mechanical failures in particular are usually preceded by characteristic symptoms over hundreds or even thousands of miles. Those components which do occasionally fail without warning are often small and easily carried in the car.

With any fault-finding, the first step is to decide where to begin investigations. Sometimes this is obvious, but on other occasions, a little detective work will be necessary. The owner who makes half a dozen haphazard adjustments or replacements may be successful in curing a fault (or its symptoms), but will be none the wiser if the fault recurs, and ultimately may have spent more time and money than was necessary. A calm and logical approach will be found to be more satisfactory in the long run. Always take into account any warning signs or abnormalities that may have been noticed in the period preceding the fault – power loss, high or low gauge readings, unusual smells,

etc – and remember that failure of components such as fuses may only be pointers to some underlying fault.

The pages which follow provide an easy reference guide to the more common problems which may occur during the operation of the car. These problems and their possible causes are grouped under headings denoting various components or systems, such as Engine, Cooling system, etc. The Chapter and/or Section which deals with the problem is also shown in brackets. Whatever the fault, certain basic principles apply. These are as follows:

Verify the fault. This is simply a matter of being sure that you know what the symptoms are before starting work. This is particularly important if you are investigating a fault for someone else, who may not have described it very accurately.

Don't overlook the obvious. For example, if the car won't start, is there fuel in the tank? (Don't take anyone else's word on this particular point, and don't trust the fuel gauge either!) If an electrical fault is indicated, look for loose or broken wires before using the test gear.

Cure the disease, not the symptom. Substituting a flat battery with a fully-charged one will get you off the hard shoulder, but if the underlying cause is not attended to, the new battery will go the same way.

Don't take anything for granted. Particularly, don't forget that a 'new' component may itself be defective (especially if it's been rattling around in the boot for months), and don't leave components out of a fault diagnosis sequence just because they are new or recently fitted. When you do finally diagnose a difficult fault, you'll probably realise that all the evidence was there from the start.

Consider what work, if any, has recently been carried out. Many faults arise through careless or hurried work. For instance, if any work has been performed under the bonnet, could some of the wiring have been dislodged or incorrectly routed, or a hose trapped? Have all the fasteners been properly tightened? Were new, genuine parts and new gaskets used? There is often a certain amount of detective work to be done in this case, as an apparently-unrelated task can have far-reaching consequences.

Diesel fault diagnosis

The majority of starting problems on small diesel engines are electrical in origin. The mechanic who is familiar with petrol engines but less so with diesel may be inclined to view the diesel's injectors and pump in the same light as the spark plugs and distributor, but this is generally a mistake.

When investigating complaints of difficult starting for someone else, make sure that the correct starting procedure is understood and is being followed. Some drivers are unaware of the significance of the preheating warning light – many modern engines are sufficiently forgiving for this not to matter in mild weather, but with the onset of winter problems begin.

As a rule of thumb, if the engine is difficult to start but runs well when it has finally got going, the problem is electrical (battery, starter motor or preheating system). If poor performance is combined with difficult starting, the problem is likely to be in the fuel system. The low pressure (supply) side of the fuel system should be checked before suspecting the injectors and injection pump. The most common fuel supply problem is air getting into the system, and any pipe from the fuel tank forwards must be scrutinised if air leakage is suspected. Normally the pump is the last item to suspect, since unless it has been tampered with, there is no reason for it to be at fault.

Engine

Engine fails to rotate when attempting to start

- ☐ Battery terminal connections loose or corroded (*Weekly checks*).
- ☐ Battery discharged or faulty (Chapter 5A).
- ☐ Broken, loose or disconnected wiring in the starting circuit (Chapter 5A).
- ☐ Defective starter solenoid or switch (Chapter 5A).
- ☐ Defective starter motor (Chapter 5A).
- ☐ Starter pinion or flywheel ring gear teeth loose or broken (Chapters 2A, 2B, 2C and 5A).
- ☐ Engine earth strap broken or disconnected (Chapter 5A).

Engine rotates, but will not start

- ☐ Fuel tank empty.
- ☐ Battery discharged (engine rotates slowly) (Chapter 5A).
- ☐ Battery terminal connections loose or corroded (*Weekly checks*).
- ☐ Ignition components damp or damaged – petrol models (Chapters 1A and 5B).
- ☐ Broken, loose or disconnected wiring in the ignition circuit – petrol models (Chapters 1A and 5B).
- ☐ Worn, faulty or incorrectly gapped spark plugs – petrol models (Chapter 1A).
- ☐ Fuel injection system fault (Chapter 4A and 4B).
- ☐ Air in fuel system – diesel models (Chapter 4B).
- ☐ Major mechanical failure (eg, timing belt/chain) (Chapter 2A, 2B, or 2C).

Engine difficult to start when cold

- ☐ Battery discharged (Chapter 5A).
- ☐ Battery terminal connections loose or corroded (*Weekly checks*).
- ☐ Worn, faulty or incorrectly gapped spark plugs – petrol models (Chapter 1A).
- ☐ Fuel injection system fault (Chapter 4A and 4B).
- ☐ Other ignition system fault – petrol models (Chapters 1A and 5B).
- ☐ Preheating system fault – diesel models (Chapter 5A).
- ☐ Low cylinder compressions (Chapter 2A, 2B, or 2C).

Engine difficult to start when hot

- ☐ Air filter element dirty or clogged (Chapter 1A or 1B).
- ☐ Fuel injection system fault (Chapter 4A and 4B).
- ☐ Low cylinder compressions (Chapter 2A, 2B, or 2C).

Starter motor noisy or excessively rough in engagement

- ☐ Starter pinion or flywheel ring gear teeth loose or broken (Chapters 2A, 2B, 2C and 5A).
- ☐ Starter motor mounting bolts loose or missing (Chapter 5A).
- ☐ Starter motor internal components worn or damaged (Chapter 5A).

Engine starts, but stops immediately

- ☐ Loose or faulty electrical connections in the ignition circuit – petrol models (Chapters 1A and 5B).
- ☐ Vacuum leak at the throttle body or intake manifold – petrol models (Chapter 4A).
- ☐ Blocked injector/fuel injection system fault (Chapter 4A or 4B).
- ☐ Faulty injector(s) – diesel models (Chapter 4B).
- ☐ Air in fuel system – diesel models (Chapter 4B).

Engine idles erratically

- ☐ Air filter element clogged (Chapter 1A or 1B).
- ☐ Vacuum leak at the throttle body, intake manifold or associated hoses – petrol models (Chapter 4A).
- ☐ Worn, faulty or incorrectly gapped spark plugs – petrol models (Chapter 1A).
- ☐ Uneven or low cylinder compressions (Chapter 2A, 2B, or 2C).
- ☐ Camshaft lobes worn (Chapter 2A, 2B, or 2C).
- ☐ Timing belt incorrectly tensioned (Chapter 2A, 2B, or 2C).
- ☐ Blocked injector/fuel injection system fault (Chapter 4A or 4B).
- ☐ Faulty injector(s) – diesel models (Chapter 4B).

Engine misfires at idle speed

- ☐ Worn, faulty or incorrectly gapped spark plugs – petrol models (Chapter 1A).
- ☐ Faulty spark plug HT leads – petrol models (Chapter 5B).
- ☐ Vacuum leak at the throttle body, intake manifold or associated hoses (Chapter 4A or 4B).
- ☐ Blocked injector/fuel injection system fault (Chapter 4A and 4B).
- ☐ Faulty injector(s) – diesel models (Chapter 4B).
- ☐ Uneven or low cylinder compressions (Chapter 2A, 2B, or 2C).
- ☐ Disconnected, leaking, or perished crankcase ventilation hoses (Chapter 4C).

Engine (continued)

Engine misfires throughout the driving speed range

- ☐ Fuel filter choked (Chapter 1A or 1B).
- ☐ Fuel pump faulty, or delivery pressure low (Chapter 4A or 4B).
- ☐ Fuel tank vent blocked, or fuel pipes restricted (Chapter 4A or 4B).
- ☐ Vacuum leak at the throttle body, intake manifold or associated hoses – petrol models (Chapter 4A).
- ☐ Worn, faulty or incorrectly gapped spark plugs – petrol models (Chapter 1A).
- ☐ Faulty spark plug HT leads, where applicable (Chapter 5B).
- ☐ Faulty injector(s) – diesel models (Chapter 4B).
- ☐ Faulty ignition coil(s) – petrol models (Chapter 5B).
- ☐ Uneven or low cylinder compressions (Chapter 2A, 2B, or 2C).
- ☐ Blocked injector/fuel injection system fault (Chapter 4A or 4B).

Engine hesitates on acceleration

- ☐ Worn, faulty or incorrectly gapped spark plugs – petrol models (Chapter 1A).
- ☐ Vacuum leak at the throttle body, intake manifold or associated hoses – petrol models (Chapter 4A).
- ☐ Blocked injector/fuel injection system fault (Chapter 4A or 4B).
- ☐ Faulty injector(s) – diesel models (Chapter 4B).

Engine stalls

- ☐ Vacuum leak at the throttle body, intake manifold or associated hoses – petrol models (Chapter 4A).
- ☐ Fuel filter choked (Chapter 1A or 1B).
- ☐ Fuel pump faulty, or delivery pressure low – petrol models (Chapter 4A).
- ☐ Fuel tank vent blocked, or fuel pipes restricted (Chapter 4A or 4B).
- ☐ Blocked injector/fuel injection system fault (Chapter 4A or 4B).
- ☐ Faulty injector(s) – diesel models (Chapter 4B).
- ☐ Air in fuel system – diesel models (Chapter 4B).

Engine lacks power

- ☐ Timing belt incorrectly fitted or tensioned (Chapter 2B, or 2C).
- ☐ Fuel filter choked (Chapter 1A or 1B).
- ☐ Fuel pump faulty, or delivery pressure low – petrol models (Chapter 4A).
- ☐ Uneven or low cylinder compressions (Chapter 2A, 2B, or 2C).
- ☐ Worn, faulty or incorrectly gapped spark plugs – petrol models (Chapter 1A).
- ☐ Vacuum leak at the throttle body, intake manifold or associated hoses – petrol models (Chapter 4A).
- ☐ Blocked injector/fuel injection system fault (Chapter 4A or 4B).
- ☐ Brakes binding (Chapters 1A or 1B and 9).
- ☐ Clutch slipping (Chapter 6).

Engine backfires

- ☐ Timing belt incorrectly fitted or tensioned (Chapter 2B, or 2C).
- ☐ Vacuum leak at the throttle body, intake manifold or associated hoses – petrol models (Chapter 4A).
- ☐ Blocked injector/fuel injection system fault (Chapter 4A or 4B).

Oil pressure warning light illuminated with engine running

- ☐ Low oil level, or incorrect oil grade (Weekly checks).
- ☐ Faulty oil pressure warning light switch (Chapter 2A, 2B, or 2C).
- ☐ Worn engine bearings and/or oil pump (Chapter 2A, 2B, 2C or 2D).
- ☐ High engine operating temperature (Chapter 3).
- ☐ Oil pressure relief valve defective (Chapter 2A, 2B, or 2C).
- ☐ Oil pick-up strainer clogged – remove sump to inspect (Chapter 2A, 2B, or 2C).

Engine runs-on after switching off

- ☐ Excessive carbon build-up in engine – remove cylinder head (Chapter 2A, 2B, or 2C).
- ☐ High engine operating temperature (Chapter 3).
- ☐ Fuel injection system fault (Chapter 4A or 4B).

Engine noises

Pre-ignition (pinking) or knocking during acceleration or under load

- ☐ Ignition timing incorrect/ignition system fault – petrol models (Chapters 1A and 5B).
- ☐ Incorrect grade of spark plug – petrol models (Chapter 1A).
- ☐ Incorrect grade of fuel (Chapter 4A).
- ☐ Vacuum leak at the throttle body, intake manifold or associated hoses – petrol models (Chapter 4A).
- ☐ Excessive carbon build-up in engine – remove cylinder head (Chapter 2A, 2B, or 2C).
- ☐ Blocked injector/fuel injection system fault – petrol models (Chapter 4A).

Whistling or wheezing noises

- ☐ Leaking intake manifold or throttle body gasket – petrol models (Chapter 4A).
- ☐ Leaking exhaust manifold gasket or pipe-to-manifold joint (Chapter 4C).
- ☐ Leaking vacuum hose (Chapters 4A, 4B, 4C and 9).
- ☐ Blowing cylinder head gasket (Chapter 2A, 2B, or 2C).

Tapping or rattling noises

- ☐ Worn valve gear or camshaft (Chapter 2A, 2B, or 2C).
- ☐ Ancillary component fault (coolant pump, alternator, etc) (Chapters 3, 5A, etc).

Knocking or thumping noises

- ☐ Worn big-end bearings (regular heavy knocking, perhaps worsening under load) (Chapter 2D).
- ☐ Worn main bearings (rumbling and knocking, perhaps less under load) (Chapter 2D).
- ☐ Piston slap (most noticeable when cold) – caused by cylinder bore/piston ring wear (Chapter 2D).
- ☐ Ancillary component fault (coolant pump, alternator, etc) (Chapters 3, 5A, etc).

Cooling system

Overheating

- [ ] Insufficient coolant in system (*Weekly checks*).
- [ ] Thermostat faulty (Chapter 3).
- [ ] Radiator core blocked, or grille restricted (Chapter 3).
- [ ] Electric cooling fan or thermo-switch faulty (Chapter 3).
- [ ] Pressure cap faulty (Chapter 3).
- [ ] Ignition system fault – petrol engines (Chapters 1A and 5B).
- [ ] Inaccurate temperature gauge sender unit (Chapter 3).
- [ ] Airlock in cooling system.

Overcooling

- [ ] Thermostat faulty (Chapter 3).
- [ ] Inaccurate temperature gauge sender unit (Chapter 3).

External coolant leakage

- [ ] Deteriorated or damaged hoses or hose clips (Chapter 1A or 1B).
- [ ] Radiator core or heater matrix leaking (Chapter 3).
- [ ] Pressure cap faulty (Chapter 3).
- [ ] Water pump seal leaking (Chapter 3).
- [ ] Boiling due to overheating (Chapter 3).
- [ ] Cylinder block core plug leaking (Chapter 2D).

Internal coolant leakage

- [ ] Leaking cylinder head gasket (Chapter 2A, 2B, or 2C).
- [ ] Cracked cylinder head or cylinder bore (Chapter 2D).

Corrosion

- [ ] Infrequent draining and flushing (Chapter 1A or 1B).
- [ ] Incorrect coolant mixture or wrong coolant type (Chapter 1A or 1B).

Fuel and exhaust systems

Excessive fuel consumption

- [ ] Air filter element dirty or clogged (Chapter 1A or 1B).
- [ ] Fuel injection system fault (Chapter 4A or 4B).
- [ ] Ignition system fault – petrol models (Chapters 1A and 5B).
- [ ] Faulty injector(s) – diesel models (Chapter 4B).
- [ ] Tyres under-inflated (*Weekly checks*).

Fuel leakage and/or fuel odour

- [ ] Damaged or corroded fuel tank, pipes or connections (Chapter 4A or 4B).
- [ ] Excessive noise or fumes from exhaust system
- [ ] Leaking exhaust system or manifold joints (Chapters 1A, 1B, or 4C).
- [ ] Leaking, corroded or damaged silencers or pipe (Chapters 1A, 1B, or 4C).
- [ ] Broken mountings causing contact (Chapter 1A or 1B).

Clutch

Pedal travels to floor – no pressure or very little resistance

- [ ] Hydraulic fluid level low/air in hydraulic system (Chapter 6).
- [ ] Broken clutch release bearing or fork (Chapter 6).
- [ ] Broken diaphragm spring in clutch pressure plate (Chapter 6).

Clutch fails to disengage (unable to select gears)

- [ ] Clutch disc sticking on transmission input shaft splines (Chapter 6).
- [ ] Clutch disc sticking to flywheel or pressure plate (Chapter 6).
- [ ] Faulty pressure plate assembly (Chapter 6).
- [ ] Clutch release mechanism worn or incorrectly assembled (Chapter 6).

Clutch slips (engine speed increases, with no increase in vehicle speed)

- [ ] Clutch disc linings excessively worn (Chapter 6).
- [ ] Clutch disc linings contaminated with oil or grease (Chapter 6).
- [ ] Faulty pressure plate or weak diaphragm spring (Chapter 6).

Judder as clutch is engaged

- [ ] Clutch disc linings contaminated with oil or grease (Chapter 6).
- [ ] Clutch disc linings excessively worn (Chapter 6).
- [ ] Faulty or distorted pressure plate or diaphragm spring (Chapter 6).
- [ ] Worn or loose engine or transmission mountings (Chapter 2A, 2B, or 2C).
- [ ] Clutch disc hub or transmission input shaft splines worn (Chapter 6).

Noise when depressing or releasing clutch pedal

- [ ] Worn clutch release bearing (Chapter 6).
- [ ] Worn or dry clutch pedal bushes (Chapter 6).
- [ ] Faulty pressure plate assembly (Chapter 6).
- [ ] Pressure plate diaphragm spring broken (Chapter 6).
- [ ] Broken clutch disc cushioning springs (Chapter 6).

Manual transmission

Noisy in neutral with engine running

- [ ] Input shaft bearings worn (noise apparent with clutch pedal released, but not when depressed) (Chapter 7A).*
- [ ] Clutch release bearing worn (noise apparent with clutch pedal depressed, possibly less when released) (Chapter 6).

Noisy in one particular gear

- [ ] Worn, damaged or chipped gear teeth (Chapter 7A).*

Difficulty engaging gears

- [ ] Clutch fault (Chapter 6).
- [ ] Worn or damaged gear linkage (Chapter 7A).
- [ ] Incorrectly adjusted gear linkage (Chapter 7A).
- [ ] Worn synchroniser units (Chapter 7A).*

Vibration

- [ ] Lack of oil (Chapter 1A or 1B).
- [ ] Worn bearings (Chapter 7A).*

Jumps out of gear

- [ ] Worn or damaged gear linkage (Chapter 7A).
- [ ] Incorrectly adjusted gear linkage (Chapter 7A).
- [ ] Worn synchroniser units (Chapter 7A).*
- [ ] Worn selector forks (Chapter 7A).*

Lubricant leaks

- [ ] Leaking differential output oil seal (Chapter 7A).
- [ ] Leaking housing joint (Chapter 7A).*
- [ ] Leaking input shaft oil seal (Chapter 7A).*

Although the corrective action necessary to remedy the symptoms described is beyond the scope of the home mechanic, the above information should be helpful in isolating the cause of the condition. This should enable the owner can communicate clearly with a professional mechanic.

Automatic transmission

Note: *Due to the complexity of the automatic transmission, it is difficult for the home mechanic to properly diagnose and service this unit. For problems other than the following, the car should be taken to a dealer service department or automatic transmission specialist. Do not be too hasty in removing the transmission if a fault is suspected, as most of the testing is carried out with the unit still fitted.*

Fluid leakage

- [ ] Automatic transmission fluid is usually dark in colour. Fluid leaks should not be confused with engine oil, which can easily be blown onto the transmission by airflow.
- [ ] To determine the source of a leak, first remove all built-up dirt and grime from the transmission housing and surrounding areas using a degreasing agent, or by steam-cleaning. Drive the car at low speed, so airflow will not blow the leak far from its source. Raise and support the car, and determine where the leak is coming from.

General gear selection problems

- [ ] Chapter 7B deals with checking and adjusting the selector cable on automatic transmissions. The following are common problems which may be caused by a poorly-adjusted cable:

  a) *Engine starting in gears other than Park or Neutral.*

  b) *Indicator panel indicating a gear other than the one actually being used.*

  c) *Car moves when in Park or Neutral.*

  d) *Poor gear shift quality or erratic gearchanges.*

Transmission fluid brown, or has burned smell

- [ ] Transmission fluid level low (Chapter 1A or 1B). If the fluid appears to have deteriorated badly it is recommended that it is renewed.

Transmission will not downshift (kickdown) with accelerator pedal fully depressed

- [ ] Low transmission fluid level (Chapter 1A or 1B).
- [ ] Incorrect selector cable adjustment (Chapter 7B).

Engine will not start in any gear, or starts in gears other than Park or Neutral

- [ ] Incorrect selector cable adjustment (Chapter 7B).

Transmission slips, shifts roughly, is noisy, or has no drive in forward or reverse gears

- [ ] There are many probable causes for the above problems, but unless there is a very obvious reason (such as a loose or corroded wiring plug connection on or near the transmission), the car should be taken to a franchise dealer for the fault to be diagnosed. The transmission control unit incorporates a self-diagnosis facility, and any fault codes can quickly be read and interpreted by a dealer with the proper diagnostic equipment.

Braking system

Note: *Before assuming that a brake problem exists, make sure that the tyres are in good condition and correctly inflated, that the front wheel alignment is correct, and that the car is not loaded with weight in an unequal manner. Apart from checking the condition of all pipe and hose connections, any faults occurring on the anti-lock braking system should be referred to a Seat dealer for diagnosis.*

Car pulls to one side under braking

☐ Worn, defective, damaged or contaminated brake pads on one side (Chapters 1A or 1B and 9).
☐ Seized or partially seized brake caliper piston (Chapters 1A or 1B and 9).
☐ A mixture of brake pad lining materials fitted between sides (Chapters 1A or 1B and 9).
☐ Brake caliper mounting bolts loose (Chapter 9).
☐ Worn or damaged steering or suspension components (Chapters 1A or 1B and 10).

Noise (grinding or high-pitched squeal) when brakes applied)

☐ Brake pad friction lining material worn down to metal backing (Chapters 1A or 1B and 9).
☐ Excessive corrosion of brake disc. This may be apparent after the car has been standing for some time (Chapters 1A or 1B and 9).
☐ Foreign object (stone chipping, etc) trapped between brake disc and shield (Chapters 1A or 1B and 9).

Brakes binding

☐ Seized brake caliper piston(s) (Chapter 9).
☐ Incorrectly adjusted handbrake mechanism (Chapter 9).
☐ Faulty master cylinder (Chapter 9).

Excessive brake pedal travel

☐ Faulty master cylinder (Chapter 9).
☐ Air in hydraulic system (Chapters 1A or 1B and 9).
☐ Faulty vacuum servo unit (Chapter 9).

Brake pedal feels spongy when depressed

☐ Air in hydraulic system (Chapters 1A or 1B and 9).
☐ Deteriorated flexible rubber brake hoses (Chapters 1A or 1B and 9).
☐ Master cylinder mounting nuts loose (Chapter 9).
☐ Faulty master cylinder (Chapter 9).

Excessive brake pedal effort required to stop car

☐ Faulty vacuum servo unit (Chapter 9).
☐ Faulty brake vacuum pump – diesel models (Chapter 9).
☐ Disconnected, damaged or insecure brake servo vacuum hose (Chapter 9).
☐ Primary or secondary hydraulic circuit failure (Chapter 9).
☐ Seized brake caliper piston(s) (Chapter 9).
☐ Brake pads incorrectly fitted (Chapters 1A or 1B and 9).
☐ Incorrect grade of brake pads fitted (Chapters 1A or 1B and 9).
☐ Brake pads contaminated (Chapters 1A or 1B and 9).

Judder felt through brake pedal or steering wheel when braking

Note: *Judder felt through the brake pedal is a normal feature of models fitted with ABS.*
☐ Excessive run-out or distortion of discs (Chapters 1A or 1B and 9).
☐ Brake pads worn (Chapters 1A or 1B and 9).
☐ Brake caliper mounting bolts loose (Chapter 9).
☐ Wear in suspension or steering components or mountings (Chapters 1A or 1B and 10).

Rear wheels locking under normal braking

☐ Rear brake pads contaminated (Chapters 1A or 1B and 9).
☐ ABS system fault (Chapter 9).

Driveshafts

Clicking or knocking noise on turns (at slow speed on full-lock)

☐ Lack of constant velocity joint lubricant, possibly due to damaged gaiter (Chapter 8).

☐ Worn outer constant velocity joint (Chapter 8).
☐ Vibration when accelerating or decelerating
☐ Worn inner constant velocity joint (Chapter 8).
☐ Bent or distorted driveshaft (Chapter 8).

Suspension and steering

Note: *Before diagnosing suspension or steering faults, be sure that the trouble is not due to incorrect tyre pressures, mixtures of tyre types, or binding brakes.*

Car pulls to one side

- ☐ Defective tyre (*Weekly checks*).
- ☐ Excessive wear in suspension or steering components (Chapters 1A or 1B and 10).
- ☐ Incorrect front wheel alignment (Chapter 10).
- ☐ Accident damage to steering or suspension components (Chapter 1A or 1B and 10).

Excessive pitching and/or rolling around corners, or during braking

- ☐ Defective shock absorbers (Chapters 1A or 1B and 10).
- ☐ Broken or weak spring and/or suspension component (Chapters 1A or 1B and 10).
- ☐ Worn or damaged anti-roll bar or mountings – where applicable (Chapter 10).

Lack of power assistance

- ☐ Incorrect power steering fluid level (*Weekly checks*).
- ☐ Restriction in power steering fluid hoses (Chapter 1A or 1B).
- ☐ Faulty power steering pump (Chapter 10).
- ☐ Faulty rack-and-pinion steering gear (Chapter 10).

Wandering or general instability

- ☐ Incorrect front wheel alignment (Chapter 10).
- ☐ Worn steering or suspension joints, bushes or components (Chapters 1A or 1B and 10).
- ☐ Roadwheels out of balance (Chapters 1A or 1B and 10).
- ☐ Faulty or damaged tyre (*Weekly checks*).
- ☐ Wheel bolts loose (refer to Chapter 10 for correct torque).
- ☐ Defective shock absorbers (Chapters 1A or 1B and 10).

Excessively stiff steering

- ☐ Lack of steering gear lubricant (Chapter 10).
- ☐ Seized track rod end balljoint or suspension balljoint Chapters 1A or 1B and 10).
- ☐ Incorrect front wheel alignment (Chapter 10).
- ☐ Steering rack or column bent or damaged (Chapter 10).

Excessive play in steering

- ☐ Worn steering column intermediate shaft universal joint (Chapter 10).
- ☐ Worn steering track rod end balljoints (Chapters 1A or 1B and 10).
- ☐ Worn rack-and-pinion steering gear (Chapter 10).
- ☐ Worn steering or suspension joints, bushes or components (Chapters 1A or 1B and 10).

Wheel wobble and vibration

- ☐ Front roadwheels out of balance (vibration felt mainly through the steering wheel) (Chapters 1A or 1B and 10).
- ☐ Rear roadwheels out of balance (vibration felt throughout the car) (Chapters 1A or 1B and 10).
- ☐ Roadwheels damaged or distorted (Chapters 1A or 1B and 10).
- ☐ Faulty or damaged tyre (*Weekly checks*).
- ☐ Worn steering or suspension joints, bushes or components (Chapters 1A or 1B and 10).
- ☐ Wheel bolts loose (Chapter 10).

Tyre wear excessive

Tyres worn on inside or outside edges

- ☐ Tyres under-inflated (wear on both edges) (*Weekly checks*).
- ☐ Incorrect camber or castor angles (wear on one edge only) (Chapter 10).
- ☐ Worn steering or suspension joints, bushes or components (Chapters 1A or 1B and 10).
- ☐ Excessively hard cornering.
- ☐ Accident damage.

Tyre treads exhibit feathered edges

- ☐ Incorrect toe setting (Chapter 10).

Tyres worn in centre of tread

- ☐ Tyres over-inflated (*Weekly checks*).

Tyres worn on inside and outside edges

- ☐ Tyres under-inflated (*Weekly checks*).

Tyres worn unevenly

- ☐ Tyres/wheels out of balance (Chapter 1A, 1B or 10).
- ☐ Excessive wheel or tyre run-out (Chapter 1A, 1B or 10).
- ☐ Worn shock absorbers (Chapters 1A or 1B and 10).
- ☐ Faulty tyre (*Weekly checks*).

Electrical system

Note: For problems associated with the starting system, refer to the faults listed under 'Engine' earlier in this Section.

Battery will not hold a charge for more than a few days

☐ Battery defective internally (Chapter 5A).
☐ Battery terminal connections loose or corroded (*Weekly checks*).
☐ Auxiliary drivebelt worn or incorrectly adjusted (Chapter 1A or 1B).
☐ Alternator not charging at correct output (Chapter 5A).
☐ Alternator or voltage regulator faulty (Chapter 5A).
☐ Short-circuit causing continual battery drain (Chapters 5A and 12).

Ignition/no-charge warning light remains illuminated with engine running

☐ Auxiliary drivebelt broken, worn, or incorrectly adjusted (Chapter 1A or 1B).
☐ Alternator brushes worn, sticking, or dirty (Chapter 5A).
☐ Alternator brush springs weak or broken (Chapter 5A).
☐ Internal fault in alternator or voltage regulator (Chapter 5A).
☐ Broken, disconnected, or loose wiring in charging circuit (Chapter 5A).

Ignition/no-charge warning light fails to come on

☐ Warning light LED defective (Chapter 12).
☐ Broken, disconnected, or loose wiring in warning light circuit (Chapter 12).
☐ Alternator faulty (Chapter 5A).

Lights inoperative

☐ Bulb blown (Chapter 12).
☐ Corrosion of bulb or bulbholder contacts (Chapter 12).
☐ Blown fuse (Chapter 12).
☐ Faulty relay (Chapter 12).
☐ Broken, loose, or disconnected wiring (Chapter 12).
☐ Faulty switch (Chapter 12).

Instrument readings inaccurate or erratic

Fuel or temperature gauges give no reading

☐ Faulty gauge sender unit (Chapters 3, 4A or 4B).
☐ Wiring open-circuit (Chapter 12).
☐ Faulty gauge (Chapter 12).

Fuel or temperature gauges give continuous maximum reading

☐ Faulty gauge sender unit (Chapters 3, 4A or 4B).
☐ Wiring short-circuit (Chapter 12).
☐ Faulty gauge (Chapter 12).

Horn inoperative, or unsatisfactory in operation

Horn operates all the time

☐ Horn push either earthed or stuck down (Chapter 12).
☐ Horn cable-to-horn push earthed (Chapter 12).

Horn fails to operate

☐ Blown fuse (Chapter 12).
☐ Cable or cable connections loose, broken or disconnected (Chapter 12).
☐ Faulty horn (Chapter 12).

Horn emits intermittent or unsatisfactory sound

☐ Cable connections loose (Chapter 12).
☐ Horn mountings loose (Chapter 12).
☐ Faulty horn (Chapter 12).

Windscreen/tailgate wipers inoperative, or unsatisfactory in operation

Wipers fail to operate, or operate very slowly

☐ Wiper blades stuck to screen, or linkage seized or binding (*Weekly checks* and Chapter 12).
☐ Blown fuse (Chapter 12).
☐ Wiring loose, broken or disconnected (Chapter 12).
☐ Faulty relay (Chapter 12).
☐ Faulty wiper motor (Chapter 12).

Wiper blades sweep over too large or too small an area of the glass

☐ Wiper arms incorrectly positioned on spindles (Chapter 12).
☐ Excessive wear of wiper linkage (Chapter 12).
☐ Wiper motor or linkage mountings loose or insecure (Chapter 12).

Wiper blades fail to clean the glass effectively

☐ Wiper blade rubbers worn or perished (*Weekly checks*).
☐ Wiper arm tension springs broken, or arm pivots seized (Chapter 12).
☐ Insufficient windscreen washer additive to adequately remove road film (*Weekly checks*).

Windscreen/tailgate washers inoperative, or unsatisfactory in operation

One or more washer jets inoperative

☐ Blocked washer jet (Chapter 1A or 1B).
☐ Disconnected, kinked or restricted fluid hose (Chapter 12).
☐ Insufficient fluid in washer reservoir (Chapter 1A or 1B).

Washer pump fails to operate

☐ Broken or disconnected wiring or connections (Chapter 12).
☐ Blown fuse (Chapter 12).
☐ Faulty washer switch (Chapter 12).
☐ Faulty washer pump (Chapter 12).

Electric windows inoperative, or unsatisfactory in operation

Window glass will only move in one direction

☐ Faulty switch (Chapter 12).

Window glass slow to move

☐ Regulator seized or damaged, or in need of lubrication (Chapter 11).
☐ Door internal components or trim fouling regulator (Chapter 11).
☐ Faulty motor (Chapter 11).

Window glass fails to move

☐ Blown fuse (Chapter 12).
☐ Faulty relay (Chapter 12).
☐ Broken or disconnected wiring or connections (Chapter 12).
☐ Faulty motor (Chapter 11).

Electrical system (continued)

Central locking system inoperative, or unsatisfactory in operation

Complete system failure

☐ Blown fuse (Chapter 12).
☐ Faulty relay (Chapter 12).
☐ Broken or disconnected wiring or connections (Chapter 12).
☐ Faulty control module (Chapter 11).

Latch locks but will not unlock, or unlocks but will not lock

☐ Faulty master switch (Chapter 11).
☐ Broken or disconnected latch operating rods or levers (Chapter 11).
☐ Faulty relay (Chapter 12).
☐ Faulty control module (Chapter 11).

One actuator fails to operate

☐ Broken or disconnected wiring or connections (Chapter 12).
☐ Faulty actuator (Chapter 11).
☐ Broken, binding or disconnected latch operating rods or levers (Chapter 11).
☐ Fault in door lock (Chapter 11).

Note: *References throughout this index are in the form* **"Chapter number"** • **"Page number"**. *So, for example, 2C•15 refers to page 15 of Chapter 2C.*

Note: *References throughout this index are in the form "***Chapter number***" • "***Page number***". So, for example, 2C•15 refers to page 15 of Chapter 2C.*

Note: *References throughout this index are in the form* "**Chapter number**" • "**Page number**". *So, for example, 2C•15 refers to page 15 of Chapter 2C.*

Note: *References throughout this index are in the form* **"Chapter number"** • **"Page number"**. *So, for example, 2C•15 refers to page 15 of Chapter 2C.*

Note: *References throughout this index are in the form* "**Chapter number**" • "**Page number**". *So, for example, 2C•15 refers to page 15 of Chapter 2C.*

Haynes Manuals – The Complete UK Car List

Title	Book No.
ALFA ROMEO Alfasud/Sprint (74 - 88) up to F *	0292
Alfa Romeo Alfetta (73 - 87) up to E *	0531
AUDI 80, 90 & Coupe Petrol (79 - Nov 88) up to F	0605
Audi 80, 90 & Coupe Petrol (Oct 86 - 90) D to H	1491
Audi 100 & 200 Petrol (Oct 82 - 90) up to H	0907
Audi 100 & A6 Petrol & Diesel (May 91 - May 97) H to P	3504
Audi A3 Petrol & Diesel (96 - May 03) P to 03	4253
Audi A4 Petrol & Diesel (95 - 00) M to X	3575
Audi A4 Petrol & Diesel (01 - 04) X to 54	4609
AUSTIN A35 & A40 (56 - 67) up to F *	0118
Austin/MG/Rover Maestro 1.3 & 1.6 Petrol (83 - 95) up to M	0922
Austin/MG Metro (80 - May 90) up to G	0718
Austin/Rover Montego 1.3 & 1.6 Petrol (84 - 94) A to L	1066
Austin/MG/Rover Montego 2.0 Petrol (84 - 95) A to M	1067
Mini (59 - 69) up to H *	0527
Mini (69 - 01) up to X	0646
Austin/Rover 2.0 litre Diesel Engine (86 - 93) C to L	1857
Austin Healey 100/6 & 3000 (56 - 68) up to G *	0049
BEDFORD CF Petrol (69 - 87) up to E	0163
Bedford/Vauxhall Rascal & Suzuki Supercarry (86 - Oct 94) C to M	3015
BMW 316, 320 & 320i (4-cyl) (75 - Feb 83) up to Y *	0276
BMW 320, 320i, 323i & 325i (6-cyl) (Oct 77 - Sept 87) up to E	0815
BMW 3- & 5-Series Petrol (81 - 91) up to J	1948
BMW 3-Series Petrol (Apr 91 - 99) H to V	3210
BMW 3-Series Petrol (Sept 98 - 03) S to 53	4067
BMW 520i & 525e (Oct 81 - June 88) up to E	1560
BMW 525, 528 & 528i (73 - Sept 81) up to X *	0632
BMW 5-Series 6-cyl Petrol (April 96 - Aug 03) N to 03	4151
BMW 1500, 1502, 1600, 1602, 2000 & 2002 (59 - 77) up to S *	0240
CHRYSLER PT Cruiser Petrol (00 - 03) W to 53	4058
CITROËN 2CV, Ami & Dyane (67 - 90) up to H	0196
Citroën AX Petrol & Diesel (87 - 97) D to P	3014
Citroën Berlingo & Peugeot Partner Petrol & Diesel (96 - 05) P to 55	4281
Citroën BX Petrol (83 - 94) A to L	0908
Citroën C15 Van Petrol & Diesel (89 - Oct 98) F to S	3509
Citroën C3 Petrol & Diesel (02 - 05) 51 to 05	4197
Citroen C5 Petrol & Diesel (01-08) Y to 08	4745
Citroën CX Petrol (75 - 88) up to F	0528
Citroën Saxo Petrol & Diesel (96 - 04) N to 54	3506
Citroën Visa Petrol (79 - 88) up to F	0620
Citroën Xantia Petrol & Diesel (93 - 01) K to Y	3082
Citroën XM Petrol & Diesel (89 - 00) G to X	3451
Citroën Xsara Petrol & Diesel (97 - Sept 00) R to W	3751
Citroën Xsara Picasso Petrol & Diesel (00 - 02) W to 52	3944
Citroen Xsara Picasso (03-08)	4784
Citroën ZX Diesel (91 - 98) J to S	1922
Citroën ZX Petrol (91 - 98) H to S	1881
Citroën 1.7 & 1.9 litre Diesel Engine (84 - 96) A to N	1379
FIAT 126 (73 - 87) up to E *	0305
Fiat 500 (57 - 73) up to M *	0090
Fiat Bravo & Brava Petrol (95 - 00) N to W	3572
Fiat Cinquecento (93 - 98) K to R	3501
Fiat Panda (81 - 95) up to M	0793
Fiat Punto Petrol & Diesel (94 - Oct 99) L to V	3251
Fiat Punto Petrol (Oct 99 - July 03) V to 03	4066
Fiat Punto Petrol (03-07) 03 to 07	4746
Fiat Regata Petrol (84 - 88) A to F	1167
Fiat Tipo Petrol (88 - 91) E to J	1625
Fiat Uno Petrol (83 - 95) up to M	0923
Fiat X1/9 (74 - 89) up to G *	0273
FORD Anglia (59 - 68) up to G *	0001

Title	Book No.
Ford Capri II (& III) 1.6 & 2.0 (74 - 87) up to E *	0283
Ford Capri II (& III) 2.8 & 3.0 V6 (74 - 87) up to E	1309
Ford Cortina Mk I & Corsair 1500 ('62 - '66) up to D*	0214
Ford Cortina Mk III 1300 & 1600 (70 - 76) up to P *	0070
Ford Escort Mk I 1100 & 1300 (68 - 74) up to N *	0171
Ford Escort Mk I Mexico, RS 1600 & RS 2000 (70 - 74) up to N *	0139
Ford Escort Mk II Mexico, RS 1800 & RS 2000 (75 - 80) up to W *	0735
Ford Escort (75 - Aug 80) up to V *	0280
Ford Escort Petrol (Sept 80 - Sept 90) up to H	0686
Ford Escort & Orion Petrol (Sept 90 - 00) H to X	1737
Ford Escort & Orion Diesel (Sept 90 - 00) H to X	4081
Ford Fiesta (76 - Aug 83) up to Y	0334
Ford Fiesta Petrol (Aug 83 - Feb 89) A to F	1030
Ford Fiesta Petrol (Feb 89 - Oct 95) F to N	1595
Ford Fiesta Petrol & Diesel (Oct 95 - Mar 02) N to 02	3397
Ford Fiesta Petrol & Diesel (Apr 02 - 07) 02 to 57	4170
Ford Focus Petrol & Diesel (98 - 01) S to Y	3759
Ford Focus Petrol & Diesel (Oct 01 - 05) 51 to 05	4167
Ford Galaxy Petrol & Diesel (95 - Aug 00) M to W	3984
Ford Granada Petrol (Sept 77 - Feb 85) up to B *	0481
Ford Granada & Scorpio Petrol (Mar 85 - 94) B to M	1245
Ford Ka (96 - 02) P to 52	3570
Ford Mondeo Petrol (93 - Sept 00) K to X	1923
Ford Mondeo Petrol & Diesel (Oct 00 - Jul 03) X to 03	3990
Ford Mondeo Petrol & Diesel (July 03 - 07) 03 to 56	4619
Ford Mondeo Diesel (93 - 96) L to N	3465
Ford Orion Petrol (83 - Sept 90) up to H	1009
Ford Sierra 4-cyl Petrol (82 - 93) up to K	0903
Ford Sierra V6 Petrol (82 - 91) up to J	0904
Ford Transit Petrol (Mk 2) (78 - Jan 86) up to C	0719
Ford Transit Petrol (Mk 3) (Feb 86 - 89) C to G	1468
Ford Transit Diesel (Feb 86 - 99) C to T	3019
Ford Transit Diesel (00-06)	4775
Ford 1.6 & 1.8 litre Diesel Engine (84 - 96) A to N	1172
Ford 2.1, 2.3 & 2.5 litre Diesel Engine (77 - 90) up to H	1606
FREIGHT ROVER Sherpa Petrol (74 - 87) up to E	0463
HILLMAN Avenger (70 - 82) up to Y	0037
Hillman Imp (63 - 76) up to R *	0022
HONDA Civic (Feb 84 - Oct 87) A to E	1226
Honda Civic (Nov 91 - 96) J to N	3199
Honda Civic Petrol (Mar 95 - 00) M to X	4050
Honda Civic Petrol & Diesel (01 - 05) X to 55	4611
Honda CR-V Petrol & Diesel (01-06)	4747
Honda Jazz (01 - Feb 08) 51 - 57	4735
HYUNDAI Pony (85 - 94) C to M	3398
JAGUAR E Type (61 - 72) up to L *	0140
Jaguar MkI & II, 240 & 340 (55 - 69) up to H *	0098
Jaguar XJ6, XJ & Sovereign; Daimler Sovereign (68 - Oct 86) up to D	0242
Jaguar XJ6 & Sovereign (Oct 86 - Sept 94) D to M	3261
Jaguar XJ12, XJS & Sovereign; Daimler Double Six (72 - 88) up to F	0478
JEEP Cherokee Petrol (93 - 96) K to N	1943
LADA 1200, 1300, 1500 & 1600 (74 - 91) up to J	0413
Lada Samara (87 - 91) D to J	1610
LAND ROVER 90, 110 & Defender Diesel (83 - 07) up to 56	3017
Land Rover Discovery Petrol & Diesel (89 - 98) G to S	3016
Land Rover Discovery Diesel (Nov 98 - Jul 04) S to 04	4606
Land Rover Freelander Petrol & Diesel (97 - Sept 03) R to 53	3929
Land Rover Freelander Petrol & Diesel (Oct 03 - Oct 06) 53 to 56	4623

Title	Book No.
Land Rover Series IIA & III Diesel (58 - 85) up to C	0529
Land Rover Series II, IIA & III 4-cyl Petrol (58 - 85) up to C	0314
MAZDA 323 (Mar 81 - Oct 89) up to G	1608
Mazda 323 (Oct 89 - 98) G to R	3455
Mazda 626 (May 83 - Sept 87) up to E	0929
Mazda B1600, B1800 & B2000 Pick-up Petrol (72 - 88) up to F	0267
Mazda RX-7 (79 - 85) up to C *	0460
MERCEDES-BENZ 190, 190E & 190D Petrol & Diesel (83 - 93) A to L	3450
Mercedes-Benz 200D, 240D, 240TD, 300D & 300TD 123 Series Diesel (Oct 76 - 85)	1114
Mercedes-Benz 250 & 280 (68 - 72) up to L *	0346
Mercedes-Benz 250 & 280 123 Series Petrol (Oct 76 - 84) up to B *	0677
Mercedes-Benz 124 Series Petrol & Diesel (85 - Aug 93) C to K	3253
Mercedes-Benz A-Class Petrol & Diesel (98-04) S to 54	4748
Mercedes-Benz C-Class Petrol & Diesel (93 - Aug 00) L to W	3511
Mercedes-Benz C-Class (00-06)	4780
MGA (55 - 62) *	0475
MGB (62 - 80) up to W	0111
MG Midget & Austin-Healey Sprite (58 - 80) up to W *	0265
MINI Petrol (July 01 - 05) Y to 05	4273
MITSUBISHI Shogun & L200 Pick-Ups Petrol (83 - 94) up to M	1944
MORRIS Ital 1.3 (80 - 84) up to B	0705
Morris Minor 1000 (56 - 71) up to K	0024
NISSAN Almera Petrol (95 - Feb 00) N to V	4053
Nissan Almera & Tino Petrol (Feb 00 - 07) V to 56	4612
Nissan Bluebird (May 84 - Mar 86) A to C	1223
Nissan Bluebird Petrol (Mar 86 - 90) C to H	1473
Nissan Cherry (Sept 82 - 86) up to D	1031
Nissan Micra (83 - Jan 93) up to K	0931
Nissan Micra (93 - 02) K to 52	3254
Nissan Micra Petrol (03-07) 52 to 57	4734
Nissan Primera Petrol (90 - Aug 99) H to T	1851
Nissan Stanza (82 - 86) up to D	0824
Nissan Sunny Petrol (May 82 - Oct 86) up to D	0895
Nissan Sunny Petrol (Oct 86 - Mar 91) D to H	1378
Nissan Sunny Petrol (Apr 91 - 95) H to N	3219
OPEL Ascona & Manta (B Series) (Sept 75 - 88) up to F *	0316
Opel Ascona Petrol (81 - 88)	3215
Opel Astra Petrol (Oct 91 - Feb 98)	3156
Opel Corsa Petrol (83 - Mar 93)	3160
Opel Corsa Petrol (Mar 93 - 97)	3159
Opel Kadett Petrol (Nov 79 - Oct 84) up to B	0634
Opel Kadett Petrol (Oct 84 - Oct 91)	3196
Opel Omega & Senator Petrol (Nov 86 - 94)	3157
Opel Rekord Petrol (Feb 78 - Oct 86) up to D	0543
Opel Vectra Petrol (Oct 88 - Oct 95)	3158
PEUGEOT 106 Petrol & Diesel (91 - 04) J to 53	1882
Peugeot 205 Petrol (83 - 97) A to P	0932
Peugeot 206 Petrol & Diesel (98 - 01) S to X	3757
Peugeot 206 Petrol & Diesel (02 - 06) 51 to 06	4613
Peugeot 306 Petrol & Diesel (93 - 02) K to 02	3073
Peugeot 307 Petrol & Diesel (01 - 04) Y to 54	4147
Peugeot 309 Petrol (86 - 93) C to K	1266
Peugeot 405 Petrol (88 - 97) E to P	1559
Peugeot 405 Diesel (88 - 97) E to P	3198
Peugeot 406 Petrol & Diesel (96 - Mar 99) N to T	3394
Peugeot 406 Petrol & Diesel (Mar 99 - 02) T to 52	3982

* Classic reprint

Title	Book No.
Peugeot 505 Petrol (79 - 89) up to G	0762
Peugeot 1.7/1.8 & 1.9 litre Diesel Engine (82 - 96) up to N	0950
Peugeot 2.0, 2.1, 2.3 & 2.5 litre Diesel Engines (74 - 90) up to H	1607
PORSCHE 911 (65 - 85) up to C	0264
Porsche 924 & 924 Turbo (76 - 85) up to C	0397
PROTON (89 - 97) F to P	3255
RANGE ROVER V8 Petrol (70 - Oct 92) up to K	0606
RELIANT Robin & Kitten (73 - 83) up to A *	0436
RENAULT 4 (61 - 86) up to D *	0072
Renault 5 Petrol (Feb 85 - 96) B to N	1219
Renault 9 & 11 Petrol (82 - 89) up to F	0822
Renault 18 Petrol (79 - 86) up to D	0598
Renault 19 Petrol (89 - 96) F to N	1646
Renault 19 Diesel (89 - 96) F to N	1946
Renault 21 Petrol (86 - 94) C to M	1397
Renault 25 Petrol & Diesel (84 - 92) B to K	1228
Renault Clio Petrol (91 - May 98) H to R	1853
Renault Clio Diesel (91 - June 96) H to N	3031
Renault Clio Petrol & Diesel (May 98 - May 01) R to Y	3906
Renault Clio Petrol & Diesel (June '01 - '05) Y to 55	4168
Renault Espace Petrol & Diesel (85 - 96) C to N	3197
Renault Laguna Petrol & Diesel (94 - 00) L to W	3252
Renault Laguna Petrol & Diesel (Feb 01 - Feb 05) X to 54	4283
Renault Mégane & Scénic Petrol & Diesel (96 - 99) N to T	3395
Renault Mégane & Scénic Petrol & Diesel (Apr 99 - 02) T to 52	3916
Renault Megane Petrol & Diesel (Oct 02 - 05) 52 to 55	4284
Renault Scenic Petrol & Diesel (Sept 03 - 06) 53 to 06	4297
ROVER 213 & 216 (84 - 89) A to G	1116
Rover 214 & 414 Petrol (89 - 96) G to N	1689
Rover 216 & 416 Petrol (89 - 96) G to N	1830
Rover 211, 214, 216, 218 & 220 Petrol & Diesel (Dec 95 - 99) N to V	3399
Rover 25 & MG ZR Petrol & Diesel (Oct 99 - 04) V to 54	4145
Rover 414, 416 & 420 Petrol & Diesel (May 95 - 98) M to R	3453
Rover 45 / MG ZS Petrol & Diesel (99 - 05) V to 55	4384
Rover 618, 620 & 623 Petrol (93 - 97) K to P	3257
Rover 75 / MG ZT Petrol & Diesel (99 - 06) S to 06	4292
Rover 820, 825 & 827 Petrol (86 - 95) D to N	1380
Rover 3500 (76 - 87) up to E *	0365
Rover Metro, 111 & 114 Petrol (May 90 - 98) G to S	1711
SAAB 95 & 96 (66 - 76) up to R *	0198
Saab 90, 99 & 900 (79 - Oct 93) up to L	0765
Saab 900 (Oct 93 - 98) L to R	3512
Saab 9000 (4-cyl) (85 - 98) C to S	1686
Saab 9-3 Petrol & Diesel (98 - Aug 02) R to 02	4614
Saab 9-3 Petrol & Diesel (02-07) 52 to 57	4749
Saab 9-5 4-cyl Petrol (97 - 04) R to 54	4156
SEAT Ibiza & Cordoba Petrol & Diesel (Oct 93 - Oct 99) L to V	3571
Seat Ibiza & Malaga Petrol (85 - 92) B to K	1609
SKODA Estelle (77 - 89) up to G	0604
Skoda Fabia Petrol & Diesel (00 - 06) W to 06	4376
Skoda Favorit (89 - 96) F to N	1801
Skoda Felicia Petrol & Diesel (95 - 01) M to X	3505
Skoda Octavia Petrol & Diesel (98 - Apr 04) R to 04	4285
SUBARU 1600 & 1800 (Nov 79 - 90) up to H *	0995

Title	Book No.
SUNBEAM Alpine, Rapier & H120 (67 - 74) up to N *	0051
SUZUKI SJ Series, Samurai & Vitara (4-cyl) Petrol (82 - 97) up to P	1942
Suzuki Supercarry & Bedford/Vauxhall Rascal (86 - Oct 94) C to M	3015
TALBOT Alpine, Solara, Minx & Rapier (75 - 86) up to D	0337
Talbot Horizon Petrol (78 - 86) up to D	0473
Talbot Samba (82 - 86) up to D	0823
TOYOTA Avensis Petrol (98 - Jan 03) R to 52	4264
Toyota Carina E Petrol (May 92 - 97) J to P	3256
Toyota Corolla (80 - 85) up to C	0683
Toyota Corolla (Sept 83 - Sept 87) A to E	1024
Toyota Corolla (Sept 87 - Aug 92) E to K	1683
Toyota Corolla Petrol (Aug 92 - 97) K to P	3259
Toyota Corolla Petrol (July 97 - Feb 02) P to 51	4286
Toyota Hi-Ace & Hi-Lux Petrol (69 - Oct 83) up to A	0304
Toyota RAV4 Petrol & Diesel (94-06) L to 55	4750
Toyota Yaris Petrol (99 - 05) T to 05	4265
TRIUMPH GT6 & Vitesse (62 - 74) up to N *	0112
Triumph Herald (59 - 71) up to K *	0010
Triumph Spitfire (62 - 81) up to X	0113
Triumph Stag (70 - 78) up to T *	0441
Triumph TR2, TR3, TR3A, TR4 & TR4A (52 - 67) up to F *	0028
Triumph TR5 & 6 (67 - 75) up to P *	0031
Triumph TR7 (75 - 82) up to Y *	0322
VAUXHALL Astra Petrol (80 - Oct 84) up to B	0635
Vauxhall Astra & Belmont Petrol (Oct 84 - Oct 91) B to J	1136
Vauxhall Astra Petrol (Oct 91 - Feb 98) J to R	1832
Vauxhall/Opel Astra & Zafira Petrol (Feb 98 - Apr 04) R to 04	3758
Vauxhall/Opel Astra & Zafira Diesel (Feb 98 - Apr 04) R to 04	3797
Vauxhall/Opel Astra Petrol (04 - 08)	4732
Vauxhall/Opel Astra Diesel (04 - 08)	4733
Vauxhall/Opel Calibra (90 - 98) G to S	3502
Vauxhall Carlton Petrol (Oct 78 - Oct 86) up to D	0480
Vauxhall Carlton & Senator Petrol (Nov 86 - 94) D to L	1469
Vauxhall Cavalier Petrol (81 - Oct 88) up to F	0812
Vauxhall Cavalier Petrol (Oct 88 - 95) F to N	1570
Vauxhall Chevette (75 - 84) up to B	0285
Vauxhall/Opel Corsa Diesel (Mar 93 - Oct 00) K to X	4087
Vauxhall Corsa Petrol (Mar 93 - 97) K to R	1985
Vauxhall/Opel Corsa Petrol (Apr 97 - Oct 00) P to X	3921
Vauxhall/Opel Corsa Petrol & Diesel (Oct 00 - Sept 03) X to 53	4079
Vauxhall/Opel Corsa Petrol & Diesel (Oct 03 - Aug 06) 53 to 06	4617
Vauxhall/Opel Frontera Petrol & Diesel (91 - Sept 98) J to S	3454
Vauxhall Nova Petrol (83 - 93) up to K	0909
Vauxhall/Opel Omega Petrol (94 - 99) L to T	3510
Vauxhall/Opel Vectra Petrol & Diesel (95 - Feb 99) N to S	3396
Vauxhall/Opel Vectra Petrol & Diesel (Mar 99 - May 02) T to 02	3930
Vauxhall/Opel Vectra Petrol & Diesel (June 02 - Sept 05) 02 to 55	4618
Vauxhall/Opel 1.5, 1.6 & 1.7 litre Diesel Engine (82 - 96) up to N	1222
VW 411 & 412 (68 - 75) up to P *	0091
VW Beetle 1200 (54 - 77) up to S	0036
VW Beetle 1300 & 1500 (65 - 75) up to P	0039

Title	Book No.
VW 1302 & 1302S (70 - 72) up to L *	0110
VW Beetle 1303, 1303S & GT (72 - 75) up to P	0159
VW Beetle Petrol & Diesel (Apr 99 - 07) T to 57	3798
VW Golf & Jetta Mk 1 Petrol 1.1 & 1.3 (74 - 84) up to A	0716
VW Golf, Jetta & Scirocco Mk 1 Petrol 1.5, 1.6 & 1.8 (74 - 84) up to A	0726
VW Golf & Jetta Mk 1 Diesel (78 - 84) up to A	0451
VW Golf & Jetta Mk 2 Petrol (Mar 84 - Feb 92) A to J	1081
VW Golf & Vento Petrol & Diesel (Feb 92 - Mar 98) J to R	3097
VW Golf & Bora Petrol & Diesel (April 98 - 00) R to X	3727
VW Golf & Bora 4-cyl Petrol & Diesel (01 - 03) X to 53	4169
VW Golf & Jetta Petrol & Diesel (04 - 07) 53 to 07	4610
VW LT Petrol Vans & Light Trucks (76 - 87) up to E	0637
VW Passat & Santana Petrol (Sept 81 - May 88) up to E	0814
VW Passat 4-cyl Petrol & Diesel (May 88 - 96) E to P	3498
VW Passat 4-cyl Petrol & Diesel (Dec 96 - Nov 00) P to X	3917
VW Passat Petrol & Diesel (Dec 00 - May 05) X to 05	4279
VW Polo & Derby (76 - Jan 82) up to X	0335
VW Polo (82 - Oct 90) up to H	0813
VW Polo Petrol (Nov 90 - Aug 94) H to L	3245
VW Polo Hatchback Petrol & Diesel (94 - 99) M to S	3500
VW Polo Hatchback Petrol (00 - Jan 02) V to 51	4150
VW Polo Petrol & Diesel (02 - May 05) 51 to 05	4608
VW Scirocco (82 - 90) up to H *	1224
VW Transporter 1600 (68 - 79) up to V	0082
VW Transporter 1700, 1800 & 2000 (72 - 79) up to V *	0226
VW Transporter (air-cooled) Petrol (79 - 82) up to Y *	0638
VW Transporter (water-cooled) Petrol (82 - 90) up to H	3452
VW Type 3 (63 - 73) up to M *	0084
VOLVO 120 & 130 Series (& P1800) (61 - 73) up to M *	0203
Volvo 142, 144 & 145 (66 - 74) up to N *	0129
Volvo 240 Series Petrol (74 - 93) up to K	0270
Volvo 262, 264 & 260/265 (75 - 85) up to C *	0400
Volvo 340, 343, 345 & 360 (76 - 91) up to J	0715
Volvo 440, 460 & 480 Petrol (87 - 97) D to P	1691
Volvo 740 & 760 Petrol (82 - 91) up to J	1258
Volvo 850 Petrol (92 - 96) J to P	3260
Volvo 940 petrol (90 - 98) H to R	3249
Volvo S40 & V40 Petrol (96 - Mar 04) N to 04	3569
Volvo S40 & V50 Petrol & Diesel (Mar 04 - Jun 07) 04 to 07	4731
Volvo S60 Petrol & Diesel (01-08)	4793
Volvo S70, V70 & C70 Petrol (96 - 99) P to V	3573
Volvo V70 / S80 Petrol & Diesel (98 - 05) S to 55	4263

DIY MANUAL SERIES

The Haynes Air Conditioning Manual	4192
The Haynes Car Electrical Systems Manual	4251
The Haynes Manual on Bodywork	4198
The Haynes Manual on Brakes	4178
The Haynes Manual on Carburettors	4177
The Haynes Manual on Diesel Engines	4174
The Haynes Manual on Engine Management	4199
The Haynes Manual on Fault Codes	4175
The Haynes Manual on Practical Electrical Systems	4267
The Haynes Manual on Small Engines	4250
The Haynes Manual on Welding	4176

* Classic reprint

All the products featured on this page are available through most motor accessory shops, cycle shops and book stores. Our policy of continuous updating and development means that titles are being constantly added to the range. For up-to-date information on our complete list of titles, please telephone: (UK) +44 1963 442030 • (USA) +1 805 498 6703 • (Sweden) +46 18 124016 • (Australia) +61 3 9763 8100

Preserving Our Motoring Heritage

< The Model J Duesenberg Derham Tourster. Only eight of these magnificent cars were ever built – this is the only example to be found outside the United States of America

Almost every car you've ever loved, loathed or desired is gathered under one roof at the Haynes Motor Museum. Over 300 immaculately presented cars and motorbikes represent every aspect of our motoring heritage, from elegant reminders of bygone days, such as the superb Model J Duesenberg to curiosities like the bug-eyed BMW Isetta. There are also many old friends and flames. Perhaps you remember the 1959 Ford Popular that you did your courting in? The magnificent 'Red Collection' is a spectacle of classic sports cars including AC, Alfa Romeo, Austin Healey, Ferrari, Lamborghini, Maserati, MG, Riley, Porsche and Triumph.

A Perfect Day Out

Each and every vehicle at the Haynes Motor Museum has played its part in the history and culture of Motoring. Today, they make a wonderful spectacle and a great day out for all the family. Bring the kids, bring Mum and Dad, but above all bring your camera to capture those golden memories for ever. You will also find an impressive array of motoring memorabilia, a comfortable 70 seat video cinema and one of the most extensive transport book shops in Britain. The Pit Stop Cafe serves everything from a cup of tea to wholesome, home-made meals or, if you prefer, you can enjoy the large picnic area nestled in the beautiful rural surroundings of Somerset.

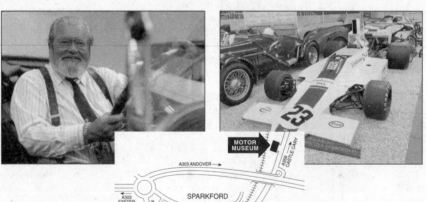

> John Haynes O.B.E., Founder and Chairman of the museum at the wheel of a Haynes Light 12.

< Graham Hill's Lola Cosworth Formula 1 car next to a 1934 Riley Sports.

The Museum is situated on the A359 Yeovil to Frome road at Sparkford, just off the A303 in Somerset. It is about 40 miles south of Bristol, and 25 minutes drive from the M5 intersection at Taunton.
Open 9.30am - 5.30pm (10.00am - 4.00pm Winter) 7 days a week, *except Christmas Day, Boxing Day and New Years Day*
Special rates available for schools, coach parties and outings Charitable Trust No. 292048